DOCUMENTARY HISTORY OF THE FIRST FEDERAL CONGRESS OF THE UNITED STATES OF AMERICA

March 4, 1789–March 3, 1791

LINDA GRANT DE PAUW, EDITOR

SPONSORED BY

THE NATIONAL HISTORICAL PUBLICATIONS AND RECORDS COMMISSION

AND

THE GEORGE WASHINGTON UNIVERSITY

U. S. Congress, 1789 - 1791. House.
III.

HOUSE

OF

REPRESENTATIVES

JOURNAL

LINDA GRANT DE PAUW, Editor

CHARLENE BANGS BICKFORD, Associate Editor

LAVONNE SIEGEL HAUPTMAN, Associate Editor

The Johns Hopkins University Press, Baltimore and London

Copyright © 1977 by The Johns Hopkins University Press

All rights reserved. No part of this book may be reproduced or transmitted in any
form or by any means, electronic or mechanical, including photocopying, recording,
xerography, or any information storage or retrieval system, without permission in
writing from the publishers.

Manufactured in the United States of America

The Johns Hopkins University Press, Baltimore, Maryland 21218
The Johns Hopkins Press Ltd., London

Library of Congress Catalog Card Number 76–25106
ISBN 0–8018–1819–2

Library of Congress Cataloging in Publication data
will be found on the last printed page of this book.

CONTENTS

JOURNAL OF THE FIRST SESSION OF THE HOUSE OF REPRESENTATIVES OF THE UNITED STATES

JOURNAL OF THE SECOND SESSION OF THE HOUSE OF REPRESENTATIVES OF THE UNITED STATES

JOURNAL OF THE THIRD SESSION OF THE HOUSE OF REPRESENTATIVES OF THE UNITED STATES

INTRODUCTION

John Beckley, the first clerk of the House of Representatives of the United States, clearly never anticipated that his official files would be scrutinized and their contents edited and published in the twentieth century. Samuel Otis, the secretary of the Senate, had the soul of a modern archivist. His colleague in the House, however, had several habits which did not prevent him from performing his duties to the satisfaction of the House of Representatives two hundred years ago, but which have often driven the staff of this editorial project to the point of exasperation.

In particular, the editors encountered two major problems in the preparation of this edition of the *House of Representatives Journal* that were not present in our earlier work on the Senate journals. First, we found a good number of omissions and some errors in the two forms of the journal—printed and manuscript—that survive. This subject will be discussed later. Second, we were forced to deal with a House archive so fragmentary that some portions of the documentary record can never be reconstructed. It has usually been assumed that the small number of official documents of the first House of Representatives that has survived to the present day was the result of the fire in Washington, set by the British in 1814, or other accidents occurring after Beckley's death in 1807. The editors have concluded, however, that most of the documents missing from the House records today were deliberately destroyed while John Beckley was clerk.

It is true that even had Beckley kept his files intact, the dangers to which they were exposed after his death might have caused considerable damage.[1] The staff of the clerk's office was not as well prepared to deal with the emergency that occurred when the British burned the Capitol as was that of the secretary of the Senate. The clerk himself had been ill and was not in Washington at the time. All but one of the junior clerks were called up by the local militia to defend the city. The single clerk who was old enough to be exempt from military service was newly hired. Evacuation of the records was delayed until the last minute, and only one oxcart was available for the operation. Nevertheless, the evacuation of House records was thought to have been reasonably successful. Contemporaries seem to have believed that the most serious loss was the current account book. Some manuscript material from early Congresses was reported to have been destroyed, but it was

---

[1] The best history of the House records over the years is Buford Rowland, "Recordkeeping Practices of the House of Representatives," *National Archives Accession*, No. 53 (1957), pp. 1–19.

described as "mostly of a private nature, consisting chiefly of petitions, and unimportant papers." The fire also destroyed all of Congress's secret journals.[2]

Other serious if less dramatic threats to the integrity of the official House files after Beckley's death were inadequate storage facilities and inadequate control of access to documents. Before the files were deposited in the National Archives in 1946, little thought was given to the care of the documents of noncurrent Congresses. After materials were no longer needed for the day-to-day business of the House, the thought was merely to get them out of the way. By the end of the nineteenth century, House files were crammed into odd corners of the Capitol from the basement to the attic. In 1899 the House file clerk described the situation:

One-half of these [the bound volumes of House records] are stored in an open gallery in the basement, exposed to dust and change of temperature, and in consequence many of the bindings are falling apart. They comprise in part the early messages of the Presidents. . . . The remainder of the bound volumes are stored in the attic with very many committee papers of the early Congresses, and are in a condition that will lead to their destruction before many years. The extreme heat in summer from the iron roof and the dampness in winter from the condensation of hot air coming against the cold iron of the roof render the place unfit for documents of such value. Portions of the shelving in the attic are of wood, and in the event of fire would be entirely inaccessible, as this attic can only be reached through this office and up three flights of narrow stairs. This stairway is used by the Architect's laborers to gain access to the roof and also by the employees of the House who raise and lower the flags.[3]

In 1901 some noncurrent House records, including copies of the contemporary printed journals for the First Congress, which were no longer used for reference after a new printing was made in 1826,[4] were transferred to the Library of Congress. Although crowding was somewhat relieved, a deputy examiner for the National Archives reported in 1937 that records of the First Federal Congress were still in the Capitol attic. If anything, the situation up there had grown even worse. When air-conditioning was installed, the workmen had torn down some of the shelves, scattered the boxes of documents "helter-skelter upon the floor in practically inaccessible places, or piled one upon another against the walls." As a final insult they had made a habit of eating their lunch surrounded by these piles of historic documents and tossing the wrappings onto the heap. The volumes of docu-

---

[2] *American State Papers: Miscellaneous*, 2:245–46, 258–59.

[3] U.S. Congress, House, *Additional Space for Files of the House of Representatives*, 56th Cong., 1st sess., 1900, H. Doc. 536, p. 2.

[4] *Journal of the House of Representatives of the United States*, 1 (Washington, D.C.: Gales and Seaton, 1826).

ments in the Library of Congress were only slightly better cared for. "Volumes are disarranged and dirty," the examiner reported, "with the leather binding smudging and with backs broken."[5]

Today, cleaned, fumigated, repaired and carefully guarded, the official records of the First House of Representatives are maintained under scientifically controlled atmospheric conditions by the professional staff of the National Archives. The Senate documents came to the Archives in 1937, but it was not until 1946 that the noncurrent records of the House were moved from their dirty vermin-infested quarters. The reason for the delay was not indifference to the older records on the part of the House or its clerk. Paradoxically, it was heightened concern for the records that delayed the transfer.

Before the transfer of the older House files to the National Archives, pilfering, loss, and what archivists call "alienation" of the official records were probably a greater threat to the integrity of the documents than the inadequate storage facilities. Certainly it was a threat to which the clerks were more sensitive. During the nineteenth century a great deal of manuscript material was casually withdrawn from the House files. When Congress authorized publication of the *American State Papers* in 1831, the editors of the series made their own markings right on the House documents and even cut many papers out of the bound manuscript books. The clerk recovered the documents from the editors in 1846 by special resolution of the House. The then substantial sum of two hundred and three dollars was expended for "stitching and pasting" them back into their proper places.[6] At least this material was eventually recovered. Many other papers, however, were withdrawn from the clerk's files by unanimous consent of the House. Until 1873, this was routinely voted at the request of any member. As the sheer mass of noncurrent documents grew, the task of preventing alienation of documents became increasingly difficult. The growth of the files was particularly rapid after the clerk began to enforce his control over the voluminous committee records in the 1870s. During this period of rapid growth, the House suddenly became alarmed about its possible loss of control over the contents of its files. In the year 1879 it established a precedent so sternly worded as to impress later clerks with the overriding urgency of keeping House documents directly responsive to the orders and rules of each succeeding House.

The precedent for maintaining rigid administrative control over House records was established in the case of Ferris Finch. Finch, a House file clerk,

---

[5] U.S. Congress, House, Committee on the Library, *Transfer of Certain Records of House of Representatives to National Archives*, 75th Cong., 1st sess., 1937, H. Rept. 917, pp. 16–17.

[6] U.S. Congress, House, *Contingent Expenses House of Representatives*, 29th Cong., 2nd sess., 1846, H. Doc. 2, pp. 188, 209.

was subpoenaed to appear as a witness at a court-martial in 1879 and to bring with him some documents that had been presented to an 1872 Military Affairs Committee hearing. In forbidding him to comply with the subpoena, the House report stated, "They [the documents] belong to the House, and are under its absolute and unqualified control. It can at any time take them from the custody of the Clerk, refuse to allow them to be inspected by any one, order them to be destroyed, or dismiss the Clerk for permitting any of them to be removed from the files without its expressed consent."[7]

Before the transfer of the noncurrent files to the National Archives, the Finch precedent probably did not make the records of the First Congress any more inaccessible to researchers than they would have been without it. Stored in dusty boxes in forgotten corners of the Capitol they would have been virtually impossible to use even if they could have been located. Once they were housed in the National Archives, however, historians and others who were interested in the legislative history of the early Congresses were inconvenienced by the administrative restrictions. They were told that only those records previously printed or made public by order of the House were open for inspection. Since 1953 all House records over fifty years old may be examined, but even now permission from the clerk is required in each instance. In 1964, House Resolution 902 authorized the "reproduction and publication" of all the First Federal Congress records for the *Documentary History of the First Federal Congress*.[8] Consequently, this and future volumes dealing with official House records will make the contents of these files easily available to the American public for the first time, while still giving full protection to the valuable manuscripts.

The dangers to which the files of the First House of Representatives were exposed in the years following Beckley's death do not entirely explain the fragmentary state of the records. Indeed, the virtually complete Senate files were subjected to similar conditions. A study of Beckley's record-keeping practices makes it clear that he was an early practitioner of what archivists today call "records management"—the disposal of excess government-produced paper. Beckley's view of what was worth keeping and what was mere wastepaper was not the same as that of modern records appraisers. The members of the early Congresses, however, appear to have been entirely satisfied with his methods. Both were satisfied to have legible, easily available reference volumes, containing transcripts of official records. They did not miss what could be considered mere rough drafts.

---

[7] U.S. Congress, House, Committee on the Judiciary, *Production of Original Papers before Court-Martial*, 46th Cong., 1st sess., 1879, H. Rept. 1, p. 5.

[8] U.S. Congress, House, *Congressional Record*, 88th Cong., 2nd sess., 1964, 110, pt. 18:23785.

There was considerable turnover in the clerk's office in the course of the First Federal Congress. In the spring of 1789 Beckley hired William Lambert as his principal clerk and George Sutton as engrossing clerk.[9] By law, the principal clerk earned three dollars a day and had greater responsibilities than the engrossing clerk, who earned only two dollars a day and was the preindustrial age's equivalent of typewriter, carbon paper, and Xerox machine.[10] The engrossing clerk was required merely to make accurate copies, in a fair round hand, of whatever was laid before him. Lambert kept his job through the second session, while Sutton worked through November 1789. Sutton was replaced by Bernard Webb, who soon was promoted to Lambert's job. In the third session Webb served as principal clerk and Beckley hired two new engrossing clerks: William C. Claiborne and Reuben Burnley.[11]

Beckley was particular about the care and storage of those papers which he thought fit to keep. In the course of his tenure, the seat of Congress was moved twice. The first move was from New York to Philadelphia at the end of the second session of the First Congress. Beckley wrote ahead to make sure that adequately furnished office space would be ready to receive the House files as soon as they arrived.[12] He was given space in the West Wing of Independence Hall that had formerly been occupied by the Pennsylvania Receiver General and Land Office. The office can no longer be seen, since the present reconstruction of the building is not entirely accurate; however, it was comparable to the office of the secretary of the Senate, which is on display today in Congress Hall. From Philadelphia, Beckley moved his files to the unfinished Capitol in Washington in 1800. Perhaps because he himself was obliged to move so often and because he remembered the many moves Congress had made during the Confederation period, Beckley kept his files easily portable. Unless these arrangements were radically changed in the seven years following his death, which seems unlikely, the sudden evacuation of 1814 should have been relatively simple to accomplish. A House select committee that examined the books and records in the clerk's office in 1802 admired the manner in which Beckley had the House documents "regularly marked, numbered and endorsed according to their

---

[9] Secretary of Treasury's Reports, 2nd Congress (November 1792), p. 59, RG 233, Records of the United States House of Representatives, DNA.

[10] An Act for allowing compensation to the members of the Senate and House of Representatives of the United States, and to the officers of both Houses, September 22, 1789, Enrolled Acts and Resolutions of the Congress of the United States, 1789–1823, RG 11, General Records of the United States Government, DNA.

[11] Secretary of Treasury's Reports, 2nd Congress (November 1792), pp. 54, 57, 59–60, RG 233, Records of the United States House of Representatives, DNA.

[12] John Beckley, November 17, 1790, Miers Fisher Papers, PHi.

respective subjects, in board files, and duly preserved in portable cases."[13] The question remains, what did Beckley keep in those portable cases? We believe they contained only such documents as had not been transcribed into equally portable bound volumes.

Both internal and external evidence suggests that Beckley routinely destroyed all original documents that he felt were superseded by revised or perfected copies. For instance, no House bills are preserved in House records in the form in which they were originally introduced, and no original engrossed House bills remain in the House records when such bills were subsequently passed by the Senate and became law. In such cases Beckley apparently felt that the enrolled act was all it was necessary to save. After all, that was the form that was law. On the other hand, if the Senate did not pass the bill, Beckley preserved the earlier engrossed form. All but four of them survive. Another gap in the House files that may be explained by Beckley's records management is the absence of all original House committee reports and most executive department reports. For almost all of these, transcribed copies prepared in Beckley's office still exist, suggesting that he disposed of the originals after a clean copy had been made and bound in leather. Except for petitions and miscellaneous papers, Beckley put his assistants to work transcribing all the important materials entrusted to his keeping, and these bound volumes are, with very few exceptions, the only House records that have survived. In accounts of the evacuation of the clerk's office in 1814, the materials removed are described as though they were mainly bound volumes and, except for the papers "mostly of a private nature," which were thought too unimportant to transcribe, the only materials lost were manuscripts waiting to be copied.[14]

It is not necessary to rely on inference from the pattern of missing records to establish Beckley's preference for clean transcriptions over scribbled originals of committee reports, bills, and even the House journal itself. In 1836 Samuel Burch, who was then principal clerk in the office of the clerk of the House, described the records management practices of earlier days:

I entered this office a youth, under John Beckley, who was the first Clerk of the House of Representatives. . . .

During the recess of Congress he put me at what was termed "recording the journal" of the preceding session, which was to write it off from the printed copy into a large bound volume. I inquired of him why it was that it was copied, when there were so many printed copies? He answered that the printed copies

---

[13] A Record of the Reports of Select Committees of the House of Representatives of the United States, 7th Congress, Vol. III, p. 234, RG 233, Records of the United States House of Representatives, DNA.

[14] American State Papers: Miscellaneous, 2:245.

would, probably, in time, disappear from use, &c.; the large manuscript volume would not.

The term "rough journal," as it was then termed, and is still termed, being the original rough draught read in the House on the morning after the day of which it narrates the proceedings, was not, and had not from the beginning, been preserved. I inquired the reason, and was answered, that the printed copy was the . . . most correct, and that, therefore, there was no use in lumbering the office with the "rough Journal," after it had been printed.

It was not until 1823 that Burch "determined, without consulting my superior," to preserve the rough journal.[15] But the practice of "recording the journal" continued for another sixteen years.

Beckley's point of view was not entirely without merit. Had his practices remained in effect, the overcrowding that threatened the total destruction of early records by the action of fire or vermin would not have occurred. And certainly the large bound volumes were easier to move quickly in case of emergency and were unlikely to be lost as loose manuscripts might be. He was even right about the probable disappearance of printed documents. As early as 1833, the compilers of the *American State Papers* found that the books of transcribed documents provided the only copy available of many important items, even those that had been printed earlier by order of Congress. Clerks in various executive departments and former Congressmen obviously felt there was no need to "lumber up" their rooms with copies of a printed document, which, all were sure, someone else must be preserving.

Finally, Beckley was probably right that it was easier to protect copies bound into a book than loose papers. The recollections of Senator William Plumer suggest that Beckley had difficulty preventing Congressmen from removing loose documents from the House records. When Plumer entered Congress in 1802, the Capitol was unfinished, and Beckley was forced to store some materials under conditions that were less than ideal. A leaky roof and the activities of workmen threatened so much damage that some Congressmen apparently felt they would be doing posterity a favor if they carried off some of the papers. "When I came here . . ." Plumer later recalled, "I was informed that each member of Congress was entitled to each document if he would take the trouble of selecting them. I accordingly began—selected & removed a considerable number when I received a message indirectly from John Beckley clerk of the House of Representatives, in whose custody the key of the chamber was, that those documents were the property of the United States & that members of Congress had no

[15] U.S. Congress, Senate, *Register of Debates in Congress*, 24th Cong., 1st sess., 1836, 12, pt. 2:1594, Samuel Burch to Walter S. Franklin, April 6, 1836.

right to them. A few days after I found one of his favorites: a member of the House selecting a number of those papers. I then renewed my search." Plumer collected documents for the Massachusetts Historical Society and for a friend in Salem but proudly observed that "neither of these two collections of documents are half so large & extensive as mine."[16]

However plausible these defenses of Beckley's records management, the fact remains that the House files today have suffered from it. In sharp contrast to the Senate files, they are badly fragmented and can be only partially reconstructed. The purpose of this volume of the *Documentary History of the First Federal Congress* is to provide, insofar as possible, an accurate text of the official House Journal and then to lay the foundation for reconstruction of the House files in later volumes of the series by identifying the materials that have survived and providing points of reference for what is missing.

As was mentioned earlier, there are both omissions and errors in the edition of the House journal printed by Francis Childs and John Swaine at the end of each session, which Beckley insisted was the "official" form, since it was printed by the order of Congress.[17] The bound manuscript journal that was copied from the printed volumes contains even more errors. We cannot positively conclude from these facts that Beckley was more careless in keeping the House journal than Otis was in keeping that of the Senate. The rough journal, which Beckley read to the House each morning, may have been free of errors. Since Otis preserved all manuscript versions, we were able to identify and correct errors introduced by his engrossing clerk or the printer by referring to his own original text in our footnotes. It has been impossible, however, for us to do this for Beckley. Yet although the printed journal of the House has far more errors than that of the Senate, the editors have been just as reluctant to make any changes at all in the contemporary form that is the basis of this edition. The errors and omissions in the originals are part of the official record; our footnoted corrections are not. In order to aid the reader, however, and to establish a clearly dated reference for each House action, so that cross-references in future volumes will be possible, we have included two forms of explanatory footnotes. We have supplied such obvious omissions as the

---

[16] Edmund Berkeley and Dorothy Smith Berkeley, *John Beckley: Zealous Partisan in a Nation Divided* (Philadelphia: The American Philosophical Society, 1973), p. 273.

[17] *Journal of the House of Representatives of the United States* (New York: Francis Childs and John Swaine, 1789), E–22208; *Journal of the House of Representatives of the United States* (New York: Francis Childs and John Swaine, 1790), E–22981; *Journal of the House of Representatives of the United States* (Philadelphia: Francis Childs and John Swaine, 1791), E–23899.

second reading of a bill for which both first and third readings are recorded, and we have identified the topics discussed when the Journal states only that the House moved into "the committee of the whole House on the state of the Union." As in earlier volumes, cross-reference notes are included to enable the reader to follow action on a particular subject from day to day without consulting the index. After the point when the bill was engrossed, we have silently corrected errors in bill titles.

The boys who copied the printed journal into bound books do not seem to have believed that they were engaged in anything except make-work. A great deal of carelessness is apparent in the transcription—often whole lines are omitted. Beckley did not have either the time or the interest to check their work carefully. So long as they did not blot a page, it could pass inspection. Nevertheless, Beckley does seem to have believed, as he later told Samuel Burch, that the manuscript journal would be the most permanent record. At several points the manuscript journal contains additions to the printed journal from which it was copied. Although the editors have not noted the engrossing clerks' numerous casual errors, we have noted what we have determined to be deliberate corrections.

Once we had determined that the contemporary printed journal should be our basic text, the editors wrestled for some time with the puzzling circumstance that several variations of the contemporary printings exist. Charles Evans noted in 1912 that the New York Public Library owned two copies of the printed journal for the first session of the First Congress that contained some variations in spelling. We identified variations between printed copies of the third-session journal. Indeed, we found some copies of the journal were even printed on larger sheets of paper than others. How many variations in the contemporary printed edition may once have existed is unknown. It was common for eighteenth-century printers to reset type when they spotted an error or when a piece of type broke. Furthermore, the House journal may have been reset one or more times. It was first printed a few sheets at a time for the use of Congressmen and other subscribers during the term. Undistributed sheets were bound together as complete books at the end of each session. The printers, however, could not afford to hold the type out of use for months at a time, nor, in a busy newspaper office, could they print up enough sheets every few days to be sure they would have 700 copies available at the end of the session to conform to the report on printing of May 28, 1789. Since an undetermined number of private individuals also purchased copies, either bound or in loose sheets, a great many combinations of different pages may have existed at one time. Only a few copies of the journal for each session survive today.

Ideally, we would have wished to use as our basic text that copy of the printed journal that was used in the clerk's office by the boys who transcribed the manuscript journal. Yet the clerk's office had at least seven copies of the journal (all of which were transferred to the Library of Congress in 1901 and have never been returned to the House records), and these copies are not identical. Fortunately, the question of which copies of the contemporary printed edition to use turned out to be entirely academic. While the printings vary, there are no substantial differences. Our policies on silent editing would produce the same text no matter which of the copies we used.

As in previous volumes of this series, we have silently edited the text to correct obvious typographical errors, to delete archaic punctuation that does not affect the sense of the text, and to adjust quotation marks for the sake of clarity. We have added appropriate running heads. We have regularized the spelling of proper names of members to conform to that used by the men themselves in contemporary signed documents. We have also attempted to confirm the spellings of petitioners' names and regularize them throughout the text. Since many of the petitioners were obscure people and most of the petitions have disappeared, it was not always possible to be sure of the correct spellings. In such cases we have left the spelling as it appears in the printed journal and listed all variations in the index. When the variation is substantial (e.g., as when the same individual is referred to as Dade and McDade), attention is called to the variation in a footnote and index entries are cross-referenced. The petitioners are indexed under name, object of petition, and state of residence when that could be determined.

This volume is the first in the *Documentary History of the First Federal Congress* to deal with official House of Representatives records. The official records include all documents produced by the order of the House or directed to the House, including documents produced or received by House committees. The *House of Representatives Journal* is the most important of these records. It is the only record that the Constitution specifically requires the House "to keep,"[18] and it is the official guide for the arrangement of all other records. Since the Journal reveals the exact disposition made by the House of every paper that came to its notice, it serves to identify documents precisely. Indeed, the terminology of the journals is taken as definitive by the National Archives whenever the endorsements on a document are not clear.

Despite the fundamental importance of the Journal, students of politics or law may well find this volume dull and barren. That cannot be helped. Members of the First Congress themselves found it dull and required the

---

[18] Article I, Section 5.

clerk to supply them with the accounts of debates published by newspapers. These lively unofficial accounts will be reproduced in later volumes of this series. The dates and documents defined in this volume and the two preceding it provide identification points that will be necessary in cross-referencing both official and unofficial materials in the rest of the series.

Since so many of the official House documents have been destroyed, we have not noted missing documents in this volume as we did in Volume I, the *Senate Legislative Journal*. It may be assumed that any document for which no location is given in a footnote has not been found. Copies from unofficial sources that are located will be reproduced in their proper place in later volumes, but they are not footnoted here. The purpose of these notes is to identify those official documents still preserved, not to reconstruct the full archive. All documents preserved in the House records in the National Archives are footnoted at the point in the journal where they are first mentioned. When the journal failed to mention the introduction of the document, we corrected the journal in a footnote when possible and cited the document at that point. When copies of a document are preserved among the official records, these are identified as well as the original if it has been preserved. If we could find neither the original of a document nor a copy in the House records, we have cited any copy available in the official Senate records. Some documents—for instance, petitions—were probably examined in the same form or even shared by both houses. When we could find no copy of a document printed by order of the House in either House or Senate records, we have identified it by Evans number.[19] When earlier bibliographers have located no copies, we have supplied the location of any copy we have found. Finally, documents mentioned in the House journal that have been printed in one of the previous volumes in this series are footnoted and cross-referenced.

The editors wish to express special thanks for their help with this volume to members of our staff: Roberta Haber, Michael Margeson, Marie McMahon, Richard Marmaro, John Rowland, and Kathryn Stafford; to George Washington University graduate fellows: Roger Davis, Nancy Granese, James Holmes, Richard Pandich, and Helen Veit; and to present and former

---

[19] We use the term "Evans number" to apply to numbers assigned to printed documents in one of two related bibliographies of early American imprints: Charles Evans, *American Bibliography*, vols. 7 and 8 (New York: Peter Smith, 1942), and Roger Bristol, *Supplement to Charles Evans' American Bibliography* (Charlottesville: University Press of Virginia, 1970). The Readex Microprint Corporation's edition of *Early American Imprints 1639–1800*, edited by Clifford Shipton, is keyed to these numbers. The index to the microprint edition is: Clifford Shipton and James Mooney, *National Index of American Imprints through 1800, The Short-Title Evans* (Worcester, Mass.: The American Antiquarian Society and Barre Publishers, 1969).

members of the National Archives and National Historical Publications and Records Commission staffs: H. B. Fant, Mary Giunta, Sara Jackson, James Masterson, George Perros, Buford Rowland, Marion Tinling, and Debra Wallace.

ASP	American State Papers
COWH	Committee of the Whole House
CtHi	Connecticut Historical Society, Hartford, Connecticut
CtY	Yale University, New Haven, Connecticut
DLC	United States Library of Congress, Washington, D.C.
DNA	United States National Archives, Washington, D.C.
E	Evans (Readex microprint) number
HR	House Records, RG 233, United States National Archives, Washington, D.C.
M	Microcopy number in United States National Archives, Washington, D.C.
M-Ar	Archives Division, Secretary of State, Boston, Massachusetts
MdHi	Maryland Historical Society, Baltimore, Maryland
MHi	Massachusetts Historical Society, Boston, Massachusetts
MSaE	Essex Institute, Salem, Massachusetts
MWA	American Antiquarian Society, Worcester, Massachusetts
NcD	Duke University, Durham, North Carolina
NHi	New York Historical Society, New York, New York
NjR	Rutgers—The State University, New Brunswick, New Jersey
OHi	Ohio State Historical Society, Columbus, Ohio
PCC	Papers of the Continental Congress, RG 360, United States National Archives, Washington, D.C.
.PHi	Historical Society of Pennsylvania, Philadelphia, Pennsylvania
RBkRm	Rare Book Room, Library of Congress, Washington, D.C.
RPJCB	John Carter Brown Library, Providence, Rhode Island
RG	Record Group, located in the United States National Archives, Washington, D.C.
	11 General Records of the United States Government
	46 Records of the United States Senate—SR
	59 General Records of the Department of State
	128 Records of Joint Committees of Congress
	217 Records of the United States Government Accounting Office
	233 Records of the United States House of Representatives—HR
	360 Records of the Continental Congress and the Constitutional Convention—PCC
RNHi	Newport Historical Society, Newport, Rhode Island
SR	Senate Records, RG 46, United States National Archives, Washington, D.C.
Vi	Virginia State Library, Archives Division, Richmond, Virginia

ACT: (1) A bill that has been passed by one or both houses of Congress. (2) A bill that has been passed by both houses of Congress and signed by the president or passed over his veto.

ADJOURNMENT SINE DIE: An adjournment without setting a time for another meeting; literally "adjournment without a day." Marks the official end of the Congress.

AMENDMENT: (1) A proposal to alter a bill, act, amendment, or resolution after it has been formally introduced. Amendments vary in importance from slight word changes to major substantive alterations. To be adopted, an amendment must be agreed to by a majority of the members voting. (2) A change in the Constitution. Such an amendment is usually proposed in the form of a joint resolution of Congress, which may originate in either house. If passed, it does not go to the president for his approval but is submitted directly to the states for ratification.

AYES AND NAYS (YEAS AND NAYS): The record of the vote on a matter by the members of the House or Senate. Article I, Section 5 of the Constitution provides that "the Yeas and Nays of the Members of either House on any question shall, at the Desire of one-fifth of those Present, be entered on the Journal."

BILL: A proposal of specific legislation presented to Congress for enactment into law. Bills may originate in either house; two exceptions, however, are those for raising revenue, which, according to the Constitution, must originate in the House of Representatives, and those for appropriating money, which customarily originate in the House. The House followed the traditional parliamentary practice that all bills must be read three times before passage. In the rules of the House for the First Congress, adopted on April 7, 1789, it was specified that "every bill shall receive three several readings in the House previous to its passage; and all bills shall be dispatched in order as they were introduced, unless where the House shall direct otherwise; but no bill shall be twice read on the same day without special order of the House." Before becoming law, a bill must be passed by both houses and approved by the president; if vetoed by the president, it must be passed over his veto by two-thirds of each house. During the First Congress, bills were not introduced by individual members. A rule of the House of the First Congress provided that "every bill shall be introduced by motion for leave, or by an order of the House on the report of a committee, and in either case a committee to prepare the same shall be appointed. In cases of a general nature one day's notice at least shall be given of the motion to bring in a bill; and every such motion may be committed."

Engrossed bill: The final copy of a bill that has passed the house of origin and is sent to the other house for further action. Such a bill bears the certification of the clerk of the House of Representatives or of the secretary of the Senate. The engrossed copy of a bill that has passed both houses, together with its engrossed amendments, is the official working copy from which an enrolled bill is prepared.

Enrolled bill: The final copy of an engrossed bill that has passed both houses and that embodies all amendments. Such a bill is on parchment and is signed by the Speaker of the House and by the president of the Senate. It bears the attestation of an officer of the house of origin, that is, the clerk of the House of Representatives or the secretary of the Senate. This final copy is then presented to the president for approval or disapproval. No bills of the First Congress were vetoed by George Washington.

CLERK OF THE HOUSE: The chief administrative officer of the House of Representatives, elected by a ballot of its members. John Beckley held this position during the First Congress.

COMMITTEE: A body of members, limited in number, that is selected under House rules or by resolution to consider some matter of business and to report thereon to the House for further action. With few exceptions, committees of the First Congress were select committees (ad hoc); when their purpose had been accomplished, they ceased to exist. In addition, the House had standing committees, which were permanently established. The committee on elections and the committee on enrolled bills were standing committees in the First Congress.

Committee of elections: The first standing committee of the House of Representatives elected by ballot of members on April 13, 1789. The committee consisted of seven members whose duty it was "to examine and report upon the certificates of election, or other credentials of the members returned to serve in this House, and to take into their consideration all such matters as shall or may come in question, and be referred to them by the House, touching returns and elections, and to report their proceedings with their opinion thereupon to the House."

Committee of the whole: A committee that is formed by the House resolving itself into a committee. At this time the speaker leaves the chair and is supplanted by another member as chairman of the committee. Any legislation favorably acted on by the committee of the whole must be reported to the House by the chairman of the committee for further action. The committee of the whole was a device to facilitate and speed the work of the House.

There were two committees of the whole: a committee of the whole House and a committee of the whole House on the state of the union.

Conference committee: A committee whose members are designated by order or resolve and whose purpose is to consider the points of conflict between the two houses on a specific bill or joint resolution in an attempt to reach an agreement. The members are referred to as "managers." Bills and resolutions that are passed by the House and the Senate with slightly different provisions need not be sent to conference; either body may agree to the other's amendments. Few bills of the First Congress went to conference.

Joint committee: A committee consisting of members of both houses and having jurisdiction over matters of common interest. Most of the joint committees of the First Congress were ad hoc; when their purpose had been accomplished, they ceased to exist.

Joint committee for enrolled bills: A committee composed of two members of the House of Representatives and one member of the Senate and charged with examining enrolled bills to assure their accuracy, with reporting thereon to both houses, with presenting the truly enrolled bill to the president, and with notifying both houses of such presentation. This standing committee dates from July 31, 1789.

CONGRESS: (1) The national legislature as a whole, including both the House and the Senate. (2) The united body of Senators and Representatives for any term of two years for which the whole body is chosen. A Congress lasts for a period of two years and is divided into sessions.

CONTINGENT FUND: A sum appropriated for miscellaneous expenses, to be drawn on for lawful contingencies.

CREDENTIALS OF REPRESENTATIVES: Certificates of election of members of the House. Properly executed certificates are prima facie evidence of the lawful election of members that entitles them to their respective seats. Article I, Section 5 of the Constitution states that "each House shall be the Judge of the Elections, Returns and Qualifications of its own Members."

JOURNAL: The official record of the proceedings of the House. Article I, Section 5 of the Constitution provides that "each House shall keep a Journal of its Proceedings, and from time to time publish the same, excepting such Parts as may in their Judgment require Secrecy." The Journal does not report speeches and debates.

LIE FOR CONSIDERATION: Action of postponing the consideration of a subject to a later date. In the case of petitions and memorials, such action often resulted in the adverse disposition of the document.

MEMORIAL: A document in the form of a petition, but differing from a petition insofar as it usually opposes a contemplated or proposed action and carries no prayer (plea). Some petitions, especially those from state legislatures, are termed "memorials."

MOTION: A proposal made to Congress for its approval or disapproval.

ORDER: A directive of the House.

ORDERS OF THE DAY: Agreement to take up certain matters on given days.

PASSED IN THE AFFIRMATIVE: Agreed to.

PASSED IN THE NEGATIVE: Disagreed to.

PETITION: A written request for action addressed to either house of Congress and containing a prayer that the action be taken. *See also* Memorial.

PRESIDENT PRO TEMPORE: The presiding officer of the Senate when the vice president is absent. John Langdon held this position during the First Congress.

PREVIOUS QUESTION: The principle of previous question was inherited from the Parliament of England where it was used as a device for removing a question from consideration.

An amended rule adopted by the Continental Congress in 1784 stated: "The previous question (which is always to be understood in this sense, that the main question be *not* now put) shall only be admitted when in the judgement of two Members, at least, the subject moved is in its nature, or from the circumstances of time or place, improper to be debated or decided, and shall therefore preclude all amendments and further debates on the subject until it is decided." (See Continental Congress Journal, July 8, 1784.) The House retained this form of the previous question except that it omitted the word *not* and thus reversed the formula. The rules of the House read: "The previous question shall be in this form: 'Shall the main question be now put?' It shall only be admitted when demanded by five members; and until it is decided shall preclude all amendment and further debate of the main question."

In the House previous question was employed to stop debate on a certain line of discussion but not necessarily on the entire bill. It was used infrequently and inconsistently.

QUORUM: A majority of the membership of the House. Article I, Section 5 of the Constitution provides that "a Majority of each [House] shall constitute a Quorum to do Business."

RECOMMIT: To return business to a committee.

RESOLUTION: Although not formally designated as such, resolutions of the First Congress fell into three categories: (1) concurrent, (2) joint, and (3) simple.

Concurrent resolution: A resolution that indicates joint action and requires the concurrence of both houses. It contains no legislation, its authority does not extend beyond Congress, and does not require presidential approval. For example, in the First Congress, this type of resolution was used (1) to establish certain joint rules between the two houses, (2) to furnish members with copies of the Journals of the Continental Congress, and (3) for the appointment of chaplains, etc.

Joint resolution: A form of proposed legislation similar to a bill but usually serving a limited purpose or being temporary in effect. A joint resolution (except a joint resolution proposing an amendment to the Constitution) requires the signature of the president or passage over his veto before it becomes law. For example, in the First Congress joint resolutions were used to direct the secretary of state to procure the statutes of the several states and to complete a survey ordered by the Continental Congress. For the most part, joint resolutions did not embrace comprehensive laws.

Simple resolution: A resolution whose authority extends only to the house in which it originates. It does not contain legislation and does not require concurrence of the other house, or presidential approval. In the First Congress, such resolutions were used to express the sentiments of the House, to establish rules of procedure, to secure information from executive departments, etc.

SECRETARY OF THE SENATE: The chief administrative officer of the Senate, elected by a ballot of its members. Samuel Otis held this position during the First Congress.

SESSION: A meeting of the Congress that continues from day to day until adjournment to a specified day or to adjournment *sine die.* The Constitution provides that "the Congress shall assemble at least once in every Year." The First Congress had three sessions: March 4, 1789–September 29, 1789; January 4, 1790–August 12, 1790; and December 6, 1790–March 3, 1791.

SPEAKER: The presiding officer of the House of Representatives, elected by a ballot of its members. During the First Congress, this position was held by Frederick Augustus Muhlenberg.

TABLE: In the First Congress, the House followed general parliamentary law and used the motion "to lay on the table" as a means to put aside a matter temporarily; the issue could later be considered at any time, if the House desired.

Ames, Fisher	Massachusetts
Ashe, John Baptista	North Carolina
Baldwin, Abraham	Georgia
Benson, Egbert	New York
Bland, Theodorick	Virginia
(Died June 1, 1790)	
Bloodworth, Timothy	North Carolina
Boudinot, Elias	New Jersey
Bourn, Benjamin	Rhode Island
Brown, John	Virginia
Burke, Aedanus	South Carolina
Cadwalader, Lambert	New Jersey
Carroll, Daniel	Maryland
Clymer, George	Pennsylvania
Coles, Isaac	Virginia
Contee, Benjamin	Maryland
Fitzsimons, Thomas	Pennsylvania
Floyd, William	New York
Foster, Abiel	New Hampshire
Gale, George	Maryland
Gerry, Elbridge	Massachusetts
Giles, William B.	Virginia
(Took his seat on December 7, 1790, after being elected to fill the vacancy caused by the death of Theodorick Bland)	
Gilman, Nicholas	New Hampshire
Goodhue, Benjamin	Massachusetts
Griffin, Samuel	Virginia
Grout, Jonathan	Massachusetts
Hartley, Thomas	Pennsylvania
Hathorn, John	New York
Hiester, Daniel Jr.	Pennsylvania
Huger, Daniel	South Carolina
Huntington, Benjamin	Connecticut
Jackson, James	Georgia
Laurance, John	New York
Lee, Richard Bland	Virginia
Leonard, George	Massachusetts
Livermore, Samuel	New Hampshire

Madison, James Jr.	Virginia
Mathews, George	Georgia
Moore, Andrew	Virginia
Muhlenberg, Frederick A.	Pennsylvania
Muhlenberg, Peter	Pennsylvania
Page, John	Virginia
Parker, Josiah	Virginia
Partridge, George	Massachusetts
Schureman, James	New Jersey
Scott, Thomas	Pennsylvania
Sedgwick, Theodore	Massachusetts
Seney, Joshua	Maryland
Sevier, John	North Carolina
Sherman, Roger	Connecticut
Silvester, Peter	New York
Sinnickson, Thomas	New Jersey
Smith, William	Maryland
Smith, William	South Carolina
Steele, John	North Carolina
Stone, Michael Jenifer	Maryland
Sturges, Jonathan	Connecticut
Sumter, Thomas	South Carolina
Thatcher, George	Massachusetts
Trumbull, Jonathan	Connecticut
Tucker, Thomas Tudor	South Carolina
Van Rensselaer, Jeremiah	New York
Vining, John	Delaware
Wadsworth, Jeremiah	Connecticut
White, Alexander	Virginia
Williamson, Hugh	North Carolina
Wynkoop, Henry	Pennsylvania

First Session: March 4, 1789–September 29, 1789

April 8–May 18	John Page
May 19–July 10	Jonathan Trumbull
July 13–August 13	Elias Boudinot
August 14	Jonathan Trumbull
August 15–September 24	Elias Boudinot

Second Session: January 4, 1790–August 12, 1790

January 9–February 22	Abraham Baldwin
February 23–March 22	Egbert Benson
March 26	Elias Boudinot
March 30–April 28	Samuel Livermore
April 29–May 2	Joshua Seney
May 4–May 10	Samuel Livermore
May 11–May 13	Joshua Seney
May 14	Elias Boudinot
May 18–June 4	Joshua Seney
June 8–June 9	Elias Boudinot
June 11–June 14	Joshua Seney
June 14–June 16	Elias Boudinot
June 21	Joshua Seney
June 22–June 24	Elias Boudinot
June 25	Joshua Seney
June 28–July 15	Elias Boudinot
July 19	Joshua Seney
July 20	Elias Boudinot
July 28–August 3	Joshua Seney
August 4–August 5	Samuel Livermore
August 7	Joshua Seney
August 9	Samuel Livermore

Third Session: December 6, 1790–March 3, 1791

December 9–December 27	Samuel Livermore
December 28–March 2	Elias Boudinot
March 2	Samuel Livermore

J O U R N A L

OF THE

HOUSE OF REPRESENTATIVES

OF THE

UNITED STATES

TO WIT:

NEW-HAMPSHIRE	DELAWARE
MASSACHUSETTS	MARYLAND
CONNECTICUT	VIRGINIA
NEW-YORK	SOUTH-CAROLINA
NEW-JERSEY	and
PENNSYLVANIA	GEORGIA

Being the eleven States that have respectively ratified the Constitution of Government for the United States, proposed by the Federal Convention, held in Philadelphia, on the 17th of September, 1787.

CONGRESS of the United States, begun and held at the city of New-York, on Wednesday the fourth of March, one thousand seven hundred and eighty-nine, pursuant to a resolution of the late Congress, made in conformity to the resolutions of the Federal Convention of the 17th of September, 1787; being the first session of the Congress, held under the Constitution aforesaid. On which day, the following members of the House of Representatives appeared and took their seats, to wit:

From Massachusetts
- George Thatcher
- Fisher Ames
- George Leonard and
- Elbridge Gerry

From Connecticut
- Benjamin Huntington
- Jonathan Trumbull and
- Jeremiah Wadsworth

From Pennsylvania
- Frederick Augustus Muhlenberg
- Thomas Hartley
- Peter Muhlenberg and
- Daniel Hiester

From Virginia
- Alexander White

From South-Carolina
- Thomas Tudor Tucker

But a quorum of the whole number not being present, the House adjourned until to-morrow morning eleven o'clock.

THURSDAY, MARCH 5, 1789

The House met according to adjournment.

Several other members, to wit, from New-Hampshire, Nicholas Gilman; from Massachusetts, Benjamin Goodhue; from Connecticut, Roger Sherman, and Jonathan Sturges; and from Pennsylvania, Henry Wynkoop, appeared and took their seats.

But a quorum of the whole number not being present,

The House adjourned until to-morrow morning eleven o'clock.

FRIDAY, MARCH 6, 1789

The House met according to adjournment.

But a quorum of the whole number not being present,

The House adjourned until to-morrow morning eleven o'clock.

SATURDAY, MARCH 7, 1789

The House met according to adjournment.
But a quorum of the whole number not being present,
The House adjourned until Monday morning eleven o'clock.

MONDAY, MARCH 9, 1789

The House met according to adjournment.
But a quorum of the whole number not being present,
The House adjourned until to-morrow morning eleven o'clock.

TUESDAY, MARCH 10, 1789

The House met according to adjournment.
But a quorum of the whole number not being present,
The House adjourned until to-morrow morning eleven o'clock.

WEDNESDAY, MARCH 11, 1789

The House met according to adjournment.
But a quorum of the whole number not being present,
The House adjourned until to-morrow morning eleven o'clock.

THURSDAY, MARCH 12, 1789

The House met according to adjournment.
But a quorum of the whole number not being present,
The House adjourned until to-morrow morning eleven o'clock.

FRIDAY, MARCH 13, 1789

The House met according to adjournment.
But a quorum of the whole number not being present,
The House adjourned until to-morrow morning eleven o'clock.

SATURDAY, MARCH 14, 1789

The House met according to adjournment.
Several other members, to wit, James Madison, junior, John Page, and Richard Bland Lee, from Virginia, appeared and took their seats:
But a quorum of the whole number not being present,
The House adjourned until Monday morning eleven o'clock.

MONDAY, March 16, 1789

The House met according to adjournment.
But a quorum of the whole number not being present,
The House adjourned until to-morrow morning eleven o'clock.

TUESDAY, March 17, 1789

The House met according to adjournment.
Another member, to wit, Samuel Griffin, from Virginia, appeared and took his seat.
But a quorum of the whole number not being present,
The House adjourned until to-morrow morning eleven o'clock.

WEDNESDAY, March 18, 1789

The House met according to adjournment.
Another member, to wit, Andrew Moore, from Virginia, appeared and took his seat.
But a quorum of the whole number not being present,
The House adjourned until to-morrow morning eleven o'clock.

THURSDAY, March 19, 1789

The House met according to adjournment.
But a quorum of the whole number not being present,
The House adjourned until to-morrow morning eleven o'clock.

FRIDAY, March 20, 1789

The House met according to adjournment.
But a quorum of the whole number not being present,
The House adjourned until to-morrow morning eleven o'clock.

SATURDAY, March 21, 1789

The House met according to adjournment.
But a quorum of the whole number not being present,
The House adjourned until Monday morning eleven o'clock.

MONDAY, March 23, 1789

The House met according to adjournment.
Two other members, to wit, Elias Boudinot, from New-Jersey, and William Smith, from Maryland, appeared and took their seats.
But a quorum of the whole number not being present,
The House adjourned until to-morrow morning eleven o'clock.

TUESDAY, March 24, 1789

The House met according to adjournment.
But a quorum of the whole number not being present,
The House adjourned until to-morrow morning eleven o'clock.

WEDNESDAY, March 25, 1789

The House met according to adjournment.
Another member, to wit, Josiah Parker, from Virginia, appeared and took his seat.
But a quorum of the whole number not being present,
The House adjourned until to-morrow morning eleven o'clock.

THURSDAY, March 26, 1789

The House met according to adjournment.
But a quorum of the whole number not being present,
The House adjourned until to-morrow morning eleven o'clock.

FRIDAY, March 27, 1789

The House met according to adjournment.
But a quorum of the whole number not being present,
The House adjourned until to-morrow morning eleven o'clock.

SATURDAY, March 28, 1789

The House met according to adjournment.
But a quorum of the whole number not being present,
The House adjourned until Monday morning eleven o'clock.

MONDAY, March 30, 1789

The House met according to adjournment.
Two other members, to wit, George Gale, from Maryland, and Theodorick Bland, from Virginia, appeared and took their seats.
But a quorum of the whole number not being present,
The House adjourned until to-morrow morning eleven o'clock.

TUESDAY, March 31, 1789

The House met according to adjournment.
But a quorum of the whole number not being present,
The House adjourned until to-morrow morning eleven o'clock.

WEDNESDAY, APRIL 1, 1789

The House met according to adjournment.

Two other members, to wit, James Schureman, from New-Jersey, and Thomas Scott, from Pennsylvania, appeared and took their seats.

And a quorum, consisting of a majority of the whole number, being present,

RESOLVED, That this House will proceed to the choice of a Speaker by ballot.

The House accordingly proceeded to ballot for a Speaker, and upon examining the ballots, a majority of the votes of the whole House was found in favor of FREDERICK AUGUSTUS MUHLENBERG, one of the representatives for the state of Pennsylvania.

Whereupon the said Frederick Augustus Muhlenberg was conducted to the chair, from whence he made his acknowledgements to the House for so distinguished an honor.

The House then proceeded in the same manner to the appointment of a Clerk, and upon examining the ballots, a majority of the votes of the whole House was found in favor of MR. JOHN BECKLEY.

On motion,

ORDERED, That the members of this House do severally deliver in their credentials at the Clerk's table.

And then the House adjourned until to-morrow morning eleven o'clock.

THURSDAY, APRIL 2, 1789

Another member, to wit, Lambert Cadwalader, from New-Jersey, appeared and took his seat.

On motion,

ORDERED, That a committee be appointed to prepare and report such standing rules and orders of proceeding as may be proper to be observed in this House:

And a committee was appointed of Mr. Gilman, Mr. Gerry, Mr. Wadsworth, Mr. Boudinot, Mr. Hartley, Mr. Smith, Mr. Lee, Mr. Tucker, Mr. Madison, Mr. Sherman, and Mr. Goodhue.

On motion,

RESOLVED, That a door-keeper and an assistant door-keeper be appointed for the service of this House.

On motion,

ORDERED, That it be an instruction to the committee appointed to prepare and report such standing rules and orders of proceeding as may be proper to be observed in this House, that they also report the duty and services of a serjeant at arms, or other proper officer for enforcing the orders of the House.[1]

And then the House adjourned until to-morrow twelve o'clock.

FRIDAY, APRIL 3, 1789

Another member, to wit, George Clymer, from Pennsylvania, appeared and took his seat.

And then the House adjourned until to-morrow twelve o'clock.

SATURDAY, APRIL 4, 1789

Another member, to wit, George Partridge, from Massachusetts, appeared and took his seat.

On motion,

The House proceeded by ballot to the appointment of a door-keeper, and upon examining the ballots, a majority of the votes of the whole House was found in favor of GIFFORD DALLEY.

ORDERED, That the said Gifford Dalley do give his attendance accordingly.

The House then proceeded in the same manner to the appointment of an assistant door-keeper, and upon examining the ballots, a majority of the votes of the whole House was found in favor of THOMAS CLAXTON.[2]

ORDERED, That the said Thomas Claxton do give his attendance accordingly.

And then the House adjourned until Monday morning eleven o'clock.

MONDAY, APRIL 6, 1789

Another member, to wit, Daniel Carroll, from Maryland, appeared and took his seat.

On motion,

---

[1] On April 7 this committee reported, and the report was printed and agreed to.

[2] Presumably Claxton, Dalley, and others requested jobs, although there is no record in the Journal of their petitions being received by the House. Petitions from (1) Thomas Claxton, for the position of messenger; (2) Abraham Mitchell, for any office; (3) David Elliot, for the position of doorkeeper or messenger; and (4) Abraham Okie, for the position of messenger are in Petitions and Memorials: Applications for jobs, RG 46, Records of the United States Senate (hereinafter, RG 46 will be referred to as SR), DNA.

ORDERED, That leave be given to bring in a bill to regulate the taking the oath or affirmation prescribed by the sixth article of the Constitution; and that Mr. White, Mr. Madison, Mr. Trumbull, Mr. Gilman, and Mr. Cadwalader, do prepare and bring in the same.[3]

On motion,

RESOLVED, That the form of the oath to be taken by the members of this House, as required by the third clause of the sixth article of the Constitution of government of the United States, be as followeth, to wit, "I, A. B. a Representative of the United States in the Congress thereof, do solemnly swear (or affirm, as the case may be) in the presence of Almighty GOD, that I will support the Constitution of the United States—so help me GOD."

A message from the Senate by Mr. Ellsworth:

MR. SPEAKER, I am charged by the Senate to inform this House that a quorum of the Senate is now formed; that a President is elected for the sole purpose of opening the certificates, and counting the votes of the Electors of the several States in the choice of a President and Vice-President of the United States; and that the Senate is now ready in the senate-chamber, to proceed in presence of this House, to discharge that duty: I have it also in further charge, to inform this House that the Senate has appointed one of its members to sit at the Clerk's table to make a list of the votes as they shall be declared, submitting it to the wisdom of this House to appoint one or more of its members for the like purpose.   And then he withdrew.

On motion,

RESOLVED, That Mr. Speaker, attended by the House, do now withdraw to the senate-chamber, for the purpose expressed in the message from the Senate, and that Mr. Parker and Mr. Hiester be appointed on the part of this House to sit at the Clerk's table with the member of the Senate, and make a list of the votes as the same shall be declared.

Mr. Speaker accordingly left the chair, and attended by the House, withdrew to the senate-chamber, and after some time returned to the House.

Mr. Speaker resumed the chair.

Mr. Parker and Mr. Hiester then delivered in at the Clerk's table a list of the votes of the Electors of the several States in the choice of a President and Vice-President of the United States, as the same were declared by the President of the Senate, in the presence of the Senate and of this House, which was ordered to be entered on the journal, and is as followeth:

---

[3] On April 14 this committee presented the Oath Bill [HR–1], which was read.

	George Washington	John Adams	Samuel Huntington	John Jay	John Hancock	Robert H. Harrison	George Clinton	John Rutledge	John Milton	James Armstrong	Edward Telfair	Benjamin Lincoln
New-Hampshire	5	5	–	–	–	–	–	–	–	–	–	–
Massachusetts	10	10	–	–	–	–	–	–	–	–	–	–
Connecticut	7	5	2	–	–	–	–	–	–	–	–	–
New-Jersey	6	1	–	5	–	–	–	–	–	–	–	–
Pennsylvania	10	8	–	–	2	–	–	–	–	–	–	–
Delaware	3	–	–	3	–	–	–	–	–	–	–	–
Maryland	6	–	–	–	–	6	–	–	–	–	–	–
Virginia	10	5	–	1	1	–	3	–	–	–	–	–
South-Carolina	7	–	–	–	1	–	–	6	–	–	–	–
Georgia	5	–	–	–	–	–	–	–	2	1	1	1
	69	34	2	9	4	6	3	6	2	1	1	1[4]

RECAPITULATION of the VOTES of the ELECTORS

His Excellency George Washington – –	69 Votes
The Honorable John Adams – – –	34
The Honorable John Jay – – – –	9
Robert H. Harrison, Esquire – – –	6
John Rutledge, Esquire – – – –	6
John Hancock, Esquire – – – –	4
George Clinton, Esquire – – – –	3
Samuel Huntington, Esquire – – –	2
John Milton, Esquire – – – – –	2
James Armstrong, Esquire – – – –	1
Edward Telfair, Esquire – – – –	1
Benjamin Lincoln, Esquire – – – –	1

On motion,

ORDERED, That a message be sent to the Senate, to inform them that it is the desire of this House that the notifications of the election of the President and Vice-President of the United States, should be made by such persons and

---

[4] The votes with related documents are in Election Records: Electoral votes, SR, DNA.

in such manner as the Senate shall be pleased to direct; and that Mr. Madison do communicate the said message.[5]

And then the House adjourned until to-morrow twelve o'clock.

TUESDAY, April 7, 1789

The Speaker laid before the House a letter from the Mayor of the city of New-York, covering certain resolutions of the Mayor, Aldermen and, Commonalty of the said city, appropriating the City-Hall for the accommodation of the General Government of the United States—which were read and ordered to lie on the table.[6]

Mr. Boudinot reported from the committee appointed to prepare such rules and orders of proceeding as may be proper to be observed in this House, that the committee had according to order prepared the same, and agreed to a report thereupon,[7] which he delivered in at the Clerk's table, where the same was read, and on a question put thereupon, agreed to by the House as followeth:

The committee to whom it was referred to prepare such standing rules and orders of proceeding as may be proper to be observed in this House, have according to order prepared the same, and agreed to the following report:

RESOLVED, That it is the opinion of this committee, that the rules and orders following, are proper to be established as the standing rules and orders of this House, to wit:

FIRST. Touching the DUTY of the SPEAKER

HE shall take the chair every day at the hour to which the House shall have adjourned on the preceding day; shall immediately call the members to order, and, on the appearance of a quorum, shall cause the journal of the preceding day to be read.

He shall preserve decorum and order; may speak to points of order in preference to other members, rising from his seat for that purpose, and shall decide questions of order, subject to an appeal to the House by any two members.

---

[5] The message is in Papers Pertaining to the Notification of the President and Vice President of Their Election, SR, DNA.

[6] The letter, addressed to the Senate, and the resolutions are in Reports and Communications, SR, DNA. A draft of the letter to the House is in the James Duane Papers, NHi. On May 9 the House was notified that the Senate had appointed a committee on the use of City Hall.

[7] A copy of the report is in A Record of the Reports of Select Committees, RG 233, Records of the United States House of Representatives (hereinafter RG 233 will be referred to as HR), DNA. E–45669.

He shall rise to put a question, but may state it sitting.

Questions shall be distinctly put in this form, viz. "As many as are of opinion that (as the question may be) say Aye:" And, after the affirmative voice is expressed—"As many as are of a contrary opinion, say No."

If the Speaker doubts, or a division be called for, the House shall divide; those in the affirmative going to the right, and those in the negative to the left of the chair: If the Speaker still doubt, or a count be required, the Speaker shall name two members, one from each side, to tell the numbers in the affirmative, which being reported, he shall then name two others, one from each side, to tell those in the negative; which being also reported, he shall rise and state the decision to the House.

The Speaker shall appoint committees; unless it be determined by the House that the committee shall consist of more than three members, in which case the appointment shall be by ballot of the House.

In all cases of ballot by the House, the Speaker shall vote; in other cases he shall not vote, unless the House be equally divided, or unless his vote, if given to the minority, will make the division equal, and in case of such equal division, the question shall be lost.

When the House adjourns, the members shall keep their seats until the Speaker go forth; and then the members shall follow.

SECONDLY. Of DECORUM and DEBATE

When any member is about to speak in debate, or deliver any matter to the House, he shall rise from his seat and respectfully address himself to Mr. Speaker.

If any member, in speaking or otherwise, transgress the rules of the House, the Speaker shall, or any member may call to order; in which case the member called to order shall immediately sit down, unless permitted to explain, and the House shall, if appealed to, decide on the case, but without debate: If there be no appeal, the decision of the chair shall be submitted to: If the decision be in favor of the member called to order, he shall be at liberty to proceed; if otherwise, and the case require it, he shall be liable to the censure of the House.

When two or more members happen to rise at once, the Speaker shall name the member who is first to speak.

No member shall speak more than twice to the same question without leave of the House; nor more than once until every member choosing to speak, shall have spoken.

Whilst the Speaker is putting any question, or addressing the House, none shall walk out of, or across the house; nor either in such case, or when a member is speaking, shall entertain private discourse, or read any printed book or paper; nor whilst a member is speaking, shall pass between him and the chair.

No member shall vote on any question, in the event of which he is immediately and particularly interested; or in any other case where he was not present when the question was put.

Every member who shall be in the House when a question is put, shall vote on the one side or the other, unless the House, for special reasons, shall excuse him.

When a motion is made and seconded, it shall be stated by the Speaker, or being in writing, it shall be handed to the chair, and read aloud by the clerk before debated.

Every motion shall be reduced to writing, if the Speaker or any member desire it.

After a motion is stated by the Speaker, or read by the clerk, it shall be deemed to be in possession of the House, but may be withdrawn at any time before decision or amendment.

When a question is under debate, no motion shall be received, unless to amend it, to commit it, for the previous question, or to adjourn.

A motion to adjourn shall be always in order, and shall be decided without debate.

The previous question shall be in this form: "Shall the main question be now put?" It shall only be admitted when demanded by five members; and until it is decided shall preclude all amendment and further debate of the main question.

On a previous question no member shall speak more than once without leave.

Any member may call for the division of a question, where the sense will admit of it.

A motion for commitment until it is decided, shall preclude all amendment of the main question.

Motions and reports may be committed at the pleasure of the House.

No new motion or proposition shall be admitted under colour of amendment, as a substitute for the motion or proposition under debate.

Committees consisting of more than three members shall be balloted for by the House; if upon such ballot the number required shall not be elected by a majority of the votes given, the House shall proceed to a second ballot, in which a plurality of votes shall prevail; and in case a greater number than are required to compose or complete the committee shall have an equal number of votes, the House shall proceed to a further ballot or ballots.

In all other cases of ballot than for committees, a majority of the votes given shall be necessary to an election; and where there shall not be such majority on the first ballot, the ballot shall be repeated until a majority be obtained.

In all cases where others than members of the House may be eligible, there shall be a previous nomination.

If a question depending be lost by adjournment of the House, and revived on the succeeding day, no member who has spoken twice on the day preceding shall be permitted again to speak without leave.

Every order, resolution or vote to which the concurrence of the Senate shall be necessary, shall be read to the House, and laid on the table, on a day preceding that in which the same shall be moved, unless the House shall otherwise expressly allow.

Petitions, memorials, and other papers addressed to the House, shall be presented through the Speaker, or by a member in his place, and shall not be debated or decided on the day of their being first read, unless where the House shall direct otherwise; but shall lie on the table to be taken up in the order they were read.

Any fifteen members (including the Speaker if there is one) shall be authorised to compel the attendance of absent members.

Upon calls of the House, or in taking the ayes and noes on any question, the names of the members shall be called alphabetically.

THIRDLY. Of BILLS

Every bill shall be introduced by motion for leave, or by an order of the House on the report of a committee, and in either case a committee to prepare the same shall be appointed. In cases of a general nature one day's notice at least shall be given of the motion to bring in a bill; and every such motion may be committed.

Every bill shall receive three several readings in the House previous to its passage; and all bills shall be dispatched in order as they were introduced, unless where the House shall direct otherwise; but no bill shall be twice read on the same day without special order of the House.

The first reading of a bill shall be for information, and if opposition be made to it, the question shall be, "Shall the bill be rejected?" If no opposition be made, or the question to reject be negatived, the bill shall go to its second reading without a question.

Upon the second reading of a bill, the Speaker shall state it as ready for commitment or engrossment, and if committed, then a question shall be whether to a select committee, or to a committee of the whole House; if to a committee of the whole House, the House shall determine on what day. But if the bill be ordered to be engrossed, the House shall appoint the day when it shall be read the third time. After commitment, and a report thereof to the House, a bill may be re-committed, or at any time before its passage.

All bills ordered to be engrossed shall be executed in a fair round hand.

The enacting stile of bills shall be, "Be it enacted by the Senators and Representatives of the United States in Congress assembled."

When a bill shall pass, it shall be certified by the clerk, noting the day of its passing at the foot thereof.

No bill amended by the Senate shall be committed.

FOURTHLY. Of COMMITTEES of the WHOLE HOUSE

It shall be a standing order of the day, throughout the session, for the House to resolve itself into a committee of the whole House on the state of the Union.

In forming a committee of the whole House, the Speaker shall leave his chair, and a chairman to preside in committee shall be appointed.

Upon bills committed to a committee of the whole House, the bill shall be first read throughout by the clerk, and then again read and debated by clauses, leaving the preamble to be last considered; the body of the bill shall not be defaced or interlined; but all amendments, noting the page and line, shall be duly entered by the clerk on a separate paper as the same shall be agreed to by the committee, and so reported to the House. After report the bill shall again be subject to be debated and amended by clauses before a question to engross it be taken.

All amendments made to an original motion in committee shall be incorporated with the motion, and so reported.

All amendments made to a report committed to a committee of the whole shall be noted and reported as in the case of bills.

All questions, whether in committee or in the House, shall be propounded in the order they were moved, except that in filling up blanks the largest sum and longest day shall be first put.

The rules of proceeding in the House shall be observed in committee so far as they may be applicable, except that limiting the times of speaking.[8]

On motion,

ORDERED, That the Chief Justice of the state of New-York be requested to attend this House, at the hour of its meeting to-morrow, for the purpose of administering to the Speaker and other Members of the House, the oath required by the Constitution, in the form agreed to yesterday.

And then the House adjourned until to-morrow morning eleven o'clock.

---

[8] On April 9 the rules committee reported again.

WEDNESDAY, April 8, 1789

Two other members, to wit, John Laurance, from New-York, and Thomas Fitzsimons, from Pennsylvania, appeared and took their seats.

The Chief Justice of the state of New-York, attended agreeably to the order of yesterday, and administered the oath required by the Constitution, in the form agreed to on Monday last, first to Mr. Speaker in his place, and then to the other members of the House present, to wit, Fisher Ames, Elias Boudinot, Theodorick Bland, Lambert Cadwalader, George Clymer, Daniel Carroll, Thomas Fitzsimons, Nicholas Gilman, Benjamin Goodhue, Elbridge Gerry, George Gale, Samuel Griffin, Benjamin Huntington, Thomas Hartley, Daniel Hiester, George Leonard, Richard Bland Lee, John Laurance, Peter Muhlenberg, James Madison, junior, Andrew Moore, George Partridge, John Page, Josiah Parker, Jonathan Sturges, Roger Sherman, James Schureman, William Smith, Thomas Scott, George Thatcher, Thomas Tudor Tucker, Henry Wynkoop, and Alexander White.

On motion,

The House according to the standing order of the day, resolved itself into a committee of the whole House on the state of the Union.

Mr. Speaker left the chair.

Mr. Page took the chair of the committee.

Mr. Speaker resumed the chair, and Mr. Page reported that the committee had, according to order, had the state of the Union under consideration, but had come to no resolution thereupon.[9]

And then the House adjourned until to-morrow morning eleven o'clock.

THURSDAY, April 9, 1789

Two other members, to wit, Egbert Benson, from New-York, and Isaac Coles, from Virginia, appeared and took their seats.

Mr. Boudinot reported from the committee to whom it was referred to prepare such further rules and orders as may be proper to be observed in this House, that the committee had, according to order, prepared the same, and agreed to a report thereupon,[10] which he delivered in at the clerk's table, where the same was read.

On motion,

ORDERED, That the said report do lie on the table.[11]

---

[9] According to the *New York Daily Gazette*, April 9, 1789, the topic discussed on this day was imposts. This subject was considered again on April 9.

[10] A copy of the report is in A Record of the Reports of Select Committees, HR, DNA.

[11] On April 13 this report was printed and considered, and part of it was recommitted.

ORDERED, That Mr. Leonard of Massachusetts have leave to be absent from the service of this House until the first Monday in May next, and Mr. Wynkoop of Pennsylvania, until this day se'nnight.

The Speaker laid before the House a letter from Oliver Ellsworth, Esquire, a member of the Senate, stating the appointment of a committee of that House to confer with a committee to be appointed on the part of this House, in preparing a system of rules to govern the two Houses in cases of conference, and to regulate the appointment of Chaplains, which was read.

On motion,

ORDERED, That a committee of five be now appointed for the purposes expressed in the communication from the member of the Senate.

The members elected Mr. Boudinot, Mr. Sherman, Mr. Tucker, Mr. Madison, and Mr. Bland.[12]

On motion,

The House, according to the standing order of the day, resolved itself into a committee of the whole House on the state of the Union.

Mr. Speaker left the chair.

Mr. Page took the chair of the committee.

Mr. Speaker resumed the chair, and Mr. Page reported that the committee had, according to order, had the state of the Union under consideration, but had come to no resolution thereupon.[13]

And then the House adjourned until to-morrow morning eleven o'clock.

FRIDAY, APRIL 10, 1789

The House met, and adjourned until to-morrow morning eleven o'clock.

SATURDAY, APRIL 11, 1789

A petition of the tradesmen, manufacturers, and others, of the town of Baltimore, in the state of Maryland, whose names are thereunto subscribed, was presented to the House and read, stating certain matters, and praying an imposition of such duties on all foreign articles which can be made in America, as will give a just and decided preference to the labors of the petitioners, and that there may be granted to them in common with the other manufacturers and mechanics of the United States, such relief as in the wisdom of Congress may appear proper.[14]

ORDERED, That the said petition be referred to the committee of the whole House on the state of the Union.

---

[12] On April 15 this committee reported.

[13] According to the *New York Daily Gazette*, April 10, 1789, the topic discussed on this day was imposts. On April 11 this subject was again discussed in the COWH.

[14] The petition is in Petitions and Memorials: Various subjects, HR, DNA.

The House then according to the standing order of the day, resolved itself into a committee of the whole House on the state of the Union.

Mr. Speaker left the chair.

Mr. Page took the chair of the committee.

Mr. Speaker resumed the chair, and Mr. Page reported that the committee had, according to order, had the state of the Union under consideration, and had come to a resolution thereupon, which he read in his place, and afterwards delivered in at the clerk's table, where the same was again twice read, and agreed to by the House, as followeth: [15]

RESOLVED, That it is the opinion of this committee, that an act ought to pass for regulating the collection of imposts and tonnage in the United States.

ORDERED, That a bill or bills be brought in pursuant to the said resolution, and that a committee, to consist of a member from each State present, be appointed to prepare and bring in the same.

The members elected, Mr. Gilman
                    Mr. Gerry
                    Mr. Sherman
                    Mr. Laurance
                    Mr. Cadwalader
                    Mr. Fitzsimons
                    Mr. Gale
                    Mr. Madison and
                    Mr. Tucker.[16]

The Speaker laid before the House a letter from the secretary of the Senate, communicating the appointment of a committee of that House, to confer with any committee to be appointed on the part of this House in making the necessary arrangements to receive the President, which was read and ordered to lie on the table.[17]

And then the House adjourned until Monday morning eleven o'clock.

MONDAY, APRIL 13, 1789

Several other members, to wit, William Floyd, from New-York, Thomas Sinnickson, from New-Jersey, Joshua Seney, from Maryland, and Aedanus Burke, Daniel Huger, and William Smith, from South-Carolina, appeared and took their seats.

On motion,

---

[15] According to the *New York Daily Gazette*, April 13, 1789, the COWH was discussing imposts, as well as the resolution on appointing a committee to prepare a collection bill. On April 14 imposts were considered again.

[16] On May 8 this committee presented a Collection Bill [HR-3], which was read.

[17] On April 13 the House appointed a committee to confer with this Senate committee, and further Senate instructions were referred to the committee.

ORDERED, That Mr. Benson, Mr. Peter Muhlenberg, and Mr. Griffin, be a committee to consider of and report to the House respecting the ceremonial of receiving the President, and that they be authorised to confer with a committee of the Senate for the purpose.

The House proceeded to consider the report from the committee appointed to prepare such further rules and orders of proceeding as may be proper to be observed in this House, which lay on the table, and the said report was read and is as followeth:

RESOLVED, That it is the opinion of this committee, that the rules and orders following ought to be established as additional standing rules and orders of this House, to wit:

1. That any member may excuse himself from serving on any committee at the time of his appointment, if he is then a member of two other committees.

2. That no member absent himself from the service of the House unless he have leave, or be sick and unable to attend.

3. Upon a call of the House, for which at least one day's notice shall be requisite, the names of the members shall be called over by the clerk, and the absentees noted, after which the names of the absentees shall be again called over; the doors shall then be shut, and those for whom no excuses, or insufficient excuses are made, may by order of the House be taken into custody.

4. It shall be the office and duty of a serjeant at arms to attend the House during its sitting, to execute the commands of the House from time to time, and all such process issued by authority thereof as shall be directed to him by the Speaker, and either by himself, or special messengers appointed by him, to take and detain in his custody, members or other persons ordered by the House to be taken or committed.

5. A proper symbol of office shall be provided for the serjeant at arms, of such form and device as the Speaker shall direct, which shall be placed on the clerk's table during the sitting of the House, but when the House is in committee, shall be placed under the table; the serjeant at arms shall moreover always bear the said symbol when executing the immediate commands of the House during its sitting, returning the same to the clerk's table when the service is performed.

6. Every member or other person ordered into custody, shall pay to the serjeant at arms   for every arrest, and   for each day's custody and releasement; also   per mile for travelling expences going and returning, unless the payment thereof shall be remitted by the House.

7. A standing committee of elections shall be appointed to consist of seven members; it shall be the duty of the said committee to examine and report upon the certificates of election, or other credentials of the members returned to serve in this House, and to take into their consideration all such matters as

shall, or may come in question and be referred to them by the House, touching returns and elections, and to report their proceedings with their opinion thereupon to the House.

8. The Clerk of the House shall take an oath for the true and faithful discharge of the duties of his office, to the best of his knowledge and abilities.

RESOLVED, That it is the opinion of this committee, that joint rules ought to be established between the two Houses to provide for the mode of communicating messages, of holding and conducting conferences, and all other cases of proceeding requiring previous mutual agreement.

The first resolution being read a second time, and debated by paragraphs, the first, second, third, seventh, and eighth clauses were, on the question put, thereupon agreed to by this House.

The fourth, fifth, and sixth clauses were severally read a second time, and ordered to be re-committed to the same committee.[18]

The second resolution was read a second time, and ordered to lie on the table.[19]

On motion,

The House proceeded to ballot for a standing committee of elections.

The members elected, Mr. Clymer, Mr. Ames, Mr. Benson, Mr. Carroll, Mr. White, Mr. Huntington, and Mr. Gilman.[20]

The Speaker laid before the House a letter from the honorable John Langdon, a member of the Senate, communicating an instruction to a committee of that House, to report if any and what arrangements are necessary for the reception of the Vice-President, which was read.

ORDERED, That the said letter be referred to the committee appointed to consider of and report to the House respecting the ceremonial of receiving the President; and that it be an instruction to the said committee, to report upon the said letter also.[21]

A petition of the shipwrights of the city of Charleston in the state of South-Carolina, was presented to the House and read, stating the distress they are in from the decline of that branch of business, and the present situation of the trade of the United States, and praying that the wisdom and policy of the National Legislature may be directed to such measures in a general regulation of trade, and the establishment of a proper navigation act, as will tend to relieve the particular distresses of the petitioners, and in common with them, those of their fellow shipwrights throughout the United States.[22]

---

[18] On April 14 the committee on House rules reported again, and the report was agreed to.

[19] On May 7 a joint committee on joint rules was appointed.

[20] On April 15 the petition of David Ramsay was referred to this committee.

[21] On April 15 this committee reported, and the report was agreed to.

[22] The petition is in Petitions and Memorials: Various subjects, SR, DNA.

ORDERED, That the said petition be referred to the committee of the whole House, on the state of the Union.

And then the House adjourned until to-morrow morning eleven o'clock.

TUESDAY, APRIL 14, 1789

Mr. White presented according to order a bill to regulate the taking the oath or affirmation prescribed by the sixth article of the Constitution, which was received and read the first time.[23]

Mr. Boudinot reported from the committee to whom was re-committed certain clauses of the report for establishing additional rules and orders of proceeding to be observed in this House, that the committee had according to order re-considered the same, and agreed to a report thereupon, which he delivered in at the clerk's table, where the same was twice read, the blanks therein filled up, and on a question put thereupon, agreed to by the House as followeth:

RESOLVED, That it is the opinion of this committee, that the rules and orders following ought to be established as additional standing rules and orders of this House, to wit:

A serjeant at arms shall be appointed to hold his office during the pleasure of the House, whose duty shall be to attend the House during its sitting, to execute the commands of the House from time to time, and all such process issued by authority thereof as shall be directed to him by the Speaker.

A proper symbol of office shall be provided for the serjeant at arms, of such form and device as the Speaker shall direct, which shall be borne by the serjeant when in the execution of his office.

The fees of the serjeant at arms shall be, for every arrest the sum of two dollars; for each day's custody and releasement one dollar; and for travelling expences, going and returning, one tenth of a dollar per mile.[24]

The House according to the standing order of the day, resolved itself into a committee of the whole House on the state of the Union.

Mr. Speaker left the chair.

Mr. Page took the chair of the committee.

Mr. Speaker resumed the chair, and Mr. Page reported that the committee had, according to order, had the state of the Union under consideration, but had come to no resolution thereupon.[25]

And then the House adjourned until to-morrow morning eleven o'clock.

---

[23] On April 16 this bill was read again.

[24] On April 24 one of the House rules was rescinded.

[25] According to the *New York Daily Gazette*, April 15, 1789, the subject discussed in the COWH was imposts. On April 15 imposts were considered again.

WEDNESDAY, April 15, 1789

A petition of David Ramsay, of the State of South-Carolina, was presented to the House and read, setting forth that he has at a great expence of time and money published a book entitled, "The History of the Revolution of South-Carolina from a British Province to an independent State;" that he has also prepared, and purposes shortly to publish another book under the title of the "History of the American Revolution," and praying that a law may pass for securing to the petitioner, his heirs and assigns for a certain term of years, the sole and exclusive right of vending and disposing of the said books within the United States.[26]

Also a petition of John Churchman, setting forth that by several year's labour, close application, and at great expence, he hath invented several different methods by which the principles of magnetic variation are so explained, that the latitude of a place being given, its longitude may be easily determined; and praying that a law may pass for vesting in the petitioner, his heirs and assigns, an exclusive right of vending of spheres, hemispheres, maps, charts, and tables on his principles of magnetism, throughout the United States, as also that he may receive the patronage of Congress to enable him to perform a voyage to Baffin's Bay, for the purpose of making magnetical experiments to ascertain the causes of the variation of the needle, and how near the longitude may be thereby ascertained.

ORDERED, That the said petitions be referred to a committee of three, and that Mr. Tucker, Mr. White, and Mr. Huntington be of the said committee.[27]

A petition of David Ramsay of the State of South-Carolina, was presented to the House and read, setting forth that Mr. William Smith, a member returned to serve in this House as one of the Representatives for the State of South-Carolina, was, at the time of his election ineligible thereto, and came within the disqualification of the third paragraph of the new Constitution, which declares "that no person shall be a Representative who shall not have been seven years a citizen of the United States;" and praying that those allegations may be enquired into by the House.

ORDERED, That the said petition be referred to the committee of elections, and that the said committee do report a proper mode of investigating and deciding thereupon.[28]

Mr. Boudinot reported from the committee appointed to confer with a committee from the Senate, respecting the mode of conducting conferences, and the appointment of Chaplains, that the committee had according to order

---

[26] The petition is in Petitions and Memorials: Various subjects, SR, DNA.

[27] On April 20 this committee reported, and the report was considered. A committee was appointed to prepare copyright and patent bills.

[28] On April 18 this committee reported on credentials and David Ramsay's petition.

met and conferred with a committee of the Senate thereupon, and had agreed to a report, which he delivered in at the clerk's table, where the same was read and ordered to lie on the table.[29]

Mr. Benson reported from the committee to whom it was referred to consider of and report to the House respecting the ceremonial of receiving the President, and to whom was also referred a letter from the chairman of a committee of the Senate to the Speaker, communicating an instruction from that House to a committee thereof to report, if any and what arrangements are necessary for the reception of the Vice-President, that the committee had according to order considered of the same, and had agreed to a report thereupon,[30] which he delivered in at the clerk's table, where the same was twice read, and on the question put thereupon, agreed to by the House as followeth:

That Mr. Osgood, the proprietor of the house lately occupied by the President of Congress, be requested to put the same and the furniture therein in proper condition for the residence and use of the President of the United States, and otherwise, at the expence of the United States to provide for his temporary accommodation.

That it will be most eligible in the first instance that a committee of three members from the Senate, and five members from the House of Representatives, to be appointed by the Houses respectively, attend to receive the President at such place as he shall embark from New-Jersey for this city, and conduct him without form to the House lately occupied by the President of Congress, and that at such time thereafter as the President shall signify it will be most convenient for him, he be formally received by both Houses.

That a committee of two members from the Senate, and three members from the House of Representatives, to be appointed by the Houses respectively, wait on the Vice-President of the United States as soon as he shall come to this city, and in the name of the Congress of the United States congratulate him on his arrival.[31]

The House then according to the standing order of the day, resolved itself into a committee of the whole House on the state of the Union.

Mr. Speaker left the chair.

Mr. Page took the chair of the committee.

---

[29] The report is in RG 128 (which is included in Senate Records for the First Congress), Records of Joint Committees of Congress (hereinafter RG 128 will be referred to as Joint Committee Reports), SR, DNA. A copy of the report is in A Record of the Reports of Select Committees, HR, DNA. On April 17 this report was printed and agreed to.

[30] A copy of the report is in A Record of the Reports of Select Committees, HR, DNA.

[31] On April 16 committees to greet the president and vice president were appointed. On the same date the Senate appointed committees to wait on the president and vice president.

Mr. Speaker resumed the chair, and Mr. Page reported that the committee had, according to order, had the state of the Union under consideration, but had come to no resolution thereupon.[32]

And then the House adjourned until to-morrow morning eleven o'clock.

THURSDAY, APRIL 16, 1789

A bill to regulate the taking the oath or affirmation prescribed by the sixth article of the Constitution, was read the second time, and ordered to be committed to a committee of the whole House on Monday next.[33]

The House proceeded by ballot to the appointment of a committee of five, to attend with a committee from the Senate, to receive the President of the United States, at such place as he shall embark from New-Jersey for this city.

The members elected, Mr. Boudinot, Mr. Bland, Mr. Tucker, Mr. Benson, and Mr. Laurance.

On motion,

ORDERED, That Mr. Gilman, Mr. Ames, and Mr. Gale, be a committee in conjunction with a committee from the Senate, to wait on the Vice-President of the United States upon his arrival in this city, and to congratulate him thereupon in the name of the Congress of the United States.

The House according to the standing order of the day, resolved itself into a committee of the whole House on the state of the Union.

Mr. Speaker left the chair.

Mr. Page took the chair of the committee.

Mr. Speaker resumed the chair, and Mr. Page reported that the committee had, according to order, had the state of the Union under consideration, but had come to no resolution thereupon.[34]

ORDERED, That Mr. Schureman have leave to be absent from the service of this House until Thursday next.

The Speaker laid before the House a letter from the honorable John Langdon, President pro tempore, of the Senate, communicating the appointment of two committees of that House, agreeably to the report of the committee of both Houses agreed to yesterday, which was read, and ordered to lie on the table.[35]

And then the House adjourned until to-morrow morning eleven o'clock.

---

[32] According to the *New York Daily Gazette*, April 16, 1789, the subject discussed was imposts. On April 16 the COWH considered imposts again.

[33] On April 20 this bill was considered in the COWH.

[34] According to the *New York Daily Gazette*, April 17, 1789, the subject discussed by the COWH was imposts. On April 17 this topic was considered again.

[35] On April 24 the committee to meet the president reported.

FRIDAY, APRIL 17, 1789

Another member, to wit, Benjamin Contee, from Maryland, appeared and took his seat.

The House, according to the standing order of the day, resolved itself into a committee of the whole House on the state of the Union.

Mr. Speaker left the chair.

Mr. Page took the chair of the committee.

Mr. Speaker resumed the chair, and Mr. Page reported that the committee had, according to order, had the state of the Union under consideration, but had come to no resolution thereupon.[36]

The Speaker laid before the House a letter from the honorable John Langdon, President pro tempore of the Senate, communicating two orders of that House, the one for regulating proceedings in cases of conference with this House, and the appointment of Chaplains, and the other appointing a committee to confer with such committee as may be appointed on the part of this House in reporting a mode of communication to be observed between the two Houses with respect to papers, bills and messages, which was read, and

On motion,

ORDERED, That Mr. Lee, Mr. Burke, and Mr. Seney, be a committee to confer with a committee of the Senate, in reporting a proper mode of communicating papers, bills, and messages, between the two Houses.[37]

The House then proceeded to consider the report of the committee appointed to confer with a committee of the Senate, for the purpose of regulating proceedings in cases of conference, and the appointment of Chaplains, which lay on the table, and the same being again read, was, on the question put thereupon, agreed to by the House as followeth:

That in every case of an amendment of a bill agreed to in one House and dissented to in the other, if either House shall request a conference, and appoint a committee for that purpose, and the other House shall also appoint a committee to confer, such committees shall at a convenient hour, to be agreed on by their Chairmen, meet in the conference-chamber, and state to each other, verbally, or in writing, as either shall chuse, the reasons of their respective Houses for and against the amendment, and confer freely thereon.

That two Chaplains, of different denominations, be appointed to Congress for the present session; the Senate to appoint one, and give notice thereof to the House of Representatives, who shall thereupon appoint the other—which

---

[36] According to the *New York Daily Gazette*, April 18, 1789, the topic being discussed was imposts. On April 18 imposts were considered again.

[37] On April 23 this committee reported.

Chaplains shall commence their services in the Houses that appoint them, but shall interchange weekly.[38]

And then the House adjourned until to-morrow morning eleven o'clock.

SATURDAY, APRIL 18, 1789

Mr. White reported from the committee of elections, that the committee had, according to order, examined the certificates and other credentials of the members returned to serve in this House, and had agreed to a report thereupon, which he delivered in at the clerk's table, where the same was twice read, and agreed to by the House as followeth:

It appears to your committee, that the credentials of the following members are sufficient to entitle them to take their seats in this House, to wit:

From New-Hampshire	Nicholas Gilman
From Massachusetts	Fisher Ames Elbridge Gerry Benjamin Goodhue George Leonard George Partridge George Thatcher
From Connecticut	Benjamin Huntington Roger Sherman Jonathan Sturges Jonathan Trumbull Jeremiah Wadsworth
From New-York	Egbert Benson William Floyd John Hathorn John Laurance Jeremiah Van Rensselaer Peter Silvester
From New-Jersey	Elias Boudinot Lambert Cadwalader James Schureman Thomas Sinnickson

---

[38] A copy of the report is in Messages from the House, SR, DNA.

From Pennsylvania	George Clymer Thomas Fitzsimons Thomas Hartley Daniel Hiester Frederick Augustus Muhlenberg, Speaker Peter Muhlenberg Thomas Scott Henry Wynkoop
From Maryland	Daniel Carroll Benjamin Contee George Gale Joshua Seney William Smith Michael Jenifer Stone
From Virginia	Theodorick Bland Isaac Coles Samuel Griffin Richard Bland Lee James Madison, junior Andrew Moore John Page Josiah Parker Alexander White
From South-Carolina	Aedanus Burke Daniel Huger William Smith Thomas Tudor Tucker

A petition of the mechanics and manufacturers of the city of New-York, whose names are thereunto subscribed, was presented to the House and read, setting forth that in the present deplorable state of trade and manufactures, they look with confidence to the operations of the new government for a restoration of both, and that relief which they have so long and anxiously desired; that they have subjoined a list of such articles as can be manufactured in the state of New-York, and humbly pray the countenance and attention of the National Legislature thereto.[39]

ORDERED, That the said petition be referred to the committee of the whole House on the state of the Union.

---

[39] The petition is in Petitions and Memorials: Various subjects, SR, DNA.

Mr. Clymer reported from the committee of elections, to whom it was referred to report a proper mode of investigating and deciding on the petition
of David Ramsay, of South-Carolina, suggesting that William Smith, returned
a member of this House, as elected within that State, was at the time of his
being elected, ineligible; that the committee had agreed to a report thereupon,
which he delivered in at the clerk's table, where the same was read, and ordered to lie on the table.[40]

The House according to the standing order of the day, resolved itself into
a committee of the whole House on the state of the Union.

Mr. Speaker left the chair.

Mr. Page took the chair of the committee.

Mr. Speaker resumed the chair, and Mr. Page reported that the committee
had, according to order, had the state of the Union under consideration, but
had come to no resolution thereupon.[41]

And then the House adjourned until Monday morning eleven o'clock.

MONDAY, APRIL 20, 1789

Two other members, to wit, Abraham Baldwin, and James Jackson, from
Georgia, appeared and took their seats.

Mr. Tucker reported from the committee to whom was referred the petitions of John Churchman and David Ramsay, that the committee had, according to order, had the said petitions under their consideration, and agreed to a
report thereupon,[42] which he delivered in at the clerk's table, where the same
was twice read, and debated by clauses.

The first clause in the words following, to wit, "That the committee have
conferred with Mr. Churchman, and find that he has made many calculations
which tend to establish his position, that there are two magnetic points which
give direction to the needle; that upon this doctrine he has endeavored to
ascertain from a given latitude, and a given variation, what must be the longitude of the place; and having applied his principles to many instances in
Cook's voyages, has found the result to correspond with considerable accuracy
with the real facts, as far as they could be determined by the reckoning of the
ship: That the object to which Mr. Churchman's labors are directed, is con-
fessedly of very high importance, and his ideas on the subject appear to be in-
genious: That with a view of applying them to practice, he has contrived a
map and a globe, whereby to shew the angles which are made by the inter-

---

[40] On April 28 petitions concerning the New Jersey elections were presented to the
House.

[41] According to the *New York Daily Gazette*, April 20, 1789, the subject discussed
was imposts. On April 20 the COWH continued this discussion.

[42] A copy of the report is in A Record of the Reports of Select Committees, HR,
DNA.

section of the real and the magnetic meridians in different parts of the earth: That he is also engaged in constructing tables for determining the longitude at sea upon magnetic principles: That the committee are of opinion that such efforts deserve encouragement, and that a law should pass to secure to Mr. Churchman, for a term of years, the exclusive pecuniary emolument to be derived from the publication of these several inventions," was again read, and on the question put thereupon, agreed to by the House.

The second clause in the words following, to wit, "With respect to the voyage proposed by Mr. Churchman to Baffin's Bay, the committee are cautious of recommending, in the present deranged state of our finances, a precipitate adoption of a measure which would be attended with considerable expence; but they are of opinion that at a future day, if Mr. Churchman's principles should be found to succeed in practice, it would be proper to give further encouragement to his ingenuity," was again read, and on a motion made, ordered to lie on the table.

The third clause in the words following, to wit, "On the subject of the petition of Doctor David Ramsay, your committee report it as their opinion, that a law should pass to secure to him the exclusive right of publishing and vending, for a term of years, the two works mentioned in the petition," was read, and on the question put thereupon, agreed to by the House.

On motion,

ORDERED, That a bill or bills be brought in, making a general provision for securing to authors and inventors the exclusive right of their respective writings and discoveries, and that Mr. Huntington, Mr. Cadwalader, and Mr. Contee, do prepare and bring in the same.[43]

The House according to the standing order of the day, resolved itself into a committee of the whole House on the state of the Union.

Mr. Speaker left the chair.

Mr. Page took the chair of the committee.

Mr. Speaker resumed the chair, and Mr. Page reported that the committee had, according to order, had the state of the Union under consideration, but had come to no resolution thereupon.[44]

The House then according to the order of the day, resolved itself into a committee of the whole House on the bill to regulate the taking the oath or affirmation prescribed in the sixth article of the Constitution.

Mr. Speaker left the chair.

Mr. Page took the chair of the committee.

Mr. Speaker resumed the chair, and Mr. Page reported that the committee

---

[43] On May 7 a petition was referred to this committee.

[44] According to the *New York Daily Gazette*, April 21, 1789, the topic under discussion was imposts. On April 21 the COWH reported resolutions on imposts and tonnage.

had, according to order, had the said bill under their consideration, and made some progress therein, but not having time to go through the same, had directed him to move the House for leave to sit again.

RESOLVED, That this House will on Wednesday next, again resolve itself into a committee of the whole House, on the said bill.[45]

And then the House adjourned until to-morrow morning eleven o'clock.

TUESDAY, APRIL 21, 1789

The House, according to the standing order of the day, resolved itself into a committee of the whole House, on the state of the Union.

Mr. Speaker left the chair.

Mr. Page took the chair of the committee.

Mr. Speaker resumed the chair, and Mr. Page reported that the committee had, according to order, had the state of the Union under consideration, and had come to several resolutions thereupon, which he delivered in at the clerk's table, where the same were read, and ordered to lie on the table.[46]

ORDERED, That Mr. Hartley have leave to be absent from the service of this House until this day six weeks.

And then the House adjourned until to-morrow morning eleven o'clock.

WEDNESDAY, APRIL 22, 1789

Another member, to wit, Peter Silvester, from New-York, appeared and took his seat.

The House, according to the order of the day, resolved itself into a committee of the whole House, on the bill to regulate the taking the oath or affirmation prescribed by the sixth article of the Constitution.

Mr. Speaker left the chair.

Mr. Page took the chair of the committee.

Mr. Speaker resumed the chair, and Mr. Page reported that the committee had, according to order, again had the said bill under consideration, and had gone through the same, and made several amendments thereto, which they had directed him to report whenever the House should think proper to receive the same.

ORDERED, That the said report be received to-morrow.[47]

And then the House adjourned until to-morrow morning eleven o'clock.

---

[45] On April 22 the COWH reported several amendments to this bill.

[46] According to the New York *Daily Advertiser*, April 22, 1789, the COWH discussed tonnage and imposts. The resolutions reported were on imposts and tonnage. On April 24 the impost resolutions were considered. The tonnage resolutions were considered on May 4.

[47] On April 23 this report was postponed.

THURSDAY, APRIL 23, 1789

Another member, to wit, John Hathorn, from New-York, appeared and took his seat.

Mr. Richard Bland Lee, reported from the committee appointed to confer with a committee of the Senate, in reporting a proper mode of communicating papers, bills, and messages, between the two Houses, that the committee had, according to order, met and conferred with a committee of the Senate thereupon, and had agreed to a report, which he delivered in at the clerk's table, where the same was read, and ordered to lie on the table.[48]

ORDERED, That the report from the committee of the whole House, on the bill to regulate the taking the oath or affirmation prescribed by the sixth article of the Constitution, be put off until to-morrow.[49]

And then the House adjourned until to-morrow morning eleven o'clock.

FRIDAY, APRIL 24, 1789

Mr. Boudinot, reported from the committee appointed to attend with a committee from the Senate, to receive the President of the United States, at the place of his embarkation from New-Jersey,[50] that the committee did, according to order, together with a committee from the Senate, attend at Elizabeth-Town, in New-Jersey, on the twenty-third instant, at which place the two committees met the President, and thence embarked for this city, where they arrived about three o'clock in the afternoon of the same day, and conducted him to the house appointed for his residence.

The House proceeded to consider the report from the committee appointed to confer with a committee of the Senate, in reporting a proper mode of communicating papers, bills, and messages, between the two Houses, which lay on the table, and the said report being twice read, was, on a motion made, ordered to be re-committed to the same committee.[51]

On motion,

RESOLVED, That so much of the standing rules and orders of this House as prescribes the enacting style of bills, be rescinded.[52]

---

[48] The report and a copy of the report are in Joint Committee Reports, SR, DNA. A copy of the report is in A Record of the Reports of Select Committees, HR, DNA. It is printed in the *Senate Legislative Journal* on April 23. On April 24 this report was considered and recommitted.

[49] On April 25 the House agreed to the amendments reported by the COWH.

[50] A copy of the report is in A Record of the Reports of Select Committees, HR, DNA.

[51] A copy of the proceedings on communication between houses, including the report, is in Messages from the House, SR, DNA. On April 28 this committee reported, and the report was agreed to.

[52] On June 9 another change in the rules was made.

The Speaker laid before the House a letter from the Vice-President of the United States, enclosing a resolution of the Senate, appointing a committee to consider and report what style or titles it will be proper to annex to the office of President and Vice-President of the United States, if any other than those given in the Constitution; also to consider of the time, place, and manner in which, and the person by whom the oath prescribed by the Constitution shall be administered to the President, and to confer thereon with such committee as this House should appoint for that purpose: Whereupon,

ORDERED, That a committee, to consist of five members, be appointed for the purpose expressed in the resolution of the Senate.

The members elected, Mr. Benson, Mr. Ames, Mr. Madison, Mr. Carroll, and Mr. Sherman.[53]

The House proceeded to consider the resolutions reported from the committee of the whole House on the state of the Union, which lay on the table, and made some progress therein.[54]

And then the House adjourned until to-morrow morning eleven o'clock.

SATURDAY, APRIL 25, 1789

The House, according to the order of the day, received the report from the committee of the whole House, to the bill to regulate the taking the oath or affirmation prescribed by the sixth article of the Constitution; and the amendments to the said bill being read and amended at the clerk's table, were agreed to by the House.

ORDERED, That the said bill, with the amendments, be engrossed, and read the third time on Monday next.[55]

Mr. Benson, from the committee appointed to consider of the time, place, and manner in which, and of the person by whom the oath prescribed by the Constitution shall be administered to the President of the United States, and to confer with a committee of the Senate for the purpose, reported as followeth:[56]

That the President hath been pleased to signify to them that any time or place which both Houses may think proper to appoint, and any manner which shall appear most eligible to them, will be acceptable to him—That requisite

---

[53] A copy of the proceedings on titles for the president and vice president is in Messages from the House, SR, DNA. On April 25 this committee reported on the presidential oath and the report was agreed to. A committee to plan an inaugural ceremony was then appointed.

[54] These resolutions were on imposts and tonnage and were considered again on April 25.

[55] On April 27 this bill was read, agreed to, and sent to the Senate.

[56] A copy of the report is in A Record of the Reports of Select Committees, HR, DNA.

preparations cannot probably be made before Thursday next—That the President be on that day formally received by both Houses in the Senate chamber —That the representatives-chamber being capable of receiving the greater number of persons, that therefore the President do take the oath in that place, and in the presence of both Houses—That after the formal reception of the President in the senate-chamber, he be attended by both Houses to the representatives-chamber, and that the oath be administered by the Chancellor of this State.

The committee farther report it as their opinion, that it will be proper that a committee of both Houses be appointed to take order for farther conducting the ceremonial.

The said report was twice read; and, on the question put thereupon, agreed to by the House.

ORDERED, That Mr. Benson, Mr. Ames, and Mr. Carroll, be a committee on the part of this House, pursuant to the said report.[57]

The House then resumed the consideration of the resolutions reported from the committee of the whole House on the state of the Union, and made a farther progress therein.[58]

The Speaker laid before the House a letter from the Vice-President of the United States, enclosing a vote of the Senate, appointing the Reverend Doctor Provoost a Chaplain to Congress, on the part of that House, which was read, and ordered to lie on the table.

And then the House adjourned until Monday morning eleven o'clock.

MONDAY, APRIL 27, 1789

An engrossed bill to regulate the taking the oath or affirmation prescribed by the sixth article of the Constitution, was read the third time, and a blank therein filled up.

RESOLVED, That the bill do pass, and that the title be, "An act to regulate the time and manner of administering certain oaths."

ORDERED, That the said bill be sent to the Senate for their concurrence, and that Mr. Speaker do transmit the same.[59]

---

[57] On April 27 a letter about the reception of the president was received from the Senate, and the committee on the inaugural ceremony made a report, which was agreed to. On May 5 the joint committee on titles reported, and the report was agreed to.

[58] The resolutions concerned imposts and tonnage and were discussed again on April 27.

[59] The letter of transmittal is in Messages from the House, SR, DNA. The Senate read this bill on April 28 and 29. On April 29 it was committed, and this committee reported amendments on May 2. These amendments are printed in the *Senate Legislative Journal* on May 4. On the same day they were agreed to. On May 5 the bill was read again and agreed to with the amendments.

On motion,

RESOLVED, That this House will on Friday next proceed by ballot to the appointment of a Chaplain to Congress, on the part of this House.[60]

The House resumed the consideration of the resolutions reported from the committee of the whole House on the state of the Union, and made a farther progress therein.[61]

The Speaker laid before the House a letter from the Vice-President of the United States, enclosing certain proceedings of the Senate touching the ceremonial of the formal reception of the President of the United States, by both Houses, which were read, and ordered to lie on the table.

Mr. Benson, from the committee of both Houses, appointed to take order for conducting the ceremonial of the formal reception of the President of the United States, reported as followeth:[62]

That it appears to the committee more eligible that the oath should be administered to the President in the outer gallery adjoining the senate-chamber, than in the representatives-chamber, and therefore submit to the respective Houses the propriety of authorising their committees to take order as to the place where the oath shall be administered to the President, the resolutions of Saturday assigning the representatives-chamber as the place, notwithstanding.

The said report being twice read,

RESOLVED, That this House doth concur in the said report, and authorise the committee to take order for the change of place thereby proposed.

The Speaker laid before the House a letter from the Vice-President of the United States, enclosing two orders of the Senate, one of the thirteenth instant, appointing a committee to confer with any committee to be appointed on the part of this House, respecting the future disposition of the papers, &c. in the office of the late Secretary of the United States;[63] the other of the twenty-seventh instant, for the attendance of both Houses, with the President of the United States, after the oath shall be administered to him, to hear divine service at St. Paul's Chapel[64]—which was read, and ordered to lie on the table.

And then the House adjourned until to-morrow morning eleven o'clock.

---

[60] On May 1 William Linn was elected chaplain.

[61] On April 28 the impost resolutions were agreed to, after being amended. A committee was appointed to prepare a bill based on these resolutions, which are printed in the Journal on April 28.

[62] A copy of the report is in A Record of the Reports of Select Committees, HR, DNA.

[63] A copy of the order is in Joint Committee Reports, SR, DNA. On April 28 the House appointed a committee to confer with this committee.

[64] On April 29 the House agreed to this resolution with amendments.

TUESDAY, APRIL 28, 1789

Mr. Richard Bland Lee, from the committee to whom was re-committed the report respecting the mode of communicating papers, bills, and messages, between the two Houses, reported as followeth:[65]

When a message shall be sent from the Senate to the House of Representatives, it shall be announced at the door of the House by the door-keeper, and shall be respectfully communicated to the Chair, by the person by whom it may be sent.

The same ceremony shall be observed when a message shall be sent from the House of Representatives to the Senate.

Messages shall be sent by such persons as a sense of propriety in each House may determine to be proper.

The said report was twice read, and, on the question put thereupon, agreed to by the House.[66]

The House resumed the consideration of the resolutions reported from the committee of the whole House on the state of the Union, and the first resolution being amended to read as followeth, to wit:

RESOLVED, That it is the opinion of this committee, that the following duties ought to be laid on goods, wares, and merchandizes, imported into the United States, to wit:

	IN CENTS
On all distilled spirits of Jamaica proof, imported from any state or kingdom in alliance with the United States, per gal.	12
On all other distilled spirits imported from any such state or kingdom, per gal.	10
On all distilled spirits of Jamaica proof, imported from any state or kingdom not in alliance with the United States, per gal. . .	15
On all other distilled spirits imported from any such state or kingdom, per gal.	12
On molasses, per gal.	6
On Madeira wine, per gal.	25
On all other wines, per gal.	15
On every gallon of beer, ale or porter, imported in casks	8
On all beer, ale, or porter, imported in bottles, per doz.	25
On malt, per bush.	10
On brown sugars, per lb.	1

[65] A copy of the report is in A Record of the Reports of Select Committees, HR, DNA. At some time on or after this date, the House ordered printed a summary entitled "Additional Standing Rules and Orders of the House of Representatives," as adopted on April 13, 14, 17, and 28, 1789. This document is E–45628.

[66] On May 9 the Senate sent an order concerning this matter to the House.

On loaf sugars, per lb.	3
On all other sugars, per lb.	$1\frac{1}{2}$
On coffee, per lb.	$1\frac{1}{2}$[67]
On cocoa, per lb.	1
On all candles of tallow, per lb.	2
On all candles of wax and spermaceti, per lb.	6
On cheese, per lb.	4
On soap, per lb.	2
On boots, per pair	50
On all shoes, slippers, or goloshoes, made of leather, per pair	7
On all shoes, or slippers, made of silk or stuff, per pair	10
On cables, for every cwt.	75
On tarred cordage, for every 112 lb.	75
On untarred do. and yarn, for every 112 lb.	90
On twine, or packthread, for every 112 lb.	200
On hemp, per cwt. after the first of December, 1789[68]	60
On all steel unwrought, for every 112 lb.	56
On all nails and spikes, per lb.	1
On salt, per bushel, except such as shall be used on fish and provisions exported	6
On manufactured tobacco, per lb.	6
On snuff, per lb.	10
On every dozen of wool or cotton cards	50
On every bushel of coal	3
On pickled fish, per barrel	75
On dried fish, per quintal	50
On all teas imported from China or India, in ships built in the United States, and belonging to a citizen or citizens thereof, as follows:	
On bohea tea, per lb.	6
On all souchong and other black teas, per lb.	10
On superior green teas, per lb.	20
On all other teas, per lb.	10
On all teas imported from any other country, or from India or China, in ships which are not the property of a citizen or citizens of the United States, as follows:	
On bohea tea, per lb.	10
On all souchong and other black teas, per lb.	15
On superior green tea, per lb.	30

---

[67] The manuscript journal correctly changes the figure to read "$2\frac{1}{2}$."
[68] The manuscript journal correctly changes this date to read "1790."

On all other green teas, per lb.   18

On all window and other glass, except black quart bottles, ten per cent. ad valorem

On all blank books

On all writing, printing, wrapping paper, paper hangings, and paste-board

On all cabinet wares

On all buttons of metal

On all saddles

On all gloves of leather

On all hats of beaver, fur, wool, or mixture of either

On all millinary

On all castings of iron, and upon slit or rolled iron

On all leather tanned or tawed, and on all manufacture of leather, except such as shall be otherwise rated

On canes, walking-sticks, and whips

On clothing ready made

On gold, silver, and plated ware, and on jewellery and paste work

On anchors and

On all wrought tin and pewter ware

Seven and an half per cent. ad valorem

On every coach, chariot, or other four wheel carriage, and on every chaise, solo, or other two wheel carriage, or parts thereof, 15 per cent. ad valorem

On all other articles, five per cent. on their value at the time and place of importation, except as follows: Tin in pigs, tin plates, lead, old pewter, brass, iron or brass wire, copper in plates, wool, dying woods, and drying drugs, (other than indigo), raw hides, beaver and all other furs, and deer skins. Provided, That a drawback of six cents per gallon, be allowed on all rum distilled in the United States, and which shall be exported without the limits thereof.

Also, That all the duties paid or secured to be paid upon goods imported, shall be returned or discharged upon such of the said goods as shall within   months be exported to any country without the limits of the United States, except so much as shall be necessary to defray the expence that may have accrued by the entry and safe keeping thereof.

RESOLVED, That this House doth concur with the committee in the said resolution, and that Mr. Clymer, Mr. White, and Mr. Baldwin, do prepare and bring in a bill or bills pursuant thereto.[69]

ORDERED, That the farther consideration of the report from the committee of the whole House be postponed until to-morrow.

---

[69] On May 5 this committee reported the Impost Bill [HR–2], which was read.

The Speaker laid before the House a letter from Matthias Ogden, referring to sundry petitions annexed thereto, from a number of citizens of New-Jersey, complaining of illegality in the late election of Representatives for that State to this House.

The said letter was read, and, together with the petitions accompanying it, ordered to lie on the table.[70]

The order of the Senate of the thirteenth instant, was read, appointing a committee to confer with any committee to be appointed on the part of this House, respecting the future disposition of the papers in the office of the late Secretary of the United States: Whereupon,

ORDERED, That Mr. Trumbull, Mr. Cadwalader, and Mr. Jackson, be a committee for that purpose.[71]

And then the House adjourned until to-morrow morning eleven o'clock.

WEDNESDAY, APRIL 29, 1789

The petitions of the citizens of New-Jersey, whose names are thereunto subscribed, complaining of the illegality of the election of Representatives to Congress for that State, as referred to in Mr. Ogden's letter of yesterday, were read: Whereupon,

ORDERED, That the said petitions be referred to the committee of elections, and that it be an instruction to the said committee, to report a proper mode of investigation and decision thereupon.

The House proceeded to consider the report from the committee of elections, (which lay on the table) on the petition of David Ramsay of the State of South-Carolina, suggesting that William Smith, returned a member of this House as elected within that State, was, at the time of his election, ineligible; and the said report being amended to read as followeth:

That in this case it will be sufficient in the first instance, that a committee take such proofs as can be obtained in this city respecting the facts stated in the petition, and report the same to the House—That Mr. Smith be permitted to be present from time to time when such proofs are taken, to examine the witnesses, and to offer counter proofs, which shall also be received by the committee, and reported to the House—That if the proofs so to be reported shall be declared by the House insufficient to verify the material facts stated in the petition, or such other facts as the House shall deem proper to be enquired into, it will then be necessary for the House to direct a farther enquiry, and especially the procuring whatever additional testimony may be

---

[70] On April 29 these petitions were referred to the committee on elections. On the same day the report from this committee on the petition of David Ramsay was agreed to.

[71] On May 12 this committee reported.

supposed to be in South-Carolina, as the case may require—That all questions arising on the proofs be decided by the House without any previous opinion thereon reported by a committee.

RESOLVED, That this House doth agree to the said report, and that it be an instruction to the committee of elections to proceed accordingly.[72]

On motion,

ORDERED, That a committee be appointed to prepare and report an estimate of the supplies requisite for the present year, and of the nett produce of the impost as agreed to by the House, and that Mr. Gerry, Mr. Smith (of Maryland) and Mr. Parker, be of the said committee.[73]

The House proceeded to consider the following resolution of the Senate, to wit:

"In Senate, April 27

"RESOLVED, That after the oath shall have been administered to the President, he, attended by the Vice-President, and the members of the Senate and House of Representatives, proceed to St. Paul's Chapel to hear divine service, to be performed by the Chaplains to Congress already appointed:"

Whereupon,

RESOLVED, That this House doth concur with the Senate in the said resolution, amended to read as followeth, to wit:

"That after the oath shall have been administered to the President, the Vice-President and members of the Senate, the Speaker and members of the House of Representatives, will accompany him to St. Paul's Chapel to hear divine service, performed by the Chaplain of Congress."[74]

ORDERED, That the clerk of this House do carry the said resolution to the Senate, and desire their concurrence.

And then the House adjourned until to-morrow morning eleven o'clock.

THURSDAY, APRIL 30, 1789

Another member, to wit, Jonathan Grout, from Massachusetts, appeared and took his seat.

And then the House adjourned until to-morrow morning eleven o'clock.[75]

---

[72] On May 12 another petition relating to the New Jersey elections was received. The committee on elections also reported again on David Ramsay's petition.

[73] On May 8 this committee was further instructed.

[74] A copy of the proceedings on the inaugural ceremony is in Messages from the House, SR, DNA.

[75] According to the New York *Daily Advertiser*, April 30, 1789, both houses had agreed to a report on the procedure for the inaugural ceremony, which was held on this day. This report was never journalized. A copy of the report is in the Office of the Financial Clerk, SR, DNA. E–45671.

FRIDAY, MAY 1, 1789

The Speaker laid before the House a copy of the Speech of the President of the United States, to both Houses of Congress, delivered yesterday in the senate-chamber, immediately after his inauguration, as followeth:

FELLOW CITIZENS OF THE SENATE, AND OF THE
HOUSE OF REPRESENTATIVES

AMONG the vicissitudes incident to life, no event could have filled me with greater anxieties, than that of which the notification was transmitted by your order, and received on the fourteenth day of the present month. On the one hand, I was summoned by my country, whose voice I can never hear but with veneration and love, from a retreat which I had chosen with the fondest predilection, and in my flattering hopes, with an immutable decision, as the asylum of my declining years; a retreat which was rendered every day more necessary as well as more dear to me, by the addition of habit to inclination, and of frequent interruptions in my health to the gradual waste committed on it by time. On the other hand, the magnitude and difficulty of the trust to which the voice of my country called me, being sufficient to awaken in the wisest and most experienced of her citizens, a distrustful scrutiny into his qualifications, could not but overwhelm with despondence, one, who, inheriting inferior endowments from nature, and unpractised in the duties of civil administration, ought to be peculiarly conscious of his own deficiencies. In this conflict of emotions, all I dare aver, is, that it has been my faithful study to collect my duty from a just appreciation of every circumstance by which it might be affected. All I dare hope, is, that, if in executing this task, I have been too much swayed by a grateful remembrance of former instances, or by an affectionate sensibility to this transcendent proof of the confidence of my fellow citizens, and have thence too little consulted my incapacity as well as disinclination, for the weighty and untried cares before me; my error will be palliated by the motives which misled me, and its consequences be judged by my country, with some share of the partiality in which they originated.

Such being the impressions under which I have, in obedience to the public summons, repaired to the present station; it would be peculiarly improper to omit, in this first official act, my fervent supplications to that Almighty Being who rules over the universe—who presides in the councils of nations—and whose providential aids can supply every human defect—that his benediction may consecrate to the liberties and happiness of the people of the United States, a government instituted by themselves for these essential purposes; and may enable every instrument employed in its administration, to execute with success the functions allotted to his charge. In tendering this homage to the Great Author of every public and private good, I assure myself that it expresses your sentiments not less than my own; nor those of my fellow citizens at large, less than either. No people can be bound to acknowledge and adore the invisible hand, which conducts the affairs of men, more than the people of the United States. Every step by which they have advanced to the character of an independent nation, seems to have been distinguished by some token of providential agency. And in the important revolution just accomplished in the system of their united government, the tranquil deliberations, and voluntary consent of so many distinct communities, from which the event has resulted, cannot be compared with the means by which most governments have been established, without some return of pious gratitude, along with a humble anticipation of the future blessings which the past seem to presage. These reflections arising out of the present crisis, have forced themselves too strongly on my mind to be suppressed. You will join with me, I trust, in thinking that there are none under the influence of which the proceedings of a new and free government can more auspiciously commence.

By the article establishing the executive department, it is made the duty of the President, "to recommend to your consideration such measures as he shall judge necessary and expedient." The circumstances under which I now meet you, will acquit me from entering into that subject, further than to refer to the great constitutional charter under which you are assembled, and which, in defining your powers, designates the objects to which your attention is to be given. It will be more consistent with those circumstances, and far more congenial with the feelings which actuate me, to substitute, in place of a recommendation of particular measures, the tribute that is due to the talents, the rectitude and the patriotism which adorn the characters selected to devise and adopt them. In these honorable qualifications, I behold the surest pledges, that as on one side no local prejudices or attachments—no separate views, nor party animosities, will misdirect the comprehensive and equal eye which ought to watch over this great assemblage of communities and interests; so on another, that the foundations of our national policy will be laid in the pure and immutable principles of private morality; and the pre-eminence of free government, be exemplified by all the attributes which can win the affections of its citizens, and command the respect of the world. I dwell on this prospect with every satisfaction which an ardent love for my country can inspire. Since there is no truth more thoroughly established, than that there exists in the economy and course of nature, an indissoluble union between virtue and happiness; between duty and advantage; between the genuine maxims of an honest and magnanimous policy, and the solid rewards of public prosperity and felicity. Since we ought to be no less persuaded that the propitious smiles of Heaven can never be expected on a nation that disregards the eternal rules of order and right which Heaven itself has ordained. And since the preservation of the sacred fire of liberty, and the destiny of the republican model of government, are justly considered as *deeply*, perhaps as *finally*, staked on the experiment entrusted to the hands of the American people.

Besides the ordinary objects submitted to your care, it will remain with your judgment to decide, how far an exercise of the occasional power delegated by the fifth article of the Constitution, is rendered expedient at the present juncture by the nature of objections which have been urged against the system, or by the degree of inquietude which has given birth to them. Instead of undertaking particular recommendations on this subject, in which I could be guided by no lights derived from official opportunities, I shall again give way to my entire confidence in your discernment and pursuit of the public good. For I assure myself that whilst you carefully avoid every alteration which might endanger the benefits of an united and effective government, or which ought to await the future lessons of experience; a reverence for the characteristic rights of freemen, and a regard for the public harmony, will sufficiently influence your deliberations on the question, how far the former can be more impregnably fortified, or the latter be safely and advantageously promoted.

To the preceding observations I have one to add, which will be most properly addressed to the House of Representatives. It concerns myself, and will therefore be as brief as possible. When I was first honored with a call into the service of my country, then on the eve of an arduous struggle for its liberties, the light in which I contemplated my duty, required that I should renounce every pecuniary compensation. From this resolution I have in no instance departed. And being still under the impressions which produced it, I must decline as inapplicable to myself, any share in the personal emoluments, which may be indispensibly included in a permanent provision for the executive department; and must accordingly pray, that the pecuniary estimates for the station in which I am placed, may, during my continuance in it, be limited to such actual expenditures as the public good may be thought to require.

Having thus imparted to you my sentiments, as they have been awakened by the occasion which brings us together, I shall take my present leave; but not without resorting once more to the benign Parent of the human race, in humble supplication, that since he has been pleased to favor the American people with opportunities for deliberating in perfect tranquility, and dispositions for deciding with unparalleled unanimity on a form of government, for the security of their union, and the advancement of their happiness; so his divine blessing may be equally *conspicuous* in the enlarged views, the temperate consultations, and the wise measures on which the success of this government must depend.

GEORGE WASHINGTON[1]

On motion,

RESOLVED, That the said speech be committed to the consideration of a committee of the whole House, immediately.

The House accordingly resolved itself into the said committee.

Mr. Speaker left the chair.

Mr. Page took the chair of the committee.

Mr. Speaker resumed the chair, and Mr. Page reported that the committee had, according to order, had the said speech under consideration, and had come to a resolution thereupon, which he delivered in at the clerk's table, where the same was twice read; and, on a question put thereupon, agreed to by the House, as followeth:

RESOLVED, That it is the opinion of this committee, that an address to the President ought to be prepared, expressing the congratulations of the House of Representatives, on the distinguished proof given him of the affection and confidence of his fellow citizens, by the unanimous suffrage which has appointed him to the high station which he fills; the approbation felt by the House of the patriotic sentiments and enlightened policy recommended by his speech; and assuring him of their disposition to concur in giving effect to every measure which may tend to secure the liberties, promote the harmony, and advance the happiness and prosperity of their country.

ORDERED, That a committee to consist of five members be appointed to prepare an address pursuant to the said resolution.

The members elected, Mr. Madison, Mr. Clymer, Mr. Sherman, Mr. Gale, and Mr. Benson.[2]

Another member, to wit, Samuel Livermore, from New-Hampshire, appeared and took his seat.

A motion was made that the House do come to the following resolution:

RESOLVED, That   per annum be the compensation to be allowed to the President of the United States, during the time for which he is elected.

And the said motion being read at the clerk's table, was ordered to be committed to a committee of the whole House on the state of the Union.[3]

---

[1] The address is in President's Messages: Annual reports, SR, DNA. E–22212, E–45726, E–45727.

[2] On May 5 this committee presented an answer to the inaugural address, which was agreed to.

[3] The subject of compensation for the president was considered in the COWH on the state of the union on May 25. On the same day the COWH was discharged from considering this topic, and a committee was appointed to bring in a bill.

The House then, according to the order of the day, proceeded by ballot to the appointment of a Chaplain to Congress on the part of this House; and upon examining the ballots, a majority of the votes of the whole House was found in favor of the REVEREND WILLIAM LINN.

ORDERED, That the Clerk of this House do acquaint the Senate therewith.

And then the House adjourned until Monday morning eleven o'clock.

MONDAY, MAY 4, 1789

A petition of the shipwrights of the town of Baltimore, in the state of Maryland, was presented to the House, and read, praying the attention of Congress to the increase of American shipping and tonnage, and the establishing a proper navigation act or acts for that purpose.

ORDERED, That the said petition be referred to the committee of the whole House on the state of the Union.

A petition of Alexander Lewis, of the state of Pennsylvania, was presented to the House, and read, setting forth that he hath discovered and constructed an easy and expeditious method of impelling boats of twenty-five tons burthen and under, through the water, against any current or stream however rapid; as also an easy method of raising a sufficient quantity of water twenty feet in height, to turn any mill; and praying that an act may pass to secure to him, his heirs, &c. for the term of twenty-one years, an exclusive right of constructing boats upon his model, in the United States.

Also a petition of Andrew Newell, and Seth Clark, of the state of Massachusetts, praying that the proper officer may be authorised to receive and examine their accounts as assistant-commissaries of issues, the lapse of time limited for that purpose by the late Congress notwithstanding.

Also a petition of Sarah Parker, of the state of Massachusetts, praying that some relief may be granted for the support of herself and a large family of children, being the widow and orphans of lieutenant colonel Moses Parker, who was wounded and made prisoner by the British troops in the battle of Charlestown, on the 17th of June 1775, and was afterwards confined in the gaol in Boston, and there died of his wounds in the month of July following.

Also a petition of Martha Walker, of Boston, in the state of Massachusetts, praying that some relief may be granted her, as the distressed widow of Thomas Walker, Esquire, late of Boston, who at the commencement of the late revolution, abandoned a very considerable property in the province of Quebec, and attached himself to the interests and fortunes of the United States.[4]

ORDERED, That the said petitions do severally lie on the table.

---

[4] On September 21 this petition was referred to a committee on claims.

The House resumed the consideration of the resolutions reported from the committee of the whole House on the state of the Union, the twenty-first ultimo, and made some progress therein.[5]

And then the House adjourned until to-morrow morning eleven o'clock.

TUESDAY, MAY 5, 1789

Mr. Benson, from the committee appointed to consider of and report what style or titles it will be proper to annex to the office of President and Vice President of the United States, if any other than those given in the Constitution, and to confer with a committee of the Senate appointed for the same purpose, reported as followeth;[6]

That it is not proper to annex any style or title to the respective styles or titles of office expressed in the Constitution.

And the said report being twice read at the clerk's table, was, on the question put thereupon, agreed to by the House.

ORDERED, That the Clerk of this House do acquaint the Senate therewith.[7]

Mr. Madison from the committee appointed to prepare an address on the part of this House to the President of the United States, in answer to his speech to both Houses of Congress, reported as followeth:[8]

The ADDRESS of the HOUSE of REPRESENTATIVES to GEORGE WASHINGTON, PRESIDENT of the UNITED STATES

SIR,

THE Representatives of the people of the United States present their congratulations on the event by which your fellow citizens have attested the preeminence of your merit. You have long held the first place in their esteem. You have often received tokens of their affection. You now possess the only proof that remained of their gratitude for your services, of their reverence for your wisdom, and of their confidence in your virtues. You enjoy the highest, because the truest honor, of being the First Magistrate, by the unanimous choice, of the freest people on the face of the earth.

We well know the anxieties with which you must have obeyed a summons from the repose reserved for your declining years, into public scenes, of which

---

[5] The resolutions under discussion concerned tonnage. On May 5 these resolutions were considered again.

[6] A copy of the report is in A Record of the Reports of Select Committees, HR, DNA.

[7] On May 9 the House was notified that the Senate had disagreed to this committee report and appointed a new committee on titles.

[8] A copy of the report is in A Record of the Reports of Select Committees, HR, DNA.

you had taken your leave for ever. But the obedience was due to the occasion. It is already applauded by the universal joy which welcomes you to your station. And we cannot doubt that it will be rewarded with all the satisfaction with which an ardent love for your fellow citizens must review successful efforts to promote their happiness.

This anticipation is not justified merely by the past experience of your signal services. It is particularly suggested by the pious impressions under which you commence your administration, and the enlightened maxims by which you mean to conduct it. We feel with you the strongest obligations to adore the invisible hand which has led the American people through so many difficulties, to cherish a conscious responsibility for the destiny of republican liberty; and to seek the only sure means of preserving and recommending the precious deposit in a system of legislation founded on the principles of an honest policy, and directed by the spirit of a diffusive patriotism.

The question arising out of the fifth article of the Constitution will receive all the attention demanded by its importance; and will, we trust be decided, under the influence of all the considerations to which you allude.

In forming the pecuniary provisions for the executive department, we shall not lose sight of a wish resulting from motives which give it a peculiar claim to our regard. Your resolution, in a moment critical to the liberties of your country, to renounce all personal emolument, was among the many presages of your patriotic services, which have been amply fulfilled; and your scrupulous adherence now to the law then imposed on yourself, cannot fail to demonstrate the purity, whilst it increases the lustre of a character which has so many titles to admiration.

Such are the sentiments which we have thought fit to address to you. They flow from our own hearts, and we verily believe that among the millions we represent, there is not a virtuous citizen whose heart will disown them.

All that remains is that we join in your fervent supplication for the blessings of Heaven on our country; and that we add our own for the choicest of these blessings on the most beloved of her citizens.

And the said address being twice read, at the clerk's table, was ordered to be committed to a committee of the whole House immediately.

The House accordingly resolved itself into the said committee.

Mr. Speaker left the chair.

Mr. Page took the chair of the committee.

Mr. Speaker resumed the chair, and Mr. Page reported that the committee had, according to order, had the said address under consideration, and made no amendment thereto.

RESOLVED UNANIMOUSLY, That this House doth agree to the said address, and that the Speaker, attended by the members of this House, do present the said address to the President.

ORDERED, That Mr. Sinnickson, Mr. Coles, and Mr. Smith, of South-Carolina, be a committee to wait on the President, to know when it will be convenient for him to receive the same.[9]

Mr. Clymer, from the committee appointed, presented according to order, a bill for laying a duty on goods, wares, and merchandizes, imported into the United States, and the same was received and read the first time.[10]

Mr. Bland, one of the Representatives from Virginia, presented to the House an application in the name and behalf of the legislature of the commonwealth of Virginia, addressed to the Congress of the United States, which was read,

Whereupon,

ORDERED, That the said application be entered on the journal, and carefully preserved by the clerk of this House, among the files in his office.

The said application is as followeth:

VIRGINIA, to wit:

In GENERAL ASSEMBLY, November 14, 1788

RESOLVED, That an application be made in the name and on behalf of the Legislature of this Commonwealth to the Congress of the United States, in the words following, to wit:

"The good people of this Commonwealth, in Convention assembled, having ratified the Constitution submitted to their consideration, this Legislature has, in conformity to that act and the resolutions of the United States in Congress assembled to them transmitted, thought proper to make the arrangements that were necessary for carrying it into effect. Having thus shown themselves obedient to the voice of their constituents, all America will find that so far as it depended on them, that plan of government will be carried into immediate operation.

"But the sense of the people of Virginia would be but in part complied with and but little regarded, if we went no farther. In the very moment of adoption, and coeval with the ratification of the new plan of government, the general voice of the Convention of this State pointed to objects no less interesting to the people we represent, and equally entitled to our attention. At the same time that, from motives of affection to our sister States, the Convention yielded their assent to the ratification, they gave the most unequivocal proofs, that they dreaded its operation under the present form.

"In acceding to the government under this impression, painful must have been the prospect, had they not derived consolation from a full expectation of

---

[9] On May 7 this committee reported.
[10] On May 6 this bill was read again.

its imperfections being speedily amended. In this resource, therefore, they placed their confidence, a confidence that will continue to support them, whilst they have reason to believe that they have not calculated upon it in vain.

"In making known to you the objections of the people of this Commonwealth to the new plan of government, we deem it unnecessary to enter into a particular detail of its defects, which they consider as involving all the great and unalienable rights of freemen. For their sense on this subject, we beg leave to refer you to the proceedings of their late Convention, and the sense of the House of Delegates as expressed in their resolutions of the thirtieth day of October, one thousand seven hundred and eighty-eight.

"We think proper, however, to declare, that, in our opinion, as those objections were not founded in speculative theory, but deduced from principles which have been established by the melancholy example of other nations in different ages; so they will never be removed, until the cause itself shall cease to exist. The sooner, therefore, the public apprehensions are quieted, and the government is possessed of the confidence of the people, the more salutary will be its operations, and the longer its duration.

"The cause of amendments we consider as a common cause, and since concessions have been made from political motives, which, we conceive, may endanger the republic, we trust, that a commendable zeal will be shown for obtaining those provisions, which, experience has taught us, are necessary to secure from danger the unalienable rights of human nature.

"The anxiety with which our countrymen press for the accomplishment of this important end, will ill admit of delay. The slow forms of congressional discussion and recommendation, if, indeed, they should ever agree to any change, would, we fear, be less certain of success. Happily for their wishes, the Constitution hath presented an alternative, by admitting the submission to a convention of the states. To this, therefore, we resort, as the source from whence they are to derive relief from their present apprehensions.

"We do, therefore, in behalf of our constituents, in the most earnest and solemn manner, make this application to Congress, that a Convention be immediately called of deputies from the several states, with full power to take into their consideration the defects of this Constitution that have been suggested by the state Conventions, and report such amendments thereto, as they shall find best suited to promote our common interests, and secure to ourselves and our latest posterity, the great and unalienable rights of mankind."

Signed   JOHN JONES, Sp. Senate,

THOMAS MATHEWS, Sp. H. Del.[11]

---

[11] On May 6 an application for amendments to the Constitution was received from New York State.

A message from the Senate, by Mr. Otis, their Secretary.

MR. SPEAKER, The Senate have passed the bill, entitled, "An act to regulate the time and manner of administering certain oaths," with amendments, to which they desire the concurrence of your House.[12] And then he withdrew.

The House resumed the consideration of the resolutions reported from the committee of the whole House on the state of the Union, the twenty-first ultimo, and made a farther progress therein.[13]

And then the House adjourned until to-morrow morning eleven o'clock.

WEDNESDAY, MAY 6, 1789

Another member, to wit, John Vining, from Delaware, appeared and took his seat.

A bill for laying a duty on goods, wares, and merchandizes, imported into the United States, was read the second time, and ordered to be committed to a committee of the whole House to-morrow.[14]

A petition of Arthur Greer, of the state of Pennsylvania, was presented to the House, and read, setting forth that he has invented a machine which he conceives has reduced to a certainty the discovery of the true longitude or departure from any given meridian north of the equator; and praying that an exclusive patent for his discovery may be granted him for the space of twenty-one years.

ORDERED, That the said petition do lie on the table.[15]

The House proceeded to consider the amendments of the Senate to the bill entitled "An act to regulate the time and manner of administering certain oaths," and the same being twice read at the clerk's table, were amended, and agreed to by the House.

ORDERED, That the clerk of this House do acquaint the Senate therewith, and desire their concurrence to the amendment to their amendments.[16]

Mr. Laurance, one of the Representatives from New-York, presented to the House an application, in the name and behalf of the legislature of that State, addressed to the Congress of the United States, which was read: Whereupon,

---

[12] On May 6 these amendments, which are printed in the *Senate Legislative Journal* for May 4, were agreed to with an amendment.

[13] The resolutions under discussion concerned tonnage. On May 6 these resolutions were considered again.

[14] On May 7 consideration of this bill was postponed. On May 8 it was considered in the COWH.

[15] On May 7 this petition was referred to the committee on copyrights and patents.

[16] On May 7 the House was notified that the Senate agreed to this amendment. The House amendment is printed in the *Senate Legislative Journal* on May 7.

ORDERED, That the said application be entered on the journal, and carefully preserved by the clerk of this House, among the files in his office.

The said application is as followeth:

STATE OF NEW-YORK

In ASSEMBLY, February 5, 1789

RESOLVED, If the honorable the Senate concur therein, that an application be made to the Congress of the United States of America, in the name and behalf of the Legislature of this State, in the words following, to wit:

The people of the state of New-York having ratified the Constitution agreed to on the seventeenth day of September, in the year of our Lord one thousand seven hundred and eighty-seven, by the Convention then assembled at Philadelphia, in the state of Pennsylvania, as explained by the said ratification, in the fullest confidence of obtaining a revision of the said Constitution by a general Convention; and in confidence, that certain powers in and by the said Constitution granted, would not be exercised, until a convention should have been called and convened for proposing amendments to the said Constitution. In compliance therefore, with the unanimous sense of the Convention of this State, who all united in opinion, that such a revision was necessary to recommend the said Constitution to the approbation and support of a numerous body of their constituents; and a majority of the members of which conceived several articles of the Constitution so exceptionable, that nothing but such confidence, and an invincible reluctance to separate from our sister States, could have prevailed upon a sufficient number to assent to it, without stipulating for previous amendments: And from a conviction that the apprehensions and discontents which those articles occasion, cannot be removed or allayed, unless an act to revise the said Constitution, be among the first that shall be passed by the new Congress, We, the Legislature of the state of New-York, do in behalf of our constituents, in the most earnest and solemn manner, make this application to the Congress, that a Convention of Deputies from the several States be called as early as possible, with full powers to take the said Constitution into their consideration, and to propose such amendments thereto, as they shall find best calculated to promote our common interests, and secure to ourselves and our latest posterity, the great and unalienable rights of mankind.

By order of the Assembly,

JOHN LANSING, Junior, Speaker

In SENATE, February 7, 1789

By order of the SENATE,

PIERRE VAN CORTLANDT, President[17]

---

[17] On June 8 a motion that the House propose amendments to the Constitution was referred to the COWH.

The House resumed the consideration of the resolutions reported from the committee of the whole House on the state of the Union, the twenty-first ultimo, and made a farther progress therein.[18]

And then the House adjourned until to-morrow morning eleven o'clock.

THURSDAY, MAY 7, 1789

Mr. Smith, of South-Carolina, from the committee appointed to wait on the President of the United States, to know when it will be convenient for him to receive the address of this House, reported,

That the committee had, according to order, waited on the President, and that he signified to them that it would be convenient to him to receive the said address, at twelve o'clock on Friday, at such place as the House shall be pleased to appoint: Whereupon,

RESOLVED, That as the chamber designed for the President's receiving the respective Houses, is not yet prepared, this House will wait on the President, to present their address, in the room adjacent to the representatives-chamber.[19]

On motion,

RESOLVED, That a committee of three members be appointed to confer with any committee to be appointed on the part of the Senate, in preparing and reporting joint rules to be established between the two Houses, for the inrollment, attestation, publication, and preservation of the acts of Congress; as also on the mode of presenting addresses, bills, votes, or resolutions, to the President of the United States.

The members appointed, Mr. Bland, Mr. Trumbull, and Mr. Vining.[20]

ORDERED, That the Clerk of this House do acquaint the Senate therewith.

ORDERED, That the petition of Arthur Greer, which lay on the table, be referred to Mr. Huntington, Mr. Cadwalader, and Mr. Contee, that they do examine the matter thereof, and report the same with their opinion thereupon to the House.[21]

The House resumed the consideration of the resolutions reported from the committee of the whole House on the state of the Union, the twenty-first ultimo, and the last resolution being amended to read as followeth:

---

[18] The resolutions under discussion concerned tonnage. On May 7 these resolutions were agreed to, and a committee was appointed to prepare a tonnage bill. The resolutions are printed in the Journal on this date.

[19] On May 8 the House reply to the inaugural address was presented to the president, and he replied.

[20] A copy of the resolution is in Messages from the House, SR, DNA.

[21] This committee is the one that was appointed on copyrights and patents on April 20. On May 13 another petition was referred to this committee.

RESOLVED, That there ought to be levied on all vessels entered or cleared in the United States, the duties following, to wit:

On all vessels built within the United States, and belonging wholly to citizens thereof, at the rate of six cents per ton.

On all vessels not built within the United States, but now belonging wholly to citizens thereof, at the rate of six cents per ton.

On all vessels belonging wholly to the subjects of powers with whom the United States have formed treaties; or partly to the subjects of such powers, and partly to citizens of the said States, at the rate of thirty cents per ton.

On all vessels belonging wholly or in part to subjects of other powers, at the rate of fifty cents per ton.

PROVIDED, That no vessel built within the United States, and belonging to a citizen or citizens thereof, whilst employed in the coasting trade, or in the fisheries, shall pay tonnage more than once in any one year; nor shall any ship or vessel built within the United States, pay tonnage on her first voyage.

PROVIDED ALSO, That no vessel be employed in the transportation of the produce or manufactures of the United States, or any of them, coastwise, except such vessels shall be built within the United States, and the property of a citizen or citizens thereof.

The same was, on the question put thereupon, agreed to by the House.

ORDERED, That a bill or bills be brought in pursuant to the said resolution, and that Mr. Wadsworth, Mr. Hiester, and Mr. Seney, do prepare and bring in the same.[22]

A message from the Senate, by Mr. Otis, their Secretary.

MR. SPEAKER, The Senate agree to the amendment proposed by this House to their third amendment to the bill, entitled, "An act to regulate the time and manner of administering certain oaths;"[23] they have also appointed a committee, agreeable to the proposition this day communicated in a message from this House.[24]   And then he withdrew.

The order of the day for the House to resolve itself into a committee of the whole House, on the bill for laying a duty on goods, wares, and merchandizes, imported into the United States, was read, and postponed until to-morrow.

And then the House adjourned until to-morrow morning eleven o'clock.

---

[22] On May 25 this committee presented a Tonnage Bill [HR–5], which was read.

[23] On May 19 a committee to examine this bill and present it to the president was appointed.

[24] The proposition suggested appointing a joint committee to confer on joint rules. On May 15 the committee reported.

FRIDAY, MAY 8, 1789

The Speaker, attended by the members of the House, withdrew to the room adjoining the representatives-chamber, and there presented to the President of the United States, the address agreed to on Tuesday last—to which he returned the following answer:

GENTLEMEN,

YOUR very affectionate address, produces emotions which I know not how to express. I feel that my past endeavors in the service of my country, are far overpaid by its goodness; and I fear much that my future ones may not fulfil your kind anticipation. All that I can promise, is, that they will be invariably directed by an honest and an ardent zeal—Of this resource my heart assures me. For all beyond, I rely on the wisdom and patriotism of those with whom I am to co-operate, and a continuance of the blessings of Heaven on our beloved country.

The Speaker and members being returned into the House;

Mr. Gerry, from the committee appointed, presented, according to order, a bill for collecting duties on goods, wares, and merchandizes, imported into the United States; and the same was received and read the first time.

ORDERED, That the clerk of this House do procure one hundred copies of the said bill to be printed for the use of the members of this House.[25]

On motion,

ORDERED, That the committee appointed on the twenty-ninth ultimo, to report an estimate of the supplies requisite for the present year, and of the nett produce of the impost, as agreed to by the House, be authorised and instructed to collect early and authentic statements of the particular articles of foreign produce and manufactures annually imported into, and of all the articles exported from the several States, and the value of such imports and exports; also the number of vessels, both foreign and domestic, entered and cleared during that time, specifying their tonnage, and the nations to which they respectively belong, specifying also the exact numbers of each particular description of vessels of each nation, and the amount of tonnage of each particular vessel.[26]

On motion,

RESOLVED, That this House will on Tuesday next proceed by ballot to the appointment of a serjeant at arms.

---

[25] On May 9 this bill was read again.

[26] A letter from the committee to the governor of Connecticut in compliance with this order is in the Miscellaneous Manuscript Collection, MWA. On July 9 this committee reported.

The House, according to the order of the day, resolved itself into a committee of the whole House, on the bill for laying a duty on goods, wares, and merchandizes, imported into the United States.

Mr. Speaker left the chair.

Mr. Page took the chair of the committee.

Mr. Speaker resumed the chair, and Mr. Page reported that the committee had, according to order, had the said bill under consideration, and made some progress therein.

RESOLVED, That this House will to-morrow again resolve itself into a committee of the whole House on the said bill.[27]

And then the House adjourned until to-morrow morning eleven o'clock.

SATURDAY, MAY 9, 1789

Another member, to wit, Jeremiah Van Rensselaer, from New-York, appeared and took his seat.

A bill for collecting duties on goods, wares, and merchandizes, imported into the United States, was read the second time, and ordered to be committed to a committee of the whole House on Monday next.[28]

ORDERED, That Mr. Boudinot have leave to be absent from the service of this House until Monday se'nnight.

A message from the Senate by Mr. Otis, their secretary.

MR. SPEAKER,   I am directed by the Senate to communicate to this House, the following order:

"In SENATE, the 7th May, 1789

"ORDERED, That when a message shall come from the House of Representatives to the Senate, and shall be announced by the door-keeper, the messenger or messengers being a member or members of the House, shall be received within the bar, the President rising, when the message is by one member, and the Senate also when it is by two or more. If the messenger be not a member of the House, he shall be received at the bar by the Secretary, and the bill or papers that he may bring, shall there be received from him by the Secretary, and be by him delivered to the President."   And then he withdrew.

The House, according to the order of the day, resolved itself into a committee of the whole House, on the bill for laying a duty on goods, wares, and merchandizes, imported into the United States.

Mr. Speaker left the chair.

---

[27] On May 9 the COWH considered this bill again.

[28] Consideration of this bill was postponed from day to day until May 18, when the bill was considered and tabled.

Mr. Page took the chair of the committee.

Mr. Speaker resumed the chair, and Mr. Page reported that the committee had, according to order, again had the said bill under consideration, and made a farther progress therein.

RESOLVED, That this House will on Monday next, again resolve itself into a committee of the whole House on the said bill.[29]

A message from the Senate by Mr. Otis, their Secretary.

MR. SPEAKER, The Senate have disagreed to the report of a committee appointed to determine what style or titles it will be proper to annex to the office of President and Vice-President of the United States, if any other than those given in the Constitution, and have appointed a committee to consider and report under what title it will be proper for the President of the United States in future to be addressed, and to confer thereon with such committee as this House may appoint for that purpose.[30] The Senate have also appointed a committee to view and report how the rooms in the city-hall shall be appropriated, and to confer with any committee this House may appoint for that purpose.[31]   And then he withdrew.

And then the House adjourned until Monday morning eleven o'clock.

MONDAY, MAY 11, 1789

On motion,

That the House do agree to the following resolution;

"RESOLVED, That this House having, on Tuesday last, adopted the report of their committee appointed to confer with a committee of the Senate, stating 'that it is not proper to annex any style or title to the respective styles or titles of office expressed in the Constitution,' and having in their address to the President of the United States on Friday last, proceeded to act pursuant thereto, deem it improper to accede to the proposition made by the Senate, as communicated by their order of the ninth instant, for appointing a committee to confer with a committee of this House in considering and reporting under what title it will be proper for the President of the United States in future to be addressed."

The previous question was demanded by five members, shall the main question be now put?   And on the question, Shall the main question be now put?

It passed in the negative.

---

[29] On May 11 the COWH considered this bill again.

[30] On May 11 the House appointed a conference committee on this topic.

[31] On May 11 the House appointed a committee to meet with this committee.

So the motion was lost.

On motion,

RESOLVED, That a committee be appointed to join with such committee as the Senate may appoint to confer on the disagreeing votes of the two Houses upon the report of their joint committee appointed to consider what titles shall be given to the President and Vice-President of the United States, if any other than those given in the Constitution. The members elected, Mr. Madison, Mr. Trumbull, Mr. Page, Mr. Benson, and Mr. Sherman.[32]

On motion,

RESOLVED, That a committee be appointed, to confer with the committee appointed by the Senate, to view and report in what manner the rooms in the city-hall shall be appropriated.

The members appointed, Mr. White, Mr. Scott, and Mr. Sturges.[33]

The House, according to the order of the day, resolved itself into a committee of the whole House on the bill for laying a duty on goods, wares, and merchandizes, imported into the United States.

Mr. Speaker left the chair.

Mr. Page took the chair of the committee.

Mr. Speaker resumed the chair, and Mr. Page reported that the committee had, according to order, again had the said bill under consideration, and made a farther progress therein.

RESOLVED, That this House will to-morrow again resolve itself into a committee of the whole House, on the said bill.[34]

The order of the day for the House to resolve itself into a committee of the whole House, on the bill for the collection of duties on goods, wares, and merchandizes, imported into the United States, was read and postponed until to-morrow.

And then the House adjourned until to-morrow morning eleven o'clock.

TUESDAY, MAY 12, 1789

The Speaker laid before the House the petition of Jedidiah Morse, stating that he has at great labor, expence and risque compiled and published a geographical and historical treatise of the United States, entitled "the American Geography, or a View of the present Situation of the United States of America" embellished and illustrated with two original maps, and praying that an

---

[32] A copy of the resolution is in Messages from the House, SR, DNA. On May 12 the Senate agreed to this conference.

[33] A copy of the resolution is in Messages from the House, SR, DNA. On June 19 the House was notified that the Senate had agreed to the report of this committee.

[34] On May 12 the COWH considered this bill again.

exclusive right may be secured to him, of publishing the same for a limited time.[35]

Also a petition of a number of the citizens of the state of New-Jersey, whose names are thereunto subscribed, in opposition to a petition of sundry other citizens of the said state, complaining of the illegality of the election of representatives from that State, returned to serve in this House.

Mr. Clymer, from the committee of elections, to whom it was referred to take proofs of the facts stated in the petition of David Ramsay, suggesting, that William Smith, elected a member of this House, within the state of South-Carolina, was, at the time when he was elected, ineligible, by reason that he had not been seven years a citizen of the United States, reported as followeth.

That Mr. Smith appeared before them, and admitted that he had subscribed, and had caused to be printed in the state gazette of South-Carolina, of the twenty-fourth of November last, the publication which accompanies this report, and to which the petitioner doth refer as proof of the facts stated in his petition—That Mr. Smith also admitted, that his father departed this life in the year one thousand seven hundred and seventy, about five months after he sent him to Great-Britain—That his mother departed this life about the year one thousand seven hundred and sixty, and that he was admitted to the bar of the supreme court in South-Carolina in the month of January, one thousand seven hundred and eighty-four.

The committee also report the following counter proofs, produced by Mr. Smith, viz. Printed copies of the following acts of the legislature of the state of South-Carolina, viz. An act, entitled, "An act to oblige every free male inhabitant of this State, above a certain age, to give assurance of fidelity and allegiance to the same, and for other purposes therein mentioned," passed the twenty-eighth of March, one thousand seven hundred and seventy-eight. An act, entitled, "An act disposing of certain estates, and banishing certain persons therein mentioned," passed the twenty-sixth of February, one thousand seven hundred and eighty-two. An act, entitled, "An act to alter and amend an act, entitled, an act for disposing of certain estates, and banishing certain persons, passed at Jacksonburgh, in the state of South-Carolina, on the twenty-sixth day of February, in the year one thousand seven hundred and eighty two," passed in March, one thousand seven hundred and eighty-three. An act, entitled, "An act to confer the right of citizenship on aliens," passed the twenty-sixth of March, one thousand seven hundred and eighty-four. Also an ordinance of the legislature of the said State, entitled, "An ordinance to dis-

---

[35] A draft of what is probably the petition received by the House is in the Morse Family Collection, CtY. On May 14 this petition was referred to the committee on copyrights and patents.

courage[36] subjects of foreign States to lend money at interest on real estates within this State," passed the twenty-sixth of March, one thousand seven hundred and eighty-four. A certified copy of an extract from an act of the legislature of that State, entitled, "An act for raising and paying into the public treasury of this State, a tax for the uses therein mentioned," passed the ninth of September, one thousand seven hundred and seventy-nine—and a printed copy of the constitution of South-Carolina—also a certificate from John Edwards, and William Hort, commissioners of the treasury of that State, under their seal of office.

ORDERED, That the said report do lie on the table.[37]

The House, according to the order of the day, proceeded by ballot to the appointment of a serjeant at arms; and, upon examining the ballots, a majority of the votes of the whole House was found in favor of MR. JOSEPH WHEATON.[38]

Mr. Trumbull, from the committee appointed to confer with any committee from the Senate, respecting the future disposition of the papers in the office of the late secretary of the United States, made a report,[39] which was read, and ordered to lie on the table.

The House, according to the order of the day, resolved itself into a committee of the whole House on the bill for laying a duty on goods, wares, and merchandizes, imported into the United States.

Mr. Speaker left the chair.

Mr. Page took the chair of the committee.

Mr. Speaker resumed the chair, and Mr. Page reported that the committee had, according to order, again had the said bill under consideration, and made a farther progress therein.

RESOLVED, That this House will to-morrow, again resolve itself into a committee of the whole House on the said bill.[40]

A message from the Senate, by Mr. Otis, their Secretary.

MR. SPEAKER, The Senate have appointed a committee to confer with the

---

[36] The manuscript journal correctly changes this word to read "encourage."

[37] On May 14 the petitions from the citizens of New Jersey were referred to the committee on elections. The report on the Ramsay petition was considered by the House on May 21.

[38] Presumably Joseph Wheaton and others requested this job, although there is no record in the Journal of their petitions being received by the House. Petitions from Joseph Wheaton, Leonard Bleecker, and William Finnie for the position of sergeant at arms are in Petitions and Memorials: Applications for jobs, SR, DNA.

[39] A draft and a clean copy of the report are in Joint Committee Reports, SR, DNA. A copy of the report is in A Record of the Reports of Select Committees, HR, DNA.

[40] On May 13 the COWH considered this bill again.

committee appointed by this House, on the disagreeing votes of the two Houses, on the subject of titles.[41]   And then he withdrew.

The order of the day for the House to resolve itself into a committee of the whole House on the bill for collecting duties on goods, wares, and merchandizes imported into the United States, was read and postponed until to-morrow.

And then the House adjourned until to-morrow morning eleven o'clock.

WEDNESDAY, MAY 13, 1789

A petition of the merchants and traders of the town of Portland, in the state of Massachusetts, was presented to the House, and read, stating that the proposed duty on molasses will operate injuriously upon all the New-England States, and be attended with pernicious consequences to manufactures; and praying that that article may remain entirely free from all imposts and duties whatever.[42]

ORDERED, That the said petition do lie on the table.

The House, according to the order of the day, resolved itself into a committee of the whole House, on the bill for laying a duty on goods, wares, and merchandizes, imported into the United States.

Mr. Speaker left the chair.

Mr. Page took the chair of the committee.

Mr. Speaker resumed the chair, and Mr. Page reported that the committee had, according to order, again had the said bill under consideration, and made a farther progress therein.

RESOLVED, That this House will to-morrow again resolve itself into a committee of the whole House on the said bill.[43]

A petition of John Fitch, of the state of Pennsylvania, was presented to the House, and read, stating, that he is the original discoverer of the principle of applying the power of steam to the purposes of navigation, and has obtained an exclusive right therein, for a term of years, in the states of Virginia, Delaware, Pennsylvania, New-Jersey, and New-York, and praying that his rights may be secured to him by law, and in such manner, upon the true principles of priority of invention, as will preclude subsequent improvers upon his prin-

---

[41] This committee did not report to the House. On May 14 the Senate resolved to conform to the House practice for addressing the president.

[42] The petition is in Petitions and Memorials: Various subjects, SR, DNA.

[43] On May 14 the COWH reported several amendments to this bill, which were agreed to by the House.

ciple from participating therein until the expiration of the term of his exclusive grants.[44]

ORDERED, That the said petition be referred to Mr. Huntington, Mr. Cadwalader, and Mr. Contee, that they do examine the matter thereof, and report the same, with their opinion thereupon, to the House.[45]

The order of the day, for the House to resolve itself into a committee of the whole House, on the bill for collecting duties on goods, wares, and merchandizes, imported into the United States, was read, and postponed until to-morrow.

And then the House adjourned until to-morrow morning eleven o'clock.

THURSDAY, MAY 14, 1789

A message from the Senate, by Mr. Otis, their Secretary.

MR. SPEAKER, The Senate have appointed a committee to confer with any committee to be appointed on the part of this House, and report what newspapers the members of Congress shall be furnished with, at the public expence.[46] And then he withdrew.

A petition of Archibald McLean, of the city of New-York, printer, was presented to the House, and read, praying to be employed to execute any part of the printing business of the United States, which Congress in their wisdom may think proper to allot him.[47]

Also a petition of the distillers, in and near the city of Philadelphia, suggesting an opinion that a greater difference in the duties on the articles of rum and molasses imported, than what is now proposed, would be of advantage to the interests of the United States, and submitting their reasons for that opinion, to the consideration of Congress.[48]

ORDERED, That the said petitions do lie on the table.

ORDERED, That the petition of Jedidiah Morse, which lay on the table, be referred to Mr. Huntington, Mr. Cadwalader, and Mr. Contee, that they do examine the matter thereof, and report the same with their opinion thereupon, to the House.[49]

---

[44] A petition from Fitch, dated April 2, 1789, and located in the William Samuel Johnson Papers, CtHi, is probably the one received in the House on this date.

[45] This committee is the one that was appointed on copyrights and patents on April 20. On May 14 two more petitions were referred to this committee.

[46] On May 15 the House appointed a committee to confer with this committee and instructed them also to consider proposals for printing. Three petitions were then referred to this committee.

[47] On May 15 this petition was referred to the committee on newspapers.

[48] The memorial is in Petitions and Memorials: Various subjects, SR, DNA.

[49] This committee is the one that was appointed on copyrights and patents on April 20.

ORDERED, That the petition of the citizens of New-Jersey, which lay on the table, be referred to the committee of elections, that they do examine the matter thereof, and report the same with their opinion thereupon, to the House.[50]

A petition of Angelhart Cruse, was presented to the House, and read, praying that an exclusive privilege may be granted him for a term of years, to construct and vend, within the United States, an improved steam engine, which he has invented, for raising of water for the purposes of manufactories, grist-mills, or the like.

ORDERED, That the said petition be referred to Mr. Huntington, Mr. Cadwalader, and Mr. Contee, that they do examine the matter thereof, and report the same with their opinion thereupon, to the House.[51]

The House, according to the order of the day, resolved itself into a committee of the whole House, on the bill for laying a duty on goods, wares, and merchandizes, imported into the United States.

Mr. Speaker left the chair.

Mr. Page took the chair of the committee.

Mr. Speaker resumed the chair, and Mr. Page reported that the committee had, according to order, again had the said bill under consideration, and gone through the same, and made several amendments thereto, which he delivered in at the clerk's table, where the same were twice read, and agreed to by the House.

ORDERED, That the said bill, with the amendments be engrossed, and read the third time to-morrow.[52]

The order of the day for the House to resolve itself into a committee of the whole House, on the bill for collecting duties on goods, wares, and merchandizes, imported into the United States, was read, and postponed until to-morrow.

And then the House adjourned until to-morrow morning eleven o'clock.

FRIDAY, MAY 15, 1789

Mr. Bland, from the committee appointed to confer with a committee of the Senate, in preparing proper rules to be established between the two Houses, for the inrollment, attestation, publication, and preservation of the

---

[50] On May 15 further petitions relating to the New Jersey elections were presented and referred to the committee on elections.

[51] This committee is the one that was appointed on copyrights and patents on April 20. On June 8 another petition was referred to this committee.

[52] On May 15 this bill was read again and recommitted to the COWH. Several amendments from the COWH were agreed to.

acts of Congress, and to regulate the mode of presenting addresses, and other acts, to the President of the United States, made a report,[53] which was read.

On motion,

ORDERED, That the said report be referred to a committee of the whole House, on Monday next.[54]

On motion,

ORDERED, That Mr. Silvester, Mr. Wynkoop, and Mr. Smith (of South-Carolina) be a committee to confer with the committee appointed by the Senate, to report what news-papers the members of Congress shall be furnished with at the public expence; and that it be an instruction to the said committee, on the part of this House, to receive proposals for printing the acts and other proceedings of Congress, and to report thereupon.[55]

The several petitions of Francis Childs and John Swaine, and of Samuel Loudon and Son, praying to be employed in the printing business of Congress, were presented to the House, and, together with the petition of Archibald McLean, presented yesterday, to the same effect, ordered to be referred to the committee last appointed.[56]

Several other petitions of the citizens of New-Jersey, praying that the election of representatives from that State, may be declared valid, were presented to the House, and ordered to be referred to the committee of elections.[57]

A petition of Baron de Glaubeck, praying the consideration of Congress for certain losses and military services, during the late war; also a petition of Bartlett Hinds, a wounded officer in the Massachusetts line of the late continental army, in behalf of himself and the continental pensioners in that State, praying relief against certain injuries which they have sustained under the operation of the acts of the late Congress, were presented to the House, and ordered to lie on the table.[58]

ORDERED, That Mr. Sherman have leave to be absent from the service of this House, until Monday se'nnight.

The order of the day for the House to resolve itself into a committee of the whole House, on the bill for collecting duties on goods, wares, and merchandizes, imported into the United States, was read and postponed until to-morrow.

---

[53] A copy of the report is in A Record of the Reports of Select Committees, HR, DNA.

[54] On May 18 this report was considered in the COWH.

[55] A copy of the order is in Messages from the House, SR, DNA.

[56] On May 16 another petition was referred to this committee, and the Senate agreed to the House instructions to the committee.

[57] A draft petition from the Minutes of the Board of Justices and Freeholders of Burlington, New Jersey, which is probably a draft of one of the petitions received on this date, is in NjR. On May 21 this committee reported on the New Jersey petitions.

[58] On July 23 another petition from Baron de Glaubeck was presented.

Mr. White, one of the representatives from Virginia, presented to the House a resolve of the Legislature of that State, of the 27th of December, 1788, offering to the acceptance of the Federal Government, ten miles square of territory, or any lesser quantity, in any part of that State, which Congress may chuse, to be occupied and possessed by the United States, as the seat of the Federal Government; which was read, and ordered to lie on the table.

An engrossed bill for laying a duty on goods, wares, and mechandizes, imported into the United States, was read the third time, and, on a motion made, ordered to be re-committed to a committee of the whole House, immediately.

The House accordingly resolved itself into the said committee.

Mr. Speaker left the chair.

Mr. Page took the chair of the committee.

Mr. Speaker resumed the chair, and Mr. Page reported, that the committee had, according to order, had the said bill under consideration, and made several amendments thereto, which he delivered in at the clerk's table, where the same were twice read, and agreed to by the House.

A motion was then made and seconded, farther to amend the said bill, by adding to the end thereof, a clause for limiting the time of its continuance; and the said motion being under debate,[59]

The House adjourned until to-morrow morning eleven o'clock.

SATURDAY, MAY 16, 1789

Mr. Seney, one of the representatives from Maryland, presented to the House, an act of the Legislature of that State, offering to the acceptance of Congress, ten miles square of territory, in any part of the said State, for the seat of the Federal Government, which was read, and ordered to lie on the table.

A petition of Duncan Campbell, of the city of New-York, was presented to the House, and read, praying that compensation may be made him, for sundry advances which he made during the late war, for the service of the United States.

ORDERED, That the said petition do lie on the table.[60]

A petition of John Fenno, was presented to the House, and read, praying to be employed in the printing service of the United States.

ORDERED, That the said petition be referred to the committee appointed yesterday, for receiving proposals for printing the acts and other proceedings of Congress.

---

[59] On May 16 an amendment to the bill was agreed to, and the bill was read again, agreed to, and sent to the Senate.

[60] On September 21 this petition was referred to a committee on claims.

The House resumed the consideration of the amendment proposed yesterday, to the bill for laying a duty on goods, wares, and merchandizes, imported into the United States, and the said amendment being amended, to read as followeth: "And be it farther enacted by the authority aforesaid, that this act shall continue and be in force until the   day of   and from thence until the end of the next succeeding session of Congress, which shall happen thereafter."

The previous question was demanded by five members, Shall the main question be now put?   And on the question, Shall the main question be now put?

It was resolved in the affirmative.

And then the main question being put, that the House do agree to the amendment proposed to the said bill,

It was resolved in the affirmative—$\begin{cases} \text{AYES } 41 \\ \text{NOES } 8 \end{cases}$

The ayes and noes being called for by one fifth of the members present.

Those who voted in the affirmative, are,

Abraham Baldwin
Egbert Benson
Theodorick Bland
Aedanus Burke
Daniel Carroll
Isaac Coles
Benjamin Contee
Thomas Fitzsimons
William Floyd
George Gale
Elbridge Gerry
Nicholas Gilman
Benjamin Goodhue
Samuel Griffin
Jonathan Grout
John Hathorn
Daniel Hiester
Benjamin Huntington
James Jackson
Richard Bland Lee
George Leonard

Samuel Livermore
James Madison, junior
Andrew Moore
Peter Muhlenberg
John Page
Josiah Parker
George Partridge
Jeremiah Van Rensselaer
Joshua Seney
Thomas Scott
William Smith (of Maryland)
William Smith (of South-Carolina)
Jonathan Sturges
Peter Silvester
Jonathan Trumbull
Thomas Tudor Tucker
John Vining
Jeremiah Wadsworth
Alexander White and
Henry Wynkoop

Those who voted in the negative, are,

Fisher Ames	John Laurance
Elias Boudinot	Roger Sherman
Lambert Cadwalader	Thomas Sinnickson and
George Clymer	George Thatcher

ORDERED, That the said bill, with the amendments, be engrossed, and read the third time, to-day.

ORDERED, That Mr. Hathorn have leave to be absent from the service of this House, until Wednesday se'nnight.

The order of the day for the House to resolve itself into a committee of the whole House, on the bill for collecting duties on goods, wares, and merchandizes, imported into the United States, was read, and postponed until Monday next.

A message from the Senate, by Mr. Otis, their Secretary.

MR. SPEAKER,   The Senate have instructed their committee appointed to confer with a committee of this House, and report what news-papers the members of Congress shall be furnished with, at the public expence, to receive proposals for printing the acts and other proceedings of Congress.[61] And then he withdrew.

An engrossed bill, for laying a duty on goods, wares, and mechandizes, imported into the United States, was read the third time, and the blanks therein filled up.

RESOLVED, That the said bill do pass, and that the title be, "An act for laying a duty on goods, wares, and merchandizes, imported into the United States."[62]

ORDERED, That the clerk of this House do carry the said bill to the Senate, and desire their concurrence.[63]

And then the House adjourned until Monday morning eleven o'clock.

MONDAY, MAY 18, 1789

A petition of John Bryce, of the city of New-York, was presented to the House and read, praying to be employed as stationer and book-binder to Congress.[64]

---

[61] On May 18 two more petitions were referred to this committee.

[62] A printed copy of the bill, annotated by the Senate, is in House Bills, SR, DNA. E-45674.

[63] The Senate read and considered this bill on May 18, 25, 28, 29, June 1, 2, 3, 4, 5, and 8. On June 8 it was committed. The bill was read again on June 9 and 10, and on June 11 the bill was read again and agreed to with forty amendments, which are printed in the *Senate Legislative Journal* for June 11. The House was notified of these amendments on June 12.

[64] The petition is in Petitions and Memorials: Applications for jobs, SR, DNA.

Also the several petitions of Edward Evelith Powers, and Thomas Greenleaf, printers, praying to be employed in the printing service of Congress:

ORDERED, That the said petitions be referred to the committee appointed
to receive proposals for printing the acts and other proceedings of Congress.[65]

The House according to the order of the day, resolved itself into a committee of the whole House, on the bill for collecting duties on goods, wares, and
merchandizes, imported into the United States.

Mr. Speaker left the chair.

Mr. Page took the chair of the committee.

Mr. Speaker resumed the chair, and Mr. Page reported that the committee
had, according to order, had the said bill under consideration, and gone
through the same, and made no amendment thereto.

On motion,

ORDERED, That the said bill do lie on the table.[66]

ORDERED, That leave be given to bring in a bill concerning the importation
of certain persons into the United States, prior to the year one thousand eight
hundred and eight, and that Mr. Parker, Mr. Sinnickson, and Mr. Muhlenberg, do prepare and bring in the same.[67]

The House, according to the order of the day, resolved itself into a committee of the whole House, on the report of the committee, appointed to confer with a committee of the Senate, in preparing joint rules to be established
between the two Houses, for the inrollment, attestation, publication, and
preservation of the acts of Congress, and to regulate the mode of presenting
addresses, and other acts, to the President of the United States.

Mr. Speaker left the chair.

Mr. Page took the chair of the committee.

Mr. Speaker resumed the chair, and Mr. Page reported that the committee
had, according to order, had the said report under consideration, and made
some progress therein.

RESOLVED, That this House will, to-morrow, again resolve itself into a
committee of the whole House, on the said report.[68]

On motion,

ORDERED, That a committee be appointed, to prepare and bring in a bill,

---

[65] On May 19 this committee reported.

[66] On May 27 the committee appointed on April 11 presented another Collection
Bill [HR–6], which was read.

[67] On September 19 this committee presented a Slave Trade Bill [HR–30], and
consideration of it was postponed until the next session.

[68] From May 19 through July 24 consideration of this bill was postponed as an
order of the day. On July 27 several resolutions on the report were agreed to and
printed. A committee was then appointed to bring in a bill for safekeeping of the
records of the United States.

providing for the actual enumeration of the inhabitants of the United States, in conformity to the Constitution, and for the purposes therein mentioned, and that Mr. Goodhue, Mr. Hiester, and Mr. Seney, be of the said committee. And then the House adjourned until to-morrow morning eleven o'clock.

TUESDAY, MAY 19, 1789

A message from the Senate by Mr. Otis, their secretary.

MR. SPEAKER, The Senate have appointed a committee, to join a committee on the part of this House, to present to the President of the United States, the bill, entitled, "an act to regulate the time and manner of administering certain oaths," after the same shall be duly engrossed, examined, and signed by the speaker of this House, and the President of the Senate. And then he withdrew.

ORDERED, That Mr. Partridge and Mr. Floyd, be appointed a committee on the part of this House, for the purpose expressed in the message from the Senate.[69]

The House, according to the order of the day, resolved itself into a committee of the whole House, on the state of the Union.

Mr. Speaker left the chair.

Mr. Trumbull took the chair of the committee.

Mr. Speaker resumed the chair, and Mr. Trumbull reported, that the committee had, according to order, had the state of the Union under consideration, but had come to no resolution thereupon.[70]

Mr. Silvester, from the committee appointed to confer with a committee of the Senate, to consider and report what news-papers the members of Congress shall be furnished with, at the public expence, and to receive proposals for printing the acts, and other proceedings of Congress, made a report, which was read, and ordered to lie on the table.[71]

The order of the day for the House to resolve itself into a committee of the whole House, on the report of the committee appointed to confer with a committee of the Senate, in preparing proper rules to be established between

[69] A copy of the House order, with the Senate resolution appointing a committee, is in Messages from the House, SR, DNA. On May 21 the speaker signed the Oath Bill [HR–1].

[70] According to the *Gazette of the United States*, May 23, 1789, the topic under discussion was executive departments. On May 20 the COWH came to a resolution on this topic.

[71] The report is in Joint Committee Reports, SR, DNA. A copy of the report is in A Record of the Reports of Select Committees, HR, DNA. On May 26 this committee reported again.

the two Houses, for the inrollment, attestation, publication, and preservation of the acts of Congress, and to regulate the mode of presenting addresses, and other acts, to the President of the United States, was read, and postponed until to-morrow.

And then the House adjourned until to-morrow morning eleven o'clock.

WEDNESDAY, MAY 20, 1789

The House, according to the order of the day, resolved itself into a committee of the whole House on the state of the Union.

Mr. Speaker left the chair.

Mr. Trumbull took the chair of the committee.

Mr. Speaker resumed the chair, and Mr. Trumbull reported, that the committee had, according to order, had the state of the Union under consideration, and had come to a resolution thereupon, which he delivered in at the clerk's table, where the same was read.

ORDERED, That the said resolution do lie on the table.[72]

The order of the day, for the House to resolve itself into a committee of the whole House, on the report of the committee appointed to confer with a committee of the Senate, in preparing proper rules to be established between the two Houses, for the inrollment, attestation, publication, and preservation of the acts of Congress, and to regulate the mode of presenting addresses, and other acts, to the President of the United States, was read, and postponed until to-morrow.

And then the House adjourned until to-morrow morning eleven o'clock.

THURSDAY, MAY 21, 1789

The House proceeded to consider the resolution reported from the committee of the whole House, on the state of the Union, yesterday, and the same being amended to read as followeth:

RESOLVED, That it is the opinion of this committee, that there ought to be established, the following executive departments, to wit; A department of foreign affairs, at the head of which shall be an officer to be called secretary to the United States for the department of foreign affairs, removable by the President. A treasury department, at the head of which shall be an officer, to be called secretary to the United States, for the treasury department, removable by the President. A department of war, at the head of which shall be an

---

[72] The resolution introduced concerned executive departments. On May 21 this resolution was agreed to, and a committee was appointed to prepare bills on it. The resolution is printed in the Journal on that date.

officer, to be called secretary to the United States for the department of war, removable by the President.

RESOLVED, That this House doth concur with the committee in the said resolution; and that a committee to consist of eleven members, be appointed to prepare and bring in a bill or bills pursuant thereto.

The members elected, Mr. Baldwin, Mr. Vining, Mr. Livermore, Mr. Madison, Mr. Benson, Mr. Burke, Mr. Fitzsimons, Mr. Boudinot, Mr. Wadsworth, Mr. Gerry, and Mr. Cadwalader.[73]

Mr. Partridge, reported from the committee appointed to examine the engrossed bill, intitled, "An act to regulate the time and manner of administering certain oaths,"[74] that the committee had, according to order, examined the same, and found it to be truly engrossed:　Whereupon,

Mr. Speaker signed the said engrossed bill.[75]

Mr. Clymer, from the committee of elections, to whom it was referred to report a proper mode of investigation and decision on the petitions of a number of the citizens of New-Jersey, complaining of the illegality of the election of the members holding seats in this House, as elected within that State, made a report, which was read, and ordered to lie on the table.[76]

The order of the day for the House to resolve itself into a committee of the whole House, on the report of the committee appointed to confer with a committee of the Senate, in preparing proper rules to be established between the two Houses, for the inrollment, attestation, publication, and preservation of the acts of Congress, and to regulate the mode of presenting addresses, and other acts, to the President of the United States, was read, and postponed until to-morrow.

The House proceeded to consider the report from the committee of elections, which lay on the table, stating the proofs of the facts charged in the petition of David Ramsay, suggesting that William Smith, elected a member of this House, within the state of South-Carolina, was, at the time when he was elected, ineligible, by reason that he had not been seven years a citizens of the United States, and made some progress therein.[77]

And then the House adjourned until to-morrow morning eleven o'clock.

---

[73] On June 2 this committee presented the War Department Bill [HR–7] and the Foreign Affairs Bill [HR–8], which were read. On June 4 the Treasury Bill [HR–9] was presented and read.

[74] The inspected enrolled bill is in Enrolled Acts and Resolutions of the Congress of the United States: 1789–1823, RG 11, General Records of the United States Government (hereinafter referred to as Enrolled Acts, RG 11), DNA. E–45715.

[75] On May 24 the vice president signed this bill. On May 25 the committee reported that this bill had been delivered to the president.

[76] On May 25 the House agreed to this report.

[77] On May 22 the House voted to seat William Smith.

FRIDAY, MAY 22, 1789

The House resumed the consideration of the report from the committee of elections, stating the proofs of the facts charged in the petition of David Ramsay, suggesting that William Smith, returned a member of this House for the state of South-Carolina, was, at the time of his election, ineligible, by reason that he had not been seven years a citizen of the United States: Whereupon, it being moved and seconded, that the House do agree to the following resolution:

RESOLVED, That it appears to this House, upon full and mature considera-tion, that the said William Smith had been seven years a citizen of the United States, at the time of his election.

It was resolved in the affirmative—$\begin{cases} \text{AYES} & 36 \\ \text{NOES} & 1 \end{cases}$

The ayes and noes being demanded by one fifth of the members present. Those who voted in the affirmative, are,

Abraham Baldwin	James Madison, junior
Egbert Benson	Andrew Moore
Elias Boudinot	Peter Muhlenberg
Lambert Cadwalader	John Page
Daniel Carroll	Jeremiah Van Rensselaer
George Clymer	Joshua Seney
Isaac Coles	James Schureman
Benjamin Contee	Thomas Scott
Thomas Fitzsimons	Thomas Sinnickson
William Floyd	William Smith (of Maryland)
Nicholas Gilman	Jonathan Sturges
Benjamin Goodhue	Peter Silvester
Daniel Hiester	George Thatcher
Benjamin Huntington	Jonathan Trumbull
John Laurance	Thomas Tudor Tucker
Richard Bland Lee	John Vining
George Leonard	Alexander White and
Samuel Livermore	Henry Wynkoop

Jonathan Grout voted in the negative.

The order of the day for the House to resolve itself into a committee of the whole House, on the report of the committee appointed to confer with a com-mittee of the Senate, in preparing joint rules to be established between the two Houses, for the inrollment, attestation, publication, and preservation, of the acts of Congress, and to regulate the mode of presenting addresses, and other acts, to the President of the United States; was read, and postponed until Monday next.

And then the House adjourned until Monday morning eleven o'clock.

MONDAY, MAY 25, 1789

Another member, to wit, Thomas Sumter, from South-Carolina, appeared and took his seat.

Mr. Partridge, from the committee appointed jointly with a committee of the Senate, to present to the President of the United States, for his approbation, the engrossed bill, entitled, "An act to regulate the time and manner of administering certain oaths," reported, that the committee did, according to order, on Friday last, wait on the President, and present him with the said engrossed bill, for his approbation.[78]

The House, according to the order of the day, resolved itself into a committee of the whole House, on the state of the Union.

Mr. Speaker left the chair.

Mr. Trumbull took the chair of the committee.

Mr. Speaker resumed the chair, and Mr. Trumbull reported that the committee had, according to order, had the state of the Union under consideration, and had come to no resolution thereupon.[79]

The House proceeded to consider the report from the committee of elections, to whom it was referred to report a proper mode of investigation and decision, on the petition of a number of the citizens of New-Jersey, complaining of the illegality of the election of the members holding seats in this House, as elected within that State; and the said report being amended, to read as followeth:

That it will be proper to appoint a committee, before whom the petitioners are to appear, and who shall receive such proofs and allegations, as the petitioners shall judge proper to offer, in support of their said petition, and who shall, in like manner, receive all proofs and allegations from persons who may be desirous to appear and be heard in opposition to the said petition, and to report to the House all such facts as shall arise from the proofs and allegations of the respective parties.

RESOLVED, That this House doth agree with the committee in the said report, and that it be an instruction to the said committee of elections to proceed accordingly.[80]

---

[78] On June 1 the president signed this bill.

[79] The topic discussed as the state of the union for this date was compensation for the president.

[80] On July 14 the committee on elections reported on these petitions again.

On motion,

RESOLVED, That a committee be appointed to confer with any committee which may be appointed by the Senate, on the proper method of receiving into either House, bills, or messages, from the President of the United States.

The members appointed, Mr. Partridge, Mr. Floyd, and Mr. Thatcher.[81]

On motion,

ORDERED, That the committee of the whole House, on the state of the Union, be discharged from further proceeding on the motion to them committed, for making a compensation to the President of the United States, for his services, and that a committee be appointed to take into consideration the subject of compensations to be made for the services of the President, Vice-President, the members of the Senate and House of Representatives, and to report thereupon.

The members appointed, Mr. Baldwin, Mr. Vining, Mr. Livermore, Mr. Madison, Mr. Benson, Mr. Burke, Mr. Fitzsimons, Mr. Boudinot, Mr. Wadsworth, Mr. Gerry, Mr. Cadwalader, and Mr. Smith, of Maryland.[82]

Mr. Wadsworth presented, according to order, a bill, imposing duties on tonnage, and the same was received, and read the first time.[83]

A petition of the shipwrights of the city of Philadelphia, whose names are thereunto subscribed, was presented to the House, and read, stating such regulations, as they conceive will tend to the advancement and increase of American shipping, and praying the attention of Congress thereto.[84]

ORDERED, That the said petition do lie on the table.

The order of the day, for the House to resolve itself into a committee of the whole House, on the report of the committee appointed to confer with a committee of the Senate, in preparing joint rules to be established between the two Houses, for the inrollment, attestation, publication, and preservation, of the acts of Congress, and to regulate the mode of presenting addresses, and other acts, to the President of the United States, was read, and postponed until to-morrow.

And then the House adjourned until to-morrow morning eleven o'clock.

TUESDAY, MAY 26, 1789

A bill, imposing duties on tonnage, was read the second time, and ordered to be committed to a committee of the whole House, to-morrow.[85]

---

[81] A copy of the resolution is in Messages from the House, SR, DNA. On May 27 the Senate notified the House that they had appointed a committee on this subject.

[82] On June 1 this committee reported.

[83] On May 26 this bill was read again.

[84] The petition is in Petitions and Memorials: Various subjects, SR, DNA.

[85] On May 27 the COWH reported amendments to this bill.

Mr. Silvester, from the committee appointed to confer with a committee of the Senate, to consider and report what news-papers the members of Congress shall be furnished with at the public expence, and to receive proposals from the printers, for printing the acts and other proceedings of Congress, made a farther report, which was read, and ordered to lie on the table.[86]

The order of the day, for the House to resolve itself into a committee of the whole House, on the report of the committee appointed to confer with a committee of the Senate, in preparing joint rules to be established between the two Houses, for the inrollment, attestation, publication, and preservation, of the acts of Congress, and to regulate the mode of presenting addresses, and other acts, to the President of the United States, was read, and postponed until to-morrow.

And then the House adjourned until to-morrow morning eleven o'clock.

WEDNESDAY, MAY 27, 1789

A message from the Senate, by Mr. Otis, their Secretary.

MR. SPEAKER,   The Senate have appointed a committee to confer with the committee appointed by this House, on the proper method of receiving into either House, bills, or messages from the President of the United States.[87] And then he withdrew.

The House, according to the order of the day, resolved itself into a committee of the whole House, on the bill, imposing duties on tonnage.

Mr. Speaker left the chair.

Mr. Trumbull took the chair of the committee.

Mr. Speaker resumed the chair, and Mr. Trumbull reported, that the committee had, according to order, had the said bill under consideration, and gone through the same, and made several amendments thereto, which they had directed him to report, when the House should think proper to receive the same.

ORDERED, That the said report be received to-morrow.[88]

Mr. Fitzsimons, from the committee appointed, presented, according to order, a bill to regulate the collection of duties, imposed on goods, wares, and

---

[86] The report is in Joint Committee Reports, SR, DNA. A copy of the report is in A Record of the Reports of Select Committees, HR, DNA. On May 28 the two reports of this committee were considered. The report concerning newspapers was disagreed to, and the report on printing was agreed to. The reports are printed in the Journal for that date.

[87] On May 29 this committee reported, and the report was agreed to.

[88] On May 28 these amendments were agreed to.

merchandizes, imported into the United States, and the same was received, and read the first time.[89]

The order of the day, for the House to resolve itself into a committee of the whole House, on the report of the committee appointed to confer with a committee of the Senate, in preparing joint rules to be established between the two Houses, for the inrollment, attestation, publication, and preservation, of the acts of Congress, and to regulate the mode of presenting addresses, and other acts, to the President of the United States, was read, and postponed until to-morrow.

And then the House adjourned until to-morrow morning eleven o'clock.

THURSDAY, MAY 28, 1789

The House proceeded to receive and consider the amendments made yesterday, by the committee of the whole House, to the bill, imposing duties on tonnage, and the said amendments were severally twice read at the clerk's table, and agreed to.

ORDERED, That the said bill, with the amendments, be engrossed, and read the third time to-morrow.[90]

The House, according to the order of the day, resolved itself into a committee of the whole House, on the state of the Union.

Mr. Speaker left the chair.

Mr. Trumbull took the chair of the committee.

Mr. Speaker resumed the chair, and Mr. Trumbull reported, that the committee had, according to order, had the state of the Union under consideration, but had come to no resolution thereupon.

ORDERED, That a committee be appointed to consider the state of the unappropriated lands in the western territory, and to report thereupon:

And a committee was appointed, of Mr. Scott, Mr. Huntington, and Mr. Sherman.[91]

On motion,

RESOLVED, That every such member of the present Congress, as is not yet furnished with a set of the journals of the late Congress, shall, on application

---

[89] The committee that prepared the Collection Bill [HR–6] is the same committee that prepared the Collection Bill [HR–3]. This committee was appointed on April 11, and its members were Nicholas Gilman, Elbridge Gerry, Roger Sherman, John Laurance, Lambert Cadwalader, Thomas Fitzsimons, George Gale, James Madison, and Thomas T. Tucker. On May 29 this bill was read again.

[90] On May 29 this bill was read again, agreed to, and sent to the Senate.

[91] According to the *New York Daily Gazette*, May 29, 1789, the topic under discussion in the COWH was a land office for the Northwest Territory. The order establishing a committee was a direct result of this discussion. On June 15 this committee reported.

to the keeper of the records, and papers, of the said late Congress, be entitled to receive a complete set of such journals.[92]

ORDERED, That the clerk of this House do carry the said resolution to the Senate, and desire their concurrence.[93]

The House proceeded to consider the two reports, one made the nineteenth instant, the other the twenty-sixth instant, by the committee appointed to confer with a committee of the Senate, to consider and report what news-papers the members of Congress shall be furnished with at the public expence, and to receive proposals for printing the acts, and other proceedings of Congress; and the first report in the words following, to wit:

"That in their opinion, public economy requires that the expence heretofore incurred by the public, of supplying every member of Congress with all the news-papers printed at the seat of Congress, should be retrenched in future: but as your committee consider the publication of news-papers to be highly beneficial in disseminating useful knowledge throughout the United States, and deserving of public encouragement, they recommend, that each member of Congress be supplied at the public expence, with one paper, leaving the choice of the same to each member, and that it be the duty of the Secretary of the Senate, and clerk of the House of Representatives, to give the necessary directions to the different printers, to furnish each member with such paper as he shall chuse," being again read, and debated:

RESOLVED, That this House doth disagree to the said report.

The other report, being again read, and amended to read as followeth:

"That it would be proper that it should be left to the Secretary of the Senate, and clerk of the House of Representatives, to contract with such person as shall engage to execute the printing and binding business, on the most reasonable terms, the paper being furnished by the said Secretary and clerk, to such person, at the public expence. That such person as they shall contract with, shall be obliged to render a state of his accounts quarterly, and that six hundred copies of the acts of Congress, and seven hundred copies of the journals be printed, and distributed to the executive and judicial, and heads of departments of the government of the United States, and the executive, legislative, and judicial, of the several states."

RESOLVED, That this House doth agree to the said report.[94]

---

[92] A copy of the resolution is in Messages from the House, SR, DNA.

[93] On June 8 the House was notified that the Senate concurred in this resolution.

[94] A copy of the House proceedings on the report of the committee on newspapers is in Joint Committee Reports, SR, DNA. In compliance with the second report, John Beckley and Samuel A. Otis, clerk of the House of Representatives and secretary of the Senate, respectively, issued a joint statement that each would choose a printer for the journals for his respective house, and that Messrs. Francis Childs and John Swaine would print the laws of Congress and Thomas Greenleaf would print other bills as

ORDERED, That the clerk of this House do acquaint the Senate therewith.[95]

The order of the day, for the House to resolve itself into a committee of the whole House, on the report of the committee appointed to confer with a committee of the Senate, in preparing joint rules to be established between the two Houses, for the inrollment, attestation, publication, and preservation of the acts of Congress, and to regulate the mode of presenting addresses, and other acts, to the President of the United States, was read, and postponed until to-morrow.

And then the House adjourned until to-morrow morning eleven o'clock.

FRIDAY, MAY 29, 1789

An engrossed bill, imposing duties on tonnage, was read the third time.

RESOLVED, That the said bill do pass, and that the title be, "An act imposing duties on tonnage."[96]

ORDERED, That the clerk of this House do carry the said bill to the Senate, and desire their concurrence.[97]

Mr. Partridge, from the committee appointed to confer with a committee of the Senate, on the proper method of receiving into either House, bills, or messages, from the President of the United States, made a report, and the said report being amended to read as followeth:

That until the public offices are established, and the respective officers appointed, any returns of bills, and resolutions, or other communications from the President, may be received by either House, under cover, directed to the President of the Senate, or Speaker of the House of Representatives, as the case may be, and transmitted by such person as the President may think proper.

---

necessary. The agreement, with a note from Beckley explaining an amendment he inserted, and a copy of the agreement as corrected are in Records of the Secretary: Letters concerning printing, SR, DNA. Filed with the previously cited agreement are the contracts with Childs and Swaine, another journal extract of the report supporting Beckley's and Otis's authority to make the contracts, and two documents, one of which is a short statement of the agreement made by Beckley and Otis with Childs and Swaine, and the other which is a draft of the contract. In addition, there is a letter from Childs and Swaine outlining their conditions for printing the laws of Congress. There is also evidence that Beckley did send copies of the House Journal to the various state legislatures. Two letters from Beckley transmitting the journals are in Executive Papers, Archives Division, Vi, and the Livingston Papers, MHi.

[95] On June 3 the Senate sent an amendment to the report on printing to the House, and it was agreed to.

[96] This bill is E–45626.

[97] The Senate read this bill on June 9, 15, 16, and 17. On June 17 it was agreed to with amendments, which are printed in the *Senate Legislative Journal* for that date. The House was notified of these amendments on June 18.

RESOLVED, That this House doth agree to the said report.[98]

ORDERED, That the clerk of this House do acquaint the Senate therewith, and desire their concurrence.[99]

A bill to regulate the collection of duties imposed on goods, wares, and merchandizes imported into the United States, was read the second time, and ordered to be committed to a committee of the whole House, on Monday next.

The order of the day for the House to resolve itself into a committee of the whole House, on the report of a committee appointed to confer with a committee of the Senate, in preparing joint rules to be established between the two Houses, for the inrollment, attestation, publication, and preservation of the acts of Congress, and to regulate the mode of presenting addresses, and other acts, to the President of the United States, was read, and postponed until Monday next.[100]

And then the House adjourned until Monday morning eleven o'clock.

---

[98] A copy of the amended report with the resolution is in Joint Committee Reports, SR, DNA. A copy of the report is in A Record of the Reports of Select Committees, HR, DNA.

[99] On June 1 the Senate notified the House that they had agreed to this report.

[100] On June 1 the COWH considered this bill.

MONDAY, JUNE 1, 1789

ORDERED, That Mr. Bland have leave to be absent from the service of this House six weeks.

A message from the Senate, by Mr. Otis, their Secretary.

MR. SPEAKER, The Senate agree to the report, on the mode of receiving into either House, bills, or other communications, from the President of the United States, as the same was amended by this House. And then he withdrew.

The House, according to the order of the day, resolved itself into a committee of the whole House, on the bill to regulate the collection of duties imposed on goods, wares, and merchandizes imported into the United States.

Mr. Speaker left the chair.

Mr. Trumbull took the chair of the committee.

Mr. Speaker resumed the chair, and Mr. Trumbull reported, that the committee had, according to order, had the said bill under consideration, and made some progress therein.

RESOLVED, That this House will, to-morrow, again resolve itself into a committee of the whole House on the said bill.[1]

A message was received from the President of the United States, notifying, that the President approves of the act, entitled, "an act to regulate the time and manner of administering certain oaths," and has this day affixed his signature thereto; and the messenger delivered in the said act, and then withdrew.

ORDERED, That the clerk of this House do acquaint the Senate therewith.

Mr. Baldwin, from the committee appointed to take into consideration the subject of compensations to be made for the services of the President, Vice-President, the members of the Senate and House of Representatives, made a report, which was read, and ordered to lie on the table.[2]

On motion,

ORDERED, That Mr. Smith (of South-Carolina), Mr. Laurance, and Mr. Ames, be a committee to prepare and bring in a bill or bills, to establish an uniform system on the subject of bankruptcies throughout the United States.

The order of the day for the House to resolve itself into a committee of the whole House, on the report of the committee appointed to confer with a committee of the Senate, in preparing joint rules to be established between the two Houses, for the inrollment, attestation, publication, and preservation of

---

[1] On June 2 the COWH considered this bill again.

[2] A copy of the report is in A Record of the Reports of Select Committees, HR, DNA. On July 13 this report was considered.

the acts of Congress, and to regulate the mode of presenting addresses, and other acts, to the President of the United States, was read, and postponed until to-morrow.

And then the House adjourned until to-morrow morning eleven o'clock.

TUESDAY, JUNE 2, 1789

ORDERED, That Mr. Floyd have leave to be absent from the service of this House, until this day fortnight.

Mr. Speaker, pursuant to the directions of the act, entitled, "An act to regulate the time and manner of administering certain oaths," proceeded to administer the oath to support the Constitution of the United States, in the form prescribed by the said act, to the following members of this House, who had not before taken a similar oath, to wit: Abraham Baldwin, Egbert Benson, Aedanus Burke, Isaac Coles, Benjamin Contee, William Floyd, Jonathan Grout, John Hathorn, James Jackson, Samuel Livermore, Jeremiah Van Rensselaer, Joshua Seney, Thomas Sinnickson, Peter Silvester, Thomas Sumter, Jonathan Trumbull, John Vining, and Jeremiah Wadsworth.

The same oath, and moreover the oath of office, prescribed by the said act, were also administered by Mr. Speaker, to the clerk.

Mr. Huger, and Mr. Smith (of South-Carolina) produced certificates under the hand of the Chief Justice of New-York, of their having taken the oath to support the Constitution of the United States, before the said Chief Justice, pursuant to a former resolution of this House.

Mr. Baldwin, from the committee appointed, presented, according to order, a bill to establish an executive department, to be denominated the department of war, which was received, and read the first time.[3]

Mr. Baldwin, from the committee appointed, presented, according to order, a bill to establish an executive department, to be denominated, the department of foreign affairs, which was received, and read the first time.[4]

The House, according to the order of the day, resolved itself into a committee of the whole House, on the bill to regulate the collection of duties imposed on goods, wares, and merchandizes imported into the United States.

Mr. Speaker left the chair.

Mr. Trumbull took the chair of the committee.

Mr. Speaker resumed the chair, and Mr. Trumbull reported, that the committee had, according to order, had the said bill under consideration, and made a further progress therein.

---

[3] On June 3 this bill was read again.
[4] On June 3 this bill was read again.

RESOLVED, That this House will to-morrow, again resolve itself into a committee of the whole House on the said bill.[5]

On motion,

ORDERED, That it be an instruction to the committee appointed the eleventh of April, to prepare and bring in a bill or bills for regulating the collection of imposts and tonnage in the United States, that they do prepare and bring in a bill, directing the mode of registering and clearing vessels, ascertaining their tonnage, and for regulating the coasting trade, pilots, and light-houses.[6]

The order of the day for the House to resolve itself into a committee of the whole House, on the report of the committee appointed to confer with a committee of the Senate, in preparing joint rules to be established between the two Houses, for the inrollment, attestation, publication, and preservation of the acts of Congress, and to regulate the mode of presenting addresses, and other acts, to the President of the United States; was read, and postponed until to-morrow.

And then the House adjourned until to-morrow morning eleven o'clock.

WEDNESDAY, JUNE 3, 1789

A message from the Senate, by Mr. Otis, their Secretary.

MR. SPEAKER,   The Senate have agreed to the amended report, for the publication of the acts of Congress, with an amendment,[7] to which they desire the concurrence of this House.   And then he withdrew.

The House proceeded to consider the amendment of the Senate to the said report, and the same being read, was agreed to.

ORDERED, That the clerk of this House do acquaint the Senate therewith.

A bill to establish an executive department, to be denominated the department of war, was read the second time, and ordered to be committed to a committee of the whole House, on Tuesday next.[8]

A bill to establish an executive department, to be denominated the department of foreign affairs, was read the second time, and ordered to be committed to a committee of the whole House, on Tuesday next.[9]

---

[5] On June 3 the COWH considered this bill again.

[6] The committee members are Nicholas Gilman, Elbridge Gerry, Roger Sherman, John Laurance, Lambert Cadwalader, Thomas Fitzsimons, George Gale, James Madison, and Thomas Tucker. On June 12 three members were added to this committee.

[7] The Senate amendment is noted on the copy of the House proceedings of May 28 in Joint Committee Reports, SR, DNA. The amendment is printed in the *Senate Legislative Journal* on June 2.

[8] From June 9–23 consideration of this bill was postponed. On June 24 amendments to it were presented from the COWH.

[9] Consideration of this bill in the COWH was postponed as an order of the day on June 9 and 10. On June 16 it was considered in the COWH.

A message from the Senate, by Mr. Otis, their secretary.

MR. SPEAKER,   The Senate are about to proceed to take the oath to support the Constitution of the United States, pursuant to the act, entitled, "An
act to regulate the time and manner of administering certain oaths," and request that the said act, to which the President of the United States affixed his
signature, may be sent to them for that purpose.   And then he withdrew.

ORDERED, That the clerk of this House do carry the said act to the Senate,
for the purpose expressed in their message.

The House, according to the order of the day, resolved itself into a committee of the whole House, on the bill to regulate the collection of duties imposed on goods, wares, and merchandizes imported into the United States.

Mr. Speaker left the chair.

Mr. Trumbull took the chair of the committee.

Mr. Speaker resumed the chair, and Mr. Trumbull reported, that the committee had, according to order, had the said bill under consideration, and
made a farther progress therein.

RESOLVED, That this House will, to-morrow, again resolve itself into a
committee of the whole House, on the said bill.[10]

The order of the day, for the House to resolve itself into a committee of the
whole House, on the report of the committee appointed to confer with a committee of the Senate, in preparing joint rules to be established between the
two Houses, for the inrollment, attestation, publication, and preservation of
the acts of Congress, and to regulate the mode of presenting addresses, and
other acts, to the President of the United States, was read, and postponed until to-morrow.

And then the House adjourned until to-morrow morning eleven o'clock.

THURSDAY, JUNE 4, 1789

The House, according to the order of the day, resolved itself into a committee of the whole House, on the bill to regulate the collection of duties imposed on goods, wares, and merchandizes imported into the United States.

Mr. Speaker left the chair.

Mr. Trumbull took the chair of the committee.

Mr. Speaker resumed the chair, and Mr. Trumbull reported, that the committee had, according to order, had the said bill under consideration, and
made a farther progress therein.

---

[10] On June 4 the COWH considered this bill again.

RESOLVED, That this House will, to-morrow, again resolve itself into a committee of the whole House on the said bill.[11]

A message from the Senate, by Mr. Otis, their Secretary.

MR. SPEAKER,   The Senate have agreed to the following resolution:

UNITED STATES OF AMERICA

IN SENATE, June 4, 1789

"RESOLVED, That in ten days after the passing of every act of Congress during the present session, or until some other regulation shall be adopted, twenty-two printed copies thereof, signed by the Secretary of the Senate, and Clerk of the House of Representatives, and certified by them to be true copies of the original acts, be lodged with the President of the United States; and that he be requested to cause to be transmitted, two of the said copies, so attested as aforesaid, to each of the Supreme Executives in the several states"— To which resolution they desire the concurrence of this House.[12]   And then he withdrew.

Mr. Baldwin, from the committee appointed, presented, according to order, a bill to establish an executive department, to be denominated the treasury department, which was received, and read the first time.[13]

The order of the day, for the House to resolve itself into a committee of the whole House, on the report of the committee appointed to confer with a committee of the Senate, in preparing joint rules to be established between the two Houses, for the inrollment, attestation, publication, and preservation of the acts of Congress, and to regulate the mode of presenting addresses, and other acts, to the President of the United States, was read, and postponed until to-morrow.

And then the House adjourned until to-morrow morning eleven o'clock.

FRIDAY, JUNE 5, 1789

ORDERED, That Mr. Wynkoop have leave to be absent from the service of this House, until this day fortnight.

The House proceeded to consider the resolution of the Senate, sent for concurrence yesterday;[14]   whereupon,

---

[11] On June 5 the COWH considered this bill again.

[12] A copy of the resolution is in Senate Joint and Concurrent Resolutions, SR, DNA. A draft of a circular letter from George Washington addressed to the executives of the states indicates his agreement to this resolution. It is in Miscellaneous Letters, M179, roll 2, RG 59, General Records of the Department of State (hereinafter referred to as RG 59), DNA. On June 5 the House agreed to this resolution.

[13] On June 5 this bill was read again.

[14] The resolution concerns sending the acts of Congress to the states.

RESOLVED, That this House doth concur with the Senate, in the said resolution.

ORDERED, That the clerk of this House do acquaint the Senate therewith.

A bill to establish an executive department, to be denominated the treasury department, was read the second time, and ordered to be committed to a committee of the whole House on Tuesday next.[15]

The House, according to the order of the day, resolved itself into a committee of the whole House, on the bill to regulate the collection of duties imposed on goods, wares, and merchandizes imported into the United States.

Mr. Speaker left the chair.

Mr. Trumbull took the chair of the committee.

Mr. Speaker resumed the chair, and Mr. Trumbull reported that the committee had, according to order, had the said bill under consideration, and made a farther progress therein.

RESOLVED, That this House will, on Monday next, again resolve itself into a committee of the whole House on the said bill.[16]

A petition of the tradesmen and manufacturers of the town of Boston, was presented to the House and read, praying the attention of Congress to the encouragement of manufactures, and the increase of American shipping, by such commercial regulations as the wisdom of the National Legislature shall judge most consistent with the interest, prosperity and happiness of this extensive empire.[17]

ORDERED, That the said petition do lie on the table.

The order of the day, for the House to resolve itself into a committee of the whole House, on the report of the committee appointed to confer with a committee of the Senate, in preparing joint rules to be established between the two Houses, for the inrollment, attestation, publication, and preservation of the acts of Congress, and to regulate the mode of presenting addresses, and other acts, to the President of the United States, was read, and postponed until Monday next.

And then the House adjourned until Monday morning eleven o'clock.

MONDAY, JUNE 8, 1789

Another member, to wit, Michael Jenifer Stone, from Maryland, appeared and took his seat; the oath to support the Constitution of the United States having been first administered to him by the Speaker, pursuant to a late act of Congress.

---

[15] From June 9–24 consideration of this bill was postponed. On June 25 the bill was considered in the COWH.

[16] On June 9 the COWH considered this bill again.

[17] The petition is in Petitions and Memorials: Various subjects, SR, DNA.

A petition of Nicholas Pike, of Newburyport, in the state of Massachusetts, was presented to the House and read, praying that an exclusive privilege may be granted him for a limited time, in the publication of a work which he has lately written, entitled, "A new and complete System of Arithmetic."

ORDERED, That the said petition be referred to Mr. Huntington, Mr. Cadwalader, and Mr. Contee, that they do examine the matter thereof, and report the same with their opinion thereupon, to the House.[18]

A message from the Senate, by Mr. Otis, their Secretary.

MR. SPEAKER,   The Senate concur in the resolution of this House, of the twenty-eighth ultimo, for furnishing each member of the present Congress with a complete set of the journals of the late Congress.   And then he withdrew.

A motion was made and seconded, that the House do come to a resolution, stating certain specific amendments, proper to be proposed by Congress, to the legislatures of the States, to become, if ratified by three-fourths thereof, part of the Constitution of the United States: Whereupon,

ORDERED, That the said motion be referred to the consideration of the committee of the whole House, on the state of the Union.[19]

The orders of the day, for the House to resolve itself into a committee of the whole House, on the bill to regulate the collection of duties imposed on goods, wares, and merchandizes imported into the United States; also on the report of the committee appointed to confer with a committee of the Senate, in preparing joint rules to be established between the two Houses, for the inrollment, attestation, publication, and preservation of the acts of Congress, and to regulate the mode of presenting addresses, and other acts, to the President of the United States, were read, and postponed until to-morrow.

And then the House adjourned until to-morrow morning eleven o'clock.

TUESDAY, JUNE 9, 1789

On motion,

The order of the day for the House to resolve itself into a committee of the whole House, on the report of the committee appointed to confer with a committee of the Senate, in preparing joint rules to be established between the two Houses, for the inrollment, attestation, publication, and preservation of the acts of Congress, and to regulate the mode of presenting addresses, and

---

[18] On June 23 this committee presented the Copyright Bill (and Patents) [HR–10], which was read.

[19] On July 21 the COWH was discharged from consideration of this motion, and the motion was committed.

other acts, to the President of the United States, was farther postponed until this day fortnight.

On motion,

RESOLVED, That so much of the standing rules and orders, as directs that upon a division of the House on any question, the members who vote in the affirmative shall go to the right, and those in the negative to the left of the chair, be rescinded; and that in future when a division is called for, those in the affirmative of the question shall rise from their seats, and those in the negative remain sitting.

The House, according to the order of the day, resolved itself into a committee of the whole House, on the bill to regulate the collection of duties imposed on goods, wares, and merchandizes imported into the United States.

Mr. Speaker left the chair.

Mr. Trumbull took the chair of the committee.

Mr. Speaker resumed the chair, and Mr. Trumbull reported, that the committee had, according to order, had the said bill under consideration, and made a farther progress therein.

RESOLVED, That this House will, to-morrow, again resolve itself into a committee of the whole House on the said bill.[20]

The several orders of the day for the House to resolve itself into a committee of the whole House, on the bills establishing executive departments of war, of foreign affairs, and of the treasury department, were read, and postponed until to-morrow.

And then the House adjourned until to-morrow morning eleven o'clock.

WEDNESDAY, JUNE 10, 1789

On motion,

The several orders of the day for the House to resolve itself into a committee of the whole House on the bills establishing executive departments of war, of foreign affairs, and of the treasury, were farther postponed until Tuesday next.

The House, according to the order of the day, resolved itself into a committee of the whole House, on the bill to regulate the collection of duties imposed on goods, wares, and merchandizes imported into the United States.

Mr. Speaker left the chair.

Mr. Trumbull took the chair of the committee.

Mr. Speaker resumed the chair, and Mr. Trumbull reported, that the committee had, according to order, had the said bill under consideration, and made a farther progress therein.

---

[20] On June 10 the COWH considered this bill again.

RESOLVED, That this House will, to-morrow, again resolve itself into a committee of the whole House, on the said bill.[21]

ORDERED, That Mr. Gale have leave to be absent from the service of this House until Tuesday fortnight.

And then the House adjourned until to-morrow morning eleven o'clock.

THURSDAY, JUNE 11, 1789

The House, according to the order of the day, resolved itself into a committee of the whole House, on the bill to regulate the collection of duties imposed on goods, wares, and merchandizes imported into the United States.

Mr. Speaker left the chair.

Mr. Trumbull took the chair of the committee.

Mr. Speaker resumed the chair, and Mr. Trumbull reported, that the committee had, according to order, had the said bill under consideration, and made a farther progress therein.

RESOLVED, That this House will to-morrow, again resolve itself, into a committee of the whole House on the said bill.[22]

And then the House adjourned until to-morrow morning eleven o'clock.

FRIDAY, JUNE 12, 1789

On motion,

ORDERED, That Mr. Vining, Mr. Stone, and Mr. Jackson, be added to the committee to whom it was referred to prepare and bring in a bill, directing the mode of registering and clearing vessels, ascertaining their tonnage, and for regulating the coasting trade, pilots, and light-houses.[23]

A message from the Senate, by Mr. Otis, their Secretary.

MR. SPEAKER, The Senate have passed the bill, entitled, "An act for laying a duty on goods, wares, and merchandizes imported into the United States," with several amendments, to which they desire the concurrence of this House.[24] And then he withdrew.

The House, according to the order of the day, resolved itself into a commit-

---

[21] On June 11 the COWH considered this bill again.

[22] On June 12 the COWH considered this bill again.

[23] On July 1 this committee presented the Lighthouses Bill [HR–12], which was read. On July 24 this committee presented the Coasting Bill [HR–16], which was read.

[24] Senate amendments are filed with the bill in House Bills, SR, DNA. The amendments are printed in the *Senate Legislative Journal* on June 11. On June 15 these amendments were considered.

tee of the whole House, on the bill to regulate the collection of duties imposed on goods, wares, and merchandizes imported into the United States.

Mr. Speaker left the chair.

Mr. Trumbull took the chair of the committee.

Mr. Speaker resumed the chair, and Mr. Trumbull reported that the committee had, according to order, had the said bill under consideration, and made a farther progress therein.

RESOLVED, That this House will, to-morrow, again resolve itself into a committee of the whole House on the said bill.[25]

And then the House adjourned until to-morrow morning eleven o'clock.

SATURDAY, JUNE 13, 1789

The House, according to the order of the day, resolved itself into a committee of the whole House, on the bill to regulate the collection of duties imposed on goods, wares, and merchandizes imported into the United States.

Mr. Speaker left the chair.

Mr. Trumbull took the chair of the committee.

Mr. Speaker resumed the chair, and Mr. Trumbull reported that the committee had, according to order, had the said bill under consideration, and made a farther progress therein.

On motion,

ORDERED, That the committee of the whole House be discharged from farther proceeding on the said bill, and that it be committed to a committee of seven.

The members elected, Mr. Goodhue, Mr. Fitzsimons, Mr. Laurance, Mr. Jackson, Mr. Burke, Mr. Livermore, and Mr. Sherman.[26]

And then the House adjourned until Monday morning eleven o'clock.

MONDAY, JUNE 15, 1789

Two other members, to wit, John Brown, from Virginia, and Theodore Sedgwick, from Massachusetts, appeared and took their seats; the oath to support the Constitution of the United States having been first administered to them by the Speaker, pursuant to a late act of Congress.

On motion,

ORDERED, That Mr. Smith, of Maryland, and Mr. Parker, be added to the committee appointed on Saturday last, and to whom was committed the bill

---

[25] On June 13 the COWH considered this bill again. The bill was then committed.
[26] On June 15 two members were added to this committee.

to regulate the collection of duties imposed on goods, wares, and merchandizes imported into the United States.[27]

Mr. Scott, from the committee appointed to consider the state of the unappropriated lands in the western territory, made a report, which was read, and ordered to be referred to the committee of the whole House on the state of the Union.[28]

The House proceeded to consider the amendments proposed by the Senate, to the bill, entitled, "An act for laying a duty on goods, wares, and merchandizes imported into the United States," and made some progress therein.[29]

And then the House adjourned until to-morrow morning eleven o'clock.

TUESDAY, JUNE 16, 1789

On motion,

RESOLVED, That seats be provided within the bar of this House for the accommodation of the President, and members of the Senate.

The House proceeded to consider the amendments of the Senate to the bill, entitled, "An act for laying a duty on goods, wares, and merchandizes imported into the United States:" Whereupon,

RESOLVED, That this House doth agree to the first, eighth, ninth, tenth, sixteenth, eighteenth, nineteenth, twentieth, twenty-first, twenty-third, thirty-first, thirty-third, thirty-fourth, thirty-fifth, thirty-sixth, thirty-seventh, thirty-eighth, thirty-ninth, and fortieth amendments;

And doth disagree to the second, fourth, fifth, sixth, seventh, eleventh, twelfth, thirteenth, fourteenth, fifteenth, seventeenth, twenty-second, twenty-fourth, twenty-fifth, twenty-sixth, twenty-seventh, twenty-eighth, twenty-ninth, thirtieth, and thirty-second amendments.

The third amendment was read, and agreed to, with an amendment, by striking out the word "July," proposed to be inserted by the Senate, and inserting in lieu thereof, the word "August."

ORDERED, That the clerk of this House do acquaint the Senate therewith.[30]

The House, according to the order of the day, resolved itself into a committee of the whole House on the bill establishing an executive department, to be denominated "the department of foreign affairs."

Mr. Speaker left the chair.

Mr. Trumbull took the chair of the committee.

---

[27] On June 29 this committee presented a third Collection Bill [HR–11], which was read.

[28] On July 13 this report was considered in the COWH.

[29] On June 16 the House agreed to some of these amendments and disagreed to others.

[30] The Senate considered the House actions on June 18, and on June 19 they insisted upon some of their amendments and receded from others.

Mr. Speaker resumed the chair, and Mr. Trumbull reported, that the committee had, according to order, had the said bill under consideration, and made some progress therein.

RESOLVED, That this House will, to-morrow, again resolve itself into a committee of the whole House on the said bill.[31]

The orders of the day, for the House to resolve itself into a committee of the whole House, on the bill establishing an executive department, to be denominated "the department of war;" also on the bill establishing an executive department, to be denominated "the treasury department," were read, and postponed until to-morrow.

And then the House adjourned until to-morrow morning eleven o'clock.

WEDNESDAY, JUNE 17, 1789

Another member, to wit, George Mathews, from Georgia, appeared and took his seat; the oath to support the Constitution of the United States having been first administered to him by the Speaker, pursuant to a late act of Congress.

The House, according to the order of the day, resolved itself into a committee of the whole House on the bill "establishing an executive department, to be denominated the department of foreign affairs."

Mr. Speaker left the chair.

Mr. Trumbull took the chair of the committee.

Mr. Speaker resumed the chair, and Mr. Trumbull reported, that the committee had, according to order, had the said bill under consideration, and made a farther progress therein.

RESOLVED, That this House will, to-morrow, again resolve itself into a committee of the whole House on the said bill.[32]

The orders of the day, for the House to resolve itself into a committee of the whole House, on the bill "establishing an executive department, to be denominated the department of war;" also on the bill "establishing an executive department, to be denominated the treasury department," were read and postponed until to-morrow.

And then the House adjourned until to-morrow morning eleven o'clock.

THURSDAY, JUNE 18, 1789

A petition of Robert Frazier, late a soldier in the continental army, was presented to the House and read, praying that compensation may be made him for military services rendered during the late war.

ORDERED, That the said petition do lie on the table.

A message from the Senate, by Mr. Otis, their Secretary.

---

[31] On June 17 the COWH considered this bill again.
[32] On June 18 the COWH considered this bill again.

MR. SPEAKER, The Senate have passed the bill, entitled, "An act imposing duties on tonnage," with several amendments, to which they desire the
concurrence of this House.[33] And then he withdrew.

ORDERED, That Mr. Floyd have leave to be absent from the service of this
House until this day fortnight.

The House, according to the orders of the day, resolved itself into a committee of the whole House, on the bill "establishing an executive department,
to be denominated the department of foreign affairs."

Mr. Speaker left the chair.

Mr. Trumbull took the chair of the committee.

Mr. Speaker resumed the chair, and Mr. Trumbull reported, that the committee had, according to order, had the said bill under consideration, and
made a farther progress therein.

RESOLVED, That this House will, to-morrow, again resolve itself into a
committee of the whole House on the said bill.[34]

The orders of the day for the House to resolve itself into a committee of
the whole House, on the bill "establishing an executive department, to be
denominated the department of war;" also, on the bill "establishing an executive department, to be denominated the treasury department," were read and
postponed until to-morrow.

And then the House adjourned until to-morrow morning eleven o'clock.

FRIDAY, JUNE 19, 1789

The House, according to the order of the day, resolved itself into a committee of the whole House on the bill "establishing an executive department,
to be denominated the department of foreign affairs."

Mr. Speaker left the chair.

Mr. Trumbull took the chair of the committee.

Mr. Speaker resumed the chair, and Mr. Trumbull reported, that the committee had, according to order, had the said bill under consideration, and
gone through the same, and made several amendments thereto, which they
had directed him to report, when the House should think proper to receive
the same.

---

[33] Annotations on the printed bill, in the Broadside Collection, Rare Book Room
(hereinafter referred to as RBkRm), DLC, correspond roughly to Senate amendments. The amendments are printed in the *Senate Legislative Journal* on June 17. On
June 24 these amendments were considered, and a conference was appointed on the
bill.

[34] On June 19 the COWH reported that they had made amendments to this bill.

ORDERED, That the said report be received on Monday next.[35]

A message from the Senate, by Mr. Otis, their Secretary.

MR. SPEAKER,   The Senate recede from the third, thirteenth, fourteenth, fifteenth, twenty-second, twenty-fourth, twenty-fifth, twenty-sixth, twenty-seventh, twenty-eighth, twenty-ninth, thirtieth, and thirty-second of their proposed amendments to the bill, entitled, "An act for laying a duty on goods, wares, and merchandizes, imported into the United States," disagreed to by this House, and do insist on their second, fourth, fifth, sixth, seventh, eleventh, twelfth, and seventeenth amendments to the same bill, also disagreed to by this House.[36] The Senate have also agreed to the report of a joint committee, appointed to view and report on the appropriation of the rooms in the city-hall, to which they desire the concurrence of this House.[37]   And then he withdrew.

The orders of the day for the House to resolve itself into a committee of the whole House on the bill "establishing an executive department, to be denominated the department of war," also on the bill "establishing an executive department, to be denominated the treasury department," were read and postponed until Monday next.

And then the House adjourned until Monday morning eleven o'clock.

MONDAY, JUNE 22, 1789

The House proceeded to consider the report of a joint committee, agreed to by the Senate on Friday last, and sent to this House for concurrence, to wit, "That the two rooms on the first floor in the south-west angle of the city-hall are not necessary for the accommodation of Congress, and that the Mayor of the city be notified thereof, that the said rooms may be occupied by such persons as the corporation may employ to take charge of the building:"   Whereupon,

RESOLVED, That this House doth agree to the said report.

The House, according to the order of the day, proceeded to consider the amendments agreed to by the committee of the whole House, on Friday last, to the bill "for establishing an executive department, to be denominated the

---

[35] On June 22 the COWH's amendments were agreed to along with two other amendments to this bill.

[36] On June 23 this Senate message was considered.

[37] A copy of the report with the House resolution is in Joint Committee Reports, SR, DNA. A copy of the report is in A Record of the Reports of Select Committees, HR, DNA. A copy of a note from John Beckley and Samuel Otis to the Mayor of New York regarding the report is in Other Records: Various papers, SR, DNA. On June 22 the House printed and agreed to this report.

department of foreign affairs;" and the said amendments being severally twice read at the clerk's table, were agreed to by the House.

A motion was made and seconded, farther to amend the said bill, by striking out the words "in case of vacancy in the said office of secretary to the United States for the department of foreign affairs," in the second enacting clause, and to insert in lieu thereof, the words "whenever the said principal officer shall be removed from office by the President of the United States, or in any other case of vacancy."

And the question being put thereupon,

It was resolved in the affirmative— $\begin{cases} \text{AYES} & 30 \\ \text{NOES} & 18 \end{cases}$

The ayes and noes being demanded by one fifth of the members present, Those who voted in the affirmative, are,

Fisher Ames	Richard Bland Lee
Abraham Baldwin	George Leonard
Egbert Benson	James Madison, junior
John Brown	Andrew Moore
Aedanus Burke	Peter Muhlenberg
Daniel Carroll	Thomas Scott
George Clymer	Theodore Sedgwick
Benjamin Contee	Joshua Seney
Thomas Fitzsimons	Thomas Sinnickson
Nicholas Gilman	William Smith (of Maryland)
Benjamin Goodhue	Peter Silvester
Samuel Griffin	George Thatcher
Thomas Hartley	Jonathan Trumbull
Daniel Hiester	John Vining and
John Laurance	Jeremiah Wadsworth

Those who voted in the negative, are,

Lambert Cadwalader	Josiah Parker
Isaac Coles	George Partridge
Elbridge Gerry	Jeremiah Van Rensselaer
Jonathan Grout	Roger Sherman
John Hathorn	William Smith (of South-Carolina)
Benjamin Huntington	Jonathan Sturges
Samuel Livermore	Thomas Sumter
George Mathews	Thomas Tudor Tucker and
John Page	Alexander White

A motion was then made and seconded, farther to amend the said bill by striking out the words "to be removable from office by the President of the United States," in the first enacting clause:

And the question being put thereupon,

It was resolved in the affirmative— $\begin{cases} \text{Ayes} & 31 \\ \text{Noes} & 19 \end{cases}$

The ayes and noes being demanded by one fifth of the members present, Those who voted in the affirmative, are,

Fisher Ames	George Mathews
Abraham Baldwin	Andrew Moore
Egbert Benson	Peter Muhlenberg
John Brown	John Page
Aedanus Burke	Josiah Parker
George Clymer	George Partridge
Isaac Coles	Jeremiah Van Rensselaer
Elbridge Gerry	Thomas Scott
Benjamin Goodhue	Roger Sherman
Samuel Griffin	Thomas Sinnickson
Jonathan Grout	William Smith (of South-Carolina)
John Hathorn	Jonathan Sturges
Benjamin Huntington	Thomas Sumter
George Leonard	John Vining and
Samuel Livermore	Alexander White
James Madison, junior	

Those who voted in the negative, are,

Elias Boudinot	James Schureman
Lambert Cadwalader	Theodore Sedgwick
Daniel Carroll	Joshua Seney
Benjamin Contee	William Smith (of Maryland)
Thomas Fitzsimons	Peter Silvester
Nicholas Gilman	George Thatcher
Thomas Hartley	Jonathan Trumbull
Daniel Hiester	Thomas Tudor Tucker and
John Laurance	Jeremiah Wadsworth
Richard Bland Lee	

Ordered, That the said bill be engrossed, and read the third time to-morrow.[38]

---

[38] On June 23 the third reading of this bill was postponed.

The orders of the day for the House to resolve itself into a committee of the whole House on the bill "establishing an executive department, to be denominated the department of war;" also on the bill "establishing an executive department, to be denominated the treasury department," were read and postponed until to-morrow.

And then the House adjourned until to-morrow morning eleven o'clock.

TUESDAY, JUNE 23, 1789

Mr. Huntington, from the committee appointed, presented, according to order, a bill to promote the progress of science and useful arts, by securing to authors and inventors the exclusive right to their respective writings and discoveries; which was received and read the first time.[39]

On motion,

ORDERED, That the third reading of the engrossed bill, entitled, "An act for establishing an executive department, to be denominated the department of foreign affairs," be put off until to-morrow.[40]

The House proceeded to consider the message sent from the Senate on Friday last, touching their amendments to the bill, entitled, "An act for laying a duty on goods, wares and merchandizes imported into the United States," and made some progress therein.[41]

The orders of the day for the House to resolve itself into a committee of the whole House, on the bill "establishing an executive department, to be denominated the department of war;" also on the bill "establishing an executive department, to be denominated the treasury department;" and also on the report of the committee, appointed to confer with a committee of the Senate, in preparing joint rules to be established between the two Houses, for the inrollment, attestation, publication, and preservation of the acts of Congress, and to regulate the mode of presenting addresses, and other acts, to the President of the United States; were read, and postponed until to-morrow.

And then the House adjourned until to-morrow morning eleven o'clock.

WEDNESDAY, JUNE 24, 1789

A bill to promote the progress of science and useful arts, by securing to authors and inventors the exclusive right to their respective writings and discoveries, was read the second time, and ordered to be committed to a committee of the whole House on Monday se'nnight.[42]

---

[39] On June 24 this bill was read again.

[40] On June 24 this bill was read, agreed to, and sent to the Senate.

[41] On June 24 this message was considered again, and a conference was appointed on the bill.

[42] This bill was postponed as an order of the day from July 6 through August 15. On August 17 it was postponed until second session.

An engrossed bill "for establishing an executive department, to be denominated the department of foreign affairs," was read the third time, and the question being put that the said bill do pass,

It was resolved in the affirmative, $\begin{cases} \text{AYES} & 29 \\ \text{NOES} & 22 \end{cases}$

The ayes and noes being demanded by one fifth of the members present, Those who voted in the affirmative, are,

Fisher Ames	Daniel Huger
Egbert Benson	John Laurance
Elias Boudinot	Richard Bland Lee
John Brown	James Madison, junior
Aedanus Burke	Andrew Moore
Lambert Cadwalader	Peter Muhlenberg
Daniel Carroll	James Schureman
George Clymer	Thomas Scott
Benjamin Contee	Theodore Sedgwick
Thomas Fitzsimons	Joshua Seney
Nicholas Gilman	Thomas Sinnickson
Benjamin Goodhue	Peter Silvester
Samuel Griffin	Jonathan Trumbull and
Thomas Hartley	John Vining
Daniel Hiester	

Those who voted in the negative, are,

Isaac Coles	George Partridge
Elbridge Gerry	Jeremiah Van Rensselaer
Jonathan Grout	Roger Sherman
John Hathorn	William Smith (of Maryland)
Benjamin Huntington	William Smith (of South-Carolina)
James Jackson	Michael Jenifer Stone
George Leonard	Jonathan Sturges
Samuel Livermore	Thomas Sumter
George Mathews	George Thatcher
John Page	Thomas Tudor Tucker and
Josiah Parker	Alexander White

RESOLVED, That the title of the said bill be, "An act for establishing an executive department, to be denominated the department of foreign affairs;"

and that the clerk of this House do carry the said bill to the Senate, and desire their concurrence.[43]

The House resumed the consideration of the message sent from the Senate on Friday last, touching their amendment to the bill, entitled "An act for laying a duty on goods, wares and merchandizes imported into the United States:" Whereupon,

RESOLVED, That this House doth recede from their disagreement to the second amendment to the said bill, and doth agree to the said second amendment with an amendment, by inserting after the words "*Senate and*" the words "House of."

RESOLVED, That this House doth insist on their disagreement to the fourth and fifth amendments to the said bill.

ORDERED, That a conference be desired with the Senate, on the subject matter of the sixth, seventh, eleventh, twelfth, and seventeenth amendments to the said bill, and that Mr. Boudinot, Mr. Fitzsimons, and Mr. Madison, be appointed managers at the said conference, on the part of this House.[44]

The House proceeded to consider the amendments of the Senate to the bill entitled, "An act imposing duties on tonnage:" Whereupon,

RESOLVED, That this House doth agree to the first, second and ninth amendments to the said bill, with amendments to the said first and ninth amendment, as follow:

In the first amendment, after the words "*Senate and*" insert "House of."

In the ninth amendment, strike out the word "*July*," and insert "August."

RESOLVED, That this House doth disagree to the third, fourth, fifth, sixth, seventh, and eighth amendments to the said bill.

ORDERED, That a conference be desired with the Senate upon the subject matter of the amendments disagreed to, and that Mr. Boudinot, Mr. Fitzsimons, and Mr. Madison, be appointed managers at the said conference on the part of this House.[45]

The House, according to the order of the day, resolved itself into a committee of the whole House, on the bill "for establishing an executive department, to be denominated the department of war."

Mr. Speaker left the chair.

---

[43] A copy of the bill is in House Bills, SR, DNA. The Senate read this bill on June 25, July 14, 15, 16, and 17. On July 17 an amendment was agreed to. On July 18 several amendments were proposed, and one was agreed to. The bill was then agreed to. The House was notified on July 20 and agreed to the Senate amendments on the same day.

[44] On June 25 the House was notified of further Senate action on these amendments and the appointment of a conference.

[45] On June 25 the House was notified that the Senate had agreed to the House amendments to their amendments and to the conference on the amendments disagreed to.

Mr. Trumbull took the chair of the committee.

Mr. Speaker resumed the chair, and Mr. Trumbull reported, that the committee had, according to order, had the said bill under consideration, and gone through the same, and made several amendments thereto, which he delivered in at the clerk's table, where the same were read and partly considered.[46]

The orders of the day for the House to resolve itself into a committee of the whole House, on the bill to "establish an executive department, to be denominated the treasury department;" also on the report of the committee appointed to confer with a committee of the Senate in preparing joint rules to be established between the two Houses, for the inrollment, attestation, publication, and preservation of the acts of Congress, and to regulate the mode of presenting addresses, and other acts, to the President of the United States, were read and postponed until to-morrow.

And then the House adjourned until to-morrow morning eleven o'clock.

THURSDAY, JUNE 25, 1789

ORDERED, That Mr. Hiester have leave to be absent from the service of this House until Monday fortnight.

A petition of Samuel Briggs, of the city of Philadelphia, was presented to the House and read, praying that an exclusive privilege may be granted him for a limited time, to construct and vend a machine which he has invented for making nails by mill-work.

ORDERED, That the said petition do lie on the table.

The House resumed the consideration of the amendments reported yesterday by the committee of the whole House, to the bill "for establishing an executive department, to be denominated the department of war;" and the same being twice read at the clerk's table, were severally agreed to by the House.

ORDERED, That the said bill, with the amendments, be engrossed, and read the third time to-morrow.[47]

The House, according to the order of the day, resolved itself into a committee of the whole House, on the bill, "establishing an executive department, to be denominated the treasury department."

Mr. Speaker left the chair.

Mr. Trumbull took the chair of the committee.

Mr. Speaker resumed the chair, and Mr. Trumbull reported, that the com-

---

[46] On June 25 these amendments were agreed to.
[47] On June 27 this bill was read again, agreed to, and sent to the Senate.

mittee had, according to order, had the said bill under consideration, and made some progress therein.

RESOLVED, That this House will, to-morrow, again resolve itself into a committee of the whole House on the said bill.[48]

A message from the Senate, by Mr. Otis, their Secretary.

MR. SPEAKER, The Senate agree to the amendment proposed by this House to their amendment to the bill, entitled, "An act for laying a duty on goods, wares and merchandizes imported into the United States;" insist on their fourth and fifth amendments to the said bill, agree to the proposed conference on the subject matter of the other amendments thereto, and have charged their managers to confer also on the said fourth and fifth amendments.[49] The Senate likewise agree to the amendments proposed by this House to their first and ninth amendments to the bill, entitled, "An act imposing duties on tonnage;" as also to the proposed conference on the subject matter of the other amendments to the said bill.[50]   And then he withdrew.

The order of the day for the House to resolve itself into a committee of the whole House on the report of the committee appointed to confer with a committee of the Senate, in preparing joint rules to be established between the two Houses for the inrollment, attestation, publication and preservation of the acts of Congress; and to regulate the mode of presenting addresses and other acts to the President of the United States, was read and postponed until to-morrow.

And then the House adjourned until to-morrow morning eleven o'clock.

FRIDAY, JUNE 26, 1789

The orders of the day for the House to resolve itself into a committee of the whole House on the bill, "establishing an executive department, to be denominated, the treasury department;" also on the report of the committee appointed to confer with a committee of the Senate, in preparing joint rules to be established between the two Houses, for the inrollment, attestation, publication, and preservation of the acts of Congress, and to regulate the mode of presenting addresses, and other acts to the President of the United States, were read, and postponed until to-morrow.

And then the House adjourned until to-morrow morning eleven o'clock.

---

[48] On June 26 and 27 consideration of this bill was postponed. On June 29 the bill was considered in the COWH.

[49] On June 27 this conference reported, and further action was taken on the amendments.

[50] On June 27 this conference reported, and the House took further action on the Senate amendments.

SATURDAY, JUNE 27, 1789

A petition of Tristram Coffin, of Nantucket, in the state of Massachusetts, was presented to the House, and read, praying that compensation may be made him for a schooner, which was taken into the service of the United States, during the late war, and burnt by the enemy.

ORDERED, That the said petition do lie on the table.[51]

An engrossed bill "for establishing an executive department, to be denominated, the department of war," was read the third time.

RESOLVED, That the said bill do pass, and that the title be, "An act to establish an executive department, to be denominated the department of war."[52]

ORDERED, That the clerk of this House do carry the said bill to the Senate, and desire their concurrence.[53]

Mr. Boudinot, from the managers appointed on the part of this House, to attend the conference with the Senate, on the subject matter of the amendments depending between the two Houses, to the bill, entitled, "An act for laying a duty on goods, wares and merchandizes, imported into the United States," made a report:[54]   Whereupon,

RESOLVED, That this House doth recede from their disagreement to the fourth, fifth, sixth, seventh, eleventh, twelfth and seventeenth amendments, and doth agree to the said amendments respectively, with amendments to the said twelfth and seventeenth amendments, as follow:

In the twelfth amendment, strike out "*sixteen*," and insert "twenty."

In the seventeenth amendment, strike out "*one*," and insert "two."[55]

Mr. Boudinot, from the managers appointed on the part of this House, to attend the conference with the Senate, on the subject matter of the amendments depending between the two Houses, to the bill, entitled, "An act imposing duties on tonnage," made a report:[56]   Whereupon,

RESOLVED, That this House doth recede from their disagreement to the third, seventh, and eighth amendments, and doth agree to the said amendments, with an amendment to the third amendment, as followeth:

In lieu of striking out the clause, as proposed by the Senate, to retain the

---

[51] On September 21 this petition was referred to a committee on claims.

[52] A printed copy of the bill, annotated by the Senate, is in House Bills, SR, DNA. E–45629.

[53] The Senate read this bill on July 6, 21, and August 3. On August 4 it was read again and agreed to with amendments, which are printed in the *Senate Legislative Journal* on that date. On August 5 the House was notified of the amendments and agreed to them.

[54] The report is in Joint Committee Reports, SR, DNA.

[55] On June 29 the House was notified that the Senate agreed to these actions on the amendments.

[56] The report is in Joint Committee Reports, SR, DNA.

same, and to add to the end thereof, the words proposed to be inserted by the Senate, amended to read thus, "On all ships or vessels, hereafter built in the United States, belonging wholly, or in part to subjects of foreign powers, at the rate of thirty cents per ton."

RESOLVED, That this House doth insist on their disagreement to the fourth, fifth, and sixth amendments.[57]

The orders of the day for the House to resolve itself into a committee of the whole House, on the bill, "establishing an executive department, to be denominated the treasury department," also on the report of the committee appointed to confer with a committee of the Senate, in preparing joint rules to be established between the two Houses, for the inrollment, attestation, publication and preservation of the acts of Congress, and to regulate the mode of presenting addresses, and other acts, to the President of the United States, were read, and postponed until Monday next.

And then the House adjourned until Monday morning eleven o'clock.

MONDAY, JUNE 29, 1789

Mr. Goodhue, from the committee to whom the bill to regulate the collection of duties imposed on goods, wares and merchandizes imported into the United States was committed, reported, that the committee had prepared an entire new bill, as an amendment and substitute to the former bill, which he delivered in at the clerk's table, where the same was read, and ordered to be committed to a committee of the whole House to-morrow.[58]

A message from the Senate by Mr. Otis their Secretary.

MR. SPEAKER, The Senate agree to the amendments proposed by this House, to their twelfth and seventeenth amendments to the bill, entitled, "an act for laying a duty on goods, wares and merchandizes imported into the United States."[59] And then he withdrew.

A petition of William Finnie, deputy quarter-master general in the southern department during the late war, was presented to the House and read, praying a reimbursement of monies expended by him in the public service.

ORDERED, That the said petition do lie on the table.[60]

---

[57] On July 1 the House was notified of further Senate action on these amendments, and the House receded from its disagreement to the third, fourth, and sixth Senate amendments.

[58] A printed copy of a bill, which probably represents the Collection Bill [HR–11] as introduced in the House, is in U.S. Laws and Statutes, 1790, RBkRm, DLC. The bill could also be either of the Collection Bills [HR–3] or [HR–6], which were forerunners of the Collection Bill [HR–11]. E–46024. On June 30 and July 1 this bill was postponed as an order of the day. On July 2 it was considered in the COWH.

[59] On July 1 a committee to examine this bill was appointed.

[60] On September 5 this petition was committed to the committee on invalid pensioners.

The House, according to the order of the day, resolved itself into a committee of the whole House, on the bill "establishing an executive department, to be denominated the treasury department."

Mr. Speaker left the chair.

Mr. Trumbull took the chair of the committee.

Mr. Speaker resumed the chair, and Mr. Trumbull reported, that the committee had, according to order, had the said bill under consideration, and made a farther progress therein.

RESOLVED, That this House will, to-morrow, again resolve itself into a committee of the whole House on the said bill.[61]

The order of the day for the House to resolve into a committee of the whole House, on the report of the committee appointed to confer with a committee of the Senate, in preparing joint rules to be established between the two Houses, for the inrollment, attestation, publication, and preservation of the acts of Congress, and to regulate the mode of presenting addresses and other acts to the President of the United States, was read and postponed until Monday se'nnight.

And then the House adjourned until to-morrow morning eleven o'clock.

TUESDAY, JUNE 30, 1789

The House, according to the order of the day, resolved itself into a committee of the whole House, on the bill "establishing an executive department, to be denominated the treasury department."

Mr. Speaker left the chair.

Mr. Trumbull took the chair of the committee.

Mr. Speaker resumed the chair, and Mr. Trumbull reported that the committee had, according to order, had the said bill under consideration, and gone through the same, and made several amendments thereto, which he delivered in at the clerk's table, where the same were twice read, and agreed to by the House.

ORDERED, That the said bill, with the amendments, do lie on the table.[62]

ORDERED, That Mr. Schureman have leave to be absent from the service of this House until Tuesday next.

The order of the day for the House to resolve itself into a committee of the whole House, on the bill to regulate the collection of duties imposed on goods, wares and merchandizes imported into the United States, was read and postponed until to-morrow.

And then the House adjourned until to-morrow morning eleven o'clock.

---

[61] On June 30 this bill was amended.

[62] On July 1 this bill was amended again.

WEDNESDAY, JULY 1, 1789

On motion,

RESOLVED, That Mr. Partridge and Mr. White be a committee, jointly with any committee which the Senate may appoint, to examine the enrolled bill, entitled, "An act for laying a duty on goods, wares and merchandizes imported into the United States;" and after it shall be signed by the Speaker of this House, and the President of the Senate, to present the same to the President of the United States for his approbation.

The House resumed the consideration of the bill establishing an executive department, to be denominated the treasury department, which lay on the table; and the same being further amended at the clerk's table, was, together with the amendments, ordered to be engrossed, and read the third time tomorrow.[1]

A message from the Senate by Mr. Otis their Secretary.

MR. SPEAKER, The Senate have appointed a committee, jointly with a committee of this House to examine the inrolled bill, entitled, "An act for laying a duty on goods, wares and merchandizes imported into the United States," and to present the same to the President of the United States for his approbation:[2] The Senate also concur in the amendment proposed by this House to their third amendment to the bill, entitled, "An act imposing duties on tonnage," so far as to admit the insertion of the words substituted by this House in lieu of others proposed by the Senate; but they do adhere to such other part of the said third amendment as was disagreed to by this House; and also do adhere to their fourth, fifth and sixth amendments to the said bill, a disagreement to which this House hath insisted on.   And then he withdrew.

The House proceeded to consider the said message, so far as relates to the amendments to the bill, entitled, "An act imposing duties on tonnage;" whereupon, it being moved and seconded that this House doth recede from their disagreement to the said third, fourth, fifth and sixth amendments as adhered to by the Senate.

It was resolved in the affirmative—$\begin{cases} \text{AYES } 31 \\ \text{NOES } 19 \end{cases}$

The ayes and noes being demanded by one fifth of the members present, Those who voted in the affirmative, are,

Fisher Ames	Aedanus Burke
Abraham Baldwin	Lambert Cadwalader
Egbert Benson	Thomas Fitzsimons

---

[1] On July 2 this bill was read again, agreed to, and sent to the Senate.
[2] On July 2 this bill was signed by the speaker and vice president.

Elbridge Gerry
Nicholas Gilman
Benjamin Goodhue
John Hathorn
Benjamin Huntington
James Jackson
John Laurance
Richard Bland Lee
Samuel Livermore
George Mathews
Andrew Moore
George Partridge
Theodore Sedgwick

Roger Sherman
Thomas Sinnickson
William Smith (of Maryland)
William Smith (of South-Carolina)
Michael Jenifer Stone
Peter Silvester
George Thatcher
Jonathan Trumbull
Thomas Tudor Tucker
Jeremiah Wadsworth
Alexander White and
Henry Wynkoop

Those who voted in the negative, are,

Elias Boudinot
John Brown
Daniel Carroll
George Clymer
Isaac Coles
Benjamin Contee
Samuel Griffin
Jonathan Grout
Thomas Hartley
James Madison, junior

Peter Muhlenberg
John Page
Josiah Parker
Jeremiah Van Rensselaer
Thomas Scott
Joshua Seney
Jonathan Sturges
Thomas Sumter and
John Vining[3]

Mr. Gerry, from the committee appointed, presented according to order, a bill for the establishment and support of light-houses, beacons and buoys; and for authorising the several states to provide and regulate pilots; which was received and read the first time.[4]

The order of the day for the House to resolve itself into a committee of the whole House, on the bill to regulate the collection of duties imposed on goods, wares and merchandizes imported into the United States, was read and postponed until to-morrow.

And then the House adjourned until to-morrow morning eleven o'clock.

---

[3] On July 2 the committee that had examined the Impost Bill [HR-2] was instructed to examine the Tonnage Bill [HR-5] also.

[4] On July 2 this bill was read again.

THURSDAY, JULY 2, 1789

Mr. Partridge reported from the committee appointed to examine the inrolled bill, entitled, "An act for laying a duty on goods, wares and merchandizes imported into the United States,"[5] that the committee had according to order, examined the same, and found it to be truly inrolled: Whereupon,

Mr. Speaker signed the said inrolled bill.[6]

An engrossed bill for "establishing an executive department, to be denominated the treasury department," was read the third time, and the blanks therein filled up.

RESOLVED, That the said bill do pass, and that the title be, "An act to establish the treasury department."[7]

ORDERED, That the clerk of this House do carry the said bill to the Senate, and desire their concurrence.[8]

A bill for the establishment and support of light-houses, beacons and buoys, and for authorising the several states to provide and regulate pilots, was read the second time, and ordered to be committed to a committee of the whole House on Wednesday next.[9]

The House, according to the order of the day, resolved itself into a committee of the whole House, on the bill, "to regulate the collection of duties imposed on goods, wares and merchandizes imported into the United States."

Mr. Speaker left the chair.

Mr. Trumbull took the chair of the committee.

Mr. Speaker resumed the chair, and Mr. Trumbull reported, that the committee had, according to order, had the said bill under consideration, and made a farther progress therein.

RESOLVED, That this House will, to-morrow, again resolve itself into a committee of the whole House on the said bill.[10]

ORDERED, That it be an instruction to the committee appointed yesterday, to examine the inrolled bill, entitled "An act for laying a duty on goods, wares and merchandizes imported into the United States;" that they do in like manner examine the inrolled bill, entitled, "An act imposing duties on tonnage."[11]

---

[5] The inspected enrolled bill is in Enrolled Acts, RG 11, DNA. E–22193, E–45693.

[6] On July 3 the committee reported that it had presented the bill to the president.

[7] A printed copy of the bill, annotated by the Senate, is in House Bills, SR, DNA. E–45631.

[8] The Senate read this bill on July 6, 21, 29, 30, and 31. On July 31 it was agreed to with several amendments, which are printed in the *Senate Legislative Journal* for that date. The House was notified of the amendments on the same day.

[9] From July 8–15 consideration of this bill was postponed. On July 16 the bill was considered in the COWH.

[10] On July 3 the COWH considered this bill again.

[11] On July 7 the House was notified that the Senate had appointed a committee to examine the Tonnage Bill [HR–5].

And then the House adjourned until to-morrow morning eleven o'clock.

FRIDAY, JULY 3, 1789

Mr. Partridge, from the committee appointed jointly with a committee of the Senate, to present to the President of the United States, for his approbation, the inrolled bill, entitled "An act for laying a duty on goods, wares and merchandizes imported into the United States," reported, that the committee did, according to order, yesterday wait on the President, and present him with the said inrolled bill for his approbation.[12]

The House, according to the order of the day, resolved itself into a committee of the whole House, on the bill to regulate the collection of duties imposed on goods, wares and merchandizes imported into the United States.

Mr. Speaker left the chair.

Mr. Trumbull took the chair of the committee.

Mr. Speaker resumed the chair, and Mr. Trumbull reported that the committee had, according to order, had the said bill under consideration, and made a farther progress therein:

RESOLVED, That this House, will, on Monday next, again resolve itself into a committee of the whole House on the said bill.[13]

And then the House adjourned until Monday morning, eleven o'clock.

MONDAY, JULY 6, 1789

A petition of Andrew Ellicott, was presented to the House and read, praying that money may be advanced to defray his expences, and to enable him to execute an act of the late Congress for determining the western boundary of the state of New-York, and to ascertain the quantity of land lying west of said boundary, and included between the northern boundary of the state of Pennsylvania and lake Erie.

ORDERED, That the said petition be referred to Mr. Page, Mr. Scott, and Mr. Baldwin, that they do examine the matter thereof, and report the same with their opinion thereupon to the House.[14]

On motion,

RESOLVED, That there be prefixed to the publication of the acts of the present session of Congress, a correct copy of the Constitution of government for the United States.[15]

---

[12] On July 6 the House was notified that the president had signed this bill on July 4.

[13] On July 6 the COWH considered this bill again.

[14] On July 8 this committee reported.

[15] A copy of the resolution is in Messages from the House, SR, DNA.

ORDERED, That the clerk of the House do carry the said resolution to the Senate, and desire their concurrence.[16]

A message was received from the President of the United States, notifying that the President approves of the act, entitled "An act for laying a duty on goods, wares and merchandizes imported into the United States," and did on the fourth instant affix his signature to the same; and the messenger delivered in the said act, and then withdrew.

ORDERED, That the clerk of this House do acquaint the Senate therewith.

The House according to the order of the day, resolved itself into a committee of the whole House on the bill to regulate the collection of duties imposed on goods, wares and merchandizes imported into the United States.

Mr. Speaker left the chair.

Mr. Trumbull took the chair of the committee.

Mr. Speaker resumed the chair, and Mr. Trumbull reported, that the committee had, according to order, had the said bill under consideration, and made a farther progress therein.

RESOLVED, That this House will, to-morrow, again resolve itself into a committee of the whole House on the said bill.[17]

ORDERED, That Mr. Wadsworth have leave to be absent from the service of this House until this day fortnight.

The order of the day for the House to resolve itself into a committee of the whole House on the bill to promote the progress of science and useful arts, by securing to authors and inventors, the exclusive right to their respective writings and discoveries, was read, and postponed until to-morrow.

And then the House adjourned until to-morrow morning ten o'clock.

TUESDAY, JULY 7, 1789

A petition of John McGarragh was presented to the House and read, praying compensation for military services rendered during the late war.

ORDERED, That the said petition do lie on the table.[18]

The House according to the order of the day resolved itself into a committee of the whole House on the bill to regulate the collection of duties imposed on goods, wares and merchandizes imported into the United States.

Mr. Speaker left the chair.

Mr. Trumbull took the chair of the committee.

Mr. Speaker resumed the chair, and Mr. Trumbull reported that the committee had, according to order, had the said bill under consideration, and made a farther progress therein.

---

[16] On July 7 the House was notified that the Senate had agreed to this resolution.

[17] On July 7 the COWH considered this bill again.

[18] On September 21 this petition was referred to the committee on claims.

RESOLVED, That this House will, to-morrow, again resolve itself into a committee of the whole House on the said bill.[19]

A message from the Senate, by Mr. Otis, their Secretary.

MR. SPEAKER, The Senate have appointed a committee on their part, jointly with a committee of this House, to examine the inrolled bill, entitled "An act imposing duties on tonnage," and after the same shall be signed by the Speaker of this House, and the President of the Senate, to present it to the President of the United States for his approbation:[20] The Senate have also agreed to the resolution of this House for prefixing to the publication of the acts of the present session of Congress, a correct copy of the constitution of the United States. And then he withdrew.

ORDERED, That Mr. Contee have leave to be absent from the service of this House until this day four weeks.

The order of the day for the House to resolve itself into a committee of the whole House on the bill to promote the progress of science and useful arts, by securing to authors and inventors, the exclusive right to their respective writings and discoveries, was read and postponed until to-morrow.

And then the House adjourned until to-morrow morning ten o'clock.

WEDNESDAY, JULY 8, 1789

Mr. Partridge from the committee appointed to examine the inrolled bill, entitled, "An act imposing duties on tonnage,"[21] reported that the committee had, according to order, examined the same, and found it to be truly inrolled: Whereupon,

Mr. Speaker signed the said inrolled bill.[22]

ORDERED, That Mr. Clymer have leave to be absent from the service of this House until Monday se'nnight.

Mr. Page, from the committee to whom was referred the petition of Andrew Ellicott, made a report, which was read, and ordered to lie on the table.[23]

The House, according to the order of the day, resolved itself into a committee of the whole House, on the bill to regulate the collection of duties imposed on goods, wares and merchandizes imported into the United States.

Mr. Speaker left the chair.

Mr. Trumbull took the chair of the committee.

---

[19] On July 8 the COWH considered this bill again.

[20] On July 8 this bill was signed by the speaker and the vice president.

[21] The inspected enrolled bill is in Enrolled Acts, RG 11, DNA. E–45700.

[22] On July 9 the committee reported that they had delivered this bill to the president.

[23] On July 20 this report was considered and recommitted.

Mr. Speaker resumed the chair, and Mr. Trumbull reported that the committee had, according to order, had the said bill under consideration, and
made a farther progress therein.

RESOLVED, That this House will, to-morrow, again resolve itself into a
committee of the whole House on the said bill.[24]

The orders of the day for the House to resolve itself into a committee of
the whole House on the bill to promote the progress of science and useful
arts, by securing to authors and inventors, the exclusive right to their respective writings and discoveries; also, on the bill for the establishment and support of light-houses, beacons and buoys, and for authorising the several states
to provide and regulate pilots, were read, and postponed until to-morrow.

And then the House adjourned until to-morrow morning ten o'clock.

THURSDAY, JULY 9, 1789

Mr. Partridge, from the committee appointed jointly with a committee of
the Senate, to present to the President of the United States, for his approbation, the inrolled bill, entitled, "An act imposing duties on tonnage," reported,
that the committee did, according to order, yesterday wait on the President,
and present him with the said inrolled bill for his approbation.[25]

Mr. Gerry, from the committee appointed to prepare and report an estimate of the supplies requisite for the present year, and of the nett produce
of the impost as agreed to by the House, made a report, which was read and
ordered to lie on the table.[26]

On motion,

The orders of the day for the House to resolve itself into a committee of
the whole House, on the bill to promote the progress of science and useful
arts, by securing to authors and inventors, the exclusive right to their respective writings and discoveries; also on the bill, for the establishment and support of light-houses, beacons and buoys, and for authorising the several States
to provide and regulate pilots, were farther postponed until Wednesday next.

The House, according to the order of the day, resolved itself into a committee of the whole House, on the bill to regulate the collection of duties imposed on goods, wares and merchandizes imported into the United States.

Mr. Speaker left the chair.

Mr. Trumbull took the chair of the committee.

Mr. Speaker resumed the chair, and Mr. Trumbull reported, that the com-

---

[24] On July 9 the COWH considered this bill again.

[25] On July 20 the president signed this bill.

[26] A copy of the report is in A Record of the Reports of Select Committees, HR,
DNA. A copy, probably made by ASP, is in Various Select Committees, HR, DNA.
E–22199. On July 24 this report was referred to the committee on ways and means.

mittee had, according to order, had the said bill under consideration, and made a farther progress therein.

RESOLVED, That this House will, to-morrow, again resolve itself into a committee of the whole House on the said bill.[27]

And then the House adjourned until to-morrow morning ten o'clock.

FRIDAY, JULY 10, 1789

The House, according to the order of the day, resolved itself into a committee of the whole House, on the bill to regulate the collection of duties, imposed on goods, wares and merchandizes imported into the United States.

Mr. Speaker left the chair.

Mr. Trumbull took the chair of the committee.

Mr. Speaker resumed the chair, and Mr. Trumbull reported that the committee had, according to order, had the said bill under consideration, and gone through the same, and made several amendments thereto, which they had directed him to report, when the House should think proper to receive the same.

ORDERED, That the said report be received to-morrow.[28]

ORDERED, That Mr. Parker have leave to be absent from the service of this House, until the second Monday in August next, and Mr. Trumbull until this day fortnight.

And then the House adjourned until to-morrow morning ten o'clock.

SATURDAY, JULY 11, 1789

A petition of David Sturges, of the county of Dutchess, in the State of New-York, was presented to the House and read, praying relief in consideration of wounds received in the service of the United States during the late war.

ORDERED, That the said petition do lie on the table.

The House proceeded to consider the amendments reported by the committee of the whole House, yesterday, to the bill to regulate the collection of duties imposed on goods, wares and merchandizes imported into the United States, and the said amendments being read and amended at the clerk's table, were agreed to by the House.

ORDERED, That the said bill, with the amendments, be engrossed and read the third time, on Tuesday next.[29]

And then the House adjourned until Monday morning eleven o'clock.

---

[27] On July 10 the COWH reported amendments to this bill.

[28] On July 11 these amendments were agreed to.

[29] On July 14 this bill was read, agreed to, and sent to the Senate.

MONDAY, JULY 13, 1789

The House, according to the standing order of the day, resolved itself into a committee of the whole House on the state of the Union.

Mr. Speaker left the chair.

Mr. Boudinot took the chair of the committee.

Mr. Speaker resumed the chair, and Mr. Boudinot reported that the committee had, according to order, had the state of the Union under consideration, but had come to no resolution thereupon.[30]

The order of the day, for the House to resolve itself into a committee of the whole House, on the report of the committee appointed to confer with a committee of the Senate, in preparing joint rules to be established between the two Houses, for the inrollment, attestation, publication and preservation of the acts of Congress, and to regulate the mode of presenting addresses, and other acts to the President of the United States, was read and postponed until to-morrow.

The House proceeded to consider the report of the committee which lay on the table, on the subject of compensations to be made to the President, Vice-President, the members of the Senate and House of Representatives, for their services, and made some progress therein.[31]

And then the House adjourned until to-morrow morning eleven o'clock.

TUESDAY, JULY 14, 1789

Mr. Ames, from the committee of elections, to whom was referred the petition of a number of the citizens of New-Jersey, complaining of the illegality of the election of the members holding seats in this House, as elected within that State, made a report, which was received and ordered to lie on the table.[32]

ORDERED, That a committee be appointed, to prepare and bring in a bill or bills, to provide for the government of the Western Territory.

And a committee was appointed, of Mr. Fitzsimons, Mr. Sedgwick and Mr. Brown.[33]

ORDERED, That a committee be appointed to prepare and bring in a bill or bills, to provide for the settlement of the accounts between the United

---

[30] According to the *New York Daily Gazette*, July 14, 1789, the topic under discussion was the establishment of a land office in the Northwest Territory. On July 22 the COWH considered this topic again, passed a resolution on it, and appointed a committee to bring in a land office bill.

[31] On July 16 this report was agreed to, and a committee was appointed to prepare a bill. The report is printed in the Journal on that date.

[32] On July 15 this report was considered.

[33] On July 16 this committee presented the Northwest Territory Bill [HR–14], which was read.

States and the individual States, agreeably to the ordinance of the late Congress.

And a committee was appointed of Mr. Baldwin, Mr. Sturges and Mr. Smith (of South-Carolina).[34]

An engrossed bill, to regulate the collection of duties imposed on goods, wares and merchandizes imported into the United States, was read the third time, and the blanks therein filled up.

RESOLVED, That the said bill do pass, and that the title be, "An act to regulate the collection of the duties imposed by law on the tonnage of ships or vessels, and on goods, wares and merchandizes imported into the United States."[35]

ORDERED, That the clerk of this House do carry the said bill to the Senate and desire their concurrence.[36]

The order of the day for the House to resolve itself into a committee of the whole House, on the report of the committee appointed to confer with a committee of the Senate, in preparing joint rules to be established between the two Houses, for the inrollment, attestation, publication and preservation of the acts of Congress, and to regulate the mode of presenting addresses, and other acts, to the President of the United States, was read, and postponed until to-morrow.

And then the House adjourned until to-morrow morning eleven o'clock.

WEDNESDAY, JULY 15, 1789

The several orders of the day for the House to resolve itself into a committee of the whole House, on the report of the committee appointed to confer with a committee of the Senate, in preparing joint rules to be established between the two Houses, for the inrollment, attestation, publication and preservation of the acts of Congress; and to regulate the mode of presenting addresses and other acts to the President of the United States; also on the bill to promote the progress of science and useful arts, by securing to authors and inventors the exclusive right to their respective writings and discoveries; and on the bill for the establishment and support of light-houses, beacons and

---

[34] On July 16 this committee presented a Settlement of Accounts Bill [HR-13], which was read.

[35] A printed copy of the bill, annotated by the Senate, is in House Bills, SR, DNA. E-45633.

[36] The Senate read this bill on July 15 and 20. It was committed on July 20, but there is no record in the *Senate Legislative Journal* of this committee reporting. On July 21 the second reading of the bill was completed, and on July 23 an amendment to the bill was defeated. On July 27 the Senate read the Collection Bill [HR-11] again and agreed to it with amendments, which are printed in the *Senate Legislative Journal* for that date. These amendments were received and agreed to by the House on July 28.

buoys, and for authorizing the several States to provide and regulate pilots, were read and postponed until to-morrow.

The House proceeded to consider the report made yesterday by the committee of elections on the petition of a number of the citizens of New-Jersey, complaining of the illegality of the election of the members holding seats in this House, as elected within that State, and the said report being twice read at the clerk's table, was debated, and ordered to lie on the table.[37]

And then the House adjourned until to-morrow morning eleven o'clock.

THURSDAY, JULY 16, 1789

A petition of John Christopher Stoebel, of the city of Philadelphia, was presented to the House and read, praying that an exclusive privilege may be granted him for a term of years, to construct and navigate boats with wheels, upon the principles of a model which he has invented to facilitate the passage of boats up and down streams and rapids without the use of oars.

ORDERED, That the said petition do lie on the table.

Mr. Baldwin from the committee appointed, presented according to order, a bill for settling the accounts between the United States, and individual States, which was received, and read the first time.[38]

The House resumed the consideration of the report of the committee, on the subject of compensations to be made to the President, Vice-President, the members of the Senate and House of Representatives for their services; and the said report being amended to read as followeth:

That there be allowed to the President of the United States, as compensation for his services, the sum of twenty five thousand dollars per annum, to be paid in equal quarterly payments at the treasury.

That there be paid in like quarterly payments to the Vice-President of the United States, five thousand dollars per annum.

That the daily pay of the members of the Senate and House of Representatives, for their attendance at the time appointed for the meeting of their respective Houses, and for the time they shall be going to, and returning therefrom, allowing the travel of twenty miles for each day, be six dollars, and of the Speaker of the House of Representatives, twelve dollars.

RESOLVED, That this House doth agree to the said report.

ORDERED, That a bill or bills be brought in pursuant thereto; and that Mr. Burke, Mr. Stone and Mr. Moore be a committee to prepare and bring in the same, with instruction to insert a clause or clauses, making provision for a

---

[37] On August 18 this committee reported. The report is printed in the Journal.
[38] On July 17 this bill was read again.

reasonable compensation to the Secretary of the Senate, and Clerk of the House of Representatives, respectively, for their services.[39]

Mr. Fitzsimons, from the committee appointed, presented according to order, a bill to provide for the government of the territory north west of the river Ohio, which was received and read the first time.[40]

The House according to the order of the day, resolved itself into a committee of the whole House on the bill for the establishment and support of light-houses, beacons and buoys, and for authorising the several States to provide and regulate pilots.

Mr. Speaker left the chair.

Mr. Boudinot took the chair of the committee.

Mr. Speaker resumed the chair, and Mr. Boudinot reported, that the committee had, according to order, had the said bill under consideration, and made some progress therein.

RESOLVED, That this House will, to-morrow, again resolve itself into a committee of the whole House on the said bill.[41]

The orders of the day, for the House to resolve itself into a committee of the whole House, on the report of the committee appointed to confer with a committee of the Senate, in preparing joint rules to be established between the two Houses for the inrollment, attestation, publication and preservation of the acts of Congress, and to regulate the mode of presenting addresses and other acts to the President of the United States; also on the bill to promote the progress of science and useful arts, by securing to authors and inventors the exclusive right to their respective writings and discoveries, were read and postponed until to-morrow.

And then the House adjourned until to-morrow morning eleven o'clock.

FRIDAY, JULY 17, 1789

A petition of Leonard Harbaugh, was presented to the House and read, praying that an exclusive privilege may be granted him for a term of years, to make, use and vend three machines which he has invented for threshing, reaping, and deepening docks, and which are calculated to facilitate labor, and aid the two great objects of agriculture and commerce.

ORDERED, That the said petition do lie on the table.

The Speaker laid before the House, a letter from Ebenezer Hazard, postmaster general of the United States, submitting the propriety of some imme-

---

[39] On July 22 this committee presented the Compensation Bill [HR–15], which was read. On the same date this committee was further instructed.

[40] On July 17 this bill was read again.

[41] On July 17 this bill was amended.

diate provision by law for the arrangement of that department,[42] which was read and ordered to be referred to Mr. Boudinot, Mr. Goodhue and Mr. Lee, that they do examine the matter thereof, and report the same with their opinion thereupon to the House.[43]

A bill for settling the accounts between the United States and individual States, was read the second time, and ordered to be committed to a committee of the whole House on Tuesday next.[44]

A bill to provide for the government of the territory north-west of the river Ohio, was read the second time, and ordered to be committed to a committee of the whole House on Monday next.[45]

The House, according to the order of the day, resolved itself into a committee of the whole House, on the bill for the establishment and support of light-houses, beacons and buoys, and for authorising the several States to provide and regulate pilots.

Mr. Speaker left the chair.

Mr. Boudinot took the chair of the committee.

Mr. Speaker resumed the chair, and Mr. Boudinot reported, that the committee had, according to order, had the said bill under consideration, and gone through the same, and made several amendments thereto, which he delivered in at the clerk's table, where the same were twice read and agreed to by the House.

ORDERED, That the said bill with the amendments be engrossed, and read the third time on Monday next.[46]

The order of the day for the House to resolve itself into a committee of the whole House, on the report of the committee appointed to confer with a committee of the Senate, in preparing joint rules to be established between the two Houses, for the inrollment, attestation, publication and preservation of the acts of Congress, and to regulate the mode of presenting addresses and other acts to the President of the United States, was read, and farther postponed until Monday se'nnight.

The order of the day for the House to resolve itself into a committee of the whole House on the bill to promote the progress of science and useful arts, by securing to authors and inventors, the exclusive right to their respective writings and discoveries, was read, and postponed until Monday next.

And then the House adjourned until Monday morning eleven o'clock.

---

[42] The letter is in Reports and Communications from the Postmaster General, HR, DNA.

[43] On August 18 this committee reported.

[44] On July 21 consideration of this bill was postponed. On July 22 the bill was considered by the COWH and recommitted.

[45] On July 20 several amendments to this bill were agreed to.

[46] On July 20 this bill was read, agreed to, and sent to the Senate.

MONDAY, JULY 20, 1789

An engrossed bill for the establishment and support of light-houses, beacons and buoys, and for authorising the several States to provide and regulate pilots, was read the third time, and the blanks therein filled up.

RESOLVED, That the said bill do pass, and that the title be, "an Act for the establishment and support of light-houses, beacons and buoys."[47]

ORDERED, That the clerk of this House do carry the said bill to the Senate and desire their concurrence.[48]

A message from the Senate by Mr. Otis their Secretary.

MR. SPEAKER,   The Senate have passed the bill, entitled, "An act for establishing an executive department, to be denominated the department of foreign affairs," with several amendments,[49] to which they desire the concurrence of this House: They have also passed a bill, entitled, "An act to establish the judicial courts of the United States,"[50] to which they desire the concurrence of this House.   And then he withdrew.

A message was received from the President of the United States, notifying that the President approves of the act, entitled, "An act imposing duties on tonnage," and has this day affixed his signature thereto: And the messenger delivered in the said act, and then withdrew.

ORDERED, That the clerk of this House do acquaint the Senate therewith.

On motion,

ORDERED, That a committee be appointed to bring in a bill or bills, providing for the establishment of hospitals for sick and disabled seamen, and for the regulation of harbours and that Mr. Smith (of South Carolina), Mr. Clymer and Mr. Carroll, do prepare and bring in the same.[51]

The House resumed the consideration of the report on the petition of Andrew Ellicott, which lay on the table: Whereupon,

ORDERED, That the said report be re-committed to the same committee.[52]

---

[47] This bill is E–45624.

[48] The Senate read this bill on July 21 and 23. On July 23 it was committed, and the committee reported amendments on July 24. The second reading of the bill was continued on July 28, 29, and 30. On July 31 the bill was read the third time and agreed to with amendments, which are printed in the *Senate Legislative Journal*. The House was notified on August 3 and agreed to the Senate amendments on the same day.

[49] Senate amendments are filed with the bill in House Bills, SR, DNA. The amendments are printed in the *Senate Legislative Journal* on July 17 and 18.

[50] The bill is in Engrossed Senate Bills and Resolutions, SR, DNA. E–45683.

[51] On August 27 this committee presented the Hospitals and Harbors Bill [HR–22], which was read.

[52] On July 23 this committee reported.

The House proceeded to consider the amendments proposed by the Senate to the bill, entitled, "An act for establishing an executive department to be denominated the department of foreign affairs," and the same being read, were agreed to.

ORDERED, That the clerk of this House do acquaint the Senate therewith.[53]

The bill sent from the Senate, entitled, "An act to establish the judicial courts of the United States," was read the first time.

ORDERED, That Mr. Sinnickson have leave to be absent from the service of this House until this day three weeks.

On motion,

The bill sent from the Senate, entitled, "An act to establish the judicial courts of the United States," was read the second time, and ordered to be committed to a committee of the whole House on Monday next.[54]

The House, according to the order of the day, resolved itself into a committee of the whole House, on the bill to provide for the government of the territory north-west of the river Ohio.

Mr. Speaker left the chair.

Mr. Boudinot took the chair of the committee.

Mr. Speaker resumed the chair, and Mr. Boudinot reported, that the committee had, according to order, had the said bill under consideration, and gone through the same, and made several amendments thereto, which he delivered in at the clerk's table, where the same were twice read, and agreed to by the House.

ORDERED, That the said bill with the amendments be engrossed, and read the third time to-morrow.[55]

The order of the day for the House to resolve itself into a committee of the whole House on the bill to promote the progress of science and useful arts, by securing to authors and inventors the exclusive right to their respective writings and discoveries, was read, and postponed until this day fortnight.

And then the House adjourned until to-morrow morning eleven o'clock.

TUESDAY, JULY 21, 1789

An engrossed bill to provide for the government of the territory north-west of the river Ohio, was read the third time.

RESOLVED, That the said bill do pass, and that the title be, "An act to provide for the government of the territory north-west of the river Ohio."[56]

---

[53] On July 21 a committee to examine this bill was appointed.

[54] From July 27 through August 22 consideration of this bill was postponed as an order of the day. On August 24 this bill was considered in the COWH.

[55] On July 21 this bill was read, agreed to, and sent to the Senate.

[56] A printed copy of the bill, annotated by the Senate, is in House Bills, SR, DNA. E-45632.

ORDERED, That the clerk of this House do carry the said bill to the Senate and desire their concurrence.[57]

On motion,

RESOLVED, That Mr. Partridge and Mr. White, be a committee jointly with any committee which the Senate shall appoint, to examine the inrolled bill, entitled, "An act for establishing an executive department, to be denominated the department of foreign affairs," and after it shall be signed by the Speaker of this House, and the President of the Senate, to present the same to the President of the United States for his approbation.[58]

On motion,

ORDERED, That the committee of the whole House, on the state of the Union, be discharged from proceeding on a motion, referred to the said committee on the eighth day of June last, stating certain specific amendments proper to be proposed by Congress to the legislatures of the States, to become, if ratified by three fourths thereof, part of the Constitution of the United States: And that the said motion, together with the amendments to the said Constitution, as proposed by the several States, be referred to a committee to consist of a member from each State, with instruction to take the subject of amendments to the Constitution of the United States generally into their consideration, and to report thereupon to the House.

The members elected,

Mr. Vining
Mr. Madison
Mr. Baldwin
Mr. Sherman
Mr. Burke
Mr. Gilman
Mr. Clymer
Mr. Benson
Mr. Goodhue
Mr. Boudinot and
Mr. Gale[59]

The order of the day for the House to resolve itself into a committee of the whole House on the bill for settling the accounts between the United States and individual States, was read, and postponed until to-morrow.

And then the House adjourned until to-morrow morning eleven o'clock.

---

[57] The Senate read this bill on July 21, 31, and August 3. On August 4 the bill was read again and agreed to with amendments, which are printed in the *Senate Legislative Journal*. The House was notified of these amendments on August 5 and agreed to them on the same day.

[58] On July 22 this bill was signed by the speaker and the vice president.

[59] On July 28 this committee reported.

WEDNESDAY, JULY 22, 1789

Mr. Burke, from the committee appointed, presented, according to order, a bill for allowing a compensation to the President and Vice-President of the United States, which was received and read the first time.[60]

ORDERED, That it be an instruction to the committee appointed to bring in a bill for making compensation to the members of the Senate and House of Representatives, that they do insert a clause or clauses, making compensation to the serjeant at arms, messengers and door-keepers of the two Houses for their services.[61]

A petition of Richard Phillips, was presented to the House and read, praying relief in consideration of indigence occasioned by military services rendered during the late war:

Also a petition of Hannah Adams, praying that an exclusive privilege may be granted her for a limited time, to publish and vend a work which she has compiled, entitled, "An alphabetical compendium of the various sects which have appeared in the world from the beginning of the christian era, to the present day, with an appendix, containing a brief account of the different schemes of religion now embraced among mankind."

ORDERED, That the said petitions do lie on the table.

The House, according to the order of the day, resolved itself into a committee of the whole House on the bill for settling the accounts between the United States and individual States.

Mr. Speaker left the chair.

Mr. Boudinot took the chair of the committee.

Mr. Speaker resumed the chair, and Mr. Boudinot reported, that the committee had, according to order, had the said bill under consideration, and gone through the same, and made no amendment thereto.

On motion,

ORDERED, That the committee of the whole House be discharged from farther proceeding on the said bill, and that it be recommitted to Mr. Baldwin, Mr. Sturges and Mr. Smith (of South-Carolina).[62]

The House, according to the standing order of the day, resolved itself into a committee of the whole House on the state of the Union.

Mr. Speaker left the chair.

Mr. Boudinot took the chair of the committee.

Mr. Speaker resumed the chair, and Mr. Boudinot reported that the committee had, according to order, had the state of the Union under considera-

---

[60] On July 23 this bill was read again.
[61] On August 4 this committee presented the Salaries-Legislatives Bill [HR–19], which was read.
[62] On July 24 this committee reported, and amendments to the bill were agreed to.

tion, and come to a resolution thereupon, which he read in his place, and then delivered in at the clerk's table, where the same was twice read, and agreed to by the House, as followeth:

RESOLVED, That an act of Congress ought to pass for establishing a Land-Office, and for regulating the terms and manner of granting vacant and unappropriated lands, the property of the United States—That the said office be under the superintendance of the Governor of the Western Territory—That the land to be disposed of, be confined to the following limits, viz.

That the tracts or parcels to be disposed of to any one person, shall not exceed   acres; that the price to be required for the same shall be   per acre; and that every person actually settled within the said limits shall be entitled to the pre-emption of a quantity not exceeding   acres, including his settlement.

ORDERED, That a bill or bills be brought in, pursuant to the said resolution; and that Mr. Scott, Mr. Silvester, and Mr. Moore, do prepare and bring in the same.[63]

A message from the Senate by Mr. Otis their Secretary.

MR. SPEAKER,   The Senate have appointed a committee on their part jointly with a committee of this House, to examine an inrolled bill, entitled, "An act for establishing an executive department, to be denominated the Department of Foreign Affairs;" and after the same shall be signed by the Speaker of this House, and the President of the Senate, to present it to the President of the United States for his approbation.   And then he withdrew.

Mr. Partridge reported from the committee appointed to examine the inrolled bill, entitled, "An act for establishing an executive department, to be denominated the Department of Foreign Affairs;"[64] that the committee had, according to order, examined the same, and found it to be truly inrolled: Whereupon,

Mr. Speaker signed the said inrolled bill.[65]

And then the House adjourned until tomorrow morning eleven o'clock.

THURSDAY, JULY 23, 1789

Mr. Partridge, from the committee appointed jointly with a committee of the Senate, to present to the President of the United States for his approbation, the enrolled bill, entitled, "An act for establishing an executive department, to be denominated the Department of Foreign Affairs," reported, that

---

[63] On July 31 this committee presented the Land Office Bill [HR–17], which was read.

[64] The inspected enrolled bill is in Enrolled Acts, RG 11, DNA. E–45691.

[65] On July 23 a motion for a bill supplementing this bill was disagreed to.

the committee did, according to order, yesterday, wait on the President, and present him with the said inrolled bill for his approbation.

A bill for allowing a compensation to the President and Vice-President of the United States, was read the second time, and ordered to be engrossed, and read the third time to-morrow.[66]

On motion,

RESOLVED, That a committee be appointed to examine into the measures taken by Congress, and the state of Virginia, respecting the lands reserved for the use of the officers and soldiers of the said state, on continental and state establishments in the cession made by the said state to the United States, of the territory northwest of the river Ohio, and to report the same to this House; and that Mr. White, Mr. Peter Muhlenberg, and Mr. Seney, be of the said committee.[67]

The House, according to the standing order of the day, resolved itself into a committee of the whole House on the state of the Union.

Mr. Speaker left the chair.

Mr. Boudinot took the chair of the committee.

Mr. Speaker resumed the chair, and Mr. Boudinot reported that the committee had, according to order, had the state of the Union under consideration, but had come to no resolution thereupon.

A motion was made and seconded, "That a committee be appointed to bring in a bill, supplementary to the act for establishing the department of Foreign Affairs, declaring that department to be hereafter denominated   , and that the principal officer in that department, shall have the custody of the records, and seal of the United States, and that such bill do contain provision for the fees of office to be taken for copies of records, and further provision for the due publication of the acts of Congress, and other matters relating to the premises, as the committee shall deem necessary to be reported to this House;"   and the question being put thereupon,

It passed in the negative.[68]

Another petition of the Baron de Glaubeck, was presented to the House and read, praying the attention of Congress to his former petition, to be compensated for certain losses and military services rendered during the late war.

ORDERED, That the said petition do lie on the table.[69]

Mr. Page, from the committee to whom was re-committed the report on the

---

[66] On July 24 this bill was read again and committed to the COWH, which reported several amendments to it.

[67] On July 31 this committee reported.

[68] The custody of the records and seal of the United States was the topic of resolutions, introduced by the committee on joint rules, which were considered on July 27. On July 27 the president signed the Foreign Affairs Bill [HR–8].

[69] On July 28 the Glaubeck petitions were committed.

memorial of Andrew Ellicott, made a report, which was read, and ordered to lie on the table.[70]

And then the House adjourned until to-morrow morning eleven o'clock.

FRIDAY, JULY 24, 1789

An engrossed bill for allowing a compensation to the President and Vice-President of the United States was read a third time, and ordered to be committed to a committee of the whole House to-day.

Mr. Gerry from the committee appointed, presented, according to order, a bill for registering and clearing vessels, ascertaining their tonnage, and for regulating the coasting trade, which was received and read the first time.[71]

Mr. Baldwin from the committee to whom was committed the bill for settling the accounts between the United States and individual states, reported that the committee had, according to order, had the said bill under consideration, and made an amendment thereto, which he read in his place, and afterwards delivered in at the clerk's table, where the same was again twice read, amended and agreed to by the House.

ORDERED, That the said bill with the amendment, be engrossed, and read the third time on Monday next.[72]

The House, according to order, resolved itself into a committee of the whole House, on the bill for allowing a compensation to the President and Vice-President of the United States.

Mr. Speaker left the chair.

Mr. Boudinot took the chair of the committee.

Mr. Speaker resumed the chair, and Mr. Boudinot reported that the committee had, according to order, had the said bill under consideration, and gone through the same, and made several amendments thereto, which he read in his place, and afterwards delivered in at the clerk's table, where the same were again read, and ordered to lie on the table.[73]

On motion,

ORDERED, That a committee of ways and means, to consist of a member from each state, be appointed, to whom it shall be referred to consider the report of a committee appointed to prepare an estimate of supplies requisite for the service of the United States the current year, and to report thereupon.

The members elected—Mr. Fitzsimons

Mr. Vining

---

[70] A copy of the report is in A Record of the Reports of Select Committees, HR, DNA. On August 10 this report was amended, agreed to, and sent to the Senate.

[71] On July 28 this bill was read again and considered in the COWH.

[72] On July 27 this bill was read, agreed to, and sent to the Senate.

[73] On August 3 these amendments were agreed to.

Mr. Livermore
Mr. Cadwalader
Mr. Laurance
Mr. Wadsworth
Mr. Jackson
Mr. Gerry
Mr. Smith (of South-Carolina)
Mr. Smith (of Maryland) and
Mr. Madison[74]

A petition of Nathaniel Gorham, of the state of Massachusetts, was presented to the House and read, setting forth, that Oliver Phelps, Esq. and the petitioner are interested by purchase from the said state of Massachusetts in certain lands, which will be materially affected by the line directed to be run between the United States and the state of New-York, and praying that such measures may be taken therein as shall be consistent with a due regard to the rights of the said Phelps and the petitioner.[75]

ORDERED, That the said petition do lie on the table.[76]

And then the House adjourned until Monday morning eleven o'clock.

MONDAY, JULY 27, 1789

An engrossed bill for settling the accounts between the United States and individual states, was read the third time, and the blanks therein filled up.

RESOLVED, That the said bill do pass, and that the title be, "An act for settling the accounts between the United States and individual States."

ORDERED, That the clerk of this House do carry the said bill to the Senate, and desire their concurrence.[77]

A message was received from the President of the United States, notifying, that the President approves of the act, entitled, "An act for establishing an executive department, to be denominated the Department of Foreign Affairs," and has this day affixed his signature thereto: And the messenger delivered in the said act, and then withdrew.

ORDERED, That the clerk of this House do acquaint the Senate therewith.

ORDERED, That the petition of Nathaniel Gorham, which lay on the table, be referred to Mr. Huntington, Mr. Jackson, and Mr. Lee, that they do ex-

---

[74] On August 4 a member was added to the committee on supplies and imposts. On September 17 the committee on ways and means was discharged.

[75] The petition is in Petitions and Memorials: Various subjects, SR, DNA.

[76] On July 27 this petition was committed.

[77] The Senate read this bill on July 27, 29, and 30. It was agreed to, and the House was notified on July 30.

amine the matter thereof, and report the same, with their opinion thereupon to the House.[78]

The House, according to the order of the day, resolved itself into a committee of the whole House, on the report of the committee appointed to confer with a committee of the Senate, in preparing joint rules to be established between the two Houses, for the inrollment, attestation, publication and preservation of the acts of Congress, and to regulate the mode of presenting addresses, and other acts to the President of the United States.

Mr. Speaker left the chair.

Mr. Boudinot took the chair of the committee.

Mr. Speaker resumed the chair, and Mr. Boudinot reported that the committee had, according to order, had the said report under consideration, and gone through the same, and come to several resolutions thereupon, which he delivered in at the clerk's table, where the same were severally twice read, and agreed to by the House, as follow:

RESOLVED, That it is the opinion of this committee, that the following ought to be established joint rules between the two Houses, to wit:

THAT while bills are on their passage between the two Houses, they shall be on paper, and under the signature of the Secretary or Clerk of each House respectively.

After a bill shall have passed both Houses, it shall be duly inrolled on parchment, by the Clerk of the House of Representatives, or the Secretary of the Senate, as the bill may have originated in the one or the other House, before it shall be presented to the President of the United States.

When bills are inrolled, they shall be examined by a joint committee of one from the Senate, and two from the House of Representatives, appointed as a standing committee for that purpose, who shall carefully compare the inrollment with the engrossed bills, as passed in the two Houses, and correcting any errors that may be discovered in the inrolled bills, make their report forthwith to the respective Houses.

After examination and report, each bill shall be signed in the respective Houses, first by the Speaker of the House of Representatives, and then by the President of the Senate.

After a bill shall have thus been signed in each house, it shall be presented by the said committee to the President of the United States for his approbation, it being first endorsed on the back of the roll, certifying in which House the same originated; which endorsement shall be signed by the Secretary or Clerk (as the case may be) of the House in which the same did originate, and shall be entered on the Journals of each House. The said committee shall

---

[78] On July 31 this committee reported.

report the day of presentation to the President, which time shall also be carefully entered on the Journal of each House.

All orders, resolutions and votes, which are to be presented to the President of the United States for his approbation, shall also in the same manner be previously inrolled, examined and signed, and shall be presented in the same manner, and by the same committee, as provided in case of bills.

That when the Senate and House of Representatives shall judge it proper to make a joint address to the President, it shall be presented to him in his audience chamber, by the President of the Senate, in the presence of the Speaker and both Houses.[79]

RESOLVED, That it is the opinion of this committee, that a committee ought to be appointed to prepare and bring in a bill or bills, to provide, without the establishment of a new department, for the safe keeping of the acts, records and seal of the United States; for the authentication of records and papers, for establishing the fees of office to be taken for commissions, and for copies of records and papers, for making out and recording commissions and prescribing their form, and to provide for the due publication of the acts of Congress.

ORDERED, That a committee be appointed pursuant to the second resolution, and that Mr. Sedgwick, Mr. Mathews and Mr. Wynkoop, be of the said committee.[80]

The order of the day for the House to resolve itself into a committee of the whole House on the bill sent from the Senate, entitled, "An act to establish the judicial courts of the United States," was read and postponed until tomorrow.

And then the House adjourned until to-morrow morning eleven o'clock.

TUESDAY, JULY 28, 1789

Mr. Vining, from the committee of eleven, to whom it was referred to take the subject of amendments to the Constitution of the United States, generally, into their consideration, and to report thereupon, made a report, which was read, and ordered to lie on the table.[81]

ORDERED, That the petitions of the Baron de Glaubeck, which lay on the table, be referred to Mr. Page, Mr. Sumter, and Mr. Hiester, that they do examine the matter thereof, and report the same with their opinion thereupon to the House.[82]

A message from the Senate by Mr. Otis, their Secretary.

---

[79] A copy of the resolution is in Messages from the House, SR, DNA. On August 8 the House was notified that the Senate had agreed to these rules.

[80] On July 31 this committee presented the Records Bill [HR–18], which was read.

[81] This report is E–22200. On August 3 this report was referred to the COWH.

[82] On July 31 this committee reported.

MR. SPEAKER, The Senate have passed the bill entitled, "An act to regulate the collection of the duties imposed by law on the tonnage of ships or vessels, and on goods, wares, and merchandizes imported into the United States," with several amendments,[83] to which they desire the concurrence of the House, and then he withdrew.

The House proceeded to consider the said amendments, and the same being read were agreed to.

ORDERED, That the clerk of the House do acquaint the Senate therewith.[84]

A bill for registering and clearing vessels, ascertaining their tonnage, and for regulating the coasting trade, was read the second time, and ordered to be committed to a committee of the whole House, immediately.

The House accordingly resolved itself into the said committee.

Mr. Speaker left the chair.

Mr. Boudinot took the chair of the committee.

Mr. Speaker resumed the chair, and Mr. Boudinot reported, that the committee had, according to order, had the said bill under consideration, and made some progress therein.

RESOLVED, That this House will to-morrow, again, resolve itself into a committee of the whole House, on the said bill.[85]

The order of the day, for the House to resolve itself into a committee of the whole House, on the bill sent from the Senate, entitled, "An act to establish the judicial courts of the United States," was read, and postponed until to-morrow.

And then the House adjourned until to-morrow morning eleven o'clock.

WEDNESDAY, JULY 29, 1789

On motion,

RESOLVED, That Mr. White and Mr. Partridge be a committee jointly with any committee which the Senate shall appoint to examine the inrolled bill, entitled, "An act to regulate the collection of the duties imposed by law on the tonnage of ships or vessels, and on goods, wares and merchandizes imported into the United States;" and after it shall be signed by the Speaker of this House, and the President of the Senate, to present the same to the President of the United States for his approbation.

The House, according to the order of the day, resolved itself into a committee of the whole House, on the bill for registering and clearing vessels, ascertaining their tonnage, and for regulating the coasting trade.

---

[83] Senate amendments are filed with and noted on the bill in House Bills, SR, DNA. The amendments are printed in the *Senate Legislative Journal* on July 27.

[84] On July 29 a joint committee to examine this enrolled bill was appointed.

[85] On July 29 the COWH considered this bill again.

Mr. Speaker left the chair.

Mr. Boudinot took the chair of the committee.

Mr. Speaker resumed the chair, and Mr. Boudinot reported that the committee had, according to order, had the said bill under their consideration, and made a further progress therein.

RESOLVED, That this House will to-morrow, again resolve itself into a committee of the whole House, on the said bill.[86]

A message from the Senate by Mr. Otis their Secretary.

MR. SPEAKER, The Senate have appointed a committee on their part, jointly with a committee of this House, to examine an inrolled bill, entitled "An act to regulate the collection of the duties imposed by law on the tonnage of ships or vessels, and on goods, wares and merchandizes imported into the United States;" and after the same shall be signed by the Speaker of this House, and the President of the Senate to present it to the President of the United States for his approbation.[87]   And then he withdrew.

The order of the day, for the House to resolve itself into a committee of the whole House, on the bill sent from the Senate, entitled, "An act to establish the Judicial Courts of the United States," was read, and postponed until to-morrow.

And then the House adjourned until to-morrow morning eleven o'clock.

THURSDAY, JULY 30, 1789

Mr. White reported from the committee appointed to examine the inrolled bill, entitled, "An act to regulate the collection of the duties imposed by law on the tonnage of ships or vessels, and on goods, wares and merchandizes imported into the United States,"[88] that the committee had, according to order, examined the same and found it to be truly inrolled: Whereupon,

Mr. Speaker signed the said inrolled bill.[89]

The House, according to the order of the day, resolved itself into a committee of the whole House, on the bill for registering and clearing vessels, ascertaining their tonnage, and for regulating the coasting trade.

Mr. Speaker left the chair.

Mr. Boudinot took the chair of the committee.

Mr. Speaker resumed the chair, and Mr. Boudinot reported that the committee had, according to order, had the said bill under consideration, and

---

[86] On July 30 amendments to this bill were reported by the COWH.

[87] On July 30 the speaker and vice president signed this bill.

[88] The inspected enrolled bill is in Enrolled Acts, RG 11, DNA. E–45713.

[89] On July 31 this bill was signed by the president.

gone through the same, and made several amendments thereto, which he delivered in at the clerk's table, where the same were read, and partly considered.[90]

A message from the Senate by Mr. Otis their Secretary.

MR. SPEAKER,   The Senate have passed the bill, entitled, "An act for settling the accounts between the United States and individual States."[91]   And then he withdrew.

The order of the day for the House to resolve itself into a committee of the whole House on the bill sent from the Senate, entitled, "An act to establish the judicial courts of the United States," was read and postponed until to-morrow.

And then the House adjourned until to-morrow morning eleven o'clock.

FRIDAY, JULY 31, 1789

Mr. White, from the committee appointed jointly with a committee of the Senate, to present to the President of the United States for his approbation, the inrolled bill, entitled, "An act to regulate the collection of the duties imposed by law on the tonnage of ships or vessels, and on goods, wares and merchandizes, imported into the United States," reported, that the committee did, yesterday, according to order, wait on the President and present him with the said inrolled bill for his approbation.

Mr. Scott, from the committee appointed, presented according to order, a bill establishing a Land Office, in, and for the Western Territory, which was received and read the first time.[92]

ORDERED, That Mr. White and Mr. Partridge be appointed a standing committee on the part of this House, jointly with any committee of the Senate, to examine the inrollments of all bills as the same shall pass the two Houses, and after being signed by the Speaker of this House, and the President of the Senate, to present them forthwith to the President of the United States, for his approbation.[93]

ORDERED, That the clerk of this House do acquaint the Senate therewith.

Mr. White, from the committee to whom it was referred to examine into the measures taken by Congress and the state of Virginia, respecting the lands reserved for the use of the officers and soldiers of the said state, on continental and state establishments, in the cession made by the said state to the United

---

[90] On July 31 these amendments were agreed to.
[91] On August 4 the speaker and the vice president signed this bill.
[92] On August 3 this bill was read again.
[93] A copy of the order is in Messages from the House, SR, DNA.

States, of the territory north-west of the river Ohio, made a report which was read, and ordered to lie on the table.[94]

Mr. Page, from the committee to whom were referred the petitions of the Baron de Glaubeck, made a report, which was read, and ordered to lie on the table.[95]

The House resumed the consideration of the amendments reported yesterday by the committee of the whole House, to the bill for registering and clearing vessels, ascertaining their tonnage, and for regulating the coasting trade, and the same being severally twice read at the clerk's table, were agreed to.

ORDERED, That the said bill with the amendments be engrossed, and read the third time on Monday next.[96]

A message was received from the President of the United States, notifying that the President approves of the act, entitled, "An act to regulate the collection of the duties imposed by law on the tonnage of ships or vessels, and on goods, wares and merchandizes imported into the United States," and has this day affixed his signature thereto: And the messenger delivered in the said act, and then withdrew.

ORDERED, That the clerk of this House do acquaint the Senate therewith.

A message from the Senate by Mr. Otis their Secretary.

MR. SPEAKER,   The Senate have passed the bill, entitled, "An act to establish the Treasury department," with several amendments, to which they desire the concurrence of this House:[97] The Senate has also appointed a standing committee on their part, jointly with the committee of this House, to examine the inrollments of all bills as the same shall pass the two Houses; and after being signed by the Speaker of this House, and the President of the Senate, to present them forthwith to the President of the United States for his approbation: And then he withdrew.

Mr. Sedgwick, from the committee appointed, presented according to or-

---

[94] A copy of the report is in A Record of the Reports of Select Committees, HR, DNA. A copy, probably made by ASP, is in Various Select Committees, HR, DNA. E–22954. On September 18 this report was considered and postponed until the next session of Congress.

[95] A copy of the report is in A Record of the Reports of Select Committees, HR, DNA. On September 21 this report was considered, and a resolution was agreed to and sent to the Senate.

[96] A printed copy of what is probably this bill at this stage is E–45680. On August 3 this bill was read again.

[97] Senate amendments are filed with and noted on the bill in House Bills, SR, DNA. Amendments are also noted in rough form on the printed bill in the Broadside Collection, RBkRm, DLC. The amendments are printed in the *Senate Legislative Journal* on July 31. On August 3 the Senate amendments were considered.

der, a bill to provide for the safe keeping of the acts, records, and seal of the United States; for the due publication of the acts of Congress; for the authentication of copies of records; for making out, and recording commissions, and prescribing their form, and for establishing the fees of office to be taken for making such commissions, and for copies of records and papers; which was received, and read the first time.[98]

Mr. Huntington, from the committee to whom was referred the memorial of Nathaniel Gorham, made a report[99] which was read, and ordered to lie on the table.

The order of the day for the House to resolve itself into a committee of the whole House on the bill sent from the Senate, entitled, "An act to establish the Judicial Courts of the United States," was read, and postponed until Monday next.

And then the House adjourned until Monday morning eleven o'clock.

---

[98] On August 3 this bill was read again.

[99] A copy of the report is in A Record of the Reports of Select Committees, HR, DNA. A copy, probably made by ASP, is in Various Select Committees, HR, DNA.

MONDAY, AUGUST 3, 1789

A message from the Senate by Mr. Otis, their Secretary.

MR. SPEAKER,   The Senate have passed the bill, entitled, "An act for the establishment and support of light-houses, beacons and buoys," with several amendments,[1] to which they desire the concurrence of this House.   And then he withdrew.

An engrossed bill for registering and clearing vessels, and regulating the coasting trade, was read the third time, and on a motion made, ordered to be re-committed to a committee of the whole House to-morrow.[2]

A bill for establishing a land-office, in, and for the western territory, was read the second time, and ordered to be committed to a committee of the whole House on Thursday next.[3]

A bill to provide for the safe keeping of the acts, records, and seal of the United States, for the due publication of the acts of Congress, for the authentication of the copies of records, for making out, and recording commissions, and prescribing their form, and for establishing the fees of office to be taken for making such commissions, and for copies of records and papers, was read the second time, and ordered to be committed to a committee of the whole House on Friday next.[4]

On motion,

RESOLVED, That this House will on Wednesday se'nnight resolve itself into a committee of the whole House to take into consideration the report from the committee of eleven, to whom it was referred, to take the subject of amendments to the Constitution of the United States, generally, into their consideration, and to report thereupon.[5]

ORDERED, That Mr. Sherman have leave to be absent from the service of this House until to-morrow se'nnight.

The House proceeded to consider the amendments proposed by the Senate, to the bill, entitled, "An act to establish the Treasury Department," and having made some progress therein, postponed the further consideration thereof until to-morrow.[6]

---

[1] The amendments are printed in the *Senate Legislative Journal* on July 31.

[2] On August 4 the COWH reported further amendments to this bill, which were agreed to.

[3] Consideration of this bill was postponed from day to day until the end of the session. No further action was taken on the bill.

[4] From August 7–24 consideration of this bill was postponed. On August 25 the COWH considered the bill.

[5] On August 13 the COWH considered this report.

[6] On August 4 the House considered these amendments again, and a resolution on the eighth amendment was agreed to.

The House proceeded to consider the amendments of the Senate to the bill, entitled, "An act for the establishment and support of light-houses, beacons, and buoys;" and the same being read, were agreed to.

ORDERED, That the clerk of this House do acquaint the Senate therewith.[7]

The House proceeded to consider the amendments reported by the committee of the whole House the 24th ult. to the bill for allowing a compensation to the President and Vice-President of the United States, and the same being severally twice read at the clerk's table, were agreed to.

ORDERED, That the said bill, with the amendments, be engrossed, and read the third time to-morrow.[8]

The orders of the day for the House to resolve itself into a committee of the whole House on the bill sent from the Senate, entitled, "An act to establish the judicial courts of the United States," and on the bill to promote the progress of science and useful arts, by securing to authors and inventors, the exclusive right to their respective writings and discoveries, were read, and postponed until to-morrow.

And then the House adjourned until to-morrow morning ten o'clock.

TUESDAY, AUGUST 4, 1789

A petition of sundry freeholders of the county of Cumberland, in the state of Pennsylvania, whose names are thereunto subscribed, was presented to the House and read, praying that the District and Circuit Judicial Courts of the United States, to be established in the said state, may be fixed at some central place therein, convenient to the citizens thereof at large.

Also a petition of Dudley Tyler, of the state of Massachusetts, praying that he may receive compensation for certain arrearages of pay due to him, as an officer in the late army of the United States, which have been unjustly detained from him.[9]

Also a petition of Christopher Colles, of the city of New-York, praying that an exclusive privilege may be granted him in the benefits of an invention which he has reduced to practice, for counting with the utmost precision, the number of revolutions or vibrations of any wheel or other part of any mechanical engine or machine.

ORDERED, That the said petitions do lie on the table.

An engrossed bill for making compensation to the President and Vice-President of the United States, was read the third time.

RESOLVED, That the said bill do pass, and that the title be, "An act for making compensation to the President and Vice-President of the United States."

---

[7] On August 6 this bill was signed by the speaker and vice president.

[8] On August 4 this bill was read, agreed to, and sent to the Senate.

[9] On September 21 this petition was referred to a committee on claims.

ORDERED, That the clerk of this House do carry the said bill to the Senate, and desire their concurrence.[10]

Mr. White, from the committee for inrolled bills, reported that the committee had examined the inrolled bill, entitled, "An act for settling the accounts between the United States and individual states,"[11] and found the same to be truly inrolled: Whereupon,

Mr. Speaker signed the said inrolled bill.[12]

ORDERED, That the clerk of this House do acquaint the Senate therewith.

Mr. Burke, from the committee appointed, presented according to order, a bill for allowing compensations to the members of the Senate and House of Representatives of the United States, and to the officers of both Houses, which was received, and read the first time.[13]

The House, according to the order of the day, resolved itself into a committee of the whole House, on the bill for registering and clearing vessels, and regulating the coasting trade.

Mr. Speaker left the chair.

Mr. Boudinot took the chair of the committee.

Mr. Speaker resumed the chair, and Mr. Boudinot reported, that the committee had, according to order, had the said bill under consideration, and gone through the same, and made several amendments thereto, which he delivered in at the clerk's table, where the same were twice read, and agreed to by the House.

ORDERED, That the said bill, with the amendments, be engrossed, and read the third time to-morrow.[14]

On motion,

RESOLVED, That a committee be appointed to join with a committee of the Senate, to be appointed for the purpose, to consider of and report when it will be convenient and proper that an adjournment of the present session of Congress should take place, and to consider and report such business now before Congress necessary to be finished before the adjournment, and such as may be conveniently postponed to the next sessions; and also to consider and report such matters not now before Congress, but which it will be necessary should be considered and determined by Congress before an adjournment.

---

[10] The Senate read this bill on August 5 and 6. On August 6 it was committed, and on August 7 this committee reported and two motions to amend the bill were disagreed to. The Senate did not consider this bill again until September 7, when the bill was agreed to with one amendment from the committee and sent to the House.

[11] The inspected enrolled bill is in Enrolled Acts, RG 11, DNA. E–45697.

[12] On August 5 the president signed this bill.

[13] On August 5 this bill was read again and considered in the COWH.

[14] On August 5 this bill was read again, agreed to, and sent to the Senate.

And a committee was appointed of Mr. Wadsworth, Mr. Carroll, and Mr. Hartley.[15]

ORDERED, That Mr. Baldwin be added to the committee appointed to prepare and report an estimate of the nett produce of the impost.[16]

The House resumed the consideration of the amendments proposed by the Senate to the bill, entitled, "An act to establish the Treasury department:" Whereupon,

RESOLVED, That this House doth agree to so much of the eighth amendment as proposes to strike out the following words in the seventh clause of the bill, to wit, "The assistant to the secretary of the Treasury shall be appointed by the President, and" and doth disagree to such other part of the said amendment as proposes to strike out the residue of the clause.

ORDERED, That the farther consideration of the said amendments be postponed until to-morrow.[17]

The orders of the day for the House to resolve itself into a committee of the whole House, on the bill sent from the Senate, entitled, "An act to establish the judicial courts of the United States;" and on the bill to promote the progress of science and useful arts, by securing to authors and inventors the exclusive right to their respective writings and discoveries, were read and postponed until to-morrow.

And then the House adjourned until to-morrow morning ten o'clock.

WEDNESDAY, AUGUST 5, 1789

ORDERED, That Mr. Contee have further leave of absence from the service of this House, until this day three weeks.

A message from the Senate by Mr. Otis their Secretary.

MR. SPEAKER,   The Senate have passed the bill, entitled, "An act to establish an executive department, to be denominated the department of War," with several amendments,[18] to which they desire the concurrence of this House. The Senate have also passed the bill, entitled, "An act to provide for the government of the territory north-west of the river Ohio," with several

---

[15] A copy of the resolution is in Messages from the House, SR, DNA. On August 6 the Senate notified the House that it had appointed a committee to meet with this committee.

[16] On August 27 this committee reported again.

[17] On August 5 these amendments were considered again, and the Senate was notified of the House actions on them.

[18] Senate amendments are noted on the bill in House Bills, SR, DNA, and in rough form on the annotated printed bill in the Broadside Collection, RBkRm, DLC. The amendments are printed in the *Senate Legislative Journal* on August 4.

amendments,[19] to which they desire the concurrence of this House. And then he withdrew.

The House proceeded to consider the amendments to the said bills, and the same being severally twice read at the clerk's table, were agreed to.

ORDERED, That the clerk of this House do acquaint the Senate therewith.[20]

Mr. White, from the committee for inrolled bills, reported, that the committee did yesterday present to the President of the United States for his approbation, the inrolled bill, entitled, "An act for settling the accounts between the United States and individual States."

The House resumed the farther consideration of the amendments proposed by the Senate to the bill, entitled, "An act to establish the Treasury department:" Whereupon,

RESOLVED, That this House doth agree to the ninth and tenth amendments to the said bill.

ORDERED, That the clerk of this House do acquaint the Senate therewith.[21]

RESOLVED, That a committee be appointed to bring in a bill to establish the salaries of the executive officers of government, with their assistants and clerks.

And a committee was appointed of Mr. Fitzsimons, Mr. Laurance, and Mr. Griffin.[22]

A bill for allowing compensation to the members of the Senate and House of Representatives of the United States, and to the officers of both Houses, was read the second time, and ordered to be committed to a committee of the whole House, to day.

An engrossed bill for registering and clearing vessels, and regulating the coasting trade, was read the third time, and the blanks therein filled up.

RESOLVED, That the said bill do pass, and that the title be, "An act for registering and clearing vessels, regulating the coasting trade, and for other purposes."[23]

ORDERED, That the clerk of this House do carry the said bill to the Senate, and desire their concurrence.[24]

---

[19] Senate amendments are filed with and noted on the bill in House Bills, SR, DNA. The amendments are printed in the *Senate Legislative Journal* on August 4.

[20] On August 6 the speaker and the vice president signed these bills.

[21] On August 6 the House was notified that the Senate insisted on its eighth amendment to this bill.

[22] On August 24 this committee presented the Salaries-Executive Bill [HR–21], which was read.

[23] A printed copy of the bill, annotated by the Senate, is in House Bills, SR, DNA. E–45645.

[24] The Senate read this bill on August 6 and 10. It was committed on August 10, and this committee reported amendments on August 17. The Senate continued reading this bill on August 20, 21, 22, and 25. On August 25 the bill was agreed to with

A message was received from the President of the United States, notifying that the President approves of the act, entitled, "An act for settling the accounts between the United States and individual States," and has this day affixed his signature thereto. And the messenger delivered in the said act, and then withdrew.

ORDERED, That the clerk of this house do acquaint the Senate therewith.

The House, according to order, resolved itself into a committee of the whole House on the bill for allowing compensation to the members of the Senate and House of Representatives of the United States, and to the officers of both Houses.

Mr. Speaker left the chair.

Mr. Boudinot took the chair of the committee.

Mr. Speaker resumed the chair, and Mr. Boudinot reported that the committee had, according to order, had the said bill under consideration, and made some progress therein.

RESOLVED, That this House will, to-morrow, again resolve itself into a committee of the whole House on the said bill.[25]

The orders of the day for the House to resolve itself into a committee of the whole House on the bill sent from the Senate, entitled, "An act to establish the judicial courts of the United States," and on the bill to promote the progress of science and useful arts, by securing to authors and inventors the exclusive right to their respective writings and discoveries, were read and postponed until to-morrow.

And then the House adjourned until to-morrow morning eleven o'clock.

THURSDAY, AUGUST 6, 1789

Mr. White from the committee for inrolled bills, reported, that the committee had examined the following inrolled bills, to wit.

A bill, entitled, "An act to establish an executive department, to be denominated the department of war."[26]

A bill, entitled, "An act to provide for the government of the territory northwest of the river Ohio."[27]   Also,

A bill, entitled, "An act for the establishment and support of light-houses, beacons, buoys, and public piers;"[28]

And had found the same to be truly inrolled: Whereupon,

---

sixty-nine amendments, which are printed in the *Senate Legislative Journal* for this date. The House was notified of these amendments and considered them on August 26.

[25] On August 6 this bill was amended in the COWH.

[26] The inspected enrolled bill is in Enrolled Acts, RG 11, DNA. E–22194.

[27] The inspected enrolled bill is in Enrolled Acts, RG 11, DNA. E–22195.

[28] The inspected enrolled bill is in Enrolled Acts, RG 11, DNA. E–45698.

Mr. Speaker signed the said inrolled bills.[29]
A message from the Senate by Mr. Otis their Secretary.

MR. SPEAKER, The Senate have appointed a committee on their part, jointly with the committee of this House, to consider of and report when it will be convenient and proper that an adjournment of the present session of Congress should take place, agreeably to the resolution of this House on Tuesday last;[30] and the Senate do insist on their eighth amendment to the bill, entitled, "An act to establish the treasury department," disagreed to in part by this House.[31]   And then he withdrew.

ORDERED, That Mr. White have leave to be absent from the service of this House for the remainder of the session.

The House, according to the order of the day, resolved itself into a committee of the whole House on the bill for allowing compensation to the members of the Senate, and House of Representatives of the United States, and to the officers of both Houses.

Mr. Speaker left the chair.

Mr. Boudinot took the chair of the committee.

Mr. Speaker resumed the chair, and Mr. Boudinot reported that the committee had, according to order, had the said bill under consideration, and gone through the same, and made several amendments thereto, which he delivered in at the clerk's table, where the same were read, and some agreed to, and others disagreed to.

ORDERED, That the said bill, with the amendments be engrossed, and read the third time to-morrow.[32]

On motion,

The order of the day for the House to resolve itself into a committee of the whole House on the bill to promote the progress of science and useful arts, by securing to authors and inventors, the exclusive right to their respective writings and discoveries, was farther postponed until Thursday next.

The order of the day for the House to resolve itself into a committee of the whole House on the bill sent from the Senate, entitled, "An act to establish the judicial courts of the United States;" also on the bill for establishing a land-office, in, and for the western territory, were read and postponed until to-morrow.

And then the House adjourned until to-morrow morning eleven o'clock.

---

[29] On August 7 the president signed all of these bills.
[30] On August 11 this committee reported.
[31] On August 10 a conference was appointed on this bill.
[32] On August 7 this bill was read again and amended in the COWH.

FRIDAY, AUGUST 7, 1789

A petition of John White, late a commissioner for settling the accounts between the United States, and the states of Pennsylvania, Delaware, and Maryland, was presented to the House and read, praying that he may receive compensation for services in that character, which, from public considerations, he was induced to render beyond the time limited by an ordinance of the late Congress.

ORDERED, That the said petition be referred to Mr. Seney, Mr. Vining and Mr. Hiester, that they do examine the matter thereof, and report the same with their opinion thereupon to the House.[33]

Mr. White from the committee for inrolled bills, reported that the committee did, yesterday, jointly with the committee of the Senate, wait on the President of the United States, and present him with the following inrolled bills for his approbation, to wit:

A bill, entitled, "An act to establish an executive department, to be denominated the department of war."

A bill, entitled, "An act to provide for the government of the territory northwest of the river Ohio." Also,

A bill, entitled, "An act for the establishment and support of light-houses, beacons, buoys, and public piers."

On motion,

ORDERED, That a committee be appointed to bring in a bill, or bills, for the further encouragement of the commerce and navigation of the United States.

And a committee was appointed of Mr. Gerry, Mr. Trumbull, and Mr. Burke.

A message in writing was received from the President of the United States, by General Knox, who delivered therewith sundry statements and papers relating to the same. And then withdrew.

The said message was then read, and is as followeth:

GENTLEMEN of the HOUSE of REPRESENTATIVES,

THE business which has been under the consideration of Congress, has been of so much importance, that I was unwilling to draw their attention from it to any other subject, but the disputes which exist between some of the United States, and several powerful tribes of Indians within the limits of the Union, and the hostilities which have in several instances been committed on the frontiers, seem to require the immediate interposition of the General Government.

I have therefore directed the several statements and papers which have

---

[33] On September 5 this committee reported.

been submitted to me on this subject by General Knox, to be laid before you for your information.

While the measures of government ought to be calculated to protect its citizens from all injury and violence, a due regard should be extended to those Indian tribes whose happiness, in the course of events, so materially depends on the national justice and humanity of the United States.

If it should be the judgment of Congress, that it would be most expedient to terminate all differences in the southern district, and to lay the foundation for future confidence, by an amicable treaty with the Indian tribes in that quarter, I think proper to suggest the consideration of the expediency of instituting a temporary commission for that purpose, to consist of three persons, whose authority should expire with the occasion.

How far such a measure, unassisted by posts, would be competent to the establishment and preservation of peace and tranquility on the frontiers, is also a matter which merits your serious consideration.

Along with this object, I am induced to suggest another, with the national importance and necessity of which I am deeply impressed; I mean some uniform and effective system for the militia of the United States. It is unnecessary to offer arguments in recommendation of a measure, on which the honor, safety, and well-being of our country so evidently, and so essentially depend.

But it may not be amiss to observe, that I am particularly anxious it should receive as early attention as circumstances will admit; because it is now in our power to avail ourselves of the military knowledge disseminated throughout the several States, by means of the many well instructed officers and soldiers of the late army, a resource which is daily diminishing by deaths and other causes.

To suffer this peculiar advantage to pass away unimproved, would be to neglect an opportunity which will never again occur, unless unfortunately we should again be involved in a long and arduous war.

GEORGE WASHINGTON

NEW-YORK, August 7, 1789[34]

On motion,

ORDERED, That the said message, with the statement and papers accompanying the same, be committed to the consideration of a committee of the whole House on the state of the Union.[35]

---

[34] The message with copies of enclosures, probably made by ASP, is in President's Messages: Transmitting reports from the Secretary of War, SR, DNA. The enclosures are in Transcribed Reports and Communications from Executive Departments, 1789–1814, (War Department, Southern Indians), Records of the Secretary, SR, DNA.

[35] On August 8 the COWH presented two resolutions on this message. Two committees were appointed to bring in bills pursuant to these resolutions.

Another message was received from the President of the United States, notifying that the President approves of the following acts, to wit:

An act, entitled, "An act to establish an executive department, to be denominated the department of war."

An act, entitled, "An act to provide for the government of the territory northwest of the river Ohio." Also,

An act, entitled, "An act for the establishment and support of light-houses, beacons, buoys, and public piers;"

And has this day affixed his signature to the same. And the messenger delivered in the said acts, and then withdrew.

ORDERED, That the Clerk of this House do acquaint the Senate therewith.

An engrossed bill for allowing compensation to the members of the Senate and House of Representatives of the United States, and to the officers of both Houses, was read the third time, and ordered to be re-committed to a committee of the whole House immediately.

The House accordingly resolved itself into the said committee.

Mr. Speaker left the chair.

Mr. Boudinot took the chair of the committee.

Mr. Speaker resumed the chair, and Mr. Boudinot reported that the committee had, according to order, had the said bill under consideration, and gone through the same, and made several amendments thereto, which he delivered in at the clerk's table, where the same were severally twice read, and agreed to by the House.

ORDERED, That the said bill with the amendments, be again engrossed, and read the third time on Monday next.[36]

A petition of David Greenleaf was presented to the House and read, praying that an exclusive privilege may be granted him to construct and build mills, within the United States, upon the principles of an invention which he has discovered for turning them by the help of a weight that is appended.

ORDERED, That the said petition do lie on the table.

The order of the day for the House to resolve itself into a committee of the whole House, on the bill sent from the Senate, entitled, "An act to establish the judicial courts of the United States;" also, on the bill for establishing a land-office, in, and for the western territory; and on the bill to provide for the safe keeping of the acts, records, and seal of the United States; for the due publication of the acts of Congress; for the authentication of the copies of records; for making out and recording commissions, and prescribing their form, and for establishing the fees of office to be taken for making such commissions, and for copies of records and papers; were read and postponed until to-morrow.

---

[36] On August 10 this bill was read, agreed to, and sent to the Senate.

And then the House adjourned until to-morrow morning eleven o'clock.

SATURDAY, AUGUST 8, 1789

A message from the Senate by Mr. Otis, their Secretary.

MR. SPEAKER, The Senate agree to the resolutions of this House of the twenty-seventh ultimo, establishing joint rules between the two houses for the inrollment of the acts of Congress, and to regulate the mode of presenting addresses to the President of the United States. And then he withdrew.

The House according to the standing order of the day, resolved itself into a committee of the whole House on the state of the Union.

Mr. Speaker left the chair.

Mr. Boudinot took the chair of the committee.

Mr. Speaker resumed the chair, and Mr. Boudinot reported, that the committee had, according to order, had the state of the Union under consideration, and come to several resolutions thereupon, which he delivered in at the clerk's table, where the same were severally twice read, and agreed to by the House, as follow:

RESOLVED, That it is the opinion of this committee, that an act ought to pass, providing for the necessary expences attending any negociations or treaties which may be held with the Indian tribes, or attending the appointment of commissioners for those purposes.

RESOLVED, That it is the opinion of this committee, that an act ought to pass, providing a proper system of regulations for the militia of the United States.

ORDERED, That a bill or bills be brought in pursuant to the first resolution, and that Mr. Clymer, Mr. Ames, and Mr. Moore, do prepare and bring in the same.[37]

ORDERED, That a bill or bills be brought in pursuant to the second resolution, and that Mr. Sumter, Mr. Hiester, and Mr. Mathews, do prepare and bring in the same.[38]

The several orders of the day, for the House to resolve itself into a committee of the whole house on the bill sent from the Senate, entitled, "An act to establish the judicial courts of the United States;" also, on the bill for establishing a land-office, in, and for the western territory; and on the bill to provide for the safe keeping of the acts, records, and seal of the United States;

---

[37] On August 10 this committee presented the Indian Treaties Bill [HR–20], which was read.

[38] On August 11 a House resolution on raising troops or militia was referred to the COWH, and two members were added to this committee.

for the due publication of the acts of Congress; for the authentication of the copies of records; for making out, and recording commissions, and prescribing their form, and for establishing the fees of office to be taken for making such commissions; and for copies of records and papers; were read, and postponed until Monday next.

And then the House adjourned until Monday morning eleven o'clock.

MONDAY, AUGUST 10, 1789

A petition of John Macpherson was presented to the House, and read, praying that an exclusive privilege may be granted him for a term of years, to make and vend lightning rods, upon an improved construction; also, conductors and umbrellas, upon a model which he has invented, making them certain preservers from lightning.

ORDERED, That the said petition do lie on the table.

An engrossed bill for allowing compensation to the members of the Senate and House of Representatives of the United States, and to the officers of both Houses, was read the third time:

And the question being put that the said bill do pass,

It was resolved in the affirmative— $\begin{cases} \text{AYES} & 30 \\ \text{NOES} & 16 \end{cases}$

The ayes and noes being demanded by one fifth of the members present, Those who voted in the affirmative, are,

Abraham Baldwin	George Mathews
Egbert Benson	Andrew Moore
John Brown	Peter Muhlenberg
Aedanus Burke	John Page
Daniel Carroll	Thomas Scott
George Clymer	Joshua Seney
Thomas Fitzsimons	William Smith (of Maryland)
George Gale	William Smith (of South-Carolina)
Samuel Griffin	Michael Jenifer Stone
Thomas Hartley	Jonathan Sturges
Daniel Hiester	Thomas Sumter
Benjamin Huntington	Jonathan Trumbull
John Laurance	Thomas Tudor Tucker
Richard Bland Lee	John Vining and
James Madison, junior	Jeremiah Wadsworth

Those who voted in the negative, are,

Fisher Ames	John Hathorn
Elias Boudinot	George Leonard
Lambert Cadwalader	Samuel Livermore
William Floyd	George Partridge
Elbridge Gerry	Jeremiah Van Rensselaer
Nicholas Gilman	Theodore Sedgwick
Benjamin Goodhue	Peter Silvester and
Jonathan Grout	George Thatcher

RESOLVED, That the title of the said bill be, "An act for allowing compensation to the members of the Senate and House of Representatives of the United States, and to the officers of both Houses," and that the clerk of this House do carry the said bill to the Senate, and desire their concurrence.[39]

The House proceeded to consider the message sent from the Senate on the fifth instant, insisting on so much of their eighth amendment to the bill, entitled, "An act to establish the treasury department," as was disagreed to by this House: Whereupon,

RESOLVED, That a conference be desired with the Senate, on the subject matter of the said eighth amendment; and that Mr. Madison, Mr. Fitzsimons, and Mr. Boudinot be appointed managers at the same, on the part of this House.[40]

A message in writing was received from the President of the United States, by General Knox, who delivered in the same, together with a statement of the troops in the service of the United States.   And then withdrew.

The said message was then read, and is as followeth:

GENTLEMEN of the HOUSE of REPRESENTATIVES,

I HAVE directed a statement of the troops in the service of the United States to be laid before you for your information.

These troops were raised by virtue of the resolves of Congress of the twentieth of October, one thousand seven hundred and eighty-six, and the third of October, one thousand seven hundred and eighty-seven, in order to protect the frontiers from the depredations of the hostile Indians; to prevent all intrusions on the public lands; and to facilitate the surveying and selling of the same for the purpose of reducing the public debt.

---

[39] A printed copy of the bill, annotated by the Senate, is in House Bills, SR, DNA. E-45634. The Senate read this bill on August 11, 12, and 25. It was committed on August 25, and this committee reported amendments to the bill on August 27. The committee report is printed in the *Senate Legislative Journal* on August 28. On the same date the report was agreed to with amendments, and several other amendments to the bill were agreed to. On August 31 the bill was further amended, read again, and agreed to. The House was notified on September 1.

[40] A copy of the resolution is in Messages from the House, SR, DNA.

As these important objects continue to require the aid of the troops, it is necessary that the establishment thereof should in all respects be conformed by law to the Constitution of the United States.

GEORGE WASHINGTON

NEW-YORK, August 10, 1789[41]

ORDERED, That the said message, with the statement accompanying the same, do lie on the table.[42]

A message from the Senate by Mr. Otis their Secretary.

MR. SPEAKER,   The Senate agree to the proposed conference on the subject matter of so much of their eighth amendment to the bill, entitled, "An act to establish the treasury department," as was disagreed to by this House, and have appointed managers at the said conference on their part.[43]   And then he withdrew.

The House proceeded to consider the report of the committee on the memorial of Andrew Ellicott, which lay on the table, and the same being amended to read as followeth:

That the survey directed by Congress in their act of June the sixth, one thousand seven hundred and eighty-eight, be made and returned to the secretary of the treasury without delay; and that the President of the United States be requested to appoint a fit person to complete the same, who shall be allowed five dollars per day, whilst actually employed in the said service, with the expences necessarily attending the execution thereof.[44]

RESOLVED, That this House doth agree to the said report.

ORDERED, That the clerk of this House do carry the said resolution to the Senate, and desire their concurrence.[45]

Mr. Clymer, from the committee appointed, presented according to order, a bill providing for the expences which may attend negociations or treaties with the Indian tribes, and the appointment of commissioners for managing the same, which was received, and read the first time.[46]

---

[41] The message with an enclosure is in President's Messages: Transmitting reports from the Secretary of War, SR, DNA. The enclosure is printed in the *Senate Legislative Journal* on August 10.

[42] On August 11 this message was committed to the COWH. A House resolution on raising troops or militia was also referred to the COWH.

[43] On August 24 this conference reported, and the House adhered to its disagreement to the eighth amendment.

[44] A copy of the amended report is in Messages from the House, SR, DNA.

[45] The Senate read this resolution on August 11. On August 14 it was read again together with two petitions relating to it. On August 19 the Senate agreed to the resolution, after defeating several motions on it. The House was notified on August 20.

[46] On August 11 this bill was read again, and amendments to it from the COWH were agreed to.

The orders of the day for the House to resolve itself into a committee of the whole House on the bill sent from the Senate, entitled, "An act to establish the judicial courts of the United States;" also, on the bill for establishing a land-office, in, and for the western territory; and on the bill to provide for the safe-keeping of the acts, records, and seal of the United States; for the due publication of the acts of Congress; for the authentication of the copies of records; for making out and recording commissions, and prescribing their form, and for establishing the fees of office to be taken for making such commissions; and for copies of records and papers, were read and postponed until to-morrow.

And then the House adjourned until to-morrow morning eleven o'clock.

TUESDAY, AUGUST 11, 1789

A bill providing for the expences which may attend negociations or treaties with the Indian tribes, and the appointment of commissioners for managing the same, was read the second time, and ordered to be committed to a committee of the whole House to-day.

A petition of Englebert Kemmena, of the city of New-York, was presented to the House and read, praying that he may receive payment for certain medicines and services, which as a surgeon he rendered to the army during the late war.[47]

Also, a petition of Atcheson Thompson, of the city of New-York, praying that he may receive payment for sundry articles of clothing and other supplies furnished to George M. White Eyes, an Indian youth of the Delaware tribe, by order of the President of the United States.

ORDERED, That the said petitions do lie on the table.

The House, according to the order of the day, resolved itself into a committee of the whole House on the bill providing for the expences which may attend negociations or treaties with the Indian tribes, and the appointment of commissioners for managing the same.

Mr. Speaker left the chair.

Mr. Boudinot took the chair of the committee.

Mr. Speaker resumed the chair, and Mr. Boudinot reported, that the committee had, according to order, had the said bill under consideration, and gone through the same, and made several amendments thereto, which he delivered in at the clerk's table, where the same were twice read, and agreed to by the House.

---

[47] On September 21 this petition was referred to a committee on claims.

ORDERED, That the said bill, with the amendments, be engrossed, and read the third time to-morrow.[48]

On motion,

ORDERED, That the message, sent from the President of the United States, by General Knox, the tenth instant, with the statement accompanying the same,[49] be referred to the consideration of a committee of the whole House on the state of the Union.

On motion, That the House do come to the following resolution:

RESOLVED, That in case of refusal of the Creek Indians to treat, or on treaty to agree to such articles and terms, as to the commissioners to be appointed shall appear necessary and just, the President of the United States shall be, and he is hereby authorised to raise, or cause to be raised, such number of troops, on the pay and establishment of the United States, or to call forth and embody such proportion of the militia of the states of South-Carolina and Georgia, as will secure and protect, by such proper posts as he may think necessary, the inhabitants of the state of Georgia from the invasion and farther inroads of the Creek Indians: PROVIDED, That the whole number of men so to be raised on the establishment of the United States, shall not exceed   nor be continued for a longer term than   . AND PROVIDED ALSO, That the whole number of the militia so to be called forth and embodied, shall not exceed   nor shall any one person be obliged to serve more than   . And the said militia when in actual service, shall be entitled to the pay and emoluments of the troops of the United States.

ORDERED, That the said motion be committed to the consideration of a committee of the whole House on the state of the Union.[50]

On motion,

ORDERED, That Mr. Peter Muhlenberg, and Mr. Wadsworth be added to the committee appointed to bring in a bill or bills providing a proper system of regulation for the militia of the United States.[51]

Mr. Wadsworth, from the committee appointed to confer with a committee of the Senate, to consider of, and report when it will be convenient and proper that an adjournment of the present session of Congress should take place, made a report, which was read, and ordered to lie on the table.[52]

The several orders of the day for the House to resolve itself into a commit-

---

[48] On August 12 this bill was read, considered, and recommitted to the COWH. A further amendment from this committee was agreed to.

[49] The message concerned the militia.

[50] On September 9 the COWH was discharged from considering the president's message of August 10, and a new committee was appointed to consider it.

[51] There is no record in the Journal of any report by this committee.

[52] A draft of the report is in Joint Committee Reports, SR, DNA. On August 24 the House passed a resolution on adjournment and sent it to the Senate.

tee of the whole House, on the bill sent from the Senate, entitled, "An act to establish the judicial courts of the United States;" also, on the bill for establishing a land-office, in, and for the western territory; and on the bill to provide for the safe keeping of the acts, records and seal of the United States; for the due publication of the acts of Congress; for the authentication of the copies of records, for making out and recording commissions, and prescribing their form, and for establishing the fees of office to be taken for making such commissions; and for copies of records and papers, were read and postponed until to-morrow.

And then the House adjourned until to-morrow morning eleven o'clock.

WEDNESDAY, AUGUST 12, 1789

An engrossed bill, providing for the expences which may attend negociations or treaties with the Indian tribes, and the appointment of commissioners for managing the same, was read the third time.

A motion was made and seconded to fill up the first blank therein with the sum of forty thousand dollars.

And the question being put thereupon,

It was resolved in the affirmative— $\begin{cases} \text{AYES } 28 \\ \text{NOES } 23 \end{cases}$

The ayes and noes being demanded by one fifth of the members present,
Those who voted in the affirmative, are,

Abraham Baldwin	Richard Bland Lee
Egbert Benson	James Madison, junior
John Brown	George Mathews
Aedanus Burke	Peter Muhlenberg
Lambert Cadwalader	John Page
George Clymer	Thomas Scott
Isaac Coles	William Smith (of South-Carolina)
Thomas Fitzsimons	Michael Jenifer Stone
George Gale	Peter Silvester
Samuel Griffin	Jonathan Trumbull
Thomas Hartley	Thomas Tudor Tucker
Benjamin Huntington	John Vining
James Jackson	Jeremiah Wadsworth and
John Laurance	Henry Wynkoop

Those who voted in the negative, are,

Fisher Ames
Elias Boudinot
Daniel Carroll
William Floyd
Elbridge Gerry
Nicholas Gilman
Jonathan Grout
John Hathorn
Daniel Hiester
George Leonard
Samuel Livermore
Andrew Moore

Josiah Parker
George Partridge
Jeremiah Van Rensselaer
James Schureman
Theodore Sedgwick
Joshua Seney
Roger Sherman
William Smith (of Maryland)
Jonathan Sturges
Thomas Sumter and
George Thatcher

On motion,

ORDERED, That the said bill be re-committed to a committee of the whole House immediately.

The House accordingly resolved itself into the said committee.

Mr. Speaker left the chair.

Mr. Boudinot took the chair of the committee.

Mr. Speaker resumed the chair, and Mr. Boudinot reported, that the committee had, according to order, had the said bill under consideration, and gone through the same, and made an amendment thereto, which he delivered in at the clerk's table, where the same was twice read, and agreed to by the House.

ORDERED, That the said bill with the amendment, be again engrossed, and read the third time to-morrow.[53]

The orders of the day for the House to resolve itself into a committee of the whole House, on the bill sent from the Senate, entitled, "An act to establish the judicial courts of the United States;" also, on the bill for establishing a land-office, in, and for the western territory; and on the bill to provide for the safe keeping of the acts, records, and seal of the United States; for the due publication of the acts of Congress; for the authentication of the copies of records; for making out and recording commissions, and prescribing their form, and for establishing the fees of office to be taken for making such commissions, and for copies of records and papers; were read and postponed until to-morrow.

And then the House adjourned until to-morrow morning eleven o'clock.

---

[53] On August 13 this bill was read again, agreed to, and sent to the Senate.

THURSDAY, August 13, 1789

An engrossed bill, providing for the expences which may attend negociations or treaties with the Indian tribes, and the appointment of commissioners for managing the same, was read the third time.

RESOLVED, That the said bill do pass, and that the title be, "An act providing for the expences which may attend negociations or treaties with the Indian tribes, and the appointment of commissioners for managing the same."

ORDERED, That the clerk of this House do carry the said bill to the Senate, and desire their concurrence.[54]

The House, according to the order of the day, resolved itself into a committee of the whole House on the report from the committee of eleven, to whom it was referred to take the subject of amendments to the Constitution of the United States generally into their consideration, and to report thereupon.

Mr. Speaker left the chair.

Mr. Boudinot took the chair of the committee.

Mr. Speaker resumed the chair, and Mr. Boudinot reported that the committee had, according to order, had the said report under consideration, and made some progress therein.

RESOLVED, That this House will, to-morrow, again resolve itself into a committee of the whole House on the said report.[55]

The several orders of the day, for the House to resolve itself into a committee of the whole house on the bill sent from the Senate, entitled, "An act to establish the judicial courts of the United States;" also, on the bill for establishing a land-office, in, and for the western territory; also, on the bill to provide for the safe keeping of the acts, records, and seal of the United States; for the due publication of the acts of Congress; for the authentication of the copies of records; for making out, and recording commissions, and prescribing their form, and for establishing the fees of office to be taken for making such commissions; and for copies of records and papers; and on the bill to promote the progress of science and useful arts, by securing to authors and inventors the exclusive right to their respective writings and discoveries, were read and postponed until to-morrow.

And then the House adjourned until Monday morning eleven o'clock.

---

[54] The Senate read this bill on August 13 and 14. It was committed on August 14, and the committee reported on August 17. The report was disagreed to, and two resolutions were disagreed to. On August 18 several amendments were disagreed to, and one was agreed to. The bill was then passed with one amendment, and the House was notified.

[55] On August 14 this report was considered again by the COWH.

FRIDAY, AUGUST 14, 1789

Another member, to wit, Abiel Foster, from New-Hampshire, appeared and took his seat; the oath to support the Constitution of the United States having been first administered to him by the Speaker, pursuant to a late act of Congress.

The House, according to the order of the day, resolved itself into a committee of the whole House, on the report from the committee of eleven, to whom it was referred to take the subject of amendments to the Constitution of the United States, generally into their consideration, and to report thereupon.

Mr. Speaker left the chair.

Mr. Trumbull took the chair of the committee.

Mr. Speaker resumed the chair, and Mr. Trumbull reported that the committee had, according to order, had the said report under consideration, and made a further progress therein.

RESOLVED, That this House will, to-morrow, again resolve itself into a committee of the whole House on the said report.[56]

The orders of the day for the House to resolve itself into a committee of the whole House, on the bill sent from the Senate, entitled, "An act to establish the judicial courts of the United States;" also, on the bill for establishing a land-office, in, and for the western territory; also, on the bill to provide for the safe keeping of the acts, records, and seal of the United States; for the due publication of the acts of Congress; for the authentication of the copies of records; for making out and recording commissions, and prescribing their form, and for establishing the fees of office to be taken for making such commissions, and for copies of records and papers; and on the bill to promote the progress of science and useful arts, by securing to authors and inventors the exclusive right to their respective writings and discoveries, were read and postponed until to-morrow.

And then the House adjourned until to-morrow morning ten o'clock.

SATURDAY, AUGUST 15, 1789

The House, according to the order of the day, resolved itself into a committee of the whole House, on the report from the committee of eleven, to whom it was referred to take the subject of amendments to the Constitution of the United States, generally into their consideration, and to report thereupon.

Mr. Speaker left the chair.

---

[56] On August 15 this bill was considered again by the COWH.

Mr. Boudinot took the chair of the committee.

Mr. Speaker resumed the chair, and Mr. Boudinot reported, that the committee had, according to order, had the said report under consideration, and made a farther progress therein.

RESOLVED, That this House will, on Monday next, again resolve itself into a committee of the whole House, on the said report.[57]

The several orders of the day, for the House to resolve itself into a committee of the whole house on the bill sent from the Senate, entitled, "An act to establish the judicial courts of the United States;" also, on the bill for establishing a land-office, in, and for the western territory; also, on the bill to provide for the safe keeping of the acts, records, and seal of the United States; for the due publication of the acts of Congress; for the authentication of the copies of records; for making out, and recording commissions, and prescribing their form, and for establishing the fees of office to be taken for making such commissions; and for copies of records and papers; and on the bill to promote the progress of science and useful arts, by securing to authors and inventors the exclusive right to their respective writings and discoveries, were read and postponed until Monday next.

And then the House adjourned until Monday morning eleven o'clock.

MONDAY, AUGUST 17, 1789

On motion,

The order of the day for the House to resolve itself into a committee of the whole House, on the bill to promote the progress of science and useful arts, by securing to authors and inventors the exclusive right to their respective writings and discoveries, was postponed until the next session of Congress.

The House, according to the order of the day, resolved itself into a committee of the whole House on the report from the committee of eleven, to whom it was referred to take the subject of amendments to the Constitution of the United States generally into their consideration, and to report thereupon.

Mr. Speaker left the chair.

Mr. Boudinot took the chair of the committee.

Mr. Speaker resumed the chair, and Mr. Boudinot reported, that the committee had, according to order, had the said report under consideration, and made a farther progress therein.

RESOLVED, That this House will, to-morrow, again resolve itself into a committee of the whole House on the said report.[58]

---

[57] On August 17 this report was considered again by the COWH.

[58] On August 18 a motion on amendments to the Constitution was defeated, and amendments to the committee report were presented from the COWH. On the same

The orders of the day for the House to resolve itself into a committee of the whole House, on the bill sent from the Senate, entitled, "An act to establish the judicial courts of the United States;" also, on the bill for establishing a land-office, in, and for the western territory; and on the bill to provide for the safe keeping of the acts, records, and seal of the United States; for the due publication of the acts of Congress; for the authentication of the copies of records; for making out and recording commissions, and prescribing their form, and for establishing the fees of office to be taken for making such commissions, and for copies of records and papers; were read and postponed until to-morrow.

And then the House adjourned until to-morrow morning eleven o'clock.

TUESDAY, AUGUST 18, 1789

Mr. Boudinot, from the committee to whom was referred a letter from the Postmaster-General, made a report, which was read, and ordered to lie on the table.[59]

On a motion made that the House do agree to the following order, to wit:

"That such of the amendments to the Constitution proposed by the several states, as are not in substance comprized in the report of the select committee appointed to consider amendments, be referred to a committee of the whole House; and that all the amendments which shall be agreed to by the committee last mentioned, be included in one report."

The previous question was demanded by five members, Shall the main question to agree to the said order be now put? And on the question, Shall the main question be now put?

It passed in the negative, $\left\{\begin{array}{l} \text{AYES} \ \ 16 \\ \text{NOES} \ \ 34 \end{array}\right.$

And so the motion was lost,

The ayes and noes being demanded by one fifth of the members present,

Those who voted in the affirmative, are,

Aedanus Burke	John Hathorn
Isaac Coles	Samuel Livermore
William Floyd	John Page
Elbridge Gerry	Josiah Parker
Samuel Griffin	Jeremiah Van Rensselaer
Jonathan Grout	Roger Sherman

day several proposed amendments to the Constitution were introduced, but a motion to refer them to the COWH was defeated.

[59] A copy of the report is in A Record of the Reports of Select Committees, HR, DNA. On August 27 this report was considered and recommitted.

Michael Jenifer Stone   Thomas Sumter and
Jonathan Sturges   Thomas Tudor Tucker

Those who voted in the negative, are,

Fisher Ames   James Madison, junior
Abraham Baldwin   Andrew Moore
Egbert Benson   Peter Muhlenberg
Elias Boudinot   George Partridge
John Brown   James Schureman
Lambert Cadwalader   Thomas Scott
Daniel Carroll   Theodore Sedgwick
George Clymer   Joshua Seney
Thomas Fitzsimons   Peter Silvester
Abiel Foster   Thomas Sinnickson
Nicholas Gilman   William Smith (of Maryland)
Benjamin Goodhue   William Smith (of South-Carolina)
Thomas Hartley   George Thatcher
Daniel Hiester   Jonathan Trumbull
Benjamin Huntington   John Vining
John Laurance   Jeremiah Wadsworth and
Richard Bland Lee   Henry Wynkoop

The House, according to the order of the day, resolved itself into a committee of the whole House, on the report from the committee of eleven, to whom it was referred to take the subject of amendments to the Constitution of the United States, generally into their consideration, and to report thereupon.

Mr. Speaker left the chair.

Mr. Boudinot took the chair of the committee.

Mr. Speaker resumed the chair, and Mr. Boudinot reported that the committee had, according to order, had the said report under consideration, and gone through the same, and made several amendments thereto, which he delivered in at the clerk's table, where the same were read, and ordered to lie on the table.

A message from the Senate by Mr. Otis, their Secretary.

MR. SPEAKER, The Senate have passed the bill, entitled, "An act providing for the expences which may attend negociations or treaties with the Indian tribes, and the appointment of commissioners for managing the same," with an amendment, to which they desire the concurrence of this House.[60] And then he withdrew.

A motion was made and seconded, that the following propositions of amendment to the Constitution of the United States, be referred to the consideration of a committee of the whole House, to wit:

ARTICLE 1. *section 2.* clause 2. At the end add these words, "nor shall any person be capable of serving as a representative more than six years in any term of eight years."

Clause 3. At the end add these words, "from and after the commencement of the year one thousand seven hundred and ninety-five, the election of senators for each state shall be annual; and no person shall be capable of serving as a senator more than five years in any term of six years."

Section 4. clause 1. Strike out the words, "But the Congress may at any time by law make or alter such regulations, except as to the places of choosing senators."

Section 5. clause 1. Amend the first part to read thus, "Each state shall be the judge (according to its own laws) of the elections of its senators and representatives to sit in Congress, and shall furnish them with sufficient credentials; but each House shall judge of the qualifications of its own members. A majority of said House shall constitute, &c."

Clause 2. Strike out these words, "and with the concurrence of two thirds expel a member;" and insert the word "and" after the word "proceedings."

Section 6. clause 2. Amend to read thus, "No person having been elected, and having taken his seat as a senator or representative, shall, during the time for which he was elected, be appointed to any civil office under the authority of the United States; and no person, &c."

Section 8. clause 1. At the end add these words, "No direct tax shall be laid, unless any state shall have neglected to furnish in due time its proportion of a previous requisition, in which case Congress may proceed to levy by direct taxation, within any state so neglecting, its proportion of such requisition, together with interest at the rate of six per cent. per annum, from the time it ought to have been furnished, and the charges of levying the same."

Clause 9. Strike out the words, "tribunals inferior to the supreme court," and insert the words, "courts of admiralty."

Clause 17. At the end add these words, "Provided that the Congress shall not have authority to make any law to prevent the laws of the states respectively in which such district or places may be, from extending to such district or places in all civil and criminal matters, in which any person without the limits of such district or places, shall be a party aggrieved."

---

[60] The amendment is printed in the *Senate Legislative Journal* on August 18. On August 19 the House agreed to this amendment.

Section 9. clause 7. Strike out the words, "without the consent of the Congress;" and amend to read thus, "shall accept of any present or emolument, or hold any office or title of any kind whatever, from any king, prince or foreign state; Provided, That this clause shall not be construed to affect the rights of those persons (during their own lives) who are now citizens of the United States, and hold foreign titles."

Section 10. clause 2. Amend the first sentence to read thus, "No state shall lay any duties on imports or exports, or any duty of tonnage, except such as shall be uniform in their operation on all foreign nations, and consistent with the existing treaties; and also uniform in their operation on the citizens of all the several states in the Union."

ARTICLE 2. *section 1.* clause 5. At the end add these words, "Nor shall any person be capable of holding the office of President of the United States, more than eight years in any term of twelve years."

Section 2. clause 1. Strike out the words, "be commander in chief," and insert, "have power to direct (agreeable to law) the operations."

Clause 3. At the end add these words, "He shall also have power to suspend from his office, for a time not exceeding twelve months, any officer whom he shall have reason to think unfit to be entrusted with the duties thereof; and Congress may by law provide for the absolute removal of officers found to be unfit for the trust reposed in them.

ARTICLE 3. *section 1.* From each sentence strike out the words, "inferior courts," and insert the words, "courts of admiralty."

Section 2. clause 1. Strike out the words, "between a state and citizens of another state, &c." to the end; and amend to read thus, "between a state and foreign states, and between citizens of the United States claiming the same lands under grants of different states."

ARTICLE 6. clause 3. Between the word, "no," and the word, "religious," insert the word, "other."

And on the question, Shall the said propositions of amendment be referred to the consideration of a committee of the whole House?

It passed in the negative.[61]

Mr. Clymer, from the committee of elections, reported, that the committee pursuant to the instruction to them contained in the resolution of the twenty-fifth of May, relative to the petition of a number of citizens of the state of New-Jersey, complaining of the illegality of the election of the members of this House, as elected within that state, do ascertain the following facts, as arising from the proofs, to wit:

1st. That the elections for members of this House held within that state, in

---

[61] On August 19 the amendments from the COWH to the committee report on constitutional amendments were considered.

consequence of an act of the legislature thereof, entitled, "An act for carrying into effect on the part of the state of New-Jersey, the Constitution of the United States, assented to, ratified and confirmed by this state, on the eighteenth day of December, one thousand seven hundred and eighty-seven," passed the twenty-first of November, one thousand seven hundred and eighty-eight, were closed in the several counties of Bergen, Morris, Monmouth, Hunterdon, Somerset, Middlesex, Sussex, Salem, Cape-May, Cumberland, Burlington and Gloucester; and the lists of the several persons voted for, and the number of votes taken for each, were received by the Governor at the respective times appearing from the said lists, and the indorsements thereon, which lists accompany this report.

2d. That the election in the county of Essex, the remaining county in the state, closed on the twenty-seventh of April, and the list was received by the Governor on the third of May.

3d. That in consequence of a summons from the Governor, (a copy whereof accompanies this report) dated the twenty-seventh of February, to four of the members of the council, a privy council, consisting of the Governor, and the four members so summoned, did assemble at Elizabethtown on the third of March, and being so assembled, Mr. Haring, another member of the council, received a note from the Governor, (a copy whereof accompanies this report) in consequence whereof Mr. Haring did then also attend the privy council as a member thereof.

4th. That the Governor then appointed another meeting of the privy council, to be held on the eighteenth of March, at which day the Governor and eleven members of the council did assemble, and did then determine from the lists of the twelve counties specified in the first fact above stated, the four members now holding seats in this House, the four persons elected members of this House within that state; against which determination of the council three of the members then present did protest; and a protest, (a copy whereof accompanies this report) was with the consent of the council delivered into the council in form on the subsequent day.

5th. That there was no determination of the Governor and privy council in the premises until the eighteenth of March.

6th. That the Governor did on the nineteenth of March issue a proclamation, (a copy whereof accompanies this report).

ORDERED, That the said report do lie on the table.[62]

The orders of the day for the House to resolve itself into a committee of the whole House, on the bill sent from the Senate, entitled, "An act to establish the judicial courts of the United States;" also, on the bill for establishing a land-office, in, and for the western territory; and, on the bill to provide for

---

[62] On September 1 this report was considered.

the safe keeping of the acts, records, and seal of the United States; for the due publication of the acts of Congress; for the authentication of the copies of records; for making out and recording commissions, and prescribing their form, and for establishing the fees of office to be taken for making such commissions, and for copies of records and papers; were read, and postponed until to-morrow.

And then the House adjourned until to-morrow morning eleven o'clock.

WEDNESDAY, AUGUST 19, 1789

A petition of Patrick Bennet, was presented to the House and read, praying compensation for certain arrears of pay due to him as a quartermaster in the late army.[63]

Also, a petition of sundry inhabitants of the port of Stonington in the state of Connecticut, whose names are thereunto subscribed, praying the attention of Congress to the fishery of the said port, by the appointment of a proper officer with power to grant permits and clearances to all vessels employed in the said fishery.

ORDERED, That the said petitions do lie on the table.

The House proceeded to consider the amendment proposed by the Senate, to the bill, entitled, "An act providing for the expences which may attend negociations or treaties with the Indian tribes, and the appointment of commissioners for managing the same;" and the same being read was agreed to.

ORDERED, That the clerk of this House do acquaint the Senate therewith.[64]

The House proceeded to consider the amendments made by the committee of the whole House to the report from the committee of eleven, to whom it was referred to take the subject of amendments to the Constitution of the United States, generally into their consideration, and having made some progress therein,

ORDERED, That the farther consideration of the said amendments be put off until to-morrow.[65]

The several orders of the day, for the House to resolve itself into a committee of the whole house on the bill sent from the Senate, entitled, "An act to establish the judicial courts of the United States;" also, on the bill for establishing a land-office, in, and for the western territory; and, on the bill to provide for the safe keeping of the acts, records, and seal of the United States; for the due publication of the acts of Congress; for the authentication of the copies of records; for making out, and recording commissions, and prescribing their form, and for establishing the fees of office to be taken for making

---

[63] On September 21 this petition was referred to a committee on claims.

[64] On August 20 this bill was signed by the speaker, vice president, and president.

[65] On August 20 the amendments were considered again.

such commissions; and for copies of records and papers; were read, and post-poned until to-morrow.

And then the House adjourned until to-morrow morning eleven o'clock.

THURSDAY, AUGUST 20, 1789

A message from the Senate by Mr. Otis, their Secretary.

MR. SPEAKER,   The Senate agree to the resolution of this House of the tenth instant, for executing the survey directed by an act of the late Congress of June the sixth, one thousand seven hundred and eighty-eight.[66]   And then he withdrew.

ORDERED, That Mr. Vining be added to the committee for inrolled bills, in the room of Mr. White, who has obtained leave of absence.

Mr. Partridge, reported from the committee for inrolled bills, that the com-mittee had examined the inrolled bill, entitled, "An act providing for the expences which may attend negociations or treaties with the Indian tribes, and the appointment of commissioners for managing the same,"[67] and had found it to be truly inrolled: Whereupon,

Mr. Speaker signed the said inrolled bill.

ORDERED, That the clerk of this House do acquaint the Senate therewith.

The House resumed the consideration of the amendments made by the committee of the whole House to the report from the committee of eleven, to whom it was referred to take the subject of amendments to the Constitution of the United States, generally into their consideration; and having made a farther progress therein,

ORDERED, That the farther consideration of the said amendments be put off until to-morrow.[68]

Mr. Partridge, from the committee for inrolled bills, reported that the com-mittee did, this day, jointly with the committee of the Senate, wait on the President of the United States, and present him with the inrolled bill, entitled, "An act providing for the expences which may attend negociations or treaties with the Indian tribes, and the appointment of commissioners for managing the same," for his approbation.

A message was received from the President of the United States, notifying that the President approves of the act, entitled, "An act providing for the

---

[66] On August 22 the speaker signed this resolution.

[67] The inspected enrolled bill is in Enrolled Acts, RG 11, DNA. E-45703, E-22196.

[68] On August 21 the amendments and the report were considered, and seventeen proposed articles of amendment were agreed to and printed. A further amendment was then considered.

expences which may attend negociations or treaties with the Indian tribes, and the appointment of commissioners for managing the same," and has this day affixed his signature thereto: And the messenger delivered in the said act, and then withdrew.

ORDERED, That the clerk of this House do acquaint the Senate therewith.

The orders of the day for the House to resolve itself into a committee of the whole House, on the bill sent from the Senate, entitled, "An act to establish the judicial courts of the United States;" also, on the bill for establishing a land-office, in, and for the western territory; and on the bill to provide for the safe keeping of the acts, records, and seal of the United States; for the due publication of the acts of Congress; for the authentication of the copies of records; for making out and recording commissions, and prescribing their form, and for establishing the fees of office to be taken for making such commissions, and for copies of records and papers; were read and postponed until to-morrow.

And then the House adjourned until to-morrow morning eleven o'clock.

FRIDAY, AUGUST 21, 1789

The House resumed the consideration of the amendments made by the committee of the whole House, to the report from the committee of eleven, to whom it was referred to take the subject of amendments to the Constitution of the United States, generally into their consideration; and the said amendments being partly agreed to, and partly disagreed to,

The House proceeded to consider the original report of the committee of eleven, consisting of seventeen articles, as now amended; whereupon the first, second, third, fourth, fifth, sixth, seventh, eighth, ninth, tenth, eleventh, twelfth, thirteenth, fourteenth, fifteenth and sixteenth articles being again read and debated, were, upon the question severally put thereupon, agreed to by the House, as follows, two-thirds of the members present concurring, to wit:

FIRST. After the first enumeration, there shall be one representative for every thirty thousand, until the number shall amount to one hundred; after which the proportion shall be so regulated by Congress, that there shall be not less than one hundred representatives, nor less than one representative for every forty thousand persons, until the number of representatives shall amount to two hundred; after which the proportion shall be so regulated, that there shall not be less than two hundred representatives, nor less than one representative for every fifty thousand persons.

SECOND. No law varying the compensation of the members to Congress shall take effect, until an election of representatives shall have intervened.

THIRD. Congress shall make no law establishing religion, or prohibiting the free exercise thereof, nor shall the rights of conscience be infringed.

FOURTH. The freedom of speech, and of the press, and the right of the people peaceably to assemble and consult for their common good, and to apply to the government for redress of grievances, shall not be infringed.

FIFTH. A well regulated militia, composed of the body of the people, being the best security of a free state, the right of the people to keep and bear arms, shall not be infringed; but no one religiously scrupulous of bearing arms, shall be compelled to render military service in person.

SIXTH. No soldier shall in time of peace be quartered in any house, without the consent of the owner; nor in time of war but in a manner to be prescribed by law.

SEVENTH. No person shall be subject, except in case of impeachment, to more than one trial or one punishment for the same offence; nor shall be compelled in any criminal case to be a witness against himself; nor be deprived of life, liberty or property, without due process of law; nor shall private property be taken for public use, without just compensation.

EIGHTH. Excessive bail shall not be required; nor excessive fines imposed; nor cruel and unusual punishments inflicted.

NINTH. The right of the people to be secure in their persons, houses, papers and effects, against unreasonable searches and seizures, shall not be violated; and no warrants shall issue, but upon probable cause, supported by oath or affirmation, and particularly describing the place to be searched, and the persons or things to be seized.

TENTH. The enumeration in this Constitution of certain rights, shall not be construed to deny or disparage others retained by the people.

ELEVENTH. No state shall infringe the right of trial by jury in criminal cases; nor the rights of conscience; nor the freedom of speech or of the press.

TWELFTH. No appeal to the supreme court of the United States shall be allowed, where the value in controversy shall not amount to one thousand dollars; nor shall any fact, triable by a jury according to the course of the common law, be otherwise re-examinable than according to the rules of common law.

THIRTEENTH. In all criminal prosecutions, the accused shall enjoy the right to a speedy and public trial; to be informed of the nature and cause of the accusation; to be confronted with the witnesses against him; to have compulsory process for obtaining witnesses in his favour; and to have the assistance of counsel for his defence.

FOURTEENTH. The trial of all crimes, (except in cases of impeachment, and in cases arising in the land or naval forces, or in the militia when in actual service in time of war or public danger) shall be by an impartial jury of the vicinage, with the requisite of unanimity for conviction, the right of challenge and other accustomed requisites; and no person shall be held to answer for a capital or otherwise infamous crime, unless on a presentment or indictment by a grand jury; but if a crime be committed in a place in the possession of an enemy, or in which an insurrection may prevail, the indictment and trial may by law be authorised in some other place within the same state.

FIFTEENTH. In suits at common law, the right of trial by jury shall be preserved.

SIXTEENTH. The powers delegated by the Constitution to the government of the United States, shall be exercised as therein appropriated, so that the legislative shall never exercise the powers vested in the executive or judicial; nor the executive the powers vested in the legislative or judicial; nor the judicial the powers vested in the legislative or executive.

The seventeenth article in the words following, to wit, "The powers not delegated by the Constitution, nor prohibited by it to the states, are reserved to the states respectively," being under debate, a motion was made, and the question being put to amend the same by inserting after the word "*not*," the word "*expressly.*"

It passed in the negative, $\begin{cases} \text{AYES} & 17 \\ \text{NOES} & 32 \end{cases}$

The ayes and noes being demanded by one fifth of the members present, Those who voted in the affirmative, are,

Aedanus Burke	Josiah Parker
Isaac Coles	George Partridge
William Floyd	Jeremiah Van Rensselaer
Elbridge Gerry	William Smith (of South-Carolina)
Jonathan Grout	Michael Jenifer Stone
John Hathorn	Thomas Sumter
James Jackson	George Thatcher and
Samuel Livermore	Thomas Tudor Tucker
John Page	

Those who voted in the negative, are,

Fisher Ames	George Clymer
Egbert Benson	Thomas Fitzsimons
Elias Boudinot	Abiel Foster
John Brown	George Gale
Lambert Cadwalader	Nicholas Gilman
Daniel Carroll	Benjamin Goodhue

Thomas Hartley
Daniel Hiester
John Laurance
Richard Bland Lee
James Madison, junior
Andrew Moore
Peter Muhlenberg
James Schureman
Thomas Scott
Theodore Sedgwick

Joshua Seney
Roger Sherman
Peter Silvester
Thomas Sinnickson
William Smith (of Maryland)
Jonathan Sturges
Jonathan Trumbull
John Vining
Jeremiah Wadsworth and
Henry Wynkoop

And then the main question being put that the House do agree to the said seventeenth article;

It was resolved in the affirmative, two-thirds of the members present concurring.

A motion was then made and seconded, to add to the said articles the following:

"Congress shall not alter, modify or interfere in the times, places or manner of holding elections of senators or representatives, except when any state shall refuse or neglect, or be unable by invasion or rebellion to make such election."

And on the question that the House do agree to the said proposed article;

It passed in the negative. $\begin{cases} \text{AYES} & 23 \\ \text{NOES} & 28 \end{cases}$

The ayes and noes being demanded by one-fifth of the members present,

Those who voted in the affirmative, are,

Aedanus Burke
Isaac Coles
William Floyd
Elbridge Gerry
Samuel Griffin
Jonathan Grout
John Hathorn
Daniel Hiester
James Jackson
Samuel Livermore
George Mathews
Andrew Moore

John Page
Josiah Parker
George Partridge
Jeremiah Van Rensselaer
Joshua Seney
Peter Silvester
William Smith (of South-Carolina)
Michael Jenifer Stone
Thomas Sumter
George Thatcher and
Thomas Tudor Tucker

Those who voted in the negative, are,

Fisher Ames   Richard Bland Lee
Egbert Benson   James Madison, junior
Elias Boudinot   Peter Muhlenberg
John Brown   James Schureman
Lambert Cadwalader   Thomas Scott
Daniel Carroll   Theodore Sedgwick
George Clymer   Roger Sherman
Thomas Fitzsimons   Thomas Sinnickson
Abiel Foster   William Smith (of Maryland)
George Gale   Jonathan Sturges
Nicholas Gilman   Jonathan Trumbull
Benjamin Goodhue   John Vining
Thomas Hartley   Jeremiah Wadsworth and
John Laurance   Henry Wynkoop

On motion,

ORDERED, That the farther consideration of amendments to the Constitution of the United States be postponed until to-morrow.[69]

The orders of the day for the House to resolve itself into a committee of the whole House, on the bill sent from the Senate, entitled, "An act to establish the judicial courts of the United States;" also, on the bill for establishing a land-office, in, and for the western territory; and on the bill to provide for the safe keeping of the acts, records, and seal of the United States; for the due publication of the acts of Congress; for the authentication of the copies of records; for making out and recording commissions, and prescribing their form, and for establishing the fees of office to be taken for making such commissions, and for copies of records and papers; were read and postponed until to-morrow.

And then the House adjourned until to-morrow morning eleven o'clock.

SATURDAY, AUGUST 22, 1789

Mr. Partridge, from the committee for inrolled bills, reported that the committee had examined the inrolled resolve for executing the survey directed by an act of the late Congress, of June the sixth, one thousand seven hundred and eighty-eight,[70] and had found the same to be truly inrolled: Whereupon,

---

[69] On August 22 further amendments to the Constitution were considered and disagreed to. A committee was appointed to arrange the articles of amendment that had been agreed to.

[70] The inspected enrolled resolution is in Enrolled Acts, RG 11, DNA. E–45723.

Mr. Speaker signed the said inrolled resolve.[71]

The several memorials of the inhabitants of Trenton, in the state of New-Jersey, and of the boroughs of Lancaster and York-town, in the state of Pennsylvania,[72] were presented to the House and read, respectively praying that the permanent seat of Congress may be established at the same.

ORDERED, That the said memorials do lie on the table.

The House, according to the order of the day, resumed the consideration of amendments to the Constitution of the United States: Whereupon,

A motion was made and seconded, to add to the amendments already agreed to, the following article, to wit:

"The Congress shall never impose direct taxes, but where the monies arising from the duties, imposts and excise, are insufficient for the public exigencies; nor then, until Congress shall have made a requisition upon the states, to assess, levy and pay their respective proportions of such requisitions: and in case any state shall neglect or refuse to pay its proportion, pursuant to such requisition, then Congress may assess and levy such state's proportion, together with interest thereon, at the rate of six per cent. per annum, from the time of payment prescribed by such requisition."

And on the question that the House do agree to the said proposed article;

It passed in the negative. $\begin{cases} \text{AYES} & 9 \\ \text{NOES} & 39 \end{cases}$

The ayes and noes being demanded by one fifth of the members present,

Those who voted in the affirmative, are,

Aedanus Burke	Samuel Livermore
Isaac Coles	Jeremiah Van Rensselaer
William Floyd	Thomas Sumter and
Jonathan Grout	Thomas Tudor Tucker
John Hathorn	

Those who voted in the negative, are,

Fisher Ames	Thomas Fitzsimons
Egbert Benson	Abiel Foster
John Brown	George Gale
Lambert Cadwalader	Elbridge Gerry
Daniel Carroll	Nicholas Gilman
George Clymer	Benjamin Goodhue

---

[71] The vice president signed this resolution on August 25, and on August 26 the House was notified that the president had signed it.

[72] The memorial from Lancaster and the petition from Trenton are in Petitions and Memorials: Various subjects, SR, DNA.

Thomas Hartley
Daniel Hiester
James Jackson
John Laurance
Richard Bland Lee
James Madison, junior
George Mathews
Andrew Moore
Peter Muhlenberg
John Page
Josiah Parker
George Partridge
James Schureman
Thomas Scott

Theodore Sedgwick
Joshua Seney
Roger Sherman
Peter Silvester
Thomas Sinnickson
William Smith (of Maryland)
William Smith (of South-Carolina)
Michael Jenifer Stone
Jonathan Sturges
George Thatcher
Jonathan Trumbull
John Vining and
Jeremiah Wadsworth

Another motion was made and seconded, further to amend the Constitution, as follows:

ARTICLE 1. *section 8*. clause 9. Strike out the words, "tribunals inferior to the supreme court," and insert the words, "courts of admiralty."

And on the question that the House do agree to the said amendment,

It passed in the negative.

Another motion was made and seconded, further to amend the Constitution, as follows:

In the third section of the sixth article, insert the word, "other," between the word "*no*," and the word "religious."

And on the question that the House do agree to the said amendment,

It passed in the negative.

Another motion was made and seconded, to add to the amendments already agreed to, the following article, to wit:

"That Congress erect no company of merchants with exclusive advantages of commerce."

And on the question that the House do agree to the said proposed article,

It passed in the negative.

Another motion was made and seconded, to add to the amendments already agreed to, the following article, to wit:

"Congress shall at no time consent that any person holding an office of trust or profit under the United States, shall accept of a title of nobility, or any other title or office from any king, prince, or foreign state."

And on the question that the House do agree to the said proposed article,

It passed in the negative.

On motion,

ORDERED, That it be referred to a committee of three, to prepare and report a proper arrangement of, and introduction to the articles of amendment to the Constitution of the United States, as agreed to by the House; and that Mr. Benson, Mr. Sherman, and Mr. Sedgwick be of the said committee.[73]

A petition of Thomasin Gordon, was presented to the House and read, praying that the accounts of her late husband, Colonel John White, of the Georgia line, deceased, may be liquidated in such manner that his child may receive in common, the benefits which have been granted to the heirs of other officers deceased.[74]

Also, a memorial of the merchants and other inhabitants of the towns of Alexandria and Dumfries, in the state of Virginia, praying that so much of the act of Congress to regulate the collection of duties, as restricts ships or vessels bound up the river Potowmack, to stop at Saint Mary's or Yeocomico, and there obtain a certified manifest of their cargoes before entry made, be repealed, or that the like regulation be made general throughout the United States.

ORDERED, That the said petition and memorial do lie on the table.[75]

The several orders of the day, for the House to resolve itself into a committee of the whole house on the bill sent from the Senate, entitled, "An act to establish the judicial courts of the United States;" also, on the bill for establishing a land-office, in, and for the western territory; and, on the bill to provide for the safe keeping of the acts, records, and seal of the United States; for the due publication of the acts of Congress; for the authentication of the copies of records; for making out, and recording commissions, and prescribing their form, and for establishing the fees of office to be taken for making such commissions; and for copies of records and papers; were read, and postponed until Monday next.

And then the House adjourned until Monday morning eleven o'clock.

MONDAY, AUGUST 24, 1789

A memorial of the merchants and other inhabitants of George-Town, Bladensburg and Piscataway, in the state of Maryland, was presented to the House and read, praying that so much of the act of Congress to regulate the collection of duties, as restricts ships or vessels bound up the river Potowmack, to stop at Saint Mary's or Yeocomico, and there obtain a manifest of their cargoes before entry made, be repealed, or that the like regulation may be made general throughout the United States.

ORDERED, That the said memorial, together with the memorial of the mer-

---

[73] On August 24 this committee made a report, which was agreed to, and the articles of amendment were sent to the Senate.

[74] On September 21 this petition was referred to a committee on claims.

[75] On August 24 this petition was committed.

chants of Alexandria and Dumfries, presented on Saturday last, be referred to Mr. Goodhue, Mr. Carroll, and Mr. Lee, that they do examine the matter thereof, and report the same with their opinion thereupon to the House.[76]

A petition of John Hurt, late a chaplain in the continental army, was presented to the House and read, praying that his claims for services in several military stations, may be liquidated and satisfied.[77]

ORDERED, That the said petition do lie on the table.[78]

Mr. Fitzsimons, from the committee appointed, presented according to order, a bill establishing the salaries of the executive officers of government, with their assistants and clerks, which was received and read the first time.[79]

Mr. Benson, from the committee appointed, reported according to order, an arrangement of the articles of amendment to the Constitution of the United States, as agreed to by the House on Friday last; also a resolution proper to be prefixed to the same, which resolution he delivered in at the clerk's table, where the same was twice read and agreed to by the House, as followeth:

RESOLVED, By the Senate and House of Representatives of the United States of America in Congress assembled, two-thirds of both Houses deeming it necessary, That the following articles be proposed to the legislatures of the several states, as amendments to the Constitution of the United States, all or any of which articles when ratified by three-fourths of the said legislatures, to be valid to all intents and purposes as part of the said Constitution.[80]

ORDERED, That the clerk of this House do carry to the Senate a fair engrossed copy of the said proposed articles of amendment, and desire their concurrence.[81]

---

[76] On August 26 this committee reported.

[77] A petition, addressed to George Washington and dated August 24, 1789, which is probably similar to that received by the House, is in item 78, M247, roll 96, RG 360, Records of the Continental Congress and the Constitutional Convention (hereinafter referred to as PCC), DNA.

[78] On September 21 this petition was referred to the committee on claims.

[79] On August 25 this bill was read again.

[80] A printed copy of the resolution and articles of amendment, annotated by the Senate, is in House Joint and Concurrent Resolutions, SR, DNA. E–22201.

[81] On August 25 the Senate read the House resolution proposing articles of amendment to the Constitution. The resolution is printed in the *Senate Legislative Journal* on that date. On September 2 the Senate considered the proposed articles and amended Article I. The Senate agreed to Articles II and III with amendments on September 3, after several other amendments had been disagreed to. The Senate debated the articles further on September 4 and agreed to Articles IV–XI with amendments to some of them. On September 7 the Senate agreed to the rest of the articles, except numbers 14 and 16, with some amendments. Several further articles of amendment were proposed and disagreed to on the same day and on September 8. On September 9 several amendments to the House articles were agreed to, and the amended articles were passed and returned to the House.

On motion,

RESOLVED, That the President of the Senate, and Speaker of the House of Representatives, do adjourn their respective Houses on the twenty-second day of September next, to meet again on the first Monday in December next.[82]

ORDERED, That the clerk of this House do carry the said resolution to the Senate, and desire their concurrence.[83]

Mr. Madison, from the managers appointed on the part of this House, to attend the conference with the Senate, on the subject matter of the amendment depending between the two Houses, to the bill entitled, "An act to establish the treasury department," made a report: Whereupon,

RESOLVED, That this House doth adhere to their disagreement to so much of the eighth amendment proposed by the Senate to the said bill, as was disagreed by this House, and insisted on by the Senate.

ORDERED, That the clerk of this House do acquaint the Senate therewith.[84]

The House, according to the order of the day, resolved itself into a committee of the whole House, on the bill sent from the Senate, entitled, "An act to establish the judicial courts of the United States."

Mr. Speaker left the chair.

Mr. Boudinot took the chair of the committee.

Mr. Speaker resumed the chair, and Mr. Boudinot reported, that the committee had, according to order, had the said bill under consideration, and made some progress therein.

RESOLVED, That this House will, to-morrow, again resolve itself into a committee of the whole House on the said bill.[85]

ORDERED, That Mr. Stone have leave to be absent from the service of this House from the first day of September next, for the remainder of the present session, and Mr. Silvester until this day three weeks.

The orders of the day for the House to resolve itself into a committee of the whole House on the bill for establishing a land-office, in, and for the western territory; also, on the bill to provide for the safe keeping of the acts, records, and seal of the United States; for the due publication of the acts of Congress; for the authentication of the copies of records; for making out and recording commissions, and prescribing their form, and for establishing the fees of office to be taken for making such commissions, and for copies of records and papers; were read, and postponed until to-morrow.

And then the House adjourned until to-morrow morning eleven o'clock.

---

[82] A copy of the resolution is in Messages from the House, SR, DNA.

[83] On August 25 the Senate notified the House that they had agreed to this resolution.

[84] On August 25 the Senate receded from the eighth amendment.

[85] From August 25–28 this bill was postponed. The bill was considered in the COWH on August 29.

TUESDAY, AUGUST 25, 1789

A bill for establishing the salaries of the executive officers of government, with their assistants and clerks, was read the second time, and ordered to be committed to a committee of the whole House on Friday next.[86]

The House, according to the order of the day, resolved itself into a committee of the whole House, on the bill to provide for the safe keeping of the acts, records, and seal of the United States; for the due publication of the acts of Congress; for the authentication of the copies of records; for making out and recording commissions, and prescribing their form, and for establishing the fees of office to be taken for making such commissions, and for copies of records and papers.

Mr. Speaker left the chair.

Mr. Boudinot took the chair of the committee.

Mr. Speaker resumed the chair, and Mr. Boudinot reported, that the committee had, according to order, had the said bill under consideration, and made some progress therein.

RESOLVED, That this House will, to-morrow, again resolve itself into a committee of the whole House on the said bill.[87]

A message from the Senate, by Mr. Otis their Secretary.

MR. SPEAKER,   The Senate recede from so much of their eighth amendment to the bill, entitled, "An act to establish the treasury department," as was disagreed to by this House, and insisted on by the Senate.[88]

The Senate have also agreed to the resolution of this House, of the twenty-fourth instant, appointing the time for an adjournment of both Houses of Congress.[89]   And then he withdrew.

The orders of the day for the House to resolve itself into a committee of the whole House, on the bill sent from the Senate, entitled, "An act to establish the judicial courts of the United States;" also, on the bill for establishing a land-office, in, and for the western territory; were read, and postponed until to-morrow.

And then the House adjourned until to-morrow morning eleven o'clock.

WEDNESDAY, AUGUST 26, 1789

The several petitions of James McLean, James Reed, and Prudent La Jeunesse, were presented to the House and read, praying that their several

---

[86] On August 28 this bill was amended.

[87] On August 26 this bill was amended.

[88] On August 27 this bill was signed by the speaker.

[89] On September 22 an order postponing the adjournment was agreed to by the House and Senate.

claims for military services, rendered during the late war, may be liquidated and satisfied.[90]

Also, a petition of Joseph Wheaton, serjeant at arms to this House, praying that an enquiry may be made into certain charges exhibited against him in an anonymous letter addressed to the Speaker.

ORDERED, That the said petitions do lie on the table.

Mr. Goodhue, from the committee to whom were referred the memorials of the merchants and other inhabitants of the towns of Alexandria and Dumfries, in the state of Virginia, and of George-Town, Bladensburg and Piscataway, in the state of Maryland, made a report, which was read, and ordered to lie on the table.[91]

Mr. Partridge, from the committee for inrolled bills, reported, that the committee did yesterday, jointly with the committee of the Senate, wait on the President of the United States, and present him with the inrolled resolve for executing the survey directed by an act of the late Congress of June the sixth, one thousand seven hundred and eighty-eight, for his approbation.

The House, according to the order of the day, resolved itself into a committee of the whole House, on the bill to provide for the safe keeping of the acts, records, and seal of the United States; for the due publication of the acts of Congress; for the authentication of the copies of records; for making out and recording commissions, and prescribing their form, and for establishing the fees of office to be taken for making such commissions, and for copies of records and papers.

Mr. Speaker left the chair.

Mr. Boudinot took the chair of the committee.

Mr. Speaker resumed the chair, and Mr. Boudinot reported, that the committee had, according to order, had the said bill under consideration, and gone through the same, and made several amendments thereto, which he delivered in at the clerk's table, where the same were read, amended, and agreed to by the House.

ORDERED, That the said bill, with the amendments, be engrossed, and read the third time to-morrow.[92]

A message was received from the President of the United States, notifying that the President approves of the resolve for executing the survey directed by an act of the late Congress, of June the sixth, one thousand seven hundred

[90] On September 21 the La Jeunesse and Reed petitions were committed to a committee on claims.

[91] A copy of the report is in A Record of the Reports of Select Committees, HR, DNA. On August 28 this report was amended, agreed to, and a committee was appointed to bring in a bill. On the same day this committee presented a Collection Bill [HR–23], which was read.

[92] On August 27 this bill was read, agreed to, and sent to the Senate.

and eighty-eight, and has this day affixed his signature thereto: And the messenger delivered in the said resolve, and then withdrew.

ORDERED, That the clerk of this House do acquaint the Senate therewith. A message from the Senate, by Mr. Otis their Secretary.

MR. SPEAKER,   The Senate have passed the bill, entitled, "An act for registering and clearing vessels, regulating the coasting trade, and for other purposes," with several amendments,[93] to which they desire the concurrence of this House.   And then he withdrew.

The House proceeded to consider the amendments proposed by the Senate to the said bill, and having made some progress therein,

ORDERED, That the farther consideration of the said amendments be put off until to-morrow.[94]

The orders of the day for the House to resolve itself into a committee of the whole House, on the bill sent from the Senate, entitled, "An act to establish the judicial courts of the United States;" also, on the bill "for establishing a land-office, in, and for the western territory," were read, and postponed until to-morrow.

And then the House adjourned until to-morrow morning eleven o'clock.

THURSDAY, AUGUST 27, 1789

Mr. Partridge reported from the committee for inrolled bills, that the committee had examined the inrolled bill, entitled, "An act to establish the treasury department,"[95] and had found the same to be truly inrolled: Whereupon,

Mr. Speaker signed the said inrolled bill.[96]

An engrossed bill to provide for the safe keeping of the acts, records, and seal of the United States; for the due publication of the acts of Congress; for the authentication of the copies of records; for making out and recording commissions, and prescribing their form, and for establishing the fees of office to be taken for making such commissions, and for copies of records and papers, was read the third time.

---

[93] Senate amendments are filed with and noted on the bill in House Bills, SR, DNA. Annotations on the printed bill, in the Broadside Collection, RBkRm, DLC, correspond roughly to Senate amendments. The amendments are printed in the *Senate Legislative Journal* on August 25.

[94] On August 27 the House agreed to these amendments with amendments.

[95] The inspected enrolled bill is in Enrolled Acts, RG 11, DNA. E–45708.

[96] On August 28 this bill was signed by the vice president, and on September 1 it was presented to the president.

RESOLVED, That the said bill do pass, and that the title be, "An act to provide for the safe keeping of the acts, records, and seal of the United States, and for other purposes."[97]

ORDERED, That the clerk of this House do carry the said bill to the Senate, and desire their concurrence.[98]

ORDERED, That Mr. Brown be added to the committee for inrolled bills.

The House resumed the consideration of the amendments proposed by the Senate to the bill, entitled, "An act for registering and clearing vessels, regulating the coasting trade, and for other purposes:"   Whereupon,

RESOLVED, That this House doth agree to all the said amendments, with amendments to the third and fifty-seventh amendments, as follow:

Third amendment. In lieu of the words proposed to be stricken out by the Senate, insert the words, "shall be in the form following, viz."

Fifty-seventh amendment. After the word "*sworn*," in the clauses proposed to be inserted by the Senate, insert the words "or affirmed."

ORDERED, That the clerk of this House do acquaint the Senate therewith.[99]

Mr. Gerry, from the committee appointed to prepare and report an estimate of the supplies requisite for the present year, made a further report, which was read, and ordered to lie on the table.[100]

Mr. Smith (of South-Carolina) from the committee appointed, presented according to order, a bill providing for the establishment of hospitals for the relief of sick and disabled seamen, and prescribing regulations for the harbours of the United States, which was received, and read the first time.[101]

On a motion made and seconded, that the House do agree to the following resolution:

"That a permanent residence ought to be fixed for the general government of the United States, at some convenient place, as near the center of wealth, population, and extent of territory, as may be consistent with convenience to the navigation of the Atlantic ocean, and having due regard to the particular situation of the western country."

---

[97] A printed copy of the bill, annotated by the Senate, is in House Bills, SR, DNA. E–45675.

[98] The Senate read this bill on August 31, September 1, and 2. On September 2 the bill was committed, and the committee reported on the third. On September 7 the report was agreed to as amendments to the bill. The amendments are printed in the *Senate Legislative Journal* for that date. The bill was then agreed to with the amendments, and the House was notified.

[99] On August 29 the Senate notified the House that it had agreed to these amendments.

[100] A copy of the report is in A Record of the Reports of Select Committees, HR, DNA. A copy, probably by ASP, is in Various Select Committees, HR, DNA. On September 24 this committee reported again.

[101] On August 28 this bill was read again.

RESOLVED, That this House will, on Thursday next, proceed to consider the said motion.[102]

The House proceeded to consider the report of the committee, to whom was referred a letter from the Postmaster-General, which lay on the table: Whereupon,

ORDERED, That the said report be re-committed to Mr. Boudinot, Mr. Goodhue, and Mr. Lee.[103]

The orders of the day for the House to resolve itself into a committee of the whole House, on the bill sent from the Senate, entitled, "An act to establish the judicial courts of the United States;" also, on the bill for establishing a land-office, in, and for the western territory, were read, and postponed until to-morrow.

And then the House adjourned until to-morrow morning eleven o'clock.

FRIDAY, AUGUST 28, 1789

A memorial of the public creditors in the state of Pennsylvania, was presented to the House and read, praying the aid and interposition of Congress on behalf of the public creditors by a permanent appropriation of adequate funds for the punctual payment of the interest of the public debt, or by the adoption of such other means as in the wisdom of Congress shall be best calculated to promote the public welfare, and render justice to the individuals who are interested.[104]

Also, a petition of the commanders of packets plying between Providence and Newport, in the state of Rhode-Island and the city of New-York, praying that so much of a late act of Congress as subjects ships or vessels of that state to the same tonnage as is imposed on foreign ships or vessels, may be suspended so far as relates to the petitioners, until the first day of December next.[105]

ORDERED, That the said memorial and petition do lie on the table.

A bill providing for the establishment of hospitals for the relief of sick and disabled seamen, and prescribing the regulations for the harbours of the United States, was read the second time, and ordered to be committed to a committee of the whole House, on the fifteenth of September next.[106]

The House proceeded to consider the report of the committee to whom

---

[102] On September 3 this motion was considered.

[103] On September 9 a resolution on this report was agreed to and sent to the Senate.

[104] The petition is in Petitions and Memorials: Various subjects, SR, DNA. On September 2 this petition was committed.

[105] On August 31 this petition was referred to a committee on the Collection Bill [HR–23].

[106] On September 15 this bill was postponed as an order of the day. On September 16 the bill was postponed to second session.

were referred the memorials of the merchants and other inhabitants of Alexandria and Dumfries, in the state of Virginia, and of George-Town, Bladensburg and Piscataway, in the state of Maryland, and the same being amended to read as followeth:

"That so much of the act, entitled, 'An act to regulate the collection of duties imposed by law on the tonnage of ships or vessels, and on goods, wares and merchandizes imported into the United States,' as obliges vessels bound up the Potowmac, to stop at Saint Mary's or Yeocomico, to report a manifest of their cargoes, ought to be suspended."

RESOLVED, That this House doth agree to the said report.

ORDERED, That a bill or bills be brought in pursuant to the said report; and that Mr. Goodhue, Mr. Carroll, and Mr. Lee, do prepare and bring in the same.

The House, according to the order of the day, resolved itself into a committee of the whole House, on the bill for establishing the salaries of the executive officers of government, with their assistants and clerks.

Mr. Speaker left the chair.

Mr. Boudinot took the chair of the committee.

Mr. Speaker resumed the chair, and Mr. Boudinot reported that the committee had, according to order, had the said bill under consideration, and gone through the same, and made several amendments thereto, which he delivered in at the clerk's table, where the same were twice read, amended, and agreed to by the House.

ORDERED, That the said bill, with the amendments, be engrossed, and read the third time to-morrow.[107]

Mr. Goodhue, from the committee appointed, presented according to order, a bill to suspend part of an act, entitled, "An act to regulate the collection of the duties imposed by law on the tonnage of ships or vessels, and on goods, wares and merchandizes imported into the United States;" which was received, and read the first time.[108]

ORDERED, That Mr. Sturges have leave to be absent from the service of this House, for the remainder of the session; and Mr. Clymer, until this day se'nnight.

The orders of the day for the House to resolve itself into a committee of the whole House, on the bill sent from the Senate, entitled, "An act to establish the judicial courts of the United States;" also, on the bill for establishing a land-office, in, and for the western territory, were read, and postponed until to-morrow.

And then the House adjourned until to-morrow morning eleven o'clock.

---

[107] On August 29 this bill was read, agreed to, and sent to the Senate.
[108] On August 29 this bill was read again.

SATURDAY, AUGUST 29, 1789

A message from the Senate, by Mr. Otis their Secretary.

MR. SPEAKER,   The Senate have agreed to the amendments made by this House to the third and fifty-seventh amendments proposed by the Senate to the bill, entitled, "An act for registering and clearing vessels, regulating the coasting trade, and for other purposes."[109]   And then he withdrew.

An engrossed bill for establishing the salaries of the executive officers of government, with their assistants and clerks, was read the third time.

And the question being put that the said bill do pass,

It was resolved in the affirmative. $\begin{cases} \text{AYES} & 27 \\ \text{NOES} & 16 \end{cases}$

The ayes and noes being demanded by one fifth of the members present, Those who voted in the affirmative, are,

Fisher Ames	George Mathews
Abraham Baldwin	Andrew Moore
Egbert Benson	Thomas Scott
Elias Boudinot	Theodore Sedgwick
John Brown	Roger Sherman
Lambert Cadwalader	Peter Silvester
George Gale	William Smith (of Maryland)
Benjamin Goodhue	William Smith (of South-Carolina)
Samuel Griffin	Jonathan Sturges
Thomas Hartley	Jonathan Trumbull
Daniel Hiester	Thomas Tudor Tucker
James Jackson	Jeremiah Wadsworth and
John Laurance	Henry Wynkoop
Richard Bland Lee	

Those who voted in the negative, are,

Isaac Coles	George Partridge
William Floyd	Jeremiah Van Rensselaer
Abiel Foster	James Schureman
Elbridge Gerry	Joshua Seney
Jonathan Grout	Thomas Sinnickson
John Hathorn	Michael Jenifer Stone
Samuel Livermore	Thomas Sumter and
Josiah Parker	George Thatcher

---

[109] On August 31 this bill was signed by the speaker and vice president.

RESOLVED, That the title of the said bill, be, "An act for establishing the salaries of the executive officers of government, with their assistants and clerks," and that the clerk of this House do carry the said bill to the Senate, and desire their concurrence.[110]

A bill to suspend part of the act, entitled, "An act to regulate the collection of the duties imposed by law on the tonnage of ships or vessels, and on goods, wares and merchandizes imported into the United States," was read the second time.

ORDERED, That the said bill be engrossed, and read the third time on Monday next.[111]

A petition of Abraham Westervelt, was presented to the House and read, praying that an exclusive patent may be granted him for manufacturing shell buttons, of different dimensions, the art of doing which he has lately discovered.

Also, a petition of sundry inhabitants of that part of the state of New-Jersey, known by the name of East-New-Jersey, praying that the district court of the United States to be held within the said state, may be fixed at Perth-Amboy, as a place most central and convenient to the inhabitants of the said state at large.

ORDERED, That the said petitions do lie on the table.

The House, according to the order of the day, resolved itself into a committee of the whole House, on the bill sent from the Senate, entitled, "An act to establish the judicial courts of the United States."

Mr. Speaker left the chair.

Mr. Boudinot took the chair of the committee.

Mr. Speaker resumed the chair, and Mr. Boudinot reported that the committee had, according to order, had the said bill under consideration, and made some progress therein.

RESOLVED, That this House will, on Monday next, again resolve itself into a committee of the whole House, on the said bill.[112]

The order of the day for the House to resolve itself into a committee of the whole House, on the bill for establishing a land-office, in, and for the western territory, was read, and postponed until Monday next.

And then the House adjourned until Monday morning ten o'clock.

---

[110] A printed copy of the bill, annotated by the Senate, is in House Bills, SR, DNA. E–45673. The Senate read this bill on August 31 and September 1. On September 7 the bill was read again and agreed to with nine amendments, which are printed in the *Senate Legislative Journal* for that date. On the same day the House was notified of the amendments.

[111] On August 31 this bill was read again and recommitted. On the same date two petitions were referred to this committee.

[112] On August 31 this bill was considered again.

MONDAY, AUGUST 31, 1789

An engrossed bill to suspend part of an act, entitled, "An act to regulate the collection of the duties imposed by law on the tonnage of ships or vessels, and on goods, wares and merchandizes imported into the United States," was read the third time; and, on motion, ordered to be committed to Mr. Goodhue, Mr. Carroll, Mr. Lee, and Mr. Bland, with instruction to the said committee, that they do insert a clause or clauses for establishing Bath and Frenchman's-Bay, in the state of Massachusetts, ports of delivery for all foreign vessels.[113]

A petition of Hugh Williamson, of the state of North-Carolina, on behalf of himself and the citizens of the said state, was presented to the House and read, praying that so much of a late act of Congress as subjects ships or vessels of that state to the same tonnage as is imposed on foreign ships or vessels, may be suspended.[114]

ORDERED, That the said petition, together with the petition of the commanders of packets plying between Providence and Newport, in the state of Rhode-Island, and the city of New-York, presented on Friday last, be referred to the committee last appointed, that they do examine the matter thereof, and report the same, with their opinion thereupon to the House.[115]

ORDERED, That Mr. Mathews have leave to be absent from the service of this House until Friday next.

The House, according to the order of the day, resolved itself into a committee of the whole House, on the bill sent from the Senate, entitled, "An act to establish the judicial courts of the United States."

Mr. Speaker left the chair.

Mr. Boudinot took the chair of the committee.

Mr. Speaker resumed the chair, and Mr. Boudinot reported that the committee had, according to order, had the said bill under consideration, and made a farther progress therein.

RESOLVED, That this House will, to-morrow, again resolve itself into a committee of the whole House, on the said bill.[116]

Mr. Partridge, from the committee for inrolled bills, reported that the committee had examined the inrolled bill, entitled, "An act for registering and clearing vessels, regulating the coasting trade, and for other purposes,"[117] and had found the same to be truly inrolled: Whereupon,

---

[113] On September 2 this committee reported on the Collection Bill [HR–23].

[114] What is apparently the original petition is in the North Carolina State Papers, NcD.

[115] This committee presented a Tonnage Bill [HR–24] on September 9, after having another petition referred to it on September 8.

[116] From September 1–7 consideration of this bill was postponed. On September 8 it was considered by the COWH.

[117] The inspected inrolled bill is in Enrolled Acts, RG 11, DNA. E–45695, E–45696.

Mr. Speaker signed the said inrolled bill.[118]

The order of the day for the House to resolve itself into a committee of the whole House, on the bill for establishing a land-office, in, and for the western territory, was read, and postponed until to-morrow.

And then the House adjourned until to-morrow morning eleven o'clock.

---

[118] On September 1 this bill was presented to the president.

TUESDAY, SEPTEMBER 1, 1789

Mr. Partridge reported from the committee for inrolled bills, that the committee did this day, jointly with the committee of the Senate, wait on the President of the United States, and present him with two inrolled bills, one entitled, "An act to establish the treasury department;" and the other entitled, "An act for registering and clearing vessels, regulating the coasting trade, and for other purposes," for his approbation.[1]

A message from the Senate, by Mr. Otis their Secretary.

MR. SPEAKER, The Senate have passed a bill, entitled, "An act for the punishment of certain crimes against the United States," to which they desire the concurrence of this House.[2] The Senate have also passed the bill, entitled, "An act for allowing a compensation to the members of the Senate and House of Representatives of the United States, and to the officers of both Houses," with several amendments, to which they desire the concurrence of this House.[3] And then he withdrew.

The House proceeded to consider the report from the committee of elections, of the eighteenth of August last, relative to the petition of a number of the citizens of the state of New-Jersey, complaining of the illegality of the election of the members holding seats in this House, as elected within that state, which lay on the table, and having made some progress therein,

ORDERED, That the farther consideration of the said report be put off until to-morrow.[4]

The orders of the day for the House to resolve itself into a committee of the whole House, on the bill for establishing a land-office, in, and for the western territory; also, on the bill sent from the Senate, entitled, "An act to establish the judicial courts of the United States," were read, and postponed until to-morrow.

And then the House adjourned until to-morrow morning eleven o'clock.

WEDNESDAY, SEPTEMBER 2, 1789

Several petitions of the inhabitants of Philadelphia, Bucks, and Montgomery counties, in the state of Pennsylvania, were presented to the House

---

[1] On September 2 the House was notified that the president had signed these bills.

[2] The bill and an amendment, which may represent in rough form the bill as sent to the House, are in Senate Bills, SR, DNA. On September 2 this bill was read.

[3] Senate amendments are filed with and noted on the bill in House Bills, SR, DNA. The amendments are printed in the *Senate Legislative Journal* on August 28 and 31. On September 2 some of these amendments were disagreed to, and the Senate was notified.

[4] On September 2 this report was considered again, and a resolution on the subject was agreed to.

and read, praying that the permanent seat of Congress may be established at the place known by the name of Old Philadelphia, on the west side of the river Delaware.

ORDERED, That the said petitions do lie on the table.

Mr. Goodhue reported from the committee to whom was committed the engrossed bill to suspend part of an act, entitled, "An act to regulate the collection of the duties imposed by law on the tonnage of ships or vessels, and on goods, wares and merchandizes imported into the United States;" that the committee had, according to order, had the said bill under consideration, and made no amendment thereto.

ORDERED, That the said bill be again engrossed, and read the third time to-morrow.[5]

On motion,

ORDERED, That the memorial of the public creditors in the state of Pennsylvania, presented on Friday last, which lay on the table, be referred to Mr. Madison, Mr. Vining, and Mr. Boudinot, that they do examine the matter thereof, and report the same with their opinion thereupon to the House.[6]

The House resumed the consideration of the report from the committee of elections, touching the petition of a number of the citizens of the state of New-Jersey, complaining of the illegality of the election of the members holding seats in this House, as elected within that state: Whereupon,

A motion being made and seconded that the House do agree to the following resolution:

RESOLVED, That it appears to this House, upon full and mature consideration, that James Schureman, Lambert Cadwalader, Elias Boudinot, and Thomas Sinnickson, were duly elected and returned to serve in this House, as representatives for the state of New-Jersey, in the present Congress of the United States.

It was resolved in the affirmative.

The House proceeded to consider the amendments proposed by the Senate to the bill, entitled, "An act for allowing a compensation to the members of the Senate and House of Representatives of the United States and to the officers of both Houses:"   Whereupon,

RESOLVED, That this House doth disagree to the first, second, and third amendments, and doth agree to all the other amendments to the said bill.

ORDERED, That the clerk of this House do acquaint the Senate therewith.

A message was received from the President of the United States, notifying that the President approves of two acts, one entitled, "An act for registering and clearing vessels, regulating the coasting trade, and for other purposes;"

---

[5] On September 3 this bill was read, agreed to, and sent to the Senate.
[6] On September 10 this committee reported.

and the other, entitled, "An act to establish the treasury department;" and has affixed his signature thereto, to wit, to the former on the first, and to the latter on the second instant: And the messenger delivered in the said acts, and then withdrew.

ORDERED, That the clerk of this House do acquaint the Senate therewith.[7]

The bill sent from the Senate, entitled, "An act for the punishment of certain crimes against the United States," was read the first time.[8]

ORDERED, That Mr. Sedgwick have leave to be absent from the service of this House for the remainder of the session.

The orders of the day for the House to resolve itself into a committee of the whole House, on the bill for establishing a land-office, in, and for the western territory, also, on the bill sent from the Senate, entitled, "An act to establish the judicial courts of the United States," were read, and postponed until to-morrow.

And then the House adjourned until to-morrow morning eleven o'clock.

THURSDAY, SEPTEMBER 3, 1789

An engrossed bill to suspend part of an act, entitled, "An act to regulate the collection of the duties imposed by law on the tonnage of ships or vessels, and on goods, wares and merchandizes imported into the United States," was read the third time, and the blanks therein filled up.

RESOLVED, That the said bill do pass, and that the title be, "An act to suspend part of an act, entitled, 'An act to regulate the collection of the duties imposed by law on the tonnage of ships or vessels, and on goods, wares and merchandizes imported into the United States.' "

ORDERED, That the clerk of this House do carry the said bill to the Senate, and desire their concurrence.[9]

The Speaker laid before the House a letter from George Walton, Esquire, Governor of the state of Georgia, inclosing returns of the imports and exports of that state.

ORDERED, That the said letter, with its enclosures, do lie on the table.

The bill sent from the Senate, entitled, "An act for the punishment of cer-

---

[7] On September 7 the Senate adhered to its first amendment to this bill.

[8] On September 3 this bill was read again.

[9] The Senate read this bill on September 7, 10, and 11. On September 11 it was committted with the Tonnage Bill [HR–24]. On September 12 this committee reported on these two bills, and the Collection Bill [HR–23] was read again and agreed to with the committee's amendments and floor amendments. On September 14 the House received the Senate amendments to this bill and agreed to them.

tain crimes against the United States," was read the second time, and ordered to be committed to a committee of the whole House on Monday se'nnight.[10]

On motion,

RESOLVED, That this House will immediately resolve itself into a committee of the whole House, to take into their consideration the motion presented on Thursday last, for establishing the permanent residence of Congress.

The House accordingly resolved itself into the said committee.

Mr. Speaker left the chair.

Mr. Boudinot took the chair of the committee.

Mr. Speaker resumed the chair, and Mr. Boudinot reported that the committee had, according to order, had the said motion under consideration, and made some progress therein.

RESOLVED, That this House will, to-morrow, again resolve itself into a committee of the whole House, on the said motion.[11]

The orders of the day for the House to resolve itself into a committee of the whole House, on the bill for establishing a land-office, in, and for the western territory; also, on the bill sent from the Senate, entitled, "An act to establish the judicial courts of the United States," were read, and postponed until to-morrow.

And then the House adjourned until to-morrow morning eleven o'clock.

FRIDAY, SEPTEMBER 4, 1789

A petition of James Gibbon, of Petersburg in Virginia, was presented to the House and read, praying that his claim for military services, rendered during the late war, may be liquidated and satisfied.

ORDERED, That the said petition do lie on the table.[12]

A petition of certain non-commissioned officers and soldiers, invalid pensioners of the state of Pennsylvania, was presented to the House and read, praying relief in consideration of the payment of their pensions being stopped by an act of the legislature of that state.

ORDERED, That the said petition, together with the petitions of sundry other invalid pensioners, presented during the present session, be referred to Mr. Hiester, Mr. Wadsworth, and Mr. Gilman, that they do examine the matter thereof, and report the same with their opinion thereupon to the House.[13]

---

[10] On September 14 and 15 consideration of this bill was postponed. On September 16 the bill was postponed to the next session.

[11] On September 4 this motion was considered again.

[12] On September 9 this petition was rejected.

[13] According to the *Gazette of the United States*, September 5, 1789, this committee was also instructed to bring in a bill. On September 5 more petitions were referred to this committee.

The House, according to the order of the day, resolved itself into a committee of the whole House, to take into their consideration the motion presented on the twenty-seventh of August last, for establishing the permanent residence of Congress.

Mr. Speaker left the chair.

Mr. Boudinot took the chair of the committee.

Mr. Speaker resumed the chair, and Mr. Boudinot reported that the committee had, according to order, had the said motion under consideration, and made a farther progress therein.

RESOLVED, That this House will, to-morrow, again resolve itself into a committee of the whole House, on the said motion.[14]

The orders of the day for the House to resolve itself into a committee of the whole House, on the bill for establishing a land-office, in, and for the western territory; also, on the bill sent from the Senate, entitled, "An act to establish the judicial courts of the United States," were read, and postponed until to-morrow.[15]

And then the House adjourned until to-morrow morning eleven o'clock.

SATURDAY, SEPTEMBER 5, 1789

Mr. Seney, from the committee to whom was referred the memorial of John White, in behalf of himself, John Wright, and Joshua Dawson, made a report, which was read, and ordered to lie on the table.[16]

A petition of Archibald McAlister, was presented to the House and read, praying that his claim for military services rendered during the late war, may be liquidated and satisfied.

ORDERED, That the said petition, together with the petitions of James Gibbon, and William Finnie, which lay on the table, be referred to Mr. Hiester, Mr. Wadsworth, and Mr. Gilman, that they do examine the matter thereof, and report the same with their opinion thereupon to the House.[17]

A memorial of the Marquis de Chartier de Lotbiniere, was presented to the House and read, stating his claim to two manors and seignories, situated at the head of Lake Champlain, and bordering on each bank of the head of the

---

[14] On September 5 the COWH reported several resolutions on this motion.

[15] Although it is not journalized, a report from the committee, to which a letter from the postmaster general was recommitted on August 27, was received on this date. A copy of the report is in A Record of the Reports of Select Committees, HR, DNA.

[16] A copy of the report is in A Record of the Reports of Select Committees, HR, DNA. On September 25 a resolution on the petition of John White was agreed to and sent to the Senate.

[17] On September 18 this committee, which was appointed on September 4, presented the Invalid Pensioners Bill [HR–29], which was read. On September 25 these petitions were referred to the secretary of the treasury.

said lake; to the possession of which the United States have succeeded by virtue of the late treaty of peace with Great-Britain, and praying that he may receive an equivalent for the same, and a just compensation for the time he has been deprived of the possession thereof.[18]

ORDERED, That the said memorial do lie on the table.[19]

The House, according to the order of the day, resolved itself into a committee of the whole House, to take into their consideration the motion presented on the twenty-seventh of August last, for establishing the permanent residence of Congress.

Mr. Speaker left the chair.

Mr. Boudinot took the chair of the committee.

Mr. Speaker resumed the chair, and Mr. Boudinot reported that the committee had, according to order, had the said motion under consideration, and gone through the same, and come to several resolutions thereupon, which he delivered in at the clerk's table, where the same were read, and partly considered.

ORDERED, That the farther consideration of the said resolutions be put off until Monday next.[20]

The orders of the day for the House to resolve itself into a committee of the whole House, on the bill for establishing a land-office, in, and for the western territory; also, on the bill sent from the Senate, entitled, "An act to establish the judicial courts of the United States," were read, and postponed until Monday next.

And then the House adjourned until Monday morning eleven o'clock.

MONDAY, SEPTEMBER 7, 1789

The Speaker laid before the House a letter from John Lamb, collector of the port of New-York, inclosing a petition from the weighers and measurers of the said port, complaining of the insufficiency of the fees allowed them by law.[21]

ORDERED, That the said letter and petition do lie on the table.

The House resumed the consideration of the resolutions reported by the

---

[18] Two petitions of Chartier de Lotbiniere, addressed to the president and dated June 18 and July 21, 1789, are in Domestic Letters, M40, roll 4, RG 59, DNA. They are concerned with the same subject and are probably similar to the petition received by Congress.

[19] On September 5 this petition was referred to the committee on invalid pensioners.

[20] On September 7 these resolutions were extensively considered, amended, and agreed to. A committee was then appointed to bring in a bill on the resolutions.

[21] A petition on this topic is in Petitions and Memorials: Applications for jobs, SR, DNA. It does not include the letter from John Lamb, but probably is the petition received by the House on this date.

committee of the whole House on Saturday last, for establishing the permanent residence of Congress: Whereupon,

The first resolution was, on the question put thereupon, agreed to by the House, in the words following:

RESOLVED, That the permanent seat of the government of the United States ought to be fixed at some convenient place as near the center of wealth, population, and extent of territory, as may be consistent with convenience to the navigation of the Atlantic ocean, and having due regard to the particular situation of the western country.

The second resolution in the words following, to wit:

"RESOLVED, That the permanent seat of the government of the United States ought to be at some convenient place on the east bank of the river Susquehannah, in the State of Pennsylvania, and that until the necessary buildings be erected for the purpose, the seat of the government ought to continue at the city of New-York," being under debate,

A motion was made and seconded, to amend the said resolution by striking out the words, "east bank of the river Susquehannah, in the state of Pennsylvania," and inserting in lieu thereof, the words, "north bank of the river Potowmac, in the state of Maryland."

And on the question that the House do agree to the said amendment,

It passed in the negative. $\begin{cases} \text{AYES} & 21 \\ \text{NOES} & 29 \end{cases}$

The ayes and noes being demanded by one fifth of the members present, Those who voted in the affirmative, are,

Abraham Baldwin	James Madison, junior
Theodorick Bland	George Mathews
John Brown	Andrew Moore
Aedanus Burke	John Page
Daniel Carroll	Josiah Parker
Isaac Coles	William Smith (of South-Carolina)
Benjamin Contee	Michael Jenifer Stone
George Gale	Thomas Sumter
Samuel Griffin	Thomas Tudor Tucker and
James Jackson	John Vining
Richard Bland Lee	

Those who voted in the negative, are,

Fisher Ames	Lambert Cadwalader
Egbert Benson	George Clymer
Elias Boudinot	Thomas Fitzsimons

William Floyd
Abiel Foster
Elbridge Gerry
Nicholas Gilman
Benjamin Goodhue
Jonathan Grout
Thomas Hartley
John Hathorn
John Laurance
Samuel Livermore
Peter Muhlenberg
George Partridge

Jeremiah Van Rensselaer
Thomas Scott
Joshua Seney
Roger Sherman
Peter Silvester
Thomas Sinnickson
William Smith (of Maryland)
George Thatcher
Jonathan Trumbull
Jeremiah Wadsworth and
Henry Wynkoop

A motion was then made and seconded, to amend the said resolution by striking out the word *"permanent;"* also, after the words, "ought to be at," to strike out to the end of the resolution, and to insert in lieu thereof, "the borough of Wilmington, in the state of Delaware."

And on the question that the House do agree to the said amendment,

It passed in the negative. $\begin{cases} \text{AYES} & 19 \\ \text{NOES} & 32 \end{cases}$

The ayes and noes being demanded by one fifth of the members present, Those who voted in the affirmative, are,

Abraham Baldwin
Theodorick Bland
Elias Boudinot
Aedanus Burke
Lambert Cadwalader
Isaac Coles
Benjamin Contee
Samuel Griffin
James Jackson
Richard Bland Lee

James Madison, junior
George Mathews
Andrew Moore
John Page
Josiah Parker
Thomas Sinnickson
William Smith (of South-Carolina)
Thomas Sumter and
John Vining

Those who voted in the negative are,

Fisher Ames
Egbert Benson
John Brown
Daniel Carroll
George Clymer
Thomas Fitzsimons

William Floyd
Abiel Foster
George Gale
Elbridge Gerry
Nicholas Gilman
Benjamin Goodhue

Jonathan Grout
Thomas Hartley
John Hathorn
Daniel Hiester
John Laurance
Samuel Livermore
Peter Muhlenberg
George Partridge
Jeremiah Van Rensselaer
Thomas Scott

Joshua Seney
Roger Sherman
Peter Silvester
William Smith (of Maryland)
Michael Jenifer Stone
George Thatcher
Jonathan Trumbull
Thomas Tudor Tucker
Jeremiah Wadsworth and
Henry Wynkoop

A motion was then made and seconded, to amend the said resolution by striking out the words, "east bank of the river Susquehannah, in the state of Pennsylvania," and inserting in lieu thereof the words, "Potowmac, Susquehannah, or Delaware."

And on the question that the House do agree to the said amendment,

It passed in the negative. $\begin{cases} \text{AYES} & 23 \\ \text{NOES} & 28 \end{cases}$

The ayes and noes being demanded by one fifth of the members present, Those who voted in the affirmative, are,

Abraham Baldwin
Theodorick Bland
Elias Boudinot
John Brown
Aedanus Burke
Lambert Cadwalader
Daniel Carroll
Isaac Coles
Benjamin Contee
Samuel Griffin
James Jackson
Richard Bland Lee

James Madison, junior
George Mathews
Andrew Moore
John Page
Josiah Parker
Thomas Sinnickson
William Smith (of South-Carolina)
Michael Jenifer Stone
Thomas Sumter
Thomas Tudor Tucker and
John Vining

Those who voted in the negative, are,

Fisher Ames
Egbert Benson
George Clymer
Thomas Fitzsimons
William Floyd
Abiel Foster

George Gale
Elbridge Gerry
Nicholas Gilman
Benjamin Goodhue
Jonathan Grout
Thomas Hartley

John Hathorn	Joshua Seney
Daniel Hiester	Roger Sherman
John Laurance	Peter Silvester
Samuel Livermore	William Smith (of Maryland)
Peter Muhlenberg	George Thatcher
George Partridge	Jonathan Trumbull
Jeremiah Van Rensselaer	Jeremiah Wadsworth and
Thomas Scott	Henry Wynkoop

A motion was then made and seconded, to amend the said resolution by striking out the words, "east bank of the river Susquehannah, in the state of Pennsylvania," and inserting in lieu thereof, the words, "banks of either side of the river Delaware, not more than eight miles above or below the lower falls of Delaware."

And on the question that the House do agree to the said amendment,

It passed in the negative. $\begin{cases} \text{AYES} & 4 \\ \text{NOES} & 46 \end{cases}$

The ayes and noes being demanded by one fifth of the members present, Those who voted in the affirmative, are,

Elias Boudinot	Elbridge Gerry and
Lambert Cadwalader	Thomas Sinnickson

Those who voted in the negative, are,

Fisher Ames	Samuel Griffin
Abraham Baldwin	Jonathan Grout
Egbert Benson	Thomas Hartley
Theodorick Bland	John Hathorn
John Brown	Daniel Hiester
Aedanus Burke	James Jackson
Daniel Carroll	John Laurance
George Clymer	Richard Bland Lee
Isaac Coles	Samuel Livermore
Benjamin Contee	James Madison, junior
Thomas Fitzsimons	George Mathews
William Floyd	Andrew Moore
Abiel Foster	Peter Muhlenberg
George Gale	John Page
Nicholas Gilman	Josiah Parker
Benjamin Goodhue	George Partridge

Jeremiah Van Rensselaer

Thomas Scott

Joshua Seney

Roger Sherman

Peter Silvester

William Smith (of Maryland)

William Smith (of South-
Carolina)

Michael Jenifer Stone

Thomas Sumter

George Thatcher

Jonathan Trumbull

Thomas Tudor Tucker

Jeremiah Wadsworth and

Henry Wynkoop

Another motion was then made and seconded, to amend the said resolution by striking out the words, "east bank," and inserting in lieu thereof, the word "banks."

And on the question that the House do agree to the said amendment,

It was resolved in the affirmative. $\begin{cases} \text{AYES} & 26 \\ \text{NOES} & 25 \end{cases}$

The ayes and noes being demanded by one fifth of the members present,

Those who voted in the affirmative, are,

Abraham Baldwin

Theodorick Bland

Elias Boudinot

John Brown

Aedanus Burke

Lambert Cadwalader

Daniel Carroll

Isaac Coles

Benjamin Contee

George Gale

Samuel Griffin

James Jackson

Richard Bland Lee

James Madison, junior

George Mathews

Andrew Moore

John Page

Josiah Parker

Joshua Seney

Thomas Sinnickson

William Smith (of Maryland)

William Smith (of South-Carolina)

Michael Jenifer Stone

Thomas Sumter

Thomas Tudor Tucker and

John Vining

Those who voted in the negative, are,

Fisher Ames

Egbert Benson

George Clymer

Thomas Fitzsimons

William Floyd

Abiel Foster

Elbridge Gerry

Nicholas Gilman

Benjamin Goodhue

Jonathan Grout

Thomas Hartley

John Hathorn

Daniel Hiester

John Laurance

Samuel Livermore

Peter Muhlenberg

George Partridge
Jeremiah Van Rensselaer
Thomas Scott
Roger Sherman
Peter Silvester

George Thatcher
Jonathan Trumbull
Jeremiah Wadsworth and
Henry Wynkoop

A motion was then made and seconded, farther to amend the said resolution by inserting after the word "*Pennsylvania*," the words, "*or Maryland.*" And on the question that the House do agree to the said amendment,

It passed in the negative. $\begin{cases} \text{AYES} & 25 \\ \text{NOES} & 26 \end{cases}$

The ayes and noes being demanded by one fifth of the members present, Those who voted in the affirmative, are,

Abraham Baldwin
Theodorick Bland
Elias Boudinot
John Brown
Aedanus Burke
Lambert Cadwalader
Daniel Carroll
Isaac Coles
Benjamin Contee
George Gale
Samuel Griffin
James Jackson
Richard Bland Lee

James Madison, junior
George Mathews
Andrew Moore
John Page
Josiah Parker
Thomas Sinnickson
William Smith (of Maryland)
William Smith (of South-Carolina)
Michael Jenifer Stone
Thomas Sumter
Thomas Tudor Tucker and
John Vining

Those who voted in the negative, are,

Fisher Ames
Egbert Benson
George Clymer
Thomas Fitzsimons
William Floyd
Abiel Foster
Elbridge Gerry
Nicholas Gilman
Benjamin Goodhue
Jonathan Grout
Thomas Hartley
John Hathorn
Daniel Hiester

John Laurance
Samuel Livermore
Peter Muhlenberg
George Partridge
Jeremiah Van Rensselaer
Thomas Scott
Joshua Seney
Roger Sherman
Peter Silvester
George Thatcher
Jonathan Trumbull
Jeremiah Wadsworth and
Henry Wynkoop

A motion was then made and seconded, farther to amend the said resolution by striking out the words, "*city of New-York*," and inserting in lieu thereof, "borough of Wilmington, in the state of Delaware."

And on the question that the House do agree to the said amendment,

It passed in the negative. $\left\{\begin{array}{l}\text{AYES } 21 \\ \text{NOES } 30\end{array}\right.$

The ayes and noes being demanded by one fifth of the members present, Those who voted in the affirmative, are,

Abraham Baldwin	James Jackson
Theodorick Bland	Richard Bland Lee
Elias Boudinot	James Madison, junior
John Brown	George Mathews
Aedanus Burke	Andrew Moore
Lambert Cadwalader	John Page
Daniel Carroll	Josiah Parker
Isaac Coles	Thomas Sinnickson
Benjamin Contee	Thomas Sumter and
George Gale	John Vining
Samuel Griffin	

Those who voted in the negative are,

Fisher Ames	Peter Muhlenberg
Egbert Benson	George Partridge
George Clymer	Jeremiah Van Rensselaer
Thomas Fitzsimons	Thomas Scott
William Floyd	Joshua Seney
Abiel Foster	Roger Sherman
Elbridge Gerry	Peter Silvester
Nicholas Gilman	William Smith (of Maryland)
Benjamin Goodhue	William Smith (of South-Carolina)
Jonathan Grout	Michael Jenifer Stone
Thomas Hartley	George Thatcher
John Hathorn	Jonathan Trumbull
Daniel Hiester	Thomas Tudor Tucker
John Laurance	Jeremiah Wadsworth and
Samuel Livermore	Henry Wynkoop

A motion was then made and seconded, farther to amend the said resolution by striking out the word "*New-York*," and inserting in lieu thereof, the word "*Philadelphia*."

And on the question that the House do agree to the said amendment,

It passed in the negative. $\begin{cases} \text{AYES } 22 \\ \text{NOES } 29 \end{cases}$

The ayes and noes being demanded by one fifth of the members present,
Those who voted in the affirmative, are,

Abraham Baldwin	James Jackson
Elias Boudinot	Richard Bland Lee
John Brown	James Madison, junior
Aedanus Burke	George Mathews
Lambert Cadwalader	Andrew Moore
Daniel Carroll	John Page
Isaac Coles	Josiah Parker
Benjamin Contee	Thomas Sinnickson
George Gale	Michael Jenifer Stone
Samuel Griffin	Thomas Sumter and
Daniel Hiester	John Vining

Those who voted in the negative, are,

Fisher Ames	Peter Muhlenberg
Egbert Benson	George Partridge
Theodorick Bland	Jeremiah Van Rensselaer
George Clymer	Thomas Scott
Thomas Fitzsimons	Joshua Seney
William Floyd	Roger Sherman
Abiel Foster	Peter Silvester
Elbridge Gerry	William Smith (of Maryland)
Nicholas Gilman	William Smith (of South-Carolina)
Benjamin Goodhue	George Thatcher
Jonathan Grout	Jonathan Trumbull
Thomas Hartley	Thomas Tudor Tucker
John Hathorn	Jeremiah Wadsworth and
John Laurance	Henry Wynkoop
Samuel Livermore	

And then the main question being put, the said second resolution, as amended, was agreed to by the House in the words following, to wit:

"RESOLVED, That the permanent seat of the government of the United States, ought to be at some convenient place on the banks of the river Susquehannah, in the state of Pennsylvania, and that until the necessary buildings be erected for the purpose, the seat of the government ought to continue at the city of New-York."

The third resolution in the words following, to wit:

"RESOLVED, That the President of the United States be authorised to appoint three commissioners to examine and report to him the most eligible situation on the banks of the Susquehannah, in the state of Pennsylvania, for the permanent seat of the government of the United States; that the said commissioners be authorised, under the direction of the President, to purchase such quantity of land as may be thought necessary, and to erect thereon, within four years, suitable buildings for the accommodation of the Congress, and of the officers of the United States; that the secretary of the treasury, together with the commissioners so to be appointed, be authorised to borrow a sum not exceeding one hundred thousand dollars, to be repaid within twenty years, with interest not exceeding the rate of five per cent. per annum, out of the duties on impost and tonnage, to be applied to the purchase of the land, and the erection of the buildings aforesaid; and that a bill ought to pass in the present session in conformity with the foregoing resolutions," being under debate,

A motion was made and seconded, to amend the same by inserting after the word "*aforesaid*," the following proviso, to wit:

"PROVIDED NEVERTHELESS, That previous to any such purchase or erection of buildings as aforesaid, the legislatures of the states of Pennsylvania and Maryland, make such provision for removing all obstructions to the navigation of the said river, between the seat of the federal government and the mouth thereof, as may be satisfactory to the President of the United States."

And on the question that the House do agree to the said amendment,

It passed in the negative. $\begin{cases} \text{AYES} & 24 \\ \text{NOES} & 25 \end{cases}$

The ayes and noes being demanded by one fifth of the members present,

Those who voted in the affirmative, are,

Abraham Baldwin	George Mathews
Elias Boudinot	Andrew Moore
John Brown	John Page
Aedanus Burke	Josiah Parker
Lambert Cadwalader	Joshua Seney
Daniel Carroll	Thomas Sinnickson
Isaac Coles	William Smith (of Maryland)
Benjamin Contee	William Smith (of South-Carolina)
George Gale	Michael Jenifer Stone
James Jackson	Thomas Sumter
Richard Bland Lee	Thomas Tudor Tucker and
James Madison, junior	John Vining

Those who voted in the negative, are,

Fisher Ames	John Laurance
Egbert Benson	Samuel Livermore
George Clymer	Peter Muhlenberg
Thomas Fitzsimons	George Partridge
William Floyd	Jeremiah Van Rensselaer
Abiel Foster	Thomas Scott
Elbridge Gerry	Roger Sherman
Nicholas Gilman	Peter Silvester
Benjamin Goodhue	George Thatcher
Jonathan Grout	Jonathan Trumbull
Thomas Hartley	Jeremiah Wadsworth and
John Hathorn	Henry Wynkoop
Daniel Hiester	

And then the main question being put, that the House do agree to the said third resolution, as reported by the committee of the whole House,

It was resolved in the affirmative. $\begin{cases} \text{AYES} \ \ 28 \\ \text{NOES} \ \ 21 \end{cases}$

The ayes and noes being demanded by one fifth of the members present, Those who voted in the affirmative, are,

Fisher Ames	Samuel Livermore
Egbert Benson	Peter Muhlenberg
George Clymer	George Partridge
Thomas Fitzsimons	Jeremiah Van Rensselaer
William Floyd	Thomas Scott
Abiel Foster	Joshua Seney
George Gale	Roger Sherman
Nicholas Gilman	Peter Silvester
Benjamin Goodhue	William Smith (of Maryland)
Jonathan Grout	Michael Jenifer Stone
Thomas Hartley	George Thatcher
John Hathorn	Jonathan Trumbull
Daniel Hiester	Jeremiah Wadsworth and
John Laurance	Henry Wynkoop

Those who voted in the negative, are,

Abraham Baldwin	John Brown
Elias Boudinot	Aedanus Burke

Lambert Cadwalader
Daniel Carroll
Isaac Coles
Benjamin Contee
Elbridge Gerry
James Jackson
Richard Bland Lee
James Madison, junior
George Mathews

Andrew Moore
John Page
Josiah Parker
Thomas Sinnickson
William Smith (of South-Carolina)
Thomas Sumter
Thomas Tudor Tucker and
John Vining

ORDERED, That a bill or bills be brought in pursuant to the foregoing resolutions, and that Mr. Ames, Mr. Laurance, and Mr. Clymer, do prepare and bring in the same.[22]

A message from the Senate, by Mr. Otis their Secretary.

MR. SPEAKER,   The Senate have passed the bill, entitled, "An act for allowing a compensation to the President and Vice-President of the United States," with several amendments, to which they desire the concurrence of this House.[23] The Senate have also passed the bill, entitled, "An act to provide for the safe keeping of the acts, records, and seal of the United States, and for other purposes," with several amendments, to which they desire the concurrence of this House.[24] The Senate have also passed the bill, entitled, "An act for establishing the salaries of the executive officers of government, with their assistants and clerks," with several amendments, to which they desire the concurrence of this House.[25] The Senate do also adhere to their first amendment to the bill, entitled, "An act for allowing compensation to the members of the Senate and House of Representatives of the United States, and to the officers of both Houses," which was disagreed to by this House; and recede from their other amendments to the said bill.[26]   And then he withdrew.

---

[22] On September 14 this committee presented the Seat of Government Bill [HR–25], which was read.

[23] The journal incorrectly says "amendments." There actually was only one amendment. The amendment is printed in the *Senate Legislative Journal* on September 7. On September 8 the House disagreed to this amendment.

[24] Senate amendments are attached to and noted on the bill in House Bills, SR, DNA. Annotations on the printed bill in the Broadside Collection, RBkRm, DLC, correspond roughly to Senate amendments. The amendments are printed in the *Senate Legislative Journal* on September 7. On September 8 these Senate amendments were agreed to.

[25] Senate amendments are noted on the bill in House Bills, SR, DNA. Annotations on the printed bill in the Broadside Collection, RBkRm, DLC, correspond roughly to these amendments. The amendments are printed in the *Senate Legislative Journal* on September 7. On September 8 the House agreed to some and disagreed to others of these amendments.

[26] On September 8 the House reconsidered the first amendment and appointed a conference on this bill.

The orders of the day for the House to resolve itself into a committee of the whole House, on the bill for establishing a land-office, in, and for the western territory; also, on the bill sent from the Senate, entitled, "An act to establish the judicial courts of the United States," were read, and postponed until to-morrow.

And then the House adjourned until to-morrow morning eleven o'clock.

TUESDAY, SEPTEMBER 8, 1789

Several petitions of the inhabitants of Providence, Newport, Bristol, Warren, and Barrington, in the state of Rhode-Island, were presented to the House and read, praying a suspension of the restrictions imposed by the late acts of Congress on the trade of that state.[27]

ORDERED, That the said petitions be referred to Mr. Goodhue, Mr. Carroll, Mr. Lee, and Mr. Bland, that they do examine the matter thereof, and report the same with their opinion thereupon to the House.[28]

A petition of sundry inhabitants of the state of New-Jersey, was presented to the House and read, praying that the seat of the federal district and circuit courts for that state may be fixed at Perth-Amboy.

Also a petition of sundry inhabitants of George-Town, in the state of Maryland, containing an offer to put themselves and fortunes under the exclusive jurisdiction of Congress, in case that town should be selected as the permanent seat of the government of the United States.

ORDERED, That the said petitions do lie on the table.

The House proceeded to consider the amendments proposed by the Senate to the bill, entitled, "An act for establishing the salaries of the executive officers of government, with their assistants and clerks;" and the same being read, some were agreed to, and others disagreed to.

ORDERED, That the clerk of this House do acquaint the Senate therewith.[29]

The House proceeded to consider the amendment proposed by the Senate, to the bill, entitled "An act for allowing a compensation to the President and Vice-President of the United States," and the same being read, was disagreed to.

ORDERED, That the clerk of this House do acquaint the Senate therewith.[30]

---

[27] A copy of the Providence petition is in the Providence Town Records, Providence City Clerk's Office, Providence, Rhode Island. A copy of the Newport petition is in the Newport Town Records, vol. I (1779–1816), RNHi.

[28] On September 9 this committee presented a Tonnage Bill [HR–24], which was read.

[29] On September 9 the House was notified of further Senate action on these amendments, and the House receded from its disagreement to two of the amendments.

[30] On September 9 a conference was appointed on this bill.

The House proceeded to consider the amendments proposed by the Senate to the bill, entitled "An Act to provide for the safe keeping of the acts, records, and seal of the United States, and for other purposes," and the same being read, were agreed to.

ORDERED, That the clerk of this House do acquaint the Senate therewith.[31]

The House proceeded to re-consider the first amendment proposed by the Senate, to the bill, entitled "An Act for allowing compensation to the Members of the Senate and House of Representatives of the United States, and to the officers of both Houses," which was disagreed to by this House, and adhered to by the Senate: Whereupon,

RESOLVED, That a conference be desired with the Senate, on the subject matter of the said amendment, and that Mr. Sherman, Mr. Tucker, and Mr. Benson, be appointed managers at the same on the part of this House.[32]

The House, according to the order of the day, resolved itself into a committee of the whole House, on the bill sent from the Senate, entitled, "An act to establish the judicial courts of the United States."

Mr. Speaker left the chair.

Mr. Boudinot took the chair of the committee.

Mr. Speaker resumed the chair, and Mr. Boudinot reported that the committee had, according to order, had the said bill under consideration, and made a farther progress therein.

RESOLVED, That this House will, to-morrow, again resolve itself into a committee of the whole House, on the said bill.[33]

The order of the day for the House to resolve itself into a committee of the whole House, on the bill for establishing a land-office, in, and for the western territory, was read, and postponed until to-morrow.

And then the House adjourned until to-morrow morning ten o'clock.

WEDNESDAY, SEPTEMBER 9, 1789

Mr. Goodhue from the committee, to whom were referred the petitions of sundry inhabitants of the States of Rhode-Island and North-Carolina, presented according to order, a bill for suspending the operations of part of an act, entitled "An act imposing duties on tonnage," which was received and read the first time.[34]

The House proceeded to consider the petition of the Marquis de Chartier de Lotbiniere, which lay on the table; whereupon,

---

[31] On September 10 this bill was signed by the speaker and vice president.

[32] On September 9 the House was notified that the Senate had appointed managers to this conference.

[33] On September 9 the COWH considered this bill again.

[34] On September 10 this bill was read again.

RESOLVED, That the said petition be rejected.

On motion,

ORDERED, That the committee of the whole House on the state of the Union, be discharged from farther proceeding on the message from the President of the United States of the 10th ultimo, and that the said message be referred to Mr. Boudinot, Mr. Trumbull, and Mr. Burke, that they do examine the matter thereof, and report the same with their opinion thereupon to the House.[35]

The House, according to the order of the day, resolved itself into a committee of the whole House, on the bill sent from the Senate, entitled "An act to establish the judicial courts of the United States."

Mr. Speaker left the chair.

Mr. Boudinot took the chair of the committee.

Mr. Speaker resumed the chair, and Mr. Boudinot reported that the committee had, according to order, had the said bill under consideration, and made a farther progress therein.

RESOLVED, That this House will, to-morrow, again resolve itself into a committee of the whole House on the said bill.[36]

A message from the Senate, by Mr. Otis, their Secretary.

MR. SPEAKER,   The Senate insist on their amendment disagreed to by this House to the bill, entitled "An act for allowing a compensation to the President and Vice-President of the United States," and desire a conference with this House on the subject matter of the same: The Senate do also agree to the conference proposed by this House on the subject matter of the first amendment of the Senate to the bill, entitled "An act for allowing compensation to the Members of the Senate and House of Representatives of the United States, and to the officers of both Houses," and have appointed managers at the said conference on their part:[37] The Senate do also recede from their second and sixth amendments, and do insist on their third and fifth amendments disagreed to by this House, to the bill, entitled, "An act for establishing the salaries of the executive officers of government, with their assistants and clerks:"   And then he withdrew.

RESOLVED, That this House doth agree to the conference desired by the Senate, on the subject matter of their amendment to the bill, entitled, "An

---

[35] The president's message of August 10 concerned the troops in the service of the United States. On September 16 a message on the militia was referred to this committee.

[36] After being postponed on September 10, this bill was again considered by the COWH on September 11.

[37] On September 10 this committee reported, and the first Senate amendment was again considered and disagreed to.

act for allowing a compensation to the President and Vice-President of the United States;" and that Mr. Baldwin, Mr. Livermore, and Mr. Goodhue, be appointed managers at the same, on the part of this House.[38]

The House proceeded to re-consider the third and fifth amendments insisted on by the Senate to the bill, entitled, "An act for establishing the salaries of the executive officers of government, with their assistants and clerks:" Whereupon,

RESOLVED, That this House doth recede from their disagreement to the said amendments.

ORDERED, That the clerk of this House do acquaint the Senate therewith.[39]

The House proceeded to consider the report of the committee, to whom was referred a letter from the post-master general, which lay on the table: Whereupon,

RESOLVED, That until further provision be made by law, the general post-office of the United States shall be conducted according to the rules and regulations prescribed by the ordinances and resolutions of the late Congress, and that contracts be made for the conveyance of the mail in conformity thereto.[40]

ORDERED, That the clerk of this House do carry the said resolution to the Senate, and desire their concurrence.[41]

On a motion made and seconded, that the House do come to the following resolution:

"That money shall not be drawn from the Treasury of the United States, unless by appropriations made, or particularly confirmed by acts of Congress, subsequent to the fourth of March last."

ORDERED, That the said motion be referred to Mr. Huntington, Mr. Burke, and Mr. Griffin, that they do examine the matter thereof, and report the same with their opinion thereupon to the House.[42]

The order of the day for the House to resolve itself into a committee of the whole House on the bill for establishing a land-office in, and for the western territory, was read and postponed until to-morrow.

And then the House adjourned until to-morrow morning eleven o'clock.

---

[38] On September 17 this conference reported, and the House adhered to its disagreement to the Senate amendment.

[39] On September 10 this bill was signed by the speaker and vice president.

[40] A copy of the resolution is in Messages from the House, SR, DNA.

[41] On September 10 the Senate committed this resolution, and on September 11 this committee reported. The Senate then voted not to concur in the House resolution and read the Post Office Bill [S-3], which was presented by the committee. This bill was read again on September 14. On September 15 it was read, agreed to, and sent to the House.

[42] On September 17 the secretary of the treasury was ordered to report on an estimate of needed appropriations.

THURSDAY, SEPTEMBER 10, 1789

Mr. Partridge reported from the committee for inrolled bills, that the committee had examined two inrolled bills, one entitled "An act to provide for the safe keeping of the acts, records, and seal of the United States, and for other purposes;"[43] and the other entitled, "An act for establishing the salaries of the executive officers of government, with their assistants and clerks,"[44] and had found the same to be truly inrolled: whereupon,

Mr. Speaker signed the said inrolled bills.[45]

Mr. White, a member from Virginia, appeared and took his seat.

A message from the Senate by Mr. Otis, their Secretary.

MR. SPEAKER,   The Senate have agreed to the resolution of this House of the 21st ult. containing certain articles to be proposed by Congress to the legislatures of the several States, as amendments to the constitution of the United States, with several amendments, to which they desire the concurrence of this House:[46]   and then he withdrew.

A bill for suspending the operation of part of an act entitled "An act imposing duties on tonnage," was read the second time.

ORDERED, That the said bill be engrossed and read the third time to-morrow.[47]

Several petitions of the inhabitants of the counties of Monmouth and Essex, in the state of New-Jersey, were presented to the House and read, praying that the seat of the federal district and circuit courts for that state may be fixed at Perth Amboy.

ORDERED, That the said petitions do lie on the table.

Mr. Sherman, from the managers appointed on the part of this House to attend the conference with the Senate on the subject matter of their first amendment to the bill entitled "An act for allowing compensation to the members of the Senate and House of Representatives of the United States, and to the officers of both Houses," made a report: Whereupon,

A motion was made and seconded, that this House do recede from their dis-

---

[43] The inspected enrolled bill is in Enrolled Acts, RG 11, DNA. E–45711.

[44] The inspected enrolled bill is in Enrolled Acts, RG 11, DNA. E–45692.

[45] On September 11 both of these bills were presented to the president, and he signed the Salaries-Executive Bill [HR–21].

[46] Senate amendments are noted on the resolution in House Joint and Concurrent Resolutions, SR, DNA. An annotated printed copy of the amendments to the Constitution, as passed by the Senate, is in the same location. A list of the Senate amendments, dated September 9, 1789, is also in the above location. On September 19 the House considered these Senate amendments.

[47] On September 11 this bill was read, agreed to, and sent to the Senate.

agreement to the said amendment, and do agree to the same with an amendment, by adding to the end of the bill the following clause:

And be it further enacted, That this act shall continue in force until the fourth day of March, in the year one thousand seven hundred and ninety-six, and no longer.

On the question being put thereupon,

It passed in the negative. $\begin{cases} \text{AYES } 24 \\ \text{NOES } 29 \end{cases}$

The ayes and noes being demanded by one fifth of the members present, Those who voted in the affirmative, are,

Fisher Ames	John Laurance
Abraham Baldwin	Richard Bland Lee
Egbert Benson	Samuel Livermore
John Brown	James Madison, junior
Lambert Cadwalader	Andrew Moore
George Clymer	Peter Muhlenberg
Thomas Fitzsimons	Thomas Scott
George Gale	Roger Sherman
Elbridge Gerry	William Smith (of South-Carolina)
Samuel Griffin	Jonathan Trumbull
Thomas Hartley	John Vining and
Benjamin Huntington	Henry Wynkoop

Those who voted in the negative, are,

Theodorick Bland	John Page
Elias Boudinot	Josiah Parker
Aedanus Burke	George Partridge
Daniel Carroll	Jeremiah Van Rensselaer
Isaac Coles	James Schureman
Benjamin Contee	Joshua Seney
William Floyd	Peter Silvester
Abiel Foster	Thomas Sinnickson
Nicholas Gilman	William Smith (of Maryland)
Benjamin Goodhue	Michael Jenifer Stone
Jonathan Grout	Thomas Sumter
John Hathorn	George Thatcher
Daniel Hiester	Thomas Tudor Tucker and
James Jackson	Alexander White
George Mathews	

RESOLVED, That this House doth adhere to their disagreement to the said amendment.[48]

Mr. Madison from the committee to whom was referred the memorial and petition of the public creditors of the state of Pennsylvania, made a report, which was read, and ordered to lie on the table.[49]

The orders of the day for the House to resolve itself into a committee of the whole House on the bill for establishing a land-office, in, and for the Western Territory; also on the bill sent from the Senate, entitled, "An act to establish the judicial courts of the United States," were read, and postponed until to-morrow.

And then the House adjourned until to-morrow morning eleven o'clock.

FRIDAY, SEPTEMBER 11, 1789

Mr. Partridge, from the committee for inrolled bills, reported that the committee did, yesterday, jointly with the committee of the Senate, wait on the President of the United States, and present him with two inrolled bills, one entitled, "An act to provide for the safe keeping of the acts, records, and seal of the United States, and for other purposes,"[50] and the other entitled, "An act for establishing the salaries of the executive officers of government, with their assistants and clerks," for his approbation.

An engrossed bill for suspending the operation of part of an act, entitled, "An act imposing duties on tonnage," was read the third time, and the blanks therein filled up.

RESOLVED, That the said bill do pass; and that the title be, "An act for suspending the operation of part of an act, entitled, 'An act imposing duties on tonnage.' "[51]

ORDERED, That the clerk of this House do carry the said bill to the Senate, and desire their concurrence.[52]

A message was received from the President of the United States, notifying that the President approves of the act, entitled, "An act for establishing the

---

[48] On September 11 the first amendment was considered again and agreed to with an amendment.

[49] A copy of the report is in A Record of the Reports of Select Committees, HR, DNA. On September 21 the House considered this report and made two resolutions on it.

[50] On September 16 the House was notified that the president had signed this bill on September 15.

[51] The bill is in Engrossed House Bills, HR, DNA.

[52] On September 11 the Senate read this bill twice and committed it with the Collection Bill [HR–23]. This committee reported on September 12. This report, which was agreed to and printed in the *Senate Legislative Journal* on this date, incorporated the provisions of [HR–24] into [HR–23]. The Senate then voted not to agree to the Tonnage Bill [HR–24].

salaries of the executive officers of government, with their assistants and clerks," and has this day affixed his signature thereto: And the messenger delivered in the said act, and then withdrew.

ORDERED, That the clerk of this House do acquaint the Senate therewith.

A motion was made and seconded, that the House do now proceed to re-consider the proceedings of yesterday, on the bill, entitled, "An act for allowing compensation to the members of the Senate and House of Representatives of the United States, and to the officers of both Houses," so far as relates to the adherence of the House, to their disagreement to the first amendment proposed by the Senate to the said bill; which motion being objected to as not in order.

Mr. Speaker declared the motion to be in order; from which decision of the chair an appeal to the judgment of the House was made by two members, and, after debate, the question being put, "Is the said motion in order?"

It was resolved in the affirmative.

And then the question on the original motion being put, "that the House do now proceed to re-consider the proceedings of yesterday, on the bill, entitled, 'An act for allowing compensation to the members of the Senate and House of Representatives of the United States, and to the officers of both Houses,' so far as relates to the adherence of the House to their disagreement to the first amendment proposed by the Senate to the said bill."

It was resolved in the affirmative. $\begin{cases} \text{AYES} & 29 \\ \text{NOES} & 25 \end{cases}$

The ayes and noes being demanded by one fifth of the members present, Those who voted in the affirmative, are,

Fisher Ames	John Laurance
Abraham Baldwin	Richard Bland Lee
Egbert Benson	Samuel Livermore
Elias Boudinot	James Madison, junior
John Brown	Andrew Moore
Aedanus Burke	Peter Muhlenberg
Lambert Cadwalader	John Page
Daniel Carroll	Thomas Scott
George Clymer	Roger Sherman
Thomas Fitzsimons	William Smith (of South-Carolina)
George Gale	Jonathan Trumbull
Elbridge Gerry	John Vining
Samuel Griffin	Jeremiah Wadsworth and
Thomas Hartley	Henry Wynkoop
Benjamin Huntington	

Those who voted in the negative, are,

Theodorick Bland	George Partridge
Isaac Coles	Jeremiah Van Rensselaer
Benjamin Contee	James Schureman
William Floyd	Joshua Seney
Abiel Foster	Peter Silvester
Nicholas Gilman	Thomas Sinnickson
Benjamin Goodhue	William Smith (of Maryland)
Jonathan Grout	Michael Jenifer Stone
John Hathorn	Thomas Sumter
Daniel Hiester	George Thatcher
James Jackson	Thomas Tudor Tucker and
George Mathews	Alexander White
Josiah Parker	

A motion was then made and seconded, that this House do recede from the adherence to their disagreement to the first amendment proposed by the Senate, to the bill, entitled, "An act for allowing compensation to the members of the Senate and House of Representatives of the United States, and to the officers of both Houses," and do agree to the same, with an amendment, by adding to the end of the bill, the following clause:

"*And be it further enacted,* That this act shall continue in force until the fourth day of March, in the year one thousand seven hundred and ninety-six, and no longer:"[53]   And the question being put thereupon;

It was resolved in the affirmative. $\begin{cases} \text{Ayes } 28 \\ \text{Noes } 26 \end{cases}$

The ayes and noes being demanded by one fifth of the members present, Those who voted in the affirmative, are,

Fisher Ames	George Gale
Abraham Baldwin	Elbridge Gerry
Egbert Benson	Samuel Griffin
Elias Boudinot	Thomas Hartley
John Brown	Benjamin Huntington
Aedanus Burke	John Laurance
Lambert Cadwalader	Richard Bland Lee
Daniel Carroll	Samuel Livermore
George Clymer	James Madison, junior
Thomas Fitzsimons	Andrew Moore

[53] A copy of the resolution and amendment is in House Joint and Concurrent Resolutions, SR, DNA.

Peter Muhlenberg
Thomas Scott
Roger Sherman
William Smith (of South-
    Carolina)

Jonathan Trumbull
John Vining
Jeremiah Wadsworth and
Henry Wynkoop

Those who voted in the negative, are,

Theodorick Bland
Isaac Coles
Benjamin Contee
William Floyd
Abiel Foster
Nicholas Gilman
Benjamin Goodhue
Jonathan Grout
John Hathorn
Daniel Hiester
James Jackson
George Mathews
John Page

Josiah Parker
George Partridge
Jeremiah Van Rensselaer
James Schureman
Joshua Seney
Peter Silvester
Thomas Sinnickson
William Smith (of Maryland)
Michael Jenifer Stone
Thomas Sumter
George Thatcher
Thomas Tudor Tucker and
Alexander White

ORDERED, That the clerk of this House do carry the said bill to the Senate, and desire their concurrence to the amendment to their amendment.[54]

The House, according to the order of the day, resolved itself into a committee of the whole House, on the bill sent from the Senate, entitled, "An act to establish the judicial courts of the United States."

Mr. Speaker left the chair.

Mr. Boudinot took the chair of the committee.

Mr. Speaker resumed the chair, and Mr. Boudinot reported that the committee had, according to order, had the said bill under consideration, and made a farther progress therein.

RESOLVED, That this House will, to-morrow, again resolve itself into a committee of the whole House on the said bill.[55]

The order of the day for the House to resolve itself into a committee of the whole House, on the bill for establishing a land-office in, and for the western territory, was read, and postponed until to-morrow.

And then the House adjourned until to-morrow morning eleven o'clock.

---

[54] On September 12 the House was notified that the Senate had agreed to this amendment to their amendment.

[55] On September 12 the COWH considered this bill again.

SATURDAY, SEPTEMBER 12, 1789

The House, according to the order of the day, resolved itself into a committee of the whole House, on the bill sent from the Senate, entitled, "An act to establish the judicial courts of the United States."

Mr. Speaker left the chair.

Mr. Boudinot took the chair of the committee.

Mr. Speaker resumed the chair, and Mr. Boudinot reported that the committee had, according to order, had the said bill under consideration, and made a farther progress therein.

RESOLVED, That this House will, on Monday next, again resolve itself into a committee of the whole House, on the said bill.[56]

A message from the Senate, by Mr. Otis their Secretary.

MR. SPEAKER,   The Senate have agreed to the amendment made by this House, to the first amendment proposed by the Senate to the bill, entitled, "An act for allowing compensation to the Members of the Senate and House of Representatives of the United States, and to the officers of both Houses:"[57] And then he withdrew.

The order of the day for the House to resolve itself into a committee of the whole House, on the bill for establishing a land-office in, and for the western territory, was read, and postponed until Monday next.

And then the House adjourned until Monday morning eleven o'clock.

MONDAY, SEPTEMBER 14, 1789

Mr. Partridge reported from the committee for inrolled bills, that the committee had examined the inrolled bill, entitled, "An act for allowing compensation to the Members of the Senate and House of Representatives of the United States, and to the officers of both Houses,"[58] and had found the same to be truly inrolled: Whereupon,

Mr. Speaker signed the said inrolled bill.[59]

The several petitions of Alexander Power, attorney in fact for the officers of Colonel Benjamin Flower's regiment of artillery and artificers;[60] and of the

---

[56] On September 14 the COWH reported amendments to this bill.

[57] On September 14 this bill was signed by the speaker and vice president.

[58] The inspected inrolled bill is in Enrolled Acts, RG 11, DNA. E–45690.

[59] On September 16 the committee on enrolled bills reported that they had presented this bill to the president.

[60] The petition is E–22813. On September 21 this petition was referred to the committee on claims.

Baron de Steuben, were presented to the House, and read, respectively pray-ing that their several claims for military services rendered during the late war, may be liquidated and satisfied;[61]

Also, a petition of the measurers of dutiable articles at the port of New-York, complaining of the insufficiency of the fees allowed them by law, and praying that an adequate compensation may be made for their services.[62]

ORDERED, That the said petitions do lie on the table.

A message from the Senate by Mr. Otis their Secretary.

MR. SPEAKER, The Senate have passed the bill, entitled, "An act to sus-pend part of an act, entitled, 'An act to regulate the collection of the duties imposed by law on the tonnage of ships or vessels, and on goods, wares, and merchandizes, imported into the United States,'" with several amendments,[63] to which they desire the concurrence of this House: And then he withdrew.

The House proceeded to consider the amendments proposed by the Senate to the said bill, and the same being read, were agreed to.

ORDERED, That the clerk of this House do acquaint the Senate therewith.[64]

The House, according to the order of the day, resolved itself into a com-mittee of the whole House on the bill sent from the Senate, entitled, "An act to establish the judicial courts of the United States."

Mr. Speaker left the chair.

Mr. Boudinot took the chair of the committee.

Mr. Speaker resumed the chair, and Mr. Boudinot reported that the com-mittee had, according to order, had the said bill under consideration, and gone through the same, and made several amendments thereto, which he de-livered in at the clerk's table, where the same were read, and ordered to lie on the table.[65]

Mr. Ames, from the committee appointed, presented according to order, a bill to establish the seat of the government of the United States, which was received, and read the first time.[66]

The orders of the day for the House to resolve itself into a committee of

---

[61] The petition with related papers is in Petitions and Memorials: Claims, SR, DNA. Additional documents, which may have been with this petition, are in Transcribed Reports and Communications from the Executive Departments, 1789–1814, Records of the Secretary, SR, DNA. On September 21 this petition was referred to a committee on claims.

[62] A petition from the measurers of the city of New York, dated July 16, 1789, may be the same as this petition. It is in Petitions and Memorials: Various subjects, SR, DNA.

[63] The amendments are printed in the *Senate Legislative Journal* on September 12.

[64] On September 15 this bill was signed by the speaker and vice president.

[65] On September 15 these amendments were considered.

[66] On September 15 this bill was read again.

the whole House, on the bill for establishing a land-office, in, and for the western territory, also, on the bill sent from the Senate, entitled, "An act for the punishment of certain crimes against the United States," were read, and postponed until to-morrow.

And then the House adjourned until to-morrow morning eleven o'clock.

TUESDAY, SEPTEMBER 15, 1789

A bill to establish the seat of the government of the United States, was read the second time, and ordered to be committed to a committee of the whole House on Thursday next.[67]

Mr. Vining, reported from the committee for inrolled bills, that the committee had examined the inrolled bill, entitled, "An act to suspend part of an act, entitled, 'An act to regulate the collection of the duties imposed by law on the tonnage of ships or vessels, and on goods, wares, and merchandizes, imported into the United States,' and for other purposes,"[68] and had found the same to be truly inrolled: Whereupon,

Mr. Speaker signed the said inrolled bill.[69]

A petition of sundry inhabitants of the county of Bergen, in the state of New-Jersey, was presented to the House and read, praying that the district court of the United States, to be held within the said state, may be at Burlington and Newark alternately.

Also, a petition of the merchants and traders of the town of Portsmouth, in the state of Virginia, praying that a naval-office may be established therein for the convenience of the trade of that port.

ORDERED, That the said petitions do lie on the table.

The House proceeded to consider the amendments reported yesterday by the committee of the whole House, to the bill sent from the Senate, entitled, "An act to establish the judicial courts of the United States," which lay on the table: Whereupon,

A motion was made and seconded, to amend the third section of the said bill, by striking out the word, "*Eastown*," and inserting in lieu thereof, the word, "*Chestertown*."

And on the question, That the House do agree to the said amendment.

It passed in the negative. $\begin{cases} \text{AYES} & 20 \\ \text{NOES} & 23 \end{cases}$

The ayes and noes being demanded by one fifth of the members present,

Those who voted in the affirmative, are,

---

[67] On September 17 several amendments to this bill were agreed to.
[68] The inspected enrolled bill is in Enrolled Acts, RG 11, DNA. E–45313.
[69] On September 16 the president signed this bill.

Egbert Benson	Josiah Parker
William Floyd	Thomas Scott
Elbridge Gerry	Joshua Seney
Benjamin Goodhue	Peter Silvester
Thomas Hartley	William Smith (of Maryland)
Daniel Hiester	William Smith (of South-Carolina)
John Laurance	George Thatcher
Samuel Livermore	Jonathan Trumbull
Andrew Moore	John Vining and
Peter Muhlenberg	Henry Wynkoop

Those who voted in the negative, are,

Abraham Baldwin	Richard Bland Lee
Theodorick Bland	James Madison, junior
John Brown	George Mathews
Lambert Cadwalader	John Page
Daniel Carroll	Jeremiah Van Rensselaer
Benjamin Contee	James Schureman
Thomas Fitzsimons	Roger Sherman
Abiel Foster	Thomas Sinnickson
George Gale	Michael Jenifer Stone
Nicholas Gilman	Thomas Sumter and
Samuel Griffin	Alexander White
John Hathorn	

And then the House having made some progress in the said amendments,

ORDERED, That the farther consideration thereof, be postponed until to-morrow.[70]

A message from the Senate, by Mr. Otis their Secretary.

MR. SPEAKER, The Senate have passed a bill, entitled, "An act for the temporary establishment of the post-office," to which they desire the concurrence of this House:[71]   And then he withdrew.

The several orders of the day for the House to resolve itself into a committee of the whole House, on the bill for establishing a land-office in, and for the western territory: Also, on the bill sent from the Senate, entitled, "An act for the punishment of certain crimes against the United States," and on the

---

[70] On September 16 several amendments to this bill were agreed to.

[71] The bill is in Engrossed Senate Bills and Resolutions, SR, DNA. On September 16 this bill was read.

bill providing for the establishment of hospitals, for the relief of sick and dis-abled seamen, and prescribing regulations for the harbours of the United States, were read, and postponed until to-morrow.

And then the House adjourned until to-morrow morning eleven o'clock.

WEDNESDAY, SEPTEMBER 16, 1789

Mr. Partridge, from the committee for inrolled bills, reported, that the com-mittee did, yesterday, jointly with the committee of the Senate, wait on the President of the United States, and present him with two inrolled bills, one entitled, "An act for allowing compensation to the members of the Senate and House of Representatives of the United States, and to the officers of both Houses,"[72] the other entitled, "An act to suspend part of an act, entitled, 'An act to regulate the collection of the duties imposed by law, on the tonnage of ships or vessels, and on goods, wares, and merchandizes imported into the United States,' and for other purposes," for his approbation.

The bill sent from the Senate, entitled, "An act for the temporary establish-ment of the post-office," was read the first time.[73]

On motion,

ORDERED, That a committee be appointed to prepare and bring in a bill for amending the act, entitled, "An act to regulate the collection of the duties imposed by law on the tonnage of ships or vessels, and on goods, wares and merchandizes imported into the United States," and that Mr. Sherman, Mr. Goodhue, and Mr. Contee, do prepare and bring in the same.[74]

On motion,

ORDERED, That a committee be appointed to prepare and bring in a bill, for establishing the salaries of the judicial department, and that Mr. Burke, Mr. Moore, and Mr. Laurance, do prepare and bring in the same.[75]

A message was received from the President of the United States, notifying that the President approves of the two acts, the one entitled, "An act to pro-vide for the safe keeping of the acts, records and seal of the United States, and for other purposes;" the other entitled, "An act to suspend part of an act, en-titled, 'An act to regulate the collection of the duties imposed by law on the tonnage of ships or vessels, and on goods, wares and merchandizes imported into the United States,' and for other purposes," and affixed his signature to

---

[72] On September 22 the president signed this bill.

[73] On September 17 this bill was read twice and agreed to.

[74] On September 17 this committee reported a Collection Bill [HR–26], which was read.

[75] On September 17 this committee presented the Salaries-Judiciary Bill [HR–28], which was read twice.

the first yesterday, and to the latter this day. And the messenger delivered in the said acts, and then withdrew.

A message in writing was received from the President of the United States, by the secretary at war, who delivered in the same, together with a letter from the governor of the western territory, therein referred to, and then withdrew.

The said message was read, and is as followeth:

GENTLEMEN of the HOUSE of REPRESENTATIVES,

THE Governor of the Western Territory has made a statement to me of the reciprocal hostilities of the Wabash Indians, and the white people inhabiting the frontiers bordering on the river Ohio, which I herewith lay before Congress.

The United States in Congress assembled, by their acts of the twenty-first day of July, one thousand seven hundred and eighty-seven, and of the twelfth day of August, one thousand seven hundred and eighty-eight, made a provisional arrangement for calling forth the militia of Virginia and Pennsylvania, in the proportions therein specified.

As the circumstances which occasioned the said arrangement continue nearly the same, I think proper to suggest to your consideration the expediency of making some temporary provision for calling forth the militia of the United States for the purposes stated in the Constitution, which would embrace the cases apprehended by the Governor of the Western Territory.

GEORGE WASHINGTON

September 16th, 1789[76]

ORDERED, That the said message be referred to Mr. Boudinot, Mr. Trumbull, and Mr. Burke, that they do examine the matter thereof, and report the same with their opinion thereupon to the House.[77]

On motion,

RESOLVED, That the orders of the day for the House to resolve itself into a committee of the whole House, on the bill sent from the Senate, entitled, "An act for the punishment of certain crimes against the United States;" also on the bill providing for the establishment of hospitals for the relief of sick and disabled seamen, and prescribing regulations for the harbours of the United States, be postponed until the next session of Congress.

The House resumed the consideration of the amendments reported by the committee of the whole House to the bill sent from the Senate, entitled, "An

---

[76] The message with an enclosure is in President's Messages: Suggesting legislation, SR, DNA.

[77] On September 17 this committee presented the Troops Bill [HR–27], which was read twice.

act to establish the judicial courts of the United States;" and the same being further amended and agreed to,

ORDERED, That the said bill, with the amendments, be read the third time to-morrow.[78]

The order of the day for the House to resolve itself into a committee of the whole House on the bill for establishing a land-office, in, and for the western territory, was read, and postponed until to-morrow.

And then the House adjourned until to-morrow morning ten o'clock.

THURSDAY, SEPTEMBER 17, 1789

The petitions of Henry Malcolm, and Charles Marckle, were presented to the House and read, respectively praying that their claims for military services rendered during the late war, may be liquidated and satisfied.

ORDERED, That the said petitions do lie on the table.[79]

Mr. Goodhue, from the committee appointed, presented according to order, a bill for amending part of an act, entitled, "An act to regulate the collection of the duties imposed by law on the tonnage of ships or vessels, and on goods, wares and merchandizes imported into the United States," which was received, and read the first time.[80]

The bill sent from the Senate, entitled, "An act for the temporary establishment of the post-office," was read the second time.

Mr. Baldwin, from the managers appointed on the part of this House, to attend a conference with the Senate, on the subject matter of the amendment depending between the two Houses to the bill, entitled, "An act for allowing a compensation to the President and Vice-President of the United States," made a report: Whereupon,

RESOLVED, That this House doth adhere to their disagreement to the said amendment.[81]

On motion,

The bill sent from the Senate, entitled, "An act for the temporary establishment of the post-office," was read the third time.

RESOLVED, That the said bill do pass.

ORDERED, That the clerk of this House do acquaint the Senate therewith.[82]

The bill sent from the Senate, entitled, "An act to establish the judicial courts of the United States," with the amendments, was read the third time.

---

[78] On September 17 this bill was read, agreed to with amendments, and returned to the Senate.

[79] On September 21 these petitions were referred to the committee on claims.

[80] On September 18 this bill was read again.

[81] On September 21 the Senate receded from the amendment disagreed to by the House.

[82] On September 18 the speaker and vice president signed this bill.

RESOLVED, That the said bill, with the amendments, do pass.

ORDERED, That the clerk of this House do acquaint the Senate therewith, and desire their concurrence to the amendments.[83]

Mr. Boudinot, from the committee appointed, presented according to order, a bill to recognize and adapt to the Constitution of the United States, the establishment of the troops raised under the resolves of the United States in Congress assembled, and for other purposes therein mentioned; which was received, and read the first time.

On motion,

The said bill was read the second time, and ordered to be committed to a committee of the whole House to-morrow.[84]

On motion,

ORDERED, That the secretary of the treasury do report to this House, an estimate of the sums requisite to be appropriated during the present session of Congress towards defraying the expences of the civil list, and of the department of war, to the end of the present year; and for satisfying such warrants as have been drawn by the late board of treasury, and which may not heretofore have been paid.[85]

Mr. Burke, from the committee appointed, presented according to order, a bill allowing certain compensation to the judges of the supreme and other courts, and to the attorney-general of the United States, which was received, and read the first time.

On motion,

The said bill was read the second time, and ordered to be committed to a committee of the whole House to-morrow.[86]

ORDERED, That the committee of ways and means be discharged from further proceeding on the business to them referred, and that it be referred to the secretary of the treasury of the United States, to consider and report thereupon.

The House, according to the order of the day, resolved itself into a committee of the whole House, on the bill to establish the seat of the government of the United States.

---

[83] The Senate committed these amendments on September 17, and this committee reported on September 19. The Senate then passed a resolution disagreeing to some House amendments and agreeing to others with an amendment to one. The House was notified of these actions on the same day.

[84] From September 18–21 consideration of this bill was postponed. On September 22 the bill was considered in the COWH and amended.

[85] On September 21 the secretary of the treasury reported, and the report was referred to a committee. On the same day the committee presented an Appropriations Bill [HR–32], which was read.

[86] On September 18 this bill was considered in the COWH, and amendments to it were reported.

Mr. Speaker left the chair.

Mr. Boudinot took the chair of the committee.

Mr. Speaker resumed the chair, and Mr. Boudinot reported that the committee had, according to order, had the said bill under consideration, and gone through the same, and made several amendments thereto, which he delivered in at the clerk's table, where the same were read, amended, and agreed to by the House.

ORDERED, That the said bill, with the amendments, do lie on the table.[87]

The order of the day for the House to resolve itself into a committee of the whole House, on the bill for establishing a land-office, in, and for the western territory, was read, and postponed until to-morrow.

And then the House adjourned until to-morrow morning ten o'clock.

FRIDAY, SEPTEMBER 18, 1789

Mr. Hiester, from the committee appointed, presented according to order, a bill making provision for the invalid pensioners of the United States, which was received and read the first time.[88]

A petition of William Hoy was presented to the House and read, setting forth that he has discovered an infallible cure for the bite of a mad dog, and praying that an adequate compensation may be made him for his labour and assiduity in the discovery, which in that case he will make public.

Also, a petition of James Rumsey, praying that an exclusive privilege may be granted him for constructing sundry engines, devices, and improvements, which he has discovered and invented for the advancement of labour and useful works, agreeable to the descriptions and models thereof accompanying his petition.

ORDERED, That the said petitions do lie on the table.

A bill for amending part of an act, entitled "An act to regulate the collection of the duties imposed by law on the tonnage of ships or vessels, and on goods, wares and merchandizes imported into the United States," was read the second time.

ORDERED, That the said bill be engrossed, and read the third time to-morrow.[89]

Mr. Vining from the committee for inrolled bills, reported that the committee had examined the inrolled bill, entitled "An act for the temporary establishment of the post-office,"[90] and had found the same to be truly inrolled: Whereupon,

---

[87] On September 21 this bill was considered again.

[88] On September 19 this bill was read again.

[89] On September 19 this bill was read, agreed to, and sent to the Senate.

[90] The inspected enrolled bill is in Enrolled Acts, RG 11, DNA. E–45699.

Mr. Speaker signed the said inrolled bill.[91]

On motion,

RESOLVED, That it shall be the duty of the secretary of state, to procure from time to time such of the statutes of the several states as may not be in his office.

ORDERED, That the clerk of this House do carry the said resolution to the Senate and desire their concurrence.

The House proceeded to consider the report of the committee to whom it was referred to examine into the measures taken by Congress and the state of Virginia respecting the lands reserved for the use of the officers and soldiers of the said state, on continental and state establishments, in the cession made by the said state to the United States, of the territory north-west of the river Ohio, which lay on the table: Whereupon,

ORDERED, that the farther consideration of the said report be postponed until the next session of Congress.[92]

The House, according to the order of the day, resolved itself into a committee of the whole House on the bill allowing certain compensation to the judges of the supreme and other courts, and to the attorney-general of the United States.

Mr. Speaker left the chair.

Mr. Boudinot took the chair of the committee.

Mr. Speaker resumed the chair, and Mr. Boudinot reported that the committee had, according to order, had the said bill under consideration, and gone through the same, and made several amendments thereto, which he delivered in at the clerk's table, where the same were read, and ordered to lie on the table.[93]

A message from the Senate, by Mr. Otis their secretary.

MR. SPEAKER,   The Senate have agreed to the resolution of this House, that the secretary of state do procure from time to time such of the statutes of the several states as may not be in his office:[94]   And then he withdrew.

The orders of the day for the House to resolve itself into a committee of the whole House, on the bill for establishing a land-office, in, and for the western territory; also on the bill to recognize and adapt to the Constitution of the United States, the establishment of the troops raised under the resolves

---

[91] On September 19 this bill was presented to the president.

[92] On January 11, 1790, the committee on unfinished business reported on this topic.

[93] On September 19 these amendments were agreed to. On the same date the bill was read, agreed to, and sent to the Senate.

[94] On September 22 this resolution was signed by the speaker and the vice president.

of the United States in Congress assembled, and for other purposes therein mentioned, were read and postponed until to-morrow.

And then the House adjourned until to-morrow morning ten o'clock.

SATURDAY, SEPTEMBER 19, 1789

An engrossed bill for amending part of an act, entitled, "An act to regulate the collection of the duties imposed by law on the tonnage of ships or vessels, and on goods, wares, and merchandizes, imported into the United States," was read the third time.

RESOLVED, That the said bill do pass, and that the title be, "An act for amending part of an act, entitled, 'An act to regulate the collection of the duties imposed by law on the tonnage of ships or vessels, and on goods, wares, and merchandizes, imported into the United States.' "[95]

ORDERED, That the clerk of this House do carry the said bill to the Senate, and desire their concurrence.[96]

A bill, making provision for the invalid pensioners of the United States, was read the second time, and ordered to be committed to a committee of the whole House on Monday next.[97]

Mr. Parker, from the committee appointed, presented according to order, a bill concerning the importation of certain persons prior to the year 1808, which was received, and read the first time.

ORDERED, That the farther consideration of the said bill be postponed until the next session of Congress.

Mr. Partridge, from the committee for inrolled bills, reported, that the committee, did this day, jointly with the committee of the Senate, wait on the President of the United States, and present him with the inrolled bill, entitled, "An act for the temporary establishment of the post-office," for his approbation.[98]

The House proceeded to consider the amendments reported by the committee of the whole House, to the bill for allowing certain compensation to the judges of the supreme and other courts, and to the attorney-general of the United States, which lay on the table; and the same being read and amended, were agreed to.

---

[95] The bill is in Engrossed House Bills, HR, DNA.

[96] The Senate read this bill twice on September 19. On September 26 it was read again and committed. This committee reported on September 28, and the Senate voted not to pass this Collection Bill [HR–26].

[97] From September 21–23 this bill was postponed. On September 24 the bill was considered in the COWH and recommitted.

[98] On September 22 the president signed this bill.

ORDERED, That the said bill, with the amendments, be engrossed, and read the third time to-day.

A message from the Senate, by Mr. Otis their Secretary.

MR. SPEAKER,   The Senate have passed a bill, entitled, "An act to regulate processes in the courts of the United States;"[99] to which they desire the concurrence of this House: And then he withdrew.

The bill sent from the Senate, entitled, "An act to regulate processes in the courts of the United States," was read the first time.

On motion,

The said bill was read the second time, and ordered to be committed to a committee of the whole House on Monday next.[100]

An engrossed bill, allowing certain compensation to the judges of the supreme and other courts, and to the attorney-general of the United States, was read the third time.

RESOLVED, That the said bill do pass, and that the title be, "An act allowing certain compensation to the judges of the supreme and other courts, and to the attorney-general of the United States."

ORDERED, That the clerk of this House do carry the said bill to the Senate, and desire their concurrence.[101]

A message from the Senate, by Mr. Otis their Secretary.

MR. SPEAKER,   The Senate agree to some, and disagree to others of the amendments proposed by this House to the bill, entitled, "An act to establish the judicial courts of the United States:"[102]   And then he withdrew.

The House proceeded to consider the amendments proposed by the Senate to the several articles of amendment to the Constitution of the United States, agreed to by this House, and sent to the Senate for their concurrence, and having made some progress therein,

---

[99] The bill with annotations is in Engrossed Senate Bills and Resolutions, SR, DNA.

[100] On September 21 and 22 consideration of this bill was postponed as an order of the day. On September 23 this bill was considered in the COWH.

[101] The Senate read this bill twice on September 19. On September 21 amendments to it were agreed to, and the bill was agreed to with these amendments. On the same day the House agreed to three of the Senate amendments and disagreed to the fourth one. The Senate then receded from this amendment.

[102] A copy of Senate resolutions and an amendment is filed with the bill in Engrossed Senate Bills and Resolutions, SR, DNA. The Senate action is printed in the *Senate Legislative Journal* on September 19. On September 21 the House agreed to the Senate action on these amendments.

ORDERED, That the farther consideration of the said amendments be postponed until Monday next.[103]

The orders of the day for the House to resolve itself into a committee of the whole House, on the bill for establishing a land-office, in, and for the western territory; also, on the bill to recognize and adapt to the Constitution of the United States, the establishment of the troops raised under the resolves of the United States in Congress assembled, and for other purposes therein mentioned, were read and postponed until Monday next.

And then the House adjourned until Monday morning ten o'clock.

MONDAY, SEPTEMBER 21, 1789

The House proceeded to reconsider such of the amendments to the bill sent from the Senate, entitled, "An act to establish the judicial courts of the United States," as were disagreed to by the Senate: Whereupon,

RESOLVED, That this House doth recede from their ninth, sixteenth, forty-first and fifty-second amendments to the said bill, and doth agree to the modification and amendment of their forty-eighth amendment as proposed by the Senate.[104]

ORDERED, That the Clerk of this House do acquaint the Senate therewith.[105]

The Speaker laid before the House a report and estimates made by the Secretary of the treasury pursuant to the order of the seventeenth instant,[106] which were read, and ordered to be referred to Mr. Wadsworth, Mr. Smith (of Maryland) and Mr. Smith (of South Carolina).

The House resumed the consideration of the amendments proposed by the Senate to the several articles of amendment to the Constitution of the United States, as agreed to by this House, and sent to the Senate for concurrence: Whereupon,

RESOLVED, That this House doth agree to the second, fourth, eighth, twelfth, thirteenth, sixteenth, eighteenth, nineteenth, twenty-fifth, and twenty-sixth amendments, and doth disagree to the first, third, fifth, sixth, seventh, ninth, tenth, eleventh, fourteenth, fifteenth, seventeenth, twentieth, twenty-first, twenty-second, twenty-third and twenty-fourth amendments proposed by the Senate to the said articles, two thirds of the members present concurring on each vote.

---

[103] On September 21 the House agreed to some of these amendments and disagreed to others. The House then appointed a conference on the amendments disagreed to. On the same day the Senate receded from its third amendment and agreed to the conference.

[104] A copy of the resolution is filed with the bill in Engrossed Senate Bills and Resolutions, SR, DNA.

[105] On September 22 this bill was signed by the speaker and vice president.

[106] This report is E–22213.

RESOLVED, That a conference be desired with the Senate on the subject matter of the amendments disagreed to, and that Mr. Madison, Mr. Sherman, and Mr. Vining, be appointed managers at the same on the part of this House.

ORDERED, That the Clerk of this House do acquaint the Senate therewith, and desire their concurrence.

ORDERED, That leave be given to bring in a bill to alter the time of the annual meeting of Congress, and that Mr. Jackson do prepare and bring in the same.

The house proceeded to consider the bill to establish the seat of government of the United States, which lay on the table with the amendments as reported by the committee of the whole House: Whereupon,

ORDERED, That the said bill, with the amendments be engrossed, and read the third time to-morrow.[107]

A message from the Senate, by Mr. Otis, their Secretary.

MR. SPEAKER,   The Senate recede from their amendment disagreed to by this House to the bill entitled, "An act for allowing a compensation to the President and Vice-President of the United States."[108] The Senate have also passed the bill, entitled, "An act for allowing certain compensation to the judges of the supreme and other courts, and to the attorney-general of the United States," with several amendments,[109] to which they desire the concurrence of the House,   and then he withdrew.

The House proceeded to consider the said amendments: Whereupon,

RESOLVED, That this House doth agree to the first, second and third amendments, and doth disagree to the fourth amendment to the said bill.

ORDERED, That the Clerk of this House do acquaint the Senate therewith.

Mr. Jackson, presented according to order, a bill to alter the time of the annual meeting of Congress, which was received and read the first time.[110]

A message from the Senate by Mr. Otis, their Secretary.

MR. SPEAKER,   The Senate have agreed to the following resolution, to which they desire the concurrence of this House, to wit:

RESOLVED, By the Senate and House of Representatives of the United States of America in Congress assembled, that it be recommended to the

---

[107] On September 22 this bill was read, agreed to, and sent to the Senate.
[108] On September 22 this bill was signed by the speaker and the vice president.
[109] A copy of the Senate resolution with amendments is in Senate Simple Resolutions and Motions, SR, DNA. The amendments are printed in the *Senate Legislative Journal* on September 21.
[110] On September 22 this bill was read again. On the same day consideration of it as the order of the day was postponed.

Legislatures of the several states, to pass laws, making it expressly the duty of the keepers of their gaols to receive and safe keep therein, all prisoners committed under the authority of the United States, until they shall be discharged by the due course of the laws thereof, under the like penalties as in the case of prisoners, committed under the authority of such states respectively; the United States to pay for the use and keeping of such gaols at the rate of fifty cents per month for each prisoner, that shall, under their authority be committed thereto, during the time such prisoners shall be therein confined; and also to support such of said prisoners as shall be committed for offences.[111]

And he delivered in the same, and then withdrew.

The House proceeded to consider the said resolution, and the same being twice read, was agreed to.

ORDERED, That the Clerk of the House do acquaint the Senate therewith.[112]

Mr. Wadsworth, from the committee appointed, presented according to order, a bill making appropriations for the service of the present year, which was received and read the first time.

On motion,

ORDERED, That all such petitions as have been presented during the present session, and lay on the table, stating any claim, or praying for the liquidation and payment of any account against the United States, be referred to Mr. Fitzsimons, Mr. Seney and Mr. Thatcher, that they do examine the matter thereof, and report the same with their opinion thereupon to the House.[113]

On motion,

A bill making appropriations for the service of the current year, was read the second time, and ordered to be committed to a committee of the whole House to-morrow.[114]

The House proceeded to consider the report of the committee, which lay on the table, on the petition of the Baron de Glaubeck: Whereupon,

RESOLVED, That the Baron de Glaubeck be allowed the pay of a captain while he commanded the legionary corps in the state of North-Carolina, to wit: From the 9th day of March, 1781, to the 24th day of August, 1782, having undertaken the command thereof, at the request, and by order of the commander in chief of the southern army.[115]

---

[111] The resolution and a copy of the resolution are in Senate Joint and Concurrent Resolutions, SR, DNA.

[112] On September 22 this resolution was signed by the speaker and the vice president.

[113] On September 25 this committee reported on the petitions of Patrick Bennet, Duncan Campbell, Tristram Coffin, Thomasin Gordon, John Hurt, Englebert Kemmena, Prudent La Jeunesse, John McGarragh, Henry Malcolm, Charles Markley, Alexander Power, James Reed, Baron de Steuben, Dudley Tyler, and Martha Walker.

[114] On September 23 the COWH considered this bill and presented an amendment, which was agreed to.

[115] A copy of the resolution is in Messages from the House, SR, DNA.

ORDERED, That the clerk of this House do carry the said resolution to the Senate, and desire their concurrence.[116]

A message from the Senate by Mr. Otis, their Secretary.

MR. SPEAKER, The Senate recede from their fourth amendment disagreed to by this House, to the bill, entitled, "An act for allowing certain compensation to the judges of the supreme and other courts, and to the attorney-general of the United States."[117] The Senate do also recede from their third amendment disagreed to by this House to the articles of amendment to the constitution of the United States, which were agreed to by this House, and sent to them for concurrence: And do insist on the other amendments to the said articles, disagreed to by this House: They have also agreed to the conference desired by this House on the subject matter of the amendments disagreed to, and have appointed managers at the same on their part:[118] And then he withdrew.

The House proceeded to consider the report which lay on the table from the committee to whom was referred the memorial and petition of the public creditors of Pennsylvania: Whereupon,

RESOLVED, That this House consider an adequate provision for the support of the public credit, as a matter of high importance to the national honor and prosperity.

RESOLVED, That the secretary of the treasury be directed to prepare a plan for that purpose, and to report the same to this House at its next meeting.

On motion,

ORDERED, That the secretary of the treasury be directed to apply to the supreme executives of the several states, for statements of their public debts; of the funds provided for the payment, in whole or in part of the principal and interest thereof; and of the amount of the loan-office certificates, or other public securities of the United States, in the state treasuries respectively; and that he report to the House such of the said documents as he may obtain, at the next session of Congress.[119]

The several orders of the day for the House to resolve itself into a committee of the whole House on the bill for establishing a land-office, in, and for

---

[116] The Senate read this resolution on September 24 and, after agreeing to it, appointed a committee to prepare a bill. On the same day this committee presented the Glaubeck Bill [S-5], which was read. The bill was read again on September 28. The bill was agreed to on September 29. On the same day it was read and agreed to by the House and signed by the speaker, vice president, and president.

[117] On September 22 this bill was signed by the speaker and vice president.

[118] On September 23 this conference reported.

[119] On January 9, 1790, the secretary of the treasury notified the House that he was ready to report on the public credit.

the western territory; also, on the bill to recognize and adapt to the Constitution of the United States, the establishment of the troops raised under the resolves of the United States in Congress assembled, and for other purposes therein mentioned; also, on the bill making provision for the invalid pensioners of the United States; and on the bill sent from the Senate, entitled, "An act to regulate processes in the courts of the United States;" were read and postponed until to-morrow.

And then the House adjourned until to-morrow morning ten o'clock.

TUESDAY, SEPTEMBER 22, 1789

Mr. Vining reported from the committee for inrolled bills, that the committee had examined two inrolled bills, one entitled, "An act for allowing a compensation to the President and Vice-President of the United States;"[120] the other entitled, "An act for allowing certain compensation to the judges of the supreme and other courts, and to the attorney-general of the United States;"[121] also, an inrolled resolve, for procuring from time to time the statutes of the several states,[122] and had found the same to be truly inrolled: Whereupon,

Mr. Speaker signed the said inrolled bills and resolve.[123]

An engrossed bill to establish the seat of government of the United States, was read the third time.

And the question being put that the said bill do pass,

It was resolved in the affirmative. $\begin{cases} \text{AYES} & 31 \\ \text{NOES} & 17 \end{cases}$

The ayes and noes being demanded by one fifth of the members present,

Those who voted in the affirmative, are,

Fisher Ames	Nicholas Gilman
Abraham Baldwin	Benjamin Goodhue
Egbert Benson	Jonathan Grout
George Clymer	Thomas Hartley
Benjamin Contee	John Hathorn
Thomas Fitzsimons	James Jackson
William Floyd	John Laurance
Abiel Foster	George Leonard
George Gale	Samuel Livermore

[120] The inspected enrolled bill is in Enrolled Acts, RG 11, DNA. E–45688.

[121] The inspected enrolled bill is in Enrolled Acts, RG 11, DNA. E–45689.

[122] The inspected enrolled resolution is in Enrolled Acts, RG 11, DNA. E–45722.

[123] On September 23 the committee on enrolled bills reported that it had presented these bills and the resolution to the president. On the same day the Salaries-Judiciary Bill [HR–28] and the resolution were signed by the president.

Peter Muhlenberg	William Smith (of Maryland)
George Partridge	Michael Jenifer Stone
Jeremiah Van Rensselaer	George Thatcher
Thomas Scott	Jonathan Trumbull
Joshua Seney	Jeremiah Wadsworth and
Roger Sherman	Henry Wynkoop
Peter Silvester	

Those who voted in the negative, are,

Theodorick Bland	Andrew Moore
Elias Boudinot	Josiah Parker
Aedanus Burke	James Schureman
Lambert Cadwalader	William Smith (of South-Carolina)
Daniel Carroll	Thomas Sumter
Isaac Coles	Thomas Tudor Tucker
Richard Bland Lee	John Vining and
James Madison, junior	Alexander White
George Mathews	

RESOLVED, That the title of the said bill be, "An act to establish the seat of government of the United States;" and that the clerk of this House do carry the said bill to the Senate, and desire their concurrence.[124]

On motion,

ORDERED, That the order of the twenty-fifth of August, directing the President of the Senate, and Speaker of the House, to adjourn their respective Houses on this day, be rescinded, and in stead thereof, that they be directed to close the present session, by adjourning their respective Houses on the twenty-sixth instant.[125]

A bill to alter the time for the annual meeting of Congress, was read the second time, and ordered to be committed to a committee of the whole House to-day.

Mr. Brown, from the committee for inrolled bills, reported that the committee had examined the inrolled bill, entitled, "An act to establish the ju-

---

[124] The bill is in Engrossed House Bills, HR, DNA. E–45630. The Senate read this bill on September 22, 23, and 24. On September 24 several amendments to the bill were considered. On September 25 the bill was considered again, and two amendments to it were agreed to. On September 26 it was read again and agreed to, and the House was notified. Documents filed with the House engrossed bill show that the Senate consolidated its amendments into an entirely new bill when sending them to the House. Thus, the House Journal refers to the Senate amendments as one "amendment." On the same day a motion to postpone consideration of the amendment to the next session was disagreed to by the House.

[125] A copy of the order is in Messages from the House, SR, DNA.

dicial courts of the United States;"[126] also, an inrolled resolve to provide for the safe keeping of prisoners committed under authority of the United States,[127] and had found the same to be truly inrolled: Whereupon,

Mr. Speaker signed the said inrolled bill and resolve.[128]

The House, according to the order of the day, resolved itself into a committee of the whole House on the bill to recognize and adapt to the Constitution of the United States, the establishment of the troops raised under the resolves of the United States in Congress assembled, and for other purposes therein mentioned.

Mr. Speaker left the chair.

Mr. Boudinot took the chair of the committee.

Mr. Speaker resumed the chair, and Mr. Boudinot reported that the committee had, according to order, had the said bill under consideration, and gone through the same, and made several amendments thereto, which he delivered in at the clerk's table, where the same were twice read, and agreed to by the House.

ORDERED, That the said bill with the amendments, be engrossed and read the third time to-morrow.[129]

A message was received from the President of the United States, notifying that the President approves of the act, entitled, "An act for allowing compensation to the members of the Senate, and House of Representatives of the United States, and to the officers of both Houses;" and has this day affixed his signature thereto: And the messenger delivered in the said act, and then withdrew.

ORDERED, That the clerk of this House do acquaint the Senate therewith.

A message from the Senate, by Mr. Otis their Secretary.

MR. SPEAKER, The Senate have agreed to the order rescinding the order of the twenty-fifth of August for the adjournment of both Houses on this day, and directing that the President of the Senate and Speaker of the House, do close the present session by adjourning their respective Houses on the twenty-sixth instant:[130] I am also directed to inform this House, that the President of the United States approves of the act, entitled, "An act for the temporary establishment of the post-office;" and has this day affixed his signature thereto: And then he withdrew.

---

[126] The inspected enrolled bill is in Enrolled Acts, RG 11, DNA. E–45707.

[127] The inspected enrolled resolution is in Enrolled Acts, RG 11, DNA. E–45721.

[128] On September 23 the committee on enrolled bills reported that it had presented this bill and resolution to the president. The resolution was signed by the president on the same day.

[129] On September 23 this bill was read again, agreed to, and sent to the Senate.

[130] On September 26 a resolution postponing the adjournment was agreed to by the Senate and House.

ORDERED, That leave be given to bring in a bill to explain and amend the act, entitled, "An act for registering and clearing vessels, regulating the coasting trade, and for other purposes;" and that Mr. Bland, Mr. Goodhue, and Mr. Benson, do prepare and bring in the same.[131]

The orders of the day for the House to resolve itself into a committee of the whole House on the bill for establishing a land-office, in, and for the western territory; on the bill making provision for the invalid pensioners of the United States; on the bill to alter the time for the annual meeting of Congress;[132] on the bill sent from the Senate, entitled, "An act to regulate processes in the courts of the United States;" also, on the bill making appropriations for the service of the present year, were read, and postponed until to-morrow.

And then the House adjourned until to-morrow morning ten o'clock.

WEDNESDAY, SEPTEMBER 23, 1789

An engrossed bill to recognize and adapt to the constitution of the United States, the establishment of the troops raised under the resolves of the United States in Congress assembled, and for other purposes therein mentioned, was read the third time, and the blanks therein filled up.

RESOLVED, That the said bill do pass, and that the title be, "An act to recognize and adapt to the constitution of the United States, the establishment of the troops raised under the resolves of the United States in Congress assembled, and for other purposes therein mentioned."

ORDERED, That the Clerk of this House do carry the said bill to the Senate, and desire their concurrence.[133]

The House according to the order of the day, resolved itself into a committee of the whole House on the bill making appropriations for the service of the present year.

Mr. Speaker left the chair.

Mr. Boudinot took the chair of the committee.

Mr. Speaker resumed the chair, and Mr. Boudinot reported that the committee had, according to order, had the said bill under consideration, and gone through the same, and made an amendment thereto, which he delivered in at the Clerk's table, where the same was twice read, and agreed to by the House.

---

[131] On September 23 this committee presented a Coasting Bill [HR–33], which was read twice.

[132] On September 23 this bill was considered and amended.

[133] The Senate read this bill on September 23 and 26. On September 26 it was committed, and this committee reported on September 28. The bill was then agreed to with the amendments reported by the committee, and the House was notified. On the same day the House agreed to all of the Senate amendments except the seventh.

ORDERED, That the said bill, with the amendment, be engrossed and read the third time to-morrow.[134]

Mr. Brown reported from the committee for inrolled bills, that the committee did yesterday, jointly with the committee of the Senate, wait on the President of the United States, and present him with the following inrolled bills for his approbation, to wit:

"An act for allowing a compensation to the President and Vice-President of the United States."[135]

"An act to establish the judicial courts of the United States."[136]

"An act for allowing certain compensation to the judges of the supreme and other courts, and to the attorney-general of the United States."

Also two inrolled resolves, one for procuring from time to time the statutes of the several states, the other to provide for the safe keeping of prisoners committed under authority of the United States.

Mr. Bland, from the committee appointed, presented, according to order, a bill to explain and amend the act, entitled, "An act for registering and clearing vessels, regulating the coasting trade, and for other purposes;" which was received and read the first time.

On motion,

The said bill was read the second time, and ordered to be engrossed, and read the third time to-morrow.[137]

On motion,

ORDERED, That the Secretary of the treasury be directed to report to the House, a particular statement of the warrants issued by the late superintendant of finance, and by the board of treasury respectively, comprised in the said Secretary's estimate of appropriations reported to the House.[138]

The House according to the order of the day, resolved itself into a committee of the whole House on the bill to alter the time for the annual meeting of Congress.

Mr. Speaker left the chair.

Mr. Boudinot took the chair of the committee.

Mr. Speaker resumed the chair, and Mr. Boudinot reported that the committee had, according to order, had the said bill under consideration, and gone through the same, and made several amendments thereto, which he de-

---

[134] On September 24 this bill was read again and recommitted to the COWH, which reported an amendment to it.

[135] On September 24 the House was notified that the president had signed this bill.

[136] On September 24 the president signed this bill.

[137] On September 24 this bill was read, agreed to, and sent to the Senate.

[138] Although the report is not journalized, the House probably received it sometime between September 25, when the report was written, and the end of first session. This report is part of E–22213, which begins with the secretary of the treasury's report of September 19, 1789.

livered in at the clerk's table, where the same were twice read, and agreed to by the House.

ORDERED, That the said bill, with the amendments be engrossed, and read the third time to-morrow.[139]

A message was received from the President of the United States, notifying that the President approves of the act, entitled, "An act for allowing certain compensation to the judges of the supreme and other courts, and to the attorney-general of the United States," also the resolve for procuring from time to time the statutes of the several states, and has this day affixed his signature to the same: And the messenger delivered in the said act, and resolve, and then withdrew.

ORDERED, That the clerk of this House do acquaint the Senate therewith.

The House, according to the order of the day, resolved itself into a committee of the whole house on the bill sent from the Senate, entitled, "An act to regulate processes in the courts of the United States."

Mr. Speaker left the chair.

Mr. Boudinot took the chair of the committee.

Mr. Speaker resumed the chair, and Mr. Boudinot reported that the committee had, according to order, had the said bill under consideration, and made some progress therein.

RESOLVED, That this House will, to-morrow, again resolve itself into a committee of the whole House on the said bill.[140]

Mr. Madison, from the managers appointed on the part of this House to attend a conference with the Senate on the subject matter of the amendments depending between the two Houses to the articles of amendment to the Constitution of the United States, agreed to by this House, and sent to the Senate for their concurrence, made a report, which was read, and ordered to lie on the table.[141]

The orders of the day for the House to resolve itself into a committee of the whole house on the bill for establishing a land-office, in, and for, the western territory; also on the bill making provision for the invalid pensioners of the United States, were read, and postponed until to-morrow.

And then the House adjourned until to-morrow morning ten o'clock.

---

[139] On September 24 this bill was read, agreed to, and sent to the Senate.

[140] On September 24 this bill was amended and agreed to with amendments, which were then sent to the Senate.

[141] A copy of the report is in House Joint and Concurrent Resolutions, SR, DNA. On September 24 the House considered this report and took further action on the Senate amendments. Articles I, III, and VIII were amended, and a resolution requesting the president to send copies of the proposed amendments to the state executives was agreed to. The Senate was notified of these actions.

THURSDAY, SEPTEMBER 24, 1789

An engrossed bill to explain and amend the act, entitled, "An act for registering and clearing vessels, regulating the coasting trade, and for other purposes," was read the third time, and a blank therein filled up.

RESOLVED, That the said bill do pass, and that the title be, "An act to explain and amend the act, entitled, 'An act for registering and clearing vessels, regulating the coasting trade, and for other purposes.' "

ORDERED, That the clerk of this House do carry the said bill to the Senate, and desire their concurrence.[142]

An engrossed bill to alter the time for the annual meeting of Congress was read the third time.

RESOLVED, That the said bill do pass, and that the title be "An act to alter the time for the next meeting of Congress."

ORDERED, That the clerk of this House do carry the said bill to the Senate, and desire their concurrence.[143]

An engrossed bill making appropriations for the service of the present year, was read the third time, and, on a motion made, ordered to be re-committed to a committee of the whole House this day.

Mr. Gerry from the committee to whom it was referred to prepare an estimate of the gross amount and net produce of the impost and tonnage duties for one year, made a report[144] which was read and ordered to lie on the table.

On motion,

ORDERED, That a committee be appointed to ascertain the amount of the compensations due to the members of this House respectively, and of the several officers thereof, together with the contingent expences of the session;

And a committee was appointed of Mr. Fitzsimons, Mr. Smith (of Maryland) and Mr. Baldwin.

A petition of Thomas Barclay, was presented to the House and read, praying that he may receive compensation for services rendered to the United States, in various public stations in Europe.

ORDERED, That the said petition do lie on the table.[145]

A message was received from the President of the United States, notifying

---

[142] The Senate read this bill on September 24 and 26. It was committed on September 26, and this committee reported an amendment on September 28. The Senate then read the bill again and agreed to it with the amendment. On the same day the House agreed to the amendment, and the bill was signed by the speaker and the vice president.

[143] On September 25 the Senate read this bill and agreed to it. The House was then notified.

[144] A copy of the report is in A Record of the Reports of Select Committees, HR, DNA. A copy, probably made by ASP, is in Various Select Committees, HR, DNA.

[145] On January 11, 1790, the committee on unfinished business reported that this petition was still on the table.

that the President approves of the act making compensation to the President and Vice-President of the United States, and has this day affixed his signature thereto: And the messenger delivered in the said act, and then withdrew.

A message from the Senate, by Mr. Otis their secretary.

MR. SPEAKER, I am directed to inform this House, that the President of the United States has returned to the Senate an act to establish the judicial courts of the United States; also a resolve to provide for the safe-keeping of prisoners committed under authority of the United States, both of which have received his approbation and signature: And then he withdrew.

The House proceeded to consider the report of a committee of conference, on the subject matter of the amendments, depending between the two Houses to the several articles of amendment to the constitution of the United States, as proposed by this House: Whereupon,

RESOLVED, That this House doth recede from their disagreement to the first, third, fifth, sixth, seventh, ninth, tenth, eleventh, fourteenth, fifteenth, seventeenth, twentieth, twenty-first, twenty-second, twenty-third, and twenty-fourth amendments, insisted on by the Senate: PROVIDED, That the two articles which by the amendments of the Senate are now proposed to be inserted as the third and eighth articles, shall be amended to read as followeth;

ARTICLE the third. "Congress shall make no law respecting an establishment of religion, or prohibiting the free exercise thereof; or abridging the freedom of speech, or of the press; or the right of the people peaceably to assemble, and to petition the government for a redress of grievances."

ARTICLE the eighth. "In all criminal prosecutions, the accused shall enjoy the right to a speedy and public trial by an impartial jury of the state and district wherein the crime shall have been committed, which district shall have been previously ascertained by law, and to be informed of the nature and cause of the accusation, to be confronted with the witnesses against him, to have compulsory process for obtaining witnesses in his favor, and to have the assistance of counsel for his defence."

AND PROVIDED ALSO, That the first article be amended by striking out the word "*less,*" in the last place of the said first article, and inserting in the lieu thereof, the word "more."[146]

On the question, that the House do agree to the alteration and amendment of the eighth article, in manner aforesaid,

It was resolved in the affirmative. $\begin{cases} \text{AYES} & 37 \\ \text{NOES} & 14 \end{cases}$

---

[146] Copies of the first, third, and eighth amendments, as agreed to, are in House Joint and Concurrent Resolutions, SR, DNA.

The ayes and noes being demanded by one fifth of the members present,
Those who voted in the affirmative, are,

Fisher Ames	Andrew Moore
Abraham Baldwin	Peter Muhlenberg
Egbert Benson	Josiah Parker
Elias Boudinot	George Partridge
John Brown	James Schureman
Lambert Cadwalader	Thomas Scott
Daniel Carroll	Joshua Seney
George Clymer	Roger Sherman
Benjamin Contee	Peter Silvester
Thomas Fitzsimons	Thomas Sinnickson
Abiel Foster	William Smith (of Maryland)
George Gale	William Smith (of South-Carolina)
Nicholas Gilman	Michael Jenifer Stone
Benjamin Goodhue	George Thatcher
Samuel Griffin	Jonathan Trumbull
Thomas Hartley	John Vining
Richard Bland Lee	Alexander White and
George Leonard	Henry Wynkoop
James Madison, junior	

Those who voted in the negative, are,

Theodorick Bland	James Jackson
Aedanus Burke	Samuel Livermore
Isaac Coles	George Mathews
William Floyd	John Page
Elbridge Gerry	Jeremiah Van Rensselaer
Jonathan Grout	Thomas Sumter and
John Hathorn	Thomas Tudor Tucker

On motion,

RESOLVED, That the President of the United States be requested to transmit to the executives of the several states which have ratified the Constitution, copies of the amendments proposed by Congress to be added thereto; and like copies to the executives of the states of Rhode-Island and North-Carolina.[147]

ORDERED, That the clerk of this House do carry the said resolution to the Senate, and desire their concurrence.[148]

---

[147] A copy of the resolution is in House Joint and Concurrent Resolutions, SR, DNA.

[148] On September 25 the House was notified that the Senate had agreed to the amendments to Articles I, III, and VIII.

The House according to the order of the day resolved itself into a committee of the whole House, on the bill making appropriations for the service of the present year.

Mr. Speaker left the chair.

Mr. Boudinot took the chair of the committee.

Mr. Speaker resumed the chair, and Mr. Boudinot reported that the committee had, according to order, had the said bill under consideration, and gone through the same and made an amendment thereto, which he read in his place, and afterwards delivered in at the clerk's table, where the same was again read, and, together with the said bill, ordered to lie on the table.[149]

The House, according to the order of the day, resolved itself into a committee of the whole House on the bill, making provision for the invalid pensioners of the United States.

Mr. Speaker left the chair.

Mr. Boudinot took the chair of the committee.

Mr. Speaker resumed the chair, and Mr. Boudinot reported that the committee had, according to order, had the said bill under consideration, and made no amendment thereto.

ORDERED, That the said bill be re-committed to Mr. Wadsworth, Mr. Hiester, and Mr. Gilman.[150]

The House according to the order of the day resolved itself into a committee of the whole House on the bill sent from the Senate, entitled, "An act to regulate processes in the courts of the United States."

Mr. Speaker left the chair.

Mr. Boudinot took the chair of the committee.

Mr. Speaker resumed the chair, and Mr. Boudinot reported that the committee had, according to order, had the said bill under consideration, and gone through the same, and made several amendments thereto, which he read in his place, and afterwards delivered in at the clerk's table, where the same were again read, and are as followeth:

Section first, line third, Strike out the words *"the President of."*

Section second, line third, After the word *"fees,"* insert *"except fees to judges."* Line fifth, after the words *"and the,"* insert *"forms and modes of."* Line eighth, after the words *"civil law,"* insert *"and the rates of the fees the same as are or were last allowed by the states respectively in the court exercising supreme jurisdiction in such causes."*

---

[149] On September 25 this amendment was agreed to. On the same day the bill was read again, agreed to, and sent to the Senate.

[150] On September 25 this committee presented an amendment to this bill, which was agreed to. On the same day the bill was read again, agreed to, and sent to the Senate.

The first amendment was read the second time, and the question being put that the House do agree to the same,

It was resolved in the affirmative. $\begin{cases} \text{AYES} & 25 \\ \text{NOES} & 18 \end{cases}$

Those who voted in the affirmative, are,

Theodorick Bland	Samuel Livermore
Aedanus Burke	James Madison, junior
Isaac Coles	George Mathews
Benjamin Contee	Andrew Moore
William Floyd	Peter Muhlenberg
Elbridge Gerry	Josiah Parker
Samuel Griffin	Thomas Scott
Jonathan Grout	Joshua Seney
Thomas Hartley	Michael Jenifer Stone
John Hathorn	Thomas Sumter
Daniel Hiester	Thomas Tudor Tucker and
James Jackson	Alexander White
Richard Bland Lee	

Those who voted in the negative, are,

Fisher Ames	John Laurance
Abraham Baldwin	George Leonard
Egbert Benson	George Partridge
George Clymer	Roger Sherman
Thomas Fitzsimons	Peter Silvester
Abiel Foster	Thomas Sinnickson
George Gale	George Thatcher
Nicholas Gilman	John Vining and
Benjamin Goodhue	Henry Wynkoop

The other amendments were severally again read, and, on the question put thereupon, agreed to by the House.

RESOLVED, That the said bill, with the amendments, do pass, and that the clerk of this House do acquaint the Senate therewith.[151]

The order of the day for the House to resolve itself into a committee of the whole House, on the bill for establishing a land-office, in, and for the western territory, was read, and postponed until to-morrow.

And then the House adjourned until to-morrow morning ten o'clock.

---

[151] A copy of the resolution with amendments is filed with the bill in Engrossed Senate Bills and Resolutions, SR, DNA. On September 25 the Senate disagreed to the first House amendment, and the House adhered to it.

FRIDAY, September 25, 1789

The House proceeded to consider the amendment agreed to by the committee of the whole House, yesterday, to the bill making appropriations for the service of the present year, which being read, was amended and agreed to.

ORDERED, That the said bill, with the amendment, be engrossed, and read the third time to-day.

The House proceeded to consider the report of a committee to whom was referred the memorial of John White, on behalf of himself, John Wright, and Joshua Dawson: Whereupon,

RESOLVED, That the said John White, late a commissioner to settle the accounts between the United States and the states of Pennsylvania, Maryland, and Delaware, and his clerks, John Wright and Joshua Dawson, be considered as in office until the thirtieth day of September, one thousand seven hundred and eighty-eight, and be paid accordingly.

ORDERED, That the clerk of this House do carry the said resolution to the Senate, and desire their concurrence.[152]

An engrossed bill making appropriations for the service of the present year, was read the third time.

RESOLVED, That the said bill do pass, and that the title be, "An act making appropriations for the service of the present year."

ORDERED, That the clerk of this House do carry the said bill to the Senate, and desire their concurrence.[153]

On motion,

RESOLVED, That a joint committee of both Houses be directed to wait upon the President of the United States to request that he would recommend to the people of the United States, a day of public thanksgiving and prayer to be observed, by acknowledging, with grateful hearts, the many signal favors of Almighty God, especially by affording them an opportunity peaceably to establish a Constitution of government for their safety and happiness.

ORDERED, That Mr. Boudinot, Mr. Sherman, and Mr. Silvester, be of the said committee on the part of this House.[154]

Mr. Hiester from the committee to whom was recommitted the bill making provision for the invalid pensioners of the United States, reported an amend-

---

[152] The Senate agreed to this resolution with amendments on September 29. The amendments are printed in the *Senate Legislative Journal*. On the same day the House agreed to the amendments, and the resolution was signed.

[153] On September 25 the Senate read this bill, and it was read again and committed on September 26. On September 28 this committee reported amendments to the bill. It was then read and agreed to with amendments. The House agreed to the amendments on the same day, and the bill was signed by the speaker and the vice president.

[154] A copy of the resolution and the order is in House Joint and Concurrent Resolutions, SR, DNA. The Senate concurred in this resolution on September 26, and the House was notified on September 28.

ment thereto, which he delivered in at the clerk's table, where the same was again read, and agreed to by the House.

ORDERED, That the said bill with the amendment be engrossed, and read the third time to-day.

Mr. Fitzsimons, from the committee to whom such of the petitions presented during the present session as state any claims against the United States, or pray for the liquidation of any account, were referred, made a report:[155] Whereupon,

RESOLVED, That the several petitions of Dudley Tyler, John Hurt, Henry Malcolm, Patrick Bennet, Charles Markley, Alexander Power, and John McGarragh, be referred to the Secretary of the department of war, and that he report thereupon to the next session of Congress; that the memorial of Baron de Steuben, and the several petitions of Duncan Campbell, Thomasin Gordon, Monsieur La Jeunesse, Englebert Kemmena, Tristram Coffin, and Martha Walker, be referred to the secretary of the treasury, to report thereupon in like manner to the next session of Congress; and that the case of Brigadier General Reed, ought to be provided for by a general law concerning invalids.[156]

An engrossed bill making provision for the invalid pensioners of the United States, was read the third time.

RESOLVED, That the said bill do pass, and that the title be, "An act making provision for the invalid pensioners of the United States."

ORDERED, That the clerk of this House do carry the said bill to the Senate, and desire their concurrence.[157]

A message from the Senate, by Mr. Otis their Secretary.

MR. SPEAKER,   The Senate agree to the amendments proposed by this House to their amendments to the several articles of amendment to the Constitution of the United States:[158]   And then he withdrew.

ORDERED, That the committee to whom were referred the several petitions of William Finnie, James Gibbon, and Archibald McAlister, be discharged

---

[155] A copy of the report is in A Record of the Reports of Select Committees, HR, DNA.

[156] On January 11, 1790, the status of these petitions was reported on by a committee on unfinished business.

[157] The Senate read and committed this bill on September 26. On September 28 this committee reported; the bill was read twice and agreed to. On the same day the bill was signed by the speaker and the vice president.

[158] On September 28 the House was notified that the Senate had agreed to the resolution requesting the president to transmit the amendments to the state executives. On the same day the articles of amendment were signed by the speaker and the vice president.

therefrom,[159] and that it be referred to the secretary of the treasury, to examine and report upon the first to the next session of Congress, and to the secretary at war, to examine and report in like manner upon the two latter.

A message from the Senate, by Mr. Otis their Secretary.

MR. SPEAKER, The Senate disagree to the first, and agree to all the other amendments proposed by this House to the bill, entitled, "An act to regulate processes in the courts of the United States:" And then he withdrew.

The House proceeded to reconsider the said first amendment: Whereupon,

RESOLVED, That this House doth adhere to the said amendment.[160]

AYES 28

NOES 22

The ayes and noes being demanded by one fifth of the members present, Those who voted in the affirmative, are,

Theodorick Bland	Richard Bland Lee
Elias Boudinot	Samuel Livermore
John Brown	James Madison, junior
Aedanus Burke	George Mathews
Daniel Carroll	Andrew Moore
Isaac Coles	Peter Muhlenberg
Benjamin Contee	John Page
William Floyd	Josiah Parker
Elbridge Gerry	Jeremiah Van Rensselaer
Jonathan Grout	Joshua Seney
Thomas Hartley	Michael Jenifer Stone
John Hathorn	Thomas Sumter
Daniel Hiester	Thomas Tudor Tucker and
James Jackson	Alexander White

Those who voted in the negative, are,

Fisher Ames	Thomas Fitzsimons
Egbert Benson	Abiel Foster
Lambert Cadwalader	George Gale
George Clymer	Nicholas Gilman

[159] This committee was appointed on September 4 to examine the petitions of invalid pensioners and claimants for military service. They presented the Invalid Pensioners Bill [HR-29] on September 18.

[160] A copy of the Senate resolution on the amendments is filed with the bill in Engrossed Bills and Resolutions, SR, DNA. The House resolution is also in the same location.

Benjamin Goodhue   Peter Silvester
John Laurance   Thomas Sinnickson
George Leonard   George Thatcher
George Partridge   Jonathan Trumbull
James Schureman   John Vining
Thomas Scott   Jeremiah Wadsworth and
Roger Sherman   Henry Wynkoop[161]

A message from the Senate, by Mr. Otis their Secretary.

MR. SPEAKER,   The Senate have passed the bill, entitled, "An act to alter the time for the next meeting of Congress:"[162]   And then he withdrew.

The order of the day for the House to resolve itself into a committee of the whole House, on the bill for establishing a land-office, in, and for the western territory, was read, and postponed until to-morrow.

And then the House adjourned until to-morrow morning nine o'clock.

SATURDAY, SEPTEMBER 26, 1789

A message from the Senate, by Mr. Otis their Secretary.

MR. SPEAKER,   The Senate have agreed to a resolution, that the late order for the adjournment of the two Houses this day, be rescinded, and that the President of the Senate, and the Speaker of this House, be authorised to close the present session by adjourning their respective Houses on Tuesday next;[163] to which they desire the concurrence of this House: And then he withdrew.

The said resolution was read and agreed to by the House.

ORDERED, That the clerk of this House do acquaint the Senate therewith.[164]

A petition of Richard Ham, of the state of South-Carolina, was presented to the House and read, praying that he may receive compensation for certain services and supplies rendered for the use of the navy of the United States, during the late war.

ORDERED, That the said petition be referred to the secretary of the treasury, with instruction to report thereupon to the next session of Congress.

A message from the Senate, by Mr. Otis their Secretary.

---

[161] On September 26 a conference was appointed on this bill.

[162] On September 28 the speaker and the vice president signed this bill.

[163] A copy of the resolution is in Senate Joint and Concurrent Resolutions, SR, DNA.

[164] On September 28 a joint committee was appointed to notify the president of the date of adjournment.

MR. SPEAKER, The Senate desire a conference with this House on the subject matter of the first amendment depending between the two Houses, to the bill, entitled, "An act to regulate processes in the courts of the United States," and have appointed managers at the same on their part: And then he withdrew.

On motion,

RESOLVED, That this House doth agree to the conference desired by the Senate, and that Mr. White, Mr. Burke, and Mr. Jackson, be appointed managers at the same on the part of this House.[165]

A message from the Senate, by Mr. Otis their Secretary.

MR. SPEAKER, The Senate have passed the bill, entitled, "An act to establish the seat of government of the United States," with an amendment,[166] to which they desire the concurrence of this House: And then he withdrew.

On a motion made and seconded, that the consideration of the Senate's amendment to the said bill be postponed until the next session of Congress.

It passed in the negative. $\begin{cases} \text{AYES} & 25 \\ \text{NOES} & 29 \end{cases}$

The ayes and noes being demanded by one fifth of the members present.

Those who voted in affirmative, are,

Abraham Baldwin	George Mathews
Theodorick Bland	Andrew Moore
John Brown	John Page
Aedanus Burke	Josiah Parker
Daniel Carroll	James Schureman
Isaac Coles	Joshua Seney
Benjamin Contee	William Smith (of Maryland)
George Gale	William Smith (of South-Carolina)
Elbridge Gerry	Michael Jenifer Stone
Samuel Griffin	Thomas Sumter
James Jackson	Thomas Tudor Tucker and
Richard Bland Lee	Alexander White
James Madison, junior	

---

[165] A copy of the Senate resolution for a conference is filed with the bill in Engrossed Senate Bills and Resolutions, SR, DNA. The House resolution is in the same location. On September 28 this conference reported. On the same day the Senate agreed to the first House amendment to this bill with amendments, which were agreed to by the House.

[166] Although the Senate agreed to several amendments, the document that was returned to the House consolidated all of the amendments into an almost completely new bill. Thus, the House Journal refers to only one amendment. A copy of the Senate amendments is filed with the bill in Engrossed House Bills, HR, DNA. The amendments are printed in the *Senate Legislative Journal* on September 24 and 25.

Those who voted in the negative, are,

Fisher Ames	George Leonard
Egbert Benson	Samuel Livermore
Elias Boudinot	Peter Muhlenberg
Lambert Cadwalader	George Partridge
George Clymer	Jeremiah Van Rensselaer
Thomas Fitzsimons	Thomas Scott
William Floyd	Roger Sherman
Abiel Foster	Peter Silvester
Nicholas Gilman	Thomas Sinnickson
Benjamin Goodhue	George Thatcher
Jonathan Grout	Jonathan Trumbull
Thomas Hartley	John Vining
John Hathorn	Jeremiah Wadsworth and
Daniel Hiester	Henry Wynkoop[167]
John Laurance	

A message in writing was received from the President of the United States, accompanied with the copy of a letter from the Governor of Rhode-Island; and the said message was read and is as followeth:

"UNITED STATES, September 26, 1789
"GENTLEMEN of the HOUSE of REPRESENTATIVES,

"HAVING yesterday received a letter written in this month by the Governor of Rhode-Island, at the request and in behalf of the General Assembly of that State, addressed to the President, the Senate, and the House of Representatives of the eleven United States of America in Congress assembled, I take the earliest opportunity of laying a copy of it before you.
                                "GEORGE WASHINGTON"[168]

ORDERED, That the said message, with the letter accompanying the same, do lie on the table.

The order of the day for the House to resolve itself into a committee of the whole House, on the bill for establishing a land-office, in, and for the western territory, was read, and postponed until Monday next.

And then the House adjourned until Monday morning ten o'clock.

---

[167] On September 28 the House agreed to the Senate amendment with an amendment. On the same day the Senate postponed consideration of the House amendment until second session.

[168] The message with the enclosure is in President's Messages: Suggesting legislation, SR, DNA.

MONDAY, September 28, 1789

A message from the Senate by Mr. Otis, their Secretary.

MR. SPEAKER, The Senate have agreed to the resolution desiring the President of the United States to recommend a day of general thanksgiving; also to the resolution desiring the President of the United States to transmit to the executives of the several States in the Union and also to the executives of the states of Rhode-Island and North-Carolina, copies of the amendments agreed to by Congress to the Constitution of the United States: they have also come to a resolution appointing a committee to join with such committee as this House shall appoint to wait upon the President of the United States and notify him of the proposed recess of Congress: And then he withdrew.

On motion,

ORDERED, That Mr. Vining, Mr. Lee, and Mr. Gilman, be a committee on the part of this House for the purpose expressed in the resolution of the Senate.[169]

The House proceeded to consider the amendment proposed by the Senate to the bill, intitled "An act to establish the seat of government of the United States."   Whereupon,

A motion being made and seconded to amend the Senate's amendment by adding to the end thereof the following words—"And provided that nothing herein contained shall be construed to affect the operation of the laws of Pennsylvania within the district ceded and accepted until Congress shall otherwise provide by law."[170]

It was resolved in the affirmative.

And then the main question being put that the House do agree to the amendment of the Senate with the foregoing amendment.

It was resolved in the affirmative. $\begin{cases} \text{AYES} & 31 \\ \text{NOES} & 24 \end{cases}$

The ayes and noes being demanded by one fifth of the members present. Those who voted in the affirmative, are,

Fisher Ames	George Clymer
Egbert Benson	Thomas Fitzsimons
Lambert Cadwalader	William Floyd

---

[169] Copies of the resolution concerning adjournment and the House order are in Senate Joint and Concurrent Resolutions, SR, DNA. On September 29 the president sent the House a message concerning adjournment. On the same date Congress adjourned.

[170] A copy of the amendment is filed with the bill in Engrossed House Bills, HR, DNA.

Abiel Foster
Elbridge Gerry
Nicholas Gilman
Benjamin Goodhue
Jonathan Grout
Thomas Hartley
John Hathorn
Daniel Hiester
Benjamin Huntington
John Laurance
George Leonard
Samuel Livermore
Peter Muhlenberg

George Partridge
Jeremiah Van Rensselaer
James Schureman
Thomas Scott
Roger Sherman
Peter Silvester
Thomas Sinnickson
George Thatcher
Jonathan Trumbull
John Vining
Jeremiah Wadsworth and
Henry Wynkoop

Those who voted in the negative, are,

Abraham Baldwin
Theodorick Bland
Elias Boudinot
John Brown
Aedanus Burke
Daniel Carroll
Isaac Coles
Benjamin Contee
George Gale
Samuel Griffin
James Jackson
Richard Bland Lee

James Madison, junior
George Mathews
Andrew Moore
John Page
Josiah Parker
Joshua Seney
William Smith (of Maryland)
William Smith (of South-Carolina)
Michael Jenifer Stone
Thomas Sumter
Thomas Tudor Tucker and
Alexander White

Mr. White, from the committee appointed to confer with a committee of the Senate, on the subject matter of the amendment depending between the two Houses, to the bill, entitled, "An act to regulate processes in the courts of the United States," reported that the committee had, according to order, met a committee of the Senate in conference on the subject to them referred, but had come to no agreement thereupon.

A message from the Senate, by Mr. Otis their Secretary.

MR. SPEAKER, The Senate have agreed to the first amendment of this House to the bill, entitled, "An act to regulate processes in the courts of the United States," with amendments,[171] to which they desire the concurrence of

---

[171] A copy of the Senate resolution with amendments is filed with the bill in Engrossed Senate Bills and Resolutions, SR, DNA. It is printed in the *Senate Legislative Journal* on September 28.

this House: The Senate have also passed the bill, entitled, "An act providing for the payment of the invalid pensioners of the United States;" also, the bill, entitled, "An act making appropriations for the service of the present year," with several amendments,[172] to which they desire the concurrence of this House: And then he withdrew.

The House proceeded to consider the said amendments, and the same being read, were agreed to.

ORDERED, That the clerk of this House do acquaint the Senate therewith.

The House proceeded to consider the amendments proposed by the Senate to the first amendment depending between the two Houses, to the bill, entitled, "An act to regulate processes in the courts of the United States."

And on the question, that the House do recede from their adherence to the said amendment, so far as to agree to the amendments to the said amendment, as proposed by the Senate,[173]

The House divided. $\begin{cases} \text{AYES} & 25 \\ \text{NOES} & 25 \end{cases}$

Whereupon Mr. Speaker declared himself with the ayes.

And so the question was determined in the affirmative.

The ayes and noes being called for by one fifth of the members present,

Those who voted in the affirmative, are,

Mr. Speaker	John Laurance
Fisher Ames	Richard Bland Lee
Abraham Baldwin	George Leonard
Egbert Benson	George Partridge
Lambert Cadwalader	James Schureman
Daniel Carroll	Thomas Scott
George Clymer	Roger Sherman
Thomas Fitzsimons	Peter Silvester
Abiel Foster	Thomas Sinnickson
George Gale	William Smith (of Maryland)
Nicholas Gilman	George Thatcher
Benjamin Goodhue	Jonathan Trumbull and
Thomas Hartley	Jeremiah Wadsworth

Those who voted in the negative, are,

Theodorick Bland	John Brown
Elias Boudinot	Aedanus Burke

---

[172] These amendments are printed in the *Senate Legislative Journal* on September 28.
[173] A copy of the resolution receding from the amendment is filed with the bill in Senate Engrossed Bills and Resolutions, SR, DNA.

Isaac Coles
Benjamin Contee
William Floyd
Elbridge Gerry
Samuel Griffin
Jonathan Grout
Daniel Hiester
James Jackson
Samuel Livermore
James Madison, junior
George Mathews

Andrew Moore
Peter Muhlenberg
John Page
Josiah Parker
Joshua Seney
William Smith (of South-Carolina)
Michael Jenifer Stone
Thomas Sumter
Thomas Tudor Tucker and
Alexander White[174]

A message from the Senate, by Mr. Otis their Secretary.

MR. SPEAKER, The Senate have passed the bill, entitled, "An act to explain and amend the act for registering and clearing vessels, regulating the coasting trade, and for other purposes," with an amendment,[175] to which they desire the concurrence of this House: And then he withdrew.

The House proceeded to consider the said amendment, and the same being read, was agreed to.

ORDERED, that the clerk of this House do acquaint the Senate therewith.
A message from the Senate, by Mr. Otis their Secretary.

MR. SPEAKER, The Senate have postponed until the next session of Congress the consideration of the amendment proposed by this House, to the amendment of the Senate to the bill, entitled, "An act to establish the seat of government of the United States;" they have also passed the bill, entitled, "An act to recognize and adapt to the Constitution of the United States, the establishment of the troops raised under the resolves of the United States in Congress assembled, and for other purposes therein mentioned," with several amendments,[176] to which they desire the concurrence of this House: And then he withdrew.

The House proceeded to consider the said amendments, and the same being read,

---

[174] According to the *Senate Legislative Journal*, this bill was signed by the speaker and vice president on September 28, and by the president on September 29. The inspected enrolled bill is in Enrolled Acts, RG 11, DNA. E–45714.

[175] A Senate committee report on this bill, with the amendment, is in Various Select Committee Reports, SR, DNA. The amendment is printed in the *Senate Legislative Journal* on September 28.

[176] The amendments are printed in the *Senate Legislative Journal* on September 28.

RESOLVED, That this House doth agree to the first, second, third, fourth, fifth, and sixth amendments.

RESOLVED, That this House doth disagree to the last amendment.

AYES 16

NOES 25

The ayes and noes being demanded by one fifth of the members present, Those who voted in the affirmative, are,

Egbert Benson	George Partridge
Daniel Carroll	Roger Sherman
George Clymer	Peter Silvester
Abiel Foster	William Smith (of Maryland)
Nicholas Gilman	Michael Jenifer Stone
John Laurance	George Thatcher
Richard Bland Lee	Jonathan Trumbull and
James Madison, junior	Jeremiah Wadsworth

Those who voted in the negative, are,

Abraham Baldwin	Samuel Livermore
Theodorick Bland	George Mathews
Elias Boudinot	Andrew Moore
Aedanus Burke	Peter Muhlenberg
Lambert Cadwalader	Jeremiah Van Rensselaer
Isaac Coles	James Schureman
Benjamin Contee	Thomas Scott
Thomas Fitzsimons	Joshua Seney
William Floyd	Thomas Sinnickson
Elbridge Gerry	Thomas Sumter
Daniel Hiester	Thomas Tudor Tucker and
James Jackson	Alexander White[177]
George Leonard	

Mr. Partridge, from the committee for inrolled bills, reported that the committee had, according to order, examined several inrolled bills, to wit: one entitled, "An act to alter the time for the next meeting of Congress;"[178] another entitled, "An act providing for the payment of the invalid pensioners of the United States;"[179] another entitled, "An act making appropriations for

---

[177] On September 9 the Senate adhered to its last amendment, and the House receded from its disagreement. On the same date the bill was signed.

[178] The inspected enrolled bill is in Enrolled Acts, RG 11, DNA. E–45706.

[179] The inspected enrolled bill is in Enrolled Acts, RG 11, DNA. E–22197, E–45704.

the service of the present year;"[180] and another entitled, "An act to explain and amend the act entitled, 'An act for registering and clearing vessels, regulating the coasting trade, and for other purposes:' "[181] Also, that the committee had examined the inrollment of the several articles of amendment to the Constitution of the United States, agreed to by Congress, to be recommended to the legislatures of the several States,[182] and had found the said bills and articles of amendment severally to be truly inrolled: Whereupon,

Mr. Speaker signed the said inrolled bills and articles of amendment.[183]

The order of the day for the House to resolve itself into a committee of the whole House, on the bill for establishing a land-office, in, and for the western territory, was read, and postponed until to-morrow.

And then the House adjourned until to-morrow morning ten o'clock.

TUESDAY, SEPTEMBER 29, 1789

Mr. Partridge, from the committee for inrolled bills, reported that the committee did, yesterday, jointly with the committee of the Senate, wait on the President of the United States, and present him with several inrolled bills, for his approbation, to wit, one entitled, "An act to alter the time for the next meeting of Congress;" another entitled, "An act providing for the payment of the invalid pensioners of the United States;" another entitled, "An act making appropriations for the service of the present year;" and another entitled, "An act to explain and amend the act, entitled, 'An act for registering and clearing vessels, regulating the coasting trade, and for other purposes.' "

Two messages in writing were received from the President of the United States, which were read, and are as follow:

"UNITED STATES, September 29, 1789
"GENTLEMEN of the HOUSE of REPRESENTATIVES,

"HIS Most Christian Majesty, by a letter dated the seventh of June last, addressed to the President and Members of the General Congress of the United States of North America, announces the much lamented death of his son, the Dauphin. The generous conduct of the French Monarch and nation towards this country, renders every event that may affect his or their prosperity, interesting to us; and I shall take care to assure him of the sensibility with which the United States participate in the affliction, which a loss so much to be regretted, must have occasioned both to him and to them.

"GEORGE WASHINGTON"[184]

---

[180] The inspected enrolled bill is in Enrolled Acts, RG 11, DNA. E–45701.
[181] The inspected enrolled bill is in Enrolled Acts, RG 11, DNA. E–45709.
[182] The articles of amendment are on display at the National Archives. E–45717. They are printed in the Appendix to the First Session of the *Senate Legislative Journal.*
[183] On September 29 the president signed the four bills.
[184] The message is in President's Messages: Suggesting legislation, SR, DNA.

"UNITED STATES, September 29, 1789
"GENTLEMEN of the HOUSE of REPRESENTATIVES,

"HAVING been yesterday informed by a joint committee of both Houses of Congress, that they had agreed to a recess, to commence this day, and to continue until the first Monday of January next, I take the earliest opportunity of acquainting you, that, considering how long and laborious this session has been, and the reasons which, I presume, have produced this resolution, it does not appear to me expedient to recommend any measures to their consideration at present.

"GEORGE WASHINGTON"[185]

ORDERED, That the said messages do lie on the table.

On motion,

ORDERED, That it shall be the duty of the Secretary of the Senate, and Clerk of the House, at the end of each session, to send a printed copy of the journals thereof respectively to the supreme executive, and to each branch of the legislature of every state.[186]

ORDERED, That the clerk of this House do carry the said order to the Senate, and desire their concurrence.

A message from the Senate, by Mr. Otis their Secretary.

MR. SPEAKER, The Senate agree to the resolve of this House for continuing John White, John Wright, and Joshua Dawson in office, with several amendments, to which they desire the concurrence of this House: The Senate do also insist on their last amendment disagreed to by this House, to the bill, entitled, "An act to recognize and adapt to the Constitution of the United States, the establishment of the troops raised under the resolves of the United States in Congress assembled, and for other purposes therein mentioned:" And then he withdrew.

The amendments proposed by the Senate to the said resolve were read, and are as follow:

Strike out the words "*thirtieth day of September, 1788*," and insert "fourth day of February, 1789."

Strike out the words "*and be paid accordingly.*"

RESOLVED, That this House doth agree to the said amendments.

ORDERED, That the clerk of this House do acquaint the Senate therewith.

The House proceeded to reconsider the last amendment proposed by the

---

[185] The message is in President's Messages: Suggesting legislation, SR, DNA.

[186] Two letters of transmittal of the Journals of the House, signed by John Beckley, are in Executive Papers, Archives Division, Vi, and the Livingston Papers, MHi.

Senate to the bill, entitled, "An act to recognize and adapt to the Constitution of the United States, the establishment of the troops raised under the resolves of the United States in Congress assembled, and for other purposes therein mentioned:" Whereupon,

RESOLVED, That this House doth recede from their disagreement to the said amendment.

ORDERED, That the clerk of this House do acquaint the Senate therewith.

A message from the Senate, by Mr. Otis their Secretary.

MR. SPEAKER, The Senate have passed a bill, entitled, "An act to allow the Baron de Glaubeck, the pay of a captain in the army of the United States,"[187] to which they desire the concurrence of this House: The Senate have also agreed to the order for transmitting a printed copy of the journals respectively to the supreme executives, and to each branch of the legislatures of every state: And then he withdrew.

The bill sent from the Senate, entitled, "An act to allow the Baron de Glaubeck the pay of a captain in the army of the United States," was read the first time.

On motion,

The said bill was read the second time: And

On motion,

The said bill was read the third time.

RESOLVED, That the said bill do pass.

ORDERED, That the clerk of this House do acquaint the Senate therewith.

A message was received from the President of the United States, notifying that the President approves of the following acts, to wit:

An act entitled, "An act to alter the time for the next meeting of Congress."

An act entitled, "An act providing for the payment of the invalid pensioners of the United States."

An act entitled, "An act making appropriations for the service of the present year:"   Also,

An act entitled, "An act to explain and amend the act, entitled, 'An act for registering and clearing vessels, regulating the coasting trade, and for other purposes;'" and has this day affixed his signature thereto: And the messenger delivered in the said acts, and then withdrew.

ORDERED, That the clerk of this House do acquaint the Senate therewith.

Mr. Partridge, reported from the committee for inrolled bills, that the committee had examined two inrolled bills, one entitled, "An act to recog-

---

[187] The bill is in Engrossed Senate Bills and Resolutions, SR, DNA.

nize and adapt to the Constitution of the United States, the establishment of the troops raised under the resolves of the United States in Congress assembled, and for other purposes therein mentioned;"[188] the other entitled, "An act to allow the Baron de Glaubeck the pay of a captain in the army of the United States;"[189] also, an inrolled resolve for continuing John White, John Wright, and Joshua Dawson, in office until the fourth of February, one thousand seven hundred and eighty-nine,[190] and had found the same to be truly inrolled:[191] Whereupon,

Mr. Speaker signed the said inrolled bills and resolve.

ORDERED, That the door keeper of this House do provide one or more stoves, and necessary fuel, for the accommodation of the House at its next session.

ORDERED, That a message be sent to the Senate, to inform them that this House having completed the business before them, are now about to proceed to close the present session by an adjournment on their part, agreeably to the order of the twenty-sixth instant; and that the clerk of this House do go with the said message.

The clerk accordingly went with the said message, and being returned,

Mr. Speaker adjourned the House until the first Monday in January next.

---

[188] The inspected enrolled bill is in Enrolled Acts, RG 11, DNA. E–45712.

[189] The inspected enrolled bill is in Enrolled Acts, RG 11, DNA. E–45705.

[190] The inspected enrolled resolution is in Enrolled Acts, RG 11, DNA. E–45720.

[191] The committee on enrolled bills also reported on the Courts Bill [S–9] on this date. The inspected enrolled bill is in Enrolled Acts, RG 11, DNA. E–45714.

SECOND SESSION

J O U R N A L

OF THE

HOUSE OF REPRESENTATIVES

OF THE

UNITED STATES

A T a session of the Congress of the United States, begun and held at the city of New-York, on Monday the fourth of January, one thousand seven hundred and ninety; being the second session of the first Congress held under the present Constitution of Government for the United States. On which day, being the day appointed by law for the meeting of the present session, the following members of the House of Representatives appeared and took their seats, to wit:

From New-Hampshire
$\left\{\begin{array}{l}\text{Abiel Foster}\\ \text{Nicholas Gilman and}\\ \text{Samuel Livermore}\end{array}\right.$

From Massachusetts
$\left\{\begin{array}{l}\text{Fisher Ames}\\ \text{Elbridge Gerry}\\ \text{Benjamin Goodhue}\\ \text{Jonathan Grout}\\ \text{George Partridge and}\\ \text{George Thatcher}\end{array}\right.$

From Connecticut
$\left\{\right.$ Roger Sherman

From New-York
$\left\{\begin{array}{l}\text{Egbert Benson}\\ \text{William Floyd and}\\ \text{John Laurance}\end{array}\right.$

From Pennsylvania
$\left\{\begin{array}{l}\text{Frederick Augustus Muhlenberg, Speaker}\\ \text{Peter Muhlenberg and}\\ \text{Thomas Scott}\end{array}\right.$

From Maryland
$\left\{\right.$ Joshua Seney

From Virginia
$\left\{\begin{array}{l}\text{John Brown}\\ \text{Isaac Coles}\\ \text{Samuel Griffin and}\\ \text{Alexander White}\end{array}\right.$

From South-Carolina
$\left\{\begin{array}{l}\text{Aedanus Burke}\\ \text{Daniel Huger}\\ \text{William Smith and}\\ \text{Thomas Tudor Tucker}\end{array}\right.$

From Georgia
$\left\{\right.$ Abraham Baldwin

But a quorum of the whole number not being present,
The House adjourned until to-morrow morning eleven o'clock.

TUESDAY, JANUARY 5, 1790

The House met according to adjournment.

Another member, to wit, Elias Boudinot from New-Jersey, appeared and took his seat.

But a quorum of the whole number not being present,

The House adjourned until to-morrow morning eleven o'clock.

WEDNESDAY, JANUARY 6, 1790

The House met according to adjournment.

Several other members, to wit, from New-Jersey, James Schureman, and from Virginia, John Page and Richard Bland Lee, appeared and took their seats.

But a quorum of the whole number not being present,

The House adjourned until to-morrow morning eleven o'clock.

THURSDAY, JANUARY 7, 1790

The House met according to adjournment.

Several other members, to wit, from Connecticut, Jonathan Sturges and Jeremiah Wadsworth; from New-York, Jeremiah Van Rensselaer; from Maryland, Daniel Carroll; and from Georgia, George Mathews, appeared and took their seats.

And a quorum of the whole number being present,

ORDERED, That a message be sent to the Senate to inform them that a quorum of this House is assembled, and ready to proceed to business; and that the Clerk of this House do go with the said message.

The Speaker laid before the House, a letter from the President of the United States, of the fourth instant, requesting, that when there shall be a sufficient number of the two Houses of Congress assembled to proceed to business, he may be informed of it; and also, at what time and place it will be convenient for Congress, that he should meet them, in order to make some oral communications at the commencement of their session[1]—which was read and ordered to lie on the table.

A message from the Senate, by Mr. Otis their Secretary.

MR. SPEAKER, The Senate have appointed a committee on their part, jointly with such committee as shall be appointed on the part of this House, to wait on the President of the United States, and notify him that a quorum

---

[1] The letter, which was addressed to the vice president, is in President's Messages: Suggesting legislation, SR, DNA. It is printed in the *Senate Legislative Journal* on January 6.

of the two Houses has assembled, and will be ready, in the senate-chamber, at such time as he shall appoint, to receive any communications which he may think proper to make: And then he withdrew.

ORDERED, That Mr. Gilman, Mr. Ames and Mr. Seney, be appointed a committee on the part of this House, for the purpose expressed in the message from the Senate.[2]

On motion,

ORDERED, That a committee be appointed to examine the journal of the last session, and to report therefrom, all such matters of business as were then depending and undetermined; and a committee was appointed, of Mr. Boudinot, Mr. Sherman and Mr. White.[3]

On motion,

RESOLVED, That two Chaplains of different denominations be appointed to Congress, for the present session; one by each House, who shall interchange weekly.[4]

ORDERED, That the Clerk of this House do carry the said resolution to the Senate, and desire their concurrence.[5]

Mr. Gilman, from the committee appointed to wait on the President of the United States, pursuant to the order of to-day, reported, that the committee had, according to order, performed that service, and that the President was pleased to say, he would attend, to make his communication to both Houses of Congress, to-morrow morning, at eleven o'clock.[6]

And then the House adjourned until to-morrow morning, half after ten o'clock.

FRIDAY, JANUARY 8, 1790

Another member, to wit, Henry Wynkoop, from Pennsylvania, appeared and took his seat.

A message from the Senate by Mr. Otis their Secretary.

MR. SPEAKER,   The Senate agree to the resolution of this House, for the appointment of two Chaplains to Congress, for the present session, and have elected the Right Reverend Doctor Samuel Provoost, on their part:[7] The Sen-

---

[2] A copy of the Senate and House orders appointing committees is in Senate Joint and Concurrent Resolutions, SR, DNA.

[3] On January 11 this committee made a report, which is printed in the Journal.

[4] A copy of the resolution is in House Joint and Concurrent Resolutions, SR, DNA.

[5] On January 8 the Senate notified the House that they had agreed to this resolution, and William Linn was elected House chaplain.

[6] On January 8 the president made his state of the union address to Congress.

[7] The Senate resolution and appointment are noted on the House resolution in House Joint and Concurrent Resolutions, SR, DNA.

ate are also now ready in the senate-chamber to attend this House in receiving the communication from the President of the United States: And then he withdrew.

Mr. Speaker, attended by the members of this House, then withdrew to the senate-chamber, for the purpose expressed in the message from the Senate; and being returned,

Mr. Speaker laid before the House a copy of the Speech delivered by the President of the United States, to both Houses of Congress, in the senate-chamber, as followeth:

FELLOW-CITIZENS of the SENATE and HOUSE of REPRESENTATIVES,

I EMBRACE with great satisfaction the opportunity which now presents itself, of congratulating you on the present favorable prospects of our public affairs. The recent accession of the important state of North-Carolina to the Constitution of the United States, (of which official information has been received)—the rising credit and respectability of our country—and the general encreasing good-will towards the Government of the Union—and the concord, peace and plenty, with which we are blessed, are circumstances, auspicious, in an eminent degree, to our national prosperity.

In resuming your consultations for the general good, you cannot but derive encouragement from the reflection, that the measures of the last session have been as satisfactory to your constituents, as the novelty and difficulty of the work allowed you to hope. Still further to realize their expectations, and to secure the blessings which a gracious Providence has placed within our reach, will, in the course of the present important session, call for the cool and deliberate exertion of your patriotism, firmness and wisdom.

Among the many interesting objects, which will engage your attention, that of providing for the common defence, will merit particular regard. To be prepared for war is one of the most effectual means of preserving peace.

A free people ought not only to be armed, but disciplined; to which end, a uniform and well digested plan is requisite: And their safety and interest require that they should promote such manufactories, as tend to render them independent on others, for essential, particularly, for military supplies.

The proper establishment of the troops which may be deemed indispensable, will be entitled to mature consideration. In the arrangements which may be made respecting it, it will be of importance to conciliate the comfortable support of the officers and soldiers, with a due regard to economy.

There was reason to hope, that the pacific measures adopted with regard to certain hostile tribes of Indians, would have relieved the inhabitants of our southern and western frontiers from their depredations. But you will perceive, from the information contained in the papers which I shall direct to be laid before you (comprehending a communication from the commonwealth of Virginia) that we ought to be prepared to afford protection to those parts of the Union; and if necessary, to punish aggressors.

The interest of the United States require, that our intercourse with other nations should be facilitated by such provisions as will enable me to fulfil my duty in that respect, in the manner which circumstances may render most conducive to the public good: And to this end, that the compensations to be made to the persons, who may be employed, should, according to the nature of their appointments, be defined by law; and a competent fund designated for defraying the expences incident to the conduct of our foreign affairs.

Various considerations also render it expedient that the terms on which foreigners may be admitted to the rights of citizens, should be speedily ascertained by a uniform rule of naturalization.

Uniformity in the currency, weights and measures of the United States, is an object of great importance and will, I am persuaded, be duly attended to.

The advancement of agriculture, commerce and manufactures, by all proper means, will not, I trust, need recommendation. But I cannot forbear intimating to you, the expediency of giving effectual encouragement as well to the introduction of new and useful inventions from abroad, as to the exertions of skill and genius in producing them at home; and of facilitating the intercourse between the distant parts of our country, by a due attention to the post-office and post-roads.

Nor am I less persuaded, that you will agree with me in opinion, that there is nothing which can better deserve your patronage, than the promotion of science and literature. Knowledge is, in every country, the surest basis of public happiness. In one, in which the measures of government receive their impression so immediately from the sense of the community, as in our's, it is proportionably essential. To the security of a free Constitution it contributes in various ways: By convincing those who are entrusted with the public administration, that every valuable end of government is best answered by the enlightened confidence of the people; and by teaching the people themselves to know and to value their own rights; to discern and provide against invasions of them; to distinguish between oppression and the necessary exercise of lawful authority; between burthens proceeding from a disregard to their convenience, and those resulting from the inevitable exigencies of society; to discriminate the spirit of liberty from that of licentiousness, cherishing the first, avoiding the last, and uniting a speedy, but temperate vigilance against encroachments, with an inviolable respect to the laws.

Whether this desirable object will be best promoted by affording aids to seminaries of learning already established—by the institution of a national university, or by any other expedients, will be well worthy of a place in the deliberations of the Legislature.

GENTLEMEN of the HOUSE of REPRESENTATIVES,

I saw with peculiar pleasure, at the close of the last session, the resolution entered into by you, expressive of your opinion that an adequate provision for the support of the public credit, is a matter of high importance to the national honor and prosperity. In this sentiment I entirely concur. And to a perfect confidence in your best endeavours to devise such a provision as will be truly consistent with the end, I add an equal reliance on the cheerful co-operation of the other branch of the Legislature. It would be superfluous to specify inducements to a measure, in which the character and permanent interests of the United States are so obviously and so deeply concerned, and which has received so explicit a sanction from your declaration.

GENTLEMEN of the SENATE and HOUSE of REPRESENTATIVES,

I have directed the proper officers to lay before you, respectively, such papers and estimates as regard the affairs particularly recommended to your consideration, and necessary to convey to you that information of the state of the Union, which it is my duty to afford.

The welfare of our country is the great object to which our cares and efforts ought to be directed. And I shall derive great satisfaction from a co-operation with you, in the pleasing, though arduous, task of ensuring to our fellow-citizens the blessings which they have a right to expect from a free, efficient and equal government.

GEORGE WASHINGTON

UNITED STATES, January 8, 1790[8]

On motion,

RESOLVED, That the said Speech be committed to the consideration of a committee of the whole House to-morrow.[9]

The House then proceeded by ballot to the appointment of a Chaplain to Congress, on the part of this House; and upon examining the ballots, a majority of the votes of the whole House was found in favor of the REVEREND DOCTOR WILLIAM LINN.

And then the House adjourned until to-morrow morning eleven o'clock.

SATURDAY, JANUARY 9, 1790

Another member, to wit, George Clymer, from Pennsylvania, appeared and took his seat.

---

[8] The speech is in President's Messages: Annual reports, SR, DNA.

[9] On January 9 the state of the union address was considered in the COWH, and a committee was appointed to prepare an answer to it.

The Speaker laid before the House a letter from the Secretary of the Treasury, stating that he is now ready to report, at such time and in such manner as the House shall be pleased to direct, a plan, which he has prepared, relative to a provision for the support of the public credit, pursuant to an order of this House of the twenty-first of September last: Whereupon,

ORDERED, That on Thursday next, this House will receive, in writing, the report of the Secretary of the department of the Treasury, agreeably to the order of the House of the twenty-first of September last.[10]

The House then, according to the order of the day, resolved itself into a committee of the whole House, on the Speech of the President of the United States to both Houses of Congress.

Mr. Speaker left the chair.

Mr. Baldwin took the chair of the committee.

Mr. Speaker resumed the chair, and Mr. Baldwin reported, that the committee had, according to order, had the said Speech under consideration, and come to a resolution thereupon, which he delivered in at the Clerk's table, where the same was twice read, and, on a question put thereupon, agreed to by the House, as followeth:

RESOLVED, That it is the opinion of this committee, that an address ought to be presented by the House to the President of the United States, in answer to his Speech to both Houses, with assurances that this House will, without delay, proceed to take into their serious consideration, the various and important matters recommended to their attention.

ORDERED, That Mr. Smith, of South-Carolina, Mr. Clymer and Mr. Laurance, be appointed a committee to prepare an address, pursuant to the said resolution.[11]

A petition of Christopher Saddler, of Nova-Scotia, in the dominion of Great-Britain, mariner, was presented to the House and read, praying to be relieved from the forfeiture of his vessel and cargo, which have been seized in the port of Boston, for a violation of the impost law of the United States, of which law the petitioner was wholly ignorant.

ORDERED, That the said petition do lie on the table.[12]

And then the House adjourned until Monday morning eleven o'clock.

MONDAY, JANUARY 11, 1790

Several other members, to wit, from Connecticut, Jonathan Trumbull; from New-York, John Hathorn; and from Virginia, Andrew Moore, appeared and took their seats.

---

[10] On January 14 the secretary of the treasury submitted his report on the public credit to the House.

[11] On January 11 this committee reported.

[12] On January 11 this petition was referred to the secretary of the treasury.

Mr. Boudinot, from the committee appointed to examine the Journal of the last session, and to report therefrom all such matters of business as were then depending and undetermined, made a report, which was read, and is as followeth:

It appears to your committee, that the several petitions of David Ramsay, John Churchman, Alexander Lewis, Arthur Greer, Jedidiah Morse, John Fitch, Angelhart Cruse, Nicholas Pike, Samuel Briggs, John Christopher Stoebel, Leonard Harbaugh, Hannah Adams, Christopher Colles, David Greenleaf, John Macpherson, Abraham Westervelt, James Rumsey, and William Hoy, respectively praying for exclusive privileges, as authors or inventors of some useful work or discovery, were ordered to lie on the table, and so remained during the session.

It further appears to your committee, that the several petitions of Martha Walker, Duncan Campbell, Tristram Coffin, William Finnie, Englebert Kemmena, Thomasin Gordon, Prudent La Jeunesse, Baron de Steuben, and Richard Ham, respectively praying to be compensated for military services, or for injuries or losses sustained during the late war, were referred to the Secretary of the Treasury, to examine and report upon to the present session.[13]

It further appears to your committee, that the several petitions of John McGarragh, Dudley Tyler, Patrick Bennet, John Hurt, James Gibbons, Archibald McAlister, Alexander Power, Attorney for Colonel Flower's regiment, Henry Malcolm and Charles Markle, respectively praying to be compensated for military services rendered during the late war, were referred to the Secretary at War, to examine and report upon to the present session.[14]

It further appears to your committee, that the several petitions of Andrew Newell and Seth Clarke, Sarah Parker, Bartlet Hinds, Robert Frazier, David Sturges, Richard Phillips, James McLean, James Reed and Thomas Barclay,[15] respectively praying that certain claims which they exhibit against the United States, may be considered and allowed, were ordered to lie on the table, and so remained during the session.

It also appears to your committee, that the petition of Joseph Wheaton, serjeant at arms to this House, praying an enquiry into the charges exhibited against him in certain anonymous letters, was ordered to lie on the table, and so remained during the session.

Your committee further report, that committees were appointed to prepare and bring in the several bills following, to wit:

---

[13] On April 6 the secretary of the treasury reported on the petition of Baron de Steuben, and on April 12 he reported on the petition of William Finnie.

[14] On January 15 the secretary of war reported on all of these petitions except that of Alexander Powers. On March 19 the secretary of war reported on the Powers petition.

[15] On February 24 the petition of Thomas Barclay was referred to a committee.

A bill to establish an uniform system, on the subject of bankruptcies throughout the United States.

A bill for the further encouragement of the commerce and navigation of the United States.

A bill providing for the actual enumeration of the inhabitants of the United States.

Also, a bill providing a proper system of regulation for the militia of the United States:

Neither of which bills were reported during the session.

It also appears to your committee, that there were postponed by this House, for further consideration, until the present session, the several bills following, to wit:

A bill to promote the progress of science and useful arts, by securing to authors and inventors the exclusive right to their respective writings and discoveries.

A bill for the establishment of hospitals for the relief of sick and disabled seamen, and prescribing regulations for the harbors of the United States.

A bill concerning the importation of certain persons prior to the year one thousand eight hundred and eight.

A bill to establish a land-office in and for the western territory.   Also,

A bill sent from the Senate, entitled, "An act for the punishment of certain crimes against the United States."

That the bill, entitled, "An act to establish the seat of government of the United States," was postponed by the Senate, for the further consideration of an amendment proposed by this House, until the present session.

And lastly: That the report of the committee appointed to examine into the measures taken by Congress, and the state of Virginia, respecting lands reserved for the officers and soldiers of the said State, was postponed by this House, for further consideration, until the present session.[16]

ORDERED, That the said report do lie on the table.[17]

Mr. Smith (of South-Carolina), from the committee appointed, presented, according to order, an Address to the President of the United States, in answer to his Speech to both Houses of Congress, which was read, and ordered to be committed to a committee of the whole House to-morrow.[18]

On motion,

ORDERED, That the petition of Christopher Saddler, presented on Saturday

---

[16] On January 28 a committee was appointed on this topic.

[17] On January 20 a joint committee was appointed by the House and Senate to confer on the unfinished business of first session.

[18] On January 12 this report was agreed to. The address is printed in the Journal. A committee was appointed to determine a time to meet with the president.

last, be referred to the Secretary of the Treasury, with instruction to examine the same, and report his opinion thereupon to the House.[19]

On motion,

ORDERED, That a committee be appointed to prepare and bring in a bill, providing for the actual enumeration of the inhabitants of the United States:

And a committee was appointed of Mr. Foster, Mr. Goodhue, Mr. Sherman, Mr. Laurance, Mr. Schureman, Mr. Clymer, Mr. Seney, Mr. White, Mr. Smith (of South-Carolina), and Mr. Baldwin.[20]

A message, in writing, was received from the President of the United States, by Mr. Lear, his private Secretary, who delivered in the same, together with the papers therein referred to, and then withdrew.

The said message and papers accompanying it, were read, and are as follow:

UNITED STATES, January 11, 1790

GENTLEMEN of the HOUSE of REPRESENTATIVES,

I HAVE directed Mr. Lear, my private Secretary, to lay before you a copy of the adoption and ratification of the Constitution of the United States, by the state of North-Carolina, together with the copy of a letter from his Excellency Samuel Johnston, President of the Convention of said State, to the President of the United States.

The originals of the papers which are herewith transmitted to you, will be lodged in the office of the Secretary of State.

GEORGE WASHINGTON

FAYETTEVILLE, STATE of NORTH-CAROLINA, 4th December, 1789

SIR,

BY order of the Convention of the people of this State, I have the honor to transmit to you the ratification and adoption of the Constitution of the United States, by the said Convention, in behalf of the people.

With sentiments of the highest consideration and respect, I have the honor to be, Sir, your most faithful and obedient servant,

(Signed) SAMUEL JOHNSTON, President of the Convention

To the PRESIDENT of the UNITED STATES

I DO certify the above to be a true copy from the original.

TOBIAS LEAR, Secretary to the President of the United States

---

[19] On January 19 the secretary reported on this petition, and the report was committed.

[20] On January 18 this committee presented the Enumeration Bill [HR–34], which was read.

A COPY of the ADOPTION and RATIFICATION of the CONSTITUTION of the UNITED STATES, by the STATE of NORTH-CAROLINA

STATE OF NORTH-CAROLINA
IN CONVENTION

WHEREAS the General Convention which met in Philadelphia, in pursuance of a recommendation of Congress, did recommend to the citizens of the United States, a Constitution or Form of Government, in the following words, viz.

"WE the People," &c.

[Here follows the Constitution of the United States, verbatim.]

RESOLVED, That this Convention, in behalf of the freemen, citizens and inhabitants of the state of North-Carolina, do adopt and ratify the said Constitution and Form of Government.

DONE in Convention, this twenty-first day of November, one thousand seven hundred and eighty-nine.

(Signed) SAMUEL JOHNSTON, President of the Convention

J. HUNT
JAS. TAYLOR } Secretaries

BY the direction of the President of the United States, I have examined and compared the foregoing with the adoption and ratification of the Constitution of the United States, by the state of North-Carolina, which was transmitted to the President of the United States, by Samuel Johnston, President of the Convention of said State, as well as the transcript of the Constitution of the United States, recited in the said ratification, which I certify to be a true copy.

TOBIAS LEAR, Secretary to the President of the United States[21]

ORDERED, That the said message and papers do lie on the table.

And then the House adjourned until to-morrow morning eleven o'clock.

TUESDAY, JANUARY 12, 1790

The House, according to the order of the day, resolved itself into a committee of the whole House, on the Address to the President of the United States, in answer to his Speech to both Houses of Congress.

Mr. Speaker left the chair.

---

[21] The message with enclosures is in President's Messages: Suggesting legislation, SR, DNA. The ratification is E–45544.

Mr. Baldwin took the chair of the committee.

Mr. Speaker resumed the chair, and Mr. Baldwin reported, that the committee had, according to order, had the said Address under consideration, and made no amendment thereto.

RESOLVED UNANIMOUSLY, That this House doth agree to the said Address, in the words following, to wit:

SIR,

THE REPRESENTATIVES of the People of the United States, have taken into consideration your Speech to both Houses of Congress, at the opening of the present session.

We reciprocate your congratulations on the accession of the state of North-Carolina; an event, which while it is a testimony of the encreasing good-will towards the Government of the Union, cannot fail to give additional dignity and strength to the American Republic, already rising in the estimation of the world, in national character and respectability.

The information that our measures of the last session have not proved dissatisfactory to our constituents, affords us much encouragement at this juncture, when we are resuming the arduous task of legislating for so extensive an empire.

Nothing can be more gratifying to the Representatives of a free People, than the reflection, that their labors are rewarded by the approbation of their fellow-citizens. Under this impression, we shall make every exertion to realize their expectations, and to secure to them those blessings which Providence has placed within their reach. Still prompted by the same desire to promote their interests which then actuated us, we shall, in the present session, diligently and anxiously pursue those measures which shall appear to us conducive to that end.

We concur with you in the sentiment, that agriculture, commerce and manufactures, are entitled to legislative protection, and that the promotion of science and literature will contribute to the security of a free government; in the progress of our deliberations, we shall not lose sight of objects so worthy of our regard.

The various and weighty matters which you have judged necessary to recommend to our attention, appear to us essential to the tranquility and welfare of the Union, and claim our early and most serious consideration. We shall proceed, without delay, to bestow on them that calm discussion which their importance requires.

We regret that the pacific arrangements pursued with regard to certain hostile tribes of Indians, have not been attended with that success which we had reason to expect from them: We shall not hesitate to concur in such further measures as may best obviate any ill effects which might be apprehended from the failure of those negociations.

Your approbation of the vote of this House, at the last session, respecting the provision for the public creditors, is very acceptable to us: The proper mode of carrying that resolution into effect, being a subject in which the future character and happiness of these States are deeply involved, will be among the first to deserve our attention.

The prosperity of the United States is the primary object of all our deliberations; and we cherish the reflection, that every measure which we may adopt for its advancement, will not only receive your cheerful concurrence, but will at the same time derive from your co-operation, additional efficacy, in ensuring to our fellow-citizens the blessings of a free, efficient and equal government.

RESOLVED, That Mr. Speaker, attended by the House, do present the said Address; and that Mr. Smith, of South-Carolina, Mr. Clymer and Mr. Laurance, be a committee to wait on the President, to know when and where it will be convenient for him to receive the same.[22]

A message, in writing, was received from the President of the United States, by the Secretary at War, accompanied by a statement of the southwestern frontier, and of the Indian department, which were partly read.[23]

And then the House adjourned until to-morrow morning eleven o'clock.

WEDNESDAY, JANUARY 13, 1790

Several other members, to wit, from Connecticut, Benjamin Huntington; from New-Jersey, Lambert Cadwalader; from Pennsylvania, Daniel Hiester; and from Maryland, William Smith, appeared and took their seats.

On motion,

ORDERED, That so much of the standing rules and orders of this House, as directs the mode of appointing committees, be rescinded; and that hereafter it be a standing rule of the House, that all committees shall be appointed by the Speaker, unless otherwise specially directed by the House, in which case they shall be appointed by ballot; and if upon such ballot, the number required shall not be elected by a majority of the votes given, the House shall

---

[22] On January 13 this committee reported.

[23] The message with a copy of the enclosures is in President's Messages: Transmitting reports from the Secretary of War, SR, DNA. The enclosures are in Reports and Communications from the Secretary of War, HR, DNA. Another copy of the enclosures is in A Record of the Reports of the Secretary of War, vol. 1, HR, DNA. Two of the documents, the instructions to (August 29, 1789) and the report of (November 17, 1789) the commissioners for southern indians, are printed in the *Senate Executive Journal* under Indian Relations—Southern. On January 13 the House completed the reading of this report and committed it.

proceed to a second ballot, in which a plurality of votes shall prevail; and in case a greater number than are required to compose or complete the committee shall have an equal number of votes, the House shall proceed to a further ballot or ballots.

The House resumed the reading of the statement of the south-western frontiers, and of the Indian department, as referred to in the President's message of yesterday; and having gone through the same.

ORDERED, That the said message and statement be referred to a committee of five, and that Mr. Wadsworth, Mr. Brown, Mr. Boudinot, Mr. Burke, and Mr. Baldwin, be of the said committee.[24]

Mr. Smith, of South-Carolina, from the committee appointed to wait on the President of the United States, to know when and where it will be convenient to him, to receive the address of this House, in answer to his speech to both Houses of Congress, reported,

That the committee had, according to order, waited on the President, and that he signified to them that it would be convenient to him to receive the said address at twelve o'clock to-morrow, at his own house.[25]

And then the House adjourned until to-morrow morning eleven o'clock.

THURSDAY, JANUARY 14, 1790

Two other members, to wit, from Massachusetts, Theodore Sedgwick; and from Pennsylvania, Thomas Hartley, appeared and took their seats.

On motion,

ORDERED, That Mr. Livermore, Mr. Ames, Mr. Laurance, Mr. Scott, and Mr. Smith (of Maryland) be added to the committee appointed yesterday, and to whom was referred the message of the President of the United States of Tuesday last, together with the statement of the southwestern frontiers, and of the Indian department.[26]

Mr. Speaker, attended by the House, then withdrew to the house of the President of the United States, and there presented to him the address of this House in answer to his speech to both Houses of Congress, to which the President made the following reply:

GENTLEMEN,

I RECEIVE with pleasure the assurances you give me, that you will diligently and anxiously pursue such measures as shall appear to you conducive to the interest of your constituents; and that an early and serious consideration will be given to the various and weighty matters recommended by me to your attention.

---

[24] On January 14 several members were added to this committee.
[25] On January 14 the House presented its address to the president and he replied.
[26] On January 20 this committee reported.

I have full confidence, that your deliberations will continue to be directed by an enlightened and virtuous zeal for the happiness of our country.

G. WASHINGTON

Mr. Speaker and the members being returned into the House,

The Speaker laid before the House a letter from the Secretary of the Treasury, accompanied with his report relative to a provision for the support of the public credit,[27] made pursuant to the order of this House of Saturday last; and the said report, with the papers therein referred to, being read,

RESOLVED, That this House will, on this day fortnight, resolve itself into a committee of the whole House, to take into consideration the said report and papers.

ORDERED, That three hundred copies of the said report and papers be forthwith struck for the use of the members of both Houses.[28]

And then the House adjourned until to-morrow morning eleven o'clock.

FRIDAY, JANUARY 15, 1790

Another member, to wit, James Jackson, from Georgia, appeared and took his seat.

A memorial of John Cochran, late receiver of continental taxes in the state of New-York, and commissioner of the loan-office for the same, was presented to the House and read, praying that a further allowance may be made him for his services and expences in the said two offices, the salary allowed by the late Congress having been very inadequate thereto. Also,

A petition of William Montgomery and Abraham Owen, praying that any exclusive privilege which Congress shall judge proper to grant to James Rumsey, as the author of certain devices and inventions, may be restricted to the plans or specifications thereof deposited by the said Rumsey in the files of Congress, in such manner that the petitioners or others may not be precluded from making or using any machinery not comprised in the said plans or specifications.

ORDERED, That the said memorial and petition do lie on the table.

The Speaker laid before the House a letter from the Secretary at War, accompanied by his reports on the several petitions of James Gibbon and Archibald McAlister, Dudley Tyler, Charles Markley, John Hurt, Patrick Bennet, Henry Malcolm, and John McGarragh, which were referred to him to ex-

---

[27] A copy of the report is in A Record of the Reports of the Secretary of the Treasury, vol. 1, HR, DNA. E–22998.

[28] Consideration of this report in the COWH was postponed as an order of the day from January 28 through February 5. On February 8 the COWH considered this report.

amine and report upon by an order of this House of the twenty-fifth of September last.[29]

The said letter and reports were read, and ordered to lie on the table.[30]

The House then, according to the standing order of the day, resolved itself into a committee of the whole House on the state of the Union.

Mr. Speaker left the chair.

Mr. Baldwin took the chair of the committee.

Mr. Speaker resumed the chair, and Mr. Baldwin reported, that the committee had, according to order, had the state of the Union under consideration, and had come to a resolution thereupon, which he delivered in at the Clerk's table, where the same was read, and is as followeth:

RESOLVED, That it is the opinion of this committee, that the several matters recommended by the President of the United States, in his speech to both Houses of Congress, relating to a provision for the national defence; to the promotion of manufactories, for essential, particularly for military supplies; to a compensation to the persons employed in the intercourse between the United States and foreign nations; to the establishing a uniform rule of naturalization; to the establishment of uniformity in the currency, weights and measures; to the advancement of the agriculture, commerce and manufactures of the United States; to the encouragement of useful inventions; to the establishment of post-offices and post-roads; and to the promotion of science and literature, ought, severally, to be referred to select committees to be appointed by the House, to prepare and bring in a bill or bills, providing for each particular purpose.

The said resolution being again read,

ORDERED, That a committee be appointed to prepare and bring in a bill or bills, providing for the national defence; and that Mr. Gilman, Mr. Peter Muhlenberg, Mr. Hiester, Mr. Mathews, and Mr. Floyd, be of the said committee.[31]

ORDERED, That a committee be appointed to prepare and bring in a bill or bills, for making compensation to persons employed in the intercourse between the United States and foreign nations; and that Mr. Sedgwick, Mr. Huntington, and Mr. Lee, be of the said committee.[32]

---

[29] Copies of all of these reports are in A Record of the Reports of the Secretary of War, vol. 1, HR, DNA.

[30] On March 19 the reports on the petitions of James Gibbon and Archibald McAlister were considered, and the petitioners were given leave to withdraw their petitions. On April 26 the petition of Charles Markley was referred to the committee to prepare the Disabled Soldiers and Seamen Bill [HR–88].

[31] On January 21 the secretary of war's plan for the militia of the United States was sent to the House. On March 17 a petition was committed to the committee to prepare a Militia Bill [HR–81].

[32] On January 19 this committee was further instructed.

ORDERED, That a committee be appointed to prepare and bring in a bill or bills, for establishing a uniform rule of naturalization; and that Mr. Hartley, Mr. Tucker, and Mr. Moore, be of the said committee.[33]

ORDERED, That it be referred to the Secretary of the Treasury to prepare and report to this House, a proper plan or plans, conformably to the recommendation of the President of the United States, in his speech to both Houses of Congress, for the encouragement and promotion of such manufactories as will tend to render the United States independent of other nations, for essential, particularly for military supplies.

ORDERED, That it be referred to the Secretary of State to prepare and report to this House, in like manner, a proper plan or plans for establishing uniformity in the currency, weights and measures of the United States.[34]

On motion,

ORDERED, That a committee be appointed to prepare and bring in a bill or bills, to make such alteration in the laws of the United States, as are necessary to conform the same to the present circumstances of the state of North-Carolina; and that Mr. Benson, Mr. Trumbull, and Mr. Cadwalader, do prepare and bring in the same.[35]

And then the House adjourned until Monday morning eleven o'clock.

MONDAY, JANUARY 18, 1790

Two other members, to wit, from New-Jersey, Thomas Sinnickson; and from Maryland, Michael Jenifer Stone, appeared and took their seats.

A petition of James Hubbs, of the state of New-Jersey, mariner, was presented to the House and read, praying to be relieved from a prosecution commenced against him at the suit of the United States, for the sum of four hundred dollars, being the penalty fixed by law for transporting goods from one district to another of the same State, without a manifest, of which law, at the time of committing the offence, he was wholly ignorant.

ORDERED, That the said petition, together with the memorial of John Cochran, presented on Friday last, be referred to the Secretary of the Treasury, with instruction to examine the same, and report his opinion thereupon to the House.

A petition of Hannibal William Dobbyn, of the kingdom of Ireland, was presented to the House and read, setting forth that he is desirous of becoming a citizen of the United States, and of making a considerable purchase of the

---

[33] On January 25 this committee presented the Naturalization Bill [HR–37], which was read.

[34] On July 13 the secretary of state reported to the House.

[35] On January 25 this committee presented the North Carolina Bill [HR–36], which was read twice.

public lands; and praying that the Secretary of the Treasury may be authorised to contract with him for that purpose.

ORDERED, That the said petition be referred to Mr. Page, Mr. Scott, and Mr. Partridge, that they do examine the matter thereof, and report the same with their opinion thereupon to the House.[36]

The Speaker laid before the House a letter from Gerard Bancker, treasurer of the state of New-York, accompanied with a copy of the laws of the said State, transmitted for the use of this House, pursuant to concurrent resolutions of the Senate and Assembly of the said State.[37]

ORDERED, That the said letter do lie on the table.

Mr. Foster, from the committee appointed, presented, according to order, a bill providing for the actual enumeration of the inhabitants of the United States, which was received and read the first time.[38]

And then the House adjourned until to-morrow morning eleven o'clock.

TUESDAY, JANUARY 19, 1790

A petition of Benjamin Bird, of Waltham in the state of Massachusetts, was presented to the House and read, praying that there may be granted to him, under such restrictions or bonds, as Congress shall require, duplicates of eight continental loan-office certificates, amounting to three thousand four hundred dollars, the property of the petitioner, and which he casually lost some time in the year one thousand seven hundred and seventy-eight. Also,

The several petitions of Nathan Fuller, of the same State, and of Salmon Burr, Lemuel Cravath, John Holbrook, Jeremiah Ryan, Ezra Smith, and Ruth Roberts, relict of Lemuel Roberts, deceased, of the state of Connecticut, praying that their respective claims for losses or injuries sustained in the service of the United States, during the late war, may be liquidated and satisfied.

ORDERED, That the said petitions do lie on the table.[39]

A bill providing for the actual enumeration of the inhabitants of the United States, was read the second time, and ordered to be committed to a committee of the whole House on Friday next.[40]

On motion,

ORDERED, That it be an instruction to the committee appointed to prepare and bring in a bill or bills, for making compensation to persons employed in the intercourse between the United States and foreign nations, to include

---

[36] On January 19 this committee reported.

[37] The letter, as sent to the Senate, is in Reports and Communications, SR, DNA.

[38] On January 19 this bill was read again.

[39] On January 20 all of these petitions, except that of Lemuel Cravath and that of John Holbrook, were referred to the secretary of war.

[40] On January 22 consideration of this bill was postponed. On January 25 it was considered in the COWH.

therein a compensation to persons who may be employed in such inter-course.[41]

Mr. Page, from the committee to whom was referred the petition of Hannibal William Dobbyn, made a report, which was read, and ordered to lie on the table.[42]

The Speaker laid before the House a letter from the Secretary of the Treasury, enclosing his report on the petition of Christopher Saddler, which was read, and ordered to be referred to Mr. Ames, Mr. Sturges, Mr. Stone, Mr. Griffin, and Mr. Wynkoop.[43]

On motion,

ORDERED, That the Secretary of the Treasury be directed to report to this House, such information as he may have obtained, respecting any difficulties which may have occurred in the execution of the several laws for collecting duties on goods, wares and merchandizes, and on tonnage, and for regulating the coasting trade, together with his opinion thereupon.[44]

And then the House adjourned until to-morrow morning eleven o'clock.

WEDNESDAY, JANUARY 20, 1790

Two other members, to wit, James Madison, junior, and Josiah Parker, from Virginia, appeared and took their seats.

ORDERED, That the several petitions of Ruth Roberts, Jeremiah Ryan, Ezra Smith, and Salmon Burr, which were presented yesterday, be referred to the Secretary at War, with instruction that he do examine the same, and report his opinion thereupon to the House.[45]

A petition of sundry inhabitants of the county of Westchester, in the state of New-York, was presented to the House and read, praying to be compensated for considerable quantities of wheat, rye, corn, oats and hay, cattle, sheep and hogs, which were taken from them during the late war, for the use of the army.

ORDERED, That the said petition do lie on the table.

---

[41] On January 21 this committee presented the Foreign Intercourse Bill [HR–35], which was read.

[42] A copy of the report is in A Record of the Reports of Select Committees, HR, DNA. On January 20 this committee report was considered, and the secretary of the treasury was ordered to report a system for the disposition of the public lands.

[43] Copies of the letter and report are in A Record of the Reports of the Secretary of the Treasury, vol. 1, HR, DNA. On January 26 this committee reported, and another committee was appointed to prepare a bill. On the same day this committee presented a Mitigation of Fines Bill [HR–38].

[44] On April 23 the secretary submitted his report on the revenue laws, and it was committed.

[45] On February 5 the secretary reported on all of these petitions except that of Jeremiah Ryan. The secretary's report on the Ryan petition was received on March 16.

The House proceeded to consider the report of the committee on the petition of Hannibal William Dobbyn: Whereupon,

ORDERED, That the said report do lie on the table; and that the Secretary of the Treasury be directed to report to this House, a uniform system for the disposition of lands the property of the United States.[46]

On motion,

ORDERED, That the state of facts respecting the western territory, reported by a committee of this House, the last session, be referred to the Secretary of the Treasury for his information.[47]

Mr. Wadsworth, from the committee to whom was referred the message from the President of the United States, with the statement of the southwestern frontier, and of the Indian department, made a report, which was read, and ordered to lie on the table.[48]

A message from the Senate by Mr. Otis their Secretary.

MR. SPEAKER,   The Senate have agreed to a resolution appointing a committee on their part, to confer with such committee as may be appointed on the part of this House, to consider and report whether or not the business begun previous to the late adjournment of Congress, shall now be proceeded in as if no adjournment had taken place; to which they desire the concurrence of this House: And then he withdrew.

The said resolution being twice read at the Clerk's table,

RESOLVED, That this House doth agree to the same, and that Mr. Sherman, Mr. Thatcher, Mr. Hartley, Mr. White, and Mr. Jackson, be a committee on the part of this House for the purpose therein mentioned.[49]

And then the House adjourned until to-morrow morning eleven o'clock.

THURSDAY, JANUARY 21, 1790

Several other members, to wit, from Massachusetts, George Leonard; from New-York, Peter Silvester; and from Pennsylvania, Thomas Fitzsimons, appeared and took their seats.

A petition of Lemuel Miller, of the state of Massachusetts, was presented to the House and read, praying to be allowed the commutation of half pay, for his services five years and five months, as a lieutenant in the army during the late war.

---

[46] On January 27 the Dobbyn petition was referred to the secretary of the treasury. On July 22 the secretary of the treasury made his report on the disposition of public lands.

[47] This committee report was presented to the House on June 15, 1789.

[48] On January 21 this committee report was considered in the COWH.

[49] Copies of the House and Senate resolutions on unfinished business are in Senate Joint and Concurrent Resolutions, SR, DNA. On January 22 this committee reported.

ORDERED, That the said petition do lie on the table.

On motion,

ORDERED, That the petition of David Sturges, which was presented at the last session, praying to be allowed a pension in consideration of a wound in his left hand, which he received in the service of the United States, during the late war, be referred to the Secretary at War, with instruction that he do examine the same, and report his opinion thereupon to the House.

A message, in writing, was received from the President of the United States, by the Secretary at War, who delivered in the same, together with the Plan therein referred to, and then withdrew.

The said message was then read, and is as followeth:

UNITED STATES, January 21, 1790

GENTLEMEN of the SENATE and HOUSE of REPRESENTATIVES,

THE Secretary of the department of War, has submitted to me certain principles to serve as a Plan for the general arrangement of the Militia of the United States.

Conceiving the subject to be of the greatest importance to the welfare of our country, and liable to be placed in various points of view, I have directed him to lay the Plan before Congress for their information, that they may make such use thereof as they shall judge proper.

G. WASHINGTON[50]

ORDERED, That the said message and plan be referred to the committee of the whole House on the state of the Union.[51]

ORDERED, That three hundred copies of the said plan be forthwith struck for the use of the members of both Houses.

Mr. Sedgwick, from the committee appointed, presented, according to order, a bill providing the means of intercourse between the United States and foreign nations, which was received and read the first time.[52]

On motion,

The report of the committee to whom was referred the message from the President of the United States, with the statement of the south-western frontier, and of the Indian department, was read the second time, and ordered to be committed to a committee of the whole House immediately.

---

[50] The message is in President's Messages: Transmitting reports from the Secretary of War, SR, DNA. The enclosures are in Transcribed Reports and Communications from the Executive Departments, 1789–1814, Records of the Secretary, SR, DNA. Another copy of the enclosures is in A Record of the Reports of the Secretary of War, vol. 1, HR, DNA. E–22987, E–22988.

[51] On April 26 the COWH was discharged from considering the secretary's plan for the militia, and the plan was committed to the committee to prepare the Militia Bill [HR–81].

[52] On January 22 this bill was read again.

The House accordingly resolved itself into the said committee.

Mr. Speaker left the chair.

Mr. Baldwin took the chair of the committee.

Mr. Speaker resumed the chair, and Mr. Baldwin reported, that the committee had, according to order, had the said report under consideration, and agreed thereto without any amendment.

The House proceeded to consider the said report, and after some time spent therein,[53]

The House adjourned until to-morrow morning eleven o'clock.

FRIDAY, JANUARY 22, 1790

The Speaker laid before the House a letter from the Secretary of the Treasury, accompanying a report made to him by the Postmaster-general, respecting the post-office, and suggesting a plan for its future establishment; which was read, and ordered to be referred to Mr. Fitzsimons, Mr. Gerry, Mr. Sinnickson, Mr. Parker, and Mr. Stone—that they do examine the matter thereof, and report the same, with their opinion thereupon, to the House.[54]

A bill providing the means of intercourse between the United States and foreign nations, was read the second time, and ordered to be committed to a committee of the whole House on Monday next.[55]

Mr. Sherman, from the committee appointed to confer with the committee appointed by the Senate, to consider and report, whether or not the business begun previous to the late adjournment of Congress, shall now be proceeded in as if no adjournment had taken place, reported,[56] that in the opinion of the committee, the business unfinished between the two Houses at the late adjournment, ought to be regarded as if it had not been passed upon by either.

ORDERED, That the said report do lie on the table.[57]

The order of the day for the House to resolve itself into a committee of the whole House, on the bill providing for the actual enumeration of the inhabitants of the United States, was read, and postponed until Monday next.

And then the House adjourned until Monday morning, eleven o'clock.

---

[53] The Journal does not record any further action on the committee report on the southwest frontiers and Indian Department, but on March 30 this committee presented the Indian Trade Bill [HR–51], which was read.

[54] This report is E–22978. On February 9 a petition from mail contractors was referred to this committee.

[55] On January 25 consideration of this bill was postponed. The bill was considered in the COWH on January 26.

[56] A copy of the report is in A Record of the Reports of Select Committees, HR, DNA.

[57] On January 25 the Senate and House agreed to a resolution on the unfinished business of first session.

MONDAY, JANUARY 25, 1790

A petition of James Price, was presented to the House, and read, praying that his claim for supplies furnished to the American army in Canada, during the late war, may be liquidated and satisfied:[58]

Also, a petition of Gabriel Allen, of the state of New-Jersey, praying that duplicates may be granted him of certain continental loan-office certificates, of which he was possessed and casually lost sometime in the year 1778.

ORDERED, That the said petitions do lie on the table.

A message, in writing, was received from the President of the United States, by Mr. Lear, his secretary, who delivered in the same, together with the papers therein referred to, and then withdrew.

The said message and papers were read, and are as follow:

UNITED STATES, January 25, 1790

GENTLEMEN of the SENATE and HOUSE of REPRESENTATIVES,

I HAVE received from his Excellency John E. Howard, Governor of the state of Maryland, an act of the legislature of Maryland, to ratify certain articles in addition to, and amendment of the Constitution of the United States of America, proposed by Congress to the legislatures of the several states; and have directed my Secretary to lay a copy of the same before you, together with the copy of a letter accompanying the above act, from his Excellency the Governor of Maryland, to the President of the United States.

The originals will be deposited in the office of the Secretary of State.

G. WASHINGTON

(Copy)

ANNAPOLIS, January 15, 1790

SIR,

I have the honor to enclose a copy of an act of the legislature of Maryland, to ratify certain articles in addition to, and amendment of the Constitution of the United States of America, proposed by Congress to the legislatures of the several States.

I have the honor to be, with the highest respect,
Sir, your most obedient servant,
(Signed)   J. E. HOWARD

His Excellency the PRESIDENT of the UNITED STATES

———————

I do certify the foregoing to be a true copy from the original letter, from John E. Howard, Governor of the State of Maryland, to the President of the United States.

TOBIAS LEAR, Secretary to the President of the United States

[58] On January 26 this petition was committed.

(Copy)

An act to ratify certain articles in addition to, and amendment of the Constitution of the United States of America, proposed by Congress to the legislatures of the several States

WHEREAS, it is provided by the fifth article of the Constitution of the United States of America, that Congress, whenever two-thirds of both Houses shall deem it necessary, shall propose amendments to the said Constitution, or on the application of the legislatures of two-thirds of the several States, shall call a convention for proposing amendments, which in either case shall be valid to all intents and purposes as part of the said Constitution, when ratified by the legislatures of three-fourths of the several States, or by conventions, in three-fourths thereof, as the one or the other mode of ratification may be proposed by the Congress. And whereas, at a session of the United States, in Congress assembled, begun and held at the city of New-York, on Wednesday, the fourth day of March, in the year of our Lord, one thousand seven hundred and eighty-nine, it was resolved by the Senate and House of Representatives of the said United States in Congress assembled, two-thirds of both Houses concurring, that the following articles be proposed to the legislatures of the several States, as amendments to the Constitution of the United States, all, or any of which articles, when ratified by three-fourths of the said legislatures, to be valid to all intents and purposes as part of the said Constitution, viz.

[Here follow the several articles of amendment, in the words agreed to by Congress.]

Be it enacted, by the General Assembly of Maryland, that the aforesaid articles, and each of them be, and they are hereby confirmed and ratified.

By the HOUSE of DELEGATES, December 17, 1789
Read and assented to,
By order,
(Signed) W. HARWOOD, Clerk

By the SENATE, December 19, 1789
Read and assented to,
By order,
H. RIDGELY, Clerk

(Signed) J. E. HOWARD $\left(\begin{smallmatrix}\text{Seal Ap-}\\\text{pendant}\end{smallmatrix}\right)$

I hereby certify that the above is a true copy from the original engrossed act, as passed by the legislature of the State of Maryland.
(Signed) T. JOHNSON, jun. Clerk Council

MARYLAND, SS.

In testimony that Thomas Johnson, jun. is clerk of the executive council of the State of Maryland, I have hereto affixed the great seal of the said State. Witness my hand, this fifteenth day of January, Anno Domini, 1790.

(Signed)   SAMUEL HARVEY HOWARD, Reg. Cur. Can.

I certify the foregoing to be a true copy of the act, transmitted to the President of the United States, by J. E. Howard, Governor of the State of Maryland.

TOBIAS LEAR, Secretary to the President of the United States[59]

ORDERED, That the said message and papers do lie on the table.

The House, according to the order of the day, resolved itself into a committee of the whole House, on the bill providing for the actual enumeration of the inhabitants of the United States.

Mr. Speaker left the chair.

Mr. Baldwin took the chair of the committee.

Mr. Speaker resumed the chair, and Mr. Baldwin reported, that the committee had, according to order, had the said bill under consideration, and made some progress therein.

RESOLVED, That this House will, to-morrow, again resolve itself into a committee of the whole House on the said bill.[60]

A message from the Senate by Mr. Otis their Secretary.

MR. SPEAKER,   The Senate have agreed to a resolution, that the business unfinished between the two Houses at the late adjournment, ought to be regarded as if it had not been passed upon by either,[61] to which they desire the concurrence of this House: And then he withdrew.

The House proceeded to consider the said resolution; and the same being twice read at the Clerk's table, was, on the question put thereupon, agreed to by the House.

ORDERED, That the Clerk of this House do acquaint the Senate therewith.

Mr. Benson, from the committee appointed, presented, according to order, a bill for giving effect to the several acts therein mentioned, in respect to the state of North-Carolina, which was received and read the first time.

---

[59] The message with enclosures is in President's Messages: Suggesting legislation, SR, DNA. The articles of amendment to the Constitution mentioned in the ratification documents are printed in the Appendix to the Second Session.

[60] On January 26 the COWH reported amendments to this bill. The bill, together with the amendments, was recommitted.

[61] A copy of the resolution is in Senate Joint and Concurrent Resolutions, SR, DNA.

Mr. Hartley, from the committee appointed, presented, according to order, a bill establishing an uniform rule of naturalization, which was received and read the first time.[62]

On motion,

The bill for giving effect to the several acts therein mentioned, in respect to the state of North-Carolina, was read the second time, and ordered to be committed to a committee of the whole House to-morrow.[63]

On motion,

ORDERED, That a committee be appointed to prepare and bring in a bill or bills, making a general provision for securing to authors and inventors the exclusive right to their respective writings and discoveries; and that Mr. Burke, Mr. Huntington, and Mr. Cadwalader, do prepare and bring in the same.[64]

The order of the day for the House to resolve itself into a committee of the whole House, on the bill providing the means of intercourse between the United States and foreign nations, was read and postponed until to-morrow.

And then the House adjourned until to-morrow morning, eleven o'clock.

TUESDAY, JANUARY 26, 1790

A petition of Rufus Lincoln, of Taunton in the state of Massachusetts, was presented to the House, and read, praying compensation for his services as a recruiting officer during the late war.

Also, a petition of the merchants and other inhabitants of the town of Portland, in the said State, praying that sundry inconveniencies which they suggest have arisen in the execution of the laws of impost, and for regulating the coasting trade, may be remedied, and the said laws amended.[65]

ORDERED, That the said petitions do lie on the table.

The House, according to the order of the day, resolved itself into a committee of the whole House, on the bill for giving effect to the several acts therein mentioned, in respect to the state of North-Carolina.

Mr. Speaker left the chair.

Mr. Baldwin took the chair of the committee.

Mr. Speaker resumed the chair; and Mr. Baldwin reported, that the committee had, according to order, had the said bill under consideration, and gone through the same, and made several amendments thereto, which he delivered in at the Clerk's table, where the same were twice read, and agreed to by the House.

---

[62] On January 26 this bill was read again.
[63] On January 26 this bill was considered in the COWH and amended.
[64] On January 28 this committee reported a Copyright Bill [HR-39], which was read. The House then further instructed the committee concerning patents.
[65] A draft of the petition is in Office of the City Clerk, Portland, Maine.

ORDERED, That the said bill, with the amendments, be engrossed, and read the third time to-morrow.[66]

A bill establishing an uniform rule of naturalization, was read the second time, and ordered to be committed to a committee of the whole House, on Tuesday next.[67]

ORDERED, That the petition of James Price, presented yesterday, be referred to Mr. Ames, Mr. Fitzsimons, and Mr. Boudinot; that they do examine the matter thereof, and report the same, with their opinion thereupon, to the House.[68]

The House, according to the order of the day, again resolved itself into a committee of the whole House, on the bill providing for the actual enumeration of the inhabitants of the United States.

Mr. Speaker left the chair.

Mr. Baldwin took the chair of the committee.

Mr. Speaker resumed the chair; and Mr. Baldwin reported, that the committee had, according to order, again had the said bill under consideration, and gone through the same, and made several amendments thereto, which he delivered in at the Clerk's table, where the same were read: Whereupon,

ORDERED, That the said bill, with the amendments, be re-committed to Mr. Foster, Mr. Goodhue, Mr. Sherman, Mr. Laurance, Mr. Schureman, Mr. Clymer, Mr. Seney, Mr. White, Mr. Smith (of South-Carolina), Mr. Baldwin, and Mr. Madison.[69]

Mr. Ames, from the committee to whom was referred the report from the Secretary of the Treasury, on the petition of Christopher Saddler, made a report,[70] which was twice read, and agreed to by the House, as followeth:

That, in the opinion of the committee, provision ought to be made by law for the remission or mitigation of fines, forfeitures and penalties, in certain cases.

ORDERED, That a bill or bills be brought in, pursuant to the said report; and that Mr. Ames, Mr. Sturges, Mr. Stone, Mr. Griffin, and Mr. Wynkoop, do prepare and bring in the same.

The House, according to the order of the day, resolved itself into a committee of the whole House, on the bill providing the means of intercourse between the United States and foreign nations.

Mr. Speaker left the chair.

---

[66] On January 27 this bill was read again, agreed to, and sent to the Senate.

[67] On February 3 this bill was considered in the COWH.

[68] On May 7 this committee reported.

[69] On February 2 this committee reported amendments to this bill, which were agreed to by the House.

[70] A copy of the report is in A Record of the Reports of Select Committees, HR, DNA.

Mr. Baldwin took the chair of the committee.

Mr. Speaker resumed the chair; and Mr. Baldwin reported, that the committee had, according to order, had the said bill under consideration, and made some progress therein.

RESOLVED, That this House will, to-morrow, again resolve itself into a committee of the whole House on the said bill.[71]

Mr. Ames, from the committee appointed, presented, according to order, a bill to provide for the remission or mitigation of fines, forfeitures and penalties in certain cases; which was received and read the first time.[72]

A message from the Senate by Mr. Otis their Secretary.

MR. SPEAKER,   I am directed by the Senate to bring to this House a letter addressed to the Congress of the United States, from Gaetan Drago de Dominico, dated Genoa, the twenty-first of September, one thousand seven hundred and eighty-nine:[73]   And he delivered in the same, and then withdrew.

And then the House adjourned until to-morrow morning eleven o'clock.

WEDNESDAY, JANUARY 27, 1790

An engrossed bill for giving effect to the several acts therein mentioned, in respect to the state of North-Carolina, was read the third time.

RESOLVED, That the said bill do pass, and that the title be, "An act for giving effect to the several acts therein mentioned, in respect to the state of North-Carolina."

ORDERED, That the Clerk of this House do carry the said bill to the Senate, and desire their concurrence.[74]

A bill to provide for the remission or mitigation of fines, forfeitures and penalties in certain cases, was read the second time, and ordered to be committed to a committee of the whole House on this day se'nnight.[75]

The House, according to the order of the day, resolved itself into a committee of the whole House on the bill providing the means of intercourse between the United States and foreign nations.

---

[71] On January 27 amendments to this bill were agreed to.

[72] On January 27 the Mitigation of Fines Bill [HR–38] was read again.

[73] The letter is printed in the Senate Legislative Journal on January 26.

[74] The Senate read this bill on January 27 and 28. On January 28 it was committed, and on February 1 this committee reported. On the same day the bill was agreed to with thirteen amendments, and the House agreed to all of the amendments with one amendment.

[75] Consideration of this bill in the COWH was postponed from February 3–5, when the bill was considered in the COWH, amended, and recommitted.

Mr. Speaker left the chair.

Mr. Baldwin took the chair of the committee.

Mr. Speaker resumed the chair; and Mr. Baldwin reported, that the committee had, according to order, had the said bill under consideration, and gone through the same, and made several amendments thereto, which he delivered in at the Clerk's table, where the same were twice read, and agreed to by the house.

ORDERED, That the said bill, with the amendments, be engrossed, and read the third time to-morrow.[76]

On motion,

RESOLVED, That the petition of Hannibal William Dobbyn, be referred to the Secretary of the Treasury, who was directed to report a general plan for the sale of the lands, the property of the United States, for his information.[77]

A petition of Ezra Stiles, in behalf of the President and Fellows of Yale College, in Connecticut, was presented to the House and read; praying that the impost duties arising on a philosophical apparatus lately purchased and imported from London, for the use of the said College, may be remitted.[78]

Also, a petition of John Wait, praying that his claim for arrearages of pay due to sundry soldiers of the late army, transferred to him, and for which he supplied them with clothing and other necessaries, may be allowed.

ORDERED, That the said petitions do lie on the table.

And then the House adjourned until to-morrow morning eleven o'clock.

THURSDAY, JANUARY 28, 1790

On motion,

The House proceeded to consider the petition of John Wait, presented yesterday: Whereupon,

RESOLVED, That the said petition be rejected.

On motion,

RESOLVED, That the order of the day for the House to resolve itself into a committee of the whole House on the report of the Secretary of the Treasury, relative to a provision for the support of the public credit, be postponed until Monday se'nnight.

A message, in writing, was received from the President of the United States, by Mr. Lear, his Secretary, who delivered in the same, together with the papers therein referred to, and then withdrew.

The said message was read, and is as followeth:

---

[76] On March 24 this bill was read again and recommitted.

[77] On March 11 the secretary was ordered to report on this petition.

[78] A draft of the petition is in the Ezra Stiles Papers, CtY.

UNITED STATES, January 28, 1790

GENTLEMEN of the SENATE and HOUSE of REPRESENTATIVES,

I HAVE directed my Secretary to lay before you the copy of an act of the legislature of Rhode-Island and Providence plantations, entitled, "An act for calling a Convention to take into consideration the Constitution proposed for the United States, passed on the seventeenth day of September, Anno Domini one thousand seven hundred and eighty-seven, by the General Convention held at Philadelphia;" together with the copy of a letter accompanying the said act, from his Excellency John Collins, Governor of the state of Rhode-Island and Providence plantations, to the President of the United States.

The originals of the foregoing act and letter, will be deposited in the office of the Secretary of State.

G. WASHINGTON[79]

ORDERED, That the said message, and papers accompanying the same, be referred to Mr. Benson, Mr. Grout, and Mr. Coles, with instruction that they do prepare and bring in a bill or bills for granting the suspension applied for by the Governor of the state of Rhode-Island and Providence plantations, in behalf of the said State.[80]

Mr. Burke, from the committee appointed, presented, according to order, a bill for securing the copy-right of books to authors and proprietors, which was received, and read the first time.[81]

On motion,

ORDERED, That it be an instruction to the committee appointed to prepare and bring in a bill or bills, for securing to authors and inventors, an exclusive right to their respective writings and discoveries, that they do insert a clause or clauses for giving effectual encouragement to the introduction of useful arts from foreign countries.[82]

On motion,

ORDERED, That a committee be appointed to examine into the measures taken by Congress, and the state of Virginia, respecting the lands reserved for the use of the officers and soldiers of the said State, on continental and state establishments, in the cession made by the said State to the United States, of the territory north-west of the river Ohio, and to report the same to this

---

[79] The message with enclosures is in President's Messages: Suggesting legislation, SR, DNA. The Rhode Island act is E–22109.

[80] Rhode Island requested the suspension of two bills, the Tonnage Bill [HR–5] and the Collection Bill [HR–11], because both bills treated Rhode Island as a foreign state.

[81] On January 29 this bill was read again.

[82] On January 29 two petitions were referred to this committee.

House; and that Mr. White, Mr. Peter Muhlenberg, and Mr. Seney, be of the said committee.[83]

And then the House adjourned until to-morrow morning eleven o'clock.

FRIDAY, JANUARY 29, 1790

The Speaker laid before the House a letter from the Treasurer of the United States, accompanying a statement of his accounts of the receipts and expenditures of the public money, from the time of his appointment, until the thirty-first of December last; which were read, and ordered to be referred to Mr. Smith (of Maryland), Mr. Moore, Mr. Smith (of South-Carolina), Mr. Rensselaer, and Mr. Clymer.[84]

A bill for securing the copy-right of books to authors and proprietors, was read the second time, and ordered to be committed to a committee of the whole House on Monday next.[85]

A petition of Aaron Putnam, of Medford in the state of Massachusetts, was presented to the House and read; praying that an exclusive privilege may be granted him in the use of an improved method of distilling, which he has discovered, whereby the spirit is rendered much more pure, and, with the same expence and time, twice the quantity produced, as in the common method.

Also, a petition of Francis Bailey, of the city of Philadelphia, printer, praying that an exclusive privilege may be granted him, in the use of an invention which he has discovered, of forming types for printing devices to surround or make parts of printed papers for any purpose, which cannot be counter-feited.[86]

ORDERED, That the said petitions be referred to the committee appointed to prepare and bring in a bill or bills, for securing to authors and inventors, the exclusive right to their respective writings and discoveries; that they do examine the matter thereof, and report the same, with their opinion thereupon, to the House.[87]

A message from the Senate by Mr. Otis their Secretary.

---

[83] On February 1 this committee reported.

[84] The letter from Samuel Meredith and the treasury accounts are in Transcribed Reports and Communications from the Executive Departments, 1789–1814, Records of the Secretary, SR, DNA. Copies of the letter and accounts are in Accounts of the Treasurer of the United States, vol. 1, HR, DNA. The letter and accounts are printed in the Appendix to the Second Session. On April 9 this committee reported.

[85] On February 1 this bill was considered in the COWH and amended.

[86] The memorial is in Petitions and Memorials: Various subjects, SR, DNA.

[87] On February 3 this committee reported on the Bailey petition. On February 8 two more petitions were referred to this committee.

MR. SPEAKER, The Senate have passed a bill, entitled, "An act for the punishment of certain crimes against the United States,"[88] to which they desire the concurrence of this House: And then withdrew.

The said bill was read the first time.[89]

A petition of Roger Alden, Deputy Secretary to the late Congress, was presented to the House, and read; praying that compensation may be made for his services, those of a clerk which he employed, and the expences of office incident to the care and custody of the records and papers of the late Congress, the great seal of the federal Union, and the seal of the admiralty, which were delivered to him on the twenty-fourth of July last, by Charles Thomson, Secretary to the late Congress, pursuant to the order of the President of the United States.

ORDERED, That the said petition be referred to Mr. Trumbull, Mr. Baldwin, and Mr. Leonard; that they do examine the matter thereof, and report the same, with their opinion thereupon, to the House.[90]

On motion,

ORDERED, That the petition of the merchants and other inhabitants of the town of Portland, in the state of Massachusetts, which was presented on Tuesday last, be referred to the Secretary of the Treasury, with instruction to examine the matter thereof, and report the same, with his opinion thereupon, to the House.

On motion,

ORDERED, That a committee be appointed to prepare and bring in a bill or bills to appropriate such a sum or sums of money as may be necessary for the payment of the civil list, with the incidental charges thereof, for the present year; and that Mr. Livermore, Mr. Silvester, and Mr. Lee, be of the said committee.[91]

And then the House adjourned until Monday morning eleven o'clock.

---

[88] The bill with annotations is in Engrossed Senate Bills and Resolutions, SR, DNA.

[89] On February 1 this bill was read again.

[90] On February 4 this committee reported.

[91] This committee was the one appointed to prepare the Appropriations Bill [HR–47]. On February 5 a resolution on the petition of Roger Alden was referred to this committee.

MONDAY, FEBRUARY 1, 1790

Another member, to wit, George Gale, from Maryland, appeared and took his seat.

The bill sent from the Senate, entitled, "An act for the punishment of certain crimes against the United States," was read a second time, and ordered to be committed to a committee of the whole House on Friday next.[1]

A petition of John McCord, of the province of Quebec, was presented to the House and read, praying to be reimbursed for supplies of money and other necessaries which he furnished to the American army, in Canada, in the year one thousand seven hundred and seventy-five.[2] Also,

A petition of John Stevens, late a captain in the army of the United States, praying that his claim to half pay, for life, under a resolution of the late Congress, may be allowed.[3]

ORDERED, That the said petitions do lie on the table.

The House, according to the order of the day, resolved itself into a committee of the whole House, on the bill for securing the copy-right of books to authors and proprietors.

Mr. Speaker left the chair.

Mr. Baldwin took the chair of the committee.

Mr. Speaker resumed the chair, and Mr. Baldwin reported, that the committee had, according to order, had the said bill under consideration, and gone through the same, and made several amendments thereto, which he delivered in at the Clerk's table, where the same were severally twice read, and agreed to by the House.

ORDERED, That the said bill, with the amendments, be engrossed, and read the third time to-morrow.[4]

Mr. White, from the committee appointed to examine into the measures taken by Congress and the state of Virginia, respecting the lands reserved for the use of the officers and soldiers of the said State, on continental and state establishments, in the cession made by the said State to the United States, of the territory north-west of the river Ohio, made a report, which was read and ordered to lie on the table.[5]

A message, in writing, was received from the President of the United States, by Mr. Lear his Secretary, who delivered in the same, together with the papers therein referred to, and then withdrew.

---

[1] Consideration of this bill in the COWH was postponed as an order of the day from February 5 through April 3. On April 5 the COWH considered this bill.

[2] On February 4 John McCord's petition was committed.

[3] On February 4 this petition was referred to the secretary of war.

[4] On February 2 this bill was read and recommitted.

[5] This report is E–22954. On April 30 this report was referred to the COWH.

The said message was read, and is as followeth:

UNITED STATES, February 1st, 1790

GENTLEMEN of the SENATE and HOUSE of REPRESENTATIVES,

I HAVE received from his Excellency Alexander Martin, Governor of the state of North-Carolina, an act of the General Assembly of that State, entitled, "An act for the purpose of ceding to the United States of America, certain western lands therein described;" and have directed my Secretary to lay a copy of the same before you, together with the copy of a letter accompanying the said act, from his Excellency Governor Martin, to the President of the United States.

The originals of the foregoing act and letter will be deposited in the office of the Secretary of State.

G. WASHINGTON[6]

ORDERED, That the said message and papers be referred to Mr. Clymer, Mr. Gale, Mr. Madison, Mr. Tucker, and Mr. Mathews.

ORDERED, That a committee be appointed to prepare and bring in a bill or bills, to prescribe the mode in which the public acts, records, and judicial proceedings in each State shall be authenticated, so as to take effect in every other State; and that Mr. Page, Mr. Jackson, and Mr. Thatcher, be of the said committee.[7]

ORDERED, That a committee be appointed to prepare and bring in a bill or bills, to provide for the invalid pensioners of the United States; and that Mr. Hiester, Mr. Partridge, and Mr. Hathorn, be of the said committee.[8]

ORDERED, That a standing committee of elections be appointed.

And a committee was appointed, of Mr. Ames, Mr. Sherman, Mr. Benson, Mr. Sinnickson, Mr. Wynkoop, Mr. White, and Mr. Stone.

A message from the Senate by Mr. Otis their Secretary.

MR. SPEAKER, The Senate have passed the bill, entitled, "An act for giving effect to the several acts therein mentioned, in respect to the state of North-Carolina," with several amendments,[9] to which they desire the concurrence of this House: And then he withdrew.

---

[6] The message with an enclosure is in President's Messages: Suggesting legislation, SR, DNA. The act from the state of North Carolina is in Deeds of Cession of Western Lands, M332, roll 7, RG 11, DNA.

[7] On April 28 this committee reported an Authentication Bill [HR–58], which was read.

[8] On June 29 this committee presented the Invalid Pensioners Bill [HR–80], which was read.

[9] A Senate committee report on this bill, with these amendments, is in Various Select Committee Reports, SR, DNA. The amendments are printed in the *Senate Legislative Journal* on February 1.

The House proceeded to consider the said amendments; and the same being severally twice read, were agreed to, with an amendment to the last amendment.[10]

ORDERED, That the Clerk of this House do acquaint the Senate therewith.[11]

And then the House adjourned until to-morrow morning eleven o'clock.

TUESDAY, FEBRUARY 2, 1790

Another member, to wit, Theodorick Bland, from Virginia, appeared and took his seat.

An engrossed bill, for securing the copy-right of books to authors and pro-prietors, was read the third time, and, on a motion made, ordered to be re-committed to Mr. Boudinot, Mr. Sherman, and Mr. Silvester.[12]

A petition of William Hassal, of the city of Philadelphia, was presented to the House, and read; praying that he may be allowed the commutation of half pay for life, in consideration of military services rendered during the late war. Also,

A petition of William and Samuel Helms, late merchants, and partners, at New-Haven, in the state of Connecticut, but now bankrupts in the island of Grenada; praying to be relieved from the payment of the impost duty on a quantity of rum, which they had compounded with their creditors to import and pay to them in the said state of Connecticut, before the act imposing the said duty was passed. Also,

A petition of the proprietors of Union-wharf, in New-Haven, in the state of Connecticut; praying that certain rates of wharfage, which were granted to them by an act of the legislature of the said state, in the year one thousand seven hundred and eighty-four, and of which they will be deprived by the operation of the laws of the United States, may be continued to them.

ORDERED, That the said petitions do lie on the table.

Mr. Foster, from the committee to whom was re-committed the bill provid-ing for the actual enumeration of the inhabitants of the United States—reported, that the committee had, according to order, had the said bill under consideration, and made several amendments thereto, which he delivered in at the Clerk's table, where the same were severally twice read, and agreed to by the House.

ORDERED, That the said bill, with the amendments, be engrossed, and read the third time to-morrow.[13]

A message from the Senate by Mr. Otis their Secretary.

---

[10] The House amendment is printed in the *Senate Legislative Journal* on February 2.

[11] On February 4 this bill was signed by the speaker and the vice president.

[12] On February 25 this committee reported a new Copyright Bill [HR–43], which was read.

[13] On February 4 this bill was read again.

MR. SPEAKER, The Senate have agreed to the amendment proposed by this House to their last amendment, to the bill, entitled, "An act for giving effect to the several acts therein mentioned, in respect to the state of North-Carolina," with an amendment,[14] to which they desire the concurrence of this House: And then he withdrew.

The House proceeded to consider the said amendment to the amendment to the amendment, and the same being read, was agreed to.

ORDERED, That the Clerk of this House do acquaint the Senate therewith.[15]

On motion,

ORDERED, That Mr. Gilman and Mr. White be appointed a committee for inrolled bills, on the part of this House, agreeable to the joint rules of the two Houses.

ORDERED, That the Clerk of this House do acquaint the Senate therewith.

The order of the day for the House to resolve itself into a committee of the whole House, on the bill establishing an uniform rule of naturalization, was read and postponed until to-morrow.

And then the House adjourned until to-morrow morning eleven o'clock.

WEDNESDAY, FEBRUARY 3, 1790

A message from the Senate by Mr. Otis their Secretary.

MR. SPEAKER, The Senate have appointed Mr. Wingate, on their part, of the committee for inrolled bills, agreeable to the joint rules of the two Houses: And then he withdrew.

Mr. Burke, from the committee to whom was referred the petition of Francis Bailey, reported,[16]

That Mr. Bailey hath communicated to the committee his invention or device to prevent the counterfeiting of public papers, which the committee are of opinion will be of great importance to the public, and therefore recommend that the said petition be referred to the Secretary of the Treasury to report thereon: Whereupon,

RESOLVED, That this House doth agree to the said report.[17]

A petition of Wilhelmus Decker, of the state of New-York, was presented

---

[14] The Senate amendment is printed in the *Senate Legislative Journal* on February 2.

[15] On February 2 the Senate agreed to the House amendment to one of their amendments with an amendment. The House agreed to this amendment on the same day.

[16] A copy of the report is in A Record of the Reports of Select Committees, HR, DNA.

[17] On February 23 the secretary of the treasury reported on the Bailey petition.

to the House, and read, praying relief in consideration of his being wounded and disabled in the service of the United States, during the late war.

ORDERED, That the said petition do lie on the table.

The House, according to the order of the day, resolved itself into a committee of the whole House, on the bill establishing an uniform rule of naturalization.

Mr. Speaker left the chair.

Mr. Baldwin took the chair of the committee.

Mr. Speaker resumed the chair, and Mr. Baldwin reported that the committee had, according to order, had the said bill under consideration, and made some progress therein.

RESOLVED, That this House will, to-morrow, again resolve itself into a committee of the whole House on the said bill.[18]

The order of the day for the House to resolve itself into a committee of the whole House on the bill to provide for the remission or mitigation of fines, forfeitures, and penalties, in certain cases, was read and further postponed until to-morrow.

And then the House adjourned until to-morrow morning eleven o'clock.

THURSDAY, FEBRUARY 4, 1790

Mr. Gilman, from the joint committee for inrolled bills, reported, that the committee had examined the inrolled bill, entitled, "An act for giving effect to the several acts therein mentioned, in respect to the state of North-Carolina, and other purposes,"[19] and had found the same to be truly inrolled: Whereupon,

Mr. Speaker signed the said inrolled bill.[20]

ORDERED, that the Clerk of this House do acquaint the Senate therewith.

A petition of Joseph Henderson, and John Carnes, junior, of Boston, executors, &c. of Edward Carnes, deceased, was presented to the House, and read, praying that payment may be made of a liquidated debt, due to their testator's estate, from the United States.

ORDERED, That the said petition do lie on the table.

Mr. Trumbull, from the committee to whom was referred the petition of Roger Alden, made a report, which was read, and ordered to lie on the table.[21]

ORDERED, That the petitions of John Stevens, and Wilhelmus Decker,

---

[18] On February 4 this bill was considered in the COWH and recommitted.

[19] The inspected enrolled bill is in Enrolled Acts, RG 11, DNA. E-46035, E-22956.

[20] On February 5 this bill was presented to the president.

[21] A copy of the report is in A Record of the Reports of Select Committees, HR, DNA. On February 5 this report was amended and agreed to. The committee was then instructed to bring in a bill. The report is printed in the Journal on the same date.

which lay on the table, be referred to the Secretary at War, with instruction to examine the same, and report his opinion thereupon to the House.[22]

ORDERED, That the petition of John McCord, which was presented on Monday last, be referred to Mr. Ames, Mr. Fitzsimons, and Mr. Boudinot, that they do examine the matter thereof, and report the same, with their opinion thereupon, to the House.[23]

The House, according to the order of the day, again resolved itself into a committee of the whole House, on the bill, establishing an uniform rule of naturalization.

Mr. Speaker left the chair.

Mr. Baldwin took the chair of the committee.

Mr. Speaker resumed the chair, and Mr. Baldwin, reported that the committee had, according to order, again had the said bill under consideration, and made a further progress therein:

On motion,

ORDERED, That the committee of the whole House, be discharged from further proceeding on the said bill; and that it be re-committed to Mr. Livermore, Mr. Sedgwick, Mr. Sherman, Mr. Laurance, Mr. Schureman, Mr. Hartley, Mr. Seney, Mr. Moore, Mr. Tucker, and Mr. Jackson.[24]

An engrossed bill, providing for the actual enumeration of the inhabitants of the United States, was read the third time, and ordered to be re-committed to a committee of the whole House, to-morrow.[25]

The order of the day, for the House to resolve itself into a committee of the whole House, on the bill to provide for the remission or mitigation of fines, forfeitures, and penalties, in certain cases, was read, and postponed until to-morrow.

And then the House adjourned until to-morrow morning eleven o'clock.

FRIDAY, FEBRUARY 5, 1790

ORDERED, That the petition of the executors of Edward Carnes, deceased, which was presented yesterday, be referred to the Secretary of the Treasury, with instruction to examine the same, and report his opinion thereupon to the House.

Mr. Gilman, from the joint committee for inrolled bills, reported that the

---

[22] On March 22 the secretary reported on the Stevens petition.

[23] On May 7 this committee reported.

[24] On February 16 this committee presented a Naturalization Bill [HR–40], which was read.

[25] On February 8 the COWH was discharged from considering this bill, and the bill was read, agreed to, and sent to the Senate.

committee did yesterday wait on the President of the United States, and present him with the inrolled bill, entitled, "An act for giving effect to the several acts therein mentioned, in respect to the State of North-Carolina, and other purposes," for his approbation.[26]

A petition of sundry citizens of the State of New-Jersey, late soldiers in the American army, was presented to the House, and read; praying that the depreciation of pay for their services in the army, may be made good to them.

Also, a petition of Isaac Sherman, of the State of Connecticut; praying that further compensation may be made for his services as an assisting surveyor to the late Geographer of the United States, in the Western Territory.

Also, a petition of William Scott, of the State of New-York; praying that his claim to a pension, in consideration of wounds received in the service of the United States, during the late war, may be allowed.

ORDERED, That the said petitions do lie on the table.

The House proceeded to consider the report of the committee on the petition of Roger Alden; which, being amended, to read as followeth:

That Mr. Alden was, on the 24th of July, 1789, appointed by the President of the United States, to take charge of the records, books, papers, and seal of the late Congress; in which employment he still continues. That for the discharge of his duty in that trust; the bringing up the books, and compleating the records of the late Congress, to be delivered over to the Secretary of State; attending to the frequent calls of the public for references to original papers; the application of members of Congress and individuals for numerous copies, extracts and authentications of unfinished business before the late Congress; receiving from the President of the United States, a variety of original papers, to be deposited in the office of the Secretary of State; affixing the seals; and other services in said office—Mr. Alden found it necessary to employ an assistant, until the fifteenth of November last, at which time he was discharged.

That a compensation, payable out of the treasury of the United States, should be allowed Mr. Alden, at the rate of one thousand dollars per annum, until the Secretary of State shall enter on the duties of his office; and that he be allowed the customary contingent expences of office: Also, that a compensation, at the rate of five hundred dollars per annum, be allowed for his assistant, during the time he was actually employed.

RESOLVED, That this House doth agree to the said report; and that it be referred to the committee appointed to prepare and bring in a bill or bills, to appropriate such a sum or sums of money as may be necessary for the payment of the civil list, to make provision accordingly.[27]

---

[26] On February 8 this bill was signed by the president.

[27] The committee on appropriations was appointed on January 29. On March 2 a report from the secretary of the treasury was referred to this committee.

The Speaker laid before the House a letter from the Secretary at War, accompanying his reports on the several petitions of Ruth Roberts, Salmon Burr, and Ezra Smith, which were read and ordered to lie on the table.[28]

The House, according to the order of the day, resolved itself into a committee of the whole House on the bill, to provide for the remission or mitigation of fines, forfeitures and penalties in certain cases.

Mr. Speaker left the chair.

Mr. Baldwin took the chair of the committee.

Mr. Speaker resumed the chair, and Mr. Baldwin reported, that the committee had, according to order, had the said bill under their consideration, and gone through the same, and made an amendment thereto, which he delivered in at the Clerk's table, where the same was twice read and agreed to by the House.

On motion,

ORDERED, That the said bill, with the amendment, be recommitted to Mr. Ames, Mr. Sturges, Mr. Stone, Mr. Griffin, and Mr. Wynkoop.[29]

The orders of the day for the House to resolve itself into a committee of the whole House, on the bill sent from the Senate, entitled, "An act for the punishment of certain crimes against the United States;" also, on the engrossed bill, providing for the actual enumeration of the inhabitants of the United States; were read and postponed until Monday next.

And then the House adjourned until Monday morning eleven o'clock.

MONDAY, FEBRUARY 8, 1790

A memorial of Robert Morris, late Superintendant of the Finances of the United States, was presented to the House and read, praying that commissioners may be appointed to make enquiry into his official conduct whilst Superintendant, in conformity to a resolution of the late Congress.[30]   Also,

A petition of sundry inhabitants of the town of Salem, in the state of Massachusetts, praying that so much of the law for regulating the coasting trade, as compels the owners of vessels employed therein to take out a licence for the same, may be amended.

ORDERED, That the said memorial and petition do lie on the table.

A petition of Nathan Read, of Salem, in the state of Massachusetts, was

---

[28] Copies of all these reports are in A Record of the Reports of the Secretary of War, vol. 1, HR, DNA. On March 24 the report on Ezra Smith's petition was committed.

[29] On March 3 this committee presented the Mitigation of Fines Bill [HR–45], which was read.

[30] The covering letter for the memorial is in Petitions and Memorials: Various subjects, SR, DNA. The memorial is in Miscellaneous Letters, M177, roll 3, RG 59, DNA. On February 10 this petition was read, printed in the Journal, and committed.

presented to the House and read, praying the aid of Congress, and an exclusive privilege for constructing sundry machines and engines, which he has invented for improving the art of distillation, for facilitating the operation of mills and other water-works, and for promoting the purposes of navigation and land carriage.

Also a petition of John Stevens, junior, praying that an exclusive privilege may be granted him for an improvement on the steam engine, which he has invented, by a new mode of generating steam.

ORDERED, That the said petitions be referred to Mr. Burke, Mr. Huntington, and Mr. Cadwalader, that they do examine the matter thereof, and report the same with their opinion thereupon to the House.[31]

On motion,

ORDERED, That the committee of the whole House, to whom the engrossed bill providing for the actual enumeration of the inhabitants of the United States, was committed, be discharged therefrom.

The said engrossed bill was then read the third time, and the blanks therein filled up.

RESOLVED, That the said bill do pass, and that the title be, "An act providing for the actual enumeration of the inhabitants of the United States."[32]

ORDERED, That the Clerk of this House do carry the said bill to the Senate, and desire their concurrence.[33]

A message was received from the President of the United States, by Mr. Lear his Secretary, notifying that the President approves of the act, entitled, "An act for giving effect to the several acts therein mentioned, in respect to the state of North-Carolina, and other purposes;" and has this day affixed his signature thereto: And the Secretary delivered in the said act, and then withdrew.

ORDERED, That the Clerk of this House do acquaint the Senate therewith.

The House, according to the order of the day, resolved itself into a committee of the whole House, on the report of the Secretary of the Treasury, relative to a provision for the support of the public credit.

Mr. Speaker left the chair.

Mr. Baldwin took the chair of the committee.

Mr. Speaker resumed the chair, and Mr. Baldwin reported, that the com-

---

[31] On February 16 this committee presented the Patents Bill [HR–41], which was read.

[32] A printed copy of the bill, annotated by the Senate, is in House Bills, SR, DNA. E–46052, E–45702.

[33] The Senate read this bill on February 9 and 12. On February 12 it was committed, and the committee reported amendments on February 16. On the same day the sixth section was recommitted. On February 17 the committee's report was agreed to, and on February 18 the bill was agreed to with twenty-nine amendments. On February 19 the House was notified that the Senate had passed the bill.

mittee had, according to order, had the said report under consideration, and made some progress therein.

RESOLVED, That this House will, to-morrow, again resolve itself into a committee of the whole House, on the said report.[34]

The order of the day for the House to resolve itself into a committee of the whole House, on the bill sent from the Senate, entitled, "An act for the punishment of certain crimes against the United States," was read and postponed until to-morrow.

And then the House adjourned until to-morrow morning eleven o'clock.

TUESDAY, FEBRUARY 9, 1790

ORDERED, That the petition of the inhabitants of the town of Salem, in the state of Massachusetts, which was presented yesterday, be referred to the Secretary of the Treasury, with instruction to examine the same, and report his opinion thereupon to the House.

A petition of Donald Campbell, of the city of New-York, was presented to the House and read, praying the attention of Congress to a representation which he made to the late Congress, against certain statements of the late Board of Treasury, on the subject of his claims against the United States.[35]

ORDERED, That the said petition do lie on the table.[36]

A petition of the contractors for conveying the mail between the cities of Philadelphia and New-York, was presented to the House and read, praying the interposition of Congress to relieve them from a tax imposed on the mail stages by the state of New-Jersey; and also in compelling a preference to the mail stages in the passage of ferries, and along the public roads.

ORDERED, That the said petition be referred to the committee to whom was referred the letter from the Secretary of the Treasury, with the report from the Postmaster-General.[37]

The House, according to the order of the day, again resolved itself into a committee of the whole House, on the report of the Secretary of the Treasury, relative to a provision for the support of the public credit.

Mr. Speaker left the chair.

Mr. Baldwin took the chair of the committee.

---

[34] According to the New York *Daily Advertiser*, February 9, 1790, Thomas Fitzsimons introduced a series of resolutions on the public debt during this meeting of the COWH. A printed copy of these resolutions is in the Broadside Collection, RBkRm, DLC. On February 9 the COWH considered this report again.

[35] The memorial with related documents is in Petitions and Memorials: Claims, SR, DNA.

[36] On February 15 this petition was committed.

[37] On February 23 this committee presented the Post Office Bill [HR–42], which was read.

Mr. Speaker resumed the chair, and Mr. Baldwin reported, that the committee had, according to order, again had the said report under consideration, and made a farther progress therein.

RESOLVED, That this House will, to-morrow, again resolve itself into a committee of the whole House on the said report.[38]

The order of the day for the House to resolve itself into a committee of the whole House, on the bill sent from the Senate, entitled, "An act for the punishment of certain crimes against the United States," was read and postponed until to-morrow.

And then the House adjourned until to-morrow morning eleven o'clock.

WEDNESDAY, FEBRUARY 10, 1790

On motion,

The memorial of Robert Morris, late Superintendant of the Finances of the United States, presented on Monday last, was read, and ordered to be inserted in the Journal, as followeth.

To the PRESIDENT, the SENATE and HOUSE of REPRESENTATIVES of the
UNITED STATES of AMERICA

The Memorial of ROBERT MORRIS, late Superintendant of the Finances of
the said United States,

Humbly Sheweth,

THAT on the twentieth day of June, one thousand seven hundred and eighty-five, and subsequent to your memorialist's resignation of his office of Superintendant, the Congress passed a resolution in the words following: "Resolved, That three commissioners be appointed, to enquire into the receipts and expenditures of public monies, during the administration of the late Superintendent of Finance, and to examine and adjust the accounts of the United States with that department, during his administration, and to report a state thereof to Congress," which resolution, to persons unacquainted with the nature of the office, and the mode of conducting the business of the department, gave occasion to the supposition, that your memorialist had accounts both difficult and important to settle with the United States, in respect to his official transactions. That though your memorialist foresaw the disagreeable consequences which might result to himself from the diffusion of such an opinion, he notwithstanding, not only forbore any representation on the subject, but scrupulously avoided every species of interference direct or indirect, lest it should be imagined, either that he was actuated by the desire of obtaining from Congress those marks of approbation, which had in re-

---

[38] On February 10 the COWH considered this report again.

peated instances, been bestowed on the servants of the public, or that he feared to meet the proposed investigation. Respect for the sovereign of the United States, concurring with motives of delicacy, to forbid even the appearance of asking, what if merited, it was to be presumed would be conferred, (as being the proper reward of services, not of solicitation) and a firm confidence in the rectitude of his conduct, leaving your memorialist no inducement to evade any enquiry into it, which it might be thought fit to institute.

That your memorialist taking it for granted, that the reasons which had produced a determination to establish a mode of enquiry into the transactions of the most important office under the government, would have ensured a prosecution of the object till it had been carried into effect, long remained in silent expectation of the appointment of commissioners, according to the resolution which had been entered into for that purpose. But it has so happened, from what cause your memorialist will not undertake to explain, that no further steps have ever been taken in relation to it; and your memorialist has remained exposed to the surmises, which the appearance of an intention to enquire into his conduct had a tendency to excite, without having been afforded an opportunity of obviating them. That the unsettled condition of certain accounts of a commercial nature between the United States, and the late house of Willing, Morris, and company, and your memorialist, prior to his appointment as Superintendant of the Finances, having been confounded with his transactions in that capacity, your memorialist has in various ways, been subjected to injurious imputations on his official conduct, the only fruits of services, which at the time they were rendered, he trusts, he may without incurring the charge of presumption, affirm, were generally esteemed both important and meritorious, and were at least rendered with ardor and zeal, with unremitted attention, and unwearied application.

That your memorialist, desirous of rescuing his reputation from the aspersions thrown upon it, came in the month of October 1788, to the city of New-York, as well for the purpose of urging the appointment of commissioners to inspect his official transactions, as for that of procuring an adjustment of the accounts which existed previous to his administration. But the first object was frustrated by the want of a sufficient number of members to make a Congress, and the last was unavoidably delayed by the preliminary investigations requisite on the part of the commissioner named by the late Board of Treasury, towards a competent knowledge of the business. That in the month of February 1789, your memorialist returned to New-York for the same purposes, but the obstacles which he had before experienced, still operated to put it out of his power to present the memorial which had been prepared by him in October, praying for an appointment of commissioners. That he was therefore obliged to confine himself to measures for the settlement of his accounts respecting the transactions antecedent to his appointment as Superintendant, which he entered upon accordingly with the Commissioner appointed by the Board of Treasury: And in which, as much progress as time and circumstances would permit, was made until the fourth of March last, when that commissioner, conceiving his authority by the organization of the new government to have ceased, declined further proceedings, and of course your memorialist was obliged to wait the establishment of the new treasury department for the further prosecution of that settlement, which has been accordingly resumed, and he hopes will speedily be accomplished. But in as much as no mode of enquiry into his official conduct has hitherto been put into operation, and as doubts of its propriety have been raised by an act of the government, your memorialist conceives himself to have a claim upon the public justice, for some method of vindicating himself, which will be unequivocal and definitive. Wherefore, and encouraged by a consciousness of the integrity of his administration, your memorialist is desirous that a strict examination should be had into his conduct while in office, in order that if he has been guilty of maladministration, it may be detected and punished; if otherwise, that his innocence may be manifested and acknowledged. Unwilling from this motive, that longer delay should attend the object of the resolution which has been recited, your memorialist humbly prays, that an appointment of Commissioners may take place to carry the said resolution into effect. And your memorialist, as in duty bound, will pray, &c.

ROBERT MORRIS

New-York, February 8, 1790

ORDERED, That the said memorial be referred to Mr. Madison, Mr. Sedgwick, and Mr. Sherman, that they do examine the matter thereof, and report the same with their opinion thereupon to the House.[39]

The House, according to the order of the day, again resolved itself into a committee of the whole House, on the report of the Secretary of the Treasury, relative to a provision for the support of the public credit.

Mr. Speaker left the chair.

Mr. Baldwin took the chair of the committee.

Mr. Speaker resumed the chair, and Mr. Baldwin reported, that the committee had, according to order, again had the said report under consideration, and made a farther progress therein.

RESOLVED, That this House will, to-morrow, again resolve itself into a committee of the whole House on the said report.[40]

The order of the day for the House to resolve itself into a committee of the

---

[39] On February 11 the Senate sent the House a resolution on the Morris petition.
[40] On February 11 the COWH considered this report again.

whole House, on the bill sent from the Senate, entitled, "An act for the punishment of certain crimes against the United States," was read and postponed until to-morrow.

And then the House adjourned until to-morrow morning eleven o'clock.

THURSDAY, FEBRUARY 11, 1790

Memorials of the people called Quakers, in their annual meetings, held at Philadelphia and New-York, in the year one thousand seven hundred and eighty-nine, were presented to the House and read, praying the attention of Congress in adopting measures for the abolition of the slave trade, and in particular in restraining vessels from being entered and cleared out, for the purposes of that trade.[41]

ORDERED, That the said memorials do lie on the table.[42]

A message from the Senate by Mr. Otis their Secretary.

MR. SPEAKER,   The Senate have agreed to a resolution, "That three commissioners be appointed by the President of the United States, to enquire into the receipts and expenditures of public monies, during the administration of the late Superintendant of Finance, and to examine and adjust the accounts of the United States, with that department, during his administration, and to report a state thereof to the President; and that five dollars per diem be allowed to each of the said commissioners, while they shall be employed in that service;"[43] to which they desire the concurrence of this House: And he delivered in the said resolution, and then withdrew.

The said resolution was read, and ordered to lie on the table.[44]

The House, according to the order of the day, again resolved itself into a committee of the whole House, on the report of the Secretary of the Treasury, relative to a provision for the support of the public credit.

Mr. Speaker left the chair.

Mr. Baldwin took the chair of the committee.

Mr. Speaker resumed the chair, and Mr. Baldwin reported, that the committee had, according to order, again had the said report under consideration, and made a farther progress therein.

RESOLVED, That this House will, to-morrow, again resolve itself into a committee of the whole House on the said report.[45]

---

[41] The memorials are in Petitions and Memorials: Various subjects, SR, DNA.

[42] On February 12 these memorials and a memorial from the Pennsylvania Society for the Abolition of Slavery were committed.

[43] The Senate committee report on the memorial of Robert Morris, with this resolution, is in Various Select Committee Reports, SR, DNA.

[44] On March 9 the House committee on the Morris petition reported.

[45] On February 15 the COWH considered this report again.

The order of the day for the House to resolve itself into a committee of the whole House, on the bill sent from the Senate, entitled, "An act for the punishment of certain crimes against the United States," was read and postponed until to-morrow.

And then the House adjourned until to-morrow morning eleven o'clock.

FRIDAY, FEBRUARY 12, 1790

A memorial of the Pennsylvania society for promoting the abolition of slavery, was presented to the House and read, praying that Congress may take such measures in their wisdom, as the powers with which they are invested will authorize, for promoting the abolition of slavery, and discouraging every species of traffic in slaves.[46]

On motion,

The memorial of the people called Quakers, at their annual meeting, held at Philadelphia, in the year one thousand seven hundred and eighty-nine, presented yesterday, was read the second time: Whereupon,

A motion being made and seconded, that the said memorial be referred to the consideration of a committee,

It was resolved in the affirmative, $\begin{cases} \text{AYES} & 43 \\ \text{NOES} & 11 \end{cases}$

The ayes and noes being demanded by one fifth of the members present, Those who voted in the affirmative, are,

Fisher Ames	John Hathorn
Egbert Benson	Daniel Hiester
Elias Boudinot	Benjamin Huntington
John Brown	John Laurance
Lambert Cadwalader	Richard Bland Lee
George Clymer	George Leonard
Thomas Fitzsimons	Samuel Livermore
William Floyd	James Madison, junior
Abiel Foster	Andrew Moore
George Gale	Peter Muhlenberg
Elbridge Gerry	John Page
Nicholas Gilman	Josiah Parker
Benjamin Goodhue	George Partridge
Samuel Griffin	Jeremiah Van Rensselaer
Jonathan Grout	James Schureman
Thomas Hartley	Thomas Scott

[46] The memorial, with covering letters from Benjamin Franklin and James Pemberton, is in Petitions and Memorials: Various subjects, SR, DNA.

Theodore Sedgwick
Joshua Seney
Roger Sherman
Thomas Sinnickson
William Smith (of Maryland)
Jonathan Sturges

George Thatcher
Jonathan Trumbull
Jeremiah Wadsworth
Alexander White and
Henry Wynkoop

Those who voted in the negative, are,

Abraham Baldwin
Theodorick Bland
Aedanus Burke
Isaac Coles
Daniel Huger
James Jackson

George Mathews
Peter Silvester
William Smith (of South-Carolina)
Michael Jenifer Stone and
Thomas Tudor Tucker

ORDERED, That the said memorial be referred to Mr. Foster, Mr. Huntington, Mr. Gerry, Mr. Laurance, Mr. Sinnickson, Mr. Hartley, and Mr. Parker; that they do examine the matter thereof, and report the same with their opinion thereupon to the House.

ORDERED, That the memorial of the people called Quakers, at their annual meeting held at New-York, in the year one thousand seven hundred and eighty-nine, as also the memorial of the Pennsylvania society for promoting the abolition of slavery, presented to-day, be referred to the committee last appointed; that they do examine the matter thereof, and report the same with their opinion thereupon to the House.[47]

A petition of Isaac Trowbridge, of the State of Connecticut, was presented to the House and read, praying to be relieved from a contract which through inadvertency he entered into with the public, for the transportation of the mail from New-York to Hartford, and which is likely to become ruinous to him.

ORDERED, That the said petition do lie on the table.

The order of the day for the House to resolve itself into a committee of the whole House on the bill sent from the Senate, entitled "An act for the punishment of certain crimes against the United States," and on the report of the Secretary of the Treasury, relative to a provision for the support of the public credit, were read and postponed until Monday next.

And then the House adjourned until Monday morning eleven o'clock.

---

[47] On April 20 this committee reported.

MONDAY, FEBRUARY 15, 1790

A petition of James Derrey, was presented to the House and read, praying compensation for military services rendered during the late war.[48]   Also,

A petition of John Stone, of Concord, in the Commonwealth of Massachusetts, praying that an exclusive privilege may be granted him for a new and expeditious method which he has invented of driving piles attached together, whereby the construction of wooden bridges over the broadest and deepest streams may be greatly facilitated.   Also,

A petition of Anna Treat, praying that some allowance or provision for her support may be granted her in consideration of the poverty and distress to which she is reduced by the loss of her son, who was slain in the service of the United States during the late war.

ORDERED, That the said petitions do lie on the table.

ORDERED, That the petition of Donald Campbell, which was presented on Tuesday last, be referred to Mr. Bland, Mr. Cadwalader, and Mr. Benson, that they do examine the matter thereof, and report the same with their opinion thereupon to the House.[49]

ORDERED, That the petition of Isaac Trowbridge, which was presented on Friday last, be referred to the Postmaster-General, with instruction to examine the same, and report his opinion thereupon to the House.

A message, in writing, was received from the President of the United States, by Mr. Lear his Secretary, who delivered in the same, together with the papers therein referred to, and then withdrew.

The said message and papers were read, and are as follow:

UNITED STATES, February 15th, 1790

GENTLEMEN of the SENATE and HOUSE of REPRESENTATIVES,

I HAVE directed my Secretary to lay before you the copy of a vote of the Legislature of the state of New-Hampshire, to accept the articles proposed in addition to, and amendment of, the Constitution of the United States of America, except the second article. At the same time will be delivered to you the copy of a letter from his Excellency the President of the state of New-Hampshire, to the President of the United States.

The originals of the abovementioned vote, and letter, will be lodged in the office of the Secretary of State.

G. WASHINGTON

---

[48] On March 1 this petition was referred to the secretary of war.
[49] On March 5 this committee reported.

(Copy)

DURHAM, in NEW-HAMPSHIRE, January 29, 1790

SIR,

I HAVE the honor to inclose you for the information of Congress, a vote of the Assembly of this State, to accept all the Articles of Amendment to the Constitution of the United States, except the second, which was rejected.

I have the honor to be,

With the most profound respect,

SIR,

Your most obedient, and

Very humble servant,

(Signed)   JOHN SULLIVAN

The PRESIDENT of the UNITED STATES

I Certify the foregoing to be a true copy of the letter to the President of the United States, from his Excellency John Sullivan.

TOBIAS LEAR, Secretary to the President of the United States

(Copy)

STATE OF NEW-HAMPSHIRE

In the HOUSE of REPRESENTATIVES, January 25, 1790

Upon reading and maturely considering the proposed Amendments to the Federal Constitution,

VOTED, To accept the whole of said Amendments, except the second Article, which was rejected.

Sent up for concurrence.

(Signed)   THOMAS BARTLETT, Speaker

In SENATE, the same day read and concurred.

(Signed)   J. PEARSON, Secretary

A true copy.

Attest.   JOSEPH PEARSON, Secretary

I certify the above to be a true copy of the copy transmitted to the President of the United States.

TOBIAS LEAR, Secretary to the President of the United States[50]

---

[50] The message with enclosures is in President's Messages: Suggesting legislation, SR, DNA.

ORDERED, That the said message and papers do lie on the table.

The House, according to the order of the day, again resolved itself into a committee of the whole House on the report of the Secretary of the Treasury, relative to a provision for the support of the public credit.

Mr. Speaker left the chair.

Mr. Baldwin took the chair of the committee.

Mr. Speaker resumed the chair, and Mr. Baldwin reported, that the committee had, according to order, again had the said report under consideration, and made a farther progress therein.

RESOLVED, That this House will, to-morrow, again resolve itself into a committee of the whole House on the said report.[51]

The order of the day for the House to resolve itself into a committee of the whole House, on the bill sent from the Senate, entitled, "An act for the punishment of certain crimes against the United States," was read, and postponed until to-morrow.

And then the House adjourned until to-morrow morning eleven o'clock.

TUESDAY, FEBRUARY 16, 1790

Mr. Livermore, from the committee to whom was recommitted a bill for establishing an uniform rule of naturalization, presented an amendatory bill to establish an uniform rule of naturalization, and to enable aliens to hold lands under certain restrictions, which was received, and read the first time.[52]

Mr. Burke, from the committee appointed, presented, according to order, a bill to promote the progress of useful arts, which was received, and read the first time.[53]

The House, according to the order of the day, again resolved itself into a committee of the whole House on the report of the Secretary of the Treasury, relative to a provision for the support of the public credit.

Mr. Speaker left the chair.

Mr. Baldwin took the chair of the committee.

Mr. Speaker resumed the chair, and Mr. Baldwin reported, that the committee had, according to order, again had the said report under consideration, and made a farther progress therein.

RESOLVED, That this House will, to-morrow, again resolve itself into a committee of the whole House on the said report.[54]

---

[51] On February 16 the COWH considered this report again.

[52] A printed copy of what is probably this bill is E–46021. On February 17 this bill was read again.

[53] A printed copy of what is probably this bill is E–46023. On February 17 this bill was read again.

[54] On February 17 the COWH considered this report again.

The order of the day for the House to resolve itself into a committee of the whole House on the bill sent from the Senate, entitled, "An act for the punishment of certain crimes against the United States," was read, and postponed until to-morrow.

And then the House adjourned until to-morrow morning eleven o'clock.

WEDNESDAY, FEBRUARY 17, 1790

A bill to establish an uniform rule of naturalization, and to enable aliens to hold lands under certain restrictions, was read the second time, and ordered to be committed to a committee of the whole House on Tuesday next.[55]

A bill to promote the progress of useful arts, was read the second time, and ordered to be committed to a committee of the whole House on Wednesday next.[56]

The several petitions of Jehoiakim McToksin, Joseph Halstead, Henry Carman, Joseph Bernard, and Moses Young, were presented to the House and read, respectively praying to be made compensation for services rendered, or for losses or injuries sustained in the service of the United States during the late war.[57]   Also,

A petition of Andrew Dunscomb, praying that he may be paid his salary for services as commissioner of accounts, from the month of November, one thousand seven hundred and eighty-four, until the month of April, one thousand seven hundred and eighty-five.   Also,

A petition of John Ingraham, praying to be relieved against the seizure of his vessel and cargo in the port of New-York, for a violation of the laws of trade, of which, at the time of committing the offence, the petitioner was entirely ignorant.

ORDERED, That the said petitions do lie on the table.

A petition of James Perry and Thomas Hayes, subjects of the King of Great-Britain, was presented to the House and read, praying to receive compensation for sundry articles of property, which were seized and taken from them in the state of New-Jersey, during the war, for the use of the army of the United States.

ORDERED, That the said petition be referred to the Secretary of the Treasury, with instruction to examine the same, and report his opinion thereupon to the House.

ORDERED, That the petition of Rufus Lincoln, which was presented on the

---

[55] On February 23 this bill was considered in the COWH.

[56] Consideration of this bill in the COWH was postponed as an order of the day from February 24 through March 3. On March 4 it was considered in the COWH.

[57] On February 18 the McToksin petition was committed.

twenty-sixth ultimo, be referred to the Secretary at War, with instruction to examine the same, and report his opinion thereupon to the House.

The House, according to the order of the day, again resolved itself into a committee of the whole House, on the report of the Secretary of the Treasury, relative to a provision for the support of the public credit.

Mr. Speaker left the chair.

Mr. Baldwin took the chair of the committee.

Mr. Speaker resumed the chair, and Mr. Baldwin reported, that the committee had, according to order, again had the said report under consideration, and made a farther progress therein.

RESOLVED, That this House will, to-morrow, again resolve itself into a committee of the whole House on the said report.[58]

The order of the day for the House to resolve itself into a committee of the whole House, on the bill sent from the Senate, entitled, "An act for the punishment of certain crimes against the United States," was read, and postponed until to-morrow.

And then the House adjourned until to-morrow morning eleven o'clock.

THURSDAY, FEBRUARY 18, 1790

ORDERED, That the petition of Anna Treat, presented on Monday last, be referred to the Secretary at War, with instruction to examine the same, and report his opinion thereupon to the House.

ORDERED, That the petition of Jehoiakim McToksin, presented yesterday, be referred to Mr. Sedgwick, Mr. Rensselaer, and Mr. Brown, that they do examine the matter thereof, and report the same, with their opinion thereupon to the House.[59]

On motion,

The order of the day for the House to resolve itself into a committee of the whole House, on the bill sent from the Senate, entitled, "An act for the punishment of certain crimes against the United States," was farther postponed until Monday se'nnight.

The House, according to the order of the day, again resolved itself into a committee of the whole House on the report of the Secretary of the Treasury, relative to a provision for the support of the public credit.

Mr. Speaker left the chair.

Mr. Baldwin took the chair of the committee.

Mr. Speaker resumed the chair, and Mr. Baldwin reported, that the com-

---

[58] On February 19 the COWH considered this report again.

[59] On March 3 this committee reported, and a resolution on McToksin's petition was referred to the committee to prepare the Appropriations Bill [HR–47].

mittee had, according to order, again had the said report under consideration, and made a farther progress therein.

RESOLVED, That this House will, to-morrow, again resolve itself into a committee of the whole House on the said report.[60]

And then the House adjourned until to-morrow morning eleven o'clock.

FRIDAY, FEBRUARY 19, 1790

A message from the Senate by Mr. Otis their Secretary.

MR. SPEAKER, The Senate have passed the bill, entitled, "An act providing for the actual enumeration of the inhabitants of the United States," with several amendments, to which they desire the concurrence of this House:[61] And then he withdrew.

The House, according to the order of the day, again resolved itself into a committee of the whole House, on the report of the Secretary of the Treasury, relative to a provision for the support of the public credit.

Mr. Speaker left the chair.

Mr. Baldwin took the chair of the committee.

Mr. Speaker resumed the chair, and Mr. Baldwin reported, that the committee had, according to order, again had the said report under consideration, and made a farther progress therein.

RESOLVED, That this House will, on Monday next, again resolve itself into a committee of the whole House on the said report.[62]

The Speaker laid before the House a letter from the Board of Commissioners for settling accounts, respecting the insufficiency of the salaries allowed by law to the clerks employed in that department, which was read, and ordered to lie on the table.[63]

And then the House adjourned until Monday morning eleven o'clock.

MONDAY, FEBRUARY 22, 1790

A petition of James McComb, was presented to the House and read, praying that an exclusive privilege may be granted him in the use of a machine which he has invented for facilitating the operation of water-mills.

---

[60] On February 18 the COWH considered this report again.

[61] Senate amendments are noted on the bill in House Bills, SR, DNA. Annotations on another printed copy of the bill, which is in the Broadside Collection, RBkRm, DLC, also correspond to Senate amendments. The amendments are printed in the *Senate Legislative Journal* on February 18. On February 22 the House agreed to all the Senate amendments except numbers twenty-two–twenty-six. On the same day the Senate receded from these amendments.

[62] On February 22 the COWH considered this report again.

[63] On February 22 this letter was committed.

ORDERED, That the said petition do lie on the table.

The House proceeded to consider the amendments proposed by the Senate to the bill, entitled, "An act providing for the actual enumeration of the inhabitants of the United States:" Whereupon,

RESOLVED, That this House doth disagree to the twenty-second, twenty-third, twenty-fourth, twenty-fifth, and twenty-sixth of the said amendments; and doth agree to all the others.

ORDERED, That the Clerk of this House do acquaint the Senate therewith.

The House, according to the order of the day, again resolved itself into a committee of the whole House, on the report of the Secretary of the Treasury, relative to a provision for the support of the public credit.

Mr. Speaker left the chair.

Mr. Baldwin took the chair of the committee.

Mr. Speaker resumed the chair, and Mr. Baldwin reported, that the committee had, according to order, again had the said report under consideration, and made a farther progress therein.

RESOLVED, That this House will, to-morrow, again resolve itself into a committee of the whole House on the said report.[64]

A message from the Senate by Mr. Otis their Secretary.

MR. SPEAKER, The Senate recede from their twenty-second, twenty-third, twenty-fourth, twenty-fifth, and twenty-sixth amendments, disagreed to by this House, to the bill, entitled, "An act providing for the actual enumeration of the inhabitants of the United States."[65] The Senate have also agreed to a resolution, "That it will be expedient for Congress, in behalf of the United States, to accept of the cession proposed by an act of the Legislature of the state of North-Carolina, entitled, 'An act for the purpose of ceding to the United States of America, certain western lands therein described,' upon the conditions therein contained; and that when a deed shall be executed for the same, Congress express their acceptance thereof by a legislative act;"[66] to which resolution they desire the concurrence of this House: And then he withdrew.

On motion,

ORDERED, That the letter from the Board of Commissioners for settling accounts, respecting the insufficiency of the salaries allowed by law to the clerks

---

[64] On February 23 the COWH considered this report again.

[65] On February 25 this bill was signed by the speaker and the vice president.

[66] The Senate committee report with the resolution is in Various Select Committee Reports, SR, DNA.

employed in that department, be referred to Mr. Gerry, Mr. Trumbull, and Mr. Gale.[67]

And then the House adjourned until to-morrow morning eleven o'clock.

TUESDAY, FEBRUARY 23, 1790

The Speaker laid before the House a letter and report from the Secretary of the Treasury, on the petition of Francis Bailey, which was read, and ordered to lie on the table.[68]

The House, according to the order of the day, again resolved itself into a committee of the whole House, on the report of the Secretary of the Treasury, relative to a provision for the support of the public credit.

Mr. Speaker left the chair.

Mr. Benson took the chair of the committee.

Mr. Speaker resumed the chair, and Mr. Benson reported, that the committee had, according to order, again had the said report under consideration, and made a farther progress therein.

RESOLVED, That this House will, to-morrow, again resolve itself into a committee of the whole House on the said report.[69]

Mr. Fitzsimons, from the committee appointed, presented, according to order, a bill for regulating the post-office of the United States, which was received, and read the first time.[70]

The House, according to the order of the day, resolved itself into a committee of the whole House, on the bill to establish an uniform rule of naturalization, and to enable aliens to hold lands under certain restrictions.

Mr. Speaker left the chair.

Mr. Benson took the chair of the committee.

Mr. Speaker resumed the chair, and Mr. Benson reported, that the committee had, according to order, had the said bill under consideration, and made some progress therein.

RESOLVED, That this House will, to-morrow, again resolve itself into a committee of the whole House on the said bill.[71]

And then the House adjourned until to-morrow morning eleven o'clock.

---

[67] On February 26 this committee reported.

[68] The report is in Reports from the Secretary of the Treasury, SR, DNA. On February 26 this report was considered, and a committee was appointed to prepare a bill on the petition. On the same day this committee presented the Bailey Bill [HR–44], which was read.

[69] On February 24 the COWH considered this report again.

[70] On February 24 this bill was read again.

[71] On February 24 this bill was again considered in the COWH.

WEDNESDAY, FEBRUARY 24, 1790

A bill for regulating the post-office of the United States, was read the second time, and ordered to be committed to a committee of the whole House, on Monday next.[72]

The several petitions of David Cook, John Ely, and David S. Franks, were presented to the House and read, praying to be compensated for losses or injuries sustained, or for services rendered during the late war.[73]   Also,

A petition of William Mumford, praying to be paid for his services as a clerk to the Commissioners for liquidating the accounts between the United States and the state of Pennsylvania.

ORDERED, That the said petitions do lie on the table.

A petition of Nathaniel Gove, of the state of Vermont, was presented to the House and read, praying relief in consideration of injuries sustained in the service of the United States during the late war.

ORDERED, That the said petition be referred to the Secretary at War, with instruction to examine the same, and report his opinion thereupon to the House.

On motion,

ORDERED, That the petition of Thomas Barclay, which was presented at the last session, praying that he may receive compensation for services rendered to the United States, in various public stations in Europe, be referred to Mr. Clymer, Mr. Page, and Mr. Sinnickson, that they do examine the matter thereof, and report the same with their opinion thereupon to the House.[74]

The House, according to the order of the day, again resolved itself into a committee of the whole House, on the report of the Secretary of the Treasury, relative to a provision for the support of the public credit.

Mr. Speaker left the chair.

Mr. Benson took the chair of the committee.

Mr. Speaker resumed the chair, and Mr. Benson reported, that the committee had, according to order, again had the said report under consideration, and made a farther progress therein.

RESOLVED, That this House will, to-morrow, again resolve itself into a committee of the whole House on the said report.[75]

The House, according to the order of the day, again resolved itself into a

---

[72] Consideration of this bill in the COWH was postponed as an order of the day from March 1 through April 12. On April 13 it was considered in the COWH.

[73] A petition similar to this Cook petition is in the George Washington Papers, series 7, vol. 7, roll 120. On February 25 the Ely and Cook petitions were referred to the secretary of war. The Franks petition was committed on February 26.

[74] On June 28 this committee reported.

[75] On February 25 the COWH considered this report again.

committee of the whole House, on the bill to establish an uniform rule of naturalization, and to enable aliens to hold lands under certain restrictions.

Mr. Speaker left the chair.

Mr. Benson took the chair of the committee.

Mr. Speaker resumed the chair, and Mr. Benson reported, that the committee had, according to order, again had the said bill under consideration, and made a farther progress therein.

RESOLVED, That this House will, to-morrow, again resolve itself into a committee of the whole House on the said bill.[76]

The order of the day, for the House to resolve itself into a committee of the whole House, on the bill to promote the progress of useful arts, was read, and postponed until to-morrow.

And then the House adjourned until to-morrow morning eleven o'clock.

THURSDAY, FEBRUARY 25, 1790

Mr. Gilman, from the joint committee for inrolled bills, reported, that the committee had examined the inrolled bill, entitled, "An act providing for the enumeration of the inhabitants of the United States,"[77] and had found the same to be truly inrolled: Whereupon,

Mr. Speaker signed the said inrolled bill.[78]

ORDERED, That the Clerk of this House do acquaint the Senate therewith.

ORDERED, That the petitions of David Cook, and John Ely, which were presented yesterday, be referred to the Secretary at War, with instruction to examine the same, and report his opinion thereupon to the House.[79]

Mr. Boudinot, from the committee to whom the bill for securing the copyright of books to authors and proprietors, was re-committed, presented an amendatory bill, for the encouragement of learning, by securing the copies of maps, charts, books, and other writings, to the authors and proprietors of such copies, during the times therein mentioned; which was received and read the first time.[80]

The several petitions of Barent Martlings, Enos Brown, Samuel Armstrong, William Mason, and Elizabeth Young, were presented to the House, and read, praying relief in consideration of losses or injuries, sustained in the service of the United States, during the late war.

Also, a petition of the weighers, measurers, and gaugers, of the district of Portland and Falmouth, in the state of Massachusetts, praying that the fees of

---

[76] The COWH considered this bill again on February 26.

[77] The inspected inrolled bill is in Enrolled Acts, RG 11, DNA. E-46053.

[78] On March 1 this bill was signed by the president.

[79] On March 8 the secretary reported on the Ely petition, and on March 16 he reported on the Cook petition.

[80] On February 26 this bill was read again.

office allowed them by law, may be augmented, and rendered more adequate to their services.

ORDERED, That the said petitions do lie on the table.

The House, according to the order of the day, again resolved itself into a committee of the whole House, on the report of the Secretary of the Treasury, relative to a provision for the support of the public credit.

Mr. Speaker left the chair.

Mr. Benson took the chair of the committee.

Mr. Speaker resumed the chair, and Mr. Benson reported, that the committee had, according to order, again had the said report under consideration, and made a farther progress therein.

RESOLVED, That this House will, to-morrow, again resolve itself into a committee of the whole House on the said report.[81]

The orders of the day, for the House to resolve itself into a committee of the whole House, on the bill to establish an uniform rule of naturalization, and to enable aliens to hold lands under certain restrictions; also, on the bill, to promote the progress of useful arts, were read, and postponed until to-morrow.

And then the House adjourned until to-morrow morning eleven o'clock.

FRIDAY, FEBRUARY 26, 1790

A bill for the encouragement of learning, by securing the copies of maps, charts, books and other writings, to the authors and proprietors of such copies, during the times therein mentioned, was read the second time, and ordered to be committed to a committee of the whole House on Wednesday next.[82]

The House proceeded to consider the report of the Secretary of the Treasury on the petition of Francis Bailey: Whereupon,

ORDERED, That a bill or bills be brought in for securing to the said Francis Bailey an exclusive privilege to the use of his invention; and that Mr. Boudinot, Mr. Sedgwick, and Mr. White, do prepare and bring in the same.

ORDERED, That the several petitions of William Mumford and Samuel Armstrong, and of the weighers, measurers, and gaugers, of the district of Portland and Falmouth, in the State of Massachusetts, which were presented yesterday, be referred to the Secretary of the Treasury, with instruction to examine the same and report his opinion thereupon to the House.

ORDERED, That the petition of David S. Franks, which was presented on Wednesday last, be referred to Mr. Hartley, Mr. Wadsworth, and Mr. Rens-

---

[81] On February 26 the COWH considered this report again.

[82] Consideration of this bill in the COWH was postponed daily from March 3 until April 29, when it was considered in the COWH and amended.

selaer, that they do examine the matter thereof, and report the same, with their opinion thereupon to the House.[83]

A petition of David Poole, of New-London, in Connecticut, was presented to the House and read, praying relief in consideration of the loss of his left arm in the service of the United States, during the late war.

ORDERED, That the said petition do lie on the table.[84]

Mr. Gerry, from the committee to whom was referred the letter from the board of commissioners for settling accounts, made a report, which was read, and ordered to lie on the table.[85]

The members from South-Carolina, presented the copies of two acts of that State, one entitled, "An act for ceding to and vesting in the United States, the light-house on Middle-Bay-Island, within the bar of Charleston harbor;" the other, "For ratifying on the part of that State, the several articles of amendment to the Constitution of the United States, proposed by Congress," which were read, and ordered to lie on the table.

The House, according to the order of the day, again resolved itself into a committee of the whole House, on the report of the Secretary of the Treasury, relative to a provision for the support of the public credit.

Mr. Speaker left the chair.

Mr. Benson took the chair of the committee.

Mr. Speaker resumed the chair, and Mr. Benson reported that the committee had, according to order, again had the said report under consideration, and made a farther progress therein.

RESOLVED, That this House will, on Monday next, again resolve itself into a committee of the whole House, on the said report.[86]

The House, according to the order of the day, again resolved itself into a committee of the whole House, on the bill to establish an uniform rule of naturalization, and to enable aliens to hold lands under certain restrictions.

Mr. Speaker left the chair.

Mr. Benson took the chair of the committee.

Mr. Speaker resumed the chair, and Mr. Benson reported, that the committee had, according to order, again had the said bill under consideration, and made a farther progress therein.

RESOLVED, That this House will, on Monday next, again resolve itself into a committee of the whole House on the said bill.[87]

---

[83] On March 11 this committee reported, and the report was tabled.

[84] On March 1 this petition was referred to the secretary of war.

[85] On March 5 this report was considered, and the same committee was ordered to bring in a bill.

[86] On March 1 the COWH considered this report again.

[87] Consideration of this bill was postponed on March 1 and 2. On March 3 the bill was considered in the COWH and amended.

Mr. Boudinot, from the committee appointed, presented, according to order, a bill to vest in Francis Bailey, the exclusive privilege of making, using, and vending to others, punches for stamping the matrices of types, and impressing marks on plates, or any other substance, to prevent counterfeits, upon a principle by him invented, for a term of years; which was received and read the first time.[88]

The order of the day, for the House to resolve itself into a committee of the whole House, on the bill to promote the progress of useful arts, was read, and postponed until Monday next.

And then the House adjourned until Monday morning eleven o'clock.

---

[88] On March 1 this bill was read again.

MONDAY, MARCH 1, 1790

Another member, to wit, Thomas Sumter, from South-Carolina, appeared and took his seat.

A message was received from the President of the United States, by the Secretary at War, who delivered in several letters and papers, being a further communication on the subject of the south-western frontier, and of the Indian department, and then withdrew.

The said letters and papers were read, and ordered to lie on the table.

A petition of Richard Wells and Josiah Hart, of the city of Philadelphia, was presented to the House and read, praying that effectual provision may be made by Congress for rendering to the petitioners, and all other creditors of the United States in a similar situation, full payment for the paper bills of credit heretofore issued by Congress, and now in the hands of the said creditors.[1]

Also, a petition of James Delaplaine, late a Lieutenant in the first Virginia regiment, praying relief, in consideration of wounds and injuries received whilst in the service of the United States.

Also, a petition of Thomas Leiper, of the city of Philadelphia, praying that duplicates may be granted him of six loan-office certificates of one thousand dollars each, which were issued to him by the Commissioner of loans in the State of Pennsylvania, and casually lost some time in the year 1779.

ORDERED, That the said petitions do lie on the table.

ORDERED, That the petitions of James Derry, and David Poole, be referred to the Secretary at War, with instruction to examine the same, and report his opinion thereupon to the House.[2]

A bill to vest in Francis Bailey the exclusive privilege of making, using, and vending to others, punches for stamping the matrices of types, and impressing marks on plates or any other substance, to prevent counterfeits, upon a principle by him invented, for a term of years, was read the second time, and ordered to be engrossed, and read the third time to-morrow.[3]

The House, according to the order of the day, again resolved itself into a committee of the whole House on the report of the Secretary of the Treasury, relative to a provision for the support of the public credit.

Mr. Speaker left the chair.

Mr. Benson took the chair of the committee.

Mr. Speaker resumed the chair, and Mr. Benson reported, that the commit-

---

[1] On March 5 this petition was committed.

[2] The secretary reported on the Poole petition on April 22 and on the Derry petition on June 25.

[3] On March 2 this bill was read again, agreed to, and sent to the Senate.

tee had, according to order, again had the said report under consideration, and made a farther progress therein.

RESOLVED, That this House will, to-morrow, again resolve itself into a committee of the whole House on the said report.[4]

A message was received from the President of the United States, by Mr. Lear, his Secretary, notifying that the President approves of the act "providing for the enumeration of the inhabitants of the United States," and has affixed his signature to the same.

The several orders of the day for the House to resolve itself into a committee of the whole House, on the bill sent from the Senate, entitled, "An act for the punishment of certain crimes against the United States;" also on the bill for regulating the post-office of the United States; on the bill to establish an uniform rule of naturalization, and to enable aliens to hold lands under certain restrictions; and on the bill to promote the progress of useful arts; were read, and postponed until to-morrow.

And then the House adjourned until to-morrow morning eleven o'clock.

TUESDAY, MARCH 2, 1790

An engrossed bill to vest in Francis Bailey the exclusive privilege of making, using, and vending to others, punches for stamping the matrices of types, and impressing marks on plates, or any other substance, to prevent counterfeits, upon a principle by him invented, for a term of years, was read the third time, and the blanks therein filled up.

RESOLVED, That the said bill do pass; and that the title be, "An act to vest in Francis Bailey the exclusive privilege of making, using, and vending to others, punches for stamping the matrices of types, and impressing marks on plates, or any other substance, to prevent counterfeits, upon a principle by him invented, for a term of years."[5]

ORDERED, That the Clerk of this House do carry the said bill to the Senate, and desire their concurrence.[6]

The Speaker laid before the House a letter from the Secretary of the Treasury, covering his further report and estimate of Extraordinaries for the services of the current year; which were read, and ordered to be referred to the

---

[4] On March 2 the COWH considered this report again.

[5] The bill is in Engrossed House Bills, HR, DNA.

[6] The Senate read this bill on March 2 and 3, and it was committed on March 3. On March 4 the committee reported and consideration of the bill was postponed until the Patent Bill [HR–41] was considered. On March 16 the Bailey Bill [HR–44] was referred to the committee on the Patents Bill [HR–41]. The Bailey Bill [HR–44] provisions became part of the Patents Bill [HR–41].

committee appointed to prepare and bring in a bill of appropriation for the support of government.[7]

On motion,

RESOLVED, That the Secretary of the Treasury be instructed to report to this House, such funds as in his opinion may be raised and applied towards the payment of the interest of the debts of individual States, should they be assumed by Congress.

ORDERED, That the Secretary of the Treasury lay before this House the amount of the duties on goods, wares and merchandize, and on tonnage, in the several States, from the time that the collection of those revenues commenced to the thirty-first of December last.[8]

A petition of Abraham Skinner, was presented to the House and read, praying to be reimbursed for monies advanced, and losses sustained by the petitioner whilst Commissary-General of Prisoners of the United States, during the late war.[9]

Also, a petition of the rope-makers in the town of Boston, praying that Congress will devise such further measures as may be effectual, to secure and improve this important branch of manufacture.

ORDERED, That the said petitions do lie on the table.

A petition of George Scriba, was presented to the House and read, praying to be permitted to purchase of the United States, a tract of Western Territory, not less than two million, and not exceeding four millions of acres, on the terms therein mentioned.

ORDERED, That the said petition be referred to the Secretary of the Treasury, for his information.

The House then, according to the order of the day, again resolved itself into a committee of the whole House, on the report of the Secretary of the Treasury, relative to a provision for the support of the public credit.

Mr. Speaker left the chair.

Mr. Benson took the chair of the committee.

Mr. Speaker resumed the chair, and Mr. Benson reported, that the committee had, according to order, again had the said report under consideration, and made a farther progress therein.

RESOLVED, That this House will, to-morrow, again resolve itself into a committee of the whole House, on the said report.[10]

---

[7] A copy of the report is in A Record of the Reports of the Secretary of the Treasury, vol. 1, HR, DNA. A copy, probably made by ASP, is in Reports and Communications from the Secretary of the Treasury, HR, DNA. E–23002. The committee on appropriations was appointed on January 29. On March 3 a resolution on the petition of Jehoiakim McToksin was referred to this committee.

[8] On March 4 the secretary submitted this report.

[9] On March 3 this petition was committed.

[10] On March 8 the COWH considered this report again.

The several orders of the day for the House to resolve itself into a committee of the whole House, on the bill sent from the Senate, entitled, "An act for the punishment of certain crimes against the United States:" Also, on the bill to establish an uniform rule of naturalization, and to enable aliens to hold lands under certain restrictions; on the bill for regulating the post-office of the United States; and on the bill to promote the progress of useful arts, were read, and postponed until to-morrow.

And then the House adjourned until to-morrow morning eleven o'clock.

WEDNESDAY, MARCH 3, 1790

Mr. Ames, from the committee to whom was re-committed the bill, to provide for the remission or mitigation of fines, forfeitures and penalties, in certain cases, presented an amendatory bill, which was received and read the first time.[11]

ORDERED, That the petition of Abraham Skinner, which was presented yesterday, be referred to Mr. Laurance, Mr. Smith (of Maryland), and Mr. Hiester, that they do examine the matter thereof, and report the same, with their opinion thereupon to the House.[12]

Mr. Sedgwick, from the committee to whom was referred the petition of Jehoiakim McToksin, reported a state of facts, together with a resolve,[13] which was twice read, and agreed to by the House, as followeth:

RESOLVED, By the Senate, and House of Representatives of the United States of America, in Congress assembled, That there be paid out of the public treasury, unto Jehoiakim McToksin, one hundred and twenty dollars, in full compensation for his services, as an interpreter and guide, in the expedition commanded by Major-General Sullivan, in the year one thousand seven hundred and seventy-nine.

ORDERED, That the said resolve be referred to the committee appointed to prepare and bring in a bill or bills, for making an appropriation for the support of government.[14]

The House, according to the order of the day, again resolved itself into a committee of the whole House, on the bill to establish an uniform rule of naturalization, and to enable aliens to hold lands under certain restrictions.

Mr. Speaker left the chair.

Mr. Benson took the chair of the committee.

Mr. Speaker resumed the chair, and Mr. Benson reported, that the commit-

---

[11] On March 4 this bill was read again.

[12] On July 27 this committee was discharged, and the petition was referred to the secretary of the treasury.

[13] A copy of the report is in A Record of the Reports of Select Committees, HR, DNA.

[14] The committee on appropriations was appointed on January 29. On March 8 this committee presented an Appropriations Bill [HR–47], which was read.

tee had, according to order, again had the said bill under consideration, and made several amendments thereto, which he delivered in at the Clerk's table, where the same were severally twice read, and agreed to by the House.

ORDERED, That the said bill, with the amendments, be engrossed, and read the third time to-morrow.[15]

A member from South-Carolina, presented to the House the proceedings of the Legislature of that State, respecting certain regulations at the post of Fort Johnson, which were read, and ordered to be referred to the Secretary of the Treasury, with instruction to examine the same, and report his opinion thereupon to the House.

The several orders of the day, for the House to resolve itself into a committee of the whole House, on the report of the Secretary of the Treasury, relative to a provision for the support of the public credit; also, on the bill sent from the Senate, entitled, "An act for the punishment of certain crimes against the United States;" on the bill for regulating the post-office of the United States; on the bill to promote the progress of useful arts; and on the bill for the encouragement of learning, by securing the copies of maps, charts, books, and other writings, to the authors and proprietors of such copies, during the times therein mentioned, were read, and postponed until to-morrow.

And then the House adjourned until to-morrow morning eleven o'clock.

THURSDAY, MARCH 4, 1790

Another member, to wit, Benjamin Contee, from Maryland, appeared and took his seat.

An engrossed bill, to establish an uniform rule of naturalization, and to enable aliens to hold lands under certain restrictions, was read the third time.

RESOLVED, That the said bill do pass, and that the title be, "An act to establish an uniform rule of naturalization."[16]

ORDERED, That the Clerk of this House, do carry the said bill to the Senate, and desire their concurrence.[17]

A bill to provide for the remission or mitigation of fines, forfeitures and penalties, in certain cases, was read the second time, and ordered to be committed to a committee of the whole House to-morrow.[18]

A petition of Catherine Wheeler, was presented to the House and read,

---

[15] On March 4 this bill was read again, agreed to, and sent to the Senate.

[16] Two printed copies of the bill, annotated by the Senate, are in House Bills, SR, DNA. E–46022.

[17] The Senate read this bill on March 4 and 8. On March 9 it was read and committed. This committee reported on March 12. The report was considered on March 15, 16, and 17. On March 18 the second reading of the bill was completed. The bill was read again and agreed to with an amendment on March 19.

[18] On March 5 this bill was considered in the COWH, and an amendment to it was agreed to.

praying relief, as the widow of an invalid soldier, who was wounded in the late war, and is since dead.

ORDERED, That the said petition do lie on the table.

A petition of Nicholas Cowenhoven and others, of Kings county, in the state of New-York, was presented to the House and read, praying to receive payment of certain claims for the board and subsistence of sundry American officers, prisoners during the late war, who were quartered on the petitioners.

ORDERED, That the said petition be referred to Mr. Laurance, Mr. Smith (of Maryland), and Mr. Hiester, that they do examine the matter thereof, and report the same, with their opinion thereupon to the House.[19]

ORDERED, That the petition of William Mason, which was presented on the twenty-fifth ultimo, be referred to the Secretary at War, with instruction to examine the same, and report his opinion thereupon to the House.

The House, according to the order of the day, resolved itself into a committee of the whole House, on the bill to promote the progress of useful arts.

Mr. Speaker left the chair.

Mr. Benson took the chair of the committee.

Mr. Speaker resumed the chair, and Mr. Benson reported, that the committee had, according to order, had the said bill under consideration, and made some progress therein.

RESOLVED, That this House will, to-morrow, again resolve itself into a committee of the whole House on the said bill.[20]

The Speaker laid before the House, a letter from the Secretary of the Treasury, covering his reports, made in pursuance of the resolution and order of the House, of the second instant, which were read, and ordered to lie on the table.[21]

The orders of the day for the House to resolve itself into a committee of the whole House, on the report of the Secretary of the Treasury, relative to a provision for the support of the public credit: Also, on the bill sent from the Senate, entitled, "An act for the punishment of certain crimes against the United States;" on the bill for regulating the post-office of the United States; and on the bill for the encouragement of learning, by securing the copies of maps, charts, books, and other writings, to the authors and proprietors of such copies, during the times therein mentioned; were read, and postponed until to-morrow.

And then the House adjourned until to-morrow morning eleven o'clock.

---

[19] On April 21 this committee reported.

[20] On March 5 this bill was considered again and amended.

[21] A copy of the report is in A Record of the Reports of the Secretary of the Treasury, vol. 1, HR, DNA. A copy of the report, probably made by ASP, is in Reports and Communications from the Secretary of the Treasury, HR, DNA. E–23003. This report concerned funding the interest on the state debts and an abstract of the revenues.

FRIDAY, MARCH 5, 1790

Mr. Foster, from the committee to whom was referred the petitions of the people called Quakers, and also of the Pennsylvania Society, for promoting the abolition of slavery, made a report, which was read, and ordered to lie on the table.[22]

ORDERED, That the petition of Richard Wells and Josiah Hart, which was presented on Monday last, be referred to Mr. Livermore, Mr. Goodhue, Mr. Sherman, Mr. Silvester, Mr. Schureman, Mr. Scott, Mr. Seney, Mr. Brown, Mr. Burke, and Mr. Jackson, that they do examine the matter thereof, and report the same, with their opinion thereupon to the House.[23]

A petition of Thomas Donnellan, of the state of Maryland, was presented to the House and read, praying that a duplicate may be granted him, of a certificate, issued in his favor, by the late quarter-master general, for three hundred and eight dollars, which certificate was accidentally burnt, with the dwelling-house of the petitioner, and all his effects, in the month of December, one thousand seven hundred and eighty-five.

ORDERED, That the said petition, together with the petitions of Gabriel Allen, and Thomas Leiper, which lay on the table, be referred to the Secretary of the Treasury, with instruction to examine the same, and report his opinion thereupon to the House.

A petition of Catherine Greene, relict of the late General Greene, was presented to the House and read, praying that an enquiry may be had on the claims and petition of her late husband, as exhibited to the late Congress, on the twenty-second of August, one thousand seven hundred and eighty-five.[24]

ORDERED, that the said petition be referred to Mr. Gerry, Mr. Boudinot, Mr. Parker, Mr. Peter Muhlenberg, and Mr. Smith (of South-Carolina), that they do examine the matter thereof, and report the same, with their opinion thereupon to the House.[25]

A memorial of the late officers of the South-Carolina line, on continental establishment, was presented to the House and read, praying that provision may be made for securing to them payment of the six months pay, granted them by certain resolutions of the late Congress, and which they have never yet received.[26]

ORDERED, That the said memorial do lie on the table.

A petition of John Rogers, in behalf of himself, James Meriwether, and

[22] On March 8 this report was considered.
[23] On July 29 this committee reported.
[24] A draft of the petition is in the Knox Papers, MHi. A copy, probably made by ASP, is in Reports of the Secretary of the Treasury, HR, DNA.
[25] On March 23 this committee reported.
[26] The petition is in the Pierce Butler Papers, PHi.

John Thurston, of the state of Virginia, was presented to the House and read, praying that the commutation of half pay may be allowed to them, as officers in a corps of dragoons, in the Illinois country during the late war, and to which they conceive themselves entitled, under the act of cession of that country, made by the said state of Virginia, to the United States.

ORDERED, That the said petition be referred to the Secretary at War, with instruction to examine the same, and report his opinion thereupon to the House.[27]

The House, according to the order of the day, resolved itself into a committee of the whole House, on the bill to provide for the remission or mitigation of fines, forfeitures and penalties, in certain cases.

Mr. Speaker left the chair.

Mr. Benson took the chair of the committee.

Mr. Speaker resumed the chair, and Mr. Benson reported, that the committee had, according to order, had the said bill under consideration, and made an amendment thereto, which he delivered in at the Clerk's table, where the same was twice read, and agreed to by the House.

ORDERED, That the said bill, with the amendment, be engrossed, and read the third time on Monday next.[28]

The House, according to the order of the day, again resolved itself into a committee of the whole House, on the bill to promote the progress of useful arts.

Mr. Speaker left the chair.

Mr. Benson took the chair of the committee.

Mr. Speaker resumed the chair, and Mr. Benson reported, that the committee had, according to order, again had the said bill under consideration, and made several amendments thereto, which he delivered in at the Clerk's table, where the same were severally twice read, and agreed to by the House.

ORDERED, That the said bill, with the amendments, be engrossed, and read the third time on Monday next.[29]

A message from the Senate by Mr. Otis their Secretary.

MR. SPEAKER, The Senate have passed a bill, entitled, "An act to accept a cession of the claims of the state of North-Carolina, to a certain district of western country," to which they desire the concurrence of this House.[30] The Senate have also agreed to a resolution, "That the respective collectors in the several ports of the United States, be directed not to grant a clearance for any

[27] On March 24 the secretary reported on this petition.

[28] On March 8 this bill was read again, agreed to, and sent to the Senate.

[29] On March 10 this bill was read again, agreed to, and sent to the Senate.

[30] The bill is in Engrossed Senate Bills and Resolutions, SR, DNA. On March 8 this bill was read.

ship or vessel, having articles on board, subject to inspection, by the laws of the State, from which such ship or vessel shall be about to depart, without having previously obtained such manifests, and other documents, as are enjoined by the said laws;" to which they desire the concurrence of this House:[31]   And then he withdrew.

The House proceeded to consider the report of the committee, to whom was referred the letter from the Commissioners for settling the accounts between the United States, and individual States: Whereupon,

ORDERED, That the said report be re-committed to the same committee, with instruction to prepare and bring in a bill or bills, pursuant thereto.[32]

The several orders of the day for the House to resolve itself into a committee of the whole House, on the report of the Secretary of the Treasury, relative to a provision for the support of the public credit; also, on the bill sent from the Senate, entitled, "An act for the punishment of certain crimes against the United States;" on the bill for regulating the post-office of the United States; and on the bill for the encouragement of learning, by securing the copies of maps, charts, books, and other writings, to the authors and proprietors of such copies, during the times therein mentioned; were read, and postponed until Monday next.

And then the House adjourned until Monday morning eleven o'clock.

MONDAY, MARCH 8, 1790

Another member, to wit, John Vining, from Delaware, appeared and took his seat.

An engrossed bill to provide for the remission or mitigation of fines, forfeitures and penalties, in certain cases, was read the third time, and a blank therein filled up.

RESOLVED, That the said bill do pass; and that the title be, "An act to provide for the remission or mitigation of fines, forfeitures and penalties, in certain cases."[33]

ORDERED, That the Clerk of this House do carry the said bill to the Senate, and desire their concurrence.[34]

---

[31] The resolution is in Senate Simple Resolutions and Motions, SR, DNA. On March 8 the House appointed a committee to prepare a bill on this resolution. On the same day this committee presented the Inspection Bill [HR–48], which was read.

[32] The members of this committee were George Gale, Elbridge Gerry, and Jonathan Trumbull. On March 8 this committee presented the Salaries of Clerks Bill [HR–46], which was read.

[33] A printed copy of the bill, annotated by the Senate, is in House Bills, SR, DNA.

[34] The Senate read this bill on March 9 and 10. On March 11 it was read and committed. On March 15 this committee reported amendments to the bill. The third

The bill sent from the Senate, entitled, "An act to accept a cession of the claims of the state of North-Carolina to a certain district of Western Territory," was read the second time, and ordered to be committed to a committee of the whole House on Thursday next.[35]

The House proceeded to consider the resolution sent from the Senate on Friday last, to prevent the exportation of goods, not duly inspected according to the laws of the several States: Whereupon,

ORDERED, That the said resolution be committed to Mr. White, Mr. Tucker, and Mr. Contee, with instruction to prepare and bring in a bill or bills pursuant thereto.

Mr. Gerry, from the committee appointed, presented, according to order, a bill for encreasing the salaries of Clerks in the office of the Commissioners for settling accounts between the United States and individual States; which was received and read the first time.[36]

Mr. Livermore, from the committee appointed, presented, according to order, a bill making appropriations for the support of government; which was received and read the first time.[37]

The Speaker laid before the House a letter and report from the Secretary at War, on the petition of John Ely, which were read, and ordered to lie on the table.[38]

The Speaker laid before the House a letter and report from the Secretary of the Treasury, on the several petitions of William Mumford, Samuel Armstrong, and the weighers, measurers and gaugers of the district of Portland and Falmouth, in the state of Massachusetts;[39] which were read, and ordered to lie on the table.

Mr. White, from the committee appointed, presented, according to order, a bill to prevent the exportation of goods not duly inspected according to the laws of the several States; which was received and read the first time.[40]

A message, in writing, was received from the President of the United

---

reading of the Mitigation of Fines Bill [HR–45] was begun on March 16 and continued on March 17, when the bill was recommitted. This committee's report was agreed to as an amendment to the bill on March 19, and the bill was agreed to on the same day.

[35] From March 11–25 this bill was postponed as an order of the day. It was considered in the COWH and amended on March 26.

[36] On March 9 this bill was read again.

[37] A printed copy of what is probably this bill is E–46019. On March 9 this bill was read again.

[38] A copy of the report is in A Record of the Reports of the Secretary of War, vol. 1, HR, DNA. On March 10 the House considered this report, and a committee was appointed to prepare a bill pursuant to the report.

[39] A copy of the report is in A Record of the Reports of the Secretary of the Treasury, vol. 1, HR, DNA.

[40] On March 9 this bill was read again.

States, by Mr. Lear his Secretary, who delivered in the same, together with the papers therein referred to, and then withdrew.

The said message and papers were read, and are as follow:

UNITED STATES, March 8, 1790
GENTLEMEN of the SENATE and HOUSE of REPRESENTATIVES,

I HAVE received from his Excellency Joshua Clayton, President of the state of Delaware, the articles proposed by Congress to the Legislatures of the several States, as Amendments to the Constitution of the United States; which articles were transmitted to him for the consideraion of the Legislature of Delaware, and are now returned, with the following resolutions annexed to them, viz.

THE GENERAL ASSEMBLY OF DELAWARE,
HAVING taken into their consideration the above Amendments proposed by Congress to the respective Legislatures of the several States,

RESOLVED, That the first article be postponed.

RESOLVED, That the General Assembly do agree to the second, third, fourth, fifth, sixth, seventh, eighth, ninth, tenth, eleventh and twelfth articles; and we do hereby assent to, ratify and confirm the same, as part of the Constitution of the United States.

In testimony whereof, We have caused the great seal of the State to be hereunto affixed, this twenty-eighth day of January, in the year of our Lord, one thousand seven hundred and ninety, and in the fourteenth year of the Independence of the Delaware State.

Signed by Order of the Council,
GEO. MITCHELL, Speaker
Signed by Order of the House of Assembly,
JEHU DAVIS, Speaker

I HAVE directed a Copy of the Letter which accompanied the said Articles, from his Excellency Joshua Clayton, to the President of the United States, to be laid before you.

The before mentioned Articles, and the Original of the Letter will be lodged in the office of the Secretary of State.

G. WASHINGTON

(Copy)
SIR,

AGREEABLY to the directions of the General Assembly of this State, I do myself the honor to inclose your Excellency the Ratification of the Articles proposed by Congress to be added to the Constitution of the United States, and am,

With every Sentiment of Esteem,
SIR,
Your Excellency's most obedient,
Humble Servant,
(Signed) JOSHUA CLAYTON

DELAWARE, February 19, 1790
His Excellency GEORGE WASHINGTON, }
  PRESIDENT of the UNITED STATES

UNITED STATES, March 8, 1790
I hereby certify that the above Letter is a true Copy from the Original.
  TOBIAS LEAR, Secretary to the President of the United States[41]

ORDERED, That the said message and papers do lie on the table.

A petition of John Watson, of the state of Connecticut, was presented to the House and read, praying further relief in consideration of wounds received in the service of the United States, during the late war.

ORDERED, That the said petition be referred to the Secretary at War, that he do examine the matter thereof, and report the same, with his opinion thereupon to the House.

A petition of David Olyphant, late Director to the Hospitals in the Southern Department, was presented to the House and read, praying that his claim to further compensation and emoluments may be examined and allowed.[42]

ORDERED, That the said petition do lie on the table.

A petition of Gifford Dalley, door-keeper to the House, was presented and read, praying compensation for services rendered during the late recess.

ORDERED, That the said petition be referred to Mr. Livermore, Mr. Lee, and Mr. Silvester; that they do examine the matter thereof, and report the same, with their opinion thereupon to the House.

The House proceeded to consider the report of the committee on the memorials of the people called Quakers, and of the Pennsylvania society for the abolition of slavery: Whereupon,

ORDERED, That the said report be referred to the consideration of the committee of the whole House on Tuesday se'nnight.[43]

The House then, according to the order of the day, again resolved itself into

---

[41] The message with enclosures is in President's Messages: Suggesting legislation, SR, DNA.

[42] The memorial is in Petitions and Memorials: Various subjects, SR, DNA.

[43] On March 16 this report was considered in the COWH.

a committee of the whole House, on the report of the Secretary of the Treasury, relative to a provision for the support of the public credit.

Mr. Speaker left the chair.

Mr. Benson took the chair of the committee.

Mr. Speaker resumed the chair, and Mr. Benson reported, that the committee had, according to order, again had the said report under consideration, and made a farther progress therein.

RESOLVED, That this House will, to-morrow, again resolve itself into a committee of the whole House on the said report.[44]

Mr. Livermore, from the committee to whom was referred the petition of Gifford Dalley, made a report, which was read, and ordered to lie on the table.[45]

ORDERED, That Mr. Clymer have leave to be absent from the service of this House until Friday se'nnight.

The several orders of the day for the House to resolve itself into a committee of the whole House, on the bill sent from the Senate, entitled, "An act for the punishment of certain crimes against the United States;" on the bill for regulating the post-office of the United States; and on the bill for the encouragement of learning, by securing the copies of maps, charts, books and other writings, to the authors and proprietors of such copies, during the times therein mentioned, were read, and postponed until to-morrow.

And then the House adjourned until to-morrow morning eleven o'clock.

TUESDAY, MARCH 9, 1790

A bill to encrease the salaries of Clerks in the office of the Commissioners for settling accounts between the United States and individual States, was read the second time, and ordered to be engrossed, and read the third time.[46]

A bill making appropriations for the support of Government, was read the second time, and ordered to be committed to a committee of the whole House on Thursday next.[47]

A bill to prevent the exportation of goods, not duly inspected according to the laws of the several States, was read the second time, and ordered to be committed to a committee of the whole House to-morrow.[48]

---

[44] On March 9 the COWH considered this report again.

[45] A copy of the report is in A Record of the Reports of Select Committees, HR, DNA. On March 10 this report was considered, and a resolution on the petition was referred to the COWH on the Appropriations Bill [HR-47].

[46] On March 10 this bill was read again, agreed to, and sent to the Senate.

[47] On March 10 a resolution on the pay of Gifford Dalley was referred to the COWH on appropriations.

[48] From March 10-25 consideration of this bill was postponed as an order of the day. On March 26 this bill was considered in the COWH, and the House agreed to an amendment to it.

A petition of William Bedlow, late Deputy-Postmaster in the city of New-York, was presented to the House and read, praying that time may be granted him to make payment of a judgment obtained against him on behalf of the United States, by the Postmaster-General, for certain arrearages due to the public.[49] Also,

A petition of John Mills, late a captain in the army of the United States, praying to be reimbursed for certain advances of recruiting money, which, during the late war, he paid on behalf of the United States.

ORDERED, That the said petitions do lie on the table.

A petition of William Oliver, of the state of New-Jersey, was presented to the House and read, praying relief in consideration of wounds received in the service of the United States, during the late war.

ORDERED, That the said petition be referred to the Secretary at War, with instruction to examine the same, and report his opinion thereupon to the House.

The House then, according to the order of the day, again resolved itself into a committee of the whole House, on the report of the Secretary of the Treasury, relative to a provision for the support of the public credit.

Mr. Speaker left the chair.

Mr. Benson took the chair of the committee.

Mr. Speaker resumed the chair, and Mr. Benson reported, that the committee had, according to order, had the said report under consideration, and made a farther progress therein.

RESOLVED, That this House will, to-morrow, again resolve itself into a committee of the whole House on the said report.[50]

Mr. Madison, from the committee to whom was referred the memorial of Robert Morris, made a report, which was read, and ordered to lie on the table.[51]

The several orders of the day for the House to resolve itself into a committee of the whole House, on the bill sent from the Senate, entitled, "An act for the punishment of certain crimes against the United States;" on the bill for regulating the post-office of the United States; and on the bill for the encouragement of learning, by securing the copies of maps, charts, books and other writings, to the authors and proprietors of such copies, during the times therein mentioned, were read, and postponed until to-morrow.

And then the House adjourned until to-morrow morning eleven o'clock.

---

[49] On March 10 this petition was committed.

[50] On March 10 the COWH considered this report again.

[51] A copy of the report is in A Record of the Reports of Select Committees, HR, DNA. On March 19 this committee report was considered, and another committee was appointed to inquire into the finances of Robert Morris's administration as superintendent of finances.

WEDNESDAY, MARCH 10, 1790

An engrossed bill to encrease the salaries of the Clerks in the office of the Commissioners for settling accounts between the United States and individual States, was read the third time.

RESOLVED, That the said bill do pass; and that the title be, "An act to encrease the salaries of the Clerks in the office of the Commissioners for settling accounts between the United States and individual States."[52]

ORDERED, That the Clerk of this House do carry the said bill to the Senate, and desire their concurrence.[53]

A petition of William McKennan, late a captain in the Delaware regiment, was presented to the House and read, praying further relief in consideration of his having been wounded and disabled in the service of his country.   Also,

A petition of Pitman Collins, of the state of Connecticut, praying to be reimbursed the value of a vessel, the property of the petitioner, which was impressed for the service of the United States, and taken by the enemy during the late war.

Also, a memorial of Anthony Walton White, late colonel of the first regiment of dragoons in the service of the United States, during the late war, praying to be reimbursed for monies advanced for the support of the said regiment.[54]

ORDERED, That the said petitions and memorial do lie on the table.

ORDERED, That the petition of John Mills, which was presented yesterday, be referred to the Secretary at War, with instruction to examine the same, and report his opinion thereupon to the House.

The House proceeded to consider the report of the Secretary of the Treasury, on the petition of Samuel Armstrong: Whereupon,

ORDERED, That the petitioner have leave to withdraw his said petition.

ORDERED, That the petition of William Bedlow, which was presented yesterday, be referred to Mr. Benson, Mr. Fitzsimons, and Mr. Ames, that they do examine the matter thereof, and report the same, with their opinion thereupon, to the House.[55]

The House proceeded to consider the report of the committee on the petition of Gifford Dalley: Whereupon,

RESOLVED, That the said Gifford Dalley be allowed for his services during the late recess, the sum of two dollars per day for ninety-six days.

ORDERED, That the said resolution be referred to the committee of the

---

[52] The bill is in Engrossed House Bills, HR, DNA.

[53] The Senate read this bill on March 11, 12, and 30. On March 30 a motion to read the bill a third time was disagreed to.

[54] On March 12 this petition was referred to the secretary of war.

[55] There is no record in the Journal of this committee reporting on the petition.

whole House, to whom is committed the bill making appropriations for the support of Government.[56]

The House proceeded to consider the report of the Secretary at War, on the petition of John Ely: Whereupon,

ORDERED, That a bill or bills be brought in pursuant to the said report; and that Mr. Trumbull, Mr. Mathews, and Mr. Burke, do prepare and bring in the same.[57]

An engrossed bill to promote the progress of useful arts, was read the third time, and the blanks therein filled up.

RESOLVED, That the said bill do pass; and that the title be, "An act to promote the progress of useful arts."[58]

ORDERED, That the Clerk of this House do carry the said bill to the Senate, and desire their concurrence.[59]

The House, according to the order of the day, again resolved itself into a committee of the whole House, on the report of the Secretary of the Treasury, relative to a provision for the support of the public credit.

Mr. Speaker left the chair.

Mr. Benson took the chair of the committee.

Mr. Speaker resumed the chair, and Mr. Benson reported, that the committee had, according to order, had the said report under consideration, and made a farther progress therein.

RESOLVED, That this House will, to-morrow, again resolve itself into a committee of the whole House, on the said report.[60]

The several orders of the day were read, and postponed until to-morrow.

And then the House adjourned until to-morrow morning eleven o'clock.

---

[56] On March 15 the Appropriations Bill [HR–47] was considered by the COWH and amended.

[57] On March 11 this committee presented the Ely Bill [HR–49], which was read.

[58] A printed copy of the bill, annotated by the Senate, is in House Bills, SR, DNA. E–46067. A petition of Richard Wells, asking that the sixth section of the Patents Bill [HR–41] be struck out, is in Petitions and Memorials, HR, DNA. Since it is dated Philadelphia, March 3, 1790, it probably reached the House after passage of the bill and was sent to the Senate. The notation on the petition "Returned to Clerk Ho. Reps. from Secretary Senate—" indicates that both Senate and House saw it, although no action seems to have been taken.

[59] The Senate read this bill on March 11 and 15. It was committed on March 15, and this committee reported on March 29 on the Patents Bill [HR–41], the Bailey Bill [HR–44], and the petition of John Fitch. The report was agreed to as amendments to the Patents Bill [HR–41]. The Bailey Bill and petition were not considered again by the Senate. The Senate agreed to the Patents Bill [HR–41] with twelve amendments on March 30. These amendments are printed in the *Senate Legislative Journal* for that date.

[60] On March 11 the COWH considered this report again.

THURSDAY, MARCH 11, 1790

A petition of George Smith, was presented to the House and read, praying relief in consideration of losses sustained in the service of the United States, during the late war.

ORDERED, That the said petition do lie on the table.

A petition of John Smith, late Postmaster in Portsmouth, Virginia, was presented to the House and read, praying that time may be granted him to make payment of certain arrearages in which he is indebted to the general post-office.

ORDERED, That the said petition be referred to Mr. Benson, Mr. Fitzsimons, and Mr. Ames, that they do examine the matter thereof, and report the same, with their opinion thereupon, to the House.

ORDERED, That the petition of William McKennan, which was presented yesterday, be referred to the Secretary at War, with instruction to examine the same, and report his opinion thereupon to the House.

ORDERED, That the petition of Pitman Collins, which was presented yesterday, be referred to the Secretary of the Treasury, with instruction to examine the same, and report his opinion thereupon to the House.

The House, according to the order of the day, again resolved itself into a committee of the whole House, on the report of the Secretary of the Treasury, relative to a provision for the support of the public credit.

Mr. Speaker left the chair.

Mr. Benson took the chair of the committee.

Mr. Speaker resumed the chair, and Mr. Benson reported, that the committee had, according to order, again had the said report under consideration, and made a farther progress therein.

RESOLVED, That this House will, to-morrow, again resolve itself into a committee of the whole House on the said report.[61]

A memorial of George Scriba, was presented to the House and read, praying that the Secretary of the Treasury may be authorised to report on a petition of the memorialist, which was presented on the second instant: Whereupon,

ORDERED, That it be an instruction to the Secretary of the Treasury, to examine and report upon the petition of the said George Scriba; and also upon the petition of Hannibal William Dobbyn, which were heretofore referred to the said Secretary for his information.

Mr. Trumbull, from the committee appointed, presented, according to order, a bill to allow compensation to John Ely, for his services and expences as

---

[61] On March 12 the COWH considered this report again.

a regimental surgeon in the late army of the United States, which was received, and read the first time.[62]

Mr. Hartley, from the committee to whom was referred the petition of David S. Franks, made a report,[63] which was read, and ordered to lie on the table.

ORDERED, That Mr. Wadsworth have leave to be absent from the service of this House until this day fortnight.

A petition of Jeremiah Ocain, of the state of Connecticut, was presented to the House and read, praying to be reimbursed the value of a sloop which was impressed from him during the late war, and taken by the enemy.[64]   Also,

A petition of Thomas Cole, praying relief in consideration of being wounded and disabled in the service of the United States, during the late war.

ORDERED, That the said petitions do lie on the table.

On motion,

The order of the day for the House to resolve itself into a committee of the whole House, on the bill sent from the Senate, entitled, "An act to accept a cession of the claims of the state of North-Carolina to a certain district of western territory," was farther postponed until Wednesday next.

ORDERED, That the petition of David Olyphant, which was presented on Monday last, be referred to the Secretary at War, with instruction to examine the same, and report his opinion thereupon to the House.

The several orders of the day were read, and postponed until to-morrow.

And then the House adjourned until to-morrow morning eleven o'clock.

FRIDAY, MARCH 12, 1790

A bill to allow compensation to John Ely, for his services and expences as a regimental surgeon in the late army of the United States, was read the second time, and ordered to be committed to a committee of the whole House on this day fortnight.[65]

ORDERED, That the petition of Anthony Walton White, which was presented on Wednesday last, be referred to the Secretary at War, with instruction to examine the same, and report his opinion thereupon to the House.[66]

The House, according to the order of the day, again resolved itself into a

---

[62] The original House bill is in House Bills, SR, DNA. On March 12 this bill was read again.

[63] A copy of the report is in A Record of the Reports of Select Committees, HR, DNA.

[64] On July 14 this petition was referred to the secretary of war.

[65] From March 26 through April 3 this bill was postponed as an order of the day. On April 5 it was considered in the COWH, and the bill was disagreed to.

[66] On July 1 the secretary reported on this petition.

committee of the whole House, on the report of the Secretary of the Treasury, relative to a provision for the support of the public credit.

Mr. Speaker left the chair.

Mr. Benson took the chair of the committee.

Mr. Speaker resumed the chair, and Mr. Benson reported, that the committee had, according to order, again had the said report under consideration, and made a farther progress therein.

RESOLVED, That this House will, to-morrow, again resolve itself into a committee of the whole House on the said report.[67]

The several orders of the day were read, and postponed until to-morrow.

And then the House adjourned until to-morrow morning eleven o'clock.

SATURDAY, MARCH 13, 1790

A petition of Stephen Guyer, of the state of Connecticut, was presented to the House and read, praying to be reimbursed the amount of a judgment and costs recovered against him, for a supply of provisions, which, as a Commissary, he obtained for the use of the late army of the United States.   Also,

The several petitions of Toney Turney, John McKenzie, James Whayland, and Cesar Edwards, of the said state of Connecticut, respectively praying relief in consideration of wounds or injuries received in the service of the United States during the late war.

ORDERED, That the said petitions do lie on the table.

ORDERED, That the memorial of the late officers of the South-Carolina line, on continental establishment, which was presented the fifth instant, be referred to the Secretary of the Treasury, with instruction to examine the same, and report his opinion thereupon to the House.

The House, according to the order of the day, again resolved itself into a committee of the whole House, on the report of the Secretary of the Treasury, relative to a provision for the support of the public credit.

Mr. Speaker left the chair.

Mr. Benson took the chair of the committee.

Mr. Speaker resumed the chair, and Mr. Benson reported, that the committee had, according to order, again had the said report under consideration, and come to several resolutions thereupon, which they had directed him to report, whenever the House should think proper to receive the same.

ORDERED, That the said report be received on Monday next.

RESOLVED, That this House will, on Monday next, again resolve itself into

---

[67] On March 13 the COWH reported several resolutions on the report on the public credit.

a committee of the whole House on the said report of the Secretary of the Treasury.[68]

The several orders of the day were read, and postponed until Monday next.

And then the House adjourned until Monday morning eleven o'clock.

MONDAY, MARCH 15, 1790

The House, according to the order of the day, resolved itself into a committee of the whole House, on the bill making appropriations for the support of government.

Mr. Speaker left the chair.

Mr. Benson took the chair of the committee.

Mr. Speaker resumed the chair, and Mr. Benson reported, that the committee had, according to order, had the said bill under consideration, and gone through the same, and made several amendments thereto, which he delivered in at the Clerk's table, where the same were severally twice read, and agreed to by the House.

ORDERED, That the said bill, with the amendments, be engrossed, and read the third time to-morrow.[69]

The several orders of the day were read, and postponed until to-morrow.

And then the House adjourned until to-morrow morning eleven o'clock.

TUESDAY, MARCH 16, 1790

An engrossed bill, making appropriations for the support of Government, was read the third time.

RESOLVED, That the said bill do pass; and that the title be, "An act making appropriations for the support of Government, for the year one thousand seven hundred and ninety."

ORDERED, That the Clerk of this House do carry the said bill to the Senate, and desire their concurrence.[70]

A message was received from the President of the United States, by the Secretary at War, who delivered in a letter and representation from the Supreme Executive Council of Pennsylvania, on the subject of Indian hostilities, committed in the county of Washington, in that State; and then withdrew.

The said letter and representation were read, and ordered to lie on the table.

A petition of the importers of hemp, and the manufacturers of cordage, in

---

[68] On March 29 the resolutions reported by the COWH are printed in the Journal. On the same day some of the resolutions were agreed to and others were tabled or recommitted.

[69] On March 16 this bill was read, agreed to, and sent to the Senate.

[70] On March 16, 17, and 18 the Senate read this bill. On March 18 the petition of James Mathers and the bill were committed. On March 22 this bill was agreed to by the Senate with three amendments, and the House was notified.

the city of New-York, was presented to the House and read, praying that the duty on hemp imported prior to December, one thousand seven hundred and ninety, may be taken off, and a prohibition laid on the importation of foreign cordage.

ORDERED, That the said petition, together with the petition of the rope-makers of the town of Boston, which was presented on the second instant, be referred to Mr. Laurance, Mr. Goodhue, and Mr. Hiester, that they do examine the matter thereof, and report the same with their opinion thereupon to the House.

A petition of Thomas Boyd, late a soldier in the Pennsylvania line of the army of the United States, was presented to the House and read, praying relief in consideration of wounds received in the service of his country.

ORDERED, That the said petition do lie on the table.

A message, in writing, was received from the President of the United States, by Mr. Lear his Secretary, who delivered in the same, together with the papers therein referred to, and then withdrew.

The said message and papers were read, and are as follow:

UNITED STATES, March 16th, 1790

GENTLEMEN of the SENATE and HOUSE of REPRESENTATIVES,

I HAVE directed my Secretary to lay before you the Copy of an Act, and the Form of Ratification of certain Articles of Amendment to the Constitution of the United States, by the Legislature of the state of Pennsylvania; together with the Copy of a Letter which accompanied the said Act, from the Speaker of the House of Assembly of Pennsylvania, to the President of the United States.

The Originals of the above will be lodged in the office of the Secretary of State.

G. WASHINGTON

(Copy)

In ASSEMBLY of PENNSYLVANIA, March 11th, 1790

SIR,

I HAVE the honor to transmit an exemplified Copy of the Act declaring the Assent of this State to certain Amendments to the Constitution of the United States, that you may be pleased to lay it before Congress.

With the greatest Respect,
I have the Honor to be,
Your obedient Servant,
(Signed)   RICHARD PETERS, Speaker

His Excellency
The PRESIDENT of the UNITED STATES

UNITED STATES, March 16th, 1790
I Certify the above to be a true Copy from the Original.
TOBIAS LEAR, Secretary to the President of the United States

(Copy)

IN GENERAL ASSEMBLY,
STATE OF PENNSYLVANIA, *to wit:*

IN pursuance of a resolution of the General Assembly of the state of Pennsylvania, being the Legislature thereof, I do hereby certify, That the paper hereunto annexed contains an exact and true Exemplification of the Act whereof it purports to be a Copy, by virtue whereof the several Amendments therein mentioned, proposed to the Constitution of the United States, were, on the part of the Commonwealth of Pennsylvania, agreed to, ratified and confirmed.

GIVEN under my Hand and the Seal of the State, this eleventh day of March, in the year of our Lord one thousand seven hundred and ninety.

(Signed)   RICHARD PETERS, Speaker

$\left(\begin{smallmatrix} \text{Seal} \\ \text{Appendant} \end{smallmatrix}\right)$

An ACT declaring the Assent of this State to certain Amendments to the Constitution of the United States

SECTION 1. WHEREAS in pursuance of the fifth article of the Constitution of the United States, certain Articles of Amendment to the said Constitution have been proposed by the Congress of the United States, for the consideration of the Legislatures of the several States: And whereas this House being the Legislature of the state of Pennsylvania, having maturely deliberated thereupon, have resolved to adopt and ratify the Articles hereafter enumerated, as part of the Constitution of the United States.

SECTION 2. *Be it enacted therefore, and it is hereby enacted by the Representatives of the Freemen of the Commonwealth of Pennsylvania, in General Assembly met, and by the authority of the same,* That the following Amendments to the Constitution of the United States, proposed by the Congress thereof, viz.

[Here follow the third, fourth, fifth, sixth, seventh, eighth, ninth, tenth, eleventh and twelfth Articles, which were proposed by Congress to the Legislatures of the several States, as Amendments to the Constitution of the United States.]

Be, and they are hereby ratified on behalf of this State, to become, when ratified by the Legislatures of three-fourths of the several States, part of the Constitution of the United States.

Signed by Order of the House,

RICHARD PETERS, Speaker

Enacted into a Law, at Philadelphia, on Wednesday the tenth day of March, in the year of our Lord one thousand seven hundred and ninety.

(Signed)   PETER ZACHARY LLOYD,

Clerk of the General Assembly

I, MATHEW IRWIN, Esquire, Master of the Rolls for the state of Pennsylvania, do certify the preceding Writing to be a true Copy (or Exemplification) of a certain Law remaining in my Office.

Witness my Hand and Seal of Office, the eleventh of March, one thousand seven hundred and ninety.

(L. S.)   (Signed)   MATHEW IRWIN, M. R.

UNITED STATES, March 16th, 1790

I do certify the foregoing to be a true Copy of the Act and Form of Ratification of certain Articles of Amendment to the Constitution of the United States, by the Legislature of Pennsylvania, as transmitted to the President of the United States.

TOBIAS LEAR, Secretary to the President of the United States[71]

ORDERED, That the said message and papers do lie on the table.

The House, according to the order of the day, resolved itself into a committee of the whole House, on the report of the committee to whom was referred the memorials of the people called Quakers, and of the Pennsylvania Society for promoting the Abolition of Slavery.

Mr. Speaker left the chair.

Mr. Benson took the chair of the committee.

Mr. Speaker resumed the chair, and Mr. Benson reported, that the committee had, according to order, had the said report under consideration, and made some progress therein.

RESOLVED, That this House will, to-morrow, again resolve itself into a committee of the whole House on the said report.[72]

The Speaker laid before the House a letter and report from the Secretary at

---

[71] The message with enclosures is in President's Messages: Suggesting legislation, SR, DNA.

[72] On March 17 the COWH considered this report again.

War, on the several petitions of David Sturges, Jeremiah Ryan, and David Cook, which were read, and ordered to lie on the table.[73]

The several orders of the day were read, and postponed until to-morrow.

And then the House adjourned until to-morrow morning eleven o'clock.

WEDNESDAY, MARCH 17, 1790

The Speaker laid before the House a letter and report from the Secretary of the Treasury, on the memorial of John Cochran,[74] which were read, and ordered to lie on the table.

The Speaker laid before the House a letter and report from the Postmaster-General, on the memorial of Isaac Trowbridge, which were read, and ordered to lie on the table.

The Speaker laid before the House a letter and reports from the Secretary at War, on the several petitions of Rufus Lincoln, John Watson, and John Mills, which were read, and ordered to lie on the table.[75]

The petitions of Samuel Carleton, and Cornelius Wynkoop, were presented to the House and read, praying relief in consideration of losses or injuries sustained in the service of the United States during the late war.

ORDERED, That the said petitions, together with the several petitions of Stephen Guyer, Toney Turney, Cesar Edwards, James Whayland, John McKenzie, Henry Carman, and William Scott, which lay on the table, be referred to the Secretary at War, with instruction to examine the same, and report his opinion thereupon to the House.

ORDERED, That the petitions of Isaac Sherman, and Andrew Dunscomb, which lay on the table, be referred to the Secretary of the Treasury, with instruction to examine the same, and report his opinion thereupon to the House.

A petition of John Frederick Amelung, proprietor of a glass manufactory at New-Bremen, in the state of Maryland, was presented to the House and read, praying that the workmen and laborers employed in the said manufactory, may be exempted from militia duty.

ORDERED, That the said petition be referred to the committee appointed to prepare and bring in a bill or bills for regulating the militia of the United States, that they do examine the matter thereof, and report the same, with their opinion thereupon, to the House.[76]

---

[73] Copies of all of these reports are in A Record of the Reports of the Secretary of War, vol. 1, HR, DNA. On April 26 the report on Jeremiah Ryan's petition was referred to the committee to prepare the Disabled Soldiers and Seamen Bill [HR–88].

[74] A copy of the report is in A Record of the Reports of the Secretary of the Treasury, vol. 1, HR, DNA.

[75] Copies of all of these reports are in A Record of the Reports of the Secretary of War, vol. 1, HR, DNA.

[76] On April 26 the secretary of war's plan for the militia was referred to this committee.

A petition of Rufus Hamilton, of the state of Massachusetts, was presented to the House and read, praying to receive compensation for certain property impressed from him during the war, for the service of the United States.

ORDERED, That the said petition do lie on the table.

The House, according to the order of the day, again resolved itself into a committee of the whole House, on the report of the committee to whom was referred the memorials of the people called Quakers, and of the Pennsylvania Society for promoting the Abolition of Slavery.

Mr. Speaker left the chair.

Mr. Benson took the chair of the committee.

Mr. Speaker resumed the chair, and Mr. Benson reported, that the committee had, according to order, again had the said report under consideration, and made a farther progress therein.

RESOLVED, That this House will, to-morrow, again resolve itself into a committee of the whole House on the said report.[77]

The several orders of the day were read, and postponed until to-morrow.

And then the House adjourned until to-morrow morning eleven o'clock.

THURSDAY, MARCH 18, 1790

A petition of Joseph Harris, of the state of New-York, was presented to the House and read, praying relief in consideration of wounds received in the service of his country, during the late war.   Also,

A petition of John Francis Vacher, of the city of New-York, praying compensation for military services rendered during the late war.

ORDERED, That the said petitions be referred to the Secretary at War, with instruction to examine the same, and report his opinion thereupon to the House.

A petition of Abraham Van Alstine, was presented to the House and read, praying to be reimbursed the value of a sum of paper money, which was placed in his hands during the late war, for public service, and has remained to the present time undisposed of.

ORDERED, That the said petition do lie on the table.

The House, according to the order of the day, again resolved itself into a committee of the whole House, on the report of the committee to whom were referred the memorials of the people called Quakers, and of the Pennsylvania Society for promoting the Abolition of Slavery.

Mr. Speaker left the chair.

Mr. Benson took the chair of the committee.

---

[77] On March 18 the COWH considered this report again.

Mr. Speaker resumed the chair, and Mr. Benson reported, that the committee had, according to order, again had the said report under consideration, and made a farther progress therein.

RESOLVED, That this House will, to-morrow, again resolve itself into a committee of the whole House on the said report.[78]

ORDERED, That Mr. Fitzsimons have leave to be absent from the service of this House until this day fortnight.

The several orders of the day were read, and postponed until to-morrow.

And then the House adjourned until to-morrow morning eleven o'clock.

FRIDAY, MARCH 19, 1790

A member from North-Carolina, to wit, Hugh Williamson, appeared, produced his credentials, and took his seat in the House; the oath to support the Constitution of the United States being administered to him by Mr. Speaker, according to law.

The Speaker laid before the House a letter and report from the Secretary of the Treasury, on the memorial of the late officers of the South-Carolina line on continental establishment,[79] which were read, and ordered to lie on the table.

The Speaker laid before the House a letter and reports from the Secretary at War, on the several petitions of Alexander Power and others, late officers in the regiment of artillery artificers; Anna Treat, and William Mason, which were read, and ordered to lie on the table.[80]

A petition of Benjamin Warren, of the state of Massachusetts, was presented to the House and read, praying relief in consideration of losses and injuries sustained during the late war.

ORDERED, That the said petition do lie on the table.

The House proceeded to consider the report of the Secretary at War, on the petitions of James Gibbons, and Archibald McAlister: Whereupon,

ORDERED, That the petitioners have leave to withdraw their said petitions.

The House proceeded to consider the report of the committee to whom was referred the memorial of Robert Morris: Whereupon,

ORDERED, That a committee of five be appointed to enquire into the receipts and expenditures of public monies during the administration of the said Robert Morris, as late Superintendant of Finance, and report to the House a state of the accounts respecting the same.

---

[78] On March 19 the COWH considered this report again.

[79] A copy of the report is in A Record of the Reports of the Secretary of the Treasury, vol. 1, HR, DNA.

[80] Copies of all of these reports are in A Record of the Reports of the Secretary of War, vol. 1, HR, DNA.

And a committee was appointed of Mr. Madison, Mr. Sherman, Mr. Sedgwick, Mr. Laurance, and Mr. Smith (of South-Carolina).[81]

The House, according to the order of the day, again resolved itself into a committee of the whole House, on the report of the committee to whom were referred the memorials of the people called Quakers, and of the Pennsylvania Society for promoting the abolition of Slavery.

Mr. Speaker left the chair.

Mr. Benson took the chair of the committee.

Mr. Speaker resumed the chair, and Mr. Benson reported, that the committee had, according to order, again had the said report under their consideration, and made a farther progress therein.

RESOLVED, That this House will, on Monday next, again resolve itself into a committee of the whole House on the said report.[82]

A message from the Senate by Mr. Otis their Secretary.

MR. SPEAKER, The Senate have passed the bill, entitled, "An act to provide for the remission or mitigation of fines, forfeitures and penalties in certain cases," with an amendment, to which they desire the concurrence of this House.[83] The Senate have also passed the bill, entitled, "An act to establish an uniform rule of naturalization," with an amendment, to which they desire the concurrence of this House:[84]   And then he withdrew.

The several orders of the day were read, and postponed until Monday next. And then the House adjourned until Monday morning eleven o'clock.

MONDAY, MARCH 22, 1790

The Speaker laid before the House a letter and report from the Secretary at War, on the petition of John Stevens, which were read, and ordered to lie on the table.[85]

A petition of Edward Thompson was presented to the House, and read,

---

[81] On February 16, 1791, this committee reported.

[82] On March 22 the COWH made several amendments to this report.

[83] The Senate committee report on this bill, with the amendment, is in Various Select Committee Reports, SR, DNA. Annotations on the bill, which is in House Bills, SR, DNA, correspond to changes incorporated into the amendment passed by the Senate. The amendment is printed in the *Senate Legislative Journal* on March 19. On March 24 the House disagreed to this Senate amendment and requested a conference on it.

[84] The Senate amendment is noted on one of the printed copies of this bill in House Bills, SR, DNA. The amendment is printed in the *Senate Legislative Journal* on March 19. On March 22 the House agreed to this Senate amendment.

[85] A copy of the report is in A Record of the Reports of the Secretary of War, vol. 1, HR, DNA. On April 26 this report was committed to the committee to prepare the Disabled Soldiers and Seamen Bill [HR–88].

praying relief in consideration of losses and injuries sustained during the late war. Also,

A memorial of John Baylor, of the state of Virginia, executor of George Baylor, deceased, praying a settlement of certain unliquidated accounts between the estate of the decedent, and the United States.

ORDERED, That the said petition and memorial do lie on the table.[86]

The House proceeded to consider the amendment proposed by the Senate, to the bill, entitled, "An act to establish an uniform rule of naturalization:" Whereupon,

RESOLVED, That this House doth agree to the said amendment.

ORDERED, That the Clerk of this House do acquaint the Senate therewith.[87]

The House, according to the order of the day, again resolved itself into a committee of the whole House on the report of the committee to whom were referred the memorials of the people called Quakers, and of the Pennsylvania Society for promoting the Abolition of Slavery.

Mr. Speaker left the chair.

Mr. Benson took the chair of the committee.

Mr. Speaker resumed the chair, and Mr. Benson reported, that the committee had, according to order, again had the said report under consideration, and made several amendments thereto, which he delivered in at the Clerk's table, where the same were read, and ordered to lie on the table.[88]

A message from the Senate by Mr. Otis their Secretary.

MR. SPEAKER, The Senate have passed the bill, entitled, "An act making appropriations for the support of government, for the year one thousand seven hundred and ninety," with several amendments, to which they desire the concurrence of this House:[89] And then he withdrew.

The several orders of the day were read, and postponed until to-morrow.

And then the House adjourned until to-morrow morning eleven o'clock.

TUESDAY, MARCH 23, 1790

A memorial of James Wilson, on behalf of the United Land-Companies of the Illinois and Wabash, was presented to the House, and read, praying to be permitted to exhibit the documents of the titles of the said companies to cer-

---

[86] On March 23 these petitions were referred to the secretary of war.

[87] On March 25 this bill was signed by the speaker and the vice president.

[88] On March 23 both the original committee report and the report of the COWH are printed in the Journal.

[89] These amendments are printed in the *Senate Legislative Journal* on March 22. On March 23 the Senate amendments were agreed to with amendments, and the Senate was notified. On the same day the Senate disagreed to one of the House amendments.

tain tracts of western lands, heretofore purchased by the said companies, under the sanction of lawful authority; and also to make proposals for obtaining the formal and regular confirmation of those titles from the United States. Also,

A petition of Adolphus Brower, of the state of New-York, praying relief in consideration of losses and injuries sustained in the service of the United States, during the late war.

ORDERED, That the said memorial and petition do lie on the table.

The petitions of Ephraim McCoy, of the state of Pennsylvania, and of Jacob Acker, of the state of New-York, were presented to the House, and read, respectively praying relief in consideration of losses or injuries sustained in the service of the United States, during the late war.

ORDERED, That the said petitions, together with the petitions of Edward Thompson, and John Baylor, executor of George Baylor, which were presented yesterday, be referred to the Secretary at War, with instruction to examine the same, and report his opinion thereupon to the House.[90]

The House proceeded to consider the amendments proposed by the Senate to the bill, entitled, "An act making appropriations for the support of government, for the year one thousand seven hundred and ninety," and the same being read, were amended[91] and agreed to.

ORDERED, That the Clerk of this House do acquaint the Senate therewith.

Mr. Livermore, from the committee to whom was referred the petition of Richard Wells and Josiah Hart, made a report, which was read, and ordered to lie on the table.[92]

A message from the Senate by Mr. Otis their Secretary.

MR. SPEAKER, The Senate disagree to the amendment proposed by this House to their last amendment to the bill, entitled, "An act making appropriations for the support of government, for the year one thousand seven hundred and ninety," and do adhere to their said amendment:[93] And then he withdrew.

On a motion made and seconded, that the House do now proceed to consider the amendments made by the committee of the whole House, and reported yesterday, to the report of the committee to whom were referred the

---

[90] On April 22 the secretary reported on the McCoy petition. On July 1 the secretary reported on John Baylor's petition.

[91] The House amendment is printed in the *Senate Legislative Journal* on March 23.

[92] A copy of the report is in A Record of the Reports of Select Committees, HR, DNA. On May 20 this committee report was committed to the COWH, which was considering the Funding Bill [HR–63].

[93] On March 24 the House reconsidered the Senate's third amendment and agreed to it.

memorials of the people called Quakers, and of the Pennsylvania Society for promoting the Abolition of Slavery.

It was resolved in the affirmative, $\begin{cases} \text{AYES} & 26 \\ \text{NOES} & 25 \end{cases}$

Whereupon the said amendments were read at the Clerk's table: And,

On a motion made and seconded, that the said report of the committee to whom were referred the memorials of the people called Quakers, and of the Pennsylvania Society for promoting the Abolition of Slavery; and also the report of the committee of the whole House, of amendments to the said report, be inserted in the Journal:

It was resolved in the affirmative, $\begin{cases} \text{AYES} & 29 \\ \text{NOES} & 25 \end{cases}$

The ayes and noes being demanded by one fifth of the members present; Those who voted in the affirmative, are,

Elias Boudinot	Richard Bland Lee
John Brown	George Leonard
Lambert Cadwalader	James Madison, junior
Benjamin Contee	Peter Muhlenberg
William Floyd	Josiah Parker
Abiel Foster	George Partridge
Elbridge Gerry	James Schureman
Nicholas Gilman	Thomas Scott
Benjamin Goodhue	Theodore Sedgwick
Samuel Griffin	Roger Sherman
Thomas Hartley	Peter Silvester
John Hathorn	Thomas Sinnickson
Daniel Hiester	John Vining and
Benjamin Huntington	Henry Wynkoop
John Laurance	

Those who voted in the negative, are,

Fisher Ames	Samuel Livermore
Abraham Baldwin	George Mathews
Egbert Benson	Andrew Moore
Theodorick Bland	John Page
Aedanus Burke	Jeremiah Van Rensselaer
Daniel Carroll	William Smith (of Maryland)
Isaac Coles	William Smith (of South-Carolina)
George Gale	Michael Jenifer Stone
Jonathan Grout	Jonathan Sturges
James Jackson	Thomas Sumter

George Thatcher   Alexander White and
Jonathan Trumbull   Hugh Williamson
Thomas Tudor Tucker

The said reports are as follow:

REPORT OF THE SPECIAL COMMITTEE

The committee to whom were referred sundry memorials from the people called Quakers; and also a memorial from the Pennsylvania Society for promoting the Abolition of Slavery, submit the following report:

THAT from the nature of the matters contained in those memorials, they were induced to examine the powers vested in Congress, under the present constitution, relating to the abolition of slavery, and are clearly of opinion,

First. That the General Government is expressly restrained from prohibiting the importation of such persons "as any of the States now existing shall think proper to admit, until the year one thousand eight hundred and eight."

Secondly. That Congress, by a fair construction of the Constitution, are equally restrained from interfering in the emancipation of slaves, who already are, or who may, within the period mentioned, be imported into, or born within any of the said States.

Thirdly. That Congress have no authority to interfere in the internal regulations of particular States, relative to the instruction of slaves in the principles of morality and religion; to their comfortable cloathing, accommodations and subsistence; to the regulation of their marriages, and the prevention of the violation of the rights thereof, or to the separation of children from their parents; to a comfortable provision in cases of sickness, age or infirmity; or to the seizure, transportation or sale of free negroes; but have the fullest confidence in the wisdom and humanity of the Legislatures of the several States, that they will revise their laws from time to time, when necessary, and promote the objects mentioned in the memorials, and every other measure that may tend to the happiness of slaves.

Fourthly. That nevertheless Congress have authority, if they shall think it necessary, to lay at any time a tax or duty, not exceeding ten dollars for each person of any description, the importation of whom shall be by any of the States admitted as aforesaid.

Fifthly. That Congress have authority to interdict, or (so far as it is or may be carried on by citizens of the United States for supplying foreigners) to regulate the African trade, and to make provision for the humane treatment of slaves, in all cases while on their passage to the United States, or to foreign ports, as far as it respects the citizens of the United States.

Sixthly. That Congress have also authority to prohibit foreigners from fitting out vessels, in any port of the United States, for transporting persons from Africa to any foreign port.

Seventhly. That the memorialists be informed, that in all cases, to which the authority of Congress extends, they will exercise it for the humane objects of the memorialists, so far as they can be promoted on the principles of justice, humanity and good policy.

REPORT OF THE COMMITTEE OF THE WHOLE HOUSE

The committee of the whole House, to whom was committed the report of the committee on the memorials of the people called Quakers, and of the Pennsylvania Society for promoting the Abolition of Slavery, report the following amendments:

STRIKE out the first clause, together with the recital thereto, and in lieu thereof insert, "That the migration or importation of such persons as any of the States now existing shall think proper to admit, cannot be prohibited by Congress, prior to the year one thousand eight hundred and eight."

Strike out the second and third clauses, and in lieu thereof insert, "That Congress have no authority to interfere in the emancipation of slaves, or in the treatment of them within any of the States; it remaining with the several States alone to provide any regulations therein, which humanity and true policy may require."

Strike out the fourth and fifth clauses, and in lieu thereof insert, "That Congress have authority to restrain the citizens of the United States from carrying on the African trade, for the purpose of supplying foreigners with slaves, and of providing by proper regulations for the humane treatment, during their passage, of slaves imported by the said citizens into the States admitting such importation."

Strike out the seventh clause.

ORDERED, That the said report of the committee of the whole House do lie on the table.

The several orders of the day were read, and postponed until to-morrow.

And then the House adjourned until to-morrow morning eleven o'clock.

WEDNESDAY, MARCH 24, 1790

A petition of Christian Khun, was presented to the House and read, praying relief in consideration of a wound received in the service of the United States, during the late war, which has disabled him from obtaining a livelihood by labor.

ORDERED, That the said petition, together with the petition of Rufus

Hamilton, which was presented on the seventeenth instant, be referred to the Secretary at War, with instruction to examine the same, and report his opinion thereupon to the House.

ORDERED, That the memorial of James Wilson, on behalf of the United Land-Companies of Illinois and Wabash, which was presented yesterday, be referred to the Secretary of the Treasury, with instruction to examine the same, and report his opinion thereupon to the House.

The Speaker laid before the House a letter and reports from the Secretary at War, on the petition of David Olyphant, and John Rogers, on behalf of himself and others, which were read, and ordered to lie on the table.[94]

The House proceeded to consider the reports of the Secretary at War, on the petitions of David Cook and Ezra Smith: Whereupon,

ORDERED, That the said reports be committed to Mr. Burke, Mr. Trumbull, and Mr. Thatcher.

The House proceeded to re-consider the third amendment adhered to by the Senate, to the bill, entitled, "An act making appropriations for the support of government, for the year one thousand seven hundred and ninety:" Whereupon,

RESOLVED, That this House doth recede from their disagreement to the said amendment.

ORDERED, That the Clerk of this House do acquaint the Senate therewith.[95]

The House proceeded to consider the amendment proposed by the Senate to the bill, entitled, "An act to provide for the remission or mitigation of fines, forfeitures and penalties in certain cases:"   Whereupon,

RESOLVED, That this House doth disagree to the said amendment, and desire a conference with the Senate on the subject matter thereof.

ORDERED, That Mr. Ames, Mr. Huntington, and Mr. Jackson, be appointed managers at the said conference, on the part of this House.[96]

Another member from North-Carolina, to wit, John Baptista Ashe, appeared, produced his credentials, and took his seat in the House, the oath to support the Constitution of the United States being administered to him by Mr. Speaker, according to law.

An engrossed bill providing the means of intercourse between the United States and foreign nations, was read the third time, and ordered to be re-committed to Mr. Sedgwick, Mr. Huntington, and Mr. Lee.[97]

---

[94] Copies of these reports are in A Record of the Reports of the Secretary of War, vol. 1, HR, DNA. A copy of the Rogers report, probably by ASP, is in Reports and Communications from the Secretary of War, HR, DNA. On April 28 the report on the petition of John Rogers and others was committed.

[95] On March 25 this bill was signed by the speaker and the vice president.

[96] On March 25 the Senate agreed to this conference.

[97] On March 31 this committee presented the Foreign Intercourse Bill [HR–52], which was read.

The several orders of the day were read, and postponed until to-morrow. And then the House adjourned until to-morrow morning eleven o'clock.

THURSDAY, MARCH 25, 1790

Mr. Gilman, from the joint committee for inrolled bills, reported, that the committee had examined two inrolled bills, one entitled, "An act to establish an uniform rule of naturalization;"[98] the other, entitled, "An act making appropriations for the support of government, for the year one thousand seven hundred and ninety,"[99] and had found the same to be truly inrolled: Whereupon,

Mr. Speaker signed the said inrolled bills.[100]

ORDERED, That the Clerk of this House do acquaint the Senate therewith.

ORDERED, That Mr. Floyd have leave to be absent from the service of this House until this day fortnight.

On motion,

ORDERED, That leave be given to bring in a bill or bills, further to suspend part of an act, entitled, "An act to regulate the collection of the duties imposed by law on the tonnage of ships or vessels, and on goods, wares and merchandizes imported into the United States;" and that Mr. Lee, Mr. Cadwalader, and Mr. Seney, do prepare and bring in the same.[101]

A petition of Mary Wooster was presented to the House, and read, praying to be allowed interest on the pension granted her by the former Congress, as widow of the late General Wooster.   Also,

A petition of Ichabod Johnson and others, late seamen and mariners in the navy of the United States, praying to be granted the wages and allowances promised them by resolutions of the late Congress.

ORDERED, That the said petitions, together with the petition of Adolphus Brower, which was presented on Tuesday last, be referred to the Secretary of the Treasury, with instruction to examine the same, and report his opinion thereupon to the House.

A message from the Senate by Mr. Otis their Secretary.

MR. SPEAKER,   The Senate agree to the conference desired by this House, on the subject matter of the amendment depending between the two Houses, to the bill, entitled, "An act to provide for the remission or mitigation of

---

[98] The inspected enrolled bill is in Enrolled Acts, RG 11, DNA.

[99] The inspected enrolled bill is in Enrolled Acts, RG 11, DNA. E–46044.

[100] On March 26 the House was notified that these bills had been delivered to the president.

[101] On March 26 this committee presented a Collection Bill [HR–50], which was read.

fines, forfeitures and penalties in certain cases;" and have appointed managers at the same on their part: [102]   And then he withdrew.

The several orders of the day were read, and postponed until to-morrow. [103] And then the House adjourned until to-morrow morning eleven o'clock.

F R I D A Y, MARCH 26, 1790

A memorial of the officers of the late navy of the United States, was presented to the House and read, praying to be allowed the half-pay and other emoluments granted to the officers of the army. [104]   Also,

A petition of the merchants and traders of the town of Portsmouth, in the state of New-Hampshire, praying that Congress will adopt measures to prevent foreigners from carrying the commodities of the continent to any part or place where the citizens of the United States are prohibited from carrying them; and also, that the District and Circuit Courts of New-Hampshire may be held in the said town of Portsmouth. [105]

ORDERED, That the said memorial and petition do lie on the table.

Mr. Lee, from the committee appointed, presented, according to order, a bill further to suspend part of an act, entitled, "An act to regulate the collection of the duties imposed by law on the tonnage of ships or vessels, and on goods, wares and merchandizes imported into the United States," which was received and read the first time. [106]

On motion,

ORDERED, That the Clerk of this House do provide a book in which each member shall enter his account of compensation, for travelling to and from the seat of government, and attendance, previous to obtaining the Speaker's certificate for the same.

The House then, according to the order of the day, resolved itself into a committee of the whole House on the bill "to prevent the exportation of goods not duly inspected according to the laws of the several States."

Mr. Speaker left the chair.

Mr. Boudinot took the chair of the committee.

Mr. Speaker resumed the chair, and Mr. Boudinot reported, that the committee had, according to order, had the said bill under consideration, and

---

[102] On April 9 this conference committee reported.

[103] In a secret session on this date the House considered and passed the Military Establishment Bill [HR–50a]. E–46036.

[104] The memorial is in Petitions and Memorials: Various subjects, SR, DNA. On March 29 this petition was committed.

[105] The petition is in Petitions and Memorials: Various subjects, SR, DNA. On March 29 the two requests in this petition were referred to separate committees.

[106] On March 29 this bill was read again.

made an amendment thereto, which he delivered in at the Clerk's table, where the same was twice read, and agreed to by the House.

ORDERED, That the said bill, with the amendment, be engrossed, and read the third time on Monday next.[107]

Mr. Gilman, from the joint committee for inrolled bills, reported, that the committee did, yesterday, wait on the President of the United States, and present him with two inrolled bills, one entitled, "An act to establish an uniform rule of naturalization;" the other entitled, "An act making appropriations for the support of government, for the year one thousand seven hundred and ninety," for his approbation.[108]

The House, according to the order of the day, resolved itself into a committee of the whole House, on the bill sent from the Senate, entitled, "An act to accept a cession of the claims of the state of North-Carolina to a certain district of western territory."

Mr. Speaker left the chair.

Mr. Boudinot took the chair of the committee.

Mr. Speaker resumed the chair, and Mr. Boudinot reported, that the committee had, according to order, had the said bill under consideration, and made an amendment thereto, which he delivered in at the Clerk's table, where the same was twice read, and agreed to by the House.

ORDERED, That the said bill, with the amendment, be read the third time on Monday next.[109]

The several orders of the day were read, and postponed until Monday next.

And then the House adjourned until Monday morning eleven o'clock.

MONDAY, MARCH 29, 1790

An engrossed bill to prevent the exportation of goods not duly inspected according to the laws of the several States, was read the third time.

RESOLVED, That the said bill do pass; and that the title be, "An act to prevent the exportation of goods not duly inspected according to the laws of the several States."

ORDERED, That the Clerk of this House do carry the said bill to the Senate, and desire their concurrence.[110]

The bill sent from the Senate, entitled, "An act to accept a cession of the

---

[107] On March 29 this bill was read, agreed to, and sent to the Senate.

[108] On March 30 the House was notified that the president had signed these bills on March 26.

[109] On March 29 this bill was read again, amended, agreed to, and returned to the Senate.

[110] On March 29, 30, and 31 the Senate read this bill, and on March 31 it was agreed to, and the House was notified.

claims of the state of North-Carolina to a cetrain district of western territory," was read the third time.

RESOLVED, That the said bill do pass, with the following amendment:

In the first line strike out the words "The honorable."[111]

ORDERED, That the Clerk of this House do acquaint the Senate therewith, and desire their concurrence to the said amendment.[112]

A bill "further to suspend part of an act, entitled 'An act to regulate the collection of the duties imposed by law on the tonnage of ships or vessels, and on goods, wares and merchandizes imported into the United States,'" was read the second time, and ordered to be committed to a committee of the whole House on Monday next.[113]

On motion,

ORDERED, That so much of the petition of the merchants and traders of the town of Portsmouth, in the state of New-Hampshire, as prays that Congress will adopt measures to prevent foreigners from carrying the commodities of this continent to any port or place where the citizens of the United States are prohibited from carrying them, be referred to Mr. Boudinot, Mr. Jackson, Mr. Tucker, Mr. Ashe, Mr. Parker, Mr. Smith of Maryland, Mr. Clymer, Mr. Vining, Mr. Benson, Mr. Sherman, Mr. Goodhue, and Mr. Foster; that they do examine the matter thereof, and report the same, with their opinion thereupon, to the House.[114]

ORDERED, That such other part of the said petition as prays that the District and Circuit Courts of New-Hampshire may be held in the said town of Portsmouth, be referred to Mr. Foster, Mr. Williamson, and Mr. Thatcher; that they do examine the matter thereof, and report the same, with their opinion thereupon, to the House.[115]

ORDERED, That the memorial of the officers of the late navy of the United States, which was presented on Friday last, be referred to Mr. Baldwin, Mr. Hartley, Mr. Laurance, Mr. Trumbull, Mr. Stone, Mr. Ashe, and Mr. Burke; that they do examine the matter thereof, and report the same, with their opinion thereupon, to the House.[116]

A petition of Moses Hazen, on behalf of himself and Andrew Lee, was presented to the House and read, praying a settlement of certain claims against the United States, as officers in the late army.

ORDERED, That the said petition do lie on the table.

---

[111] A copy of the resolution with the amendment is filed with the bill in Engrossed Senate Bills and Resolutions, SR, DNA.

[112] On March 29 the Senate agreed to this amendment with an amendment.

[113] On April 5 this bill was considered in the COWH.

[114] On April 16 this committee reported.

[115] On April 7 this committe reported.

[116] On May 13 this committee reported.

Mr. Benson, from the committee of the whole House, on the report of the Secretary of the Treasury, relative to a provision for the support of the public credit, reported, according to order, the resolutions agreed to by the committee on the thirteenth instant, as follow:

1. RESOLVED, That adequate provision ought to be made for fulfilling the engagements of the United States, in respect to their foreign debt.

2. RESOLVED, That permanent funds ought to be appropriated for the payment of interest on, and the gradual discharge of the domestic debt of the United States.

3. RESOLVED, That the arrears of interest, including indents issued in payment thereof, ought to be provided for on the same terms with the principal of the said debt.

4. RESOLVED, That the debts of the respective States, ought, with the consent of the creditors, to be assumed and provided for by the United States. And that effectual provision be at the same time made for liquidating and crediting to the States, the whole of their respective expenditures during the war, as the same have been or may be stated for the purpose; and that in such liquidation the best evidence shall be received that the nature of the case will permit.

5. RESOLVED, That it is adviseable to endeavour to effect a new modification of the domestic debt, including that of the particular States, with the voluntary consent of the creditors, by a loan, upon terms mutually beneficial to them and to the United States.

6. RESOLVED, That for the purpose expressed in the last preceding resolution, subscriptions towards a loan ought to be opened, to the amount of the said domestic debt, including that of the respective States, upon the terms following, to wit:

That for every hundred dollars subscribed, payable in the said debt (as well interest as principal) the subscriber be entitled, at his option, either

To have two-thirds funded at an annuity, or yearly interest of six per cent. redeemable at the pleasure of the government, by payment of the principal; and to receive the other third in lands in the Western Territory, at the rate of twenty cents per acre. Or,

To have sixty-six dollars and two-thirds of a dollar funded immediately, at an annuity, or yearly interest of six per cent. irredeemable by any payment exceeding   per annum, on account both of principal and interest; and to have, at the end of   years,   , funded at the like interest and rate of redemption.

7. RESOLVED, That immediate provision ought to be made for the present debt of the United States; and that the faith of government ought to be pledged to make provision, at their next session, for so much of the debts of

the respective States, as shall have been subscribed upon any of the terms expressed in the last resolution.

8. RESOLVED, That the funds which shall be appropriated according to the second of the foregoing resolutions, be applied, in the first place, to the payment of interest on the sums subscribed towards the proposed loan; and that if any part of the said domestic debt shall remain unsubscribed, the surplus of the said funds be applied, by a temporary appropriation, to the payment of interest on the unsubscribed part, so as not to exceed, for the present, four per cent. per annum; but this limitation shall not be understood to impair the right of the non-subscribing creditors to the residue of the interest on their respective debts: And in case the aforesaid surplus should prove insufficient to pay the non-subscribing creditors, at the aforesaid rate of four per cent. that the faith of government be pledged to make good such deficiency.

The first, second and third resolutions were severally read a second time, and, on the question put thereupon, agreed to by the House.

The fourth resolution was read a second time, and on a motion made, ordered to be re-committed to the same committee. AYES 29: NOES 27.

ORDERED, That the fifth, sixth, seventh and eighth resolutions do lie on the table.[117]

A message from the Senate by Mr. Otis their Secretary.

MR. SPEAKER, The Senate have agreed to the amendment proposed by this House to the bill, entitled, "An act to accept a cession of the claims of the state of North-Carolina to a certain district of western territory," with an amendment, to which they desire the concurrence of this House:[118] And then he withdrew.

The several orders of the day were read, and postponed until to-morrow.

And then the House adjourned until to-morrow morning eleven o'clock.

TUESDAY, MARCH 30, 1790

A petition of Christopher Colles, of the city of New-York, was presented to the House and read, praying to be employed by Congress in a Survey and Publication of the Roads of the United States.[119]

---

[117] On March 30 the fifth through the eighth resolutions were recommitted to the COWH, and the report on public credit was considered again by the COWH.

[118] A copy of the Senate resolution with the amendment is filed with the bill in Engrossed Senate Bills and Resolutions, SR, DNA. The amendment is printed in the *Senate Legislative Journal* on March 29. According to the *Senate Legislative Journal*, the Senate amendment was agreed to on March 30. On April 1 this bill was signed by the speaker and the vice president.

[119] The memorial with a copy of a letter from Christopher Colles to the postmaster general is in Petitions and Memorials, HR, DNA.

ORDERED, That the said petition be referred to the Postmaster-General, with instruction to examine the same, and report his opinion thereupon to the House.[120]

A petition of Stephen Steward, junior, administrator of John Steward, deceased, late a Colonel in the Maryland line of the army of the United States, was presented to the House and read, praying a settlement of certain unliquidated accounts between the estate of the decedent and the United States.[121]

Also, a petition of Leonard Young, of the state of Delaware, praying relief in consideration of wounds received in the service of the United States, during the late war, which have disabled him from procuring a livelihood by labor.

ORDERED, That the said petitions be referred to the Secretary at War, with instruction to examine the same, and report his opinion thereupon to the House.

ORDERED, That the petition of Moses Hazen, on behalf of himself and Andrew Lee, which was presented yesterday, be referred to the Secretary of the Treasury, with instruction to examine the same, and report his opinion thereupon to the House.

Mr. Wadsworth, from the committee appointed, presented, according to order, a bill "to regulate trade and intercourse with the Indian Tribes," which was received and read the first time.[122]

A message was received from the President of the United States, by Mr. Lear his Secretary, notifying that the President has approved of two acts, one entitled, "An act to establish an uniform rule of naturalization;" the other, entitled, "An act making appropriations for the support of government, for the year one thousand seven hundred and ninety," and affixed his signature to the same on the twenty-sixth instant.

The House resumed the consideration of the fifth, sixth, seventh and eighth resolutions reported yesterday from the committee of the whole House, on the report of the Secretary of the Treasury, relative to a provision for the support of the public credit: Whereupon,

ORDERED, That the said resolutions be severally re-committed to the same committee.

The House then, according to the order of the day, resolved itself into a committee of the whole House on the report of the Secretary of the Treasury, relative to a provision for the support of the public credit.

Mr. Speaker left the chair.

---

[120] On April 27 the postmaster general's report on this petition was received and read.

[121] On July 1 the secretary reported on the Steward petition.

[122] On March 31 this bill was read again.

Mr. Livermore took the chair of the committee.

Mr. Speaker resumed the chair, and Mr. Livermore reported, that the committee had, according to order, had the said report under consideration, and made some progress therein.

RESOLVED, That this House will, to-morrow, again resolve itself into a committee of the whole House on the said report.[123]

A message from the Senate by Mr. Otis their Secretary.

MR. SPEAKER, The Senate have passed the bill, entitled, "An act to promote the progress of useful arts," with several amendments, to which they desire the concurrence of this House;[124] and then he withdrew.

A member from North-Carolina, presented to the House the proceedings of a Convention of that State, recommending certain Amendments to the Constitution of the United States,[125] which were read, and ordered to lie on the table.

The several orders of the day were read, and postponed until to-morrow.

And then the House adjourned until to-morrow morning eleven o'clock.

WEDNESDAY, MARCH 31, 1790

A bill to regulate trade and intercourse with the Indian Tribes, was read the second time, and ordered to be committed to a committee of the whole House on Wednesday next.[126]

A message from the Senate by Mr. Otis their Secretary.

MR. SPEAKER, The Senate have passed the bill, entitled, "An act to prevent the exportation of goods not duly inspected according to the laws of the several States;"[127] and then he withdrew.

Memorials of the manufacturers of tobacco and snuff in the cities of Philadelphia and New-York, were presented to the House and read, praying the attention of Congress to the encouragement of the said manufactories, and that no duties may be imposed on manufactured snuff and tobacco exported.

ORDERED, That the said memorials do lie on the table.

The House, according to the order of the day, again resolved itself into a

---

[123] On March 31 the COWH considered this report again.

[124] Senate amendments are filed with and noted on the bill in House Bills, SR, DNA. The amendments are printed in the *Senate Legislative Journal* on March 30. On April 3 the House agreed to all of these Senate amendments except the tenth.

[125] These proceedings are E–22039.

[126] On April 11 this bill was considered in the COWH.

[127] On April 1 this bill was signed by the speaker and the vice president.

committee of the whole House on the report of the Secretary of the Treasury, relative to a provision for the support of the public credit.

Mr. Speaker left the chair.

Mr. Livermore took the chair of the committee.

Mr. Speaker resumed the chair, and Mr. Livermore reported, that the committee had, according to order, again had the said report under consideration, and made a farther progress therein.

RESOLVED, That this House will, to-morrow, again resolve itself into a committee of the whole House on the said report.[128]

Mr. Sedgwick, from the committee to whom was re-committed the bill "providing the means of intercourse between the United States and foreign nations," presented an amendatory bill to the same effect, which was received, and read the first time.[129]

The several orders of the day were read and postponed until to-morrow.

And then the House adjourned until to-morrow morning eleven o'clock.

---

[128] On April 1 the COWH considered this report again.
[129] On April 1 this bill was read again.

THURSDAY, APRIL 1, 1790

An amendatory bill "providing the means of intercourse between the United States and foreign nations," was read the second time, and ordered to be committed to a committee of the whole House on Thursday next.[1]

The several petitions of Stephen Califfe, of Ichabod Spencer, for himself and others, and of Josiah Harris for himself and others,[2] were presented to the House and read, respectively praying relief in consideration of losses or injuries sustained in the service of the United States during the late war.

ORDERED, That the said petitions be referred to the Secretary at War, with instruction to examine the same, and report his opinion thereupon to the House.[3]

ORDERED, That Mr. Wynkoop have leave to be absent from the service of this House until this day se'nnight.

A petition of Jacob Purdy, of the state of New-York, was presented to the House and read, praying relief in consideration of the loss of certain continental loan-office certificates, which were taken from him during the late war, by a party of the British enemy.

ORDERED, That the said petition be referred to the Secretary of the Treasury, with instruction to examine the same, and report his opinion thereupon to the House.

Mr. Gilman, from the joint committee for inrolled bills, reported, that the committee had examined two inrolled bills, one entitled, "An act to prevent the exportation of goods not duly inspected according to the laws of the several States;"[4] the other entitled, "An act to accept a cession of the claims of the state of North-Carolina, to a certain district of western territory;"[5] and had found the same to be truly inrolled: Whereupon,

Mr. Speaker signed the said inrolled bills.[6]

ORDERED, That the Clerk of this House do acquaint the Senate therewith.

The House, according to the order of the day, again resolved itself into a committee of the whole House on the report of the Secretary of the Treasury, relative to a provision for the support of the public credit.

Mr. Speaker left the chair.

Mr. Livermore took the chair of the committee.

Mr. Speaker resumed the chair, and Mr. Livermore reported, that the com-

---

[1] This bill was postponed as an order of the day from April 8–27, when the COWH considered it and reported several amendments.

[2] This petition was submitted in behalf of the children of John Harris.

[3] On April 22 the secretary of war reported on Stephen Califfe's petition.

[4] The inspected inrolled bill is in Enrolled Acts, RG 11, DNA.

[5] The inspected inrolled bill is in Enrolled Acts, RG 11, DNA.

[6] On April 2 the committee on enrolled bills reported on presenting these bills to the president.

mittee had, according to order, again had the said report under their consideration, and made a farther progress therein.

RESOLVED, That this House will, to-morrow, again resolve itself into a committee of the whole House on the said report.[7]

A message, in writing, was received from the President of the United States, by Mr. Lear his Secretary, who delivered in the same, together with the papers therein referred to, and then withdrew.

The said message and papers were read, and are as follow:

UNITED STATES, April 1, 1790

GENTLEMEN of the SENATE and HOUSE of REPRESENTATIVES,

I HAVE directed my private Secretary to lay before you a copy of the Adoption, by the Legislature of South-Carolina, of the Articles proposed by Congress to the Legislatures of the several States as Amendments to the Constitution of the United States; together with the copy of a letter from the Governor of the state of South-Carolina, to the President of the United States, which have lately come to my hands.

The Originals of the foregoing will be lodged in the office of the Secretary of State.

G. WASHINGTON

(Copy)

CHARLESTON, January 28th, 1790

SIR,

I HAVE the honor to transmit you the entire Adoption, by the Legislature of this State, of the Amendments proposed to the Constitution of the United States.

I am,
With the most perfect Esteem and Respect,
Your most obedient Servant,
(Signed)   CHARLES PINCKNEY

To the PRESIDENT of the UNITED STATES

(Copy)

In the HOUSE of REPRESENTATIVES, January 18th, 1790

THE House took into consideration the report of the committee to whom was referred the resolution of the Congress of the United States of the fourth day of March, one thousand seven hundred and eighty-nine, proposing Amendments to the Constitution of the United States, viz. [Here follow the several Articles of Amendment, in the words agreed to by Congress.] which being read through, was agreed to: Whereupon,

---

[7] On April 12 the COWH considered this report again.

RESOLVED, That this House do adopt the said several Articles, and that they become a part of the Constitution of the United States.

RESOLVED, That the resolutions be sent to the Senate for their concurrence.

By Order of the House,

JACOB READ, Speaker of the House of Representatives

In the SENATE, January 19th, 1790

RESOLVED, That this House do concur with the House of Representatives in the foregoing Resolutions.

By Order of the Senate,

D. DE SAUSSURE, President of the Senate[8]

ORDERED, That the said message and papers do lie on the table.

The several orders of the day were read, and postponed until to-morrow.

And then the House adjourned until to-morrow morning eleven o'clock.

FRIDAY, APRIL 2, 1790

Mr. Gilman, from the joint committee for inrolled bills, reported, that the committee did, yesterday, wait on the President of the United States, and present him with two inrolled bills; one entitled, "An act to prevent the exportation of goods not duly inspected according to the laws of the several States;" the other, entitled, "An act to accept a cession of the claims of the state of North-Carolina, to a certain district of western territory," for his approbation.[9]

The several orders of the day were read, and postponed until to-morrow.

And then the House adjourned until to-morrow morning eleven o'clock.

SATURDAY, APRIL 3, 1790

On motion,

ORDERED, That the printers accounts for newspapers furnished for the use of Congress, be referred to Mr. Benson, Mr. Wadsworth and Mr. Livermore, with instruction to report a provision for payment of the same, and also a proper mode of regulating the future supply of newspapers for the use of both Houses.[10]

The House proceeded to consider the amendments proposed by the Senate to the bill, entitled, "An act to promote the progress of useful arts:" Whereupon,

---

[8] The message with enclosures is in President's Messages: Suggesting legislation, SR, DNA. The articles of amendment to the Constitution mentioned in the ratification documents are printed in the Appendix to the Second Session.

[9] On April 3 the House was notified that the president had signed these bills on April 2.

[10] On April 9 this committee reported.

RESOLVED, That this House doth disagree to the tenth amendment, and doth agree to all the others.

ORDERED, That the Clerk of this House do acquaint the Senate therewith.[11]

A message was received from the President of the United States, by Mr. Lear his Secretary, notifying that the President has approved of the act entitled, "An act to prevent the exportation of goods not duly inspected according to the laws of the several States," and affixed his signature to the same on the second instant.

A message from the Senate by Mr. Otis their Secretary.

MR. SPEAKER,   I am directed by the Senate to inform this House, that the President of the United States has approved of the act, entitled, "An act to accept a cession of the claims of the State of North-Carolina to a certain district of western territory," and affixed his signature thereto on the second instant;   and then he withdrew.

On a motion made and seconded, that the Secretary of State be authorized to employ one additional Clerk, with a salary of eight hundred dollars per annum;

ORDERED, That the said motion be committed to Mr. Vining, Mr. Sherman, and Mr. Lee, with instruction to prepare and bring in a bill or bills pursuant thereto.[12]

A petition of James Warren, was presented to the House and read, praying the settlement of an unliquidated claim against the United States.

ORDERED, That the said petition be referred to the Secretary of the Treasury, with instruction to examine the same, and report his opinion thereupon to the House.

The several orders of the day were read, and postponed until Monday next. And then the House adjourned until Monday morning eleven o'clock.

MONDAY, APRIL 5, 1790

The petitions of Thomas Simpson, and John Garnett, were presented to the House and read, praying relief in consideration of wounds received in the service of the United States during the late war, which have disabled them from obtaining a livelihood by labor.

ORDERED, That the said petitions be referred to the Secretary at War, with instruction to examine the same, and report his opinion thereupon to the House.

---

[11] On April 5 the Senate receded from its tenth amendment to the Patents Bill [HR–41].

[12] On April 13 this committee presented the Salaries-Executive Bill [HR–54], which was read.

On motion,

ORDERED, That the petition of Ezra Stiles, on behalf of the President and fellows of Yale College in Connecticut, which was presented on the twenty-seventh of January last, be referred to the Secretary of the Treasury, with instruction to examine the same, and report his opinion thereupon to the House.

The House, according to the order of the day, resolved itself into a committee of the whole House on the bill, further to suspend part of an act, entitled, "An act to regulate the collection of the duties imposed by law on the tonnage of ships or vessels, and on goods, wares, and merchandizes imported into the United States."

Mr. Speaker left the chair.

Mr. Livermore took the chair of the committee.

Mr. Speaker resumed the chair, and Mr. Livermore reported, that the committee had, according to order, had the said bill under consideration, and made no amendment thereto.

ORDERED, That the said bill be engrossed, and read the third time tomorrow.[13]

The House, according to the order of the day, resolved itself into a committee of the whole House, on the bill "to allow compensation to John Ely, for his services and expences as a Regimental Surgeon in the late armies of the United States."

Mr. Speaker left the chair.

Mr. Livermore took the chair of the committee.

Mr. Speaker resumed the chair, and Mr. Livermore reported, that the committee had, according to order, had the said bill under consideration, and made several amendments thereto, which he delivered in at the Clerk's table, where the same were twice read, and agreed to by the House.

And then the question being put, that the said bill, with the amendments, be engrossed, and read the third time;

It passed in the negative; and so the bill was rejected.[14]

A message, in writing, was received from the President of the United States, by Mr. Lear his Secretary, as followeth:

UNITED STATES, April 5th, 1790

GENTLEMEN of the SENATE and HOUSE of REPRESENTATIVES,

I HAVE directed my private Secretary to lay before you copies of three acts of the Legislature of the State of New-York, which have been transmitted to me by the Governor thereof, viz.

---

[13] On April 6 this bill was read, agreed to, and sent to the Senate.

[14] On April 21 another committee to prepare a bill to compensate John Ely was appointed.

"An act declaring it to be the duty of the sheriffs of the several counties within this State to receive, and safe keep such prisoners as shall be committed under the authority of the United States."

"An act for vesting in the United States of America, the light-house, and lands thereunto belonging, at Sandy-Hook."

"An act ratifying certain articles in addition to, and amendment of the Constitution of the United States of America, proposed by Congress."

A copy of a letter, accompanying said acts, from the Governor of the State of New-York, to the President of the United States, will, at the same time, be laid before you, and the Originals deposited in the office of the Secretary of State.

G. WASHINGTON[15]

The letter and papers accompanying the said message, were read, and ordered to lie on the table.

A message from the Senate by Mr. Otis their Secretary.

MR. SPEAKER,   The Senate recede from their tenth amendment, disagreed to by this House, to the bill, entitled, "An act to promote the progress of useful arts;"[16]   and then he withdrew.

Mr. Burke, from the committee appointed, presented, according to order, a bill for the relief of a certain description of officers therein mentioned, which was received and read the first time.[17]

On motion,

ORDERED, That the exemplification of the act of the Legislature of the State of New-York, entitled, "An act for vesting in the United States of America, the light-house and lands thereunto belonging at Sandy-Hook," referred to in the message of to-day, from the President of the United States, be committed to Mr. Page, Mr. Benson, and Mr. Seney, with instruction to examine the same, and report their opinion thereupon to the House.

The House, according to the order of the day, resolved itself into a committee of the whole House on the bill sent from the Senate, entitled, "An act for the punishment of certain crimes against the United States."

Mr. Speaker left the chair.

Mr. Livermore took the chair of the committee.

---

[15] The message with enclosures is in President's Messages: Suggesting legislation, SR, DNA. The act ratifying amendments to the Constitution is printed in the Appendix to the Second Session.

[16] On April 7 this bill was signed by the speaker.

[17] The appointment of the committee to prepare this bill (Officers Bill [HR–53]) is not mentioned in the House Journal. On April 6 this bill was read again.

Mr. Speaker resumed the chair, and Mr. Livermore reported, that the committee had, according to order, had the said bill under consideration, and made some progress therein.

RESOLVED, That this House will, to-morrow, again resolve itself into a committee of the whole House on the said bill.[18]

The several orders of the day were read, and postponed until to-morrow.

And then the House adjourned until to-morrow morning, eleven o'clock.

TUESDAY, APRIL 6, 1790

An engrossed bill, further to suspend part of an act, entitled, "An act to regulate the collection of the duties imposed by law on the tonnage of ships or vessels, and on goods, wares and merchandizes imported into the United States," was read the third time, and the blanks therein filled up.

RESOLVED, That the said bill do pass, and that the title be, "An act further to suspend part of an act, entitled, 'An act to regulate the collection of the duties imposed by law on the tonnage of ships or vessels, and on goods, wares and merchandizes imported into the United States.'"

ORDERED, That the Clerk of this House do carry the said bill to the Senate, and desire their concurrence.[19]

A bill for the relief of a certain description of officers therein mentioned, was read the second time, and ordered to be committed to a committee of the whole House on Tuesday next.[20]

A petition of Joseph Henderson, was presented to the House and read, praying compensation for services rendered to the United States during the late war, as a paymaster in the navy.

ORDERED, That the said petition be referred to the Secretary of the Treasury, with instruction to examine the same, and report his opinion thereupon to the House.

A petition of David Steele, was presented to the House and read, praying relief in consideration of wounds received in the service of the United States during the late war, which have disabled him from procuring a livelihood by labor.

---

[18] On April 6 the COWH considered this bill again.

[19] On April 7 the Senate read this bill, and on April 8 it was read and committed. The committee's report was accepted as an amendment, and the bill was passed with two amendments on April 9. On the same date the House received the Senate amendments and agreed to them.

[20] Consideration of this bill in the COWH was postponed as an order of the day from April 13–19. On April 20 the Officers Bill [HR–53] was considered in the COWH and amended.

ORDERED, That the said petition be referred to the Secretary at War, with instruction to examine the same, and report his opinion thereupon to the House.[21]

The Speaker laid before the House a letter and report from the Secretary of the Treasury, on the memorial of the Baron de Steuben, which were read, and ordered to lie on the table.[22]

The House, according to the order of the day, again resolved itself into a committee of the whole House on the bill sent from the Senate, entitled, "An act for the punishment of certain crimes against the United States."

Mr. Speaker left the chair.

Mr. Livermore took the chair of the committee.

Mr. Speaker resumed the chair, and Mr. Livermore reported, that the committee had, according to order, again had the said bill under consideration, and made a farther progress therein.

RESOLVED, That this House will, to-morrow, again resolve itself into a committee of the whole House on the said bill.[23]

Another member from North-Carolina, to wit: Timothy Bloodworth, appeared, produced his credentials, and took his seat in the House; the oath to support the Constitution of the United States being administered to him by Mr. Speaker, according to law.

The several orders of the day were read, and postponed until to-morrow.

And then the House adjourned until to-morrow morning, eleven o'clock.

WEDNESDAY, APRIL 7, 1790

A petition of Elizabeth Rockwell, widow of William Rockwell, late of Norwich, in Connecticut, was presented to the House and read, praying that her claim, as administratrix of the said William Rockwell, for his services in the late navy of the United States, may be liquidated and satisfied.

ORDERED, That the said petition be referred to the Secretary of the Treasury, with instruction to examine the same, and report his opinion thereupon to the House.

A petition of Nathaniel Fox, was presented to the House, and read, praying to be placed on the list of pensioners as a deranged and wounded officer of the late army of the United States.

---

[21] On April 22 the secretary reported on this petition.

[22] A copy of the report is in A Record of the Reports of the Secretary of the Treasury, vol. 2, HR, DNA. A copy, probably made by ASP, is in Reports and Communications from the Secretary of the Treasury, HR, DNA. On April 10 this report was read again.

[23] On April 7 the COWH considered this bill again.

ORDERED, That the said petition be referred to the Secretary at War, with instruction to examine the same, and report his opinion thereupon to the House.

A member from South-Carolina, presented to the House a letter addressed to him from John H. Mitchell of the said State, reciting certain proposals of Matthew Boulton, of the Kingdom of Great-Britain, for supplying the United States with copper coinage to any amount that government shall think fit to contract with him for, upon the terms therein mentioned.[24]

ORDERED, That the said letter and proposals be referred to the Secretary of State, with instruction to examine the same, and report his opinion thereupon to the House.

Mr. Foster, from the committee to whom was referred that part of the petition of the merchants and traders of the town of Portsmouth, in the state of New-Hampshire, which prays that the Circuit and District Courts of the said State may be held at Portsmouth, made a report,[25] which was read, and ordered to lie on the table.

The House, according to the order of the day, again resolved itself into a committee of the whole House on the bill sent from the Senate, entitled, "An act for the punishment of certain crimes against the United States."

Mr. Speaker left the chair.

Mr. Livermore took the chair of the committee.

Mr. Speaker resumed the chair, and Mr. Livermore reported, that the committee had, according to order, again had the said bill under consideration, and made a farther progress therein.

RESOLVED, That this House will, to-morrow, again resolve itself into a committee of the whole House on the said bill.[26]

Mr. Gilman, from the joint committee for inrolled bills, reported, that the committee had examined the inrolled bill, entitled, "An act to promote the progress of useful arts,"[27] and had found the same to be truly inrolled: Whereupon,

Mr. Speaker signed the said inrolled bill.[28]

ORDERED, That the Clerk of this House do acquaint the Senate therewith.

The several orders of the day were read, and postponed until to-morrow.

And then the House adjourned until to-morrow morning eleven o'clock.

---

[24] A copy of the letter is in Reports of the Secretary of State to the President and Congress, RG 59, DNA.

[25] A copy of the report is in A Record of the Reports of Select Committees, HR, DNA.

[26] On April 8 the COWH considered this bill again.

[27] The inspected enrolled bill is in Enrolled Acts, RG 11, DNA.

[28] On April 8 this bill was signed by the vice president. On April 9 the committee on enrolled bills reported that they had presented this bill to the president.

THURSDAY, APRIL 8, 1790

A petition of Elisha Curtis, on behalf of himself and others, was presented to the House and read, praying payment of a claim against the United States;[29] Also, a petition of Basil Middleton, to the same effect.

ORDERED, That the said petitions be referred to the Secretary at War, with instruction to examine the same, and report his opinion thereupon to the House.[30]

The House, according to the order of the day, again resolved itself into a committee of the whole House, on the bill sent from the Senate, entitled, "An act for the punishment of certain crimes against the United States."

Mr. Speaker left the chair.

Mr. Livermore took the chair of the committee.

Mr. Speaker resumed the chair, and Mr. Livermore reported, that the committee had, according to order, again had the said bill under consideration, and made a farther progress therein.

RESOLVED, That this House will, to-morrow, again resolve itself into a committee of the whole House on the said bill.[31]

The several orders of the day were read, and postponed until to-morrow.

And then the House adjourned until to-morrow morning eleven o'clock.

FRIDAY, APRIL 9, 1790

Mr. Gilman, from the joint committee for inrolled bills, reported, that the committee did, yesterday, wait on the President of the United States, and present him with the inrolled bill, entitled, "An act to promote the progress of useful arts," for his approbation.[32]

A memorial of sundry merchants and traders, of the town of Newburyport, in the state of Massachusetts, was presented to the House and read, setting forth the inconveniences under which they labor from the operation of the laws of trade of the United States, and praying relief therein.

ORDERED, That the said memorial be referred to the Secretary of the Treasury, with instruction to examine the same, and report his opinion thereupon to the House.

A petition of the proprietors of the Beverly Cotton Manufactory, in the state of Massachusetts, was presented to the House and read, praying the patronage of government to their undertaking, and that an additional impost may be laid on the importation of cotton goods.

---

[29] This petition was presented in behalf of the children of Robert Lewis.

[30] On April 23 the secretary reported on the Middleton petition.

[31] On April 9 the COWH reported amendments to this bill, which were agreed to by the House.

[32] On April 10 the president signed this bill.

ORDERED, That the said petition be referred to Mr. Goodhue, Mr. Wadsworth, Mr. Silvester, Mr. Clymer, and Mr. Gale, that they do examine the matter thereof, and report the same, with their opinion thereupon, to the House.[33]

Mr. Benson, from the committee to whom it was referred to report a provision for payment of the printers accounts for newspapers, furnished for the use of Congress; and also a proper mode of regulating the future supply of newspapers for the use of both Houses, made a report, which was read, and ordered to lie on the table.[34]

Mr. Smith (of Maryland), from the committee to whom were referred the accounts of the Treasurer of the United States, made a report,[35] which was read, and ordered to lie on the table.

The House, according to the order of the day, again resolved itself into a committee of the whole House, on the bill sent from the Senate, entitled, "An act for the punishment of certain crimes against the United States."

Mr. Speaker left the chair.

Mr. Livermore took the chair of the committee.

Mr. Speaker resumed the chair, and Mr. Livermore reported, that the committee had, according to order, again had the said bill under consideration, and made several amendments thereto, which he delivered in at the Clerk's table, where the same were severally twice read, amended, and agreed to by the House.

ORDERED, That the said bill, with the amendments, be read the third time to-morrow.[36]

A message from the Senate by Mr. Otis their Secretary.

MR. SPEAKER,   The Senate have passed the bill, entitled, "An act further to suspend part of an act, entitled, 'An act to regulate the collection of the duties imposed by law on the tonnage of ships or vessels, and on goods, wares and merchandizes imported into the United States,'" with several amendments,[37] to which they desire the concurrence of this House: And then he withdrew.

The House proceeded to consider the said amendments, and the same being read, were agreed to.

---

[33] On April 21 this committee reported.

[34] A copy of the report is in A Record of the Reports of Select Committees, HR, DNA. On April 14 part of this report was agreed to and part was disagreed to.

[35] A copy of the report is in A Record of the Reports of Select Committees, HR, DNA.

[36] On April 10 this bill was read again and agreed to with amendments.

[37] The amendments are printed in the *Senate Legislative Journal* on April 9.

ORDERED, That the Clerk of this House do acquaint the Senate therewith.[38]

Mr. Ames, from the managers appointed on the part of this House, to attend the conference with the Senate, on the subject matter of the amendments depending between the two Houses to the bill, entitled, "An act to provide for the remission or mitigation of fines, forfeitures and penalties in certain cases," reported, that the committee had, according to order, met the managers on the part of the Senate, in the conference-chamber, and freely discussed the subject matter of the said amendments, but had come to no agreement thereupon.[39]

The several orders of the day were read, and postponed until to-morrow.

And then the House adjourned until to-morrow morning eleven o'clock.

S A T U R D A Y, APRIL 10, 1790

A message was received from the President of the United States, by Mr. Lear his Secretary, notifying that the President has approved of the act, entitled, "An act to promote the progress of useful arts," and affixed his signature to the same this day.

The bill sent from the Senate, entitled, "An act for the punishment of certain crimes against the United States," with the amendments, was read the third time.

RESOLVED, That the said bill, with the amendments, do pass.[40]

ORDERED, That the Clerk of this House do acquaint the Senate therewith, and desire their concurrence to the said amendments.[41]

ORDERED, That the several petitions of Enos Brown, Barent Martlings, and James Delaplaine, which lay on the table, be referred to the Secretary at War, with instruction to examine the same, and report his opinion thereupon to the House.

On motion,

The report of the Secretary of the Treasury, on the memorial of Baron de Steuben, was read the second time, and ordered to be taken into consideration on Monday se'nnight.[42]

The House, according to the order of the day, resolved itself into a com-

---

[38] On April 13 this bill was signed by the speaker and vice president.

[39] On April 12 the House adhered to its disagreement to the Senate amendment.

[40] A copy of the resolution with the amendments is filed with the bill in Engrossed Senate Bills and Resolutions, SR, DNA. The amendments are printed in the *Senate Legislative Journal* on April 14.

[41] The Senate considered the House amendments on April 13. On April 14 they agreed to some of the House amendments and disagreed to others. The Senate resolution on these amendments is printed in the *Senate Legislative Journal* on this date. The House was notified of the Senate actions on April 15.

[42] On April 19 a committee was appointed to bring in a bill on the Steuben petition.

mittee of the whole House, on the bill to regulate trade and intercourse with the Indian tribes.

Mr. Speaker left the chair.

Mr. Livermore took the chair of the committee.

Mr. Speaker resumed the chair, and Mr. Livermore reported, that the committee had, according to order, had the said bill under consideration, and made some progress therein.

RESOLVED, That this House will, on Monday next, again resolve itself into a committee of the whole House on the said bill.[43]

The several orders of the day were read, and postponed until Monday next.

And then the House adjourned until Monday morning eleven o'clock.

MONDAY, APRIL 12, 1790

The House proceeded to re-consider the amendment proposed by the Senate to the bill, entitled, "An act to provide for the remission or mitigation of fines, forfeitures and penalties, in certain cases:" Whereupon,

RESOLVED, That this House doth adhere to their disagreement to the said amendment.

ORDERED, That the Clerk of this House do acquaint the Senate therewith.

ORDERED, That Mr. Cadwalader and Mr. Sedgwick, have leave to be absent from the service of this House until this day fortnight, and Mr. Schureman until Friday next.

The House, according to the order of the day, resolved itself into a committee of the whole House, on the report of the Secretary of the Treasury, relative to a provision for the support of the public credit.

Mr. Speaker left the chair.

Mr. Livermore took the chair of the committee.

Mr. Speaker resumed the chair, and Mr. Livermore reported, that the committee had, according to order, again had the said report under consideration, and made a farther progress therein.

RESOLVED, That this House will, to-morrow, again resolve itself into a committee of the whole House, on the said report.[44]

The Speaker laid before the House, a letter and reports from the Secretary of the Treasury, on the petitions of William Finnie and James Warren, which were read, and ordered to lie on the table.[45]

---

[43] Consideration of the Indian Trade Bill [HR–51] was postponed as an order of the day from April 12–27. On April 28 it was considered in the COWH and then recommitted to the committee which presented it, with several members added.

[44] On April 15 the COWH considered this report again.

[45] Copies of these reports are in A Record of the Reports of the Secretary of the Treasury, vol. 1, HR, DNA. A copy, probably made by ASP, is in Reports and Communications from the Secretary of the Treasury, HR, DNA.

The several orders of the day were read, and postponed until to-morrow. And then the House adjourned until to-morrow morning eleven o'clock.

TUESDAY, APRIL 13, 1790

The petitions of Caleb Brewster and Jacobus Wynkoop, were presented to the House and read, respectively praying relief in consideration of losses or injuries sustained in the service of the United States during the late war.

ORDERED, That the said petitions be referred to the Secretary at War, with instruction to examine the same, and report his opinion thereupon to the House.[46]

Mr. Vining, from the committee appointed, presented, according to order, a bill supplemental to the act for establishing the salaries of the executive officers of government, with their assistants and clerks, which was received, and read the first time.[47]

Mr. Gilman, from the joint committee for inrolled bills, reported, that the committee had examined the inrolled bill, entitled, "An act further to suspend part of an act, entitled, 'An act to regulate the collection of the duties imposed by law on the tonnage of ships or vessels, and on goods, wares and merchandizes imported into the United States,' and to amend the said act,"[48] and had found the same to be truly inrolled: Whereupon,

Mr. Speaker signed the said inrolled bill.[49]

ORDERED, That the Clerk of this House do acquaint the Senate therewith.

A petition of Joseph Beale, was presented to the House and read, praying compensation for losses and damages, which he sustained by the American army during the late war.   Also,

A petition of Thomas Wickes, praying compensation for services rendered to the United States during the late war.

ORDERED, That the said petitions be referred to the Secretary of the Treasury, with instruction to examine the same, and report his opinion thereupon to the House.

The House, according to the order of the day, resolved itself into a committee of the whole House on the bill for regulating the post-office of the United States.

Mr. Speaker left the chair.

Mr. Livermore took the chair of the committee.

Mr. Speaker resumed the chair, and Mr. Livermore reported, that the committee had, according to order, had the said bill under consideration, and made some progress therein.

---

[46] On June 23 the secretary of war reported on the Brewster petition.
[47] On April 14 this bill was read again.
[48] The inspected enrolled bill is in Enrolled Acts, RG 11, DNA. E–22962.
[49] On April 14 this bill was presented to the president.

RESOLVED, That this House will, to-morrow, again resolve itself into a committee of the whole House on the said bill.[50]

The several orders of the day were read, and postponed until to-morrow.

And then the House adjourned until to-morrow morning eleven o'clock.

WEDNESDAY, APRIL 14, 1790

A petition of Samuel Jones and Thomas Crawford, was presented to the House and read, praying payment of a claim against the United States. Also,

A petition of Joseph McGibbons, praying to be placed on the list of pensioners, in consideration of military services rendered to the United States during the late war.

ORDERED, That the said petitions be referred to the Secretary at War, with instruction to examine the same, and report his opinion thereupon to the House.[51]

Mr. Gilman, from the joint committee for inrolled bills, reported, that the committee did, this day, wait on the President of the United States, and present him with the inrolled bill, entitled, "An act further to suspend part of an act, entitled, 'An act to regulate the collection of the duties imposed by law on the tonnage of ships or vessels, and on goods, wares and merchandizes imported into the United States,' and to amend the said act," for his approbation.[52]

A petition of Henry Emanuel Lutterloh, was presented to the House and read, praying to be allowed the pay and emoluments of a Colonel, in consideration of military services rendered to the United States during the late war.

ORDERED, That the said petition be referred to the Secretary at War, with instruction to examine the same, and report his opinion thereupon to the House.[53]

A member from Massachusetts, presented to the House a representation from the Legislature of that State to Congress, relative to the present state of the whale and cod-fisheries, together with sundry petitions accompanying the same,[54] which were read, and ordered to lie on the table.

The House proceeded to consider the report of the committee, to whom it was referred to report a provision for the payment of the printers accounts

---

[50] On April 14 the COWH considered this bill again.

[51] On April 22 the secretary reported on these petitions.

[52] On April 15 the president signed this bill, and the House was notified.

[53] On May 20 the secretary of war reported on the Lutterloh petition.

[54] A draft of the Massachusetts representation and the accompanying petitions are in Resolves, 1789, Chapter 169, M-Ar.

for newspapers furnished for the use of Congress; and also a proper mode of regulating the future supply of newspapers for the use of both Houses: Whereupon,

The first part of the said report in the words following, to wit, "That the said accounts ought to be deemed as a part of the contingent expences of the session, and to be audited and paid as such," was, on the question put thereupon, agreed to by the House.

The second part of the said report, in the words following, to wit, "That there be no future supply of newspapers for the use of the members of either House of Congress, at the public expence" was, on the question put thereupon, disagreed to by the House.

A bill supplemental to the act for establishing the salaries of the executive officers of government, with their assistants and clerks, was read the second time, and ordered to be committed to a committee of the whole House tomorrow.[55]

The House, according to the order of the day, again resolved itself into a committee of the whole House, on the bill for regulating the post-office of the United States.

Mr. Speaker left the chair.

Mr. Livermore took the chair of the committee.

Mr. Speaker resumed the chair, and Mr. Livermore reported, that the committee had, according to order, again had the said bill under consideration, and made a farther progress therein.

RESOLVED, That this House will, to-morrow, again resolve itself into a committee of the whole House on the said bill.[56]

A message from the Senate by Mr. Otis their Secretary.

MR. SPEAKER,   The Senate have passed a bill, entitled, "An act for the government of the territory of the United States south of the river Ohio;"[57] to which they desire the concurrence of this House: And then he withdrew.

The said bill was read the first time.[58]

The several orders of the day were read, and postponed until to-morrow.

And then the House adjourned until to-morrow morning eleven o'clock.

---

[55] Consideration of this bill in the COWH was postponed as an order of the day from April 15–28. On April 29 the COWH reported amendments to the bill, which were agreed to.

[56] Consideration of this bill in the COWH was postponed as an order of the day from April 15–26. On April 27 the bill was recommitted, together with the postmaster general's report of the same date.

[57] The bill is in Engrossed Senate Bills and Resolutions, SR, DNA. E–46040.

[58] On April 15 this bill was read again.

THURSDAY, April 15, 1790

Ordered, That Mr. Hartley have leave to be absent from the service of this House until this day fortnight.

A message was received from the President of the United States, notifying that the President has approved of the act, entitled, "An act further to suspend part of an act, entitled, 'An act to regulate the collection of the duties imposed by law on the tonnage of ships or vessels, and on goods, wares and merchandizes imported into the United States,' and to amend the said act," and affixed his signature to the same this day.

A message from the Senate by Mr. Otis their Secretary.

Mr. Speaker,   The Senate agree to some, and disagree to others, of the amendments proposed by this House to the bill, entitled, "An act for the punishment of certain crimes against the United States:"[59]   And then he withdrew.

The bill sent from the Senate, entitled, "An act for the government of the territory of the United States south of the river Ohio," was read the second time, and ordered to be committed to a committee of the whole House tomorrow.[60]

The Speaker laid before the House a letter and report from the Secretary of State, on the letter of John H. Mitchell, which was referred to him, reciting certain proposals for supplying the United States with copper coinage,[61] which were read, and ordered to lie on the table.

Ordered, That the Postmaster-General be directed to return to this House, the route by which the mail is carried within the United States, distinguishing those which are called cross-posts; also distinguishing those cross-posts which have been productive to the revenue, (if any such) and those which have been expensive beyond the revenue derived from them; also all the places at which post-offices are now kept, or ought to be kept, and an estimate of the emoluments to each of the post-office keepers.[62]

---

[59] A copy of the Senate resolution with a Senate amendment to a House amendment is filed with the bill in Engrossed Senate Bills and Resolutions, SR, DNA. The amendment is printed in the *Senate Legislative Journal* on April 14. On April 19 the House receded from the amendments disagreed to by the Senate and agreed to a Senate amendment.

[60] From April 16–27 consideration of this bill as an order of the day was postponed. On April 28 it was considered in the COWH and amended at the clerk's table.

[61] A copy of the letter and a copy of the report are in A Record of the Reports of the Secretary of State, vol. 1, HR, DNA. E–23001. A copy of the report, probably made by ASP, is in Reports and Communications from the Secretary of State, HR, DNA.

[62] On April 27 the postmaster general submitted this report, and on the same day it was committed, together with the Post Office Bill [HR–42].

ORDERED, that it be an instruction to the Secretary of the Treasury, to prepare and report to this House a proper plan or plans for the establishment of a national mint.[63]

On a motion made and seconded, that the House do now, according to the order of the day, resolve itself into a committee of the whole House on the report of the Secretary of the Treasury, relative to a provision for the support of the public credit.

It was resolved in the Affirmative, $\begin{cases} \text{AYES } 33 \\ \text{NOES } 23 \end{cases}$

The ayes and noes being demanded by one fifth of the members present, Those who voted in the affirmative, are,

John Baptista Ashe	James Madison, junior
Abraham Baldwin	George Mathews
John Brown	Andrew Moore
Daniel Carroll	Peter Muhlenberg
George Clymer	John Page
Isaac Coles	Josiah Parker
Benjamin Contee	Jeremiah Van Rensselaer
Thomas Fitzsimons	Thomas Scott
William Floyd	Joshua Seney
George Gale	Thomas Sinnickson
Samuel Griffin	William Smith (of Maryland)
Thomas Hartley	Thomas Sumter
John Hathorn	Thomas Tudor Tucker
Daniel Hiester	Alexander White
James Jackson	Hugh Williamson and
John Laurance	Henry Wynkoop
Richard Bland Lee	

Those who voted in the negative, are,

Fisher Ames	Benjamin Goodhue
Egbert Benson	Jonathan Grout
Theodorick Bland	Benjamin Huntington
Timothy Bloodworth	George Leonard
Elias Boudinot	Samuel Livermore
Aedanus Burke	George Partridge
Abiel Foster	Roger Sherman
Elbridge Gerry	Peter Silvester
Nicholas Gilman	William Smith (of South-Carolina)

[63] On January 28, 1791, the secretary reported.

Jonathan Sturges   John Vining and
George Thatcher   Jeremiah Wadsworth
Jonathan Trumbull

The House accordingly resolved itself into the said committee.

Mr. Speaker left the chair.

Mr. Livermore took the chair of the committee.

Mr. Speaker resumed the chair, and Mr. Livermore reported, that the committee had, according to order, again had the said report under consideration, and made a farther progress therein.

RESOLVED, That this House will, to-morrow, again resolve itself into a committee of the whole House on the said report.[64]

The several orders of the day were read, and postponed until to-morrow.

And then the House adjourned until to-morrow morning eleven o'clock.

FRIDAY, APRIL 16, 1790

A petition of the manufacturers of mustard in the city of Philadelphia, was presented to the House and read, praying the patronage of Congress to that manufacture, and that an additional duty may be imposed on imported mustard. Also,

A petition of the manufacturers of tobacco and snuff in the town of Baltimore, praying the attention of Congress to the encouragement of the said manufactories, and that no duties may be imposed on manufactured snuff and tobacco exported. Also,

A petition of Darby Oram, praying compensation for services rendered in the navy of the United States, during the late war.

ORDERED, That the said petitions do lie on the table.

ORDERED, That a committee be appointed to prepare and bring in a bill or bills for mitigating or releasing the forfeitures and penalties accruing under the revenue laws, in certain cases therein to be mentioned; and that Mr. Boudinot, Mr. Goodhue, and Mr. Huntington, be of the said committee.[65]

A petition of Jonathan Hampton, of the state of New-Jersey, was presented to the House and read, praying relief against a seizure of certain furniture and effects, the property of the petitioner, made under the act to regulate the collection of duties within the United States.

ORDERED, That the said petition be referred to the committee last appointed, that they do examine the matter thereof, and report the same, with their opinion thereupon, to the House.

---

[64] On April 16 the COWH considered this report again.

[65] On April 27 this committee presented the Mitigation of Forfeitures Bill [HR-57], which was read.

Mr. Boudinot, from the committee to whom was referred so much of the petition of the merchants and traders of the town of Portsmouth, in the state of New-Hampshire, as prays that Congress will adopt measures to prevent foreigners from carrying the commodities of this continent to any port or place, where the citizens of the United States are prohibited from carrying them, made a report, which was read, and ordered to lie on the table.[66]

The House, according to the order of the day, again resolved itself into a committee of the whole House on the report of the Secretary of the Treasury, relative to a provision for the support of the public credit.

Mr. Speaker left the chair.

Mr. Livermore took the chair of the committee.

Mr. Speaker resumed the chair, and Mr. Livermore reported, that the committee had, according to order, again had the said report under consideration and made a farther progress therein.

RESOLVED, That this House will, on Monday next, again resolve itself into a committee of the whole House on the said report.[67]

ORDERED, That Mr. Leonard have leave to be absent from the service of this House until this day three weeks.

The several orders of the day were read, and postponed until Monday next.

And then the House adjourned until Monday morning eleven o'clock.

MONDAY, APRIL 19, 1790

A petition of Peter Smith, of Stamford, in the state of Connecticut, was presented to the House and read, praying to be placed on the list of invalids as a wounded soldier in the service of the United States during the late war.

ORDERED, That the said petition be referred to the Secretary at War, with instruction to examine the same, and report his opinion thereupon to the House.

ORDERED, That the petition of Darby Oram, which was presented on Friday last, be referred to the Secretary of the Treasury, with instruction to examine the same, and report his opinion thereupon to the House.

ORDERED, That Mr. Brown have leave to be absent from the service of this House until this day se'nnight.

The House proceeded to re-consider their amendments disagreed to by the Senate, to the bill, entitled, "An act for the punishment of certain crimes against the United States:"   Whereupon,

RESOLVED, That this House do recede from their amendments disagreed to by the Senate, to the nineteenth, twentieth and twenty-sixth sections; and do

---

[66] A copy of the report is in A Record of the Reports of Select Committees, HR, DNA. On May 3 this committee report was ordered committed to the COWH.

[67] On April 20 the COWH considered this report again.

agree to the amendment proposed by the Senate to their amendment to the twenty-eighth section of the said bill.[68]

ORDERED, That the Clerk of this House do acquaint the Senate therewith.[69]

Another member, from North-Carolina, to wit, John Steele, appeared, produced his credentials, and took his seat in the House; the oath to support the constitution of the United States being administered to him by Mr. Speaker according to law.

The House, according to the order of the day, proceeded to take into consideration the report of the Secretary of the Treasury, on the memorial of the Baron de Steuben: Whereupon,

ORDERED, That a committee be appointed to prepare and bring in a bill or resolution, in conformity to the said report; and a committee was appointed of Mr. Gerry, Mr. Wadsworth, Mr. Vining, Mr. Smith (of South-Carolina) and Mr. Laurance.[70]

ORDERED, That Mr. Trumbull have leave to be absent from the service of this House until this day fortnight.

The several orders of the day were read, and postponed until to-morrow.

And then the House adjourned until to-morrow morning eleven o'clock.

TUESDAY, APRIL 20, 1790

A petition of Pattin Jackson, was presented to the House and read, praying to be allowed the commutation of full pay, in consideration of military services as a Lieutenant in the army of the United States during the late war.

ORDERED, That the said petition do lie on the table.

On motion,

RESOLVED, That a committee be appointed to enquire what further measures are necessary for making an effectual and speedy settlement of the accounts of the several States with the United States, and to prepare and bring in a bill or bills pursuant thereto;

And a committee was appointed of Mr. Fitzsimons, Mr. Williamson, Mr. Smith (of Maryland), Mr. Schureman, and Mr. Sturges.[71]

Mr. Bland, from the committee to whom was referred the memorial of Donald Campbell, made a report, which was read, and ordered to lie on the table.[72]

---

[68] A copy of the resolution is filed with the bill in Engrossed Senate Bills and Resolutions, SR, DNA.

[69] On April 22 this bill was signed by the speaker and the vice president.

[70] On April 30 this committee presented the Steuben Bill [HR–60], which was read.

[71] On May 27 this committee presented the Settlement of Accounts Bill [HR–69], which was read twice.

[72] A copy of the report is in A Record of the Reports of Select Committees, HR, DNA. On July 14 this report was considered, and a resolution to pay Campbell back wages was defeated. The petition was then rejected.

The House, according to the order of the day, resolved itself into a committee of the whole House on the bill for the relief of a certain description of officers therein mentioned.

Mr. Speaker left the chair.

Mr. Livermore took the chair of the committee.

Mr. Speaker resumed the chair, and Mr. Livermore reported, that the committee had, according to order, had the said bill under consideration, and made an amendment thereto, which he delivered in at the Clerk's table, where the same was twice read, and agreed to by the House.

ORDERED, That the said bill, with the amendment, be engrossed, and read the third time to-morrow.[73]

The Speaker laid before the House a letter and report of the Secretary at War, on the petition of Nathaniel Gove,[74] which were read, and ordered to lie on the table.

The House, according to the order of the day, again resolved itself into a committee of the whole House on the report of the Secretary of the Treasury, relative to a provision for the support of the public credit.

Mr. Speaker left the chair.

Mr. Livermore took the chair of the committee.

Mr. Speaker resumed the chair, and Mr. Livermore reported, that the committee had, according to order, again had the said report under consideration, and made a farther progress therein.

RESOLVED, That this House will, to-morrow, again resolve itself into a committee of the whole House on the said report.[75]

The several orders of the day were read, and postponed until to-morrow.

And then the House adjourned until to-morrow morning eleven o'clock.

WEDNESDAY, APRIL 21, 1790

An engrossed bill for the relief of a certain description of officers therein mentioned, was read the third time.

RESOLVED, That the said bill do pass, and that the title be, "An act for the relief of a certain description of officers therein mentioned."[76]

ORDERED, That the Clerk of this House do carry the said bill to the Senate, and desire their concurrence.[77]

---

[73] On April 21 this bill was read again, agreed to, and sent to the Senate.

[74] A copy of the report is in A Record of the Reports of the Secretary of War, vol. 1, HR, DNA.

[75] On April 21 the COWH considered this report again.

[76] The bill is in Engrossed House Bills, HR, DNA.

[77] The Senate read this bill on April 21 and 22. It was committed on April 22 and the committee reported the next day. The Senate then voted not to read the bill a third time.

Mr. Goodhue, from the committee to whom was referred the petition of the proprietors of the Beverly cotton manufactory, made a report[78] which was read, and ordered to lie on the table.

Mr. Laurance, from the committee to whom was referred the petition of Nicholas Cowenhoven and others, made a report, which was read, and ordered to lie on the table.[79]

ORDERED, That a committee be appointed to prepare and bring in a bill or bills, allowing compensation to Colonel John Ely; and a committee was appointed of Mr. Partridge, Mr. Huntington and Mr. Mathews.[80]

A petition of John Wiley, was presented to the House and read, praying to be reimbursed for monies advanced in the service of the United States during the late War.[81]

ORDERED, That the said petition be referred to the Secretary of the Treasury, with instruction to examine the same, and report his opinion thereupon to the House.

The House, according to the order of the day, resolved itself into a committee of the whole House on the report of the Secretary of the Treasury, relative to a provision for the support of the public credit.

Mr. Speaker left the chair.

Mr. Livermore took the chair of the committee.

Mr. Speaker resumed the chair, and Mr. Livermore reported, that the committee had, according to order, again had the said report under consideration, and made a farther progress therein.

RESOLVED, That this House will, to-morrow, again resolve itself into a committee of the whole House on the said report.[82]

A message from the Senate by Mr. Otis their Secretary.

MR. SPEAKER,   The Senate have passed the bill, entitled, "An act for regulating the military establishment of the United States," with several amendments, to which they desire the concurrence of this House:[83]   And then he withdrew.

---

[78] A copy of the report is in A Record of the Reports of Select Committees, HR, DNA.

[79] A copy of the report is in A Record of the Reports of Select Committees, HR, DNA. On June 23 the Cowenhoven petition and committee report were referred to the secretary of the treasury.

[80] On April 22 this committee presented the Ely Bill [HR–56], which was read.

[81] The petition is in Miscellaneous Treasury Accounts, No. 3787, RG 217, Records of the United States General Accounting Office, (hereinafter referred to as RG 217), DNA.

[82] On April 22 the COWH considered this report again.

[83] Senate amendments are in House Bills, SR, DNA. They are printed in the *Senate Legislative Journal* on April 21. Because the House considered the Military Establishment Bill [HR–50a] in secret session, it has not been mentioned in the Journal before this point. On April 22 the House agreed to all the Senate amendments to this bill with one amendment.

The several orders of the day were read, and postponed until to-morrow. And then the House adjourned until to-morrow morning eleven o'clock.

THURSDAY, APRIL 22, 1790

The Speaker laid before the House, a letter and reports from the Secretary at War, on the several petitions of William McKennan, Joseph Harris, Samuel Jones, Thomas Crawford, David Poole, Joseph McGibbon, Stephen Califfe, Ephraim McCoy, Christian Khun, and David Steele, which were read, and ordered to lie on the table.[84]

ORDERED, That the petitions of Catherine Wheelan, and Pattin Jackson, which lay on the table, be referred to the Secretary at War, with instruction to examine the same, and report his opinion thereupon to the House.

The House being informed of the decease of Benjamin Franklin, a citizen whose native genius was not more an ornament to human nature, than his various exertions of it have been precious to science, to freedom, and to his country, do resolve, as a mark of the veneration due to his memory, that the members wear the customary badge of mourning for one month.

Mr. Partridge, from the committee appointed, presented according to order, a bill to allow compensation to John Ely, for his attendance as a physician and surgeon on the prisoners of the United States, which was received, and read the first time.[85]

Mr. Gilman, from the joint committee for inrolled bills, reported, that the committee had examined the inrolled bill, entitled, "An act for the punishment of certain crimes against the United States,"[86] and had found the same to be truly inrolled: Whereupon,

Mr. Speaker signed the said inrolled bill.[87]

ORDERED, That the Clerk of this House do acquaint the Senate therewith.

ORDERED, That a committee be appointed to prepare and bring in a bill or bills for the relief of disabled soldiers and seamen;

And a committee was appointed of Mr. Williamson, Mr. Parker, and Mr. Peter Muhlenberg.[88]

The House proceeded to consider the amendments proposed by the Senate, to the bill, entitled, "An act for regulating the military establishment of the United States:"   Whereupon,

---

[84] Copies of all of these reports are in A Record of the Reports of the Secretary of War, vol. 1, HR, DNA. On April 26 the Poole, McGibbon, Califfe, McCoy, Khun, and Steele petitions were referred to the committee on the Disabled Soldiers and Seamen Bill [HR–88].

[85] On April 23 this bill was read again.

[86] The inspected enrolled bill is in Enrolled Acts, RG 11, DNA. E–46041.

[87] On April 29 this bill was presented to the president.

[88] On April 26 several reports on petitions by the secretary of war were referred to this committee.

RESOLVED, That this House do agree to all the said amendments, with an amendment to the eighth amendment to the fifth section of the said bill, as follows:

In lieu of the word *"eighteen,"* proposed to be inserted by the Senate, insert *"twenty-four."*

ORDERED, That the Clerk of this House do acquaint the Senate therewith.[89]

The House, according to the order of the day, again resolved itself into a committee of the whole House on the report of the Secretary of the Treasury, relative to a provision for the support of the public credit.

Mr. Speaker left the chair.

Mr. Livermore took the chair of the committee.

Mr. Speaker resumed the chair, and Mr. Livermore reported, that the committee had, according to order, again had the said report under consideration, and made a farther progress therein.

RESOLVED, That this House will, to-morrow, again resolve itself into a committee of the whole House on the said report.[90]

The several orders of the day were read, and postponed until to-morrow.

And then the House adjourned until to-morrow morning eleven o'clock.

FRIDAY, APRIL 23, 1790

A bill to allow compensation to John Ely, for his attendance as a physician and surgeon on the prisoners of the United States, was read the second time, and ordered to be committed to a committee of the whole House, on this day week.[91]

The Speaker laid before the House a letter from the Secretary of the Treasury, covering a report made pursuant to the order of the House of Representatives on the nineteenth of January last, respecting difficulties which have occurred in the execution of the several laws for collecting duties on goods, wares and merchandizes, and on tonnage, and for regulating the coasting trade, which was read, and ordered to be committed to Mr. Goodhue, Mr. Laurance, Mr. Boudinot, Mr. Fitzsimons, and Mr. Lee.[92]

---

[89] On April 23 the House was notified that the Senate had agreed to the House amendment to one of their amendments.

[90] On April 26 the COWH was discharged from considering the part of this report relating to assumption of state debts. The COWH then proceeded to consider the report again and reported several resolutions, which were agreed to by the House. A committee was then appointed to bring in bills pursuant to these resolutions, which are printed in the Journal on that date.

[91] On April 30 this bill was considered.

[92] The report is in Alexander Hamilton's Reports, HR, DNA. A copy of the report is in A Record of the Reports of the Secretary of the Treasury, vol. 1, HR, DNA. A copy of the report, probably made by ASP, is in Reports and Communications from the Secretary of the Treasury, HR, DNA. Filed in official records is a note from

The Speaker laid before the House a letter and reports from the Secretary at War, on the petitions of Thomas Simpson, Basil Middleton, and Cornelius Wynkoop, which were read, and ordered to lie on the table.[93]

A message from the Senate by Mr. Otis their Secretary.

MR. SPEAKER, The Senate agree to the amendment proposed by this House to their eighth amendment of the fifth section of the bill, entitled, "An act for regulating the military establishment of the United States:"[94]   And then he withdrew.

A petition and remonstrance of the merchants of George Town and Bladensburg, in the state of Maryland, was presented to the House and read, stating sundry inconveniences under which they labor from the operation of the laws of trade, and praying relief therein.

ORDERED, That the said petition and remonstrance do lie on the table.

The House proceeded to consider the report of the Secretary of the Treasury, on the petition of James Warren: Whereupon,

A motion being made and seconded, "That the sum of three hundred eighty-four dollars, and ninety-two cents, be allowed and paid to Major General James Warren, in full for so much short paid him upon a warrant of Congress on the state of Massachusetts in the year one thousand seven hundred and eighty-one."

It passed in the negative.

ORDERED, That the Secretary of the department of War, be directed to lay before the House an account of the troops, (including the militia) and also of the ordnance stores furnished from time to time by the several States, towards the support of the late war: And that the commissioners for settling the accounts of the United States with the respective States, be directed to lay before the House an abstract of the claims of the several States against the United States, specifying the principles on which the claims are founded.

ORDERED, That the Secretary of the Treasury be directed to report the sums of money, including indents and paper money of every kind reduced to specie value, which have been received from or paid to the several States by Congress, from the commencement of the revolution to the present period.

ORDERED, That the commissioners for settling accounts between the United

---

John Beckley to Samuel Otis requesting that this report be sent to the House. It is in Messages from the House, SR, DNA. On April 28 the petition of Jean Boand was referred to this committee.

[93] Copies of all of these reports are in A Record of the Reports of the Secretary of War, vol. 1, HR, DNA. A copy of the Simpson report, probably made by ASP, is in Reports and Communications from the Secretary of War, HR, DNA. On May 10 the secretary's report on Basil Middleton's petition was committed.

[94] On April 27 this bill was signed by the speaker.

States and individual States, report the amount of such claims of the States as have been offered to them since the time expired for receiving claims, specifying the principles on which the claims are founded, and distinguishing them from other claims.[95]

The several orders of the day were read, and postponed until Monday next. And then the House adjourned until Monday morning eleven o'clock.

MONDAY, APRIL 26, 1790

The Speaker laid before the House a letter and reports from the Secretary at War, on the several petitions of William Oliver, Edward Thompson, Leonard Young, and Peter Smith, which were read, and ordered to lie on the table.[96]

A petition of Isaac Spencer, executor, &c. of Joseph Spencer, deceased, was presented to the House and read, praying the settlement and payment of a debt due to the estate of the decedent from the United States.   Also,

A petition of Messrs. Bertier and Company, of the city of Philadelphia, merchants, praying relief against a seizure of sundry goods, the property of the petitioners, for a supposed violation of the laws of trade.[97]

ORDERED, That the said petitions do lie on the table.

The House proceeded to consider the report of the Secretary at War, on the petition of Nathaniel Gove: Whereupon,

ORDERED, That the said report, together with the several other reports of the said Secretary at War, on the petitions of Charles Markley, Jeremiah Ryan, John Stevens, David Poole, Joseph McGibbon, Stephen Califfe, Ephraim McCoy, Christian Khun, and David Steele, be referred to the committee appointed to prepare and bring in a bill or bills for the relief of disabled soldiers and seamen, with instruction to the said committee, to insert a clause or clauses making provision for the said petitioners respectively, pursuant to the tenor of the said report.[98]

A petition of Benjamin Harwood, of the state of Maryland, was presented to the House and read, praying compensation for services rendered to the United States during the late war.

ORDERED, That the said petition be referred to the Secretary of the Treasury, with instruction to examine the same, and report his opinion thereupon to the House.

---

[95] On April 30 the commissioners' report was submitted to the House.

[96] A copy of the report on all of these petitions is in A Record of the Reports of the Secretary of War, vol. 1, HR, DNA.

[97] The petition is in Petitions and Memorials: Claims, SR, DNA.

[98] On May 26 more reports of the secretary of war were referred to the committee to prepare the Disabled Soldiers and Seamen Bill [HR–88].

ORDERED, That the committee of the whole House on the state of the Union, be discharged from further proceeding on the plan of the Secretary at War for the general arrangement of the militia of the United States, and that the said plan be referred to the committee appointed to prepare and bring in a bill or bills providing for the national defence.[99]

On a motion made and seconded, that the House do agree to the following order, to wit:

"That the committee of the whole House on the report of the Secretary of the Treasury, relative to a provision for the support of the public credit, be for the present discharged from proceeding on so much of the said report as relates to an assumption of the State debts."

The previous question was demanded by five members, Shall the main question to agree to the said order be now put? And on the question, Shall the main question be now put?

It was resolved in the affirmative, $\begin{cases} \text{AYES} & 32 \\ \text{NOES} & 18 \end{cases}$

And then the main question being put, that the House do agree to the said order,

It was resolved in the affirmative, $\begin{cases} \text{AYES} & 32 \\ \text{NOES} & 18 \end{cases}$

The ayes and noes being called for by one fifth of the members present, Those who voted in the affirmative, are,

John Baptista Ashe	Andrew Moore
Abraham Baldwin	Peter Muhlenberg
Timothy Bloodworth	John Page
John Brown	Josiah Parker
Daniel Carroll	Jeremiah Van Rensselaer
George Clymer	James Schureman
Isaac Coles	Thomas Scott
Benjamin Contee	Joshua Seney
Thomas Fitzsimons	Thomas Sinnickson
William Floyd	William Smith (of Maryland)
Nicholas Gilman	John Steele
Samuel Griffin	Michael Jenifer Stone
James Jackson	Thomas Sumter
Richard Bland Lee	Alexander White
James Madison, junior	Hugh Williamson and
George Mathews	Henry Wynkoop

---

[99] On April 27 more members were added to this committee.

Those who voted in the negative, are,

Fisher Ames	Samuel Livermore
Theodorick Bland	Roger Sherman
Elias Boudinot	Peter Silvester
Aedanus Burke	William Smith (of South-Carolina)
Abiel Foster	Jonathan Sturges
Elbridge Gerry	George Thatcher
Benjamin Goodhue	Thomas Tudor Tucker
Jonathan Grout	John Vining and
Benjamin Huntington	Jeremiah Wadsworth

The House, according to the order of the day, resolved itself into a committee of the whole House on the report of the Secretary of the Treasury, relative to a provision for the support of the public credit.

Mr. Speaker left the chair.

Mr. Livermore took the chair of the committee.

Mr. Speaker resumed the chair, and Mr. Livermore reported, that the committee had, according to order, again had the said report under consideration, and come to several resolutions thereupon, which he delivered in at the Clerk's table, where the same were severally twice read, and agreed to by the House, as follow:

RESOLVED, That it is advisable to endeavor to effect a new modification of the domestic debt, with the voluntary consent of the creditors, by a loan, upon terms mutually beneficial to them and to the United States.

RESOLVED, That for the purpose expressed in the last preceding resolution, subscriptions towards a loan ought to be opened, to the amount of the said domestic debt, upon the terms following, to wit:

That for every hundred dollars subscribed, payable in the said debt (as well interest as principal) the subscriber be entitled at his option, either

To have two thirds funded at an annuity or yearly interest of six per cent. redeemable at the pleasure of the government, by payment of the principal, and to receive the other third in lands in the western territory, at the rate of twenty cents per acre.   Or,

To have the whole sum funded at an annuity or yearly interest of four per cent. irredeemable by any payment exceeding six dollars per annum on account both of principal and interest, and to receive as a compensation for the reduction of interest, fifteen dollars and eighty cents payable in lands as in the preceding case: Or,

To have sixty-six dollars and two-thirds of a dollar funded immediately, at an annuity or yearly interest of six per cent. irredeemable by any payment exceeding six dollars per annum, on account both of principal and interest;

and to have at the end of seven years, thirty-three dollars and one-third of a dollar, funded at the like interest and rate of redemption.

RESOLVED, That immediate provision ought to be made for the present debt of the United States.

RESOLVED, That the funds which shall be appropriated according to the second of the foregoing resolutions, be applied, in the first place, to the payment of interest on the sums subscribed towards the proposed loan; and that if any part of the said domestic debt shall remain unsubscribed, the surplus of the said funds be applied, by a temporary appropriation, to the payment of interest on the unsubscribed part, so as not to exceed, for the present, four per cent. per annum; but this limitation shall not be understood to impair the right of the non-subscribing creditors to the residue of the interest on their respective debts: And in case the aforesaid surplus should prove insufficient to pay the non-subscribing creditors, at the aforesaid rate of four per cent., that the faith of government be pledged to make good such deficiency.

ORDERED, That a bill or bills be brought in pursuant to the said resolutions, as also, to the resolutions reported from the said committee, and agreed to by the House on the 29th ultimo, and that Mr. Stone, Mr. White, Mr. Sherman, Mr. Clymer, and Mr. Gilman, do prepare and bring in the same.[100]

RESOLVED, That this House will, to-morrow, again resolve itself into a committee of the whole House on the said report.

The several orders of the day were read, and postponed until to-morrow.

And then the House adjourned until to-morrow morning eleven o'clock.

TUESDAY, APRIL 27, 1790

The Speaker laid before the House a letter and reports from the Post-master-General, on the petition of Christopher Colles;[101] and also on the several matters submitted to him by an order of the House of the fifteenth instant,[102] which were read, and ordered to lie on the table.

---

[100] According to the *Gazette of the United States*, May 8, 1790, and the manuscript journal, this committee presented the Funding Bill [HR–63] on May 6, and the bill was read twice. On May 19 the COWH considered this bill. On April 27 the plan for public credit was again considered by the COWH, and further resolutions on it were agreed to. A committee was then appointed to prepare bills from the resolutions, which are printed in the Journal for that date.

[101] The report is in Reports and Communications from the Postmaster General, HR, DNA. A copy, probably made by ASP, is in the above location. On May 31 the Colles petition was referred to the committee that the Post Office Bill [HR–42] had been recommitted to.

[102] The House order requested the postmaster general to report on the route by which the mail was carried. A letter and reports on post roads and returns of post offices are in Reports and Communications from the Postmaster General, HR, DNA. A copy of the accompanying letter from the postmaster general, probably made by ASP, is in the same location. Notes made by the postmaster general and dated April 24

Mr. Boudinot, from the committee appointed, presented, according to order, a bill to provide for mitigating or remitting the forfeitures and penalties accruing under the revenue laws, in certain cases therein mentioned, which was received and read the first time.[103]

The House, according to the order of the day, again resolved itself into a committee of the whole House, on the report of the Secretary of the Treasury, relative to a provision for the support of the public credit.

Mr. Speaker left the chair.

Mr. Livermore took the chair of the committee.

Mr. Speaker resumed the chair, and Mr. Livermore reported, that the committee had, according to order, again had the said report under consideration, and come to several resolutions thereupon, which he delivered in at the Clerk's table, where the same were severally twice read, and agreed to by the House, as follow:

RESOLVED, That from and after the ____ day of ____ next, in lieu of the duties now payable upon wines and distilled spirits imported into the United States, there shall be paid the following rates:

Upon every gallon of Madeira wine called London particular, thirty-five cents:

Upon every gallon of other Madeira wine, thirty cents:

Upon every gallon of Sherry wine, twenty-five cents:

Upon every gallon of other wine, twenty cents:

Upon every gallon of distilled spirits, more than ten per cent. below proof, according to Dicas's hydrometer, twenty cents:

Upon every gallon of those spirits under five and not more than ten per cent. below proof, according to the same hydrometer, twenty-one cents:

Upon every gallon of those spirits of proof and not more than five per cent. below proof, according to the same hydrometer, twenty-two cents:

Upon every gallon of those spirits above proof, but not exceeding twenty per cent. according to the same hydrometer, twenty-five cents:

Upon every gallon of those spirits more than twenty and not more than forty per cent. above proof, according to the same hydrometer, thirty cents:

Upon every gallon of those spirits more than forty per cent. above proof, according to the same hydrometer, forty cents:

RESOLVED, That from and after the ____ day of ____ in lieu of the duties now payable upon teas and coffee imported into the United States, there shall be paid,

Upon every pound of hyson tea, forty cents:

---

may have been received in the House on this date. These notes, which are in the above location, probably concern the Post Office Bill [HR–42], which was under discussion at this time.

[103] On April 28 this bill was read again and considered in the COWH.

Upon every pound of other green tea, twenty-four cents:

Upon every pound of souchong or other black tea, other than bohea, twenty cents:

Upon every pound of bohea tea, twelve cents:

Upon every pound of coffee, five cents.

RESOLVED, That from and after the   day of   there be paid upon spirits distilled within the United States, from molasses, sugar, or other foreign manufacture:

Upon every gallon of those spirits more than ten per cent. below proof, according to Dicas's hydrometer, eleven cents:

Upon every gallon of those spirits under five and not more than ten per cent. below proof, according to the same hydrometer, twelve cents:

Upon every gallon of those spirits of proof, and not more than five per cent. below proof, according to the same hydrometer, thirteen cents:

Upon every gallon of those spirits above proof, but not exceeding twenty per cent. according to the same hydrometer, fifteen cents:

Upon every gallon of those spirits more than twenty and not more than forty per cent. above proof, according to the same hydrometer, twenty cents:

Upon every gallon of those spirits more than forty per cent. above proof, according to the same hydrometer, thirty cents.

RESOLVED, That from and after the   day of   there be paid upon spirits distilled within the United States, in any city, town or village, from materials the growth or production of the United States,

Upon every gallon, more than ten per cent. below proof, according to Dicas's hydrometer, nine cents:

Upon every gallon of those spirits, under five, and not more than ten per cent. below proof, according to the same hydrometer, ten cents:

Upon every gallon of those spirits, of proof, and not more than five per cent. below proof, according to the same hydrometer, eleven cents:

Upon every gallon of those spirits, above proof, but not exceeding twenty per cent. according to the same hydrometer thirteen cents:

Upon every gallon of those spirits, more than twenty, and not more than forty per cent. above proof, according to the same hydrometer, seventeen cents:

Upon every gallon of those spirits, more than forty per cent. above proof, according to the same hydrometer, twenty-five cents:

And upon all stills employed in distilling spirits from materials of the growth or production of the United States, in any other place than a city, town or village, there be paid the yearly sum of sixty cents, for every gallon, English wine measure, of the capacity of each still, including its head; or cents per gallon for all spirits distilled from grain; or   cents per gallon for all spirits distilled from fruit.

ORDERED, That a bill or bills be brought in pursuant to the said resolutions, and that Mr. Fitzsimons, Mr. Huntington, Mr. Jackson, Mr. Contee, and Mr. Bloodworth do prepare and bring in the same.[104]

RESOLVED, That this House will, to-morrow, again resolve itself into a committee of the whole House on the said report.

A message from the Senate by Mr. Otis their Secretary.

MR. SPEAKER, The Senate have passed a bill, entitled, "An act to continue in force, an act passed at the last session of Congress, entitled, 'An act to regulate processes in the courts of the United States,'" to which they desire the concurrence of this House:[105]   And then he withdrew.

Mr. Gilman, from the joint committee for inrolled bills, reported, that the committee had examined the inrolled bill, entitled, "An act for regulating the military establishment of the United States,"[106] and had found the same to be truly inrolled: Whereupon,

Mr. Speaker signed the said inrolled bill.[107]

ORDERED, That the Clerk of this House do acquaint the Senate therewith.

The House, according to the order of the day, resolved itself into a committee of the whole House, on the bill providing the means of intercourse between the United States and foreign nations.

Mr. Speaker left the chair.

Mr. Livermore took the chair of the committee.

Mr. Speaker resumed the chair, and Mr. Livermore reported, that the committee had, according to order, had the said bill under consideration, and made several amendments thereto, which he delivered in at the Clerk's table, where the same were read, and, together with the said bill, ordered to lie on the table.[108]

ORDERED, That Mr. Thatcher, Mr. Wadsworth, Mr. Benson, Mr. Boudinot,

---

[104] On April 30 a petition concerning duties on paints was referred to this committee. On May 5 this committee presented the Duties on Distilled Spirits Bill [HR–64], which was read twice. On May 11 they presented the Duties on Wines Bill [HR–62], which was read.

[105] The bill is in Engrossed Senate Bills and Resolutions, SR, DNA. According to the New York *Daily Advertiser*, April 28, 1790, the House read this bill on this date. On April 28 the bill was read for the second time.

[106] The inspected enrolled bill is in Enrolled Acts, RG 11, DNA. E–22958.

[107] The vice president signed this bill on April 28, and it was presented to the president on April 29.

[108] On April 29 these amendments were agreed to.

Mr. Sumter, Mr. Seney, and Mr. Parker, be added to the committee appointed to prepare and bring in a bill or bills providing for the national defence.[109]

ORDERED, That the committee of the whole House, to whom was committed the bill for regulating the post-office of the United States, be discharged from further proceeding thereon, and that the said bill, together with the report of the postmaster-general on the several matters submitted to him by an order of the House of the fifteenth instant, be referred to Mr. Livermore, Mr. Ames, Mr. Huntington, Mr. Silvester, Mr. Wynkoop, Mr. Smith (of Maryland), Mr. Moore, Mr. Steele, Mr. Tucker, Mr. Baldwin, and Mr. Vining.[110]

On motion,

ORDERED, That the copy of an act of the Legislature of the state of South-Carolina, entitled, "An act for ceding to and vesting in the United States, the light-house on Middle-Bay Island, within the bar of Charleston harbour," which lay on the table, be referred to the Secretary of the Treasury, with instruction to examine the same, and report his opinion thereupon to the House.

ORDERED, That the petitions of John Holbrook, and Lemuel Cravath, which were presented on the nineteenth of January last, be referred to the Secretary of the Treasury, with instruction to examine the same, and report his opinion thereupon to the House.

The several orders of the day were read and postponed until to-morrow.

And then the House adjourned until to-morrow morning eleven o'clock.

WEDNESDAY, APRIL 28, 1790

A bill to provide for mitigating or remitting the forfeitures and penalties accruing under the revenue laws, in certain cases therein mentioned, was read the second time, and ordered to be committed to a committe of the whole House to-day.

The bill sent from the Senate, entitled, "An act to continue in force an act passed at the last session of Congress, entitled, 'An act to regulate processes in the courts of the United States,' " was read the second time.[111]

A petition of Jean Boand, of the city of New-York, was presented to the House and read, praying relief against the payment of double tonnage, which has been exacted from him under what he conceives to be a misconstruction of the laws of trade.

---

[109] On July 1 this committee presented the Militia Bill [HR–81], which was read twice.

[110] On May 31 a report on the petition of Christopher Colles was referred to this committee.

[111] On April 29 this bill was read again and agreed to.

ORDERED, That the said petition be referred to the committee to whom was referred the report of the Secretary of the Treasury, of the twenty-third instant, respecting difficulties which have occurred in the execution of the several laws for collecting duties on goods, wares and merchandizes, and on tonnage, and for regulating the coasting trade; that they do examine the matter thereof, and report the same, with their opinion thereupon, to the House.[112]

ORDERED, That the committee to whom was referred the act of the Legislature of the state of New-York, entitled, "An act ceding the light-house and land at Sandy-Hook to the United States," be discharged from further proceeding thereon, and that the said act be referred to the Secretary of the Treasury, with instruction to take order pursuant thereto.

The House, according to the order of the day, resolved itself into a committee of the whole House, on the bill to provide for mitigating or remitting the forfeitures and penalties accruing under the revenue laws, in certain cases therein mentioned.

Mr. Speaker left the chair.

Mr. Livermore took the chair of the committee.

Mr. Speaker resumed the chair, and Mr. Livermore reported, that the committee had, according to order, had the said bill under consideration, and made no amendment thereto.

ORDERED, That the said bill be engrossed, and read the third time to-morrow.[113]

The House, according to the order of the day, resolved itself into a committee of the whole House, on the bill sent from the Senate, entitled, "An act for the government of the territory of the United States south of the river Ohio."

Mr. Speaker left the chair.

Mr. Livermore took the chair of the committee.

Mr. Speaker resumed the chair, and Mr. Livermore reported, that the committee had, according to order, had the said bill under consideration, and made no amendment thereto.

The said bill was then amended at the Clerk's table, and, together with the amendments, ordered to be read the third time to-morrow.[114]

Mr. Page, from the committee appointed, presented, according to order, a bill, "to prescribe the mode in which the public acts, records and judicial

---

[112] On April 30 a petition from the inhabitants of Gloucester County, New Jersey was referred to this committee.

[113] On April 29 this bill was read again, agreed to, and sent to the Senate.

[114] On April 29 this bill was read again, agreed to, and returned to the Senate for concurrence in the amendments.

proceedings in each State shall be authenticated, so as to take effect in every other State," which was received and read the first time.[115]

The House, according to the order of the day, resolved itself into a committee of the whole House, on the bill "to regulate trade and intercourse with the Indian tribes."

Mr. Speaker left the chair.

Mr. Livermore took the chair of the committee.

Mr. Speaker resumed the chair, and Mr. Livermore reported, that the committee had, according to order, had the said bill under consideration, and made some progress therein.

On motion,

ORDERED, That the committee of the whole House be discharged from farther proceeding on the said bill, and that it be re-committed to Mr. Wadsworth, Mr. Brown, Mr. Boudinot, Mr. Burke, Mr. Baldwin, Mr. Livermore, Mr. Ames, Mr. Laurance, Mr. Scott, Mr. Smith (of Maryland), Mr. Sumter, and Mr. Steele.[116]

ORDERED, That the report of the Secretary at War of the twenty-fourth of March last, on the petition of John Rogers, on behalf of himself and others, be referred to Mr. Brown, Mr. Page, and Mr. Silvester.[117]

The several orders of the day were read, and postponed until to-morrow.

And then the House adjourned until to-morrow morning eleven o'clock.

THURSDAY, APRIL 29, 1790

A bill to prescribe the mode in which the public acts, records and judicial proceedings in each State shall be authenticated, so as to take effect in every other State, was read the second time, and ordered to be committed to a committee of the whole House to-morrow.[118]

An engrossed bill "to provide for mitigating or remitting the forfeitures and penalties accruing under the revenue laws, in certain cases therein mentioned," was read the third time.

RESOLVED, That the said bill do pass, and that the title be, "An act to provide for mitigating or remitting the forfeitures and penalties accruing under the revenue laws, in certain cases therein mentioned."[119]

---

[115] On April 29 this bill was read again.

[116] On May 14 this committee presented the Indian Trade Bill [HR–65], which was read.

[117] On May 19 this committee was discharged, and the petition was returned to the secretary of war.

[118] On April 30 an amendment to this bill was agreed to.

[119] This bill is E–46068.

ORDERED, That the Clerk of this House do carry the said bill to the Senate, and desire their concurrence.[120]

The bill sent from the Senate, entitled, "An act for the government of the territory of the United States, south of the river Ohio," with the amendments, was read the third time.

RESOLVED, That the said bill, with the amendments, do pass, and that the title be, "An act for the government of the territory of the United States, south-east of the river Ohio."[121]

ORDERED, That the Clerk of this House do acquaint the Senate therewith, and desire their concurrence to the said amendments.[122]

Mr. Gilman, from the joint committee for inrolled bills, reported, that the committee did, this day, wait on the President of the United States, and present him with two inrolled bills, one entitled, "An act for the punishment of certain crimes against the United States;" the other entitled, "An act for regulating the military establishment of the United States," for his approbation.[123]

The bill sent from the Senate, entitled, "An act to continue in force an act passed at the last session of Congress, entitled, 'An act to regulate processes in the courts of the United States,'" was read the third time.

RESOLVED, That the said bill do pass.

ORDERED, That the Clerk of this House do acquaint the Senate therewith.[124]

A petition of the manufacturers of cordage in the city of Philadelphia, was presented to the House and read, praying that a further duty may be imposed on the importation of foreign cordage.

ORDERED, That the said petition do lie on the table.

A petition of James Read, was presented to the House and read, praying for the settlement of a claim against the United States.

ORDERED, That the said petition be referred to the Secretary of the Treasury, with instruction to examine the same, and report his opinion thereupon to the House.

ORDERED, That a bill or bills be brought in to authorize the issuing certificates to a certain description of invalid officers; and that Mr. Burke, Mr. Contee, and Mr. Coles, do prepare and bring in the same.[125]

---

[120] The Senate read this bill on April 30 and May 3. On May 4 the bill was read again and agreed to with amendments.

[121] A copy of the resolution with amendments is filed with the bill in Engrossed Senate Bills and Resolutions, SR, DNA.

[122] The Senate disagreed to all of the House amendments on May 4, and the House was notified.

[123] The president signed both of these bills on April 30.

[124] On May 10 this bill was signed by the speaker and the vice president.

[125] On April 30 this committee presented the Invalid Officers Bill [HR–59], which was read.

ORDERED, That a bill or bills be brought in for the government and regulation of seamen in the merchants' service; and that Mr. Fitzsimons, Mr. Smith (of Maryland), and Mr. Sturges, do prepare and bring in the same.[126]

ORDERED, That a committee be appointed to consider and report whether any, and what additional rules are necessary for regulating the proceedings of this House; and that the said committee do confer with any committee to be appointed on the part of the Senate, to consider and report whether any, and what further regulations are necessary for conducting the business between the two Houses; and a committee was appointed of Mr. Sherman, Mr. Smith (of South-Carolina), and Mr. Vining.[127]

The House, according to the order of the day, resolved itself into a committee of the whole House, on the bill supplemental to the act for establishing the salaries of the executive officers of government, with their assistants and clerks.

Mr. Speaker left the chair.

Mr. Seney took the chair of the committee.

Mr. Speaker resumed the chair, and Mr. Seney reported, that the committee had, according to order, had the said bill under consideration, and made several amendments thereto, which he delivered in at the Clerk's table, where the same were severally twice read, and agreed to by the House.

ORDERED, That the said bill, with the amendments, be engrossed, and read the third time to-morrow.[128]

The House proceeded to consider the amendments reported yesterday from the committee of the whole House, to the bill providing the means of intercourse between the United States and foreign nations, and the same being read, were agreed to.

ORDERED, That the said bill, with the amendments, be engrossed, and read the third time to-morrow.[129]

The House, according to the order of the day, resolved itself into a committee of the whole House, on the bill for the encouragement of learning, by securing the copies of maps, charts, books and other writings, to the authors and proprietors of such copies, during the times therein mentioned.

Mr. Speaker left the chair.

Mr. Seney took the chair of the committee.

Mr. Speaker resumed the chair, and Mr. Seney reported, that the committee had, according to order, had the said bill under consideration, and made sev-

[126] On May 3 this committee presented the Merchant Seamen Bill [HR–61], which was read twice.

[127] On June 9 this committee reported.

[128] On April 30 this bill was read again, agreed to, and sent to the Senate.

[129] On April 30 this bill was read again, agreed to, and sent to the Senate.

eral amendments thereto, which he delivered in at the Clerk's table, where the same were severally twice read, and agreed to by the House.

ORDERED, That the said bill, with the amendments, be engrossed, and read the third time to-morrow.[130]

The orders of the day were read, and postponed until to-morrow.

And then the House adjourned until to-morrow morning eleven o'clock.

FRIDAY, APRIL 30, 1790

An engrossed bill, "supplemental to the act for establishing the salaries of the executive officers of government, with their assistants and clerks," was read the third time.

RESOLVED, That the said bill do pass, and that the title be, "An act supplemental to the act for establishing the salaries of the executive officers of government, with their assistants and clerks."[131]

ORDERED, That the Clerk of this House do carry the said bill to the Senate, and desire their concurrence.[132]

An engrossed bill, providing the means of intercourse between the United States and foreign nations, was read the third time.

RESOLVED, That the said bill do pass, and that the title be, "An act providing the means of intercourse between the United States and foreign nations."[133]

ORDERED, That the Clerk of this House do carry the said bill to the Senate, and desire their concurrence.[134]

An engrossed bill for the encouragement of learning, by securing the copies of maps, charts, books and other writings, to the authors and proprietors of such copies, during the times therein mentioned, was read the third time, and the blanks therein filled up.

RESOLVED, That the said bill do pass, and that the title be, "An act for the encouragement of learning, by securing the copies of maps, charts, books and

---

[130] On April 30 this bill was read again, agreed to, and sent to the Senate.

[131] This bill is E–46057.

[132] The Senate read this bill on this same day and committed it after a second reading on May 4. On May 12 the committee reported, and on May 13 the report was accepted as amendments to the bill. The Senate passed the bill with amendments on May 14 and notified the House.

[133] This bill is E–46054.

[134] The Senate read this bill on April 30 and May 3. On May 3 the bill was committed, and the committee reported on May 7. The report was considered, and the bill was recommitted on May 10. On May 25 the committee reported an amendment, which was agreed to. On May 26 the bill was agreed to with the amendment. The House was notified on May 27. On the same day the House disagreed to the Senate amendment.

other writings, to the authors and proprietors of such copies, during the times therein mentioned."[135]

ORDERED, That the Clerk of this House do carry the said bill to the Senate, and desire their concurrence.[136]

A petition of Joseph Hardison, on behalf of Benjamin Hardison, of Lebanon in the state of Massachusetts, was presented to the House and read, praying compensation for military services rendered, and injuries sustained by the said Benjamin, during the late war.

Also, a petition of John Wilson, praying to be placed on the list of invalids, as a wounded soldier in the service of the United States during the late war.

ORDERED, That the said petitions be referred to the Secretary at War, with instruction to examine the same, and report his opinion thereupon to the House.

A petition of sundry inhabitants of Morris county, in the state of New-Jersey, was presented to the House and read, praying that additional duties may be imposed on the importation of copperas, vitriol, Spanish brown, Venetian red, and yellow ochre paints.

ORDERED, That the said petition be referred to Mr. Fitzsimons, Mr. Huntington, Mr. Jackson, Mr. Contee and Mr. Bloodworth, to whom it was referred to prepare and bring in a bill or bills imposing additional duties.[137]

The petitions of sundry inhabitants of Gloucester county, in the state of New-Jersey, were presented to the House and read, praying that a port of entry and delivery may be established at the mouth of great Eggharbour river, in the said county.

ORDERED, That the said petitions be referred to Mr. Goodhue, Mr. Laurance, Mr. Boudinot, Mr. Fitzsimons and Mr. Lee, to whom was referred the report of the Secretary of the Treasury of the twenty-third instant.[138]

A message was received from the President of the United States, notifying that the President has approved of the act, entitled, "An act for regulating the military establishment of the United States," and affixed his signature thereto this day.

The Speaker laid before the House a letter and report of the Commissioners for settling accounts between the United States and individual States, made pursuant to an order of the House of the twenty-third instant, which were read and ordered to lie on the table.

---

[135] A printed copy of the bill, annotated by the Senate, is in House Bills, SR, DNA. E–46037.

[136] The Senate read this bill on April 30. On May 3 it was read and committed. On May 28 this committee reported, and the bill was read again and agreed to.

[137] This committee is the same one that was appointed on April 27 to bring in a bill from the resolutions on public credit.

[138] On May 3 a petition from the merchants of Alexandria, Virginia was referred to this committee.

ORDERED, That leave be given to bring in a bill or bills to alter one of the places of holding District Courts in the State of Pennsylvania; and that Mr. Boudinot, Mr. Scott, and Mr. Seney do prepare and bring in the same.

Mr. Burke, from the committee appointed, presented, according to order, a bill to authorize the issuing of certificates to a certain description of invalid officers, which was received and read the first time.[139]

ORDERED, That a committee be appointed to report a catalogue of books necessary for the use of Congress, together with an estimate of the expence thereof; and that Mr. Gerry, Mr. Burke, and Mr. White, be of the said committee.[140]

The House, according to the order of the day, resolved itself into a committee of the whole on the bill to prescribe the mode in which the public acts, records and judicial proceedings in each State, shall be authenticated, so as to take effect in every other State.

Mr. Speaker left the chair.

Mr. Seney took the chair of the committee.

Mr. Speaker resumed the chair, and Mr. Seney reported, that the committee had, according to order, had the said bill under consideration, and made an amendment thereto, which he delivered in at the Clerk's table, where the same was twice read, and agreed to by the House.

ORDERED, That the said bill, with the amendment, be engrossed, and read the third time on Monday next.[141]

The House, according to the order of the day, resolved itself into a committee of the whole House on the bill to allow compensation to John Ely, for his attendance as a physician and surgeon on the prisoners of the United States.

Mr. Speaker left the chair.

Mr. Seney took the chair of the committee.

Mr. Speaker resumed the chair, and Mr. Seney reported, that the committee had, according to order, had the said bill under consideration, and made no amendment thereto.

ORDERED, That the said bill be engrossed, and read the third time on Monday next.[142]

Mr. Gerry, from the committee appointed, presented, according to order, a bill for finally adjusting and satisfying the claims of Frederick William de Steuben, which was received and read the first time.[143]

RESOLVED, That a committee of this House be appointed to join with a

---

[139] On May 3 this bill was read again.
[140] On June 23 this committee reported.
[141] On May 3 this bill was read again, agreed to, and sent to the Senate.
[142] On May 3 the bill was read again, agreed to, and sent to the Senate.
[143] On May 3 this bill was read.

committee to be appointed by the Senate, to consider and report their opinion on the question, When, according to the Constitution, the terms for which the President, Vice-President, Senators and Representatives have been respectively chosen, shall be deemed to have commenced? And also to consider of and report their opinion on such other matters as they shall conceive have relation to this question.

And a committee was appointed of Mr. Benson, Mr. Clymer, Mr. Huntington, Mr. Moore and Mr. Carroll.[144]

On motion,

ORDERED, That the report of the committee appointed to examine into the measures taken by Congress, and the state of Virginia, respecting the lands reserved for the use of the officers and soldiers of the said State, on continental and state establishments, in the cession made by the said State to the United States, of the territory north-west of the river Ohio, be committed to the committee of the whole House on the state of the Union.[145]

ORDERED, That Mr. Mathews have leave to be absent from the service of this House until Wednesday next.

The order of the day was read, and postponed until to-morrow.

And then the House adjourned until Monday morning eleven o'clock.

---

[144] On May 4 the House was notified that the Senate had agreed to this resolution.
[145] On June 28 the House made a resolution on this topic, and a committee was appointed to bring in a bill.

MONDAY, MAY 3, 1790

An engrossed bill to prescribe the mode in which "the public acts, records and judicial proceedings in each State shall be authenticated, so as to take effect in every other State," was read the third time.

RESOLVED, That the said bill do pass, and that the title be, "An act to prescribe the mode in which the public acts, records and judicial proceedings in each State shall be authenticated, so as to take effect in every other State."[1]

ORDERED, That the Clerk of this House do carry the said bill to the Senate, and desire their concurrence.[2]

An engrossed bill, "to allow compensation to John Ely, for his attendance as a physician and surgeon on the prisoners of the United States," was read the third time.

RESOLVED, That the said bill do pass, and that the title be, "An act to allow compensation to John Ely, for his attendance as a physician and surgeon on the prisoners of the United States."[3]

ORDERED, That the Clerk of this House do carry the said bill to the Senate, and desire their concurrence.[4]

A bill to authorise the issuing of certificates to a certain description of invalid officers, was read the second time, and ordered to be engrossed, and read the third time to-morrow.[5]

A bill for finally adjusting and satisfying the claims of Frederick William de Steuben, was read the second time, and ordered to be committed to a committee of the whole House to-morrow.[6]

A petition of Joel Knapp, was presented to the House and read, praying to be placed on the list of pensioners, as a wounded soldier in the service of the United States during the late war.

Also a petition of Thomas McFall, to the same effect.

Also a petition of Joseph Ransom, praying that the pension heretofore granted him, in consideration of wounds received in the service of the United States, may be continued, and that certain arrearages thereof now due may be made good to him.

ORDERED, That the said petitions be referred to the Secretary at War, with instruction to examine the same, and report his opinion thereupon to the House.

---

[1] This bill is E–46064.

[2] The Senate read this bill on May 3, 4, and 5 and agreed to it on May 5. On the same date the House was notified of the Senate action.

[3] A printed copy of the bill is in House Bills, SR, DNA. E–46060.

[4] The Senate read this bill on May 3 and 4 and committed it on May 4. On May 12 the committee reported, and the Senate resolved not to read this bill again.

[5] On May 4 this bill was read again, agreed to, and sent to the Senate.

[6] On May 4 this bill was considered in the COWH.

A petition of the coachmakers of the city of Philadelphia, was presented to the House and read, praying the patronage of Congress to that manufacture, and that a tax on carriages manufactured in America, may not be imposed.

ORDERED, That the said petition do lie on the table.

A petition of the merchants, mechanics, and others of the town of Alexandria, was presented to the House and read, praying a repeal of so much of the act, entitled, "An act to regulate the collection of the duties imposed by law on the tonnage of ships or vessels, and on goods, wares and merchandizes imported into the United States," as obliges ships or vessels bound up the river Potowmac, to come to, and deposit manifests of their cargoes at Saint Mary's, or Yeocomico, before they proceed to their port of delivery.

ORDERED, That the said petition be referred to Mr. Goodhue, Mr. Laurance, Mr. Boudinot, Mr. Fitzsimons and Mr. Lee, to whom was referred the report of the Secretary of the Treasury of the twenty-third ultimo.[7]

Mr. Fitzsimons, from the committee appointed, presented, according to order, a bill for the government and regulation of seamen in the merchant service,[8] which was received and read the first time.

On motion,

The said bill was read the second time, and ordered to be committed to a committee of the whole House on this day week.[9]

ORDERED, That the report of the committee to whom was referred so much of the petition of the merchants and traders of Portsmouth, in New-Hampshire, as prays that Congress will adopt measures to prevent foreigners from carrying the commodities of this continent to any port or place where the citizens of the United States are prohibited from carrying them, be committed to a committee of the whole House on Friday next.[10]

ORDERED, That the report and statements from the Treasury Department, of the receipts and expenditures of the public monies, from the establishment of the said department to the thirty-first day of December last, which were laid before the House on the 29th of January, be annexed to and published with the journal of this House for the present session.[11]

ORDERED, That the petitions of Thomas Coles, Nathan Fuller, and William Hassall, which lay on the table, be referred to the Secretary at War, with in-

---

[7] On May 26 a petition of the merchants and traders on the North Potomac River, Maryland, was referred to this committee.

[8] A printing of what is probably this bill is E–46018.

[9] From May 10–26 this bill was postponed as an order of the day. On May 27 the COWH was discharged from consideration of the bill, and a committee was appointed on the bill.

[10] On May 10 this committee report was considered in the COWH.

[11] On June 25 further reports from the treasurer of the United States were presented to the House.

struction to examine the same, and report his opinion thereupon to the House.

The order of the day was read, and postponed until to-morrow.

And then the House adjourned until to-morrow morning eleven o'clock.

TUESDAY, MAY 4, 1790

An engrossed bill to authorize the issuing of certificates to a certain description of invalid officers, was read the third time, and the blanks therein filled up.

RESOLVED, That the said bill do pass, and that the title be, "An act to authorize the issuing of certificates to a certain description of invalid officers."[12]

ORDERED, That the Clerk of this House do carry the said bill to the Senate, and desire their concurrence.[13]

A message from the Senate by Mr. Otis their Secretary.

MR. SPEAKER, I am directed by the Senate to inform this House that the President of the United States did, on the thirtieth of last month, affix his signature to the act, entitled, "An act for the punishment of certain crimes against the United States." The Senate have appointed committees on their part, to confer with committees appointed by this House, pursuant to resolutions of Friday last.[14] The Senate have also passed a bill, entitled, "An act for giving effect to the act therein mentioned, in respect to the state of North-Carolina, and to amend the said act,"[15] to which they desire the concurrence of this House: And then he withdrew.

The said bill was read the first time.[16]

A petition of Stephen Moore, of the state of North-Carolina, was presented to the House and read, praying to receive compensation for the use and value of a certain tract of land at West-Point, in the state of New-York, on which are erected the fortifications and arsenals of the United States.

ORDERED, That the said petition be referred to the Secretary of the Treasury, with instruction to examine the same, and report his opinion thereupon to the House.[17]

---

[12] The bill is in Engrossed House Bills, HR, DNA.

[13] The Senate read this bill on May 4 and 5. On May 5 it was committed, and the committee reported on July 7. On the same day the bill was read again and disagreed to.

[14] The resolutions referred to concern terms of federally elected officials. On May 12 this committee reported.

[15] The bill is in Engrossed Senate Bills and Resolutions, SR, DNA.

[16] On May 5 this bill was read again.

[17] On June 10 the secretary reported on this petition, and the report was committed.

The House, according to the order of the day, resolved itself into a committee of the whole House on the bill for finally adjusting and satisfying the claims of Frederick William de Steuben.

Mr. Speaker left the chair.

Mr. Livermore took the chair of the committee.

Mr. Speaker resumed the chair, and Mr. Livermore reported that the committee had, according to order, had the said bill under consideration, and made some progress therein.

RESOLVED, That this House will, to-morrow, again resolve itself into a committee of the whole House on the said bill.[18]

A message from the Senate by Mr. Otis their Secretary.

MR. SPEAKER,   The Senate disagree to the amendments proposed by this House to the bill, entitled, "An act for the government of the territory of the United States, south of the river Ohio."[19] The Senate have also passed the bill, entitled, "An act to provide for mitigating or remitting the forfeitures and penalties accruing under the revenue laws in certain cases therein mentioned," with several amendments, to which they desire the concurrence of this House:[20]   And then he withdrew.

The order of the day was read, and postponed until to-morrow.

And then the House adjourned until to-morrow morning eleven o'clock.

WEDNESDAY, MAY 5, 1790

The bill sent from the Senate, entitled, "An act for giving effect to the act therein mentioned in respect to the state of North-Carolina, and to amend the said act," was read the second time, and ordered to be committed to a committee of the whole House to-morrow.[21]

The House proceeded to reconsider their amendments to the bill sent from the Senate, entitled, "An act for the government of the territory of the United States south of the river Ohio," which were read: Whereupon,

RESOLVED, That this House do recede from their amendments to the said bill.[22]

ORDERED, That the Clerk of this House do acquaint the Senate therewith.

---

[18] On May 10 this bill was signed by the speaker and the vice president.

[19] On May 5 the House receded from its amendments to this bill.

[20] The amendments are printed in the *Senate Legislative Journal* on May 4. On May 5 the House agreed to the Senate amendments.

[21] This bill was postponed as an order of the day on May 6. On May 7 this bill was considered in the COWH and amended.

[22] On May 5 the COWH considered this bill again.

The House proceeded to consider the amendments proposed by the Senate to the bill, entitled, "An act to provide for mitigating or remitting the forfeitures and penalties accruing under the revenue laws in certain cases therein mentioned." Whereupon,

RESOLVED, That this House do agree to the said amendments.

ORDERED, That the Clerk of this House do acquaint the Senate therewith.[23]

A petition of Benjamin Kuffe was presented to the House and read, praying to receive compensation for military services rendered to the United States during the late war.

ORDERED, That the said petition be referred to the Secretary at War, with instruction to examine the same, and report his opinion thereupon to the House.

Mr. Fitzsimons, from the committee appointed, presented, according to order, a bill for repealing, after the last day of   next, the duties heretofore laid upon distilled spirits imported from abroad, and laying others in their stead, and also upon spirits distilled within the United States, as well to discourage the excessive use of those spirits, and promote agriculture, as to provide for the support of the public credit, and for the common defence and general welfare, which was received and read the first time.

On motion,

The said bill was read the second time, and ordered to be committed to a committee of the whole House on Tuesday next.[24]

A message from the Senate by Mr. Otis their Secretary.

MR. SPEAKER,   The Senate have passed the bill, entitled, "An act to prescribe the mode in which the public acts, records and judicial proceedings in each State, shall be authenticated so as to take effect in every other State:"[25] And then he withdrew.

The House, according to the order of the day, again resolved itself into a committee of the whole House on the bill for adjusting and satisfying the claims of Frederick William de Steuben.

Mr. Speaker left the chair.

Mr. Livermore took the chair of the committee.

Mr. Speaker resumed the chair, and Mr. Livermore reported, that the committee had, according to order, again had the said bill under consideration, and made a farther progress therein.

---

[23] On May 10 this bill was signed by the speaker and vice president.

[24] This bill was postponed as an order of the day from May 11 to June 8, when it was considered in the COWH.

[25] On May 10 this bill was signed by the speaker and the vice president.

RESOLVED, That this House will, to-morrow, again resolve itself into a committee of the whole House on the said bill.[26]

ORDERED, That the Secretary of the Treasury report to the House the amount of tonnage-duties paid in each of the States from the first of September to the first of January last, distinguishing the foreign from the domestic tonnage.[27]

The order of the day was read, and postponed until to-morrow.

And then the House adjourned until to-morrow morning eleven o'clock.

THURSDAY, MAY 6, 1790

A memorial of Nathaniel Twining, was presented to the House and read, praying relief for certain losses and injuries which he has sustained in consequence of a contract entered into with the late Postmaster-General, for the conveyance of the mail.[28]   Also,

A petition of Francis Mentges, late a Lieutenant-Colonel in the Pennsylvania line, praying compensation for certain extra military services rendered during the late war.[29]

ORDERED, That the said petitions do lie on the table.

The House, according to the order of the day, resolved itself into a committee of the whole House, on the bill for finally adjusting and satisfying the claims of Frederick William de Steuben.

Mr. Speaker left the chair.

Mr. Livermore took the chair of the committee.

Mr. Speaker resumed the chair, and Mr. Livermore reported, that the committee had, according to order, had the said bill under consideration, and made no amendments thereto.

ORDERED, That the said bill do lie on the table.[30]

The orders of the day were read, and postponed until to-morrow.

And then the House adjourned until to-morrow morning eleven o'clock.

---

[26] On May 6 the COWH considered this bill again.

[27] On May 11 the secretary submitted this report.

[28] On May 7 this petition was committed.

[29] On May 13 this petition was committed.

[30] On May 7 the Steuben Bill [HR–60] was amended from the floor. The manuscript journal correctly inserts the following paragraph after the above order:

Mr. Stone, from the Committee appointed, presented according to order, a Bill making provision for the debt of the United States, which was received, and read the first time. On motion, The said Bill was read the second time, and ordered to be committed to a Committee of the whole House on Wednesday next.

A printed copy of what is probably this bill (Funding Bill [HR–63]) is E–46020. On May 19 this bill was considered in the COWH.

FRIDAY, MAY 7, 1790

The House, according to the order of the day, resolved itself into a committee of the whole House, on the bill sent from the Senate, entitled, "An act for giving effect to the act therein mentioned in respect to the state of North-Carolina, and to amend the said act."

Mr. Speaker left the chair.

Mr. Livermore took the chair of the committee.

Mr. Speaker resumed the chair, and Mr. Livermore reported that the committee had, according to order, had the said bill under consideration, and made several amendments thereto, which he delivered in at the Clerk's table, where the same were severally twice read, amended, and agreed to by the House.

ORDERED, That the said bill, with the amendments, be read the third time on Monday next.[31]

On a motion made and seconded, that the House do come to the following resolution, to wit,

RESOLVED, That the Secretary of War be, and he is hereby directed to cause accurate lists to be forthwith published in the newspapers of the states of Virginia and North-Carolina, of all the officers and soldiers who are entitled to receive certain arrears of pay due to the lines of the army of the said States, for which money was granted and appropriated by Congress at their last session; and that the payment be made to the said officers and soldiers, or where dead, to their legal representatives, under the same regulations as have been adopted for the payment of invalid pensioners, in pursuance of an act passed at the last session of Congress, intituled, "An act providing for the payment of the invalid pensioners of the United States," and that no claim of any assignee, under any transfer or power to receive the same, be admitted as valid, to entitle any person to receive any part of the said arrears of pay due to the officers or soldiers of the said lines, except as aforesaid.

ORDERED, That the said motion be committed to Mr. Bland, Mr. Williamson, and Mr. Burke.[32]

The House proceeded to consider the bill for finally adjusting and satisfying the claims of Frederick William de Steuben, which lay on the table: Whereupon,

A motion being made and seconded to amend the first section, by striking out from the word "assembled," in the second line to the end thereof, as followeth:

That for the final adjustment and satisfaction of the claims of Frederick

---

[31] On May 10 this bill was read again, agreed to with amendments, and returned to the Senate.

[32] On May 14 this committee reported.

William de Steuben, and as well to indemnify him for his sacrifices and expences in coming to the United States, as to compensate him for his services
to them during the late war (pursuant to the conference between him and a
committee of Congress in the year one thousand seven hundred and seventy-
eight, set forth in the documents accompanying his memorial), there be allowed to the said Frederick William de Steuben,

The pay and other emoluments of Major-General, and Inspector-General,
specified in the several acts of Congress relating to him, from the tenth day
of March, in the year one thousand seven hundred and seventy-eight, to the
fifteenth day of April, in the year one thousand seven hundred and eighty-
four:

An annuity *for life*, of two thousand seven hundred and six dollars, to commence on the first day of October, in the year one thousand seven hundred
and seventy-seven:

And   thousand acres of land in the western territory of the United
States, to be located in such manner as shall be hereafter prescribed by law:
PROVIDED, That the foregoing allowances shall not be construed to include
either half-pay, or the commutation for half-pay;

It was resolved in the affirmative, $\begin{cases} \text{AYES } 28 \\ \text{NOES } 21 \end{cases}$

The ayes and noes being demanded by one fifth of the members present,
Those who voted in the affirmative, are,

John Baptista Ashe	Jeremiah Van Rensselaer
Abraham Baldwin	James Schureman
Timothy Bloodworth	Joshua Seney
Elias Boudinot	Roger Sherman
John Brown	Peter Silvester
Benjamin Contee	Thomas Sinnickson
William Floyd	William Smith (of Maryland)
Abiel Foster	John Steele
Nicholas Gilman	Michael Jenifer Stone
Benjamin Goodhue	Jonathan Sturges
Jonathan Grout	George Thatcher
Samuel Livermore	Thomas Tudor Tucker
Andrew Moore	Alexander White and
Peter Muhlenberg	Hugh Williamson

Those who voted in the negative, are,

Fisher Ames	Theodorick Bland
Egbert Benson	Aedanus Burke

Lambert Cadwalader   John Laurance
Daniel Carroll   Richard Bland Lee
George Clymer   James Madison, junior
Thomas Fitzsimons   John Page
George Gale   Thomas Scott
Samuel Griffin   William Smith (of South-Carolina)
Daniel Hiester   John Vining and
Daniel Huger   Henry Wynkoop
Benjamin Huntington

A motion was then made and seconded, to insert in lieu of the said words so stricken out, the following clause, to wit:

That in order to make full and adequate compensation to Frederick William de Steuben, as well for the sacrifices and eminent services made and rendered to the United States during the late war, as for the commutation or half-pay, promised by the resolutions of Congress, there be paid to the said Frederick William de Steuben, the sum of seven thousand dollars, in addition to the monies already received by him, and also an annuity of   dollars during life, to commence on the first of January last, to be paid in quarterly payments, at the Treasury of the United States, which several sums shall be considered in full discharge of all claims and demands whatever of the said Frederick William de Steuben, against the United States.

And on the question put thereupon,

It was resolved in the affirmative.

And then the said bill being further amended at the Clerk's table, was, together with the amendments, ordered to be engrossed, and read the third time on Monday next.[33]

Mr. Ames, from the committee to whom were referred the petitions of James Price and John McCord, made a report, which was read, and ordered to lie on the table.[34]

ORDERED, That the memorial of Nathaniel Twining, which lay on the table, be referred to Mr. Burke, Mr. Lee, and Mr. Vining, with instruction to examine the matter thereof, and report the same, with their opinion thereupon to the House.[35]

The orders of the day were read, and postponed until Monday next.

And then the House adjourned until Monday morning eleven o'clock.

---

[33] On May 10 this bill was read again, amended, agreed to, and sent to the Senate.

[34] A copy of the report on the petition of James Price is in A Record of the Reports of Select Committees, HR, DNA. On June 1 the report on the petition of John McCord was considered, and a committee was appointed to prepare a bill to compensate him.

[35] On May 20 this committee reported.

MONDAY, MAY 10, 1790

Mr. Gilman, from the joint committee for inrolled bills, reported, that the committee had examined the following inrolled bills, to wit:

"An act to provide for the mitigation or remission of forfeitures and penalties accruing under the revenue laws, in certain cases therein mentioned."[36]

"An act to prescribe the mode in which the public acts, records, and judicial proceedings in each State shall be authenticated, so as to take effect in every other State."[37]

"An act to continue in force an act passed at the last session of Congress, intituled, 'An act to regulate processes in the courts of the United States.' "[38]

"An act for the government of the territory of the United States, south of the river Ohio,"[39] and had found the same to be truly inrolled: Whereupon, Mr. Speaker signed the said inrolled bills.[40]

ORDERED, That the Clerk of this House do acquaint the Senate therewith.

The bill sent from the Senate, intituled, "An act for giving effect to the act therein mentioned in respect to the State of North-Carolina, and to amend the said act," with the amendments, was read the third time.

RESOLVED, That the said bill, with the amendments, do pass.[41]

ORDERED, That the Clerk of this House do acquaint the Senate therewith, and desire their concurrence to the said amendments.[42]

An engrossed bill "for finally adjusting and satisfying the claims of Frederick William de Steuben," was read the third time.

A motion was made, and the question being put, to fill up the blank in the said bill for granting an annuity during life to the said Frederick William de Steuben, with the sum of two thousand seven hundred and six dollars,

It passed in the negative. $\begin{cases} \text{AYES} & 25 \\ \text{NOES} & 30 \end{cases}$

The ayes and noes being demanded by one fifth of the members present, Those who voted in the affirmative, are,

Fisher Ames	Theodorick Bland
Egbert Benson	Lambert Cadwalader

---

[36] The inspected enrolled bill is in Enrolled Acts, RG 11, DNA.

[37] The inspected enrolled bill is in Enrolled Acts, RG 11, DNA. E–22968.

[38] The inspected enrolled bill is in Enrolled Acts, RG 11, DNA.

[39] The inspected enrolled bill is in Enrolled Acts, RG 11, DNA. E–22960, E–46039.

[40] On May 26 the committee on enrolled bills reported that they had presented these bills to the president on May 25. The president signed all of the bills on May 26.

[41] A copy of the resolution with amendments is filed with the bill in Engrossed Senate Bills and Resolutions, SR, DNA. These amendments are printed in the *Senate Legislative Journal* on May 11.

[42] On May 11 the House was notified that the Senate had agreed to some of these amendments and disagreed to others.

Daniel Carroll
Isaac Coles
Thomas Fitzsimons
George Gale
Elbridge Gerry
Thomas Hartley
Daniel Hiester
Daniel Huger
Benjamin Huntington
John Laurance
Richard Bland Lee

James Madison, junior
Peter Muhlenberg
John Page
Thomas Scott
William Smith (of South-Carolina)
Jonathan Trumbull
Thomas Tudor Tucker
John Vining
Jeremiah Wadsworth and
Henry Wynkoop

Those who voted in the negative, are,

John Baptista Ashe
Abraham Baldwin
Timothy Bloodworth
Elias Boudinot
John Brown
Benjamin Contee
William Floyd
Abiel Foster
Nicholas Gilman
Benjamin Goodhue
Samuel Griffin
Jonathan Grout
John Hathorn
Samuel Livermore
George Mathews

Andrew Moore
Josiah Parker
George Partridge
Jeremiah Van Rensselaer
James Schureman
Joshua Seney
Roger Sherman
Peter Silvester
Thomas Sinnickson
William Smith (of Maryland)
John Steele
Michael Jenifer Stone
Jonathan Sturges
Alexander White and
Hugh Williamson

A motion was then made, and the question being put to fill up the said blank with the sum of two thousand dollars,

It was resolved in the affirmative.

And then the main question being put, that the said bill do pass,

It was resolved in the affirmative, $\begin{cases} \text{AYES} & 34 \\ \text{NOES} & 21 \end{cases}$

The ayes and noes being demanded by one fifth of the members present, Those who voted in the affirmative, are,

Fisher Ames
Egbert Benson
Theodorick Bland

Elias Boudinot
Lambert Cadwalader
Daniel Carroll

Isaac Coles
Benjamin Contee
Thomas Fitzsimons
George Gale
Elbridge Gerry
Samuel Griffin
Thomas Hartley
Daniel Hiester
Daniel Huger
Benjamin Huntington
John Laurance
Richard Bland Lee
Samuel Livermore
James Madison, junior

Andrew Moore
Peter Muhlenberg
John Page
Josiah Parker
Thomas Scott
Roger Sherman
William Smith (of Maryland)
William Smith (of South-Carolina)
Jonathan Trumbull
Thomas Tudor Tucker
John Vining
Jeremiah Wadsworth
Alexander White and
Henry Wynkoop

Those who voted in the negative, are,

John Baptista Ashe
Abraham Baldwin
Timothy Bloodworth
John Brown
William Floyd
Abiel Foster
Nicholas Gilman
Benjamin Goodhue
Jonathan Grout
John Hathorn
George Mathews

George Partridge
Jeremiah Van Rensselaer
James Schureman
Joshua Seney
Peter Silvester
Thomas Sinnickson
John Steele
Michael Jenifer Stone
Jonathan Sturges and
Hugh Williamson

RESOLVED, That the title of the said bill be "An act for finally adjusting and satisfying the claims of Frederick William de Steuben."

ORDERED, That the Clerk of this House do carry the said bill to the Senate, and desire their concurrence.[43]

The petitions of Thomas McKinstry, of Joseph Tucker, Thomas Hollis Condy, Robert Williams and Samuel Armstrong, and of Lewis I. Costigin, were presented to the House and read, respectively praying relief in consideration of military services rendered, or for losses or injuries sustained during the late war.

---

[43] The Senate read this bill on May 10 and 11. On May 11 it was committed, and this committee reported on May 24. The report was considered on May 25. It is printed in the *Senate Legislative Journal* on that date. On May 26 the report was disagreed to, and other amendments to the bill were considered on the same day and on May 27. The bill was agreed to with amendments by the Senate on May 27.

ORDERED, That the said petitions be referred to the Secretary at War, with instruction to examine the same, and report his opinion thereupon to the House.

A petition of Thomas Jenkins and Company, was presented to the House and read, praying that the payment of the duties on certain goods imported by the petitioners may be remitted, for the reasons therein alleged.

ORDERED, That the said petition be referred to Mr. Silvester, Mr. Hartley, and Mr. Tucker, that they do examine the matter thereof, and report the same, with their opinion thereupon, to the House.[44]

ORDERED, That the report of the Secretary at War, on the petition of Basil Middleton, which lay on the table, be committed to Mr. Parker, Mr. Tucker, and Mr. Bloodworth.[45]

ORDERED, That Mr. Boudinot have leave to be absent from the service of this House until this day se'nnight.

The House, according to the order of the day, resolved itself into a committee of the whole House on the report of the committee to whom was referred so much of the petition of the merchants and traders of the town of Portsmouth, in the state of New-Hampshire, as prays that Congress will adopt measures to prevent foreigners from carrying the commodities of the continent, to any port or place where the citizens of the United States, are prohibited from carrying them.

Mr. Speaker left the chair.

Mr. Livermore took the chair of the committee.

Mr. Speaker resumed the chair, and Mr. Livermore reported, that the committee had, according to order, had the said report under consideration, and made some progress therein.

RESOLVED, That this House will, to-morrow, again resolve itself into a committee of the whole House on the said report.[46]

The orders of the day were read, and postponed until to-morrow.

And then the House adjourned until to-morrow morning eleven o'clock.

TUESDAY, MAY 11, 1790

A petition of John Stiller, was presented to the House and read, praying to be placed on the list of pensioners, in consideration of wounds received in the service of the United States during the late war.

ORDERED, That the said petition be referred to the Secretary at War, with instruction to examine the same, and report his opinion thereupon to the House.

---

[44] On May 14 this committee reported.

[45] On June 28 this committee reported. The Journal for that date incorrectly states that the report is on the petition of Francis Mentges.

[46] On May 12 the COWH considered this report again.

Mr. Fitzsimons, from the committee appointed, presented, according to order, a bill, repealing, after the last day of   next, the duties heretofore laid upon wines imported from foreign ports or places, and laying others in their stead, which was received, and read the first time.[47]

The Speaker laid before the House a letter from the Secretary of the Treasury, covering a report of the tonnage duties received in each of the States, between the first day of September and the first day of January last,[48] made pursuant to an order of the House of the fifth instant, which were read, and ordered to lie on the table.

The House, according to the order of the day, again resolved itself into a committee of the whole House, on the report of the committee to whom was referred so much of the petition of the merchants and traders of the town of Portsmouth, in the state of New-Hampshire, as prays that Congress will adopt measures to prevent foreigners from carrying the commodities of this continent to any port or place where the citizens of the United States are prohibited from carrying them.

Mr. Speaker left the chair.

Mr. Seney took the chair of the committee.

Mr. Speaker resumed the chair, and Mr. Seney reported, that the committee had, according to order, again had the said report under consideration, and made a farther progress therein.

RESOLVED, That this House will, to-morrow, again resolve itself into a committee of the whole House on the said report.[49]

The Speaker laid before the House a letter from the Secretary at War, covering a report made pursuant to an order of the House of the twenty-third ultimo, stating an account of the troops (including the militia) and also of the ordnance stores furnished from time to time by the several States, towards the support of the late war,[50] which were read, and ordered to lie on the table.

The Speaker laid before the House a letter from the Secretary of the Treasury, covering a report made pursuant to an order of the House of the twenty-third ultimo, stating the sums of money, including indents and paper money of every kind reduced to specie value, which have been received from, or paid

---

[47] A printing of what is probably this bill is E–46313. On May 12 this bill was read again.

[48] A copy of the report is in A Record of the Reports of the Secretary of the Treasury, vol. 1, HR, DNA. A copy of the report, probably made by ASP, is in Reports and Communications from the Secretary of the Treasury, HR, DNA.

[49] On May 11 the COWH considered this report again.

[50] A copy of the statement is in A Record of the Reports of the Secretary of War, HR, DNA. A copy, probably made by ASP, is in Reports and Communications from the Secretary of War, HR, DNA. A copy of the accompanying letter is in the Knox Papers, MHi.

to, the several States by Congress, from the commencement of the revolution to the present period,[51] which were read, and ordered to lie on the table.

A message from the Senate by Mr. Otis their Secretary.

MR. SPEAKER,   The Senate have agreed to some, and disagreed to others, of the amendments proposed by this House to the bill sent from the Senate, intituled, "An act for giving effect to the act therein mentioned, in respect to the state of North-Carolina, and to amend the said act:"[52]   And then he withdrew.

The orders of the day were read, and postponed until to-morrow.

And then the House adjourned until to-morrow morning eleven o'clock.

WEDNESDAY, MAY 12, 1790

A bill repealing, after the last day of   next, the duties heretofore laid upon wines imported from foreign ports or places, and laying others in their stead, was read the second time, and ordered to be committed to a committee of the whole House on Monday next.[53]

A petition of Abraham Scribner, and Thomas Cable, was presented to the House, and read, praying payment for the hire and value of a vessel the property of the petitioners, which was impressed into the transport-service of the United States, in the year one thousand seven hundred and seventy-six, and taken by the enemy.

ORDERED, That the said petition be referred to the Secretary of the Treasury, with instruction to examine the same, and report his opinion thereupon to the House.

The House proceeded to re-consider such of their amendments proposed to the bill sent from the Senate, intituled, "An act for giving effect to the act therein mentioned, in respect to the state of North-Carolina, and to amend the said act," as were disagreed to by the Senate: Whereupon,

RESOLVED, That a conference be desired with the Senate, on the subject matter of the said amendments, and that Mr. White, Mr. Steele, Mr. Foster, Mr. Livermore and Mr. Williamson, be appointed managers at the said conference on the part of this House.[54]

---

[51] A copy of the report, probably made by ASP, is in Reports and Communications from the Secretary of the Treasury, HR, DNA.

[52] A copy of the Senate resolution on amendments is filed with the bill in Engrossed Senate Bills and Resolutions, SR, DNA. It is printed in the *Senate Legislative Journal* on May 11. On May 12 the House requested a conference on the amendments disagreed to by the Senate. On the same day the Senate agreed to this conference.

[53] This bill was not considered again by the House.

[54] A copy of the resolution with committee appointments is filed with the bill in Engrossed Senate Bills and Resolutions, SR, DNA.

The House, according to the order of the day, again resolved itself into a committee of the whole House, on the report of the committee to whom was referred so much of the petition of the merchants and traders of the town of Portsmouth, in the state of New-Hampshire, as prays that Congress will adopt measures to prevent foreigners from carrying the commodities of this continent to any port or place where the citizens of the United States are prohibited from carrying them.

Mr. Speaker left the chair.

Mr. Seney took the chair of the committee.

Mr. Speaker resumed the chair, and Mr. Seney reported, that the committee had, according to order, again had the said report under consideration, and made a farther progress therein.

RESOLVED, That this House will, to-morrow, again resolve itself into a committee of the whole House on the said report.[55]

A message from the Senate by Mr. Otis their Secretary.

MR. SPEAKER, The Senate agree to the conference desired by this House, on the subject-matter of the amendments to the bill sent from the Senate, intituled, "An act for giving effect to the act therein mentioned, in respect to the state of North-Carolina, and to amend the said act," and have appointed managers on their part:[56] And then he withdrew.

Mr. Benson from the joint committee of both Houses appointed to consider and report their opinion on the question, "When, according to the Constitution, the terms for which the President, Vice-President, Senators and Representatives have been respectively chosen, shall be deemed to have commenced," and also to consider of and report their opinion on, such other matters as they shall conceive to have relation to this question, made a report, which was read and ordered to lie on the table.[57]

The orders of the day were read, and postponed until to-morrow.

And then the House adjourned until to-morrow morning eleven o'clock.

THURSDAY, MAY 13, 1790

A petition of sundry persons of the denomination of people called Quakers, in the state of North-Carolina, was presented to the House and read, praying relief against the operation of an act of the Legislature of the said State, by

---

[55] On May 13 the COWH considered this report again.

[56] A copy of the Senate resolution with committee appointments for the conference is filed with the bill in Engrossed Senate Bills and Resolutions, SR, DNA. On May 14 this committee reported.

[57] On May 14 the House was notified that the Senate had agreed to this report.

which they are deprived of the right of pre-emption to certain lands which they held under the laws thereof.

ORDERED, That the said petition be referred to Mr. Hiester, Mr. Ashe, and Mr. Gale, that they do examine the matter thereof, and report the same with their opinion thereupon to the House.[58]

ORDERED, That the petition of Francis Mentges, which lay on the table, be referred to Mr. Stone, Mr. Wadsworth, and Mr. Page, that they do examine the matter thereof, and report the same, with their opinion thereupon to the House.[59]

A petition of Abel Turney, was presented to the House and read, praying to be placed on the list of invalids, in consideration of a wound received in the service of the United States during the late war.

ORDERED, That the said petition be referred to the Secretary at War, with instruction to examine the same, and report his opinion thereupon to the House.

The House, according to the order of the day, resolved itself into a committee of the whole House, on the report of the committee to whom was referred so much of the petition of the merchants and traders of the town of Portsmouth in the state of New-Hampshire, as prays that Congress will adopt measures to prevent foreigners from carrying the commodities of this continent to any port or place where the citizens of the United States are prohibited from carrying them.

Mr. Speaker left the chair.

Mr. Seney took the chair of the committee.

Mr. Speaker resumed the chair, and Mr. Seney reported, that the committee had, according to order, again had the said report under consideration, and made a farther progress therein.

RESOLVED, That this House will, to-morrow, again resolve itself into a committee of the whole House on the said report.[60]

Mr. Baldwin, from the committee, to whom was referred the memorial of the officers of the late navy of the United States, made a report, which was read, and ordered to lie on the table.[61]

The orders of the day were read, and postponed until to-morrow.

And then the House adjourned until to-morrow morning eleven o'clock.

---

[58] On July 17 this committee reported. The Journal for this date refers to the Quakers as Dunkards.

[59] On May 20 this committee reported.

[60] On May 14 the House agreed to a resolution on this report. The resolution was then referred to a committee to prepare a bill.

[61] A copy of the report is in A Record of the Reports of Select Committees, HR, DNA. On June 24 this report was considered in the COWH, and the House disagreed to it. The petition was then rejected.

FRIDAY, MAY 14, 1790

The House, according to the order of the day, again resolved itself into a committee of the whole House, on the report of the committee to whom was referred so much of the petition of the merchants and traders of the town of Portsmouth, in New-Hampshire, as prays that Congress will adopt measures to prevent foreigners from carrying the commodities of this continent to any port or place where the citizens of the United States are prohibited from carrying them.

Mr. Speaker left the chair.

Mr. Boudinot took the chair of the committee.

Mr. Speaker resumed the chair, and Mr. Boudinot reported, that the committee had, according to order, again had the said report under consideration, and come to a resolution thereupon, which he delivered in at the Clerk's table, where the same was again twice read, and agreed to by the House, as followeth:

RESOLVED, That the tonnage on all foreign built bottoms, belonging to nations not in commercial treaty with the United States, be raised to the sum of one dollar per ton, from and after the first day of January next; and that from and after the   day of   the tonnage on all such vessels be raised to   and that from and after the   day of   no such vessel be permitted to export from the United States, any unmanufactured article being the growth or produce thereof. Provided that this resolution shall not be extended to the vessels of any nation, which permits the importation of fish, other salted provision, grain, and lumber in vessels of the United States.

ORDERED, That a bill or bills be brought in pursuant to the said resolution, and that Mr. Madison, Mr. Sedgwick, and Mr. Hartley, do prepare and bring in the same.[62]

A message from the Senate by Mr. Otis their Secretary.

MR. SPEAKER, The Senate have agreed to the report of the joint committee, appointed to consider and report their opinion on the question, "When, according to the Constitution, the terms for which the President, Vice-President, Senators and Representatives, have been respectively chosen, shall be deemed to have commenced?" and also to consider and report their opinion on such other matters as they should conceive to have relation to this question:[63] They have also passed the bill, intituled, "An act for the encouragement of learning, by securing the copies of maps, charts, books and other writings, to the authors and proprietors of such copies, during the times

---

[62] On May 17 this committee presented the Trade and Navigation Bill [HR-66].
[63] On May 17 this joint committee report was ordered committed to the COWH.

therein mentioned," with several amendments, to which they desire the concurrence of this House:[64]   And then he withdrew.

Mr. Bland, from the committee to whom was referred a motion of the seventh instant, respecting the arrears of pay due to a part of the troops of the Virginia, North-Carolina, and South-Carolina lines, made a report, which was read, and ordered to lie on the table.[65]

A petition of sundry persons, citizens of the United States, captured by the Algerines, and now in slavery in Algiers, was presented to the House and read, praying the interposition of Congress in their behalf, and that effectual measures may be adopted for liberating them from slavery, and restoring them to their country.

ORDERED, That the said petition be referred to the Secretary of State, with instruction to examine the same, and report his opinion thereupon to the House.

Mr. Wadsworth, from the committee appointed, presented, according to order, an amendatory bill to regulate the trade and intercourse with the Indian tribes, which was received and read the first time.[66]

Mr. White, from the managers appointed on the part of this House, to attend the conference with the Senate on the subject matter of the amendments depending between the two Houses to the bill sent from the Senate, intituled, "An act for giving effect to the act therein mentioned, in respect to the state of North-Carolina, and to amend the said act," made a report, which was read, and ordered to lie on the table.[67]

Mr. Silvester, from the committee to whom was referred the petition of Thomas Jenkins and others, made a report which was read and ordered to lie on the table.[68]

The orders of the day were read, and postponed until Monday next.

And then the House adjourned until Monday morning eleven o'clock.

---

[64] Senate amendments are noted on the bill in House Bills, SR, DNA. The amendments are printed in the *Senate Legislative Journal* on May 14. On May 17 the Senate amendments were agreed to by the House.

[65] A copy of the report is in A Record of the Reports of Select Committees, HR, DNA. On May 17 several resolutions reported by this committee were agreed to with amendments by the House and sent to the Senate.

[66] On May 17 this bill was read again.

[67] The report is in Joint Committee Reports, SR, DNA. The report is printed in the *Senate Legislative Journal* on May 18. On May 17 the House considered this report and took further action on their amendments to this bill.

[68] On May 17 this report was considered, and the committee was ordered to bring in a bill.

MONDAY, MAY 17, 1790

An amendatory bill to regulate trade and intercourse with the Indian tribes, was read the second time, and ordered to be committed to a committee of the whole House, on Wednesday next.[69]

Mr. Madison, from the committee appointed, presented, according to order, a bill concerning the navigation and trade of the United States, which was received and read the first time.[70]

A member, in his place, presented to the House a representation from the commissioners of pilotage in the state of South-Carolina, which was read, and ordered to be referred to the Secretary of the Treasury.

The House proceeded to consider the report of the committee to whom was referred the petition of Thomas Jenkins and others: Whereupon,

ORDERED, That the said report be committed to Mr. Silvester, Mr. Hartley, and Mr. Tucker, with instruction to prepare and bring in a bill or bills pursuant thereto.[71]

The House proceeded to consider the report of the managers appointed on the part of this House, to attend the conference with the Senate, on the subject matter of the amendments depending between the two Houses, to the bill sent from the Senate, intituled, "An act for giving effect to the act therein mentioned, in respect to the state of North-Carolina, and to amend the said act:"   Whereupon,

RESOLVED, That this House do recede from their first amendment, and in lieu thereof, propose to strike out, in the last line of the third section, the words, "And Hillsborough alternately, beginning at the first."

RESOLVED, That this House do insist on their second amendment.[72]

ORDERED, That the Clerk of this House do acquaint the Senate therewith.[73]

The House proceeded to consider the amendments of the Senate, to the bill, intituled, "An act for the encouragement of learning, by securing the copies of maps, charts, books and other writings, to the authors and proprietors of such copies during the times therein mentioned:"   Whereupon,

RESOLVED, That this House do agree to the said amendments.

---

[69] Consideration of this bill by the COWH was postponed from May 19 through June 21. On June 22 it was considered in the COWH and amended. An amendment from the floor was disagreed to.

[70] This bill is E–46016. On May 18 this bill was read again.

[71] On May 20 this committee presented the Jenkins Bill [HR–67], which was read.

[72] A copy of the resolutions with the amendment is filed with the bill in Engrossed Senate Bills and Resolutions, SR, DNA.

[73] On May 18 the Senate agreed to the conference report. On the same day the Senate agreed to the above amendment to the first House amendment and adhered to their disagreement to the second House amendment. The House was notified on May 19.

ORDERED, That the Clerk of this House do acquaint the Senate therewith.[74]
On motion,

ORDERED, That the report of the committee appointed to join with a committee of the Senate, to consider and report their opinion on the question, "When, according to the Constitution, the terms for which the President, Vice-President, Senators and Representatives have been respectively chosen, shall be deemed to have commenced?" and also, to consider of, and report their opinion on, such other matters as they shall conceive to have relation to this question, be committed to a committee of the whole House to-morrow.[75]

The House proceeded to consider the resolutions reported by the committee to whom was referred a motion of the seventh instant, respecting the arrears of pay due to a part of the troops of the Virginia, North-Carolina, and South-Carolina lines: Whereupon,

RESOLVED, That this House do agree to the said resolutions, amended to read as follow:

RESOLVED, That the President of the United States be requested to cause to be forthwith transmitted to the executives of the states of Virginia, North-Carolina and South-Carolina, a complete list of the officers, non-commissioned officers and privates of the lines of those States respectively, who are entitled to receive arrears of pay due for services in the army, in the years one thousand seven hundred and eighty-two, and one thousand seven hundred and eighty-three, annexing the particular sum that is due to each individual, with a request to the executives of the said States, to make known to the claimants in the most effectual manner, that the said arrears are ready to be discharged on proper application.

RESOLVED, That the President of the United States be requested to cause the Secretary of the Treasury to take the necessary steps for paying, (within the said States respectively), the money appropriated by Congress on the twenty-ninth day of September, one thousand seven hundred and eighty-nine, for the discharging the arrears of pay due to the troops of the lines of the said States respectively.

RESOLVED, That the Secretary of the Treasury, in cases where the payment has not been made to the original claimant, in person, or to his representative, be directed to take order for making the payment to the original claimant, or to such person or persons only as shall produce a power of attorney, duly attested by two justices of the peace, of the county in which such person or persons reside, authorizing him or them to receive a certain specified sum.

---

[74] On May 25 this bill was signed by the speaker and the vice president.

[75] On May 18 this report was considered in the COWH. The report is printed in the Journal as agreed to. A committee was then appointed to bring in a bill pursuant to the report.

ORDERED, That the Clerk of this House do carry the said resolutions to the Senate and desire their concurrence.[76]

The orders of the day were read, and postponed until to-morrow.

And then the House adjourned until to-morrow morning eleven o'clock.

TUESDAY, MAY 18, 1790

A bill concerning the navigation and trade of the United States, was read the second time, and ordered to be committed to a committee of the whole House to-morrow.[77]

A petition of Mary Katherine Goddard, of the town of Baltimore, was presented to the House and read, praying payment of a claim against the United States.[78] Also,

A memorial of Dominique L. Eglize, praying an augmentation of the pension heretofore granted him, in consideration of imprisonment and sufferings during the late war.

Also a petition of Richard Phillips, praying payment of a claim against the United States.

ORDERED, That the said petitions and memorial be referred to the Secretary of the Treasury, with instruction to examine the same, and report his opinion thereupon to the House.

A memorial of William Taylor, was presented to the House and read, praying to be allowed the commutation of full pay in lieu of half-pay for life, as an officer in the late army of the United States.   Also,

A petition of Timothy Hosmer, praying to be allowed the depreciation of pay as a surgeon in the hospital of the eastern department, during the late war.

ORDERED, That the said petition and memorial be referred to the Secretary at War, with instruction to examine the same, and report his opinion thereupon to the House.

The Speaker laid before the House a letter and report from the Secretary at War, on the petition of Samuel Carleton,[79] which was read, and ordered to lie on the table.

The House, according to the order of day, resolved itself into a committee of the whole House, on the report of the committee appointed to confer with

---

[76] The Senate received and considered these resolutions on May 18. On May 19 they were committed, and on May 20 this committee reported. The resolutions were agreed to with several amendments, and the House was notified on May 21.

[77] Consideration of this bill in the COWH was postponed as an order of the day from May 19 through June 24. On June 25 it was considered in the COWH.

[78] The petition with copies of related documents is in Petitions and Memorials: Applications for jobs, SR, DNA.

[79] A copy of the report is in A Record of the Reports of the Secretary of War, vol. 1, HR, DNA.

a committee of the Senate, to consider and report their opinion on the question, "When, according to the Constitution, the terms for which the President, Vice-President, Senators and Representatives, have been respectively chosen, shall be deemed to have commenced?" and also to consider of, and report their opinion on, such other matters as they shall conceive to have relation to this question.

Mr. Speaker left the chair.

Mr. Seney took the chair of the committee.

Mr. Speaker resumed the chair, and Mr. Seney reported, that the committee had, according to order, had the said report under consideration, and made no amendment thereto.

RESOLVED, That this House do agree to the said report, amended to read as followeth:

That the terms for which the President, Vice-President, Senate and House of Representatives of the United States, were respectively chosen, did, according to the Constitution, commence on the fourth of March, one thousand seven hundred and eighty-nine: And so the Senators of the first class, and the Representatives will not, according to the Constitution, be entitled, by virtue of the same election by which they hold seats in the present Congress, to seats in the next Congress, which will be assembled after the third of March one thousand seven hundred and ninety one: And further, That whenever a vacancy shall happen in the Senate or House of Representatives, and on election to fill such vacancy, the person elected, will not, according to the Constitution, be entitled, by virtue of such election, to hold a seat beyond the time for which the Senator or Representative in whose stead such person shall have been elected, would, if the vacancy had not happened, have been entitled to hold a seat.

That it will be advisable for the Congress to pass a law or laws, for determining, agreeable to the provision in the first section of the second article of the Constitution, the time when the electors shall, in the year which will terminate on the third of March, one thousand seven hundred and ninety-three, and so in every fourth year thereafter, be chosen, and the day on which they shall give their votes, for declaring what officer shall, in case of vacancy, both in the office of President and Vice-President, act as President; for assigning a public office, where the lists mentioned in the second paragraph of the first section of the second article of the Constitution, shall, in case of vacancy in the office of President of the Senate, or his absence from the seat of government, be in the mean time deposited; and for directing the mode in which such lists shall be transmitted.[80]

---

[80] A copy of the report as agreed to is in A Record of the Reports of Select Committees, HR, DNA. E–22979.

ORDERED, That a bill or bills be brought in pursuant to the last paragraph of the said report, and that Mr. Benson, Mr. Clymer, Mr. Huntington, Mr. Moore, and Mr. Carroll, do prepare and bring in the same.[81]

The several orders of the day were read, and postponed until to-morrow.

And then the House adjourned until to-morrow morning eleven o'clock.

WEDNESDAY, MAY 19, 1790

The House, according to the order of the day, resolved itself into a committee of the whole House, on the bill making provision for the debt of the United States.

Mr. Speaker left the chair.

Mr. Seney took the chair of the committee.

Mr. Speaker resumed the chair, and Mr. Seney reported, that the committee had, according to order, had the said bill under consideration, and made some progress therein.

RESOLVED, That this House will, to-morrow, again resolve itself into a committee of the whole House on the said bill.[82]

A message from the Senate by Mr. Otis their Secretary.

MR. SPEAKER, The Senate recede from their disagreement to the first amendment proposed by this House to the bill sent from the Senate, intituled, "An act for giving effect to the act therein mentioned, in respect to the state of North-Carolina, and to amend the said act," and agree to the said amendment, as amended by this House: They do adhere to their disagreement to the second amendment proposed by this House to the said bill:[83] The Senate have also passed a bill, intituled, "An act to prevent bringing goods, wares and merchandizes from the state of Rhode-Island and Providence Plantations into the United States, and to authorize a demand of money from the said State,"[84] to which they desire the concurrence of this House: And then he withdrew.

The said bill was read the first time.[85]

ORDERED, That the committee to whom was referred the report of the Secretary at War, on the petition of John Rogers, in behalf of himself and others,

---

[81] On August 9 the above resolutions were ordered sent to the states.

[82] On May 20 the COWH considered this bill again.

[83] A copy of the Senate resolutions on amendments is filed with the bill in Engrossed Senate Bills and Resolutions, SR, DNA. On May 20 the House appointed a committee to bring in a new North Carolina judiciary bill.

[84] Two annotated bills, one of which is printed, and Senate amendments are in Senate Bills, SR, DNA. These bills, together with the annotations and amendments, may represent in rough form the bill as sent to the House.

[85] On May 20 this bill was read again.

be discharged from further proceeding thereon; and that the said petition be again referred to the Secretary at War, with instruction further to examine the same, and report his opinion thereupon to the House.[86]

The orders of the day were read, and postponed until to-morrow.

And then the House adjourned until to-morrow morning eleven o'clock.

THURSDAY, MAY 20, 1790

The bill sent from the Senate, intituled, "An act to prevent bringing goods, wares and merchandizes from the state of Rhode-Island and Providence Plantations into the United States, and to authorize a demand of money from the said State," was read the second time, and ordered to be committed to a committee of the whole House on Monday se'nnight.[87]

The House proceeded to re-consider their second amendment proposed to the bill sent from the Senate, intituled, "An act for giving effect to the act therein mentioned, in respect to the state of North-Carolina, and to amend the said act," their disagreement to which the Senate do adhere to: Whereupon,

RESOLVED, That this House do adhere to the said amendment.

ORDERED, That the Clerk of this House do acquaint the Senate therewith.

ORDERED, That a committee be appointed to prepare and bring in a bill or bills to extend the "act to establish the judicial courts of the United States," to the state of North-Carolina; and a committee was appointed of Mr. Williamson, Mr. Gerry, and Mr. Steele.[88]

Mr. Burke, from the committee to whom was referred the memorial of Nathaniel Twining, made a report, which was read, and ordered to lie on the table.[89]

Mr. Stone, from the committee to whom was referred the petition of Francis Mentges, made a report, which was read, and ordered to lie on the table.[90]

The Speaker laid before the House a letter and report from the Secretary at War, on the petition of Henry Emanuel Lutterloh, which were read, and ordered to lie on the table.[91]

---

[86] On June 22 the secretary reported on this petition.

[87] On June 1, after being notified that Rhode Island had ratified the Constitution, the House discharged the COWH from considering this bill.

[88] On May 21 this committee presented the North Carolina Judiciary Bill [HR–68], which was read twice.

[89] A copy of the report is in A Record of the Reports of Select Committees, HR, DNA. On May 28 the House agreed to a resolution on this report, and a committee was appointed to bring in a bill.

[90] On July 14 this committee reported again. The petition apparently had been recommitted without notation of this action in the Journal.

[91] A copy of this report is in A Record of the Reports of the Secretary of War, vol. 1, HR, DNA. A copy of the report, probably made by ASP, is in Reports and Com-

ORDERED, That the report of the committee to whom was referred the petition of Richard Wells and Josiah Hart, be referred to the committee of the whole House, to whom is committed the bill making provision for the debt of the United States.

The House, according to the order of the day, again resolved itself into a committee of the whole House, on the bill making provision for the debt of the United States.

Mr. Speaker left the chair.

Mr. Seney took the chair of the committee.

Mr. Speaker resumed the chair, and Mr. Seney reported, that the committee had, according to order, again had the said bill under consideration, and made a farther progress therein.

RESOLVED, That this House will, to-morrow, again resolve itself into a committee of the whole House on the said bill.[92]

Mr. Silvester, from the committee appointed, presented, according to order, a bill for the relief of Thomas Jenkins and company, which was received, and read the first time.[93]

The several orders of the day were read, and postponed until to-morrow.

And then the House adjourned until to-morrow morning ten o'oclock.

FRIDAY, MAY 21, 1790

A bill for the relief of Thomas Jenkins and company, was read the second time, and ordered to be engrossed, and read the third time on Monday next.[94]

Mr. Williamson, from the committee appointed, presented, according to order, a bill for giving effect to an act, intituled, "An act to establish the judicial courts of the United States," within the state of North-Carolina, which was received, and read the first time.

On motion,

The said bill was read the second time, and ordered to be engrossed, and read the third time on Monday next.[95]

The House, according to the order of the day, again resolved itself into a committee of the whole House, on the bill making provision for the debt of the United States.

Mr. Speaker left the chair.

Mr. Seney took the chair of the committee.

---

munications from the Secretary of War, HR, DNA. Although there is no record in the Journal of a committee being appointed on the Lutterloh petition, a committee reported on it on July 21.

[92] On May 21 the COWH considered this bill again.

[93] On May 21 this bill was read again.

[94] On May 24 this bill was read again, agreed to, and sent to the Senate.

[95] On May 24 this bill was read again, agreed to, and sent to the Senate.

Mr. Speaker resumed the chair, and Mr. Seney reported, that the committee had, according to order, again had the said bill under consideration, and made a farther progress therein.

RESOLVED, That this House will, on Monday next, again resolve itself into a committee of the whole House on the said bill.[96]

A message from the Senate by Mr. Otis their Secretary.

MR. SPEAKER,   The Senate have agreed to the resolutions of this House, of the seventeenth instant, respecting the arrears of pay due to a part of the troops of the Virginia, North-Carolina and South-Carolina lines, for the years one thousand seven hundred and eighty-two, and one thousand seven hundred and eighty-three, with several amendments, to which they desire the concurrence of this House:[97]   And then he withdrew.

The several orders of the day were read, and postponed until Monday next. And then the House adjourned until Monday morning, ten o'clock.

MONDAY, MAY 24, 1790

An engrossed bill for the relief of Thomas Jenkins and company, was read the third time.

RESOLVED, That the said bill do pass, and that the title be "An act for the relief of Thomas Jenkins and company."

ORDERED, That the Clerk of this House do carry the said bill to the Senate, and desire their concurrence.[98]

An engrossed bill for giving effect to an act, intituled, "An act to establish the judicial courts of the United States," within the state of North-Carolina, was read the third time.

RESOLVED, That the said bill do pass, and that the title be "An act for giving effect to an act, intituled, 'An act to establish the judicial courts of the United States,' within the state of North-Carolina."

ORDERED, That the Clerk of this House do carry the said bill to the Senate, and desire their concurrence.[99]

---

[96] On May 24 the COWH considered this bill again.

[97] The Senate committee report on these resolutions, with amendments, is in Various Select Committee Reports, SR, DNA. The amendments are printed in the *Senate Legislative Journal* on May 21. On May 24 the House agreed to the Senate amendments.

[98] The Senate read this bill on May 24, 27, and 28. On May 28 the bill was committed. On June 1 the committee reported, and the Senate agreed to the bill.

[99] The Senate read this bill on May 24, 27, and 28. It was agreed to and returned to the House on May 28.

The Speaker laid before the House a letter from the Secretary at War, covering his reports on the several petitions of Wilhelmus Decker, Enos Brown, Henry Carman, John Garnett, John Wilson, Abel Turney, John Stiller, Jacob Acker, Joel Knapp, Thomas Cole, Barent Martling, and Thomas McKinstry, which were read, and ordered to lie on the table.[100]

A petition of William Hardy and Joseph Bedford, was presented to the House and read, praying compensation for services rendered to the United States.

ORDERED, That the said petition, together with the petition of Isaac Spencer, executor of Joseph Spencer, deceased, which lay on the table, be referred to the Secretary of the Treasury, with instruction to examine the same, and report his opinion thereupon to the House.

A petition of John Wood was presented to the House and read, praying compensation for services rendered, and injuries sustained in the service of the United States, during the late war.

ORDERED, That the said petition do lie on the table.

The House proceeded to consider the amendments proposed by the Senate to the resolutions of this House of the seventeenth instant, respecting the arrears of pay due to a part of the troops of the Virginia, North-Carolina and South-Carolina lines: Whereupon,

RESOLVED, That this House do agree to the said amendments.

ORDERED, That the Clerk of this House do acquaint the Senate therewith.[101]

The House, according to the order of the day, again resolved itself into a committee of the whole House, on the bill making provision for the debt of the United States.

Mr. Speaker left the chair.

Mr. Seney took the chair of the committee.

Mr. Speaker resumed the chair, and Mr. Seney reported, that the committee had, according to order, again had the said bill under consideration, and made a farther progress therein.

RESOLVED, That this House will, to-morrow, again resolve itself into a committee of the whole House on the said bill.[102]

The several orders of the day were read, and postponed until to-morrow.

And then the House adjourned until to-morrow morning ten o'clock.

---

[100] A copy of the report on all of these petitions is in A Record of the Reports of the Secretary of War, vol. 1, HR, DNA.

[101] On May 25 this resolution was signed by the speaker and vice president.

[102] On May 25 the COWH considered this bill again. The first twelve sections were reported out of the COWH, which was discharged from further consideration of the Funding Bill [HR-63].

TUESDAY, MAY 25, 1790

Mr. Gilman, from the joint committee for inrolled bills, reported, that the committee had examined an inrolled bill, intituled, "An act for the encouragement of learning, by securing the copies of maps, charts and books, to the authors and proprietors of such copies, during the times therein mentioned;"[103] also, an inrolled resolve, respecting the arrears of pay due to a part of the troops of the Virginia and North-Carolina lines, for the years one thousand seven hundred and eighty-two, and one thousand seven hundred and eighty-three;[104] and had found the same to be truly inrolled: Whereupon,

Mr. Speaker signed the said inrolled bill and resolve.[105]

ORDERED, That the Clerk of this House do acquaint the Senate therewith.

The Speaker laid before the House a letter and reports from the Secretary at War, on the several petitions of Nathan Fuller, Nathaniel Fox, and of Joseph Tucker, Thomas Hollis Condy, Robert Williams and Samuel Armstrong, which were read, and ordered to lie on the table.[106]

A petition of Jacob Bailey was presented to the House and read, praying the settlement of a claim against the United States, and also to be compensated for services rendered during the late war.

ORDERED, That the said petition be referred to the Secretary of the Treasury, with instruction to examine the same, and report his opinion thereupon to the House.

The House, according to the order of the day, again resolved itself into a committee of the whole House, on the bill making provision for the debt of the United States.

Mr. Speaker left the chair.

Mr. Seney took the chair of the committee.

Mr. Speaker resumed the chair, and Mr. Seney reported, that the committee had, according to order, again had the said bill under consideration, and agreed to the first twelve sections thereof, with amendments, which they had instructed him now to report, and to pray that the committee of the whole House be discharged from the farther consideration of the said bill.[107]

The several orders of the day were read, and postponed until to-morrow.

And then the House adjourned until to-morrow morning ten o'clock.

---

103 The inspected enrolled bill is in Enrolled Acts, RG 11, DNA. E–46038.

104 The inspected enrolled resolution is in Enrolled Acts, RG 11, DNA. E–22985.

105 On May 28 the committee on enrolled bills reported that the bill and resolution had been presented to the president.

106 Copies of all of these reports are in A Record of the Reports of the Secretary of War, vol. 1, HR, DNA. A copy of the report on the petitions of Tucker, Condy, Williams, and Armstrong is in Reports and Communications from the Secretary of War, HR, DNA.

107 On May 26 amendments to this bill were considered and some were agreed to.

WEDNESDAY, MAY 26, 1790

Mr. Gilman, from the joint committee for inrolled bills, reported, that the committee did, yesterday, wait on the President of the United States, and present him with four inrolled bills; one intituled, "An act to prescribe the mode, in which the public acts, records, and judicial proceedings, in each State, shall be authenticated, so as to take effect in every other State;" another, intituled, "An act to provide for mitigating or remitting the forfeitures and penalties, accruing under the revenue laws, in certain cases therein mentioned;" another, intituled, "An act to continue in force, an act, passed at the last session of Congress, intituled, 'An act to regulate processes in the Courts of the United States;'" and another, intituled, "An act for the government of the territory of the United States, south of the River Ohio," for his approbation.

A petition of sundry merchants of the town of Wilmington in the State of North-Carolina, was presented to the House, and read, praying relief, against the payment of certain duties, which they conceive were unjustly exacted from them, under the operation of a law of the said State.[108]

ORDERED, That the said petition, together with the petition of John Wood, which lay on the table, be referred to the Secretary of the Treasury, with instruction to examine the same, and report his opinion thereupon to the House.

The several petitions of Walter Miles, Samuel Garretson, and Christian Wolfe, were presented to the House, and read, respectively praying relief, in consideration of services rendered, or for losses or injuries sustained during the late war.

ORDERED, That the said petitions be referred to the Secretary at War, with instruction to examine the same, and report his opinion thereupon to the House.[109]

ORDERED, That such of the reports of the Secretary at War, on the petitions of invalid or wounded officers and soldiers, as lie on the table, be referred to the committee appointed to prepare and bring in a bill or bills, for the relief of disabled soldiers and seamen.[110]

A petition of John Frederick Amelung, proprietor of a glass manufactory, at New Bremen, in the state of Maryland, was presented to the House, and read, praying the patronage of Congress to his undertaking, and that govern-

---

[108] The petition is in Petitions and Memorials: Claims, SR, DNA.

[109] On June 28 the secretary reported on these petitions. On the same day a House resolution concerning the Wolfe and Garretson petitions was referred to the committee to prepare the Disabled Soldiers and Seamen Bill [HR–88].

[110] On June 28 a resolution on several petitions was referred to this committee.

ment will assist him with a loan of money, or other means to further the same.[111]

ORDERED, That the said petition be referred to Mr. Carroll, Mr. Hiester, Mr. Boudinot, Mr. Gale, and Mr. Vining, that they do examine the matter thereof, and report the same, with their opinion thereupon to the house.[112]

A petition of Enos Hitchcock, of the state of Rhode-Island, was presented to the House and read, praying that the privilege of a late law, may be extended to him, for securing the copy-right of a book which he has lately published, intituled, "Memoirs of the Bloomsgrove Family."

ORDERED, That the said petition be referred to Mr. Ames, Mr. Benson, and Mr. Boudinot, that they do examine the matter thereof, and report the same, with their opinion thereupon, to the House.

A petition of the merchants and traders, on North Potowmack River, in the state of Maryland, was presented to the House, and read, praying that the River Wicomico, at Lewellinsburg, may be appointed a port of delivery.

ORDERED, That the said petition be referred to the committee, appointed to prepare and bring in a bill or bills, to amend the laws of revenue.[113]

A message was received from the President of the United States, by Mr. Lear, his Secretary, notifying, that the President has approved of two acts, one, intituled, "An act to prescribe the mode, in which the public acts, records, and judicial proceedings in each State, shall be authenticated, so as to take effect in every other State;" the other, intituled, "An act to provide for mitigating or remitting the forfeitures and penalties accruing under the revenue laws, in certain cases therein mentioned;" and affixed his signature to the same, this day.

The House proceeded to consider the report made yesterday, by the committee of the whole House, on the bill, making provision for the debt of the United States: Whereupon,

ORDERED, That the said committee be discharged from further proceeding on the said bill.

And then the amendments, proposed by the said committee, to the first, second, fourth, eighth, and twelfth sections of the said bill, being severally read at the Clerk's table, were, on the question put thereupon, agreed to by the House.

The following amendment to the third section, being under consideration, to wit:

To the end of the section, add, "Those which shall be issued for the bills

---

[111] The petition is in Petitions and Memorials: Various subjects, SR, DNA.
[112] On June 2 this committee reported.
[113] On June 14 a petition from the tanners of Philadelphia was also referred to this committee.

of credit, issued by the authority of the United States in Congress assembled, at the rate of one hundred dollars in the said bills, for one dollar in specie."

A motion was made, and the question being put, to amend the said amendment, by striking out the words, "*one hundred*,"

It was resolved in the affirmative.

A motion was then made, and the question being put, to insert, in lieu of the words so stricken out, the words "*seventy-five*,"

It was resolved in the affirmative, $\begin{cases} \text{AYES} & 31 \\ \text{NOES} & 25 \end{cases}$

The ayes and noes being demanded by one fifth of the members present, Those who voted in the affirmative, are,

Fisher Ames	Benjamin Huntington
Egbert Benson	George Leonard
Elias Boudinot	Samuel Livermore
Aedanus Burke	George Partridge
Lambert Cadwalader	Jeremiah Van Rensselaer
Thomas Fitzsimons	James Schureman
William Floyd	Theodore Sedgwick
Abiel Foster	Roger Sherman
George Gale	Peter Silvester
Elbridge Gerry	William Smith (of Maryland)
Nicholas Gilman	Jonathan Sturges
Benjamin Goodhue	Thomas Sumter
Samuel Griffin	George Thatcher
Jonathan Grout	Thomas Tudor Tucker and
John Hathorn	Henry Wynkoop
Daniel Huger	

Those who voted in the negative, are,

John Baptista Ashe	James Madison, junior
Abraham Baldwin	George Mathews
Timothy Bloodworth	Andrew Moore
Daniel Carroll	Peter Muhlenberg
Isaac Coles	John Page
Benjamin Contee	Thomas Scott
Thomas Hartley	Joshua Seney
Daniel Hiester	Thomas Sinnickson
James Jackson	William Smith (of South-Carolina)
John Laurance	John Steele
Richard Bland Lee	Michael Jenifer Stone

Jonathan Trumbull   Hugh Williamson
Alexander White and

A motion was then made, and the question being put, further to amend the
said amendment, by adding thereto the following proviso: "Provided, that
interest shall be computed on the said bills, from the   day of
1781,"

It passed in the negative, $\begin{cases} \text{AYES} & 15 \\ \text{NOES} & 42 \end{cases}$

The ayes and noes being demanded by one fifth of the members present,
Those who voted in the affirmative, are,

Fisher Ames   George Leonard
Abiel Foster   Samuel Livermore
Elbridge Gerry   George Partridge
Nicholas Gilman   Theodore Sedgwick
Benjamin Goodhue   Thomas Sumter
Jonathan Grout   George Thatcher and
John Hathorn   Thomas Tudor Tucker
Daniel Huger

Those who voted in the negative, are,

John Baptista Ashe   Richard Bland Lee
Abraham Baldwin   James Madison, junior
Egbert Benson   George Mathews
Timothy Bloodworth   Andrew Moore
Elias Boudinot   Peter Muhlenberg
Aedanus Burke   John Page
Lambert Cadwalader   Josiah Parker
Daniel Carroll   Jeremiah Van Rensselaer
Isaac Coles   James Schureman
Benjamin Contee   Thomas Scott
Thomas Fitzsimons   Joshua Seney
William Floyd   Roger Sherman
George Gale   Peter Silvester
Samuel Griffin   Thomas Sinnickson
Thomas Hartley   William Smith (of Maryland)
Daniel Hiester   William Smith (of South-Carolina)
Benjamin Huntington   John Steele
James Jackson   Michael Jenifer Stone
John Laurance   Jonathan Sturges

| Jonathan Trumbull | Hugh Williamson and |
| Alexander White | Henry Wynkoop |

And then the main question being put, that the House do agree to the amendment to the said third section as before amended,

It was resolved in the affirmative.

The said bill was then further amended at the Clerk's table, and, together with the amendments, ordered to lie on the table.[114]

The several orders of the day were read, and postponed until to-morrow.

And then the House adjourned until to-morrow morning ten o'clock.

THURSDAY, MAY 27, 1790

Mr. Fitzsimons, from the committee appointed, presented, according to order, a bill to provide for the settlement of the accounts between the United States, and the individual States,[115] which was received, and read the first time.

On motion,

The said bill was read the second time, and ordered to be committed to a committee of the whole House on Monday next.[116]

A message from the Senate by Mr. Otis their Secretary.

MR. SPEAKER, I am directed to inform this House, that the President of the United States did yesterday affix his signature to two acts which originated in the Senate; one intituled, "An act to continue in force an act passed at the last session of Congress, intituled, 'An act to regulate processes in the courts of the United States;'" and the other intituled, "An act for the government of the territory of the United States south of the river Ohio." The Senate have passed the bill, intituled, "An act providing the means of intercourse between the United States and foreign nations," with an amendment,[117] to which they desire the concurrence of this House. And then he withdrew.

The House proceeded to consider the bill which lay on the table, making provision for the debt of the United States; and the same being further amended at the Clerk's table, was, together with the amendments thereto, ordered to be engrossed, and read the third time on Monday next.[118]

The House proceeded to consider the amendment proposed by the Senate

---

[114] On May 27 further amendments to the Funding Bill [HR–63] were agreed to.
[115] A printing of what is probably this bill is E–45663.
[116] On June 1 this bill was considered in the COWH.
[117] This amendment is filed with the conference report on the bill in Joint Committee Reports, SR, DNA.
[118] On June 2 this bill was read again, agreed to, and sent to the Senate.

to the bill, intituled, "An act providing the means of intercourse between the United States and foreign nations," as followeth:

Strike out "That the President shall not allow to any minister plenipotentiary, a greater sum than at the rate of nine thousand dollars per annum, as a compensation for all his personal services and expences; nor a greater sum for the same, than three thousand dollars, to a charge des affaires; nor a greater sum than one thousand three hundred and fifty dollars for the same, to any of their secretaries; and that each of the ministers aforesaid, and their secretaries, shall be entitled to one quarter's salary, after receiving leave to return, or a recall from the court to which they may respectively be appointed. And provided also." Whereupon,

RESOLVED, That this House do disagree to the said amendment, $\begin{cases} \text{AYES} & 18 \\ \text{NOES} & 38 \end{cases}$

The ayes and noes being demanded by one fifth of the members present, Those who voted in the affirmative, are,

Fisher Ames	John Laurance
Egbert Benson	Richard Bland Lee
Lambert Cadwalader	Josiah Parker
George Gale	George Partridge
Benjamin Goodhue	William Smith (of South-Carolina)
Samuel Griffin	Michael Jenifer Stone
Thomas Hartley	Jonathan Trumbull
Daniel Hiester	John Vining and
Benjamin Huntington	Henry Wynkoop

Those who voted in the negative, are,

Abraham Baldwin	John Hathorn
Timothy Bloodworth	Daniel Huger
Elias Boudinot	James Jackson
John Brown	George Leonard
Aedanus Burke	Samuel Livermore
Daniel Carroll	James Madison, junior
Isaac Coles	George Mathews
Benjamin Contee	Andrew Moore
Thomas Fitzsimons	Peter Muhlenberg
William Floyd	John Page
Abiel Foster	Jeremiah Van Rensselaer
Elbridge Gerry	James Schureman
Nicholas Gilman	Thomas Scott
Jonathan Grout	Theodore Sedgwick

Joshua Seney	Thomas Sumter
Roger Sherman	George Thatcher
Peter Silvester	Thomas Tudor Tucker
Thomas Sinnickson	Alexander White and
John Steele	Hugh Williamson[119]

A message from the Senate by Mr. Otis their Secretary.

MR. SPEAKER, The Senate have passed the bill, intituled, "An act for finally adjusting and satisfying the claims of Frederick William de Steuben," with several amendments, to which they desire the concurrence of this House:[120]   And then he withdrew.

ORDERED, That the committee of the whole House, to whom was committed the bill for the government and regulation of seamen in the merchant's service, be discharged from further proceeding thereon; and that the said bill be committed to Mr. Gilman, Mr. Goodhue, Mr. Fitzsimons, Mr. Smith (of Maryland), and Mr. Parker.[121]

On a motion made and seconded,

"That a committee be appointed to examine into, and report the decisions of the several States respectively, upon the amendments to the Constitution of the United States, heretofore proposed by Congress; and that the committee be authorized to report what other and further amendments to the said Constitution, are necessary to be recommended by Congress at present."

A division of the said motion was called for: Whereupon,

The first part of the said motion, in the words following, to wit: "That a committee be appointed to examine into, and report the decisions of the several States respectively, upon the amendments to the Constitution heretofore proposed by Congress," was, on the question put thereupon, agreed to by the House.

The latter part of the said motion in the words following, to wit: "And that the committee be authorized to report what other and further amendments to the said Constitution, are necessary to be recommended by Congress at present," was, on the question put thereupon, disagreed to by the House.

ORDERED, That Mr. Steele, Mr. Moore, and Mr. Contee, be appointed a committee, pursuant to the first part of the said motion.

The several orders of the day were read, and postponed until to-morrow.

And then the House adjourned until to-morrow morning ten o'clock.

---

[119] On May 28 the Senate adhered to its amendment to the Foreign Intercourse Bill [HR–52]. On the same day the House reconsidered the amendment and insisted on its disagreement.

[120] On May 28 the House agreed to these Senate amendments.

[121] On June 17 this committee reported amendments to the bill.

FRIDAY, MAY 28, 1790

Mr. Gilman, from the joint committee for inrolled bills, reported, that the committee did, yesterday, wait on the President of the United States, and present him with an inrolled bill, intituled, "An act for the encouragement of learning, by securing the copies of maps, charts and books, to the authors and proprietors of such copies, during the times therein mentioned;" also, an inrolled resolve, respecting the arrears of pay due to a part of the troops of the Virginia and North-Carolina lines, for the years one thousand seven hundred and eighty-two, and one thousand seven hundred and eighty-three, for his approbation.[122]

On a motion made and seconded, that the House do agree to certain resolutions, making provision for the payment of the debts of the individual States,

ORDERED, That the said resolutions be committed to a committee of the whole House on Monday se'nnight.

The House proceeded to consider the amendments proposed by the Senate to the bill, intituled, "An act for finally adjusting and satisfying the claims of Frederick William de Steuben," which are as follow:

Line third. Strike out the words "*as well.*"

Lines fourth and fifth. Strike out the words "*as for the commutation or half pay promised by the resolutions of Congress.*"

Line sixth. Strike out the words "*the sum of seven thousand dollars in addition to the monies already received by him, and also.*"

Line seventh. After the word "*thousand,*" insert "five hundred."

Whereupon,

The first, second and third amendments, were, on the question severally put thereupon, agreed to by the House.

The last amendment to insert the words "*five hundred,*" in addition to the sum of two thousand dollars, being the amount of the annuity proposed to be granted by the said bill, was, on the question put thereupon, agreed to by the House:

AYES 32

NOES 25

The ayes and noes being demanded by one fifth of the members present, Those who voted in the affirmative, are,

Fisher Ames	Aedanus Burke
Egbert Benson	Lambert Cadwalader
Elias Boudinot	Daniel Carroll

---

[122] The president signed the Copyright Bill [HR–43] on May 31 and the resolution on June 7.

George Clymer
Isaac Coles
Benjamin Contee
Thomas Fitzsimons
William Floyd
George Gale
Elbridge Gerry
Thomas Hartley
Daniel Hiester
Daniel Huger
Benjamin Huntington
John Laurance
Richard Bland Lee

Samuel Livermore
Andrew Moore
Peter Muhlenberg
John Page
Josiah Parker
Thomas Scott
Peter Silvester
William Smith (of South-Carolina)
Jonathan Trumbull
Thomas Tudor Tucker
John Vining
Alexander White and
Henry Wynkoop

Those who voted in the negative, are,

John Baptista Ashe
Abraham Baldwin
Timothy Bloodworth
John Brown
Abiel Foster
Nicholas Gilman
Benjamin Goodhue
Samuel Griffin
Jonathan Grout
John Hathorn
James Jackson
George Leonard
George Mathews

George Partridge
Jeremiah Van Rensselaer
James Schureman
Joshua Seney
Roger Sherman
Thomas Sinnickson
John Steele
Michael Jenifer Stone
Jonathan Sturges
Thomas Sumter
George Thatcher and
Hugh Williamson[123]

The House proceeded to consider the report of the committee to whom was referred the memorial of Nathaniel Twining: Whereupon,

RESOLVED, That the penalty incurred by Nathaniel Twining, in consequence of the failure of his contract, as executed with the late Postmaster-General, for transporting the mail by means of carriages from Georgetown to Charleston, and from thence to Savannah, from the month of September, one thousand seven hundred and eighty-seven, until the first of January, one thousand seven hundred and eighty-eight, be remitted; and that he be allowed out

---

[123] The Journal does not record the signing of the Steuben Bill [HR–60] by the speaker. The speaker signed the bill on June 1, and the vice president signed it on June 2. On June 3 the committee on enrolled bills reported that they had presented this bill to the president on June 2.

of the treasury of the United States, the sum of five hundred and sixty-seven dollars, and forty-one cents; and also, the additional sum of eight dollars for having transported the mail from the Head of Elk to Philadelphia, after the first day of January, one thousand seven hundred and eighty-eight, as appears by sufficient vouchers.

ORDERED, That a committee be appointed to prepare and bring in a bill or bills pursuant to the said resolution:

And a committee was appointed of Mr. Burke, Mr. Lee, and Mr. Vining.[124]

A message from the Senate by Mr. Otis their Secretary.

MR. SPEAKER, The Senate have passed the bill, intituled, "An act supplemental to the act for establishing the salaries of the executive officers of government, with their assistants and clerks;"[125] also, the bill, intituled, "An act for giving effect to an act, intituled, 'An act to establish the judicial courts of the United States,' within the state of North-Carolina."[126] And they do insist on their amendment disagreed to by this House, to the bill, intituled, "An act providing the means of intercourse between the United States and foreign nations:" And then he withdrew.

The House proceeded to re-consider the amendment proposed by the Senate to the bill, intituled, "An act providing the means of intercourse between the United States and foreign nations:" Whereupon,

A motion was made, and the question being put, that the House do recede from their disagreement to the said amendment,

It passed in the negative, $\begin{cases} \text{AYES} & 16 \\ \text{NOES} & 37 \end{cases}$

The ayes and noes being demanded by one fifth of the members present,
Those who voted in the affirmative, are,

Fisher Ames	Richard Bland Lee
Egbert Benson	Josiah Parker
Lambert Cadwalader	George Partridge
George Clymer	William Smith (of South-Carolina)
Benjamin Goodhue	Michael Jenifer Stone
Samuel Griffin	Jonathan Trumbull
Benjamin Huntington	John Vining and
John Laurance	Henry Wynkoop

---

[124] On June 3 this committee presented the Twining Bill [HR–72], which was read.
[125] The Journal does not record the signing of this bill by the speaker and the vice president. The *Senate Legislative Journal* records the vice president's signing on June 2. On June 3 it was presented to the president.
[126] The Journal does not mention the signing of this bill by the speaker. It was signed by the vice president on June 2 and presented to the president on June 3.

Those who voted in the negative, are,

John Baptista Ashe	George Mathews
Abraham Baldwin	Andrew Moore
Timothy Bloodworth	John Page
Aedanus Burke	Jeremiah Van Rensselaer
Isaac Coles	James Schureman
Benjamin Contee	Thomas Scott
Thomas Fitzsimons	Joshua Seney
William Floyd	Roger Sherman
Abiel Foster	Peter Silvester
Elbridge Gerry	Thomas Sinnickson
Nicholas Gilman	William Smith (of Maryland)
Jonathan Grout	John Steele
Thomas Hartley	Jonathan Sturges
John Hathorn	Thomas Sumter
Daniel Huger	George Thatcher
James Jackson	Thomas Tudor Tucker
George Leonard	Alexander White and
Samuel Livermore	Hugh Williamson
James Madison, junior	

RESOLVED, That this House do insist on their disagreement to the said amendment.

ORDERED, That the Clerk of this House do acquaint the Senate therewith.[127] The several orders of the day were read, and postponed until Monday next. And then the House adjourned until Monday morning ten o'clock.

MONDAY, MAY 31, 1790

ORDERED, That the report of the Postmaster-General, on the petition of Christopher Colles, be referred to the committee to whom was recommitted the bill for regulating the post-office of the United States, with instruction to insert a clause or clauses pursuant to the said report.[128]

On a motion made and seconded, that the House do now proceed to take into consideration a motion which lay on the table, in the words following, to wit:

"RESOLVED, That Congress shall meet and hold their next session at   ."

It was resolved in the affirmative, $\begin{cases} \text{AYES} & 32 \\ \text{NOES} & 27 \end{cases}$

---

[127] On May 31 a conference committee on this bill was appointed by the Senate and House.

[128] On June 7 this committee presented a new Post Office Bill [HR–74], which was read twice.

The ayes and noes being demanded by one fifth of the members present, Those who voted in the affirmative, are,

John Baptista Ashe
Abraham Baldwin
John Brown
Lambert Cadwalader
Daniel Carroll
George Clymer
Isaac Coles
Benjamin Contee
Thomas Fitzsimons
George Gale
Nicholas Gilman
Samuel Griffin
Thomas Hartley
Daniel Hiester
James Jackson
Richard Bland Lee

James Madison, junior
George Mathews
Andrew Moore
Peter Muhlenberg
John Page
Josiah Parker
Thomas Scott
Joshua Seney
Thomas Sinnickson
John Steele
Michael Jenifer Stone
Thomas Sumter
John Vining
Alexander White
Hugh Williamson and
Henry Wynkoop

Those who voted in the negative, are,

Fisher Ames
Egbert Benson
Timothy Bloodworth
Elias Boudinot
Aedanus Burke
William Floyd
Abiel Foster
Elbridge Gerry
Benjamin Goodhue
Jonathan Grout
Daniel Huger
Benjamin Huntington
John Laurance
George Leonard

Samuel Livermore
George Partridge
Jeremiah Van Rensselaer
James Schureman
Theodore Sedgwick
Roger Sherman
Peter Silvester
William Smith (of Maryland)
William Smith (of South-Carolina)
Jonathan Sturges
George Thatcher
Jonathan Trumbull and
Thomas Tudor Tucker

Whereupon the House proceeded to consider the said motion, which being read, a motion was made and seconded, to amend the same by inserting after the word "RESOLVED," the words "That a permanent seat for the government of the United States ought to be fixed at some convenient place on the banks of the river Delaware, and"

And the said motion being objected to, as not in order,

Mr. Speaker declared the motion not to be in order:

From which opinion of the chair, an appeal was made to the House by two members.

And on the question being taken, "Is the said motion in order?"

The ayes and noes being demanded by one fifth of the members present,

There appeared, $\left\{ \begin{array}{l} \text{AYES} \quad 29 \\ \text{NOES} \quad 29 \end{array} \right.$ —as follow:

Those who voted in the affirmative, are,

Egbert Benson	George Partridge
Elias Boudinot	Jeremiah Van Rensselaer
Aedanus Burke	James Schureman
Isaac Coles	Theodore Sedgwick
William Floyd	Joshua Seney
Abiel Foster	Roger Sherman
Elbridge Gerry	Peter Silvester
Benjamin Goodhue	William Smith (of Maryland)
John Hathorn	William Smith (of South-Carolina)
Benjamin Huntington	Michael Jenifer Stone
John Laurance	Jonathan Sturges
Richard Bland Lee	George Thatcher
George Leonard	Jonathan Trumbull and
Samuel Livermore	Thomas Tudor Tucker
James Madison, junior	

Those who voted in the negative, are,

Fisher Ames	James Jackson
John Baptista Ashe	George Mathews
Abraham Baldwin	Andrew Moore
Timothy Bloodworth	Peter Muhlenberg
John Brown	John Page
Lambert Cadwalader	Josiah Parker
George Clymer	Thomas Scott
Benjamin Contee	Thomas Sinnickson
Thomas Fitzsimons	John Steele
George Gale	Thomas Sumter
Nicholas Gilman	John Vining
Samuel Griffin	Alexander White
Jonathan Grout	Hugh Williamson and
Thomas Hartley	Henry Wynkoop
Daniel Hiester	

Whereupon Mr. Speaker declared himself with those who voted in the negative:

And so the said motion was decided not to be in order.

Another motion was then made and seconded, to commit the said original motion to the consideration of a committee of the whole House, and on the question for commitment,

It passed in the negative.

Another motion was then made and seconded, to fill up the blank in the said original motion, with the words "the city of New-York;" and on the question thereupon,

It passed in the negative, $\begin{cases} \text{AYES} & 25 \\ \text{NOES} & 35 \end{cases}$

The ayes and noes being demanded by one fifth of the members present,

Those who voted in the affirmative, are,

Fisher Ames	Samuel Livermore
Egbert Benson	George Partridge
Timothy Bloodworth	Jeremiah Van Rensselaer
Elias Boudinot	James Schureman
Aedanus Burke	Theodore Sedgwick
William Floyd	Roger Sherman
Abiel Foster	Peter Silvester
Elbridge Gerry	William Smith (of South-Carolina)
Jonathan Grout	Jonathan Sturges
John Hathorn	George Thatcher
Daniel Huger	Jonathan Trumbull and
Benjamin Huntington	Thomas Tudor Tucker
John Laurance	

Those who voted in the negative, are,

John Baptista Ashe	Benjamin Goodhue
Abraham Baldwin	Samuel Griffin
John Brown	Thomas Hartley
Lambert Cadwalader	Daniel Hiester
Daniel Carroll	James Jackson
George Clymer	Richard Bland Lee
Isaac Coles	George Leonard
Benjamin Contee	James Madison, junior
Thomas Fitzsimons	George Mathews
George Gale	Andrew Moore
Nicholas Gilman	Peter Muhlenberg

John Page

Josiah Parker

Thomas Scott

Joshua Seney

Thomas Sinnickson

William Smith (of Maryland)

John Steele

Michael Jenifer Stone

Thomas Sumter

John Vining

Alexander White

Hugh Williamson and

Henry Wynkoop

Another motion was then made and seconded, to fill up the blank in the said original motion, with the words, "the city of Philadelphia;" to which motion an amendment being moved and seconded, to add the words "or Baltimore."

It passed in the negative, $\begin{cases} \text{AYES} & 22 \\ \text{NOES} & 38 \end{cases}$

The ayes and noes being demanded by one fifth of the members present, Those who voted in the affirmative, are,

Egbert Benson

Timothy Bloodworth

Aedanus Burke

William Floyd

Elbridge Gerry

Jonathan Grout

John Hathorn

Daniel Huger

James Jackson

John Laurance

George Partridge

Jeremiah Van Rensselaer

Joshua Seney

Peter Silvester

William Smith (of Maryland)

William Smith (of South-Carolina)

Michael Jenifer Stone

Jonathan Sturges

Thomas Sumter

George Thatcher

Jonathan Trumbull and

Thomas Tudor Tucker

Those who voted in the negative, are,

Fisher Ames

John Baptista Ashe

Abraham Baldwin

Elias Boudinot

John Brown

Lambert Cadwalader

Daniel Carroll

George Clymer

Isaac Coles

Benjamin Contee

Thomas Fitzsimons

Abiel Foster

George Gale

Nicholas Gilman

Benjamin Goodhue

Samuel Griffin

Thomas Hartley

Daniel Hiester

Benjamin Huntington

Richard Bland Lee

George Leonard

Samuel Livermore

James Madison, junior	Theodore Sedgwick
George Mathews	Roger Sherman
Andrew Moore	Thomas Sinnickson
Peter Muhlenberg	John Steele
John Page	John Vining
Josiah Parker	Alexander White
James Schureman	Hugh Williamson and
Thomas Scott	Henry Wynkoop

And then the question being put, to fill up the blank in the said original motion, with the words "the city of Philadelphia."

It was resolved in the affirmative, $\begin{cases} \text{AYES} & 38 \\ \text{NOES} & 22 \end{cases}$

The ayes and noes being demanded by one fifth of the members present, Those who voted in the affirmative, are,

John Baptista Ashe	James Madison, junior
Abraham Baldwin	George Mathews
Elias Boudinot	Andrew Moore
John Brown	Peter Muhlenberg
Lambert Cadwalader	John Page
Daniel Carroll	Josiah Parker
George Clymer	George Partridge
Isaac Coles	Thomas Scott
Benjamin Contee	Joshua Seney
Thomas Fitzsimons	Thomas Sinnickson
George Gale	William Smith (of Maryland)
Nicholas Gilman	John Steele
Benjamin Goodhue	Michael Jenifer Stone
Samuel Griffin	Thomas Sumter
Thomas Hartley	George Thatcher
Daniel Hiester	John Vining
James Jackson	Alexander White
Richard Bland Lee	Hugh Williamson and
George Leonard	Henry Wynkoop

Those who voted in the negative, are,

Fisher Ames	Abiel Foster
Egbert Benson	Elbridge Gerry
Timothy Bloodworth	Jonathan Grout
Aedanus Burke	John Hathorn
William Floyd	Daniel Huger

Benjamin Huntington	Roger Sherman
John Laurance	Peter Silvester
Samuel Livermore	William Smith (of South-Carolina)
Jeremiah Van Rensselaer	Jonathan Sturges
James Schureman	Jonathan Trumbull and
Theodore Sedgwick	Thomas Tudor Tucker

The main question being then put, that the House do agree to the said original motion as amended, in the words following, to wit:

"RESOLVED, That Congress shall meet and hold their next session at the city of Philadelphia."

It was resolved in the affirmative.

ORDERED, That the Clerk of this House do carry the said resolution to the Senate, and desire their concurrence.[129]

The Speaker laid before the House a letter and reports from the Secretary at War, on the several petitions of Jacobus Wynkoop, and of John McKenzie, James Whayland, Toney Turney, and Cesar Edwards, which were read, and ordered to lie on the table.[130]

A message was received from the President of the United States, by Mr. Lear his Secretary, notifying that the President approves of the act, intituled, "An act for the encouragement of learning, by securing the copies of maps, charts and books, to the authors and proprietors of such copies, during the times therein mentioned;" and has this day affixed his signature thereto.

A message from the Senate by Mr. Otis their Secretary.

MR. SPEAKER, The Senate desire a conference with this House on the subject matter of their amendment disagreed to by this House, to the bill, intituled, "An act providing the means of intercourse between the United States and foreign nations;" and have appointed managers at the said conference on their part: And then he withdrew.

RESOLVED, That this House do agree to the conference desired by the Senate as aforesaid; and that Mr. Gerry, Mr. White, and Mr. Williamson, be appointed managers at the same on the part of this House.

ORDERED, That the Clerk of this House do acquaint the Senate therewith.[131]

---

[129] On June 2 the Senate committed this resolution with the Residence Bill [S–12]. On June 8 the Senate disagreed to the resolution.

[130] Copies of these reports are in A Record of the Reports of the Secretary of War, vol. 1, HR, DNA.

[131] On June 23 the House was notified that the Senate had receded from part of its amendment to the Foreign Intercourse Bill [HR–52] and made a further amendment to the bill.

A petition of William Gould, was presented to the House and read, praying the settlement of a claim against the United States, from the estate of his deceased father, David Gould, late a senior surgeon in the hospital department.

ORDERED, That the said petition be referred to the Secretary at War, with instruction to examine the same, and report his opinion thereupon to the House.[132]

The several orders of the day were read, and postponed until to-morrow.

And then the House adjourned until to-morrow morning ten o'clock.

---

[132] On June 21 the secretary reported on the petition.

TUESDAY, JUNE 1, 1790

The Speaker laid before the House a letter and report from the Secretary at War, on the petition of William Hassall,[1] which were read, and ordered to lie on the table.

The House, according to the order of the day, resolved itself into a committee of the whole House, on the bill to provide for the settlement of the accounts between the United States and the individual States.

Mr. Speaker left the chair.

Mr. Seney took the chair of the committee.

Mr. Speaker resumed the chair, and Mr. Seney reported, that the committee had, according to order, had the said bill under consideration, and made some progress therein.

RESOLVED, That this House will, to-morrow, again resolve itself into a committee of the whole House on the said bill.[2]

A message, in writing, was received from the President of the United States, by Mr. Lear his Secretary, as followeth:

UNITED STATES, June 1, 1790

GENTLEMEN of the SENATE and HOUSE of REPRESENTATIVES,

HAVING received official information of the accession of the state of Rhode-Island and Providence Plantations to the Constitution of the United States, I take the earliest opportunity of communicating the same to you, with my congratulations on this happy event, which unites under the General Government all the states which were originally confederated; and have directed my Secretary to lay before you a copy of the letter from the President of the Convention of the state of Rhode-Island to the President of the United States.

G. WASHINGTON[3]

The House being informed that Theodorick Bland, one of the members for the state of Virginia, died this morning.

ORDERED, That such of the members of the said State as are now present, be appointed a committee to take order for superintending the funeral of the said Theodorick Bland, and that this House will attend the same.

ORDERED, That a committee be appointed to prepare and bring in a bill or bills for giving effect to the laws of the United States within the state of

---

[1] A copy of the report is in A Record of the Reports of the Secretary of War, vol. 1, HR, DNA.

[2] On June 2 the COWH considered this bill again.

[3] The message and enclosure are in President's Messages: Suggesting legislation, SR, DNA. The letter from the president of the Rhode Island convention is printed in the *Senate Legislative Journal* on June 1.

Rhode-Island and Providence Plantations; and that Mr. Sedgwick, Mr. Benson, and Mr. Tucker, do prepare and bring in the same.[4]

ORDERED, That the committee of the whole House be discharged from further proceeding on the bill sent from the Senate, intituled, "An act to prevent bringing goods, wares and merchandizes, from the state of Rhode-Island and Providence Plantations into the United States; and to authorize a demand of money from the said State."

A message from the Senate by Mr. Otis their Secretary.

MR. SPEAKER,   The Senate have passed the bill, intituled, "An act for the relief of Thomas Jenkins and Company:"[5]   And then he withdrew.

The House proceeded to consider the report of the committee to whom was referred the petition of John McCord: Whereupon,

RESOLVED, That there be paid to the said John McCord the sum of one thousand dollars, in full for all claims, either of rations or lands, as a Canadian sufferer or refugee.

ORDERED, That a bill or bills be brought in pursuant to the said resolution, and that Mr. Ames, Mr. Fitzsimons, and Mr. Boudinot, do prepare and bring in the same.[6]

On a motion made and seconded,

RESOLVED, That all treaties made, or which shall be made and promulged under the authority of the United States, shall from time to time be published and annexed to their code of laws by the Secretary of State.

ORDERED, That the Clerk of this House do carry the said resolution to the Senate, and desire their concurrence.[7]

The several orders of the day were read, and postponed until to-morrow.

And then the House adjourned until to-morrow morning ten o'clock.

WEDNESDAY, JUNE 2, 1790

An engrossed bill making provision for the payment of the debts of the United States, was read the third time, and the blanks therein filled up.

RESOLVED, That the said bill do pass, and that the title be "An act making provision for the debt of the United States."[8]

---

[4] On June 2 this committee presented the Rhode Island Bill [HR–71], which was read. They also presented the Rhode Island Judiciary Bill [HR–73], which was read on June 4. On June 7 this committee presented the Rhode Island Enumeration Bill [HR–75], which was read.

[5] On June 3 this bill was signed by the speaker and the vice president.

[6] On June 2 this committee presented the McCord Bill [HR–70], which was read.

[7] On June 3 the House was notified that the Senate had agreed to this resolution.

[8] This bill is E–46049.

ORDERED, That the Clerk of this House do carry the said bill to the Senate, and desire their concurrence.[9]

Mr. Carroll, from the committee to whom was referred the petition of John Frederick Amelung, made a report, which was read, and ordered to be taken into consideration to-morrow.[10]

Mr. Boudinot, from the committee appointed, presented, according to order, a bill to satisfy the claims of John McCord against the United States, which was received and read the first time.[11]

On motion,

RESOLVED UNANIMOUSLY, That the members of this House, from a sincere desire of shewing every mark of respect due to the memory of THEODORICK BLAND, deceased, late a member thereof, will go in mourning for him one month, by the usual mode of wearing a crape round the left arm.

The House, according to the order of the day, again resolved itself into a committee of the whole House, on the bill to provide for the settlement of the accounts between the United States and individual States.

Mr. Speaker left the chair.

Mr. Seney took the chair of the committee.

Mr. Speaker resumed the chair, and Mr. Seney reported, that the committee had, according to order, again had the said bill under consideration, and made a farther progress therein.

RESOLVED, That this House will, to-morrow, again resolve itself into a committee of the whole House on the said bill.[12]

Mr. Sedgwick, from the committee appointed, presented, according to order, a bill for giving effect to the laws of the United States within the state

[9] The Senate read and considered this bill on June 2, 3, 7, 9, 10, and 11. On June 11 it was committed. On June 14 Oliver Ellsworth presented a motion for the assumption of state debts to the Senate. The committee on the bill reported on June 15. The report was considered on June 16, 17, 18, and 21 and agreed to as amendments to the bill on June 22. From June 23 through July 15 the third reading of the bill was postponed. On July 2 Ellsworth's motion for assumption was committed, and this committee reported on July 12. After being debated on the following day and on July 14, the report of the committee on Ellsworth's motion was recommitted on July 15 with the Funding Bill [HR–63]. On July 16 this committee's report was presented and agreed to. This report was then recommitted, together with the bill and the first report on Mr. Ellsworth's motion, with instructions to conform the bill to the last two reports. On July 17 the revised bill was reported by the committee. On July 19 the committee's report was agreed to. The bill was further amended on July 19, 20, and 21. After agreeing to the bill as amended, the Senate returned it to the House on July 21.

[10] A copy of the report is in A Record of the Reports of Select Committees, HR, DNA. A copy, probably made by ASP, is in Various Select Committees, HR, DNA. On June 3 this report was disagreed to. It is printed in the Journal on that date.

[11] On June 3 this bill was read again.

[12] On June 3 the COWH considered this bill again.

of Rhode-Island and Providence Plantations, which was received and read the first time.[13]

The several orders of day were read, and postponed until to-morrow.

And then the House adjourned until to-morrow morning ten o'clock.

THURSDAY, JUNE 3, 1790

A bill to satisfy the claims of John McCord against the United States, was read the second time, and ordered to be engrossed, and read the third time to-morrow.[14]

A bill for giving effect to the laws of the United States within the state of Rhode-Island and Providence Plantations, was read the second time, and ordered to be engrossed, and read the third time to-morrow.[15]

A message from the Senate by Mr. Otis their Secretary.

MR. SPEAKER,   The Senate have agreed to the resolution for the publication of treaties made under the authority of the United States:[16]   And then he withdrew.

The House proceeded to consider the report of the committee on the petition of John Frederick Amelung: Whereupon, the resolution reported by the said committee in the words following, to wit, "That the Secretary of the Treasury of the United States be authorized to make a loan not exceeding eight thousand dollars to the said John Frederick Amelung, he giving satisfactory security for the reimbursement of the same within   years," was, on the question put thereupon, disagreed to by the House.

Mr. Burke, from the committee appointed, presented, according to order, a bill for the relief of Nathaniel Twining in certain cases, which was received and read the first time.[17]

Mr. Gilman, from the joint committee for inrolled bills, reported, that the committee did this day wait on the President of the United States, and present for his approbation, three inrolled bills; one intituled, "An act for finally adjusting and satisfying the claims of Frederick William de Steuben;"[18] another intituled, "An act for giving effect to an act, intituled, 'An act to establish the judicial courts of the United States,' within the state of North-Carolina;"[19] and another intituled, "An act supplemental to the act for

---

[13] On June 3 this bill was read again.
[14] On June 4 this bill was read again, agreed to, and sent to the Senate.
[15] On June 4 this bill was read again, agreed to, and sent to the Senate.
[16] On June 10 this resolution was signed by the speaker and the vice president.
[17] On June 4 this bill was read again and recommitted.
[18] The inspected inrolled bill is in Enrolled Acts, RG 11, DNA. E–46033.
[19] The inspected inrolled bill is in Enrolled Acts, RG 11, DNA.

establishing the salaries of the executive officers of government, with their assistants and clerks:"[20] Also, that the committee had examined an inrolled bill, intituled, "An act for the relief of Thomas Jenkins and company,"[21] and had found the same to be truly inrolled: Whereupon,

Mr. Speaker signed the said inrolled bill.[22]

ORDERED, That the Clerk of this House do acquaint the Senate therewith.

The House, according to the order of the day, again resolved itself into a committee of the whole House, on the bill to provide for the settlement of the accounts between the United States and the individual States.

Mr. Speaker left the chair.

Mr. Seney took the chair of the committee.

Mr. Speaker resumed the chair, and Mr. Seney reported, that the committee had, according to order, again had the said bill under consideration, and made a farther progress therein.

RESOLVED, That this House will, to-morrow, again resolve itself into a committee of the whole House on the said bill.[23]

The several orders of the day were read, and postponed until to-morrow.

And then the House adjourned until to-morrow morning ten o'clock.

FRIDAY, JUNE 4, 1790

An engrossed bill for giving effect to the laws of the United States within the state of Rhode-Island and Providence Plantations, was read the third time, and the blanks therein filled up.

RESOLVED, That the said bill do pass; and that the title be, "An act for giving effect to the several acts therein mentioned, in respect to the state of Rhode-Island and Providence Plantations."

ORDERED, That the Clerk of this House do carry the said bill to the Senate, and desire their concurrence.[24]

An engrossed bill to satisfy the claims of John McCord against the United States, was read the third time.

RESOLVED, That the said bill do pass; and that the title be, "An act to satisfy the claims of John McCord against the United States."

---

[20] The inspected enrolled bill is in Enrolled Acts, RG 11, DNA. E–46056. On June 4 the president signed these three bills.

[21] The inspected enrolled bill is in Enrolled Acts, RG 11, DNA.

[22] On June 14 the committee on enrolled bills reported on presenting this bill to the president. The president signed this bill on the same day.

[23] On June 4 the COWH considered this bill again and was discharged from further consideration of it.

[24] On June 4, 7, and 9 the Senate read this bill, and on June 9 it was agreed to with an amendment. On the same day the House concurred in the amendment.

ORDERED, That the Clerk of this House do carry the said bill to the Senate, and desire their concurrence.[25]

A petition of Jacob Smith, was presented to the House and read, praying relief in consideration of wounds received in the service of the United States during the late war, which have disabled him from procuring a livelihood by labor.

ORDERED, That the said petition be referred to the Secretary at War, with instruction to examine the same, and report his opinion thereupon to the House.

A bill for the relief of Nathaniel Twining in certain cases, was read the second time, and ordered to be committed to Mr. Burke, Mr. Lee and Mr. Vining.[26]

The House, according to the order of the day, again resolved itself into a committee of the whole House, on the bill to provide for the settlement of the accounts between the United States and the individual States.

Mr. Speaker left the chair.

Mr. Seney took the chair of the committee.

Mr. Speaker resumed the chair, and Mr. Seney reported, that the committee had, according to order, again had the said bill under consideration, and made a farther progress therein.

On motion,

ORDERED, That the committee of the whole House be discharged from further proceeding thereon, and that the said bill do lie on the table.[27]

A message was received from the President of the United States, by Mr. Lear his Secretary, notifying that the President approves of the following acts: One intituled, "An act for finally adjusting and satisfying the claims of Frederick William de Steuben;" another intituled, "An act for giving effect to an act, intituled, 'An act to establish the judicial courts of the United States,' within the state of North-Carolina;" and another intituled, "An act supplemental to the act for establishing the salaries of the executive officers of government, with their assistants and clerks;" and did this day affix his signature thereto.

ORDERED, That the Clerk of this House do acquaint the Senate therewith.

Mr. Sedgwick, from the committee appointed, presented, according to order, a bill for giving effect to an act, intituled, "An act to establish the

[25] The Senate read this bill on June 4 and 7. On June 7 it was committed, and on June 18 the committee reported amendments, which were agreed to. On June 21 the Senate read this bill again, agreed to it with amendments, and notified the House.

[26] On June 8 this committee reported.

[27] On June 7 this bill was amended.

judicial courts of the United States," within the state of Rhode-Island and Providence Plantations, which was received and read the first time.[28]

The several orders of the day were read, and postponed until Monday next. And then the House adjourned until Monday morning ten o'clock.

MONDAY, JUNE 7, 1790

A bill for giving effect to an act, intituled, "An act to establish the judicial courts of the United States," within the state of Rhode-Island and Providence Plantations, was read the second time, and ordered to be engrossed, and read the third time to-morrow.[29]

A message was received from the President of the United States, by Mr. Lear his Secretary, notifying that the President did this day approve and sign the resolutions respecting the arrears of pay due to a part of the troops of the Virginia and North-Carolina lines, for the years one thousand seven hundred and eighty-two, and one thousand seven hundred and eighty-three.

The House proceeded to consider the bill to provide for the settlement of the accounts between the United States and the individual States; and the same being further amended at the Clerk's table, was, together with the amendments, ordered to lie on the table.[30]

Mr. Livermore, from the committee to whom was re-committed the bill for regulating the post-office of the United States, presented, according to order, an amendatory bill to establish the post-office and post roads within the United States, which was received and read the first time.

On motion,

The said bill was read the second time, and ordered to be committed to a committee of the whole House on Thursday next.[31]

Mr. Sedgwick, from the committee appointed, presented, according to order, a bill for giving effect to an act "providing for the enumeration of the inhabitants of the United States," in respect to the state of Rhode-Island and Providence Plantations, which was received and read the first time.[32]

The several orders of the day were read and postponed until to-morrow. And then the House adjourned until to-morrow morning ten o'clock.

TUESDAY, JUNE 8, 1790

An engrossed bill for giving effect to an act, intituled, "An act to establish the judicial courts of the United States," within the state of Rhode Island and

---

[28] On June 7 this bill was read again.
[29] On June 8 this bill was read again, agreed to, and sent to the Senate.
[30] On June 8 this bill was further amended.
[31] Consideration of this bill in the COWH was postponed as an order of the day on June 10 and 11. On June 14 the bill was considered in the COWH.
[32] On June 8 this bill was read again and ordered recommitted.

Providence Plantations, was read the third time, and the blanks therein filled up.

RESOLVED, That the said bill do pass, and that the title be, "An act for giving effect to an act, inittuled 'An act to establish the judicial courts of the United States,' within the state of Rhode-Island and Providence Plantations."

ORDERED, That the Clerk of this House do carry the said bill to the Senate, and desire their concurrence.[33]

A bill for giving effect to an act, "providing for the enumeration of the inhabitants of the United States," in respect to the state of Rhode-Island and Providence Plantations, was read the second time, and ordered to be committed to Mr. Williamson, Mr. Scott, and Mr. Baldwin, with instruction to insert a clause or clauses to provide for administering the necessary oaths for more effectually procuring a full census of the inhabitants of the United States.[34]

On motion,

RESOLVED, That a committee be appointed to join with a committee of the Senate to be appointed for the purpose, to consider of, and report when it will be convenient and proper that an adjournment of the present Congress should take place, and consider and report such business now before Congress, necessary to be finished before the adjournment, and such as may be conveniently postponed; and also to consider and report such matters not now before Congress, but which it will be necessary should be considered and determined by Congress before an adjournment.

And a committee was appointed of Mr. Wadsworth, Mr. Carroll, and Mr. Hartley.[35]

The House proceeded to consider the bill to provide for the settlement of the accounts between the United States and the individual States, which lay on the table, and the same being further amended at the Clerk's table, was, together with the amendments, ordered to be engrossed, and read the third time to-morrow.[36]

A message from the Senate by Mr. Otis their Secretary.

MR. SPEAKER,   The Senate disagree to the resolution of this House of the thirty-first ultimo, "That Congress shall meet and hold their next session at the city of Philadelphia:"[37]   And then he withdrew.

---

[33] The Senate read this bill on June 10, 11, and 14. On June 14 the bill was agreed to with an amendment, which was agreed to by the House on the same day.

[34] On June 22 this committee reported amendments to the bill.

[35] A copy of the resolution is in Messages from the House, SR, DNA. On June 21 the House was notified that the Senate had appointed a committee to meet with this committee.

[36] On June 9 this bill was read again, and a new committee was appointed on it.

[37] On June 10 another resolution adjourning to Philadelphia was agreed to, and motions on this resolution were disagreed to.

Mr. Burke, from the committee to whom was committed the bill for the relief of Nathaniel Twining in certain cases, made a report, which was read, and ordered to lie on the table.[38]

The House, according to the order of the day, resolved itself into a committee of the whole House, on the bill for repealing after the last day of next, the duties heretofore laid upon distilled spirits imported from abroad, and laying others in their stead, and also upon spirits distilled within the United States, as well to discourage the excessive use of those spirits, and promote agriculture, as to provide for the support of the public credit, and for the common defence and general welfare.

Mr. Speaker left the chair.

Mr. Boudinot took the chair of the committee.

Mr. Speaker resumed the chair, and Mr. Boudinot reported, that the committee had, according to order, had the said bill under consideration, and made some progress therein.

RESOLVED, That this House will, to-morrow, again resolve itself into a committee of the whole House on the said bill.[39]

The several orders of the day were read, and postponed until to-morrow.

And then the House adjourned until to-morrow morning ten o'clock.

WEDNESDAY, JUNE 9, 1790

An engrossed bill to provide for the settlement of the accounts between the United States and the individual States, was read the third time, and ordered to be committed to Mr. Fitzsimons, Mr. Williamson, Mr. Sedgwick, Mr. Wadsworth, and Mr. Madison.[40]

A message from the Senate by Mr. Otis their Secretary.

MR. SPEAKER, The Senate have passed the bill, intituled, "An act for giving effect to the several acts therein mentioned, in respect to the state of Rhode-Island and Providence Plantations," with an amendment,[41] to which they desire the concurrence of this House: And then he withdrew.

The House proceeded to consider the said amendment; and the same being read, was agreed to.

ORDERED, That the Clerk of this House do acquaint the Senate therewith.[42]

---

[38] On June 14 this report was considered, and the bill was amended.

[39] On June 9 this bill was considered in the COWH.

[40] On June 17 this committee presented a new Settlement of Accounts Bill [HR–77], which was read twice.

[41] The amendment is printed in the *Senate Legislative Journal* on June 9.

[42] On June 10 this bill was signed by the speaker and the vice president.

The House, according to the order of the day, again resolved itself into a committee of the whole House, on the bill repealing, after the last day of next, the duties heretofore laid upon distilled spirits imported from abroad, and laying others in their stead, and also upon spirits distilled within the United States, as well to discourage the excessive use of those spirits, and promote agriculture, as to provide for the support of the public credit, and for the common defence and general welfare.

Mr. Speaker left the chair.

Mr. Boudinot took the chair of the committee.

Mr. Speaker resumed the chair, and Mr. Boudinot reported, that the committee had, according to order, again had the said bill under consideration, and made a farther progress therein.

RESOLVED, That this House will, to-morrow, again resolve itself into a committee of the whole House on the said bill.[43]

Mr. Sherman, from the committee appointed to consider and report whether any, and what additional rules are necessary for regulating the proceedings of this House; and also to confer with a committee of the Senate, to consider and report whether any, and what further regulations are necessary for conducting the business between the two Houses, made a report, which was read, and ordered to lie on the table.[44]

The several orders of the day were read, and postponed until to-morrow.

And then the House adjourned until to-morrow morning ten o'clock.

THURSDAY, JUNE 10, 1790

Mr. Gilman, from the joint committee for inrolled bills, reported, that the committee had examined an inrolled bill, entituled, "An act for giving effect to the several acts therein mentioned, in respect to the state of Rhode-Island and Providence Plantations;"[45] also an inrolled resolve for the publication of treaties, made under the authority of the United States,[46] and had found the same to be truly inrolled: Whereupon,

Mr. Speaker signed the said inrolled bill and resolve.[47]

ORDERED, That the Clerk of this House do acquaint the Senate therewith.

The Speaker laid before the House, a letter and report from the Secretary

---

[43] On June 11 this bill was considered again in the COWH.

[44] An annotated draft of the report is in Joint Committee Reports, SR, DNA. The report, as amended by the Senate, is printed in the *Senate Legislative Journal* on June 10. A copy of the report is in A Record of the Reports of Select Committees, HR, DNA. On June 11 the House was notified that the Senate had agreed to the part of the report concerning joint rules.

[45] The inspected enrolled bill is in Enrolled Acts, RG 11, DNA. E–22957.

[46] The inspected enrolled resolution is in Enrolled Acts, RG 11, DNA.

[47] The bill and resolution were presented to the president on June 11, and on June 14 the president signed them.

of the Treasury, on the petition of Stephen Moore, which were read, and ordered to be committed to Mr. Laurance, Mr. Steele, and Mr. Brown.[48]

A petition of Stephen Steele, of the city of New-York, was presented to the House and read, praying the liquidation and settlement of a claim against the United States: Also,

A petition of the tanners in and near the city of Philadelphia, praying that so much of the act, intituled, "An act for laying a duty on goods, wares, and merchandizes imported into the United States," as exempts raw hides from impost may be explained and amended.[49]

ORDERED, That the said petitions do lie on the table.

On a motion made and seconded that the House do now proceed to take into consideration, a motion which lay on the table, in the words following, to wit:

"RESOLVED, That when the two Houses shall adjourn to close the present session, the President of the Senate, and Speaker of the House of Representatives do adjourn their respective Houses, to meet, and hold their next session in the city of Philadelphia."

It was resolved in the affirmative, $\begin{cases} \text{AYES} & 32 \\ \text{NOES} & 29 \end{cases}$

The ayes and noes being demanded by one fifth of the members present,

Those who voted in the affirmative, are,

John Baptista Ashe	Richard Bland Lee
Abraham Baldwin	James Madison, junior
John Brown	George Mathews
Lambert Cadwalader	Andrew Moore
Daniel Carroll	Peter Muhlenberg
George Clymer	John Page
Isaac Coles	Josiah Parker
Benjamin Contee	Thomas Scott
Thomas Fitzsimons	Joshua Seney
George Gale	Thomas Sinnickson
Nicholas Gilman	William Smith (of Maryland)
Samuel Griffin	John Steele
Thomas Hartley	Michael Jenifer Stone
Daniel Hiester	Thomas Sumter

[48] A copy of the report is in A Record of the Reports of the Secretary of the Treasury, vol. 1, HR, DNA. A copy, probably made by ASP, is in Reports and Communications from the Secretary of the Treasury, HR, DNA. On June 15 this committee presented the West Point Bill [HR–76], which was read.

[49] The petition is in Petitions and Memorials: Various subjects, SR, DNA. On June 14 this petition was referred to the committee to revise the revenue laws.

John Vining   Hugh Williamson and
Alexander White   Henry Wynkoop

Those who voted in the negative, are,

Fisher Ames   George Leonard
Egbert Benson   Samuel Livermore
Timothy Bloodworth   George Partridge
Elias Boudinot   Jeremiah Van Rensselaer
Aedanus Burke   James Schureman
William Floyd   Theodore Sedgwick
Abiel Foster   Roger Sherman
Elbridge Gerry   Peter Silvester
Benjamin Goodhue   William Smith (of South-Carolina)
Jonathan Grout   Jonathan Sturges
John Hathorn   George Thatcher
Daniel Huger   Jonathan Trumbull
Benjamin Huntington   Thomas Tudor Tucker and
James Jackson   Jeremiah Wadsworth
John Laurance

The said original motion was then read at the Clerk's table: Whereupon,
A motion being made and seconded, to commit the same to the consideration of a committee of the whole House,

It passed in the negative, $\begin{cases} \text{AYES } 28 \\ \text{NOES } 33 \end{cases}$

The ayes and noes being demanded by one fifth of the members present,
Those who voted in the affirmative, are,

Fisher Ames   Samuel Livermore
Egbert Benson   George Partridge
Elias Boudinot   Jeremiah Van Rensselaer
Aedanus Burke   James Schureman
William Floyd   Theodore Sedgwick
Abiel Foster   Roger Sherman
Elbridge Gerry   Peter Silvester
Benjamin Goodhue   William Smith (of Maryland)
Jonathan Grout   William Smith (of South-Carolina)
John Hathorn   Jonathan Sturges
Daniel Huger   George Thatcher
Benjamin Huntington   Jonathan Trumbull
John Laurance   Thomas Tudor Tucker and
George Leonard   Jeremiah Wadsworth

Those who voted in the negative, are,

John Baptista Ashe	James Madison, junior
Abraham Baldwin	George Mathews
John Brown	Andrew Moore
Timothy Bloodworth	Peter Muhlenberg
Lambert Cadwalader	John Page
Daniel Carroll	Josiah Parker
George Clymer	Thomas Scott
Isaac Coles	Joshua Seney
Benjamin Contee	Thomas Sinnickson
Thomas Fitzsimons	John Steele
George Gale	Michael Jenifer Stone
Nicholas Gilman	Thomas Sumter
Samuel Griffin	John Vining
Thomas Hartley	Alexander White
Daniel Hiester	Hugh Williamson and
James Jackson	Henry Wynkoop
Richard Bland Lee	

Another motion was then made and seconded, to amend the said original motion by striking out the words "city of Philadelphia," and inserting in lieu thereof, the words "town of Baltimore;" and the said motion being under debate, an adjournment was called for:[50]   Whereupon,

The several orders of the day were farther postponed until to-morrow.

And then the House adjourned until to-morrow morning ten o'clock.

FRIDAY, JUNE 11, 1790

A message from the Senate by Mr. Otis their Secretary.

MR. SPEAKER, The Senate have agreed to the report of the joint committee appointed to consider and report whether any, and what further regulations are necessary for conducting the business between the two Houses: And then he withdrew.

On a motion made and seconded, that the House do now, according to the order of the day, resolve itself into a committee of the whole House, on the bill for repealing, after the last day of   next, the duties heretofore laid upon distilled spirits imported from abroad, and laying others in their stead;

---

[50] On June 11 a resolution to move Congress to Baltimore for the third session was agreed to and sent to the Senate.

and also upon spirits distilled within the United States, as well to discourage the excessive use of those spirits, and promote agriculture, as to provide for the support of the public credit, and for the common defence and general welfare.

It passed in the negative, $\begin{cases} \text{AYES } 26 \\ \text{NOES } 31 \end{cases}$

The ayes and noes being demanded by one fifth of the members present, Those who voted in the affirmative, are,

Fisher Ames	George Leonard
Egbert Benson	Samuel Livermore
Elias Boudinot	Jeremiah Van Rensselaer
Aedanus Burke	James Schureman
William Floyd	Theodore Sedgwick
Abiel Foster	Roger Sherman
Elbridge Gerry	Peter Silvester
Benjamin Goodhue	William Smith (of Maryland)
John Hathorn	William Smith (of South-Carolina)
Daniel Huger	Jonathan Sturges
Benjamin Huntington	George Thatcher
James Jackson	Jonathan Trumbull and
John Laurance	Jeremiah Wadsworth

Those who voted in the negative, are,

John Baptista Ashe	James Madison, junior
Abraham Baldwin	George Mathews
Timothy Bloodworth	Andrew Moore
John Brown	Peter Muhlenberg
Lambert Cadwalader	John Page
Daniel Carroll	Josiah Parker
George Clymer	Thomas Scott
Isaac Coles	Joshua Seney
Benjamin Contee	Thomas Sinnickson
Thomas Fitzsimons	John Steele
George Gale	Michael Jenifer Stone
Nicholas Gilman	John Vining
Samuel Griffin	Alexander White
Jonathan Grout	Hugh Williamson and
Thomas Hartley	Henry Wynkoop
Daniel Hiester	

A motion being then made and seconded, that the House do now proceed to take into consideration the resolution which was under discussion yesterday, respecting the adjournment of Congress to the city of Philadelphia,

It was resolved in the affirmative: Whereupon,

A motion was made and seconded, to amend the said resolution by striking out the words "city of Philadelphia," and inserting in lieu thereof, the words "town of Baltimore;"   and the question being put thereupon,

It was resolved in the affirmative, $\begin{cases} \text{AYES} & 31 \\ \text{NOES} & 28 \end{cases}$

The ayes and noes being demanded by one fifth of the members present,

Those who voted in the affirmative, are,

Fisher Ames	George Partridge
Egbert Benson	Jeremiah Van Rensselaer
Timothy Bloodworth	Theodore Sedgwick
Aedanus Burke	Joshua Seney
William Floyd	Roger Sherman
Abiel Foster	Peter Silvester
Elbridge Gerry	William Smith (of Maryland)
Benjamin Goodhue	William Smith (of South-Carolina)
Jonathan Grout	Michael Jenifer Stone
John Hathorn	Jonathan Sturges
Daniel Huger	Thomas Sumter
Benjamin Huntington	George Thatcher
James Jackson	Jonathan Trumbull
John Laurance	Thomas Tudor Tucker and
George Leonard	Jeremiah Wadsworth
Samuel Livermore	

Those who voted in the negative, are,

John Baptista Ashe	Thomas Hartley
Abraham Baldwin	Daniel Hiester
John Brown	Richard Bland Lee
Lambert Cadwalader	James Madison, junior
Daniel Carroll	George Mathews
George Clymer	Andrew Moore
Isaac Coles	Peter Muhlenberg
Benjamin Contee	John Page
Thomas Fitzsimons	Josiah Parker
George Gale	Thomas Scott
Nicholas Gilman	Thomas Sinnickson
Samuel Griffin	John Steele

John Vining   Hugh Williamson and
Alexander White   Henry Wynkoop

The main question being then put, that the House do agree to the said resolution, amended to read as followeth:

"RESOLVED, That when the two Houses shall adjourn to close the present session, the President of the Senate, and Speaker of the House of Representatives, do adjourn their respective Houses to meet and hold their next session at the town of Baltimore."[51]

It was resolved in the affirmative, $\begin{cases} \text{AYES} & 53 \\ \text{NOES} & 6 \end{cases}$

The ayes and noes being demanded by one fifth of the members present, Those who voted in the affirmative, are,

Fisher Ames   Samuel Livermore
John Baptista Ashe   James Madison, junior
Abraham Baldwin   George Mathews
Egbert Benson   Andrew Moore
Timothy Bloodworth   Peter Muhlenberg
John Brown   John Page
Aedanus Burke   Josiah Parker
Lambert Cadwalader   George Partridge
Daniel Carroll   Jeremiah Van Rensselaer
George Clymer   Thomas Scott
Isaac Coles   Theodore Sedgwick
Benjamin Contee   Joshua Seney
William Floyd   Roger Sherman
Abiel Foster   Peter Silvester
George Gale   Thomas Sinnickson
Elbridge Gerry   William Smith (of Maryland)
Benjamin Goodhue   William Smith (of South-Carolina)
Samuel Griffin   John Steele
Jonathan Grout   Michael Jenifer Stone
Thomas Hartley   Jonathan Sturges
John Hathorn   Thomas Sumter
Daniel Hiester   George Thatcher
Daniel Huger   Jonathan Trumbull
Benjamin Huntington   John Vining
James Jackson   Jeremiah Wadsworth and
John Laurance   Alexander White
George Leonard

---

[51] A copy of the resolution is in Messages from the House, SR, DNA.

Those who voted in the negative, are,

Thomas Fitzsimons	Thomas Tudor Tucker
Nicholas Gilman	Hugh Williamson and
James Schureman	Henry Wynkoop

ORDERED, That the Clerk of this House do carry the said resolution to the Senate, and desire their concurrence.[52]

A message, in writing, was received from the President of the United States, by Mr. Lear his Secretary, as followeth:

UNITED STATES, June 11, 1790

GENTLEMEN of the SENATE and HOUSE of REPRESENTATIVES,

I HAVE directed my Secretary to lay before you a Copy of the Ratification of the Amendments to the Constitution of the United States, by the state of North-Carolina, together with an Extract from a Letter accompanying said Ratification, from the Governor of the state of North-Carolina to the President of the United States.

GEORGE WASHINGTON[53]

The papers accompanying the said message were read, and ordered to lie on the table.

The House, according to the order of the day, again resolved itself into a committee of the whole House, on the bill for repealing, after the last day of next, the duties heretofore laid upon distilled spirits imported from abroad, and laying others in their stead; and also upon spirits distilled within the United States, as well to discourage the excessive use of those spirits, and promote agriculture, as to provide for the support of the public credit, and for the common defence and general welfare.

Mr. Speaker left the chair.

Mr. Seney took the chair of the committee.

Mr. Speaker resumed the chair, and Mr. Seney reported, that the committee had, according to order, again had the said bill under consideration, and made a farther progress therein.

RESOLVED, That this House will, on Monday next, again resolve itself into a committee of the whole House on the said bill.[54]

The several orders of the day were read, and postponed until Monday next.

And then the House adjourned until Monday morning ten o'clock.

---

[52] The Senate never considered this resolution, but a provision for the temporary residence of Congress eventually became part of the Residence Bill [S-12].

[53] The message with enclosures is in President's Messages: Suggesting legislation, SR, DNA. The enclosures are printed in the Appendix to the Second Session.

[54] On June 14 the COWH reported amendments to the bill. The amendments were agreed to and the bill tabled.

MONDAY, JUNE 14, 1790

The House proceeded to consider the report of the committee to whom was committed the bill for the relief of Nathaniel Twining, in certain cases; and the said bill being amended at the Clerk's table, was, together with the amendment, ordered to be engrossed, and read the third time to-morrow.[55]

Mr. Gilman, from the joint committee for inrolled bills, reported, that the committee did, on Friday last, wait on the President of the United States, and present for his approbation two inrolled bills; one intituled, "An act for giving effect to the several acts therein mentioned, in respect to the state of Rhode-Island and Providence Plantations;" the other intituled, "An act for the relief of Thomas Jenkins and Company;" also, an inrolled resolve for the publication of treaties made, or to be made, under the authority of the United States.

ORDERED, That the petition of Stephen Steele, which was presented on Thursday last, be referred to the Secretary of the Treasury, with instruction to examine the same, and report his opinion thereupon to the House.

ORDERED, That the petition of the tanners in and near the city of Philadelphia, which lay on the table, be referred to the committee appointed to prepare and bring in a bill or bills to amend the several laws for the collection of duties on imports and tonnage.[56]

A message was received from the President of the United States, by Mr. Lear his Secretary, notifying that the President did, this day, approve and sign two acts; one intituled, "An act for giving effect to the several acts therein mentioned, in respect to the state of Rhode-Island and Providence Plantations;" the other intituled, "An act for the relief of Thomas Jenkins and Company;" also a Resolve for the publication of treaties made, or to be made, under the authority of the United States.

The House, according to the order of the day, again resolved itself into a committee of the whole House, on the bill for repealing, after the last day of   next, the duties heretofore laid upon distilled spirits imported from abroad, and laying others in their stead; also upon spirits distilled within the United States, as well to discourage the excessive use of those spirits, and promote agriculture, as to provide for the support of the public credit, and for the common defence and general welfare.

Mr. Speaker left the chair.

Mr. Seney took the chair of the committee.

Mr. Speaker resumed the chair, and Mr. Seney reported, that the committee

---

[55] On June 15 this bill was read, agreed to, and sent to the Senate.

[56] On June 22 this committee presented a Tonnage Bill [HR–78], which was read twice. On June 28 a petition from the inspectors of Boston and Charlestown, Massachusetts, was referred to this committee.

had, according to order, again had the said bill under consideration, and made several amendments thereto, which they had directed him to report when the House should think proper to receive the same.

On a motion made and seconded, that the House do now proceed to take the said amendments into consideration,

It was resolved in the affirmative, $\begin{cases} \text{AYES } 30 \\ \text{NOES } 24 \end{cases}$

The ayes and noes being demanded by one fifth of the members present, Those who voted in the affirmative, are,

John Baptista Ashe	Samuel Livermore
Abraham Baldwin	James Madison, junior
John Brown	George Mathews
Lambert Cadwalader	Andrew Moore
George Clymer	James Schureman
Benjamin Contee	Joshua Seney
Thomas Fitzsimons	Roger Sherman
William Floyd	Thomas Sinnickson
Abiel Foster	William Smith (of Maryland)
George Gale	Michael Jenifer Stone
Nicholas Gilman	Thomas Sumter
Samuel Griffin	John Vining
Thomas Hartley	Alexander White
Daniel Hiester	Hugh Williamson and
James Jackson	Henry Wynkoop

Those who voted in the negative, are,

Fisher Ames	Josiah Parker
Timothy Bloodworth	George Partridge
Elias Boudinot	Jeremiah Van Rensselaer
Aedanus Burke	Theodore Sedgwick
Isaac Coles	Peter Silvester
Elbridge Gerry	William Smith (of South-Carolina)
Benjamin Goodhue	John Steele
Jonathan Grout	Jonathan Sturges
Daniel Huger	George Thatcher
John Laurance	Jonathan Trumbull
George Leonard	Thomas Tudor Tucker and
John Page	Jeremiah Wadsworth

Whereupon,

The said amendments were severally read at the Clerk's table, and, on the question put thereupon, agreed to by the House.

ORDERED, That the said bill, with the amendments, do lie on the table.[57]
A message from the Senate by Mr. Otis their Secretary.

MR. SPEAKER,   The Senate have passed the bill, intituled, "An act for
giving effect to an act, intituled, 'An act to establish the judicial courts of the
United States,' within the state of Rhode-Island and Providence Plantations,"
with an amendment,[58] to which they desire the concurrence of this House:
And then he withdrew.

The House proceeded to consider the said amendment; and the same being
read, was agreed to.

ORDERED, That the Clerk of this House do acquaint the Senate therewith.[59]

The House, according to the order of the day, resolved itself into a committee of the whole House, on the bill to establish the post-office and post-roads
within the United States.

Mr. Speaker left the chair.

Mr. Boudinot took the chair of the committee.

Mr. Speaker resumed the chair, and Mr. Boudinot reported, that the committee had, according to order, had the said bill under consideration, and
made some progress therein.

RESOLVED, That this House will, to-morrow, again resolve itself into a
committee of the whole House on the said bill.[60]

The several orders of the day were read, and postponed until to-morrow.

And then the House adjourned until to-morrow morning ten o'clock.

TUESDAY, JUNE 15, 1790

An engrossed bill for the relief of Nathaniel Twining, in certain cases, was
read the third time.

RESOLVED, That the said bill do pass; and that the title be, "An act for the
relief of Nathaniel Twining."

ORDERED, That the Clerk of this House do carry the said bill to the Senate,
and desire their concurrence.[61]

---

[57] On June 18 one amendment to this bill was disagreed to, while others were
agreed to.

[58] The amendment is printed in the *Senate Legislative Journal* on June 14.

[59] On June 16 this bill was signed by the speaker and the vice president.

[60] On June 15 the COWH considered this bill again.

[61] The Senate read this bill on June 15 and 16, and on June 16 it was committed.
On June 17 the Twining petition was referred to this committee, which reported on
June 23. The Senate rejected this report on June 24. The committee's report is printed
in the *Senate Legislative Journal* for this day. On June 25 the Twining Bill [HR–72]
was read again and agreed to.

The House, according to the order of the day, again resolved itself into a committee of the whole House, on the bill to establish the post-office and post-roads within the United States.

Mr. Speaker left the chair.

Mr. Boudinot took the chair of the committee.

Mr. Speaker resumed the chair, and Mr. Boudinot reported, that the committee had, according to order, again had the said bill under consideration, and made a farther progress therein.

RESOLVED, That this House will, to-morrow, again resolve itself into a committee of the whole House on the said bill.[62]

Mr. Laurance, from the committee appointed, presented, according to order, a bill to authorize the purchase of a tract of land for the use of the United States, which was received and read the first time.[63]

The several orders of the day were read, and postponed until to-morrow.

And then the House adjourned until to-morrow morning ten o'clock.

WEDNESDAY, JUNE 16, 1790

Mr. Gilman, from the joint committee for inrolled bills, reported, that the committee had examined an inrolled bill, intituled, "An act for giving effect to an Act intituled, 'An act to establish the judicial courts of the United States,' within the state of Rhode-Island and Providence Plantations,"[64] and had found the same to be truly inrolled: Whereupon,

Mr. Speaker signed the said inrolled bill.[65]

ORDERED, That the Clerk of this House do acquaint the Senate therewith.

A bill to authorize the purchase of a tract of land for the use of the United States, was read the second time, and ordered to be engrossed, and read the third time to-morrow.[66]

A petition of Hannah Douglass, widow of William Douglass, deceased, late a colonel in the army of the United States, was presented to the House and read, praying that the provision directed by a resolve of Congress to be made for widows of officers who died in the service, may be granted to her.

ORDERED, That the said petition be referred to the Secretary at War, with instruction to examine the same, and report his opinion thereupon to the House.

A petition of Adam Caldwell, was presented to the House and read, praying relief against an imprisonment under which he is now suffering for a violation of the laws of trade of the United States.

---

[62] On June 16 the COWH reported amendments to this bill.

[63] On June 16 this bill was read again.

[64] The inspected enrolled bill is in Enrolled Acts, RG 11, DNA.

[65] On June 22 this bill was presented to the president.

[66] On June 17 this bill was read again, agreed to, and sent to the Senate.

ORDERED, That the said petition do lie on the table.[67]

The House, according to the order of the day, again resolved itself into a committee of the whole House on the bill to establish the post-office and post-roads within the United States.

Mr. Speaker left the chair.

Mr. Boudinot took the chair of the committee.

Mr. Speaker resumed the chair, and Mr. Boudinot reported, that the committee had, according to order, again had the said bill under consideration, and made several amendments thereto, which he delivered in at the Clerk's table, where the same were read, and partly considered.

ORDERED, That the said bill, with the amendments, do lie on the table.[68]

Another member from North-Carolina, to wit, John Sevier, appeared, produced his credentials, and took his seat in the House; the oath to support the Constitution of the United States, being administered to him by Mr. Speaker, according to law.

A message, in writing, was received from the President of the United States, by Mr. Lear his Secretary, as followeth:

UNITED STATES, June 16, 1790

GENTLEMEN of the SENATE and HOUSE of REPRESENTATIVES,

THE ratification of the Constitution of the United States of America, by the state of Rhode-Island and Providence Plantations, was received by me last night, together with a letter to the President of the United States, from the President of the Convention.

I have directed my Secretary to lay before you a copy of each.

GEORGE WASHINGTON[69]

The letter and papers accompanying the said message were read, and ordered to lie on the table.

The several orders of the day were read, and postponed until to-morrow.

And then the House adjourned until to-morrow morning ten o'clock.

THURSDAY, JUNE 17, 1790

An engrossed bill to authorize the purchase of a tract of land for the use of the United States, was read the third time.

RESOLVED, That the said bill do pass, and that the title be, "An act to authorize the purchase of a tract of land for the use of the United States."

---

[67] On June 17 a committee was appointed to bring in a bill on this petition.

[68] On June 17 the amendments from the COWH were agreed to.

[69] The message with enclosures is in President's Messages: Suggesting legislation, SR, DNA. The enclosures are E–22847. They are printed in the Appendix to the Second Session.

ORDERED, That the Clerk of this House do carry the said bill to the Senate, and desire their concurrence.[70]

On motion,

ORDERED, That a committee be appointed to consider, whether any and what fees, perquisites or other emoluments shall be annexed to the offices of Consul and Vice-Consul.

And a committee was appointed of Mr. Gerry, Mr. Boudinot, and Mr. Huntington.[71]

ORDERED, That the petition of Adam Caldwell, which was presented yesterday, be referred to Mr. Vining, Mr. Scott, and Mr. Sevier, with instruction to prepare and bring in a bill or bills pursuant to the prayer thereof.[72]

A petition of William Peery, was presented to the House and read, praying the liquidation and settlement of a claim against the United States.

ORDERED, That the said petition be referred to the Secretary of the Treasury, with instruction to examine the same, and report his opinion thereupon to the House.

Mr. Fitzsimons, from the committee to whom was committed the engrossed bill, to provide for the settlement of the accounts between the United States, and the individual States, reported an amendatory bill, which was received and read the first time.

On motion,

The said bill was read the second time, and ordered to be committed to a committee of the whole House, on Monday next.[73]

Mr. Gilman, from the committee to whom was committed the bill for the government and regulation of seamen in the merchants service, reported sundry amendments thereto, which were read, and ordered to lie on the table.[74]

The House resumed the consideration of the amendments reported yesterday by the committee of the whole House, to the bill to establish the post-office and post-roads within the United States; and the same being severally read at the Clerk's table, were, on the question put thereupon, agreed to by the House.

ORDERED, That the said bill, with the amendments, be engrossed, and read the third time to-morrow.[75]

---

[70] The Senate read this bill on June 17 and 18. On June 18 it was committed with the petition of Stephen Moore. On June 25 this committee reported, and a part of this bill was agreed to. The bill was read again and agreed to on June 28. The House was notified on June 29.

[71] On July 1 this committee reported.

[72] On August 6 this committee presented the Caldwell Bill [HR–99], which was read twice.

[73] On June 21 this bill was amended, and a further amendment was disagreed to.

[74] On June 25 the committee's amendments were agreed to.

[75] On June 21 this bill was read again, agreed to, and sent to the Senate.

The several orders of the day were read, and postponed until to-morrow. And then the House adjourned until to-morrow morning ten o'clock.

FRIDAY, JUNE 18, 1790

The petitions of John Chappel and Ely Gladhill, were presented to the House and read, respectively praying relief in consideration of wounds and injuries sustained in the service of the United States, during the late war.

ORDERED, That said petitions be referred to the Secretary at War, with instruction to examine the same, and report his opinion thereupon to the House.

A petition of Mary McCullen, widow of James McCullen, deceased, was presented to the House and read, praying the settlement of a claim against the United States, from the estate of her deceased husband.

ORDERED, That the said petition be referred to the Secretary of the Treasury, with instruction to examine the same, and report his opinion thereupon to the House.

A petition of John Foster, was presented to the House and read, praying a grant of lands, or other relief, in consideration of losses and injuries sustained during the late war.

ORDERED, That the said petition do lie on the table.

On motion,

The House proceeded to consider the bill which lay on the table, for repealing, after the last day of   next, the duties heretofore laid upon distilled spirits imported from abroad, and laying others in their stead; and also upon spirits distilled within the United States, as well to discourage the excessive use of those spirits, and promote agriculture, as to provide for the support of the public credit, and for the common defence and general welfare: Whereupon,

A motion being made and seconded to amend the said bill by striking out the twelfth and thirteenth sections, and also such other parts thereof as impose an excise duty on all spirits distilled within the United States,

It passed in the negative, $\begin{cases} \text{AYES} & 19 \\ \text{NOES} & 35 \end{cases}$

The ayes and noes being demanded by one fifth of the members present, Those who voted in the affirmative, are,

Aedanus Burke	Jonathan Grout
Isaac Coles	Daniel Hiester
Elbridge Gerry	Daniel Huger
Benjamin Goodhue	Andrew Moore
Samuel Griffin	Peter Muhlenberg

John Page
Josiah Parker
Theodore Sedgwick
William Smith (of South-
    Carolina)

John Steele
Thomas Sumter
George Thatcher
Thomas Tudor Tucker and
Alexander White

Those who voted in the negative, are,

Fisher Ames
John Baptista Ashe
Abraham Baldwin
Egbert Benson
Timothy Bloodworth
Elias Boudinot
John Brown
Lambert Cadwalader
Daniel Carroll
Benjamin Contee
Thomas Fitzsimons
William Floyd
Abiel Foster
George Gale
Nicholas Gilman
Thomas Hartley
John Hathorn
Benjamin Huntington

James Jackson
John Laurance
George Leonard
Samuel Livermore
George Mathews
Jeremiah Van Rensselaer
Thomas Scott
Joshua Seney
John Sevier
Roger Sherman
Peter Silvester
Thomas Sinnickson
Michael Jenifer Stone
Jonathan Trumbull
Jeremiah Wadsworth
Hugh Williamson and
Henry Wynkoop

The said bill was then further amended at the Clerk's table, when an adjournment being called for,[76]

The several orders of the day were farther postponed until Monday next.

And then the House adjourned until Monday morning ten o'clock.

MONDAY, JUNE 21, 1790

An engrossed bill to establish the post-office and post-roads within the United States, was read the third time, and the blanks therein filled up.

RESOLVED, That the said bill do pass, and that the title be, "An act to establish the post-office and post-roads within the United States."[77]

---

[76] On June 21 the Duties on Distilled Spirits Bill [HR–62] was disagreed to.

[77] A printed copy of the bill, annotated by the Senate, is in House Bills, SR, DNA.

ORDERED, That the Clerk of this House do carry the said bill to the Senate, and desire their concurrence.[78]

The Speaker laid before the House a letter and reports from the Secretary at War, on the several petitions of the representatives of John Harris, Robert Lewis[79] and David Gould, deceased, and also on the petition of Hannah Douglass, widow of the late Colonel William Douglass; which were read, and ordered to lie on the table.[80]

A petition of Joseph Packwood, was presented to the House and read, praying the liquidation and settlement of a claim against the United States.

ORDERED, That the said petition be referred to the Secretary of the Treasury, with instruction to examine the same, and report his opinion thereupon to the House.

The House resumed the consideration of the bill for repealing, after the last day of   next, the duties heretofore laid upon distilled spirits imported from abroad, and laying others in their stead; and also upon spirits distilled within the United States, as well to discourage the excessive use of those spirits, and promote agriculture, as to provide for the support of the public credit, and for the common defence and general welfare;

And, on the question that the said bill, with the amendments, be engrossed, and read the third time,

It passed in the negative, $\left\{ \begin{array}{l} \text{AYES} \quad 23 \\ \text{NOES} \quad 35 \end{array} \right.$

The ayes and noes being demanded by one fifth of the members present, Those who voted in the affirmative, are,

John Brown	Abiel Foster
Lambert Cadwalader	George Gale
Daniel Carroll	Nicholas Gilman
Benjamin Contee	Samuel Griffin
Thomas Fitzsimons	Thomas Hartley
William Floyd	Daniel Hiester

---

[78] The Senate read this bill on June 22, 23, and 24. It was committed on June 24, and on June 30 this committee reported amendments. The report was considered on July 2 and agreed to on July 3. The Senate considered the Post Office Bill [HR–74] again on July 5, and on July 6 it was agreed to with amendments, which are printed in the *Senate Legislative Journal* on this date. On July 7 the House was notified of the amendments.

[79] This petition was submitted in behalf of the children of Robert Lewis by Elisha Curtis on April 8.

[80] A copy of the report on all of these petitions is in A Record of the Reports of the Secretary of War, vol. 1, HR, DNA. A copy of the report, probably made by ASP, is in Reports and Communications from the Secretary of War, HR, DNA. On June 22 the House considered the section of the report on Gould's petition, agreed to a resolution on the petition, and appointed a committee to bring in a bill on it.

Richard Bland Lee
Samuel Livermore
James Madison, junior
Peter Muhlenberg
Joshua Seney
Roger Sherman

Thomas Sinnickson
William Smith (of Maryland)
John Vining
Alexander White and
Hugh Williamson

Those who voted in the negative, are,

Fisher Ames
John Baptista Ashe
Abraham Baldwin
Egbert Benson
Timothy Bloodworth
Aedanus Burke
Isaac Coles
Elbridge Gerry
Benjamin Goodhue
Jonathan Grout
John Hathorn
Daniel Huger
Benjamin Huntington
James Jackson
John Laurance
George Leonard
George Mathews
Andrew Moore

John Page
Josiah Parker
George Partridge
Jeremiah Van Rensselaer
Thomas Scott
Theodore Sedgwick
John Sevier
Peter Silvester
William Smith (of South-Carolina)
John Steele
Michael Jenifer Stone
Jonathan Sturges
Thomas Sumter
George Thatcher
Jonathan Trumbull
Thomas Tudor Tucker and
Jeremiah Wadsworth

And so the said bill was rejected.

ORDERED, That a committee be appointed to report a plan making provision for the payment of interest on the debts of the United States.

And a committee was appointed of Mr. Fitzsimons, Mr. Madison, Mr. Sedgwick, Mr. Sherman, and Mr. Tucker.[81]

A message from the Senate by Mr. Otis their Secretary.

MR. SPEAKER, The Senate have appointed a committee on their part, to join with the committee appointed by this House to consider and report when it will be convenient and proper that an adjournment of the present session of Congress should take place, pursuant to the resolution of this House of the eighth instant:[82] The Senate have also passed the bill, intituled,

---

[81] On June 29 this committee reported.
[82] On June 28 this committee reported.

"An act to satisfy the claims of John McCord against the United States," with several amendments to which they desire the concurrence of this House:[83] And then he withdrew.

The House, according to order of the day, resolved itself into a committee of the whole House, on the bill to provide for the settlement of the accounts between the United States and the individual States.

Mr. Speaker left the chair.

Mr. Seney took the chair of the committee.

Mr. Speaker resumed the chair, and Mr. Seney reported, that the committee had, according to order, had the said bill under consideration, and made several amendments thereto, which he delivered in at the Clerk's table, where the same were severally twice read, and agreed to by the House.

A motion being then made and seconded, further to amend the said bill by striking out in the fifth section, the words "the rule for apportioning to the States the expences of the war, shall be the same that is prescribed by the Constitution of the United States, for the apportionment of representation and direct taxes, and according to the first enumeration which shall be made."

It passed in the negative, $\begin{cases} \text{AYES} & 10 \\ \text{NOES} & 45 \end{cases}$

The ayes and noes being demanded by one fifth of the members present,

Those who voted in the affirmative, are,

John Baptista Ashe	John Hathorn
Abraham Baldwin	James Jackson
William Floyd	John Laurance
Abiel Foster	Samuel Livermore and
Nicholas Gilman	Theodore Sedgwick

Those who voted in the negative, are,

Fisher Ames	Isaac Coles
Egbert Benson	Benjamin Contee
Timothy Bloodworth	Thomas Fitzsimons
Elias Boudinot	George Gale
John Brown	Benjamin Goodhue
Aedanus Burke	Samuel Griffin
Lambert Cadwalader	Jonathan Grout
Daniel Carroll	Daniel Hiester

[83] The Senate committee report on this bill, with an amendment, is in Various Select Committee Reports, SR, DNA. The Senate agreed to only one amendment to this bill. The amendment is printed in the *Senate Legislative Journal* on June 21. On June 22 the House agreed to the Senate amendment.

Daniel Huger
Benjamin Huntington
George Leonard
James Madison, junior
Andrew Moore
Peter Muhlenberg
John Page
George Partridge
Jeremiah Van Rensselaer
James Schureman
Thomas Scott
Joshua Seney
John Sevier
Roger Sherman
Peter Silvester

Thomas Sinnickson
William Smith (of Maryland)
William Smith (of South-Carolina)
John Steele
Michael Jenifer Stone
Jonathan Sturges
Thomas Sumter
George Thatcher
Jonathan Trumbull
Thomas Tudor Tucker
John Vining
Jeremiah Wadsworth
Alexander White and
Hugh Williamson

ORDERED, That the said bill, with the amendments be engrossed, and read the third time to-morrow.[84]

The several orders of the day, were farther postponed until to-morrow.

And then the House adjourned until to-morrow morning, ten o'clock.

TUESDAY, JUNE 22, 1790

An engrossed bill to provide for the settlement of the accounts between the United States and the individual States, was read the third time, and the blanks therein filled up.

RESOLVED, That the said bill do pass, and that the title be, "An act to provide more effectually for the settlement of the accounts between the United States and the individual States."[85]

ORDERED, That the Clerk of this House do carry the said bill to the Senate, and desire their concurrence.[86]

Mr. Gilman, from the joint committee for inrolled bills, reported, that the committee did this day wait on the President of the United States, and presented for his approbation an inrolled bill, intituled, "An act for giving effect to an act, intituled, 'An act to establish the judicial courts of the United States,' within the state of Rhode-Island and Providence Plantations."[87]

---

[84] On June 22 this bill was read again, agreed to, and sent to the Senate.

[85] A printed copy of the bill, annotated by the Senate, is in House Bills, SR, DNA. E–46028.

[86] The Senate read this bill on June 23 and 30. On July 1 it was committed, and this committee reported amendments on July 3. These amendments were agreed to on July 6. The bill was committed again on July 7, and the amendments reported by this committee were agreed to on July 8. On July 9 the bill was read again and agreed to with amendments, which are printed in the *Senate Legislative Journal* for this date.

[87] On June 23 the president signed this bill.

Mr. Goodhue, from the committee appointed,[88] presented, according to order, a bill imposing duties on the tonnage of ships or vessels, which was received and read the first time.

On motion,

The said bill was read the second time, and ordered to be committed to a committee of the whole House to-morrow.[89]

The Speaker laid before the House a letter and reports from the Secretary at War, on the several petitions of John Rogers, Pattin Jackson, James Delaplaine, Jacob Smith, Thomas McFall, and Benjamin Keefe; also a statement respecting sundry petitions transmitted to him by the Governor of Virginia, which reports and statement were read, and ordered to lie on the table.[90]

The House proceeded to consider the report of the Secretary at War, on the petition of the representative of David Gould, deceased: Whereupon,

RESOLVED, That provision ought to be made for paying to such of the orphan children of the late Doctor David Gould, who died in service during the late war, as were living at the time of his death, or their legal representatives, the sum of one thousand six hundred and eighty dollars, being the amount of the half pay of a Captain for seven years, the same being the ratio established as the half pay of a surgeon, by the resolves of Congress of the seventeenth of January, one thousand seven hundred and eighty-one.

ORDERED, That a bill or bills be brought in pursuant to the said resolution, and that Mr. Seney, Mr. Hiester, and Mr. Moore, do prepare and bring in the same.[91]

Mr. Williamson, from the committee to whom was committed the bill for giving effect to the act, "providing for the enumeration of the inhabitants of the United States," in respect to the state of Rhode-Island and Providence Plantations, reported sundry amendments thereto, which were read and ordered to lie on the table.[92]

The House proceeded to consider the amendment proposed by the Senate to the bill, intituled, "An act to satisfy the claims of John McCord against the United States," and the same being read, was agreed to.

---

[88] This committee is the one on laws of revenue, which was appointed on April 23. The members were Elias Boudinot, Thomas Fitzsimons, Benjamin Goodhue, Richard B. Lee, and John Laurance.

[89] On June 23 the COWH reported an amendment to this bill. The amendment was agreed to by the House.

[90] Copies of these reports and the statement are in A Record of the Reports of the Secretary of War, vol. 1, HR, DNA. A copy of the report on the Rogers petition, probably made by ASP, is in Reports and Communications from the Secretary of War, HR, DNA. When the Keefe petition was received on May 5, it was referred to as the petition of Benjamin Kuffe. No documents have been located to verify which spelling is correct.

[91] On June 23 this committee presented the Gould Bill [HR–79], which was read.

[92] On June 28 the amendments reported by the committee were disagreed to.

ORDERED, That the Clerk of this House do acquaint the Senate therewith.[93]

ORDERED, That the petition of the inhabitants of the county of Westchester, in the state of New-York, which lay on the table, be referred to the Secretary at War, with instruction to examine the same, and report his opinion thereupon to the House.

The House proceeded to consider the report of the Secretary at War, on the petition of William Oliver, which lay on the table: Whereupon,

RESOLVED, That the said petition be rejected.

The House, according to the order of the day, resolved itself into a committee of the whole House, on the bill to regulate trade and intercourse with the Indian tribes.

Mr. Speaker left the chair.

Mr. Boudinot took the chair of the committee.

Mr. Speaker resumed the chair, and Mr. Boudinot reported, that the committee had, according to order, had the said bill under consideration, and made several amendments thereto, which he delivered in at the Clerk's table, where the same were severally twice read, and agreed to by the House.

A motion being then made and seconded, further to amend the said bill by striking out the fourth section, in the words following, to wit:

"And be it further enacted, That a sum not exceeding   thousand dollars, be appropriated out of the monies arising from duties on imports and tonnage, subject to the orders of the President of the United States, to be laid out in goods and articles of trade, suitable for supplying the wants and necessities of the Indians, and to be vended and retailed to them through the agency of the said Superintendants, and persons to be licensed by them for that purpose, in such manner, and conformably to such regulations as the President of the United States shall establish."

It passed in the negative, $\begin{cases} \text{AYES} & 26 \\ \text{NOES} & 27 \end{cases}$

The ayes and noes being demanded by one fifth of the members present, Those who voted in the affirmative, are,

John Baptista Ashe	Daniel Hiester
Timothy Bloodworth	Daniel Huger
Isaac Coles	Benjamin Huntington
William Floyd	James Jackson
Abiel Foster	George Leonard
Elbridge Gerry	Samuel Livermore
Benjamin Goodhue	Josiah Parker
John Hathorn	Jeremiah Van Rensselaer

[93] On June 29 this bill was signed by the speaker and the vice president.

James Schureman
Theodore Sedgwick
Joshua Seney
John Sevier
Roger Sherman

Peter Silvester
Michael Jenifer Stone
Jonathan Sturges
Thomas Sumter and
Thomas Tudor Tucker

Those who voted in the negative, are,

Fisher Ames
Abraham Baldwin
Egbert Benson
Elias Boudinot
John Brown
Lambert Cadwalader
Benjamin Contee
Thomas Fitzsimons
George Gale
Nicholas Gilman
Samuel Griffin
Thomas Hartley
John Laurance
Richard Bland Lee

James Madison, junior
George Mathews
Andrew Moore
Peter Muhlenberg
John Page
Thomas Scott
Thomas Sinnickson
William Smith (of Maryland)
William Smith (of South-Carolina)
John Steele
Jonathan Trumbull
Jeremiah Wadsworth and
Alexander White

ORDERED, That the said bill, with the amendments, be engrossed, and read the third time to-morrow.[94]

The several orders of the day were farther postponed until to-morrow.

And then the House adjourned until Monday morning ten o'clock.

WEDNESDAY, JUNE 23, 1790

An engrossed bill to regulate trade and intercourse with the Indian tribes, was read the third time, and the blanks therein filled up.

RESOLVED, That the said bill do pass, and that the title be, "An act to regulate trade and intercourse with the Indian tribes."[95]

ORDERED, That the Clerk of this House do carry the said bill to the Senate, and desire their concurrence.[96]

Mr. Seney, from the committee appointed, presented according to order,

---

[94] On June 23 this bill was read again, agreed to, and sent to the Senate.

[95] A printed copy of the bill, annotated by the Senate, is in House Bills, SR, DNA. E–46015.

[96] The Senate read this bill on June 23 and July 2. On July 2 it was committed, and on July 8 the committee's report was agreed to as amendments to the bill. On July 9 the bill was agreed to with amendments. These amendments are printed in the *Senate Legislative Journal* for this date. The amendments were sent to the House on July 9.

a bill to satisfy the claim of the representatives of David Gould, deceased, against the United States, which was received, and read the first time.[97]

Mr. Gerry, from the committee, appointed to report a catalogue of books, necessary for the use of Congress, together with an estimate of the expence thereof, made a report,[98] which was read, and ordered to lie on the table.

A petition of Archibald Crary, of East-Greenwich, in the state of Rhode-Island, in behalf of himself and the officers and soldiers of the late Rhode-Island brigade, was presented to the House and read, praying that the same pay and allowances may be granted them, as to other officers and soldiers in the service of the United States, during the late war.

ORDERED, That the said petition be referred to the Secretary at War, with instruction to examine the same, and report his opinion thereupon to the House.

On motion,

ORDERED, That John Stone, who presented a petition to this House on the fifteenth of February last, have leave to withdraw the same.

A petition of Elias Hasket Derby, was presented to the House and read, praying further time, or other relief, in the payment of duties accruing on a cargo of teas imported from China, by the petitioner.

ORDERED, That the said petition do lie on the table.[99]

A message was received from the President of the United States, by Mr. Lear his Secretary, notifying, that the President did, this day, approve and sign the act, intituled, "An act for giving effect to an act, intituled, 'An act to establish the judicial courts of the United States,' within the state of Rhode-Island and Providence Plantations."[100]

The House, according to the order of the day, resolved itself into a committee of the whole House on the bill imposing duties on the tonnage of ships or vessels.

Mr. Speaker left the chair.

Mr. Boudinot took the chair of the committee.

Mr. Speaker resumed the chair, and Mr. Boudinot reported, that the committee had, according to order, had the said bill under consideration, and made an amendment thereto, which he delivered in at the Clerk's table, where the same was twice read, and agreed to by the House.

ORDERED, That the said bill, with the amendment, be engrossed, and read the third time to-morrow.[101]

---

[97] On June 24 this bill was read again.

[98] A copy of the report is in A Record of the Reports of Select Committees, HR, DNA.

[99] On June 24 this petition was committed.

[100] The message is in Committee on Enrolled Bills, SR, DNA.

[101] On June 24 this bill was read again, agreed to, and sent to the Senate.

The Speaker laid before the House a letter and reports from the Secretary at War, on the petitions of Caleb Brewster, and Joseph Ransom, which were read, and ordered to lie on the table.[102]

The House proceeded to consider the report of the committee to whom was referred the petition of Nicholas Cowenhoven and others: Whereupon,

ORDERED, That the said petition and report be referred to the Secretary of the Treasury, with instruction to examine the same, and report his opinion thereupon to the House.

A message from the Senate by Mr. Otis their Secretary.

MR. SPEAKER, The Senate recede in part from their amendment disagreed to by this House, to the bill, intituled, "An act providing the means of intercourse between the United States and foreign nations," and have agreed to a further amendment to the said bill, to which they desire the concurrence of this House:[103]   And then he withdrew.

The several orders of the day were farther postponed until to-morrow.

And then the House adjourned until to-morrow morning ten o'clock.

THURSDAY, JUNE 24, 1790

An engrossed bill imposing duties on the tonnage of ships or vessels, was read the third time, and the blanks therein filled up.

RESOLVED, That the said bill do pass, and that the title be, "An act imposing duties on the tonnage of ships or vessels."[104]

ORDERED, That the Clerk of this House do carry the said bill to the Senate, and desire their concurrence.[105]

A bill to satisfy the claim of the representatives of David Gould, deceased, against the United States, was read the second time and ordered to be engrossed, and read the third time to-morrow.[106]

---

[102] Copies of these reports are in A Record of the Reports of the Secretary of War, vol. 1, HR, DNA. The report on the Ransom petition includes a statement of arrearages due to invalid pensioners. A copy of the report on the Brewster petition, probably made by ASP, is in Reports and Communications from the Secretary of War, HR, DNA. On June 28 a resolution to place Caleb Brewster on the pensioners list was agreed to and referred to the committee that was preparing the Disabled Soldiers and Seamen Bill [HR–88].

[103] These Senate actions are part of the conference report on this bill. The report is printed in the *Senate Legislative Journal* on June 23. On June 24 the conference committee on this bill reported.

[104] This bill is E–22964.

[105] The Senate read this bill on June 24 and 29. On June 29 it was committed. The committee reported on July 12, and the bill was agreed to without amendments.

[106] On June 25 this bill was read again, agreed to, and sent to the Senate.

ORDERED, That the petition of Elias Hasket Derby, which was presented yesterday, be referred to Mr. Goodhue, Mr. Fitzsimons, and Mr. Smith (of Maryland), that they do examine the matter thereof, and report the same, with their opinion thereupon, to the House.[107]

On motion,

ORDERED, That the petition of Abraham Van Alstine, which was presented the eighteenth of March last, be referred to the Secretary of the Treasury, with instruction to examine the same, and report his opinion thereupon to the House.

The House proceeded to consider the report of the committee to whom was referred the memorial of the officers of the late navy of the United States: Whereupon,

RESOLVED, That the said report be committed to a committee of the whole House immediately.

The House accordingly resolved itself into the said committee.

Mr. Speaker left the chair.

Mr. Boudinot took the chair of the committee.

Mr. Speaker resumed the chair, and Mr. Boudinot reported, that the committee had, according to order, had the said report under consideration, and directed him to report as the opinion of the committee that the said report be disagreed to: Whereupon,

RESOLVED, That this House do concur with the committee of the whole House in their disagreement to the said report, and that the said memorial of the officers of the late navy of the United States be rejected.

A petition of John Brandon, was presented to the House and read, praying the liquidation and settlement of a claim against the United States.

ORDERED, That the said petition be referred to the Secretary of the Treasury, with instruction to examine the same, and report his opinion thereupon to the House.

Mr. Gerry, from the managers appointed on the part of this House, to attend the conference with the Senate on the subject matter of the amendments depending between the two Houses, to the bill, intituled, "An act providing the means of intercourse between the United States and foreign nations," made a report, which was read, and ordered to lie on the table.[108]

The several orders of the day were farther postponed until to-morrow.

And then the House adjourned until to-morrow morning ten o'clock.

---

[107] On June 28 this committee reported.

[108] The report on the conference is in Joint Committee Reports, SR, DNA. The report is printed in the *Senate Legislative Journal* on June 23. On June 25 the House agreed to the amendments to this bill, proposed by the Senate on June 23, with two amendments. The Senate agreed to the House amendments on June 25.

FRIDAY, JUNE 25, 1790

An engrossed bill to satisfy the claim of the representatives of David Gould, deceased, against the United States, was read the third time, and a blank therein filled up.

RESOLVED, That the said bill do pass; and that the title be, "An act to satisfy the claim of the representatives of David Gould, deceased, against the United States."

ORDERED, That the Clerk of this House do carry the said bill to the Senate, and desire their concurrence.[109]

The Speaker laid before the House a letter and reports from the Secretary at War, on the several petitions of Timothy Hosmer, John Chappel, Ely Gladhill, James Derry, and Benjamin Hardison, which were read, and ordered to lie on the table.[110]

A petition of Sarah Stirling, widow of the late Earl of Stirling, was presented to the House and read, praying to receive the allowance of seven years half pay due to her deceased husband, as a Major-General in the service of the United States, during the late war.[111]

ORDERED, That the said petition be referred to the Secretary at War, with instruction to examine the same, and report his opinion thereupon to the House.[112]

The House proceeded to consider the amendments last proposed on the part of the Senate to the bill, intituled, "An act providing the means of intercourse between the United States and foreign nations:"   Whereupon,

RESOLVED, That this House do agree to the said amendments, with the following amendments, to wit:

Line ninth, strike out the word "person," and in lieu thereof insert "the Minister Plenipotentiary or Charge des Affaires."

Line nineteenth, strike out "*any of their Secretaries,*" and in lieu thereof insert "the Secretary of any Minister Plenipotentiary."

ORDERED, That the Clerk of this House do acquaint the Senate therewith, and desire their concurrence to the said amendments.

The House proceeded to consider the amendments reported by the committee to whom was committed the bill for the government and regulation of

---

[109] On June 25 and 29 the Senate read this bill. On June 29 it was committed, and on July 5 this committee reported. On July 6 the Senate voted not to concur in the Gould Bill [HR–79].

[110] Copies of these reports are in A Record of the Reports of the Secretary of War, vol. 1, HR, DNA. On June 28 a resolution on the Derry, Hardison, and other petitions was agreed to and referred to the committee to prepare the Disabled Soldiers and Seamen Bill [HR–88].

[111] The petition is in Petitions and Memorials: Claims, SR, DNA. Sarah Stirling's full name is Sarah Alexander, Lady Stirling.

[112] On July 27 the secretary reported on this petition.

seamen in the merchants service; and the said amendments being severally twice read at the Clerk's table, were agreed to by the House.

ORDERED, That the said bill, with the amendments, be engrossed, and read the third time on Monday next.[113]

The House, according to the order of the day, resolved itself into a committee of the whole House on the bill concerning the trade and navigation of the United States.

Mr. Speaker left the chair.

Mr. Seney took the chair of the committee.

Mr. Speaker resumed the chair, and Mr. Seney reported, that the committee had, according to order, had the said bill under consideration, and made some progress therein.

RESOLVED, That this House will, on Monday next, again resolve itself into a committee of the whole House on the said bill.[114]

A message from the Senate by Mr. Otis their Secretary.

MR. SPEAKER, The Senate agree to the amendments proposed by this House to their amendments to the bill, intituled, "An act providing the means of intercourse between the United States and foreign nations:"[115] The Senate have also passed the bill, intituled, "An act for the relief of Nathaniel Twining:"[116] And then he withdrew.

The Speaker laid before the House a letter from Samuel Meredith, Treasurer of the United States, together with a statement of his accounts of the receipts and expenditures of public monies, from the first of January to the thirty-first of March last, which were read, and ordered to lie on the table.[117]

The orders of the day were farther postponed until Monday next.

And then the House adjourned until Monday morning ten o'clock.

MONDAY, JUNE 28, 1790

An engrossed bill for the government and regulation of seamen in the merchants service, was read the third time.

---

[113] On June 28 this bill was read again, agreed to, and sent to the Senate.

[114] Consideration of this bill in the COWH was postponed as an order of the day on June 28. On June 29 the COWH considered this bill again, after a motion to discharge the committee from further consideration of it was defeated.

[115] On June 29 this bill was signed by the speaker and the vice president.

[116] On June 29 this bill was signed by the speaker and the vice president.

[117] The letter and the treasury accounts are in Transcribed Reports and Communications from the Executive Departments, 1789–1814, Records of the Secretary, SR, DNA. Copies of the letter and accounts are in Accounts of the Treasurer of the United States, vol. 1, HR, DNA. On August 2 a further statement of accounts by the treasurer of the United States was submitted to the House and committed.

RESOLVED, That the said bill do pass; and that the title be, "An act for the government and regulation of seamen in the merchants service."[118]

ORDERED, That the Clerk of this House do carry the said bill to the Senate, and desire their concurrence.[119]

The Speaker laid before the House a letter and reports from the Secretary at War, on the several petitions of Christian Wolfe, Samuel Garretson, Catherine Wheelan, John F. Vacher, Walter Miles, William Taylor, Ichabod Spencer, Stephen Guyer, Rufus Hamilton, and Lewis I. Costigin, which were read and ordered to lie on the table.[120]

Mr. Wadsworth, from the committee appointed to join with a committee of the Senate, to consider and report when it will be convenient and proper that an adjournment of the present session of Congress should take place, and to consider and report such business now before Congress necessary to be finished before the adjournment, and such as may be conveniently postponed; and also to consider and report such matters not now before Congress, but which it will be necessary should be considered and determined by Congress before an adjournment, made a report, which was read, and ordered to lie on the table.[121]

Mr. Clymer, from the committee, to whom was referred the petition of Thomas Barclay, made a report, which was read, and ordered to lie on the table.[122]

The House proceeded to consider the amendments reported by the committee to whom was committed the bill for giving effect to an act, intituled, "An act providing for the enumeration of the inhabitants of the United States," in respect to the state of Rhode-Island and Providence Plantations, and the said amendments being severally twice read at the Clerk's table, were disagreed to by the House.

ORDERED, That the said bill be engrossed, and read the third time tomorrow.[123]

Mr. Goodhue, from the committee to whom was referred the petition of Elias Hasket Derby, made a report, which was read, and ordered to lie on the table.[124]

---

[118] A printed copy of this bill is in the Broadside Collection, RBkRm, DLC.

[119] The Senate read this bill on June 28 and July 1. It was committed on July 1, and the committee reported amendments on July 7. On July 8 the bill was read again and agreed to with the amendments. On July 9 the House was notified of this action.

[120] Copies of these reports are in A Record of the Reports of the Secretary of War, vol. 1, HR, DNA.

[121] A draft and a clean copy of the report are in Joint Committee Reports, SR, DNA. On July 15 the House considered this report and agreed to a resolution to adjourn on July 27.

[122] On July 1 this report was recommitted.

[123] On June 29 this bill was read again, agreed to, and sent to the Senate.

[124] A copy of the report is in A Record of the Reports of Select Committees, HR,

The House, according to the standing order of the day, resolved itself into a committee of the whole House on the state of the Union.

Mr. Speaker left the chair.

Mr. Boudinot took the chair of the committee.

Mr. Speaker resumed the chair, and Mr. Boudinot reported, that the committee had, according to order, had the state of the Union under consideration, and come to a resolution thereupon, which he delivered in at the Clerk's table, where the same was twice read, and agreed to by the House, as followeth:

RESOLVED, That the resolution of Congress of the seventeenth of July, one thousand, seven hundred and eighty-eight, respecting the lands reserved for the Virginia troops on continental and state establishments, pursuant to the cession made by the said State to the United States, of the territory north-west of the river Ohio, ought to be repealed.

ORDERED, That the said resolution be referred to Mr. Brown, Mr. Boudinot, Mr. White, Mr. Huntington, and Mr. Benson, with instruction to prepare and bring in a bill or bills for carrying into effect the reservations contained in the deed of cession made by the state of Virginia to the United States of the territory north-west of the river Ohio.[125]

The House proceeded to consider the reports of the Secretary at War, on the petitions of James Derry, Benjamin Hardison, Christian Wolfe, Samuel Garretson, and Caleb Brewster: Whereupon,

RESOLVED, That the commissioner of army accounts be authorized to settle the accounts of pay of the said James Derry and Benjamin Hardison, and to issue his certificates for the same, in conformity to the reports of the said Secretary of War; and that the said Caleb Brewster, Christian Wolfe, and Samuel Garretson, respectively, be placed on the list of pensioners, from the time, and in the manner also reported by the said Secretary.

ORDERED, That it be an instruction to the committee appointed to prepare and bring in a bill or bills for the relief of disabled soldiers and seamen, that they do insert a clause or clauses pursuant to the said resolution.[126]

A petition of the inspectors of dutiable articles at the ports of Boston and Charlestown, in the state of Massachusetts, was presented to the House and read, complaining of the insufficiency of the fees allowed by law for their services, and praying a farther compensation for the same.

DNA. On June 29 the House agreed to a resolution on this report, and the resolution was referred to the committee on the revenue laws.

[125] On July 15 this committee presented the Virginia Cession Bill [HR–15], which was read twice.

[126] On July 16 this committee presented the Disabled Soldiers and Seamen Bill [HR–88], which was read.

ORDERED, That the said petition be referred to the committee appointed to prepare and bring in a bill or bills to amend the laws of revenue.[127]

Mr. Parker, from the committee to whom was referred the petition of Francis Mentges, made a report, which was read and ordered to lie on the table.[128]

A memorial of Louis Pierre Lombart de la Neuville, brigadier-general of the late army of the United States, and lieutenant-colonel in the service of his Most Christian Majesty, was presented to the House and read, praying the liquidation and settlement of a claim for military services rendered during the late war.

ORDERED, That the said memorial do lie on the table.

The orders of the day were read, and postponed until to-morrow.

And then the House adjourned until to-morrow morning ten o'clock.

TUESDAY, JUNE 29, 1790

An engrossed bill for giving effect to an act providing for the enumeration of the inhabitants of the United States, in respect to the state of Rhode-Island and Providence Plantations, was read the third time, and a blank therein filled up.

RESOLVED, That the said bill do pass; and that the title be, "An act for giving effect to an act, intituled, 'An act providing for the enumeration of the inhabitants of the United States,' in respect to the state of Rhode-Island and Providence Plantations."

ORDERED, That the Clerk of this House do carry the said bill to the Senate, and desire their concurrence.[129]

Mr. Gilman, from the committee for inrolled bills, reported that the committee had examined three inrolled bills, one intituled, "An act providing the means of intercourse between the United States and foreign nations;"[130] another, intituled, "An act to satisfy the claims of John McCord against the United States;"[131] and another intituled, "An act for the relief of Nathaniel Twining,"[132] and had found the same to be truly inrolled: Whereupon,

Mr. Speaker signed the said inrolled bills.[133]

---

[127] On June 29 a resolution concerning duties on teas was referred to this committee.

[128] The name of Francis Mentges is in error. The report is on the petition of Basil Middleton. A copy of the report is in A Record of the Reports of Select Committees, HR, DNA.

[129] The Senate read this bill on June 29 and 30, and on July 1 the bill was read again and agreed to.

[130] The inspected enrolled bill is in Enrolled Acts, RG 11, DNA. E-46055.

[131] The inspected enrolled bill is in Enrolled Acts, RG 11, DNA. E-46074.

[132] The inspected enrolled bill is in Enrolled Acts, RG 11, DNA.

[133] On June 30 these bills were presented to the president.

ORDERED, That the clerk of this House do acquaint the Senate therewith.

A message from the Senate by Mr. Otis their Secretary.

MR. SPEAKER,   The Senate have passed the bill, intituled, "An act to authorize the purchase of a tract of land for the use of the United States:"[134] And then he withdrew.

Mr. Fitzsimons, from the committee appointed to report a plan making provision for the payment of interest on the debts of the United States, made a report, which was read, and ordered to be committed to a committee of the whole House to-morrow.[135]

The House proceeded to consider the report of the committee to whom was referred the petition of Elias Hasket Derby: Whereupon,

RESOLVED, That for the duty on all teas, which have been imported from China in the present year, or which shall hereafter be imported, it shall be at the option of the importer, either to deposit such teas with the officer of the customs where the same shall be entered, or to give bond therefor with sureties to the satisfaction of the officer, payable at the expiration of twelve months from the time of entry: PROVIDED, That where the teas shall be deposited as aforesaid, they shall be kept at the risk and expence of the importer, who shall pay the duties thereon as the same shall be delivered: AND PROVIDED, That if the whole of the duties shall not be paid within eighteen months, the officer with whom such tea is deposited shall dispose of the same, or so much thereof, at public auction, as may be sufficient to pay the duties.

ORDERED, That the said resolution be referred to the committee appointed to prepare and bring in a bill or bills to amend the laws of revenue.[136]

A petition of Jacob Rash, of Lenox, in the state of Massachusetts, was presented to the House and read, praying that duplicates may be granted him of certain certificates of final settlement, amounting to two hundred and sixty-five dollars, the property of the petitioner, which were destroyed by fire in the year one thousand seven hundred and eighty-five.

ORDERED, That the said petition be referred to the Secretary of the Treasury, with instruction to examine the same, and report his opinion thereupon to the House.

On a motion made and seconded, that the committee of the whole House be discharged from further proceeding on the bill concerning the trade and navigation of the United States,

---

[134] On July 2 this bill was signed by the speaker and the vice president.

[135] This report is E–46026. On June 30 this report was considered in the COWH.

[136] On July 8 this committee presented the Collection Bill [HR–82], which was read twice. On July 22 this committee presented a Coasting Bill [HR–89], which was read twice.

It passed in the negative.

The House then, according to the order of the day, again resolved itself into a committee of the whole House on the said bill.

Mr. Speaker left the chair.

Mr. Boudinot took the chair of the committee.

Mr. Speaker resumed the chair, and Mr. Boudinot reported, that the committee had, according to order, again had the said bill under consideration, and made a farther progress therein.

RESOLVED, That this House will, to-morrow, again resolve itself into a committee of the whole House on the said bill.[137]

Mr. Hiester, from the committee appointed, presented, according to order, a bill further to provide for the payment of the invalid pensioners of the United States, which was received and read the first time.[138]

The orders of the day were farther postponed until to-morrow.

And then the House adjourned until to-morrow morning ten o'clock.

WEDNESDAY, JUNE 30, 1790

A bill further to provide for the payment of the invalid pensioners of the United States, was read the second time, and ordered to be engrossed, and read the third time to-morrow.[139]

Mr. Gilman, from the joint committee for inrolled bills, reported, that the committee did, this day, wait on the President of the United States, and present for his approbation, three inrolled bills, one intituled, "An act providing the means of intercourse between the United States and foreign nations;" another, intituled, "An act to satisfy the claims of John McCord against the United States," and another, intituled, "An act for the relief of Nathaniel Twining."[140]

The House, according to the order of the day, again resolved itself into a committee of the whole House on the bill concerning the trade and navigation of the United States.

Mr. Speaker left the chair.

Mr. Boudinot took the chair of the committee.

Mr. Speaker resumed the chair, and Mr. Boudinot reported, that the committee had, according to order, again had the said bill under consideration, and made a farther progress therein.

---

[137] On June 30 the COWH considered this bill again.
[138] On June 30 this bill was read again.
[139] On July 1 this bill was read again, agreed to, and sent to the Senate.
[140] On July 1 the president signed all of these bills.

RESOLVED, That this House will, to-morrow, again resolve itself into a committee of the whole House on the said bill.[141]

A message, in writing, was received from the President of the United States, by Mr. Lear his Secretary, as followeth:

UNITED STATES, June 30th, 1790

GENTLEMEN of the SENATE and HOUSE of REPRESENTATIVES,

AN act of the legislature of the state of Rhode-Island and Providence Plantations, for ratifying certain articles as amendments to the Constitution of the United States, was yesterday put into my hands, and I have directed my Secretary to lay a copy of the same before you.

G. WASHINGTON[142]

The papers accompanying the said message, were read, and ordered to lie on the table.

A petition of Thomas Ruston, in behalf of the managers of a cotton manufactory in the city of Philadelphia, was presented to the House and read, praying the attention of Congress to that branch of manufacture, and that an additional duty may be laid on the importation of cotton cloths.

ORDERED, That the said petition do lie on the table.

The House, according to the order of the day, resolved itself into a committee of the whole House on the report of the committee making provision for the payment of interest on the debts of the United States.

Mr. Speaker left the chair.

Mr. Boudinot took the chair of the committee.

Mr. Speaker resumed the chair, and Mr. Boudinot reported, that the committee had, according to order, had the said report under consideration, and made some progress therein.

RESOLVED, That this House will, to-morrow, again resolve itself into a committee of the whole House on the said report.[143]

The orders of the day were farther postponed until to-morrow.

And then the House adjourned until to-morrow morning ten o'clock.

---

[141] The House did not consider this bill again.

[142] The message with enclosures is in President's Messages: Suggesting legislation, SR, DNA. The enclosures are printed in the Appendix to the Second Session. The ratification is E–22845.

[143] On July 1 the COWH reported several resolutions on this report.

THURSDAY, JULY 1, 1790

An engrossed bill further to provide for the payment of the invalid pensioners of the United States, was read the third time.

RESOLVED, That the said bill do pass; and that the title be "An act further to provide for the payment of the invalid pensioners of the United States."

ORDERED, That the Clerk of this House do carry the said bill to the Senate, and desire their concurrence.[1]

A petition of John Fitch was presented to the House and read, praying that an exclusive right may be granted him to the use of steam to navigation in the United States, for a limited time.[2]

ORDERED, That the said petition do lie on the table.

Mr. Boudinot, from the committee appointed, presented, according to order, a bill more effectually to provide for the national defence, by establishing a uniform militia throughout the United States, which was received, and read the first time.

On motion,

The said bill was read the second time, and ordered to be committed to a committee of the whole House on the state of the Union.[3]

A message was received from the President of the United States, by Mr. Lear his Secretary, notifying that the President did this day approve and sign three acts; one intituled, "An act providing the means of intercourse between the United States and foreign nations;" another intituled, "An act to satisfy the claims of John McCord against the United States;" and another intituled, "An act for the relief of Nathaniel Twining."

A petition of Peter Anspach, of the city of New-York, in behalf of Timothy Pickering, late quartermaster-general of the armies of the United States, was presented to the House and read, praying the liquidation and settlement of a claim of the said Timothy Pickering against the United States.[4]

ORDERED, That the said petition be referred to the Secretary of the Treasury, with instruction to examine the same, and report his opinion thereupon to the House.

Mr. Gerry, from the committee appointed to consider and report whether any, and what fees, perquisites or other emoluments shall be annexed to the

---

[1] The Senate read this bill on July 2, 6, and 7. On July 7 the bill was agreed to with an amendment. The House was notified of this action on July 8.

[2] The petition is in Petitions and Memorials: Various subjects, SR, DNA.

[3] This bill was not considered again.

[4] A draft of the petition is in the Timothy Pickering Papers, MSaE.

offices of consul and vice-consul, made a report, which was read, and ordered to lie on the table.[5]

A message from the Senate by Mr. Otis their Secretary.

MR. SPEAKER, The Senate have passed the bill, intituled, "An act for giving effect to an act, intituled, 'An act providing for the enumeration of the inhabitants of the United States,' in respect to the state of Rhode-Island and Providence Plantations:"[6] And then he withdrew.

The Speaker laid before the House a letter and reports from the Secretary at War, on the several petitions of John Baylor, Anthony Walton White, and Stephen Steward, which were read, and ordered to lie on the table.[7]

The House proceeded to consider the report of the committee to whom was referred the memorial of Thomas Barclay: Whereupon,

ORDERED, That the said report be re-committed to Mr. Page, Mr. Clymer, and Mr. Sinnickson.[8]

The House, according to the order of the day, again resolved itself into a committee of the whole House, on the report of the committee making provision for the payment of interest on the debts of the United States.

Mr. Speaker left the chair.

Mr. Boudinot took the chair of the committee.

Mr. Speaker resumed the chair, and Mr. Boudinot reported, that the committee had, according to order, again had the said report under consideration, and come to several resolutions thereupon, which he delivered in at the Clerk's table, where the same were read, and ordered to lie on the table.[9]

The orders of the day were farther postponed until to-morrow.

And then the House adjourned until to-morrow morning ten o'clock.

FRIDAY, JULY 2, 1790

Mr. Gilman, from the joint committee for inrolled bills, reported, that the committee had examined two inrolled bills; one intituled, "An act for giving effect to an act, intituled, 'An act providing for the enumeration of

---

[5] A copy of the report is in A Record of the Reports of Select Committees, HR, DNA. On July 2 this committee report was considered, and a committee was appointed to bring in a bill on this topic. On the same day this committee was further instructed.

[6] On July 2 this bill was signed by the speaker and the vice president.

[7] A copy of the report on these three petitions is in A Record of the Reports of the Secretary of War, vol. 1, HR, DNA. On July 2 these reports were considered and committed.

[8] On July 24 this committee reported again.

[9] On July 2 these resolutions, which are printed in the Journal, were agreed to, and a committee was appointed to prepare a bill on them.

the inhabitants of the United States,' in respect to the state of Rhode-Island and Providence Plantations;"[10] the other intituled, "An act to authorize the purchase of a tract of land for the use of the United States,"[11] and had found the same to be truly inrolled; Whereupon,

Mr. Speaker signed the said inrolled bills.[12]

ORDERED, That the Clerk of this House do acquaint the Senate therewith.

A petition of Jabez Champlin, of Newport, in the state of Rhode-Island, was presented to the House and read, praying the liquidation and settlement of a claim against the United States.

ORDERED, That the said petition be referred to the Secretary of the Treasury, with instruction to examine the same, and report his opinion thereupon to the House.

A message from the Senate by Mr. Otis their Secretary.

MR. SPEAKER, The Senate have passed the bill, intituled, "An act for establishing the temporary and permanent seat of the government of the United States,"[13] to which they desire the concurrence of this House: And then he withdrew.

The said bill was read the first time.

On motion,

The said bill was read the second time, and ordered to be committed to a committee of the whole House on Tuesday next.[14]

The House proceeded to consider the resolutions reported yesterday from the committee of the whole House, making provision for the payment of interest on the debts of the United States: Whereupon,

RESOLVED, That an addition of thirty-three and one third cents be made to every one hundred cents of the duties now payable upon goods, wares and merchandizes imported into the United States.

That in addition to the foregoing there be levied and collected upon the following articles,

		CENTS
Distilled spirits ....per gallon.........		$1\frac{2}{3}$
Madeira wine ....per gallon.........		8
Other wines ....per gallon.........		5

[10] The inspected enrolled bill is in Enrolled Acts, RG 11, DNA. E–46034.

[11] The inspected enrolled bill is in Enrolled Acts, RG 11, DNA. E–46062.

[12] These bills were presented to the president on July 2 and signed by him on July 5.

[13] The bill is in Engrossed Senate Bills and Resolutions, SR, DNA.

[14] On July 16 the COWH considered this bill.

Molasses	per gallon	$\frac{1}{6}$
Bohea tea	per pound	2
Souchong and other black teas	per pound	$4\frac{1}{2}$
Hyson tea	per pound	$5\frac{1}{3}$
Other green teas	per pound	$4\frac{3}{4}$
Coffee	per pound	$\frac{3}{4}$
Brown sugar	per pound	$\frac{1}{6}$
Loaf sugar	per pound	1
All other sugars	per pound	$\frac{1}{2}$
Pepper	per pound	5
Pimento	per pound	3
Nutmegs	per pound	25
Mace	per pound	25
Cinnamon	per pound	20
Cloves	per pound	$12\frac{1}{2}$
Cassia	per pound	10

RESOLVED, That after the   day of   the discount of ten per cent. of the duties on goods, wares and merchandize imported in ships or vessels, the property of a citizen or citizens of the United States, be discontinued, and that an addition of ten per cent. be made to the duties on goods, wares or merchandize imported in any other ship or vessel.

ORDERED, That a bill or bills be brought in pursuant to the said resolutions; and that Mr. Fitzsimons, Mr. Tucker, and Mr. Sherman, do prepare and bring in the same.[15]

The House proceeded to consider the report of the committee appointed to consider and report whether any, and what fees, perquisites, or other emoluments shall be annexed to the offices of consul and vice-consul: Whereupon,

RESOLVED, That it shall and may be lawful for all consuls and vice-consuls of the United States, for every protest or deposition, relative to letters of attorney, goods, wares and merchandize, bills of exchange, and other marine and mercantile affairs and transactions, with a certificate thereof, under their hands and seals, respectively, to receive the sum of   dollars.

That citizens of the United States, appointed to reside in foreign ports and places, as consuls or vice-consuls of the United States, shall be enabled to own any ships or vessels in their own names, or in partnership with any other citizen of the United States, residing within the said States, and be entitled to all the privileges and advantages, in respect to such ships or vessels, as if

---

[15] On July 13 this committee presented a Ways and Means Bill [HR-83], which was read.

such consuls or vice-consuls, respectively owning said ships or vessels, actually resided within any port or place within the United States.

ORDERED, That a bill or bills be brought in pursuant to the said resolution, and that Mr. Gerry, Mr. Boudinot, Mr. Huntington, Mr. Wadsworth, and Mr. Goodhue, do prepare and bring in the same.

ORDERED, That it be referred to the said committee, to report a provision, "That in foreign ports, where the laws of the kingdom or state make it necessary that vessels should enter by the medium of a consul, and where the laws of such kingdom or state have determined that certain fees shall be paid to such consuls, the consul of the United States shall be authorized to receive such fees; and also to report what further provision may in the opinion of the said committee, be necessary for consuls and vice-consuls of the United States.[16]

The House proceeded to consider the reports of the Secretary at War, made yesterday, on the several petitions of John Baylor, Anthony Walton White, and Stephen Steward: Whereupon,

ORDERED, That the said reports be committed to Mr. Baldwin, Mr. Steele, and Mr. Foster.[17]

ORDERED, That Mr. Benson have leave to be absent from the service of this House until this day fortnight.

The orders of the day were farther postponed until Monday next.

And then the House adjourned until Monday morning ten o'clock.

MONDAY, JULY 5, 1790

A petition of the persons confined for debt in the gaol of the city and county of New-York, was presented to the House and read, praying that a general bankrupt law may be passed, upon such principles as will tend to relieve the petitioners, and all others in a similar situation.

ORDERED, That the said petition do lie on the table.

A petition of John Stewart and John Davidson, of the city of Annapolis, in the state of Maryland, was presented to the House and read, praying that the duty on a quantity of salt imported by the petitioners, and which was casually destroyed in the month of April last, may be remitted to them.

ORDERED, That the said petition be referred to Mr. Stone, Mr. Silvester, and Mr. Coles, that they do examine the matter thereof, and report the same, with their opinion thereupon to the House.[18]

---

[16] On July 15 this committee presented the Consuls and Vice Consuls Bill [HR–86], which was read twice.

[17] On July 16 this committee reported.

[18] On July 24 this committee reported and was ordered to prepare a bill pursuant to the House resolution on the report.

The several orders of the day were farther postponed until to-morrow.
And then the House adjourned until to-morrow morning ten o'clock.

TUESDAY, JULY 6, 1790

Mr. Gilman, from the joint committee for inrolled bills, reported, that the committee did, on the second instant, wait on the President of the United States, and present for his approbation two inrolled bills, one intituled, "An act to authorize the purchase of a tract of land, for the use of the United States;" the other, intituled, "An act for giving effect to an act, intituled, 'An act providing for the enumeration of the inhabitants of the United States,' in respect to the state of Rhode-Island and Providence Plantations."

The House, according to the order of the day, resolved itself into a committee of the whole House, on the bill sent from the Senate, intituled, "An act for establishing the temporary and permanent seat of the government of the United States."

Mr. Speaker left the chair.

Mr. Boudinot took the chair of the committee.

Mr. Speaker resumed the chair, and Mr. Boudinot reported, that the committee had, according to order, had the said bill under consideration, and made some progress therein.

RESOLVED, That this House will, to-morrow, again resolve itself into a committee of the whole House on the said bill.[19]

A message was received from the President of the United States, by Mr. Lear his Secretary, notifying that the President did, yesterday, approve and sign two acts; one, intituled, "An act for giving effect to an act, intituled, 'An act providing for the enumeration of the inhabitants of the United States,' in respect to the state of Rhode-Island and Providence Plantations;" the other, intituled, "An act to authorize the purchase of a tract of land, for the use of the United States."

The several orders of the day, were farther postponed until to-morrow.

And then the House adjourned until to-morrow morning ten o'clock.

WEDNESDAY, JULY 7, 1790

A message from the Senate by Mr. Otis their Secretary.

MR. SPEAKER,   The Senate have disagreed to the bill, intituled, "An act to satisfy the claim of the representatives of David Gould, deceased, against the United States." The Senate have also passed the bill, intituled, "An act to establish the post-office and post-roads within the United States," with several

---

[19] On July 7 the COWH considered this bill again.

amendments, to which they desire the concurrence of this House:[20]   And then he withdrew.

The House, according to the order of the day, again resolved itself into a committee of the whole House, on the bill sent from the Senate, intituled, "An act for establishing the temporary and permanent seat of the government of the United States."

Mr. Speaker left the chair.

Mr. Boudinot took the chair of the committee.

Mr. Speaker resumed the chair, and Mr. Boudinot reported, that the committee had, according to order, again had the said bill under consideration, and made a farther progress therein.

RESOLVED, That this House will, to-morrow, again resolve itself into a committee of the whole House on the said bill.[21]

The several orders of the day were farther postponed until to-morrow.

And then the House adjourned until to-morrow morning ten o'clock.

THURSDAY, JULY 8, 1790

A message from the Senate by Mr. Otis their Secretary.

MR. SPEAKER,   The Senate have disagreed to the bill, intituled, "An act to authorize the issuing of certificates to a certain description of invalid officers:" The Senate have also passed the bill, intituled, "An act further to provide for the payment of the invalid pensioners of the United States," with an amendment, to which they desire the concurrence of this House:[22]   And then he withdrew.

The House, according to the order of the day, again resolved itself into a committee of the whole House, on the bill sent from the Senate, intituled, "An act for establishing the temporary and permanent seat of the government of the United States."

Mr. Speaker left the chair.

Mr. Boudinot took the chair of the committee.

Mr. Speaker resumed the chair, and Mr. Boudinot reported, that the com-

---

[20] The Senate committee report on this bill, with amendments, is in Various Select Committee Reports, SR, DNA. Senate amendments are filed with and noted on the bill in House Bills, SR, DNA. The amendments are printed in the *Senate Legislative Journal* on July 6. On July 8 the House considered these amendments.

[21] On July 8 the COWH considered this bill again.

[22] The amendment is printed in the *Senate Legislative Journal* on July 7. On July 9 the House agreed to this Senate amendment.

mittee had, according to order, again had the said bill under consideration, and gone through the same, and made no amendment thereto.

ORDERED, That the said bill do lie on the table.[23]

Mr. Goodhue, from the committee appointed,[24] presented, according to order, a bill to regulate the collection of the duties imposed by law on goods, wares and merchandizes imported into the United States, and on the tonnage of ships or vessels, which was received, and read the first time.

On motion,

The said bill was read the second time, and ordered to be committed to a committee of the whole House on Monday next.[25]

The House proceeded to consider the amendments proposed by the Senate to the bill, intituled, "An act to establish the post-office and post-roads within the United States," and made some progress therein.

ORDERED, That the farther consideration of the said amendments be put off until to-morrow.[26]

The several orders of the day were farther postponed until to-morrow.

And then the House adjourned until to-morrow morning ten o'clock.

FRIDAY, JULY 9, 1790

The House proceeded to consider the amendment proposed by the Senate to the bill, intituled, "An act further to provide for the payment of the invalid pensioners of the United States," and the same being read, was agreed to.

ORDERED, That the Clerk of this House do acquaint the Senate therewith.[27]

A message from the Senate by Mr. Otis their Secretary.

MR. SPEAKER,   The Senate have passed the bill, intituled, "An act for the government and regulation of seamen in the merchants service," with several amendments, to which they desire the concurrence of this House:[28]   And then he withdrew.

---

[23] On July 9 this bill was considered on the House floor, and several motions to amend it were disagreed to by roll call vote. On the same day the bill was agreed to by the House.

[24] This committee is the committee on laws of revenue, which was appointed on April 23. The members were Elias Boudinot, Thomas Fitzsimons, Benjamin Goodhue, Richard B. Lee, and John Laurance.

[25] On July 12 the COWH reported amendments to this bill.

[26] On July 10 the House agreed to some of the Senate amendments and disagreed to others.

[27] On July 12 this bill was signed by the speaker and vice president.

[28] The Senate committee report on this bill, with amendments, is in Various Select Committee Reports, SR, DNA. The amendments are printed in the *Senate Legislative Journal* on July 8. On July 10 the House agreed to some of these Senate amendments and disagreed to one.

The House proceeded to consider the bill sent from the Senate, intituled, "An act for establishing the temporary and permanent seat of the government of the United States," which lay on the table: Whereupon,

A motion being made and seconded, to amend the said bill by striking out in the first section, the words "Potowmack, at some place between the mouths of the eastern branch and Connogocheque," and inserting in lieu thereof, the words "Delaware, at a place not more than eight miles above, and sixty miles below the falls thereof."

It passed in the negative, $\begin{cases} \text{AYES} & 22 \\ \text{NOES} & 39 \end{cases}$

The ayes and noes being demanded by one fifth of the members present, Those who voted in the affirmative, are,

Fisher Ames	George Leonard
Egbert Benson	Samuel Livermore
Elias Boudinot	George Partridge
William Floyd	Jeremiah Van Rensselaer
Abiel Foster	James Schureman
Elbridge Gerry	Theodore Sedgwick
Benjamin Goodhue	Roger Sherman
Jonathan Grout	Peter Silvester
John Hathorn	Jonathan Sturges
Benjamin Huntington	Jonathan Trumbull and
John Laurance	Jeremiah Wadsworth

Those who voted in the negative, are,

John Baptista Ashe	Daniel Hiester
Abraham Baldwin	James Jackson
Timothy Bloodworth	Richard Bland Lee
John Brown	James Madison, junior
Aedanus Burke	George Mathews
Lambert Cadwalader	Andrew Moore
Daniel Carroll	Peter Muhlenberg
George Clymer	John Page
Isaac Coles	Josiah Parker
Benjamin Contee	Thomas Scott
Thomas Fitzsimons	Joshua Seney
George Gale	John Sevier
Nicholas Gilman	Thomas Sinnickson
Samuel Griffin	William Smith (of Maryland)
Thomas Hartley	William Smith (of South-Carolina)

John Steele   John Vining
Michael Jenifer Stone   Alexander White
Thomas Sumter   Hugh Williamson and
George Thatcher   Henry Wynkoop
Thomas Tudor Tucker

Another motion was then made and seconded, to amend the said bill by striking out in the said first section, the words "on the river Potowmack, at some place between the mouths of the eastern branch and Connogocheque," and inserting in lieu thereof, the words "in the state of Pennsylvania, including Germantown:" And on the question thereupon,

It passed in the negative, $\begin{cases} \text{AYES} & 22 \\ \text{NOES} & 39 \end{cases}$

The ayes and noes being demanded by one fifth of the members present, Those who voted in the affirmative, are,

Fisher Ames   John Laurance
Egbert Benson   George Leonard
Elias Boudinot   Samuel Livermore
William Floyd   George Partridge
Abiel Foster   Jeremiah Van Rensseiaer
Elbridge Gerry   James Schureman
Nicholas Gilman   Theodore Sedgwick
Benjamin Goodhue   Roger Sherman
Jonathan Grout   Peter Silvester
John Hathorn   Jonathan Sturges and
Benjamin Huntington   Jeremiah Wadsworth

Those who voted in the negative, are,

John Baptista Ashe   Samuel Griffin
Abraham Baldwin   Thomas Hartley
Timothy Bloodworth   Daniel Hiester
John Brown   James Jackson
Aedanus Burke   Richard Bland Lee
Lambert Cadwalader   James Madison, junior
Daniel Carroll   George Mathews
George Clymer   Andrew Moore
Isaac Coles   Peter Muhlenberg
Benjamin Contee   John Page
Thomas Fitzsimons   Josiah Parker
George Gale   Thomas Scott

Joshua Seney
John Sevier
Thomas Sinnickson
William Smith (of Maryland)
William Smith (of South-
Carolina)
John Steele
Michael Jenifer Stone

Thomas Sumter
George Thatcher
Jonathan Trumbull
Thomas Tudor Tucker
John Vining
Alexander White
Hugh Williamson and
Henry Wynkoop

Another motion was then made and seconded, to amend the said bill by striking out in the said first section, the words "on the river Potowmack, at some place between the mouths of the eastern branch and Connogocheque," and inserting in lieu thereof, the words, "between the rivers Susquehannah and Potowmack, at the most healthy and convenient place, having due regard to the navigation of the Atlantic ocean, and the situation of the western territory:" And on the question thereupon,

It passed in the negative, $\begin{cases} \text{AYES} & 25 \\ \text{NOES} & 36 \end{cases}$

The ayes and noes being demanded by one fifth of the members present, Those who voted in the affirmative, are,

Fisher Ames
Egbert Benson
Elias Boudinot
William Floyd
Abiel Foster
Elbridge Gerry
Benjamin Goodhue
Jonathan Grout
John Hathorn
Benjamin Huntington
John Laurance
George Leonard
Samuel Livermore

George Partridge
Jeremiah Van Rensselaer
James Schureman
Theodore Sedgwick
Joshua Seney
Peter Silvester
William Smith (of Maryland)
William Smith (of South-Carolina)
Jonathan Sturges
George Thatcher
Jonathan Trumbull and
Jeremiah Wadsworth

Those who voted in the negative, are,

John Baptista Ashe
Abraham Baldwin
Timothy Bloodworth
John Brown
Aedanus Burke

Lambert Cadwalader
Daniel Carroll
George Clymer
Isaac Coles
Benjamin Contee

Thomas Fitzsimons
George Gale
Nicholas Gilman
Samuel Griffin
Thomas Hartley
Daniel Hiester
James Jackson
Richard Bland Lee
James Madison, junior
George Mathews
Andrew Moore
Peter Muhlenberg
John Page

Josiah Parker
Thomas Scott
John Sevier
Roger Sherman
Thomas Sinnickson
John Steele
Michael Jenifer Stone
Thomas Sumter
Thomas Tudor Tucker
John Vining
Alexander White
Hugh Williamson and
Henry Wynkoop

Another motion was then made and seconded, to amend the said bill by striking out in the said first section, the words "on the river Potowmack, at some place between the mouths of the eastern branch and Connogocheque," and inserting in lieu thereof, the words "in the state of Maryland, including the town of Baltimore."

A division of the motion was called for; and on the question for striking out in the said first section, the words "on the river Potowmack, at some place between the mouths of the eastern branch and Connogocheque,"

It passed in the negative, $\begin{cases} \text{AYES} & 26 \\ \text{NOES} & 34 \end{cases}$

The ayes and noes being demanded by one fifth of the members present, Those who voted in the affirmative, are,

Fisher Ames
Egbert Benson
Elias Boudinot
William Floyd
Abiel Foster
Elbridge Gerry
Benjamin Goodhue
Jonathan Grout
John Hathorn
Benjamin Huntington
John Laurance
George Leonard
Samuel Livermore

George Partridge
Jeremiah Van Rensselaer
James Schureman
Theodore Sedgwick
Joshua Seney
Roger Sherman
Peter Silvester
William Smith (of Maryland)
William Smith (of South-Carolina)
Jonathan Sturges
George Thatcher
Jonathan Trumbull and
Jeremiah Wadsworth

Those who voted in the negative, are,

John Baptista Ashe
Abraham Baldwin
Timothy Bloodworth
John Brown
Lambert Cadwalader
Daniel Carroll
George Clymer
Isaac Coles
Benjamin Contee
Thomas Fitzsimons
George Gale
Nicholas Gilman
Samuel Griffin
Thomas Hartley
Daniel Hiester
James Jackson
Richard Bland Lee

James Madison, junior
George Mathews
Andrew Moore
Peter Muhlenberg
John Page
Josiah Parker
Thomas Scott
John Sevier
Thomas Sinnickson
John Steele
Michael Jenifer Stone
Thomas Sumter
Thomas Tudor Tucker
John Vining
Alexander White
Hugh Williamson and
Henry Wynkoop

And so the said motion to amend was negatived.

Another motion was then made and seconded, to amend the said bill, by striking out in the third section, the words "purchase, or" and on the question thereupon,

It passed in the negative, $\begin{cases} \text{AYES } 26 \\ \text{NOES } 35 \end{cases}$

The ayes and noes being demanded by one fifth of the members present, Those who voted in the affirmative, are,

Fisher Ames
Egbert Benson
Elias Boudinot
William Floyd
Abiel Foster
Elbridge Gerry
Benjamin Goodhue
Jonathan Grout
John Hathorn
Benjamin Huntington
John Laurance
George Leonard
Samuel Livermore

George Partridge
Jeremiah Van Rensselaer
James Schureman
Theodore Sedgwick
Joshua Seney
Roger Sherman
Peter Silvester
William Smith (of Maryland)
William Smith (of South-Carolina)
Jonathan Sturges
George Thatcher
Jonathan Trumbull and
Jeremiah Wadsworth

Those who voted in the negative, are,

John Baptista Ashe
Abraham Baldwin
Timothy Bloodworth
John Brown
Aedanus Burke
Lambert Cadwalader
Daniel Carroll
George Clymer
Isaac Coles
Benjamin Contee
Thomas Fitzsimons
George Gale
Nicholas Gilman
Samuel Griffin
Thomas Hartley
Daniel Hiester
James Jackson
Richard Bland Lee

James Madison, junior
George Mathews
Andrew Moore
Peter Muhlenberg
John Page
Josiah Parker
Thomas Scott
John Sevier
Thomas Sinnickson
John Steele
Michael Jenifer Stone
Thomas Sumter
Thomas Tudor Tucker
John Vining
Alexander White
Hugh Williamson and
Henry Wynkoop

Another motion was then made and seconded, to amend the said bill, by inserting after the word "purchase," in the third section, the words "with such money only as may be granted to the President of the United States, in the manner herein after provided;" and on the question thereupon,

It passed in the negative, $\begin{cases} \text{AYES} & 26 \\ \text{NOES} & 33 \end{cases}$

The ayes and noes being demanded by one fifth of the members present, Those who voted in the affirmative are,

Fisher Ames
Egbert Benson
Elias Boudinot
Aedanus Burke
William Floyd
Abiel Foster
Elbridge Gerry
Jonathan Grout
John Hathorn
Benjamin Huntington
John Laurance
George Leonard
Samuel Livermore

George Partridge
Jeremiah Van Rensselaer
James Schureman
Theodore Sedgwick
Joshua Seney
Roger Sherman
Peter Silvester
William Smith (of Maryland)
William Smith (of South-Carolina)
Jonathan Sturges
George Thatcher
Jonathan Trumbull and
Jeremiah Wadsworth

Those who voted in the negative, are,

John Baptista Ashe
Abraham Baldwin
John Brown
Lambert Cadwalader
Daniel Carroll
George Clymer
Isaac Coles
Benjamin Contee
Thomas Fitzsimons
George Gale
Nicholas Gilman
Samuel Griffin
Thomas Hartley
Daniel Hiester
James Jackson
Richard Bland Lee
James Madison, junior

George Mathews
Andrew Moore
Peter Muhlenberg
John Page
Josiah Parker
Thomas Scott
John Sevier
Thomas Sinnickson
John Steele
Michael Jenifer Stone
Thomas Sumter
Thomas Tudor Tucker
John Vining
Alexander White
Hugh Williamson and
Henry Wynkoop

Another motion was then made and seconded, to amend the said bill by adding to the end of the third section the words following: "*Provided*, That the purchases and buildings aforesaid shall not exceed the sum of dollars:"   And on the question thereupon,

It passed in the negative, $\begin{cases} \text{AYES } 26 \\ \text{NOES } 32 \end{cases}$

The ayes and noes being demanded by one fifth of the members present, Those who voted in the affirmative, are,

Fisher Ames
Egbert Benson
Elias Boudinot
Aedanus Burke
William Floyd
Abiel Foster
Elbridge Gerry
Jonathan Grout
John Hathorn
Benjamin Huntington
John Laurance
George Leonard
Samuel Livermore

Jeremiah Van Rensselaer
James Schureman
Theodore Sedgwick
Joshua Seney
Roger Sherman
Peter Silvester
William Smith (of Maryland)
William Smith (of South-Carolina)
Jonathan Sturges
George Thatcher
Jonathan Trumbull and
Jeremiah Wadsworth

Those who voted in the negative, are,

John Baptista Ashe	George Mathews
John Brown	Andrew Moore
Lambert Cadwalader	Peter Muhlenberg
Daniel Carroll	John Page
George Clymer	Josiah Parker
Isaac Coles	Thomas Scott
Benjamin Contee	John Sevier
Thomas Fitzsimons	Thomas Sinnickson
George Gale	John Steele
Nicholas Gilman	Michael Jenifer Stone
Samuel Griffin	Thomas Sumter
Thomas Hartley	Thomas Tudor Tucker
Daniel Hiester	John Vining
James Jackson	Alexander White
Richard Bland Lee	Hugh Williamson and
James Madison, junior	Henry Wynkoop

Another motion was then made and seconded to amend the said bill by striking out the fifth section, in the words following, to wit:

"*And be it enacted*, That prior to the first Monday in December next, all offices attached to the seat of the government of the United States, shall be removed to, and until the said first Monday in December, in the year one thousand eight hundred, shall remain at the city of Philadelphia, in the state of Pennsylvania, at which place the session of Congress next ensuing the present shall be held," and on the question thereupon,

It passed in the negative, $\begin{cases} \text{AYES } 28 \\ \text{NOES } 33 \end{cases}$

The ayes and noes being demanded by one fifth of the members present, Those who voted in the affirmative, are,

Fisher Ames	Benjamin Huntington
Egbert Benson	John Laurance
Timothy Bloodworth	George Leonard
Elias Boudinot	Samuel Livermore
Aedanus Burke	George Partridge
William Floyd	Jeremiah Van Rensselaer
Abiel Foster	James Schureman
Elbridge Gerry	Theodore Sedgwick
Jonathan Grout	Joshua Seney
John Hathorn	Roger Sherman

Peter Silvester   George Thatcher
William Smith (of Maryland)   Jonathan Trumbull
William Smith (of South-   Thomas Tudor Tucker and
    Carolina)   Jeremiah Wadsworth
Jonathan Sturges

Those who voted in the negative, are,

John Baptista Ashe   James Madison, junior
Abraham Baldwin   George Mathews
John Brown   Andrew Moore
Lambert Cadwalader   Peter Muhlenberg
Daniel Carroll   John Page
George Clymer   Josiah Parker
Isaac Coles   Thomas Scott
Benjamin Contee   John Sevier
Thomas Fitzsimons   Thomas Sinnickson
George Gale   John Steele
Nicholas Gilman   Michael Jenifer Stone
Benjamin Goodhue   Thomas Sumter
Samuel Griffin   John Vining
Thomas Hartley   Alexander White
Daniel Hiester   Hugh Williamson and
James Jackson   Henry Wynkoop
Richard Bland Lee

Another motion was then made and seconded, to amend the said bill, by
striking out, in the fifth section, the words "December next," and inserting
in lieu thereof, the words "May, one thousand seven hundred and ninety-
two,"   and on the question thereupon,

It passed in the negative, $\begin{cases} \text{AYES } 28 \\ \text{NOES } 32 \end{cases}$

The ayes and noes being demanded by one fifth of the members present,
Those who voted in the affirmative, are,

Fisher Ames   Elbridge Gerry
Egbert Benson   Jonathan Grout
Timothy Bloodworth   John Hathorn
Elias Boudinot   Benjamin Huntington
Aedanus Burke   John Laurance
William Floyd   George Leonard
Abiel Foster   Samuel Livermore

George Partridge
Jeremiah Van Rensselaer
James Schureman
Theodore Sedgwick
Joshua Seney
Roger Sherman
Peter Silvester

William Smith (of Maryland)
William Smith (of South-Carolina)
Jonathan Sturges
George Thatcher
Jonathan Trumbull
Thomas Tudor Tucker and
Jeremiah Wadsworth

Those who voted in the negative, are,

John Baptista Ashe
Abraham Baldwin
John Brown
Lambert Cadwalader
Daniel Carroll
George Clymer
Isaac Coles
Benjamin Contee
Thomas Fitzsimons
George Gale
Nicholas Gilman
Samuel Griffin
Thomas Hartley
Daniel Hiester
James Jackson
Richard Bland Lee

James Madison, junior
George Mathews
Andrew Moore
Peter Muhlenberg
John Page
Josiah Parker
Thomas Scott
John Sevier
Thomas Sinnickson
John Steele
Michael Jenifer Stone
Thomas Sumter
John Vining
Alexander White
Hugh Williamson and
Henry Wynkoop

Another motion was then made and seconded, to amend the said bill, by striking out in the fifth section, the word "December," and inserting in lieu thereof, the word "May," and on the question thereupon,

It passed in the negative, $\begin{cases} \text{AYES } 28 \\ \text{NOES } 33 \end{cases}$

The ayes and noes being demanded by one fifth of the members present, Those who voted in the affirmative, are,

Fisher Ames
Egbert Benson
Timothy Bloodworth
Elias Boudinot
Aedanus Burke
William Floyd
Abiel Foster

Elbridge Gerry
Jonathan Grout
John Hathorn
Benjamin Huntington
John Laurance
George Leonard
Samuel Livermore

George Partridge	William Smith (of Maryland)
Jeremiah Van Rensselaer	William Smith (of South-Carolina)
James Schureman	Jonathan Sturges
Theodore Sedgwick	George Thatcher
Joshua Seney	Jonathan Trumbull
Roger Sherman	Thomas Tudor Tucker and
Peter Silvester	Jeremiah Wadsworth

Those who voted in the negative, are,

John Baptista Ashe	James Madison, junior
Abraham Baldwin	George Mathews
John Brown	Andrew Moore
Lambert Cadwalader	Peter Muhlenberg
Daniel Carroll	John Page
George Clymer	Josiah Parker
Isaac Coles	Thomas Scott
Benjamin Contee	John Sevier
Thomas Fitzsimons	Thomas Sinnickson
George Gale	John Steele
Nicholas Gilman	Michael Jenifer Stone
Benjamin Goodhue	Thomas Sumter
Samuel Griffin	John Vining
Thomas Hartley	Alexander White
Daniel Hiester	Hugh Williamson and
James Jackson	Henry Wynkoop
Richard Bland Lee	

Another motion was then made and seconded, to amend the said bill, by striking out in the fifth section, the words "at which place the session of Congress next ensuing the present shall be held," and on the question thereupon,

It passed in the negative, $\begin{cases} \text{AYES} & 26 \\ \text{NOES} & 33 \end{cases}$

The ayes and noes being demanded by one fifth of the members present,
Those who voted in the affirmative, are,

Fisher Ames	Abiel Foster
Egbert Benson	Elbridge Gerry
Elias Boudinot	Jonathan Grout
Aedanus Burke	John Hathorn
William Floyd	Benjamin Huntington

John Laurance
George Leonard
Samuel Livermore
George Partridge
Jeremiah Van Rensselaer
Theodore Sedgwick
Joshua Seney
Roger Sherman

Peter Silvester
William Smith (of Maryland)
William Smith (of South-Carolina)
Jonathan Sturges
George Thatcher
Jonathan Trumbull
Thomas Tudor Tucker and
Jeremiah Wadsworth

Those who voted in the negative, are,

John Baptista Ashe
Abraham Baldwin
Timothy Bloodworth
John Brown
Lambert Cadwalader
Daniel Carroll
George Clymer
Isaac Coles
Benjamin Contee
Thomas Fitzsimons
George Gale
Nicholas Gilman
Samuel Griffin
Thomas Hartley
Daniel Hiester
James Jackson
Richard Bland Lee

James Madison, junior
George Mathews
Andrew Moore
Peter Muhlenberg
John Page
Josiah Parker
Thomas Scott
John Sevier
Thomas Sinnickson
John Steele
Michael Jenifer Stone
Thomas Sumter
John Vining
Alexander White
Hugh Williamson and
Henry Wynkoop

Another motion was then made and seconded, to amend the said bill, by adding to the end of the fifth section, the following proviso, to wit: "*Provided nevertheless*, That whenever the President of the United States shall receive authentic information that the public buildings aforesaid, are so far completed as to be fit for the reception of both Houses of Congress, all offices attached to the seat of government shall be removed thereto, any thing herein contained to the contrary notwithstanding," and on the question thereupon,

It passed in the negative, {AYES 13
{NOES 48

The ayes and noes being demanded by one fifth of the members present,
Those who voted in the affirmative, are,

Egbert Benson
Timothy Bloodworth
William Floyd
Elbridge Gerry
Jonathan Grout
John Laurance
Jeremiah Van Rensselaer

Joshua Seney
Peter Silvester
William Smith (of Maryland)
William Smith (of South-Carolina)
George Thatcher and
Thomas Tudor Tucker

Those who voted in the negative, are,

Fisher Ames
John Baptista Ashe
Abraham Baldwin
Elias Boudinot
John Brown
Aedanus Burke
Lambert Cadwalader
Daniel Carroll
George Clymer
Isaac Coles
Benjamin Contee
Thomas Fitzsimons
Abiel Foster
George Gale
Nicholas Gilman
Benjamin Goodhue
Samuel Griffin
Thomas Hartley
John Hathorn
Daniel Hiester
Benjamin Huntington
James Jackson
Richard Bland Lee
George Leonard

Samuel Livermore
James Madison, junior
George Mathews
Andrew Moore
Peter Muhlenberg
John Page
Josiah Parker
George Partridge
James Schureman
Thomas Scott
Theodore Sedgwick
John Sevier
Roger Sherman
Thomas Sinnickson
John Steele
Michael Jenifer Stone
Jonathan Sturges
Thomas Sumter
Jonathan Trumbull
John Vining
Jeremiah Wadsworth
Alexander White
Hugh Williamson and
Henry Wynkoop

A motion was then made and seconded, that the said bill be read the third time on Monday next; and on the question thereupon,

It passed in the negative.

Another motion was then made and seconded, that the said bill be read the third time to-morrow; and on the question thereupon,

It passed in the negative.

A motion was then made and seconded, to adjourn;   and on the question thereupon,

It passed in the negative.

A motion being then made and seconded, that the said bill be now read the third time;

It was resolved in the affirmative: Whereupon,

The said bill was read the third time.

And then the main question being put, that the said bill do pass,

It was resolved in the affirmative, $\begin{cases} \text{AYES} \;\; 32 \\ \text{NOES} \;\; 29 \end{cases}$

The ayes and noes being demanded by one fifth of the members present,

Those who voted in the affirmative, are,

John Baptista Ashe	James Madison, junior
Abraham Baldwin	George Mathews
Timothy Bloodworth	Andrew Moore
John Brown	Peter Muhlenberg
Lambert Cadwalader	John Page
Daniel Carroll	Josiah Parker
George Clymer	Thomas Scott
Isaac Coles	John Sevier
Benjamin Contee	Thomas Sinnickson
Thomas Fitzsimons	John Steele
George Gale	Michael Jenifer Stone
Samuel Griffin	Thomas Sumter
Thomas Hartley	John Vining
Daniel Hiester	Alexander White
James Jackson	Hugh Williamson and
Richard Bland Lee	Henry Wynkoop

Those who voted in the negative, are,

Fisher Ames	John Hathorn
Egbert Benson	Benjamin Huntington
Elias Boudinot	John Laurance
Aedanus Burke	George Leonard
William Floyd	Samuel Livermore
Abiel Foster	George Partridge
Elbridge Gerry	Jeremiah Van Rensselaer
Nicholas Gilman	James Schureman
Benjamin Goodhue	Theodore Sedgwick
Jonathan Grout	Joshua Seney

Roger Sherman   Jonathan Sturges
Peter Silvester   George Thatcher
William Smith (of Maryland)   Jonathan Trumbull
William Smith (of South-   Thomas Tudor Tucker and
    Carolina)   Jeremiah Wadsworth[29]

A message from the Senate, by Mr. Otis, their Secretary.

MR. SPEAKER,   The Senate have passed the bill, intituled "An act to regulate trade and intercourse with the Indian tribes," with several amendments, to which they desire the concurrence of this House:[30] The Senate have also passed the bill, intituled "An act to provide more effectually for the settlement of the accounts between the United States and the individual states," with several amendments, to which they desire the concurrence of this House:[31]   And then he withdrew.

The orders of the day were farther postponed until to-morrow.
And then the House adjourned until to-morrow morning eleven o'clock.

SATURDAY, JULY 10, 1790

The House proceeded to consider the amendments proposed by the Senate, to the bill, intituled "An act to regulate trade and intercourse with the Indian tribes," and the same being read, were agreed to.

ORDERED, That the Clerk of this House do acquaint the Senate therewith.[32]

The House proceeded to consider the amendments proposed by the Senate, to the bill, intituled "An act for the government and regulation of seamen

---

[29] On July 12 the speaker and vice president signed the Residence Bill [S–12].

[30] A copy of the amendments is in Senate Joint and Concurrent Resolutions, SR, DNA. The Senate committee report on this bill, with amendments, is in Various Select Committee Reports, SR, DNA. Senate amendments are also noted on the bill in House Bills, SR, DNA. The amendments are printed in the *Senate Legislative Journal* on July 9. On July 10 the House agreed to the Senate amendments and notified the Senate.

[31] The Senate committee report on this bill, with amendments, is in Various Select Committee Reports, SR, DNA. Senate amendments are filed with and noted on the bill in House Bills, SR, DNA. In the same location there is a Senate printing of this bill marked to conform to the bill as amended and passed by the Senate. The amendments are printed in the *Senate Legislative Journal* on July 9. On July 13 these amendments were considered.

[32] On July 12 the Senate notified the House that a mistake had been made in the list of Senate amendments sent to the House, and one amendment had been omitted. On the same day the House disagreed to this amendment, and the Senate insisted upon it.

in the merchants service," and the same being read, some were agreed to, and others disagreed to.[33]

ORDERED, That the Clerk of this House do acquaint the Senate therewith.[34]

The House resumed the consideration of the amendments proposed by the Senate, to the bill, intituled "An act to establish the post-office and post-roads within the United States," and the same being read, some were agreed to, and others disagreed to.

ORDERED, That the Clerk of this House do acquaint the Senate therewith.[35]

The several orders of the day were farther postponed until Monday next. And then the House adjourned until Monday morning ten o'clock.

MONDAY, JULY 12, 1790

A petition of the Clerks employed in the office of the Paymaster and Commissioner of army accounts, was presented to the House and read, praying that the salaries granted them by law may be augmented and made equal to those of the clerks in other executive departments of the United States.[36]

ORDERED, That the said petition do lie on the table.[37]

The petitions of Thomas Hart and Aquila Giles were presented to the House and read, respectively praying the liquidation and settlement of a claim against the United States.

ORDERED, That the said petitions be referred to the Secretary of the Treasury, with instruction to examine the same, and report his opinion thereupon to the House.

A petition of Thaddeus Beebe was presented to the House and read, praying to be placed on the list of invalids, in consideration of the loss of his sight, and other injuries sustained in the service of the United States during the late war.

ORDERED, That the said petition be referred to the Secretary at War, with instruction to examine the same, and report his opinion thereupon to the House.

A petition of Seth Harding was presented to the House and read, praying compensation for sundry services rendered in the navy of the United States, during the late war.

---

[33] According to other entries in this Journal and the *Senate Legislative Journal*, only one amendment was disagreed to.

[34] On July 12 the Senate receded from the amendment disagreed to by the House.

[35] On July 12 the Senate insisted upon the amendments disagreed to by the House and requested a conference.

[36] A petition of clerks in the office of the paymaster general and commissioner of army accounts, dated September 3, 1789, which probably is an earlier version of this petition, is in Petitions and Memorials: Various subjects, SR, DNA.

[37] On July 14 this petition was committed.

ORDERED, That the said petition be referred to Mr. Sturges, Mr. Hartley, and Mr. Burke, that they do examine the matter thereof, and report the same, with their opinion thereupon, to the House.[38]

Mr. Gilman, from the joint committee for inrolled bills, reported that the committee had examined two inrolled bills, one intituled, "An act further to provide for the payment of the invalid pensioners of the United States,"[39] the other intituled, "An act for establishing the temporary and permanent seat of the government of the United States,"[40] and had found the same to be truly inrolled: Whereupon,

Mr. Speaker signed the said inrolled bills.[41]

It being discovered that a mistake had been made in the message from the Senate on Friday last, respecting the amendments to the bill, intituled, "An act to regulate trade and intercourse with the Indian tribes," whereby an amendment proposed on the part of the Senate for striking out the fourth section of the said bill, in the words following, to wit:

"Sec. 4. *And be it further enacted*, That a sum not exceeding ten thousand dollars, be appropriated out of the monies arising from duties on imports and tonnage, subject to the orders of the President of the United States, to be laid out in goods and articles of trade, suitable for supplying the wants and necessities of the Indians, and to be vended and retailed to them through the agency of the said superintendants, and persons to be licensed by them for that purpose, in such manner, and conformably to such regulations, as the President of the United States shall establish," had been omitted.[42]

The House proceeded to consider the said amendment: Whereupon,

RESOLVED, That this House do disagree to the said amendment.

ORDERED, That the Clerk of this House do acquaint the Senate therewith.

The House, according to the order of the day, resolved itself into a committee of the whole House on the bill to regulate the collection of the duties, imposed on goods, wares and merchandize, imported into the United States, and on the tonnage of ships or vessels.

Mr. Speaker left the chair.

Mr. Boudinot took the chair of the committee.

Mr. Speaker resumed the chair, and Mr. Boudinot reported, that the committee had, according to order, had the said bill under consideration, and

---

[38] On July 27 this committee reported, and the House agreed to a resolution on part of the report and tabled the other part of it.

[39] The inspected enrolled bill is in Enrolled Acts, RG 11, DNA. E–46043.

[40] The inspected enrolled bill is in Enrolled Acts, RG 11, DNA. E–46032.

[41] On July 13 the committee on enrolled bills reported on presenting these bills to the president.

[42] A letter from Samuel A. Otis to the speaker, pointing out this error, is in Other Records: Various papers, SR, DNA.

made several amendments thereto, which they had directed him to report, when the House should think proper to receive the same.

ORDERED, That the said report be received to-morrow.[43]

A message from the Senate by Mr. Otis, their Secretary.

MR. SPEAKER,   The Senate have passed the bill, intituled, "An act imposing duties on the tonnage of ships or vessels;"[44] the Senate do also recede from their amendment disagreed to by this House, to the bill, intituled, "An act for the government and regulation of seamen, in the merchants service."[45] They do insist on their third amendment disagreed to by this House to the bill, intituled, "An act to regulate trade and intercourse with the Indian tribes:"[46] And they do also insist on their amendments disagreed to by this House, to the bill, intituled, "An act to establish the post-office and posts roads within the United States;" desire a conference with this House, on the subject matter of the said amendments, and have appointed managers at the same on their part:[47]   And then he withdrew.

The several orders of the day were farther postponed until to-morrow.

And then the House adjourned until to-morrow morning ten o'clock.

TUESDAY, JULY 13, 1790

Mr. Gilman, from the joint committee for inrolled bills, reported, that the committee did, on Monday last, wait on the President of the United States, and present for his approbation, two inrolled bills; one intituled, "An act further to provide for the payment of the invalid pensioners of the United States;" the other intituled, "An act for establishing the temporary and permanent seat of the government of the United States."[48]

The Speaker laid before the House a letter from the Secretary of State, covering his report of a proper plan or plans for establishing uniformity in the Currency, Weights, and Measures of the United States,[49] made pursuant

---

[43] On July 13 the COWH's amendments were agreed to by the House, and the bill was further amended.

[44] On July 17 this bill was signed by the speaker and the vice president and presented to the president.

[45] On July 17 this bill was signed by the speaker and the vice president and presented to the president.

[46] On July 13 the House adhered to its disagreement to the Senate amendment and requested a conference.

[47] On July 13 the House agreed to a conference on the Post Office Bill [HR–74].

[48] On July 16 the president signed both of these bills.

[49] Copies of the letter and the report are in A Record of the Reports of the Secretary of State, vol. 1, HR, DNA. E–22994, E–22995, E–22996, E–22997, E–23910.

to the order of this House, of the fifteenth of January last, which was read, and ordered to lie on the table.

Mr. Fitzsimons from the committee appointed, presented according to order, "A bill, making further provision for the payment of the debts of the United States," which was received, and read the first time.[50]

The House proceeded to consider the message from the Senate, desiring a conference on the subject matter of the amendments depending between the two Houses, to the bill, intituled, "An act to establish the post-office and post roads within the United States:" Whereupon,

RESOLVED, That this House do agree to the said conference, and that Mr. Gerry, Mr. Steele, Mr. Hartley, Mr. Vining and Mr. Burke, be appointed managers at the same, on the part of this House.

ORDERED, That the Clerk of this House do acquaint the Senate therewith.[51]

The House proceeded to re-consider the amendment disagreed to by this House, and insisted on by the Senate, to the bill, intituled, "An act to regulate trade and intercourse with the Indian tribes:" Whereupon,

RESOLVED, That this House do insist on their disagreement to the said amendment, and that a conference be desired with the Senate on the subject matter thereof.

ORDERED, That Mr. Madison, Mr. Scott, and Mr. Moore, be appointed managers at the said conference, on the part of this House.[52]

The House proceeded to consider the amendments made by the committee of the whole House, to the bill, "to regulate the collection of the duties imposed by law, on goods, wares and merchandize imported into the United States, and on the tonnage of ships or vessels;" which being read, were agreed to.

The said bill was then further amended at the Clerk's table, and, together with the amendments, ordered to be engrossed, and read the third time on Thursday next.[53]

The House proceeded to consider the amendments proposed by the Senate, to the bill, intituled, "An act providing more effectually for the settlement of the accounts between the United States and the individual States;" and made some progress therein.[54]

The several orders of the day were farther postponed until to-morrow.

And then the House adjourned until to-morrow morning ten o'clock.

---

[50] On July 14 this bill was read again.

[51] On July 22 the conference on the Post Office Bill [HR-74] reported, and the House took several actions on the Senate amendments.

[52] On July 14 the Senate agreed to a conference on this bill.

[53] On July 17 this bill was read again, agreed to, and sent to the Senate.

[54] On July 14 the House disagreed to all of the Senate amendments and requested a conference on them.

WEDNESDAY, JULY 14, 1790

A petition of Lemuel Sherman, was presented to the House and read, praying compensation for military services rendered during the late war:

Also a petition of Joseph Pannill, to the same effect.

ORDERED, That the said petitions, together with the petition of Jeremiah Ocain, which was presented on the eleventh of March last, be referred to the Secretary at War, with instruction to examine the same, and report his opinion thereupon to the House.[55]

The several petitions of John R. Livingston, Philip Verplank, and Peter Pra Van Zandt, were presented to the House and read, respectively praying the liquidation and settlement of a claim against the United States.

ORDERED, That the said petitions be referred to the Secretary of the Treasury, with instruction to examine the same, and report his opinion thereupon to the House.

A bill, making further provision for the payment of the debts of the United States, was read the second time, and ordered to be committed to a committee of the whole House, to-morrow.[56]

A message from the Senate by Mr. Otis, their Secretary.

MR. SPEAKER, The Senate have agreed to the conference desired by this House, on the subject matter of the amendment depending between the two Houses, to the bill, intituled, "An act to regulate trade and intercourse with the Indian tribes," and have appointed managers at the same on their part:[57] And then he withdrew.

The House proceeded to consider the amendments proposed by the Senate, to the bill, intituled, "An act to provide more effectually for the settlement of the accounts between the United States and the individual States:" Whereupon,

RESOLVED, That this House do disagree to all the said amendments, and desire a conference with the Senate on the subject matter thereof.

ORDERED, That Mr. Sedgwick, Mr. Wadsworth, Mr. Boudinot, Mr. Fitzsimons and Mr. Williamson, be appointed managers at the said conference, on the part of this House.

ORDERED, That the Clerk of this House do acquaint the Senate therewith.[58]

---

[55] The secretary reported on the Pannill petition on February 15, 1791, and on that of Sherman and that of Ocain on February 21, 1791.

[56] On July 15 this bill was considered in the COWH.

[57] On July 19 the conference on the Indian Trade Bill [HR–65] reported, and the House receded from its disagreement to the Senate amendment.

[58] On July 15 the House was notified that the Senate had agreed to this conference.

ORDERED, That a committee be appointed to prepare and bring in a bill or bills to amend the act, "for the establishment and support of light-houses, beacons, buoys and public piers;" and a committee was appointed of Mr. Smith (of South-Carolina), Mr. Sinnickson, and Mr. Foster.

The House proceeded to consider the report of the committee, to whom was referred the memorial of Donald Campbell, and the resolution reported by the said committee, in the words following, to wit: "That there be allowed to Donald Campbell, late a deputy quarter-master-general, in the American army, two and a half per cent. in addition to the two and a half per cent. which has been already allowed to him as a commission, on the purchase and distribution of cloathing to the troops in Canada, by order of general Schuyler," was, on the question put thereupon, disagreed to by the House.

A motion was then made and seconded, that the House do agree to the following resolution.

"RESOLVED, That Donald Campbell is entitled to the pay, subsistence and forage of a colonel in the army of the United States, from the date of his commission until the   day of   and, that he also, during the said time, is entitled to the pay, subsistence and forage allowed during the said time to a deputy quarter-master-general in a separate department."

And on the question thereupon, it passed in the negative.

RESOLVED, That the petition of the said Donald Campbell be rejected.

Mr. Stone, from the committee to whom was re-committed the petition of Francis Mentges, made a report, which was read, and ordered to lie on the table.[59]

The House proceeded to consider the memorial of Louis Pierre Lombart de la Neuville, which lay on the table: Whereupon,

ORDERED, That the memorialist have leave to withdraw his said memorial.

Mr. Smith (of South-Carolina), from the committee appointed, presented, according to order, a bill to amend the act "for the establishment and support of light-houses, beacons, buoys and public piers," which was received, and read the first time.

On motion,

The said bill was read the second time, and ordered to be engrossed, and read the third time to-morrow.[60]

On motion,

ORDERED, That the petition of the clerks employed in the office of the pay-master-general and commissioner of army accounts, which was presented yesterday, be referred to Mr. Vining, Mr. Hiester, and Mr. Gilman, that they

---

[59] On July 27 this report was considered, and a resolution on the Mentges petition was agreed to and sent to the Senate.

[60] On July 15 this bill was read again, agreed to, and sent to the Senate.

do examine the matter thereof, and report the same, with their opinion thereupon to the House.[61]

The several orders of the day were farther postponed until to-morrow.

And then the House adjourned until to-morrow morning eleven o'clock.

THURSDAY, JULY 15, 1790

An engrossed "bill to amend the act for the establishment and support of light-houses, beacons, buoys and public piers," was read the third time.

RESOLVED, That the said bill do pass, and that the title be, "An act to amend the act for the establishment and support of light-houses, beacons, buoys and public piers."

ORDERED, That the Clerk of this House do carry the said bill to the Senate, and desire their concurrence.[62]

A message from the Senate by Mr. Otis their Secretary.

MR. SPEAKER, The Senate agree to the conference desired by this House, on the subject matter of the amendments depending between the two Houses, to the bill, intituled, "An act to provide more effectually for the settlement of the accounts between the United States and the individual states," and have appointed managers at the same, on their part:[63] And then he withdrew.

The House proceeded to consider the report of the joint committee of the two Houses, appointed to consider and report their opinion when it will be convenient and proper that an adjournment of the present session of Congress should take place: Whereupon,

RESOLVED, That in the opinion of this House, the business now depending before the two Houses, may be finished by Tuesday the twenty-seventh instant: and that it will be convenient and proper that an adjournment of the present session of Congress should take place on that day.[64]

ORDERED, That the Clerk of this House do carry the said resolution to the Senate, and desire their concurrence.[65]

Mr. Brown, from the committee appointed, presented, according to order, a bill to enable the officers and soldiers of the Virginia line on continental

---

[61] On July 17 this committee reported, and the report was amended and agreed to as a resolution, which was sent to the Senate.

[62] The Senate read the Lighthouses Bill [HR–84] on July 16, 17, and 19. On July 19 it was agreed to, and the House was notified.

[63] On July 21 this conference reported, and the House took further action on the Senate amendments.

[64] A copy of the resolution and a Senate copy of the same are in Messages from the House, SR, DNA.

[65] On August 6 another resolution on adjournment was agreed to.

establishment, to obtain titles to certain lands lying north-west of the river Ohio, between Little Miami and Sciota, which was received, and read the first time.

On motion,

The said bill was read the second time, and ordered to be committed to a committee of the whole House on Monday next.[66]

Mr. Gerry, from the committee appointed, presented, according to order, an amendatory bill for establishing the fees and perquisites to be received by Consuls and Vice-Consuls of the United States in foreign parts, and for other purposes therein mentioned, which was received and read the first time.

On motion,

The said bill was read the second time, and ordered to be committed to a committee of the whole House on Monday next.[67]

The House, according to the order of the day, resolved itself into a committee of the whole House, on the bill making further provision for the payment of the debts of the United States.

Mr. Speaker left the chair.

Mr. Boudinot took the chair of the committee.

Mr. Speaker resumed the chair, and Mr. Boudinot reported, that the committee had, according to order, had the said bill under consideration, and made no amendment thereto.

ORDERED, That the said bill do lie on the table.[68]

The several orders of the day were farther postponed until to-morrow.

And then the House adjourned until to-morrow morning eleven o'clock.

FRIDAY, JULY 16, 1790

A message was received from the President of the United States, by Mr. Lear his Secretary, notifying that the President did, this day, approve and sign the act, intituled, "An act further to provide for the payment of the invalid pensioners of the United States."[69]

ORDERED, That the Clerk of this House do acquaint the Senate therewith.

A petition of John F. Amelung, proprietor of the glass manufactory in the state of Maryland, was presented to the House and read, praying a grant of land, or other encouragement, to enable him to extend his undertaking upon a plan, which shall be equal to the supply of the United States.[70]

ORDERED, That the said petition be referred to the Secretary of the Treas-

---

[66] On July 19 this bill was considered in the COWH.
[67] On July 19 this bill was considered in the COWH.
[68] On July 16 this bill was amended.
[69] The message is in Committee on Enrolled Bills, SR, DNA.
[70] The petition is in Petitions and Memorials: Various subjects, SR, DNA.

ury, with instruction to examine the same, and report his opinion thereupon to the House.

The House proceeded to consider the bill making further provision for the payment of the debts of the United States, which lay on the table, and the said bill being amended at the Clerk's table, was, together with the amendments, ordered to be engrossed, and read the third time on Monday next.[71]

A message from the Senate by Mr. Otis their Secretary.

MR. SPEAKER, I am directed to inform this House, that the President of the United States did, this day, affix his signature to an act, which originated in the Senate, intituled, "An act for establishing the temporary and permanent seat of the government of the United States:" And then he withdrew.

Mr. Baldwin, from the committee to whom were referred the reports of the Secretary at War, on the petitions of John Baylor, Anthony Walton White, and Stephen Steward, made a report, which was read, and ordered to lie on the table.[72]

Mr. Williamson, from the committee appointed, presented, according to order, a bill for the relief of disabled soldiers and seamen, and of certain other persons, lately in the service of the United States, which was received, and read the first time.[73]

A petition of William Gordon, was presented to the House and read, praying the settlement of a claim against the United States, which is due to the estate of John White, deceased, on which the petitioner has administered: Whereupon,

A motion being made and seconded, that the said petition be referred to the Secretary of the Treasury,

It passed in the negative.

The several orders of the day, were farther postponed until to-morrow.

And then the House adjourned until to-morrow morning eleven o'clock.

SATURDAY, JULY 17, 1790

A petition of Simon Wilmer Wilson, of Kent county, in the state of Delaware, was presented to the House and read, praying the liquidation and settlement of a claim against the United States.

---

[71] On July 19 this bill was read again, agreed to, and sent to the Senate.

[72] A copy of the report is in A Record of the Reports of Select Committees, HR, DNA. On July 20 this report was considered, and the petitions were again referred to the secretary of war.

[73] On July 17 this bill was read again.

ORDERED, That the said petition be referred to the Secretary of the Treasury, with instruction to examine the same, and report his opinion thereupon to the House.

A message from the Senate by Mr. Otis their Secretary.

MR. SPEAKER, The Senate have passed the bill, intituled, "An act providing for holding a treaty or treaties, to establish peace with certain Indian tribes," with an amendment,[74] to which they desire the concurrence of this House: And then he withdrew.

The House proceeded to consider the said amendment, and the same being read, was agreed to.

ORDERED, That the Clerk of this House do acquaint the Senate herewith.[75]

Mr. Hiester, from the committee to whom was referred the petition of a number of citizens of the state of North-Carolina, called Dunkards, made a report,[76] which was read, and ordered to lie on the table.

An engrossed bill, to regulate the collection of the duties imposed by law, on goods, wares and merchandize imported into the United States, and on the tonnage of ships or vessels, was read the third time, and the blanks therein filled up.

RESOLVED, That the said bill do pass, and that the title be, "An act to provide more effectually for the collection of the duties imposed by law, on goods wares and merchandize imported into the United States, and on the tonnage of ships or vessels."

ORDERED, That the Clerk of this House do carry the said bill to the Senate, and desire their concurrence.[77]

Mr. Gilman from the joint committee for inrolled bills, reported, that the committee had examined two inrolled bills, one intituled, "An act for the government and regulation of seamen in the merchants service,"[78] the other

---

[74] The Senate committee report on this bill, with the amendment, is in Various Select Committee Reports, SR, DNA. The amendment is printed in the *Senate Legislative Journal* on July 17.

[75] The House had considered the Indian Treaty Bill [HR–50b] in secret session up until this point. This is the first mention of this bill in the Journal. On July 20 this bill was signed by the speaker and the vice president.

[76] A copy of the report is in A Record of the Reports of Select Committees, HR, DNA. This petition is the one from the Quakers, which was received on May 13.

[77] On July 20 the Senate committed this bill, and on July 22 the committee reported. On the same day the second reading was begun, and the House sent the Senate papers relating to the bill. On July 23 the second reading was continued, and the bill was recommitted for further amendments. On July 26 amendments to the bill were agreed to, and the third reading was begun. On July 27 the Senate agreed to the bill with amendments and returned it to the House. The House agreed to the amendments on the same day.

[78] The inspected enrolled bill is in Enrolled Acts, RG 11, DNA. E–23849, E–22959.

intituled, "An act imposing duties on the tonnage of ships or vessels;"[79] and had found the same to be truly inrolled: Whereupon,

Mr. Speaker signed the said inrolled bills.

ORDERED, That the Clerk of this House do acquaint the Senate therewith.

A petition of Abraham Hunt, late captain in the first Massachusetts regiment, on continental establishment, was presented to the House and read, praying to receive the commutation of five years full pay, in lieu of half pay, in consideration of military services rendered during the late war.

ORDERED, That the said petition be referred to the Secretary at war, with instruction to examine the same, and report his opinion thereupon to the House.

Mr. Vining, from the committee to whom was referred the petition of the clerks in the office of the paymaster-general and commissioner of army accounts, made a report, which was twice read at the Clerk's table, amended, and agreed to by the House, as followeth.

RESOLVED, That the clerks in the office of the commissioner of army accounts, are entitled to receive for their services, a sum not exceeding five hundred dollars, to be paid in the same manner and at the same rate, as the salary allowed to the clerks in the department of Treasury; and that the Auditor and Comptroller, be authorized to adjust the accounts of the clerks in the said office, upon the same principles as those of the Treasury department, agreeably to the appropriation by law.

ORDERED, That the Clerk of this House do carry the said resolution to the Senate, and desire their concurrence.[80]

Mr. Gilman, from the joint committee for inrolled bills, reported, that the committee did, this day, wait on the President of the United States, and present for his approbation, two inrolled bills, one intituled, "An act for the government and regulation of seamen, in the merchants service;" the other intituled, "An act imposing duties on the tonnage of ships or vessels."[81]

"A bill, for the relief of disabled soldiers and seamen, and of certain other persons, lately in the service of the United States," was read the second time, and ordered to be committed to a committee of the whole House, on Monday next.[82]

The several orders of the day were farther postponed until Monday next.

And then the House adjourned until Monday morning eleven o'clock.

---

[79] The inspected enrolled bill is in Enrolled Acts, RG 11, DNA. E–22963.

[80] The Senate read this resolution on July 20 and committed it after consideration on July 21. On July 23 the committee reported, and on July 24 the Senate considered the report and agreed to the resolution. On July 26 the House was notified of the Senate agreement.

[81] On July 20 the president signed both of these bills.

[82] On July 19 the bill was amended.

MONDAY, JULY 19, 1790

An engrossed bill further to provide for the payment of the debts of the United States, was read the third time, and the blanks therein filled up. And then the question being put that the said bill do pass.

It was resolved in the affirmative, $\begin{cases} \text{AYES} & 40 \\ \text{NOES} & 15 \end{cases}$

The ayes and noes being demanded by one fifth of the members present, Those who voted in the affirmative, are,

John Baptista Ashe	George Mathews
Abraham Baldwin	Andrew Moore
Timothy Bloodworth	Peter Muhlenberg
John Brown	John Page
Aedanus Burke	Josiah Parker
Lambert Cadwalader	Jeremiah Van Rensselaer
Daniel Carroll	Thomas Scott
George Clymer	Joshua Seney
Isaac Coles	John Sevier
Benjamin Contee	Roger Sherman
Thomas Fitzsimons	Peter Silvester
William Floyd	Thomas Sinnickson
Nicholas Gilman	John Steele
Thomas Hartley	Jonathan Sturges
Daniel Hiester	Thomas Sumter
Benjamin Huntington	Thomas Tudor Tucker
James Jackson	John Vining
John Laurance	Alexander White
Samuel Livermore	Hugh Williamson and
James Madison, junior	Henry Wynkoop

Those who voted in the negative, are,

Fisher Ames	George Partridge
Egbert Benson	Theodore Sedgwick
Abiel Foster	William Smith (of Maryland)
George Gale	William Smith (of South-Carolina)
Elbridge Gerry	George Thatcher
Benjamin Goodhue	Jonathan Trumbull and
Jonathan Grout	Jeremiah Wadsworth
George Leonard	

RESOLVED, That the title of the said bill be, "An act further to provide for the payment of the debts of the United States," and that the Clerk of this House do carry the said bill to the Senate, and desire their concurrence.[83]

A message from the Senate, by Mr. Otis their Secretary.

MR. SPEAKER, The Senate have passed the bill, intituled, "An act to amend the act for establishment and support of light-houses, beacons, buoys, and public piers:"[84] And then he withdrew.

Mr. Madison, from the managers appointed on the part of this House to attend the conference with the Senate on the subject matter of the third amendment proposed by the Senate, and depending between the two Houses to the bill, intituled, "An act to regulate trade and intercourse with the Indian tribes," made a report: Whereupon,

RESOLVED, That this House do recede from their disagreement to the said amendment, and do agree with the Senate therein.

ORDERED, That the Clerk of this House do acquaint the Senate therewith.[85]

The House according to the order of the day, resolved itself into a committee of the whole House on the bill for the relief of disabled soldiers and seamen, and of certain other persons lately in the service of the United States.

Mr. Speaker left the chair.

Mr. Seney took the chair of the committee.

Mr. Speaker resumed the chair, and Mr. Seney reported that the committee had, according to order, had the said bill under consideration, and made an amendment thereto, which he delivered in at the Clerk's table, where the same was read, and agreed to by the House.

ORDERED, That the said bill, with the amendment, do lie on the table.[86]

The House, according to the order of the day, resolved itself into a committee of the whole House on the bill to enable the officers and soldiers of the Virginia line on continental establishment, to obtain titles to certain lands lying north-west of the river Ohio, between the Little Miami and Sciota.

Mr. Speaker left the chair.

---

[83] A printed copy of the bill is in House Bills, SR, DNA. E–46027. The Senate read this bill on July 20 and 21. On July 21 it was committed. This committee reported several amendments on August 2. The committee report was considered on August 3 and 4. On August 4 the report is printed in the *Senate Legislative Journal*. It was agreed to, and several motions to amend the bill were disagreed to. On August 5 the bill was further amended, agreed to, and returned to the House. The House considered the Senate amendments on the same day.

[84] On July 20 this bill was signed by the speaker and vice president.

[85] On July 20 the Indian Trade Bill [HR–65] was signed by the speaker and vice president.

[86] On July 27 this amendment was agreed to.

Mr. Seney took the chair of the committee.

Mr. Speaker resumed the chair, and Mr. Seney reported that the committee had, according to order, had the said bill under consideration, and made no amendment thereto.

ORDERED, That the said bill be engrossed, and read the third time to-morrow.[87]

The House, according to the order of the day, resolved itself into a committee of the whole House on the bill for establishing the fees and perquisites to be received by Consuls and Vice-Consuls of the United States in foreign parts, and for other purposes therein mentioned.

Mr. Speaker left the chair.

Mr. Seney took the chair of the committee.

Mr. Speaker resumed the chair, and Mr. Seney reported that the committee had, according to order, had the said bill under consideration, and made some progress therein.

RESOLVED, That this House will, to-morrow, again resolve itself into a committee of the whole House on the said bill.[88]

The several orders of the day were farther postponed until to-morrow.

And then the House adjourned until to-morrow morning eleven o'clock.

TUESDAY, JULY 20, 1790

Mr. Gilman, from the joint committee for inrolled bills, reported, that the committee had examined three inrolled bills, one intituled, "An act providing for holding a treaty or treaties to establish peace with certain Indian tribes."[89] Another intituled, "An act to amend the act for the establishment and support of light-houses, beacons, buoys, and public piers;"[90] and another intituled, "An act to regulate trade and intercourse with the Indian tribes,"[91] and had found the same to be truly inrolled: Whereupon,

Mr. Speaker signed the said inrolled bills.[92]

ORDERED, That the Clerk of this House do acquaint the Senate therewith.

An engrossed bill to enable the officers and soldiers of the Virginia line on continental establishment, to obtain titles to certain lands lying north-west of the river Ohio, between the Little-Miami and Sciota, was read the third time:

RESOLVED, That the said bill do pass, and that the title be "An Act to en-

---

[87] On July 20 this bill was read again, agreed to, and sent to the Senate.

[88] On July 20 this bill was considered again in the COWH and amended by the House.

[89] The inspected enrolled bill is in Enrolled Acts, RG 11, DNA. E–22966, E–46051.

[90] The inspected enrolled bill is in Enrolled Acts, RG 11, DNA. E–22967.

[91] The inspected enrolled bill is in Enrolled Acts, RG 11, DNA. E–22972.

[92] On July 21 the committee on enrolled bills reported on presenting these bills to the president.

able the officers and soldiers of the Virginia line on continental establishment, to obtain titles to certain lands lying north-west of the river Ohio, between the Little-Miami and Sciota."

ORDERED, That the Clerk of this House do carry the said bill to the Senate, and desire their concurrence.[93]

A message was received from the President of the United States by Mr. Lear his Secretary, notifying, that the President did, this day, approve and sign two acts: one intituled, "An act for the government and regulation of seamen in the merchants service," the other intituled, "An act imposing duties on the tonnage of ships or vessels."

The House, according to the order of the day, again resolved itself into a committee of the whole House on the bill for establishing the fees and perquisites to be received by Consuls and Vice-Consuls of the United States in foreign parts, and for other purposes therein mentioned.

Mr. Speaker left the chair.

Mr. Boudinot took the chair of the committee.

Mr. Speaker resumed the chair, and Mr. Boudinot reported that the committee had, according to order, again had the said bill under consideration, and made several amendments thereto, which he delivered in at the Clerk's table, where the same were severally twice read, and agreed to by the House.

ORDERED, That the said bill, with the amendments, be engrossed, and read the third time to-morrow.[94]

A petition of Nathaniel Tracey, was presented to the House and read, praying the liquidation and settlement of a claim against the United States.[95]

ORDERED, That the said petition be referred to the Secretary of the Treasury, with instruction to examine the same, and report his opinion thereupon to the House.

A petition of John Falconer, was presented to the House and read, praying compensation for property taken and destroyed by the American army, during the late war.

ORDERED, That the said petition be referred to the Secretary at War, with

---

[93] The Senate read this bill on July 20 and 21, and on July 21 it was committed. This committee reported the bill without amendments on July 22. The second reading of this bill continued on July 24, 27, and 28. It was recommitted on July 28. On August 3 the bill was amended, and on August 6 an amendment that changed practically the entire text of the bill was proposed. The *Senate Legislative Journal* does not note any action on this amendment, which is printed on August 6. On August 7 a committee report on the bill was agreed to, and the bill was agreed to with amendments. On the same day the House agreed to the amendments.

[94] On July 21 this bill was read again, agreed to, and sent to the Senate.

[95] A petition for a law of bankruptcy, which may be the same as this petition, is in Petitions and Memorials: Various subjects, SR, DNA.

instruction to examine the same, and report his opinion thereupon to the House.

The House proceeded to consider the report of the committee to whom were committed the reports of the Secretary at War on the several petitions of John Baylor, Anthony Walton White, and Stephen Steward: Whereupon,

ORDERED, That the said petitions be again referred to the Secretary at War, with instruction to receive and examine such evidence as may be adduced in support of them, and to report the same, with his opinion on the merit of each of them to the House.[96]

The several orders of the day were farther postponed until to-morrow.

And then the House adjourned until to-morrow morning, eleven o'clock.

WEDNESDAY, JULY 21, 1790

Mr. Gilman, from the joint committee for inrolled bills, reported, that the committee did yesterday, wait on the President of the United States, and present for his approbation, three inrolled bills, one intituled, "An act providing for holding a treaty or treaties to establish peace with certain Indian tribes," another intituled, "An act to amend the act for the establishment and support of light-houses, beacons, buoys, and public piers," and another, intituled, "An act to regulate trade and intercourse with the Indian tribes."[97]

An engrossed bill for establishing the fees and perquisites to be received by Consuls and Vice-Consuls of the United States in foreign parts, and for other purposes therein mentioned, was read the third time.

RESOLVED, That the said bill do pass, and that the title be, "An act concerning Consuls and Vice-Consuls of the United States in foreign parts."[98]

ORDERED, That the Clerk of this House do carry the said bill to the Senate, and desire their concurrence.[99]

A petition of John Tucker, clerk of the supreme court of the United States, was presented to the House and read, praying that the expence of procuring seals for the supreme and circuit courts of the United States, may be defrayed.

ORDERED, That the said petition do lie on the table.

Mr. Sedgwick from the managers appointed on the part of this House, to attend the conference with the Senate on the subject matter of the amendments depending between the two Houses to the bill, intituled, "An act pro-

---

[96] On February 21, 1791, the secretary reported on these petitions.

[97] The president signed all of these bills on July 22.

[98] The bill is in Engrossed House Bills, HR, DNA.

[99] The Senate read this bill on July 21 and 26. On July 26 the bill was committed, and on August 2 further consideration was postponed to third session.

viding more effectually for the settlement of the accounts between the United States and the individual states," made a report:[100]   Whereupon,

RESOLVED, That this House do insist on so much of their disagreement to the first amendment, as proposes to strike out the second section of the bill, and the words, "And be it further enacted," in the third section; and do agree to such other part of the said amendment, as proposes to strike out all the words in the first section, from the word "assembled," to the end thereof, with an amendment, to insert in lieu of the words so stricken out, the following words. "That a board, to consist of three commissioners, be, and hereby is established, to settle the accounts between the United States and the individual States; and the determination of a majority of the said commissioners, on the claims submitted to them, shall be final and conclusive; and they shall have power to employ such number of clerks as they may find necessary."

RESOLVED, That this House do insist on their disagreement to the second and sixth amendments, and do recede from their disagreement to the third, fourth, fifth, and seventh amendments.

RESOLVED, That this House do disagree to the amendment proposed by the conferees, in the third line of the third section, for striking out the word "July," and inserting in lieu thereof, the word "April."[101]

ORDERED, That the Clerk of this House do acquaint the Senate therewith.[102]

Mr. Williamson, from the committee to whom was referred the petition of Henry Emanuel Lutterloh, made a report, which was read, and ordered to lie on the table.[103]

A message from the Senate by Mr. Otis, their Secretary.

MR. SPEAKER,   The Senate have passed the bill, intituled, "An act making provision for the debt of the United States," with several amendments, to which they desire the concurrence of this House:[104]   And then he withdrew.

The several orders of the day were farther postponed until to-morrow.
And then the House adjourned until to-morrow morning eleven o'clock.

---

[100] The annotated report is in Joint Committee Reports, SR, DNA.

[101] A copy of these resolutions is in Messages from the House, SR, DNA.

[102] On July 23 the Senate took several actions on their amendments. These actions are noted in the *Senate Legislative Journal*. The House was notified on July 24.

[103] On August 2 the House considered this report, and Henry Lutterloh was given leave to withdraw his petition.

[104] Senate amendments are filed with and noted on an annotated printed copy of the bill in House Bills, SR, DNA. This bill was printed by the Senate on July 17, 1790, as a result of their committee's report. Senate amendments are printed in the *Senate Legislative Journal* on July 19 and 20. On July 22 the Senate amendments to the Funding Bill [HR–63] were considered.

THURSDAY, JULY 22, 1790

Mr. Goodhue, from the committee appointed,[105] presented according to order, a bill for registering ships or vessels, for regulating those employed in the coasting trade and fisheries, and for other purposes, which was received, and read the first time.

On motion,

The said bill was read the second time, and ordered to be committed to a committee of the whole House, on Monday next.[106]

A message was received from the President of the United States, by Mr. Lear his Secretary, notifying that the President, did this day approve and sign three acts; one intituled, "An act providing for holding a treaty or treaties to establish peace with certain Indian tribes;" another intituled, "An act to amend the act for the establishment and support of light-houses, beacons, buoys, and public piers;" and another intituled, "An act to regulate trade and intercourse with the Indian tribes."

The Speaker laid before the House a letter from the Secretary of the Treasury, covering his report of a uniform system for the disposition of lands the property of the United States, made pursuant to an order of the House of the twentieth of January last, which were read, and ordered to lie on the table.[107]

Mr. Gerry, from the managers appointed on the part of this House to attend a conference with the Senate on the subject matter of the amendments depending between the two Houses to the bill, intituled, "An act to establish the post-office and post roads within the United States," made a report.[108] Whereupon,

RESOLVED, That this House do adhere to their disagreement to the first amendment.

AYES 35

NOES 20

The ayes and noes being demanded by one fifth of the members present; Those who voted in the affirmative, are,

John Baptista Ashe	John Brown
Abraham Baldwin	Aedanus Burke
Timothy Bloodworth	George Clymer

---

[105] This committee is the committee on laws of revenue, which was appointed on April 23. The members were Elias Boudinot, Thomas Fitzsimons, Benjamin Goodhue, Richard B. Lee, and John Laurance.

[106] On July 27 further consideration of this bill was postponed to third session.

[107] A copy of the report is in A Record of the Reports of the Secretary of the Treasury, vol. 1, HR, DNA. A copy of the report, probably made by ASP, is in Reports and Communications from the Secretary of the Treasury, HR, DNA. E–23004. On July 28 this report was considered in the COWH.

[108] The annotated report is in Joint Committee Reports, SR, DNA.

Isaac Coles
Benjamin Contee
Thomas Fitzsimons
William Floyd
George Gale
Elbridge Gerry
Samuel Griffin
Thomas Hartley
Daniel Hiester
Benjamin Huntington
James Jackson
Samuel Livermore
James Madison, junior
George Mathews
Peter Muhlenberg

John Page
Josiah Parker
Thomas Scott
Joshua Seney
John Sevier
Roger Sherman
Peter Silvester
John Steele
Michael Jenifer Stone
Jonathan Sturges
Thomas Sumter
Thomas Tudor Tucker
John Vining and
Alexander White

Those who voted in the negative, are,

Fisher Ames
Egbert Benson
Elias Boudinot
Lambert Cadwalader
Abiel Foster
Nicholas Gilman
Benjamin Goodhue
Jonathan Grout
John Laurance
George Leonard

George Partridge
Jeremiah Van Rensselaer
James Schureman
Theodore Sedgwick
William Smith (of Maryland)
William Smith (of South-Carolina)
George Thatcher
Jonathan Trumbull
Jeremiah Wadsworth and
Henry Wynkoop

RESOLVED, That this House do recede from their disagreement to the second amendment; also do insist on their disagreement to the amendments to the twenty-fourth and thirty-first sections, with the following exceptions, to wit:

Twenty-fourth section, second line, after the word "persons," insert in a parenthesis, "(other than printers of newspapers)."

Thirty-first section, strike out the words "agreeable to his report on the petition of Christopher Colles."

RESOLVED, That this House do recede from their disagreement to, and do agree with the senate in their first amendment to the eleventh section; also to the amendment for striking out the thirteenth section, and to the amendment for striking out the twenty-third section, with the following amendment, to wit.

Insert, in lieu of the words proposed to be inserted by the Senate, the words following.

"That it shall be the duty of the postmaster-general, to permit any printer of newspapers within the United States, to send and receive newspapers by the post, subject to a postage of one quarter of a cent for each newspaper."[109]

ORDERED, That the Clerk of this House do acquaint the Senate therewith.[110]

The House proceeded to consider the amendments proposed by the Senate, to the bill, intituled, "An act making provision for the debt of the United States," and made some progress therein.

ORDERED, That the farther consideration of the said amendments be put off until to-morrow.[111]

The several orders of the day were farther postponed until to-morrow.

And then the House adjourned until to-morrow morning eleven o'clock.

FRIDAY, JULY 23, 1790

The House resumed the consideration of the amendments proposed by the Senate to the bill intituled, "An act making provision for the debt of the United States," and made a farther progress therein.[112]

The several orders of the day were farther postponed until to-morrow.

And then the House adjourned until to-morrow morning eleven o'clock.

SATURDAY, JULY 24, 1790

A message from the Senate by Mr. Otis, their Secretary.

MR. SPEAKER, The Senate recede from some, and agree to the amendments proposed by this House, to other of their amendments to the bill, intituled, "An act to provide more effectually for the settlement of the accounts between the United States and the individual States:"[113] And then he withdrew.

Mr. Stone, from the committee, to whom was referred the petition of John Stewart and John Davidson, made a report:[114] Whereupon,

---

[109] A copy of these resolutions is in Messages from the House, SR, DNA.

[110] On July 26 the Senate notified the House that they had insisted upon some of their amendments and receded from others.

[111] On July 23 these amendments were considered again.

[112] On July 24 the House agreed to several of the Senate amendments and made several amendments to one of the Senate amendments.

[113] On July 26 this bill was signed by the speaker and the vice president.

[114] A copy of the report is in A Record of the Reports of Select Committees, HR, DNA.

RESOLVED, That the duty on thirteen hundred and twenty-five bushels of salt imported by the petitioners into the port of Annapolis, some time in the month of April last, and which was casually destroyed by a flood, shall be remitted.

ORDERED, That a bill or bills be brought in pursuant to the said resolution, and that Mr. Stone, Mr. Silvester, and Mr. Coles do prepare and bring in the same.[115]

On motion,

RESOLVED, That the expence of procuring seals for the supreme and circuit courts of the United States, shall be defrayed out of the money appropriated by an act of the present session, for defraying the contingent charges of government.[116]

ORDERED, That the Clerk of this House do carry the said resolution to the Senate, and desire their concurrence.[117]

The House resumed the consideration of the amendment proposed by the Senate to the bill, intituled, "An act making provision for the debt of the United States:" Whereupon,

RESOLVED, That this House do agree to the first, second, third, fourth, fifth, sixth, seventh, eighth, ninth, tenth, eleventh, twelfth, and thirteenth amendments, with amendments to the said seventh amendment, as follow.

In the clauses proposed to be inserted by the Senate, in lieu of the fourth section,

Line twelfth. Strike out "seven," and insert "eight."

Line seventeenth. Strike out "twenty-six dollars and eighty-eight cents," and insert "thirty-three dollars and one third of a dollar."

Line nineteenth. Strike out "eight hundred," and insert "seven hundred and ninety-seven."

Line twenty-third. Strike out "seven," and insert "eight."

Line fortieth. Strike out "three," and insert "four."[118]

And then the last amendment proposed by the Senate, for adding to the end of the said bill, sundry clauses, "making a provision for the debt of the United States," being under consideration,

A motion was made and seconded, that the House do disagree to the said amendment; and on the question to disagree,

---

[115] On July 27 this committee reported the Stewart and Davidson Bill [HR–90], which was read twice.

[116] A copy of the resolution is in House Joint and Concurrent Resolutions, SR, DNA.

[117] On July 26 the House was notified that the Senate had concurred in this resolution with an amendment.

[118] A printed copy of the House resolution and amendments, annotated by the Senate, is filed with the bill in House Bills, SR, DNA. A manuscript copy of the resolution is included.

It passed in the negative, $\begin{cases} \text{AYES} & 29 \\ \text{NOES} & 32 \end{cases}$

The ayes and noes being demanded by one fifth of the members present, Those who voted in the affirmative, are,

John Baptista Ashe	George Mathews
Abraham Baldwin	Andrew Moore
Timothy Bloodworth	Peter Muhlenberg
John Brown	John Page
Isaac Coles	Josiah Parker
Benjamin Contee	Jeremiah Van Rensselaer
William Floyd	Thomas Scott
Nicholas Gilman	Joshua Seney
Samuel Griffin	John Sevier
Thomas Hartley	William Smith (of Maryland)
John Hathorn	John Steele
Daniel Hiester	Michael Jenifer Stone
James Jackson	Thomas Sumter and
Samuel Livermore	Hugh Williamson
James Madison, junior	

Those who voted in the negative, are,

Fisher Ames	George Leonard
Egbert Benson	George Partridge
Elias Boudinot	James Schureman
Aedanus Burke	Theodore Sedgwick
Lambert Cadwalader	Roger Sherman
Daniel Carroll	Peter Silvester
George Clymer	Thomas Sinnickson
Thomas Fitzsimons	William Smith (of South-Carolina)
Abiel Foster	Jonathan Sturges
George Gale	George Thatcher
Elbridge Gerry	Jonathan Trumbull
Benjamin Goodhue	Thomas Tudor Tucker
Jonathan Grout	John Vining
Benjamin Huntington	Jeremiah Wadsworth
John Laurance	Alexander White and
Richard Bland Lee	Henry Wynkoop

The House then proceeded to consider the said amendment by clauses, and made some progress therein.

ORDERED, That the farther consideration of the said amendment be post-poned until Monday next.[119]

Mr. Clymer, from the committee to whom was re-committed the memorial of Thomas Barclay, made a report, which was read, and ordered to lie on the table.[120]

The several orders of the day, were farther postponed until Monday next. And then the House adjourned until Monday morning, eleven o'clock.

MONDAY, JULY 26, 1790

Mr. Gilman, from the joint committee for inrolled bills, reported, that the committee had examined an inrolled bill, intituled, "An act to provide more effectually for the settlement of the accounts between the United States, and the individual States,"[121] and had found the same to be truly inrolled: Whereupon,

Mr. Speaker signed the said inrolled bill.[122]

A message from the Senate by Mr. Otis their Secretary.

MR. SPEAKER,   The Senate do adhere to their first amendment, a disagree-ment to which this House has adhered to, to the bill, intituled, "An act to establish the post-office and post-roads within the United States;" they do also insist on some, and recede from other of their amendments to the said bill, a disagreement to which this House hath insisted on:[123] The Senate have also agreed to a resolution respecting the pay of the clerks in the office of the commissioner of army accounts;[124] and to the resolution for defraying the expence of procuring seals for the supreme and circuit courts of the United States, with an amendment to the said last resolution, to which they desire the concurrence of this House:[125]   And then he withdrew.

---

[119] On July 26 the House considered the Senate amendments to the Funding Bill [HR–63] again. After amending one of the Senate amendments, the House notified the Senate of their actions on the Senate amendments.

[120] A copy of the report is in A Record of the Reports of Select Committees, HR, DNA. A copy, probably made by ASP, is in Select Committee on Claims, HR, DNA. On July 27 a resolution on this report was agreed to, and a committee to bring in a bill on the resolution was appointed.

[121] The inspected enrolled bill is in Enrolled Acts, RG 11, DNA. E–22969.

[122] On July 28 the House was notified that this bill had been presented to the president on July 27.

[123] The Senate also passed an amendment to one of the House amendments. The amendment is printed in the *Senate Legislative Journal* on July 24. On July 28 the House appointed a committee to bring in a new post office bill. This committee presented the Post Office Bill [HR–92] on the same day. This bill was then read twice.

[124] On July 27 this resolution was signed by the speaker and vice president.

[125] The House apparently agreed to this Senate amendment. On July 27 the speaker and the vice president signed the resolution.

A petition of William Harris, was presented to the House and read, praying compensation for property taken and destroyed in the service of the
United States, during the late war.

Also a petition of Henry Bass, praying that a duplicate may be granted him
of a continental loan-office certificate for six hundred dollars, signed by Dirck
Ten Broeck, commissioner for the state of New-York, dated the thirteenth of
March one thousand seven hundred and eighty, which was the property of
the petitioner, and by him casually lost;

ORDERED, That the said petitions be referred to the Secretary of the Treasury, with instruction to examine the same, and report his opinion thereupon
to the House.

The House resumed the consideration of the amendments proposed by the
Senate to the bill intituled, "An act making provision for the debt of the
United States:" Whereupon

The last amendment for adding to the end of the bill sundry clauses "making a provision for the debts of the respective States," being under consideration,

A motion was made and seconded to amend the said amendment by adding to the end of the first clause or section thereof, the following proviso, to
wit:

"*Provided always, and be it further enacted*, That if the total amount of
the sums which shall be subscribed to the said loan in the debt of any State
within the time limited for receiving subscription thereto, shall exceed the
sum by this act allowed to be subscribed within such State, the certificates and
credits granted to their respective subscribers, shall bear such proportion to
the sums by them respectively subscribed, as the total amount of the said
sums shall bear to the whole sum so allowed to be subscribed in the debt of
such State within the same; and every subscriber to the said loan, shall, at the
time of subscribing, deposit with the commissioner the certificates or notes
to be loaned by him:"   And on the question thereupon,

It was resolved in the affirmative.

Another motion was then made and seconded, further to amend the said
amendment, by adding to the end of the said first clause or section thereof,
the following proviso:

"*And provided*, That the original holders of certificates in the several states
shall have the exclusive right of subscribing for the space of six months from
the time in which the offices shall be opened in the States respectively, and
that the whole of their claims shall be funded."   And on the question thereupon,

It passed in the negative, $\left\{\begin{array}{l} \text{AYES} \ \ 15 \\ \text{NOES} \ \ 45 \end{array}\right.$

The ayes and noes being demanded by one fifth of the members present, Those who voted in the affirmative, are,

John Baptista Ashe
Timothy Bloodworth
John Brown
Isaac Coles
James Jackson
James Madison, junior
George Mathews
Peter Muhlenberg

John Page
Josiah Parker
Thomas Scott
Joshua Seney
John Steele
Thomas Sumter and
Hugh Williamson

Those who voted in the negative, are,

Fisher Ames
Abraham Baldwin
Egbert Benson
Elias Boudinot
Aedanus Burke
Lambert Cadwalader
Daniel Carroll
George Clymer
Benjamin Contee
Thomas Fitzsimons
William Floyd
Abiel Foster
George Gale
Elbridge Gerry
Nicholas Gilman
Benjamin Goodhue
Samuel Griffin
Jonathan Grout
Thomas Hartley
John Hathorn
Daniel Huger
Benjamin Huntington
Richard Bland Lee

George Leonard
Samuel Livermore
Andrew Moore
George Partridge
Jeremiah Van Rensselaer
James Schureman
Theodore Sedgwick
John Sevier
Roger Sherman
Peter Silvester
Thomas Sinnickson
William Smith (of Maryland)
William Smith (of South-Carolina)
Michael Jenifer Stone
Jonathan Sturges
George Thatcher
Jonathan Trumbull
Thomas Tudor Tucker
John Vining
Jeremiah Wadsworth
Alexander White and
Henry Wynkoop

RESOLVED, That the second clause or section of the said amendment be amended as followeth.

Line thirteenth, strike out "seven," and insert "eight."

Lines eighteenth and nineteenth, strike out "twenty-six dollars and eighty-eight cents," and insert "thirty-three dollars and one third of a dollar."

Line twenty-first, strike out "eight hundred," and insert "seven hundred and ninety-seven."

Line twenty-fifth, strike out "seven," and insert "eight."

Line thirty-first, strike out "three," and insert "four."[126]

A motion was then made and seconded, further to amend the said amendment, by striking out the fourth clause or section thereof, in the words following, to wit:

"*And be it further enacted,* That if the whole sum allowed to be subscribed in the debt or certificates of any State as aforesaid, shall not be subscribed within the time for that purpose limited, such State shall be entitled to receive, and shall receive from the United States, an interest per centum per annum, upon so much of the said sum as shall not have been so subscribed equal to that which would have accrued on the deficiency had the same been subscribed, in trust for the non-subscribing creditors of such State, who are holders of certificates or notes issued on account of services or supplies towards the prosecution of the late war, and the defence of the United States, or of some part thereof, to be paid in like manner as the interest on the stock which may be created by virtue of the said loan and to continue until there shall be a settlement of accounts between the United States, and the individual States; and in case a balance shall then appear in favor of such State, until provision shall be made for the said balance."   And on the question thereupon,

It passed in the negative, $\begin{cases} \text{AYES} & 13 \\ \text{NOES} & 47 \end{cases}$

The ayes and noes being demanded by one fifth of the members present, Those who voted in the affirmative, are,

Abraham Baldwin	Samuel Livermore
Timothy Bloodworth	George Mathews
John Brown	Andrew Moore
Isaac Coles	Jeremiah Van Rensselaer
Benjamin Contee	John Sevier and
Nicholas Gilman	Hugh Williamson
James Jackson	

Those who voted in the negative, are,

John Baptista Ashe	Egbert Benson
Fisher Ames	Elias Boudinot

---

[126] A printed copy of the House resolution and amendments, annotated by the Senate, is filed with the bill in House Bills, SR, DNA. An incomplete manuscript copy of the resolution is included. Another copy of the printing is in Other Records: Yeas and nays, SR, DNA.

Aedanus Burke
Lambert Cadwalader
Daniel Carroll
George Clymer
Thomas Fitzsimons
William Floyd
Abiel Foster
George Gale
Elbridge Gerry
Benjamin Goodhue
Samuel Griffin
Jonathan Grout
Thomas Hartley
John Hathorn
Daniel Hiester
Benjamin Huntington
John Laurance
Richard Bland Lee
George Leonard
James Madison, junior
Peter Muhlenberg
John Page

Josiah Parker
George Partridge
James Schureman
Theodore Sedgwick
Joshua Seney
Roger Sherman
Peter Silvester
Thomas Sinnickson
William Smith (of Maryland)
William Smith (of South-Carolina)
John Steele
Michael Jenifer Stone
Jonathan Sturges
Thomas Sumter
George Thatcher
Jonathan Trumbull
Thomas Tudor Tucker
John Vining
Jeremiah Wadsworth
Alexander White and
Henry Wynkoop

And then the main question being put, that the House do agree to the said last amendment proposed by the Senate for adding to the end of the said bill sundry clauses "making a provision for the debts of the respective States," as now amended,

It was resolved in the affirmative, $\begin{cases} \text{AYES} & 34 \\ \text{NOES} & 28 \end{cases}$

The ayes and noes being demanded by one fifth of the members present, Those who voted in the affirmative, are,

Fisher Ames
Egbert Benson
Elias Boudinot
Aedanus Burke
Lambert Cadwalader
Daniel Carroll
George Clymer
Thomas Fitzsimons
Abiel Foster

George Gale
Elbridge Gerry
Benjamin Goodhue
Jonathan Grout
Daniel Huger
Benjamin Huntington
John Laurance
Richard Bland Lee
George Leonard

George Partridge
James Schureman
Theodore Sedgwick
Roger Sherman
Peter Silvester
Thomas Sinnickson
William Smith (of South-
    Carolina)
Jonathan Sturges

Thomas Sumter
George Thatcher
Jonathan Trumbull
Thomas Tudor Tucker
John Vining
Jeremiah Wadsworth
Alexander White and
Henry Wynkoop

Those who voted in the negative, are,

John Baptista Ashe
Abraham Baldwin
Timothy Bloodworth
John Brown
Isaac Coles
Benjamin Contee
William Floyd
Nicholas Gilman
Samuel Griffin
Thomas Hartley
John Hathorn
Daniel Hiester
James Jackson
Samuel Livermore

James Madison, junior
George Mathews
Andrew Moore
Peter Muhlenberg
John Page
Josiah Parker
Jeremiah Van Rensselaer
Thomas Scott
Joshua Seney
John Sevier
William Smith (of Maryland)
John Steele
Michael Jenifer Stone and
Hugh Williamson[127]

The several orders of the day were farther postponed until to-morrow.
And then the House adjourned until to-morrow morning, eleven o'clock.

TUESDAY, JULY 27, 1790

Mr. Gilman, from the joint committee for inrolled bills, reported, that the committee had examined two inrolled resolves, one "respecting the pay of the clerks in the office of the commissioner of army accounts;"[128] the other "for defraying the expence of procuring seals for the supreme, circuit, and district courts of the United States,"[129] and had found the same to be truly inrolled: Whereupon,

---

[127] On July 27 the Senate considered the House amendments to their amendments to the Funding Bill [HR–63], and on July 28 they agreed to all but four of the House amendments. The House was notified of this action on July 29. On the same day the House receded from its disagreement to the four amendments insisted upon by the Senate.

[128] The inspected enrolled resolution is in Enrolled Acts, RG 11, DNA. E–46075.

[129] The inspected enrolled resolution is in Enrolled Acts, RG 11, DNA.

Mr. Speaker signed the said inrolled resolves.

ORDERED, That the Clerk of this House do acquaint the Senate therewith.[130]

Mr. Sturges, from the committee to whom was referred the petition of Seth Harding made a report: Whereupon,

RESOLVED, That there be allowed to the said Seth Harding, at the rate of sixty dollars per month, for three months and ten days pay as a captain, for services in the navy of the United States, during the late war.

ORDERED, That the residue of the said report, for granting to the said Seth Harding, the commutation of half pay, and bounty of land, agreeable to his rank in the American navy, do lie on the table.

The House proceeded to consider the report of the committee, to whom was re-committed a report on the petition of Francis Mentges: Whereupon,

RESOLVED, That the said memorialist be allowed his extra expences, for superintending the hospitals at Williamsburg, Hanover-town, and Petersburg, by order of the commander in chief of the army of the United States, from the fifth of November, one thousand seven hundred and eighty-one, to the twentieth of March, one thousand seven hundred and eighty-two, and that the auditor do settle his account accordingly.[131]

ORDERED, That the Clerk of this House do carry the said resolution to the Senate, and desire their concurrence.[132]

Mr. Stone, from the committee appointed, presented, according to order, a bill for the relief of John Stewart and John Davidson, which was received, and read the first time.

On motion,

The said bill was read the second time, and ordered to be engrossed and read the third time to-morrow.[133]

The Speaker laid before the House a letter from the Secretary at War, covering his report on the petition of Sarah Stirling; also a report of the arrearages due to the widows and orphans of officers, who died in the service of the United States, during the late war, which were read, and ordered to lie on the table.[134]

---

[130] On July 28 the House was notified that these resolutions had been presented to the president.

[131] A copy of the resolution is in House Joint and Concurrent Resolutions, SR, DNA.

[132] On July 29 the Senate read and committed this resolution. This committee reported on August 3. On August 6 this report was considered, and the Mentges resolution was disagreed to. On August 7 the House was notified of this disagreement.

[133] On July 28 this bill was read again, agreed to, and sent to the Senate.

[134] Copies of these reports are in A Record of the Reports of the Secretary of War, vol. 1, HR, DNA. On August 2 the House made a resolution on the report on the Stirling petition, and a committee was appointed to bring in a bill pursuant to the resolution.

ORDERED, That the committee to whom was referred the petition of Abraham Skinner, be discharged from farther proceeding thereon, and that the said petition be referred to the Secretary of the Treasury, with instruction to examine the same, and report his opinion thereupon to the House.[135]

On motion,

ORDERED, That the farther consideration of the bill for registering ships or vessels, for regulating those employed in the coasting trade and fisheries, and for other purposes, be postponed until the next session of Congress.

The House proceeded to consider the report of the committee, to whom was re-committed a report on the memorial of Thomas Barclay: Whereupon,

RESOLVED, That in the settlement of the accounts of the said Thomas Barclay, he be allowed, exclusive of expences charged by him in his said account, viz. As consul in France for three years, the salary appointed by Congress to that office: That on all goods purchased and shipped by him in Holland, for the United States, he be allowed a commission of two and a half per centum: That on the value of all the supplies of goods for the United States, re-packed and shipped by him in Holland, and in various ports in France, he be allowed one per centum: That as commissioner for settling the accounts of receipts and expenditures of public monies in Europe, for four years, he be allowed at the rate of fifteen hundred dollars per annum: That as agent for negociating and concluding a commercial treaty with Morocco, he be allowed two thousand dollars.

ORDERED, That a bill or bills be brought in, pursuant to the said resolution, and that Mr. Stone, Mr. Clymer, and Mr. Page, do prepare and bring in the same.[136]

The House proceeded to consider the amendment reported by the committee of the whole House, to the bill, for the relief of disabled soldiers and seamen, and of certain other persons, lately in the service of the United States, which lay on the table, and the said amendment being twice read at the Clerk's table, was agreed to by the House.

ORDERED, That the said bill, with the amendment, be engrossed, and read the third time to-morrow.[137]

The several orders of the day, were farther postponed until to-morrow.

And then the House adjourned until to-morrow morning, eleven o'clock.

---

[135] On August 7 a resolution on the claim of Abraham Skinner was agreed to, and a committee was appointed to prepare a bill.

[136] On July 28 this committee presented the Barclay Bill [HR–91], which was read twice and amended on the same day.

[137] On July 28 this bill was read again, agreed to, and sent to the Senate.

WEDNESDAY, JULY 28, 1790

Mr. Gilman, from the joint committee for inrolled bills, reported, that the committee did, yesterday, wait on the President of the United States, and present, for his approbation, an inrolled bill, intituled, "An act to provide more effectually for the settlement of the accounts between the United States, and the individual States;" also, two inrolled resolves, one respecting the pay of the clerks in the office of the commissioner of army accounts; the other for defraying the expence of procuring seals for the supreme, circuit, and district courts of the United States.[138]

An engrossed bill, for the relief of John Stewart and John Davidson, was read the third time.

RESOLVED, That the said bill do pass, and that the title be, "An act for the relief of John Stewart and John Davidson."

ORDERED, That the Clerk of this House do carry the said bill to the Senate, and desire their concurrence.[139]

An engrossed bill, for the relief of disabled soldiers and seamen, and of certain other persons lately in the service of the United States, was read the third time.

RESOLVED, That the said bill do pass, and that the title be, "An act for the relief of disabled soldiers and seamen, lately in the service of the United States, and of certain other persons."

ORDERED, That the Clerk of this House do carry the said bill to the Senate, and desire their concurrence.[140]

A message from the Senate by Mr. Otis, their Secretary.

MR. SPEAKER, The Senate have passed the bill, intituled, "An act to provide more effectually for the collection of the duties, imposed by law, on goods, wares, and merchandize, imported into the United States, and on the tonnage of ships or vessels," with several amendments,[141] to which they desire the concurrence of this House: And then he withdrew.

---

[138] On August 2 the president signed the two resolves. The Settlement of Accounts Bill [HR–77] was signed on August 5.

[139] On July 29 the Senate read this bill twice and committed it. On July 30 the committee reported, and the bill was read again and agreed to.

[140] On July 29 the Senate read this bill twice and committed it. On August 2 a petition was referred to this committee, and a committee report was presented. After being amended according to the report, the bill was read again on August 2. On August 5 the bill was considered again. The *Senate Legislative Journal* for August 6 prints the committee report. It is stated that the Senate agreed to the committee report on this date. Although no recommitment is noted in the Journal, there could have been a second report on the bill. It is also possible that the August 2 entry, noting Senate agreement to the committee report, is incorrect. On August 6 the Senate agreed to the bill as amended, after reading it again.

[141] Senate amendments are in House Bills, SR, DNA. The amendments are printed in the *Senate Legislative Journal* on July 27.

The House proceeded to consider the said amendments, and the same being read, were agreed to.

ORDERED, That the Clerk of this House do acquaint the Senate therewith.[142]

A petition of Robert Connelly, late a serjeant in the first New-York regiment, was presented to the House and read, praying compensation for loss of sight, and other injuries sustained in the service of the United States, during the late war.

ORDERED, That the said petition be referred to the Secretary at War, with instruction to examine the same, and report his opinion thereupon to the House.

ORDERED, That a committee be appointed to prepare and bring in a bill or bills to continue in force, for a limited time, an act intituled, "An act for the temporary establishment of the post-office."

And a committee was appointed of Mr. Sedgwick, Mr. Smith (of South Carolina), and Mr. Huntington.

Mr. Clymer from the committee appointed, presented according to order, a bill to compensate Thomas Barclay for various public services, which was received and read the first time.

On motion,

The said bill was read the second time, and ordered to be committed to a committee of the whole House immediately.

The House accordingly resolved itself into the said committee.

Mr. Speaker left the chair.

Mr. Seney took the chair of the committee.

Mr. Speaker resumed the chair, and Mr. Seney reported, that the committee had, according to order, had the said bill under consideration, and made several amendments thereto, which he delivered in at the Clerk's table, where the same were severally twice read and agreed to by the House.

ORDERED, That the said bill, with the amendments, be engrossed, and read the third time to-morrow.[143]

Mr. Sedgwick from the committee appointed, presented according to order, a bill to continue in force for a limited time, an act, intituled, "An act for the temporary establishment of the post-office," which was received and read the first time.

On motion,

The said bill was read the second time, and ordered to be engrossed, and read the third time to-morrow.[144]

---

[142] On August 2 this bill was signed.
[143] On July 29 this bill was read again, agreed to, and sent to the Senate.
[144] On July 29 this bill was read again, agreed to, and sent to the Senate.

ORDERED, That the report of the Secretary of the Treasury, of a uniform system for the disposition of lands the property of the United States, be referred to the consideration of the committee of the whole House on the state of the union.

The several orders of the day were farther postponed until to-morrow.

And then the House adjourned until to-morrow morning eleven o'clock.

THURSDAY, JULY 29, 1790

A message from the Senate by Mr. Otis their Secretary.

MR. SPEAKER, The Senate do agree to some and disagree to others of the amendments proposed by this House to their amendments to the bill intituled, "An act making provision for the debt of the United States:"[145] And then he withdrew.

The House proceeded to consider the said message: Whereupon,

A motion being made and seconded, that the House do recede from their disagreement to the third amendment proposed to the seventh amendment of the Senate to the said bill,

It was resolved in the affirmative, $\left\{\begin{array}{l}\text{AYES } 33 \\ \text{NOES } 27\end{array}\right.$

The ayes and noes being demanded by one fifth of the members present,

Those who voted in the affirmative, are,

John Baptista Ashe	Richard Bland Lee
Abraham Baldwin	George Leonard
John Brown	Samuel Livermore
Aedanus Burke	Peter Muhlenberg
Lambert Cadwalader	George Partridge
Daniel Carroll	Thomas Scott
George Clymer	Theodore Sedgwick
Thomas Fitzsimons	Roger Sherman
William Floyd	Thomas Sinnickson
George Gale	William Smith (of South-Carolina)
Benjamin Goodhue	Michael Jenifer Stone
Samuel Griffin	George Thatcher
Jonathan Grout	Thomas Tudor Tucker
Thomas Hartley	John Vining
Daniel Hiester	Henry Wynkoop and
Daniel Huger	Hugh Williamson
Benjamin Huntington	

---

[145] These Senate actions are noted on the printed House amendments filed with the bill in House Bills, SR, DNA.

Those who voted in the negative, are,

Fisher Ames	John Page
Egbert Benson	Josiah Parker
Timothy Bloodworth	Jeremiah Van Rensselaer
Isaac Coles	James Schureman
Benjamin Contee	Joshua Seney
Abiel Foster	John Sevier
Elbridge Gerry	Peter Silvester
Nicholas Gilman	William Smith (of Maryland)
John Hathorn	John Steele
James Jackson	Jonathan Sturges
John Laurance	Thomas Sumter
James Madison, junior	Jonathan Trumbull and
George Mathews	Alexander White
Andrew Moore	

Another motion being then made and seconded, that the House do recede from their disagreement to the fifth amendment proposed to the seventh amendment of the Senate to the said bill:

It was resolved in the affirmative, $\begin{cases} \text{AYES} & 33 \\ \text{NOES} & 27 \end{cases}$

The ayes and noes being demanded by one fifth of the members present, Those who voted in the affirmative, are,

John Baptista Ashe	George Leonard
Abraham Baldwin	Samuel Livermore
John Brown	Peter Muhlenberg
Aedanus Burke	George Partridge
Lambert Cadwalader	James Schureman
Daniel Carroll	Thomas Scott
George Clymer	Theodore Sedgwick
Thomas Fitzsimons	Roger Sherman
William Floyd	Peter Silvester
George Gale	Thomas Sinnickson
Benjamin Goodhue	William Smith (of South-Carolina)
Jonathan Grout	Michael Jenifer Stone
Thomas Hartley	George Thatcher
Daniel Hiester	Thomas Tudor Tucker
Daniel Huger	Hugh Williamson and
Benjamin Huntington	Henry Wynkoop
Richard Bland Lee	

Those who voted in the negative, are,

Fisher Ames   Andrew Moore
Egbert Benson   John Page
Timothy Bloodworth   Josiah Parker
Isaac Coles   Jeremiah Van Rensselaer
Benjamin Contee   Joshua Seney
Abiel Foster   John Sevier
Elbridge Gerry   William Smith (of Maryland)
Nicholas Gilman   John Steele
Samuel Griffin   Jonathan Sturges
John Hathorn   Thomas Sumter
James Jackson   Jonathan Trumbull
John Laurance   John Vining and
James Madison, junior   Alexander White
George Mathews

RESOLVED, That this House do recede from their third and fifth amendments proposed to the last amendment of the Senate to the said bill.

ORDERED, That the Clerk of this House do acquaint the Senate therewith.[146]

An engrossed bill to continue in force for a limited time, an act intituled, "An act for the temporary establishment of the post-office," was read the third time.

RESOLVED, That the said bill do pass, and that the title be, "An act to continue in force for a limited time, an act intituled, 'An act for the temporary establishment of the post-office.'"

ORDERED, That the Clerk of this House do carry the said bill to the Senate, and desire their concurrence.[147]

An engrossed bill to compensate Thomas Barclay for various public services, was read the third time.

RESOLVED, That the said bill do pass, and that the title be, "An act to compensate Thomas Barclay for various public services."

ORDERED, That the Clerk of this House do carry the said bill to the Senate, and desire their concurrence.[148]

Mr. Steele, from the committee appointed to examine into the proceedings

[146] On August 2 this bill was signed.
[147] The Senate read this bill on July 29 and 30. On July 30 it was agreed to.
[148] The Senate read this bill on July 29 and 30. On July 30 it was committed, and the committee reported amendments to the bill on August 3. On August 5 the amendments, which are printed in the *Senate Legislative Journal*, were agreed to. On August 6 the bill was read and agreed to by the Senate with the amendments, and the House was notified.

of the several States, on the subject of the amendments proposed by Congress, to the Constitution of the United States, made a report,[149] which was read, and ordered to lie on the table.

Mr. Gerry, from the committee to whom was referred the petition of Catherine Greene, made a report, which was read and ordered to lie on the table.[150]

A petition of John J. Miller, of the city of Philadelphia, was presented to the House and read, praying that he may be permitted to supply from his gun-powder works, all such quantities of gun-powder, as the demands of government may require.

ORDERED, That the said petition be referred to the Secretary at War, with instruction to examine the same, and report his opinion thereupon to the House.

ORDERED, That Mr. Sedgwick have leave to be absent from the service of this House for the remainder of the session.

The several orders of the day were farther postponed until to-morrow.

And then the House adjourned until to-morrow morning eleven o'clock.

FRIDAY, JULY 30, 1790

A petition of Francis Dade, was presented to the House and read, praying compensation for military services rendered during the late war.

ORDERED, That the said petition be referred to the Secretary at War, with instruction to examine the same, and report his opinion thereupon to the House.

The several petitions of Benjamin Brown, Simon Nathan, and John Griffith, were presented to the House and read, respectively praying the liquidation and settlement of a claim against the United States.

ORDERED, That the said petitions be referred to the Secretary of the Treasury, with instruction to examine the same, and report his opinion thereupon to the House.

A message from the Senate by Mr. Otis their Secretary.

MR. SPEAKER,   The Senate have passed the bill, intituled, "An act for the relief of John Stewart and John Davidson;" the Senate have also passed the bill, intituled, "An act to continue in force for a limited time, an act intituled, 'An act for the temporary establishment of the post-office:' "[151]   And then he withdrew.

---

[149] A copy of the report is in A Record of the Reports of Select Committees, HR, DNA.

[150] On July 30 this report was considered, and the Greene petition was referred to the secretary of the treasury.

[151] On August 2 these bills were signed.

The House proceeded to consider the report of the committee to whom was referred the petition of Catherine Greene: Whereupon,

ORDERED, That the said petition be referred to the Secretary of the Treasury, with instruction to examine the same, and report his opinion thereupon to the House forthwith.

The House, according to the standing order of the day, resolved itself into a committee of the whole House on the state of the Union.

Mr. Speaker left the chair.

Mr. Seney took the chair of the committee.

Mr. Speaker resumed the chair, and Mr. Seney reported, that the committee had, according to order, had the state of the Union under consideration, but had come to no resolution thereupon.

ORDERED, That a committee be appointed to prepare and bring in a bill or bills making provision for the officers of the judicial courts of the United States, and for jurors and witnesses attending the same.

And a committee was appointed, of Mr. Benson, Mr. Vining, and Mr. Smith (of South-Carolina).[152]

The several orders of the day were farther postponed until Monday next.

And then the House adjourned until Monday morning eleven o'clock.

---

[152] On August 5 this committee was discharged.

MONDAY, August 2, 1790

Mr. Gilman, from the joint committee for inrolled bills, reported, that the committee had examined four inrolled bills; one intituled, "An act to provide more effectually for the collection of the duties imposed by law on goods, wares and merchandize imported into the United States, and on the tonnage of ships or vessels;"[1] another intituled, "An act for the relief of John Stewart and John Davidson;"[2] another intituled, "An act to continue in force for a limited time an act intituled, 'An act for the temporary establishment of the post-office;'"[3] and another intituled, "An act making provision for the debt of the United States;"[4] and had found the same to be truly inrolled: Whereupon,

Mr. Speaker signed the said inrolled bills.

ORDERED, That the Clerk of this House do acquaint the Senate therewith.

ORDERED, That a committee be appointed to prepare and bring in a bill or bills, declaring the assent of Congress to certain acts of the states of Maryland, Georgia, and Rhode-Island and Providence Plantations, for raising a duty on the tonnage of ships or vessels entering the ports of Patapsco, Savannah, and Providence.

And a committee was appointed of Mr. Ames, Mr. Jackson, and Mr. Seney.[5]

A petition of Robert Provoost, was presented to the House and read, praying compensation for military services performed during the late war. Also,

A petition of Richard Lloyd, praying compensation for services as late agent to General Hazen's regiment.

ORDERED, That the said petitions be referred to the Secretary at War, with instruction to examine the same, and report his opinion thereupon to the House.

The House proceeded to consider the report of the Secretary at War, on the petition of Sarah Stirling: Whereupon,

RESOLVED, That there be paid to Sarah Stirling, the widow of the late Major-General Lord Stirling, the sum of six thousand nine hundred and seventy-two dollars, being the half pay of a Major-General in the late American army for the term of seven years.

ORDERED, That a bill or bills be brought in pursuant to the said resolution; and that Mr. Boudinot, Mr. Thatcher and Mr. Ashe, do prepare and bring in the same.[6]

---

[1] The inspected enrolled bill is in Enrolled Acts, RG 11, DNA. E–22970.

[2] The inspected enrolled bill is in Enrolled Acts, RG 11, DNA. E–22961.

[3] The inspected enrolled bill is in Enrolled Acts, RG 11, DNA. E–46063.

[4] The inspected enrolled bill is in Enrolled Acts, RG 11, DNA. E–46048.

[5] On August 3 this committee presented the Navigation Bill [HR–93], which was read twice, considered in the COWH, and amended.

[6] On August 4 this committee presented the Stirling Bill [HR–96], which was read.

Mr. Gilman, from the joint committee for inrolled bills, reported, that the committee did, this day, wait on the President of the United States, and present for his approbation four inrolled bills; one intituled, "An act to provide more effectually for the collection of the duties imposed by law on goods, wares and merchandize imported into the United States, and on the tonnage of ships or vessels;" another intituled, "An act for the relief of John Stewart and John Davidson;" another intituled, "An act to continue in force for a limited time an act intituled, 'An act for the temporary establishment of the post-office;'" and another intituled, "An act making provision for the debt of the United States."

The Speaker laid before the House a letter from the Treasurer of the United States, together with a statement of his accounts of the receipts and expenditures of public monies, from the first of April to the thirtieth of June last inclusive,[7] which were read: Whereupon,

ORDERED, That the said statement, together with the statement for the preceding quarter, be referred to Mr. Smith (of South-Carolina), Mr. Hiester, and Mr. Parker, with instruction to examine the same, and report thereupon to the House.[8]

The House proceeded to consider the report of the committee to whom was referred the report of the Secretary at War on the petition of Henry Emanuel Lutterloh: Whereupon,

RESOLVED, That this House do disagree to the said report, and that the petitioner have leave to withdraw his said petition.

The several orders of the day were farther postponed until to-morrow.

And then the House adjourned until to-morrow morning eleven o'clock.

TUESDAY, AUGUST 3, 1790

A petition of the officers of the late Massachusetts line of the American army, in behalf of themselves, and the soldiers of the said line, was presented to the House and read, praying that further and adequate compensation may be made them for military services rendered during the late war.[9]

ORDERED, That the said petition do lie on the table.

A petition of Moses Rawlings, of the state of Maryland, was presented to the House and read, praying compensation for military services rendered during the late war.

---

[7] The letter and the accounts are in Transcribed Reports and Communications from the Executive Departments, 1789–1814, Records of the Secretary, SR, DNA. Copies of the letter and accounts are in Accounts of the Treasurer of the United States, vol. 1, HR, DNA.

[8] On August 9 this committee reported.

[9] A draft of the petition is in Massachusetts Miscellany, Manuscript Division, DLC. E–45621.

ORDERED, That the said petition be referred to the Secretary at War, with instruction to examine the same, and report his opinion thereupon to the House.

On a motion made and seconded, that the House do agree to the following resolution,

"RESOLVED, That the states of Virginia and North-Carolina be permitted to enter into a compact for the purpose of opening a navigable canal between the waters of Pasquotank river in North-Carolina, and those of the south branch of Elizabeth river in Virginia, by incorporating a company, or by such other means as they shall find best for that purpose."

ORDERED, That the said motion be committed to Mr. Parker, Mr. Williamson, Mr. Burke, Mr. Steele, and Mr. Wadsworth.

ORDERED, That a committee be appointed to prepare and bring in a bill or bills, making further provision for the debt of the United States, so far as respects the assumption of the debt of the state of Georgia.

And a committee was appointed of Mr. Jackson, Mr. Page, and Mr. Trumbull.

Mr. Ames, from the committee appointed, presented, according to order, a bill declaring the assent of Congress to certain acts of the states of Maryland, Georgia, and Rhode-Island and Providence Plantations, for raising a duty on the tonnage of ships or vessels entering the ports of Patapsco, Savannah, and Providence, which was received, and read the first time.

On motion,

The said bill was read the second time, and ordered to be committed to a committee of the whole House immediately.

The House accordingly resolved itself into the said committee.

Mr. Speaker left the chair.

Mr. Seney took the chair of the committee.

Mr. Speaker resumed the chair, and Mr. Seney reported, that the committee had, according to order, had the said bill under consideration, and made several amendments thereto, which he delivered in at the Clerk's table, where the same were severally twice read, and agreed to by the House.

ORDERED, That the said bill, with the amendments, be engrossed, and read the third time to-morrow.[10]

Mr. Jackson, from the committee appointed, presented, according to order, a bill making further provision for the debt of the United States, so far as respects the assumption of the debt of the state of Georgia, which was received and read the first time.[11]

---

[10] On August 4 the Navigation Bill [HR–93] was read, agreed to, and sent to the Senate.

[11] On August 4 this bill was read again, considered in the COWH, and rejected.

The several orders of the day were farther postponed until to-morrow.
And then the House adjourned until to-morrow morning eleven o'clock.

WEDNESDAY, AUGUST 4, 1790

An engrossed bill declaring the assent of Congress to certain acts of the states of Maryland, Georgia, and Rhode-Island and Providence Plantations, for raising a duty on the tonnage of ships or vessels entering the ports of Patapsco, Savannah, and Providence, was read the third time, and the blanks therein filled up.

RESOLVED, That the said bill do pass; and that the title be, "An act declaring the assent of Congress to certain acts of the States of Maryland, Georgia, and Rhode-Island and Providence Plantations."

ORDERED, That the Clerk of this House do carry the said bill to the Senate, and desire their concurrence.[12]

A message was received from the President of the United States, by Mr. Lear his Secretary, notifying that the President did, on the second instant, approve and sign two inrolled resolves; one respecting the pay of the clerks in the office of the commissioner of army accounts; the other for defraying the expence of procuring seals for the supreme, circuit and district courts of the United States: And also did on this day approve and sign four acts, to wit: "An act making provision for the debt of the United States;" "An act to provide more effectually for the collection of the duties imposed by law on goods, wares and merchandize imported into the United States, and on the tonnage of ships or vessels;" "An act to continue in force for a limited time, an act intituled, 'An act for the temporary establishment of the post-office;' " and "An act for the relief of John Stewart and John Davidson."[13]

ORDERED, That the Clerk of this House do acquaint the Senate therewith.

On motion,

ORDERED, That leave be given to bring in a bill or bills for adding two commissioners to the board established for settling the accounts between the United States and the individual States; and that Mr. Madison, Mr. Vining, and Mr. Wadsworth, do prepare and bring in the same.

A bill making further provision for the debt of the United States, so far as respects the assumption of the debt of the state of Georgia, was read the second time, and ordered to be committed to a committee of the whole House immediately.

---

[12] The Senate read this bill on August 5 and 6. It was committed on August 6. On August 9 this committee reported an amendment to the bill, which was agreed to. The bill was then read the third time and passed with the amendment. On the same day the House agreed to the amendment.

[13] The message is in Committee on Enrolled Bills, SR, DNA.

The House accordingly resolved itself into the said committee.

Mr. Speaker left the chair.

Mr. Livermore took the chair of the committee.

Mr. Speaker resumed the chair, and Mr. Livermore reported, that the committee had, according to order, had the said bill under consideration, and made several amendments thereto, which he delivered in at the Clerk's table, where the same were severally twice read, and agreed to by the House.

And then the question being put, that the said bill, with the amendments, be engrossed, and read the third time,

It passed in the negative.

And so the said bill was rejected.

Mr. Madison, from the committee appointed, presented, according to order, a bill for adding two commissioners to the board established for settling the accounts between the United States and the individual States, which was received and read the first time.

On motion,

The said bill was read the second time, and ordered to be committed to a committee of the whole House to-day.

Mr. Boudinot, from the committee appointed, presented, according to order, a bill making an appropriation for discharging the claim of Sarah Alexander, the widow of the late Major-General Lord Stirling, who died in the service of the United States, which was received and read the first time.[14]

The House then, according to order, resolved itself into a committee of the whole House on the bill for adding two commissioners to the board established for settling the accounts between the United States and the individual States.

Mr. Speaker left the chair.

Mr. Livermore took the chair of the committee.

Mr. Speaker resumed the chair, and Mr. Livermore reported, that the committee had, according to order, had the said bill under consideration, and made an amendment thereto, which he delivered in at the Clerk's table, where the same was twice read, and agreed to by the House.

And on the question, that the said bill, with the amendment, be engrossed, and read the third time,

It was resolved in the affirmative, $\begin{cases} \text{AYES} & 36 \\ \text{NOES} & 19 \end{cases}$

The ayes and noes being demanded by one fifth of the members present,

Those who voted in the affirmative, are,

---

[14] On August 5 this bill was read again and considered in the COWH.

Fisher Ames
John Baptista Ashe
Abraham Baldwin
Egbert Benson
Timothy Bloodworth
John Brown
Aedanus Burke
Daniel Carroll
George Clymer
Isaac Coles
Thomas Fitzsimons
George Gale
Nicholas Gilman
Samuel Griffin
Jonathan Grout
Thomas Hartley
Daniel Hiester
Benjamin Huntington

Richard Bland Lee
James Madison, junior
George Mathews
Andrew Moore
Peter Muhlenberg
John Page
Josiah Parker
George Partridge
Thomas Scott
Joshua Seney
John Sevier
Michael Jenifer Stone
Thomas Sumter
Jonathan Trumbull
Thomas Tudor Tucker
Jeremiah Wadsworth
Alexander White and
Henry Wynkoop

Those who voted in the negative, are,

Elias Boudinot
Lambert Cadwalader
William Floyd
Abiel Foster
Elbridge Gerry
John Hathorn
James Jackson
John Laurance
Samuel Livermore
Jeremiah Van Rensselaer

James Schureman
Roger Sherman
Peter Silvester
Thomas Sinnickson
William Smith (of Maryland)
William Smith (of South-Carolina)
John Steele
Jonathan Sturges and
George Thatcher[15]

The several orders of the day were farther postponed until to-morrow.
And then the House adjourned until to-morrow morning eleven o'clock.

THURSDAY, AUGUST 5, 1790

A bill making an appropriation for discharging the claim of Sarah Alexander, the widow of the late Major-General Lord Stirling, who died in the service of the United States, was read the second time, and ordered to be committed to a committee of the whole House to-day.

---

[15] On August 5 the Settling of Accounts Bill [HR–95] was read again, agreed to, and sent to the Senate.

On motion,

RESOLVED, That the Secretary of the Treasury, under the direction of the President of the United States, do take measures for finishing the light-house at Portland Head, in the district of Maine: PROVIDED the expence in finishing the same, do not exceed fifteen hundred dollars.

ORDERED, That a bill or bills be brought in pursuant to the said resolution; and that Mr. Thatcher, Mr. Partridge, and Mr. Trumbull, do prepare and bring in the same.

ORDERED, That the committee appointed to prepare and bring in a bill making provision for the officers of the Supreme Court of the United States, and for jurors and witnesses attending the same, be discharged from farther proceeding thereon.

ORDERED, That the Attorney-General report to this House, at the next session of Congress, on such matters relative to the administration of justice under the authority of the United States, as may require to be remedied: And that he also report such provisions in the respective cases as he shall deem adviseable.

A message was received from the President of the United States, by Mr. Lear his Secretary, notifying that the President did this day approve and sign an act, intituled, "An act to provide more effectually for the settlement of the accounts between the United States and the individual states."

ORDERED, That the Clerk of this House do acquaint the Senate therewith.

An engrossed bill for adding two commissioners to the board established for settling the accounts between the United States and the individual states, was read the third time.

RESOLVED, That the said bill do pass, and that the title be "An act for adding two commissioners to the board established for settling the accounts between the United States and the individual states."[16]

ORDERED, That the Clerk of this House do carry the said bill to the Senate and desire their concurrence.[17]

On a motion made and seconded, that a committee be appointed to prepare and report a bill to repeal, for a limited time, the fifth section of the act, intituled, "An act for establishing the temporary and permanent seat of the government of the United States."

The previous question was demanded by five members, "Shall the main question to agree to the said motion, be now put;" and on the question, "Shall the main question be now put."

It passed in the negative, $\begin{cases} \text{AYES} & 23 \\ \text{NOES} & 35 \end{cases}$

---

[16] The bill is in Engrossed House Bills, HR, DNA.

[17] On August 5 the Senate read this bill, and on August 6 they voted not to read it a second time. The House was notified of this action on August 7.

The ayes and noes being called for by one fifth of the members present, Those who voted in the affirmative, are,

Egbert Benson
Timothy Bloodworth
Aedanus Burke
William Floyd
Abiel Foster
Elbridge Gerry
Jonathan Grout
John Hathorn
Daniel Huger
Benjamin Huntington
John Laurance
George Leonard

Samuel Livermore
Jeremiah Van Rensselaer
James Schureman
John Sevier
Peter Silvester
William Smith (of Maryland)
William Smith (of South-Carolina)
Jonathan Sturges
George Thatcher
Jonathan Trumbull and
Jeremiah Wadsworth

Those who voted in the negative, are,

Fisher Ames
John Baptista Ashe
Abraham Baldwin
John Brown
Lambert Cadwalader
Daniel Carroll
George Clymer
Isaac Coles
Thomas Fitzsimons
George Gale
Nicholas Gilman
Benjamin Goodhue
Thomas Hartley
Daniel Hiester
James Jackson
Richard Bland Lee
James Madison, junior
George Mathews

Andrew Moore
Peter Muhlenberg
John Page
Josiah Parker
George Partridge
Thomas Scott
Joshua Seney
Roger Sherman
Thomas Sinnickson
John Steele
Michael Jenifer Stone
Thomas Sumter
Thomas Tudor Tucker
John Vining
Alexander White
Henry Wynkoop and
Hugh Williamson

And so the said motion was lost.

A petition of Alexander Macomb and William Edgar, was presented to the House and read, praying to be released from a contract entered into with the United States, for the purchase of a quantity of western lands.

ORDERED, That the said petition be referred to the Secretary of the Treas-

ury, with instruction to examine the same, and report his opinion thereupon to the House.

The House then, according to order, resolved itself into a committee of the whole House on the bill making an appropriation for discharging the claim of Sarah Alexander, the widow of the late major-general Lord Stirling, who died in the service of the United States.

Mr. Speaker left the chair.

Mr. Livermore took the chair of the committee.

Mr. Speaker resumed the chair, and Mr. Livermore reported, that the committee had, according to order, had the said bill under consideration, and made no amendment thereto.

ORDERED, That the said bill be engrossed, and read the third time tomorrow.[18]

Mr. Thatcher, from the committee appointed, presented, according to order, a bill, authorizing the Secretary of the Treasury to finish a light-house on Portland-head, in the district of Maine, which was received and read the first time.

On motion, the said bill was read the second time, and ordered to be committed to a committee of the whole House immediately.

The House accordingly resolved itself into the said committee.

Mr. Speaker left the chair.

Mr. Livermore took the chair of the committee.

Mr. Speaker resumed the chair, and Mr. Livermore reported that the committee had, according to order, had the said bill under consideration, and made no amendment thereto.

ORDERED, That the said bill be engrossed and read the third time tomorrow.[19]

On motion,

RESOLVED, That a surveyor-general for the United States be appointed, who shall forthwith proceed to the completion of the surveys of all lands heretofore sold under the authority of the late Congress.

ORDERED, That a bill or bills be brought in pursuant to the said resolution, and that Mr. Smith (of South-Carolina), Mr. Page, and Mr. White, do prepare and bring in the same.[20]

A message from the Senate by Mr. Otis their Secretary.

MR. SPEAKER,   The Senate have passed the bill, intituled, "An act making further provision for the payment of the debts of the United States," with

---

[18] On August 6 this bill was read, agreed to, and sent to the Senate.

[19] On August 6 this bill was read again, agreed to, and sent to the Senate.

[20] On August 6 this committee presented the Surveyor General Bill [HR–98], which was read.

several amendments,[21] to which they desire the concurrence of this House: And then he withdrew.

The House proceeded to consider the said amendments, and made some progress therein.

ORDERED, That the farther consideration of the said amendments be put off until to-morrow.[22]

The several orders of the day were farther postponed until to-morrow.

And then the House adjourned until to-morrow morning ten o'clock.

FRIDAY, AUGUST 6, 1790

An engrossed bill making an appropriation for discharging the claim of Sarah Alexander, the widow of the late major-general Lord Stirling, who died in the service of the United States, was read the third time.

RESOLVED, That the said bill do pass, and that the title be, "An act making an appropriation for discharging the claim of Sarah Alexander, the widow of the late major-general Lord Stirling, who died in the service of the United States."

ORDERED, That the Clerk of this House do carry the said bill to the Senate, and desire their concurrence.[23]

An engrossed bill, authorizing the Secretary of the Treasury to finish the light-house on Portland-head, in the district of Maine, was read the third time.

RESOLVED, That the said bill do pass, and that the title be, "An act authorizing the Secretary of the Treasury to finish the light-house on Portland-head, in the district of Maine."

ORDERED, That the Clerk of this House do carry the said bill to the Senate and desire their concurrence.[24]

On motion,

---

[21] The Senate committee report on this bill, with amendments, is in Various Select Committee Reports, SR, DNA. The report is printed in the *Senate Legislative Journal* on August 4, and further amendments to the bill are printed on August 5. The bill, as amended by the Senate committee, was ordered to be reprinted on August 2. This bill, with annotations which represent the amendments agreed to in the Senate on August 5, is in House Bills, SR, DNA.

[22] On August 6 the House agreed to all of the Senate amendments with several amendments to the second amendment. A further amendment was disagreed to.

[23] On August 6 the Senate read this bill twice and committed it. On August 7 this committee reported extensive amendments to this bill, which are printed in the *Senate Legislative Journal*. On the same day the amendments and the bill were agreed to. On August 9 the House was notified of the Senate amendments, and they were agreed to.

[24] The Senate read this bill on August 6. On August 7 it was read twice and agreed to.

RESOLVED, That the President of the Senate, and Speaker of the House of Representatives be authorized to close the present session, by adjourning their respective Houses on Tuesday next, to meet again on the first Monday of December next.

ORDERED, That the Clerk of this House do carry the said resolution to the Senate, and desire their concurrence.[25]

ORDERED, That the Secretary of the Treasury be directed to report early in the next session, proper and effectual means of discharging the arrearages due to the invalid pensioners of the United States, and to the widows and representatives of the deceased officers and soldiers in the late American army.

Mr. Smith (of South-Carolina), from the committee appointed, presented, according to order, a bill providing for the appointment of a surveyor-general for the United States, which was received and read the first time.[26]

The House resumed the consideration of the amendments proposed by the Senate, to the bill, intituled, "An act making further provision for the payment of the debts of the United States:" Whereupon,

RESOLVED, That this House do agree to all the said amendments, with amendments to the second amendment, as follow:

Page 2d, line 21st, strike out "under," and insert "more than."

Page 4th, line 27th, strike out "all goods, wares and merchandizes (except teas) from China or India, in ships or vessels not of the United States."

Page 6th, line 32d, insert as an additional clause, "all coaches, chariots, phaetons, chaises, chairs, solos, or other carriages, or parts of carriages, fifteen and an half per centum ad valorem."

Same page and line prefix to the last clause, "and five per centum ad valorem upon," and strike out the words "five per centum ad valorem" at the end of the same.

Another motion was made and seconded, further to amend the said amendment by striking out the words "twelve cents" for the duty upon salt: And on the question thereupon,

It passed in the negative, $\left\{ \begin{array}{l} \text{AYES } 28 \\ \text{NOES } 30 \end{array} \right.$

The ayes and noes being demanded by one fifth of the members present, Those who voted in the affirmative, are,

John Baptista Ashe	Isaac Coles
Abraham Baldwin	Abiel Foster
Timothy Bloodworth	Benjamin Goodhue
John Brown	Jonathan Grout
Aedanus Burke	John Hathorn

---

[25] On August 7 the Senate agreed to this resolution.
[26] On August 7 this bill was read again and disagreed to.

Daniel Huger
James Jackson
George Leonard
James Madison, junior
George Mathews
Andrew Moore
Peter Muhlenberg
George Partridge
Thomas Scott

Joshua Seney
John Sevier
William Smith (of South-Carolina)
John Steele
Thomas Sumter
George Thatcher
Thomas Tudor Tucker
Alexander White and
Hugh Williamson

Those who voted in the negative, are,

Fisher Ames
Egbert Benson
Elias Boudinot
Lambert Cadwalader
Daniel Carroll
George Clymer
Thomas Fitzsimons
William Floyd
George Gale
Elbridge Gerry
Samuel Griffin
Thomas Hartley
Benjamin Huntington
John Laurance
Richard Bland Lee

Samuel Livermore
John Page
Josiah Parker
Jeremiah Van Rensselaer
James Schureman
Roger Sherman
Peter Silvester
Thomas Sinnickson
William Smith (of Maryland)
Michael Jenifer Stone
Jonathan Sturges
Jonathan Trumbull
John Vining
Jeremiah Wadsworth and
Henry Wynkoop[27]

A message, in writing, was received from the President of the United States, by Mr. Lear, his Secretary, as followeth:

UNITED STATES, August 6th, 1790

GENTLEMEN of the SENATE and HOUSE of REPRESENTATIVES,

I have directed my Secretary to lay before you a copy of an exemplified copy of a law, to ratify, on the part of the state of New-Jersey, certain amendments to the Constitution of the United States, together with a copy of a letter, which accompanied said ratification, from the honorable Elisha Lawrence, Esquire, Vice-President of the state of New-Jersey, to the President of the United States.

GEORGE WASHINGTON[28]

[27] On August 7 the Senate agreed to the House amendments to their second amendment to the Ways and Means Bill [HR–83].

[28] The message with enclosures is in President's Messages: Suggesting legislation, SR, DNA. The enclosures are printed in the Appendix to the Second Session.

The letter and papers accompanying the said message, were read, and ordered to lie on the table.

Mr. Vining, from the committee appointed, presented, according to order, a bill for the relief of Adam Caldwell, which was received, and read the first time.

On motion,

The said bill was read the second time, and ordered to be committed to a committee of the whole House to-morrow.[29]

A message from the Senate by Mr. Otis their Secretary.

MR. SPEAKER,   The Senate have passed the bill, intituled, "An act to compensate Thomas Barclay, for various public services," with several amendments, to which they desire the concurrence of this House:[30]   And then he withdrew.

The several orders of the day were farther postponed until to-morrow.

And then the House adjourned until to-morrow morning ten o'clock.

SATURDAY, AUGUST 7, 1790

A bill for the appointment of a Surveyor-General for the United States, was read the second time; and on the question that the said bill be engrossed and read the third time,

It passed in the negative.

And so the said bill was rejected.

The Speaker laid before the House a letter and report from the Secretary of the Treasury, accompanied with statements of additional sums necessary to be provided for the support of government by farther appropriations,[31] which were read, and ordered to be referred to the committee of the whole House on the state of the Union.

A message from the Senate by Mr. Otis their Secretary.

MR. SPEAKER,   The Senate have disagreed to the resolution of this House respecting the claim of Francis Mentges; also to the bill, intituled, "An act

---

[29] On August 7 this bill was considered in the COWH and amended.

[30] The Senate committee report on this bill, with amendments, is in Various Select Committee Reports, SR, DNA. The report is printed in the *Senate Legislative Journal* on August 5. There is no further mention of this bill in the Journal. It never became a law.

[31] The report with the statements is in Alexander Hamilton's Reports, HR, DNA. A copy of the report with the statements is in A Record of the Reports of the Secretary of the Treasury, vol. 1, HR, DNA. A copy of the report, probably made by ASP, is in Reports and Communications from the Secretary of the Treasury, HR, DNA.

for adding two commissioners to the board established for settling the accounts between the United States and individual States:" The Senate have also passed the bill, intituled, "An act for the relief of disabled soldiers and seamen, lately in the service of the United States, and of certain other persons," with several amendments, to which they desire the concurrence of this House:[32] And then he withdrew.

The Speaker laid before the House a letter from the Secretary of the Treasury, covering his report on the subject matter of sundry petitions, praying a renewal of continental loan-office certificates destroyed through accident,[33] which were read, and ordered to lie on the table.

The House then, according to the standing order of the day, resolved itself into a committee of the whole House on the state of the Union.

Mr. Speaker left the chair.

Mr. Seney took the chair of the committee.

Mr. Speaker resumed the chair, and Mr. Seney reported, that the committee had, according to order, had the state of the Union under consideration, and come to several resolutions thereupon, which he delivered in at the Clerk's table, where the same were severally twice read, and agreed to by the House, as follow:

RESOLVED, That the sum of fifty thousand dollars, out of the monies arising from the duties on imports and tonnage, be reserved and appropriated for satisfying demands against the United States, not otherwise specially provided for; and that an act for that purpose ought to be passed the present session.

RESOLVED, That out of the monies reserved during the present session for the support of government, from the duties on imports and tonnage, a sum

---

[32] The Senate committee report on this bill, with amendments, is in Various Select Committee Reports, SR, DNA. The amendments are printed in the *Senate Legislative Journal* on August 6. With the amendments the House probably also received supporting documents, including the papers of Seth Boardman and the reports of the New York commissioners of invalids on the cases of Jacob Newkirk, Daniel Culver, Severinus Koch, Joseph Shuttlief, William White, Edward Scott, David Weaver, and George Schell. These documents are in Petitions and Memorials, HR, DNA. They were probably sent to the House in compliance with a communication from the Senate on June 15, 1790, which stated:

The Senate will decline in future ~~the~~ taking up any bills etc. ~~in future~~ without the original ~~papers~~ petitions & other documents on which ~~they~~ the Bills or Resolves originated, are ~~sent to~~ communicated.

A draft of the message is in Records of the Secretary: Concerning newspapers, SR, DNA. On August 9 the House agreed to these Senate amendments.

[33] A copy of the report, which is also on the petition of Jacob Rash, is in A Record of the Reports of the Secretary of the Treasury, vol. 1, HR, DNA. A copy, probably made by ASP, is in Reports and Communications from the Secretary of the Treasury, HR, DNA.

not exceeding thirty-eight thousand eight hundred ninety-two dollars and seventy-five cents, be appropriated for the payment of the debts contracted by Abraham Skinner late commissary of prisoners, for the subsistence of the officers of the late army while in captivity.

RESOLVED, That provision by law should be immediately made for the appropriation of the surplus sum which shall remain in the treasury after all the appropriations, made during the present session, shall be satisfied, in conformity to the tenor of the report of the Secretary of the Treasury.

ORDERED, That a bill or bills be brought in pursuant to the said resolutions, and that Mr. Fitzsimons, Mr. Vining, Mr. Madison, Mr. Ames, and Mr. Benson, do prepare and bring in the same.[34]

A message from the Senate by Mr. Otis their Secretary.

MR. SPEAKER, The Senate have agreed to the amendments proposed by this House to their amendments to the bill, intituled, "An act making further provision for the payment of the debts of the United States."[35] The Senate have also passed the bill, intituled, "An act authorising the Secretary of the Treasury to finish the light-house on Portland-Head, in the district of Maine."[36] Also the bill, intituled, "An act to enable the officers and soldiers of the Virginia line, on continental establishment, to obtain titles to certain lands lying north-west of the river Ohio, between the Little Miami and Sciota," with several amendments,[37] to which they desire the concurrence of this House: And then he withdrew.

The House proceeded to consider the said amendments, and the same being read, were agreed to.

ORDERED, That the Clerk of this House do acquaint the Senate therewith.[38]

The House, according to the order of the day, resolved itself into a committee of the whole House on the bill for the relief of Adam Caldwell.

Mr. Speaker left the chair.

Mr. Seney took the chair of the committee.

Mr. Speaker resumed the chair, and Mr. Seney reported, that the committee

---

[34] On August 9 this committee presented the Special Appropriations Bill [HR–100] and the Sinking Fund Bill [HR–101]. On the same day these bills were read, amended, agreed to, and sent to the Senate.

[35] On August 9 this bill was signed by the speaker and the vice president and presented to the president.

[36] On August 9 this bill was signed by the speaker and the vice president and presented to the president.

[37] The amendments are printed in the *Senate Legislative Journal* on August 3, 6, and 7.

[38] On August 9 the Virginia Cession Bill [HR–85] was signed by the speaker and the vice president and presented to the president.

had, according to order, had the said bill under consideration, and made several amendments thereto, which he delivered in at the Clerk's table, where the same were severally twice read, and agreed to by the House.

ORDERED, That the said bill, with the amendments, be engrossed, and read the third time on Monday next.[39]

A message from the Senate by Mr. Otis their Secretary.

MR. SPEAKER, The Senate have agreed to the resolution of this House, of the sixth instant, authorizing the Speaker of the House of Representatives, and the President of the Senate to close the present session of Congress, by adjourning their respective Houses on Tuesday next, to meet again the first Monday in December next:[40] And then he withdrew.

ORDERED, That Mr. Partridge have leave to be absent from the service of this House for the reminder of the session.

The several orders of the day were farther postponed until Monday next.

And then the House adjourned until Monday morning ten o'clock.

MONDAY, AUGUST 9, 1790

An engrossed bill for the relief of Adam Caldwell, was read the third time.

RESOLVED, That the said bill do pass, and that the title be, "An act for the relief of Adam Caldwell."[41]

ORDERED, That the Clerk of this House do carry the said bill to the Senate and desire their concurrence.[42]

Mr. Gilman from the joint committee for inrolled bills reported, that the committee had examined three inrolled bills, one intituled, "An act making further provision for the payment of the debts of the United States;"[43] another intituled, "An act to enable the officers and soldiers of the Virginia line on continental establishment, to obtain titles to certain lands lying north-west of the river Ohio, between the Little Miami and Sciota;"[44] and another intituled, "An act authorizing the Secretary of the Treasury to finish the lighthouse on Portland-head, in the district of Maine,"[45] and had found the same to be truly inrolled: Whereupon,

Mr. Speaker signed the said inrolled bills.

---

[39] On August 9 this bill was read a third time, passed, and sent to the Senate.

[40] On August 9 a committee to inform the president of the proposed recess of Congress was appointed.

[41] The bill is in Engrossed House Bills, HR, DNA.

[42] The Senate read this bill on August 9 and 11 and postponed it to third session.

[43] The inspected enrolled bill is in Enrolled Acts, RG 11, DNA. E–22965, E–46046.

[44] The inspected enrolled bill is in Enrolled Acts, RG 11, DNA. E–46065.

[45] The inspected enrolled bill is in Enrolled Acts, RG 11, DNA. E–22955.

ORDERED, That the Clerk of this House do acquaint the Senate therewith.

Mr. Fitzsimons, from the committee appointed, presented, according to order, a bill making certain appropriations therein mentioned, which was received and read the first time.

On motion,

The said bill was read the second time, and ordered to be committed to a committee of the whole House to-day.

The House proceeded to consider the amendments proposed by the Senate to the bill, intituled, "An act for the relief of disabled soldiers and seamen lately in the service of the United States, and of certain other persons;" and the same being read, were agreed to.

ORDERED, That the Clerk of this House do acquaint the Senate therewith.[46]

Mr. Fitzsimons, from the committee appointed, presented, according to order, a bill making provision for the reduction of the public debt, which was received and read the first time.

On motion,

The said bill was read the second time, and ordered to be committed to a committee of the whole House to-day.

A message from the Senate by Mr. Otis their Secretary.

MR. SPEAKER, The Senate have passed the bill, intituled, "An act making an appropriation for discharging the claim of Sarah Alexander, the widow of the late major-general Lord Stirling, who died in the service of the United States," with several amendments,[47] to which they desire the concurrence of this House: And then he withdrew.

The House proceeded to consider the said amendments, and the same being read, were agreed to.

ORDERED, That the Clerk of this House do acquaint the Senate therewith.[48]

The House then, according to order, resolved itself into a committee of the whole, on the bill making provision for the reduction of the public debt.

Mr. Speaker left the chair.

Mr. Livermore took the chair of the committee.

Mr. Speaker resumed the chair, and Mr. Livermore reported, that the committee had, according to order, had the said bill under consideration, and

---

[46] On August 10 this bill was signed by the speaker and vice president and delivered to the president.

[47] The Senate committee report on this bill, with the amendments, is in Various Select Committee Reports, SR, DNA. The report is printed in the *Senate Legislative Journal* on August 7.

[48] On August 10 this bill was signed by the speaker and the vice president and presented to the president.

made several amendments thereto, which he delivered in at the Clerk's table, where the same were severally twice read, and agreed to by the House.

ORDERED, That the said bill, with the amendments, be engrossed, and read the third time to-day.

Mr. Gilman, from the joint committee for inrolled bills, reported, that the committee did, this day, wait on the President of the United States, and present for his approbation three inrolled bills; one intituled, "An act making further provision for the payment of the debts of the United States;" another intituled, "An act to enable the officers and soldiers of the Virginia line, on continental establishment, to obtain titles to certain lands lying north-west of the river Ohio, between the Little Miami and Sciota;" and another intituled, "An act authorizing the Secretary of the Treasury to finish the light-house on Portland-head, in the district of Maine."[49]

Mr. Smith (of South-Carolina), from the committee appointed to examine the accounts of the Treasurer of the United States for the two last quarters, reported[50] that the committee had examined the same, and found them to agree with the several certified statements thereon, by the Auditor, admitted by the Comptroller of the Treasury, and registered by the Register.

ORDERED, That the said report do lie on the table.

A message from the Senate by Mr. Otis their Secretary.

MR. SPEAKER, The Senate have passed a bill, intituled, "An act to alter the times of holding the circuit courts in the states of South-Carolina and Georgia,"[51] to which they desire the concurrence of this House: The Senate have also passed the bill, intituled, "An act declaring the assent of Congress to certain acts of the states of Maryland, Georgia, and Rhode-Island and Providence Plantations," with an amendment,[52] to which they desire the concurrence of this House: And then he withdrew.

The House proceeded to consider the said amendment, and the same being read was agreed to.

ORDERED, That the Clerk of this House do acquaint the Senate therewith.[53]

On motion,

RESOLVED, That Mr. Gilman, Mr. White, and Mr. Smith (of South-Carolina), be a committee to join with such committee as the Senate shall appoint

---

[49] The president signed these three bills on August 10.

[50] A copy of this report is in A Record of the Reports of Select Committees, HR, DNA.

[51] The bill with annotations is in Engrossed Senate Bills and Resolutions, SR, DNA.

[52] The amendment is printed in the *Senate Legislative Journal* on August 9.

[53] On August 10 this bill was signed by the speaker and vice president and presented to the president.

to wait on the President of the United States, and notify him of the proposed recess of Congress.[54]

ORDERED, That the Secretary of the Treasury be directed to prepare and report to this House on the second Monday of December next, such further provision as may, in his opinion, be necessary for establishing the public credit.[55]

The bill sent from the Senate, intituled, "An act to alter the times of holding the circuit courts in the states of South-Carolina and Georgia," was read the first time.

On motion,

The said bill was read the second time and ordered to be committed to a committee of the whole House to-day.

RESOLVED, That all surveys of lands in the Western Territory, made under the direction of the late geographer Thomas Hutchins, agreeably to contracts for a part of the said lands made with the late Board of Treasury, be returned to, and perfected by the Secretary of the Treasury, so as to compleat the said contracts; and that the said Secretary be, and he is hereby authorized to direct the making and compleating any other surveys that remain to be made, so as to comply on the part of the United States with the several contracts aforesaid.

ORDERED, That the Clerk of this House do carry the said resolution to the Senate and desire their concurrence.[56]

The House, according to order, resolved itself into a committee of the whole House on the bill sent from the Senate, intituled, "An act to alter the times of holding the circuit courts in the states of South-Carolina and Georgia."

Mr. Speaker left the chair.

Mr. Livermore took the chair of the committee.

Mr. Speaker resumed the chair, and Mr. Livermore reported, that the committee had, according to order, had the said bill under consideration, and made several amendments thereto, which he delivered in at the Clerk's table, where the same were severally twice read and agreed to by the House.

The said bill, with the amendments,[57] was then read the third time and passed.

ORDERED, That the Clerk of this House do acquaint the Senate therewith.[58]

---

[54] On August 10 another resolution postponing the adjournment was agreed to.

[55] On December 13, 1790, the secretary reported.

[56] On August 10 the House was notified that the Senate had agreed to this resolution.

[57] A copy of the amendments is filed with the bill in Engrossed Senate Bills and Resolutions, SR, DNA.

[58] On August 10 the House was notified that the Senate had agreed to the House

An engrossed bill making provision for the reduction of the public debt, was read the third time.

RESOLVED, That the said bill do pass, and that the title be, "An act making provision for the reduction of the public debt."[59]

ORDERED, That the Clerk of this House do carry the said bill to the Senate, and desire their concurrence.[60]

The House then, according to order, resolved itself into a committee of the whole House on the bill making certain appropriations therein mentioned.

Mr. Speaker left the chair.

Mr. Livermore took the chair of the committee.

Mr. Speaker resumed the chair, and Mr. Livermore reported, that the committee had, according to order, had the said bill under consideration and made an amendment thereto, which he delivered in at the Clerk's table, where the same was twice read, and agreed to by the House.

ORDERED, That the said bill, with the amendment, be engrossed and read the third time to-day.

ORDERED, That the representation from the general court of the commonwealth of Massachusetts, on the subject of the whale and cod fisheries, together with the several papers accompanying the same, which lay on the table, be referred to the Secretary of State, with instruction to examine the matter thereof, and report his opinion thereupon to the next session of Congress.

ORDERED, That the Speaker of this House do transmit to the executive authority of each state, an authentic copy of the resolution of the eighteenth of May last, on the report of the committee to whom it was referred, to consider and report their opinion on the question, "when, according to the constitution, the terms, for which the President, Vice-President, Senators and Representatives have been respectively chosen, shall be deemed to have commenced."

An engrossed bill making certain appropriations therein mentioned, was read the third time.

RESOLVED, That the said bill do pass, and that the title be, "An act making certain appropriations therein mentioned."

---

amendments to this bill. On the same day the bill was signed by the speaker and vice president and sent to the president.

[59] A printed copy of the bill, annotated by the Senate, is in House Bills, SR, DNA.

[60] The Senate read this bill on August 9 and 10. On August 10 several amendments to the bill were agreed to, and the bill was passed. The House was notified of the amendments on August 11 and agreed to them on the same day. The speaker and the vice president also signed this bill on August 11.

ORDERED, That the Clerk of this House do carry the said bill to the Senate, and desire their concurrence.[61]

The Speaker laid before the House a letter and report of the Secretary of the Treasury, on the petition of Moses Hazen, which were read and ordered to lie on the table.

The several orders of the day were farther postponed until to-morrow.

And then the House adjourned until to-morrow morning ten o'clock.

TUESDAY, AUGUST 10, 1790

A message was received from the President of the United States, by Mr. Lear his Secretary, notifying that the President did, this day, approve and sign three acts, to wit:

An act making further provision for the payment of the debts of the United States.

An act to enable the officers and soldiers of the Virginia line on continental establishment to obtain titles to certain lands lying north-west of the river Ohio, between the Little Miami and Sciota.

An act authorizing the Secretary of the Treasury to finish the light-house on Portland-head, in the district of Maine.[62]

ORDERED, That the Clerk of this House do acquaint the Senate therewith.

A message from the Senate by Mr. Otis their Secretary.

MR. SPEAKER, The Senate have agreed to the amendments proposed by this House to the bill sent from the Senate, intituled, "An act to alter the time of holding the circuit courts of the United States in the states of South-Carolina and Georgia, and providing that the district court of Pennsylvania shall in future be held in the city of Philadelphia only." The Senate have also agreed to the resolution respecting the completion of certain surveys directed by a resolution of the late Congress.[63] And then he withdrew.

Mr. Gilman, from the joint committee for inrolled bills, reported that the committee had examined four inrolled bills; one, intituled, "An act for the relief of disabled soldiers and seamen lately in the service of the United States, and of certain other persons;"[64] another, intituled, "An act for the relief of the persons therein mentioned or described;"[65] another, intituled, "An act

---

[61] The Senate read this bill on August 10 and 11. It was also amended and agreed to on August 11. The House agreed to the amendments on the same day, and the bill was also signed by the speaker and vice president.

[62] The message is in Committee on Enrolled Bills, SR, DNA.

[63] On August 11 this bill was signed by the speaker and the vice president.

[64] The inspected enrolled bill is in Enrolled Acts, RG 11, DNA. E-46042.

[65] The inspected enrolled bill is in Enrolled Acts, RG 11, DNA.

declaring the assent of Congress to certain acts of the states of Maryland, Georgia, and Rhode-Island and Providence Plantations;"[66] and another, intituled, "An act to alter the time of holding the circuit courts of the United States in the states of South-Carolina and Georgia, and providing that the district court of Pennsylvania shall, in future, be held in the city of Philadelphia only,"[67] and found them to be truly inrolled: Whereupon,

Mr. Speaker signed the said inrolled bills.

A message from the Senate by Mr. Otis their Secretary.

MR. SPEAKER, The Senate have come to a resolution that the resolution of the sixth instant, authorizing the Speaker of the House of Representatives and President of the Senate to close the present session, by adjourning their respective Houses on this day, be repealed, and that instead thereof they be authorized to adjourn their respective Houses on the twelfth instant, to meet again on the first Monday in December next;[68] to which they desire the concurrence of this House. And then he withdrew.

The House proceeded to consider the said resolution, and the same being read, was agreed to.[69]

ORDERED, That the clerk of this House do acquaint the Senate therewith.

Mr. Gilman, from the joint committee for inrolled bills, reported, that the committee did, this day, wait on the President of the United States, and present for his approbation four inrolled bills, to wit; one, intituled, "An act for the relief of disabled soldiers and seamen, lately in the service of the United States, and of certain other persons;" another, intituled, "An act declaring the assent of Congress to certain acts of the states of Maryland, Georgia, and Rhode-Island and Providence Plantations;" another, intituled, "An act for the relief of the persons therein mentioned or described;" and another, intituled, "An act to alter the times of holding the circuit courts of the United States in the states of South-Carolina and Georgia, and providing that the district court of Pennsylvania shall in future be held in the city of Philadelphia only."[70]

The several orders of the day were farther postponed until to-morrow.

And then the House adjourned until to-morrow morning ten o'clock.

---

[66] The inspected enrolled bill is in Enrolled Acts, RG 11, DNA.

[67] The inspected enrolled bill is in Enrolled Acts, RG 11, DNA. E–46061. A list of these enrolled bills is in Committee on Enrolled Bills, SR, DNA.

[68] A copy of the resolution is in Senate Joint and Concurrent Resolutions, SR, DNA.

[69] On August 11 the House was notified that the Senate members of the committee to notify the president of the proposed adjournment had been appointed. On the same day this committee reported.

[70] The president signed all of these bills on August 11.

WEDNESDAY, August 11, 1790

A message from the Senate by Mr. Otis their Secretary.

MR. SPEAKER, The Senate have appointed a committee on their part, jointly with the committee appointed by this House to wait on the President of the United States, and notify him of the proposed recess of Congress. The Senate have also passed the bill, intituled, "An act making provision for the reduction of the public debt," with several amendments,[71] to which they desire the concurrence of this House: And then he withdrew.

The House proceeded to consider the said amendments; and the same being read, were agreed to.

ORDERED, That the Clerk of this House do acquaint the Senate therewith.

A message from the Senate by Mr. Otis their Secretary.

MR. SPEAKER,   I am directed to inform this House, that the President of the United States did this day approve and sign an act which originated in the Senate, intituled, "An act to alter the times for holding the circuit courts of the United States, in the states of South-Carolina and Georgia, and providing that the district court of Pennsylvania shall in future be held in the city of Philadelphia only:"   And then he withdrew.

On motion,

RESOLVED, UNANIMOUSLY, That the thanks of this House be given to the Corporation of the City of New-York, for the elegant and convenient accommodations provided for Congress; and that Mr. Speaker be desired to communicate this resolve to the Mayor of the said City, and to signify to him that it is the wish of the House, that the Corporation will permit such articles of furniture, &c. now in the City-Hall, as have been provided by Congress, to remain for the use of that building.[72]

Mr. Gilman, from the joint committee appointed to notify the President of the United States of the proposed recess of Congress, reported, that the committee had, according to order, performed that service.

A message from the Senate by Mr. Otis their Secretary.

MR. SPEAKER,   The Senate have passed the bill, intituled, "An act making

---

[71] Senate amendments are noted on the bill in House Bills, SR, DNA. The amendments are printed in the *Senate Legislative Journal* on August 10.

[72] Copies of the resolution and the letter sent to the mayor of New York are in Senate Simple Resolutions and Motions, SR, DNA.

certain appropriations therein mentioned," with several amendments,[73] to which they desire the concurrence of this House: And then he withdrew.

The House proceeded to consider the said amendments; and the same being read, were agreed to.

ORDERED, That the Clerk of this House do acquaint the Senate therewith.

Mr. Gilman, from the joint committee for inrolled bills, reported, that the committee had examined two inrolled bills; one intituled, "An act making provision for the reduction of the public debt;"[74] the other intituled, "An act making certain appropriations therein mentioned;"[75] also, an inrolled resolve respecting the completion of certain surveys directed by a resolution of the late Congress,[76] and had found the same to be truly inrolled: Whereupon,

Mr. Speaker signed the said inrolled bills and resolve.[77]

ORDERED, That the Clerk of this House do acquaint the Senate therewith.

The several orders of the day were farther postponed until to-morrow.

And then the House adjourned until to-morrow morning nine o'clock.

THURSDAY, AUGUST 12, 1790

Mr. Gilman, from the joint committee for inrolled bills, reported, that the committee did, yesterday, wait on the President of the United States, and present for his approbation two inrolled bills; one intituled, "An act making certain appropriations therein mentioned;" the other intituled, "An act making provision for the reduction of the public debt;" also, an inrolled resolve respecting the completion of certain surveys, directed by a resolution of the late Congress.

A message was received from the President of the United States, by Mr. Lear his Secretary, notifying that the President did, on the eleventh instant, approve and sign three acts; one intituled, "An act declaring the assent of Congress to certain acts of the states of Maryland, Georgia, and Rhode-Island and Providence Plantations;" another intituled, "An act for the relief of disabled soldiers and seamen lately in the service of the United States, and of certain other persons;" and another intituled, "An act for the relief of the persons therein mentioned or described;" also, that the President did this day approve and sign two acts; one intituled, "An act making certain appropriations therein mentioned;" the other intituled, "An act making provision for

---

[73] Although the Journal used the plural "amendments," the Senate apparently passed only one amendment to this bill. A Senate amendment is in House Bills, SR, DNA. The amendment is printed in the *Senate Legislative Journal* on August 11.

[74] The inspected enrolled bill is in Enrolled Acts, RG 11, DNA. E–46050.

[75] The inspected enrolled bill is in Enrolled Acts, RG 11, DNA. E–46045.

[76] The inspected enrolled resolution is in Enrolled Acts, RG 11, DNA. E–46074.

[77] On August 12 the president signed the bills and resolution.

the reduction of the public debt;" also, an inrolled resolve respecting the completion of certain surveys, directed by a resolution of the late Congress.[78]

ORDERED, That a message be sent to the Senate, to inform them that this House having completed the business before them, are now about to proceed to close the present session by an adjournment on their part, agreeably to the order of the tenth instant; and that the Clerk of this House do go with the said message.

The Clerk accordingly went with the said message; and being returned, A message was received from the Senate by Mr. Otis their Secretary.

MR. SPEAKER,   I am directed to inform this House, that the Senate having completed the legislative business before them, are now ready to close the present session by an adjournment on their part: And then he withdrew.

Mr. Speaker then adjourned the House until the first Monday in December next.

---

[78] The message is in Committee on Enrolled Bills, SR, DNA.

APPENDIX to the SECOND SESSION

RATIFICATION of the CONSTITUTION of the UNITED STATES
BY the STATE of NORTH-CAROLINA

UNITED STATES, January 11, 1790

GENTLEMEN of the HOUSE of REPRESENTATIVES,

I HAVE directed Mr. Lear, my private Secretary, to lay before you a copy of the adoption and ratification of the Constitution of the United States by the state of North-Carolina, together with a copy of a letter from his Excellency Samuel Johnston, President of the Convention of said State, to the President of the United States.

The originals of the papers which are herewith transmitted to you will be lodged in the office of the Secretary of State.

G. WASHINGTON

FAYETTE-VILLE, STATE of NORTH-CAROLINA, December 4, 1789

SIR,

BY order of the Convention of the people of this State, I have the honor to transmit to you the ratification and adoption of the Constitution of the United States by the said Convention, in behalf of the people.

With sentiments of the highest consideration and respect, I have the honor to be, Sir, your most faithful and obedient servant,

(Signed) SAMUEL JOHNSTON, President of the Convention

To the PRESIDENT of the UNITED STATES

I DO certify the above to be a true copy from the original.

TOBIAS LEAR, Secretary to the President of the United States

A COPY of the ADOPTION and RATIFICATION of the CONSTITUTION of the UNITED STATES by the STATE of NORTH-CAROLINA

STATE OF NORTH-CAROLINA
IN CONVENTION

WHEREAS the General Convention which met in Philadelphia in pursuance of a recommendation of Congress, did recommend to the citizens of the United States, a constitution or form of government in the following words, viz. We the People, &c.

[Here follows the Constitution of the United States, verbatim.]

RESOLVED, That this Convention, in behalf of the freemen, citizens and inhabitants of the State of North-Carolina, do adopt and ratify the said Constitution and form of government.

Done in Convention this 21st day of November, 1789.

(Signed) SAMUEL JOHNSTON, President of the Convention

J. HUNT, JAMES TAYLOR, Secretaries

BY the direction of the President of the United States, I have examined and compared the foregoing with the adoption and ratification of the Constitution of the United States by the State of North-Carolina, which was transmitted to the President of the United States by Samuel Johnston, President of the Convention of said State—as well as the transcript of the Constitution of the United States recited in the said ratification, which I certify to be a true copy.

TOBIAS LEAR, Secretary to the President of the United States

RATIFICATION OF THE CONSTITUTION OF THE UNITED STATES BY THE STATE OF RHODE-ISLAND AND PROVIDENCE PLANTATIONS

UNITED STATES, June 16th, 1790

GENTLEMEN of the SENATE and HOUSE of REPRESENTATIVES,

THE ratification of the Constitution of the United States of America, by the state of Rhode-Island and Providence Plantations, was received by me last night, together with a letter to the President of the United States, from the President of the Convention. I have directed my Secretary to lay before you a copy of each.

G. WASHINGTON

RHODE-ISLAND

NEWPORT, June 9th, 1790

SIR,

I HAD, on the twenty-ninth ultimo, the satisfaction of addressing you, after the ratification of the Constitution of the United States of America by the Convention of this State. I have now the honor of inclosing the Ratification as then agreed upon by the Convention of the people of this State. The Legislature is now in session in this town; an appointment of Senators will undoubtedly take place in the present week, and from what appears to be the sense of the legislature, it may be expected that the gentlemen who may be appointed, will immediately proceed to take their seats in the Senate of the United States.

I have the honor to be, with great respect,

Sir, your obedient humble servant,

(Signed)   DANIEL OWEN, President

PRESIDENT of the UNITED STATES

[The Constitution of the United States of America precedes the following Ratification]

RATIFICATION of the CONSTITUTION by the CONVENTION of the STATE of RHODE-ISLAND and PROVIDENCE PLANTATIONS

WE, the delegates of the people of the state of Rhode-Island and Providence Plantations, duly elected and met in Convention, having maturely considered the Constitution for the United States of America, agreed to, on the seventeenth day of September, in the year one thousand seven hundred and eighty-seven, by the Convention then assembled at Philadelphia, in the commonwealth of Pennsylvania, (a copy whereof precedes these presents) and having also seriously and deliberately considered the present situation of this State, do declare and make known,

First. That there are certain natural rights, of which men, when they form a social compact, cannot deprive or divest their posterity, among which are the enjoyment of life and liberty, with the means of acquiring, possessing and protecting property, and pursuing and obtaining happiness and safety.

Second. That all power is naturally vested in, and consequently derived from the people; that magistrates, therefore, are their trustees and agents, and at all times amenable to them.

Third. That the powers of government may be reassumed by the people, whensoever it shall become necessary to their happiness. That the rights of the States respectively to nominate and appoint all state officers, and every other power, jurisdiction and right, which is not by the said Constitution clearly delegated to the Congress of the United States, or to the departments of government thereof, remain to the people of the several States or their respective state governments, to whom they may have granted the same; and that those clauses in the said Constitution which declare that Congress shall not have or exercise certain powers, do not imply that Congress is entitled to any powers not given by the said Constitution; but such clauses are to be construed as exceptions to certain specified powers, or as inserted merely for greater caution.

Fourth. That religion, or the duty which we owe to our Creator, and the manner of discharging it, can be directed only by reason and conviction, and not by force or violence, and therefore all men have an equal, natural and un-alienable right to the exercise of religion, according to the dictates of con-science; and that no particular religious sect or society ought to be favoured or established, by law, in preference to others.

Fifth. That the legislative, executive and judiciary powers of government should be separate and distinct; and that the members of the two first may be restrained from oppression, by feeling and participating the public burthens, they should at fixed periods be reduced to a private station, return into the mass of the people, and the vacancies be supplied by certain and regular elec-tions, in which all or any part of the former members to be eligible, or in-eligible, as the rules of the Constitution of government and the laws shall direct.

Sixth. That elections of representatives in legislature ought to be free and frequent, and all men having sufficient evidence of permanent common in-terest with, and attachment to the community, ought to have the right of suffrage; and no aid, charge, tax or fee, can be set, rated or levied upon the people without their own consent, or that of their representatives so elected, nor can they be bound by any law to which they have not in like manner consented for the public good.

Seventh. That all power of suspending laws, or the execution of laws, by any authority, without the consent of the representatives of the people in the legislature, is injurious to their rights, and ought not to be exercised.

Eighth. That in all capital and criminal prosecutions, a man hath a right to demand the cause and nature of his accusation, to be confronted with the ac-cusers and witnesses, to call for evidence and be allowed counsel in his favour, and to a fair and speedy trial by an impartial jury of his vicinage, without whose unanimous consent he cannot be found guilty, (except in the government of the land and naval forces) nor can he be compelled to give evidence against himself.

Ninth. That no freeman ought to be taken, imprisoned or disseised of his freehold, liberties, privileges or franchises, or outlawed, or exiled, or in any manner destroyed or deprived of his life, liberty or property, but by the trial by jury, or by the law of the land.

Tenth. That every freeman restrained of his liberty, is entitled to a remedy, to enquire into the lawfulness thereof, and to remove the same if unlawful, and that such remedy ought not to be denied or delayed.

Eleventh. That in controversies respecting property, and in suits between man and man, the ancient trial by jury, as hath been exercised by us and our ancestors, from the time whereof the memory of man is not to the contrary, is one of the greatest securities to the rights of the people, and ought to remain sacred and inviolable.

Twelfth. That every freeman ought to obtain right and justice, freely and without sale, completely and without denial, promptly and without delay; and that all establishments or regulations contravening these rights are oppressive and unjust.

Thirteenth. That excessive bail ought not to be required, nor excessive fines imposed, nor cruel or unusual punishments inflicted.

Fourteenth. That every person has a right to be secure from all unreasonable searches and seizures of his person, his papers or his property; and therefore, that all warrants to search suspected places, or seize any person, his papers or his property, without information upon oath or affirmation of sufficient cause, are grievous and oppressive; and that all general warrants (or such in which the place or person suspected are not particularly designated) are dangerous and ought not to be granted.

Fifteenth. That the people have a right peaceably to assemble together to consult for their common good, or to instruct their representatives; and that every person has a right to petition or apply to the legislature for redress of grievances.

Sixteenth. That the people have a right to freedom of speech, and of writing and publishing their sentiments. That freedom of the press is one of the greatest bulwarks of liberty, and ought not to be violated.

Seventeenth. That the people have a right to keep and bear arms; that a well regulated militia, including the body of the people capable of bearing arms, is the proper, natural and safe defence of a free state; that the militia shall not be subject to martial law, except in time of war, rebellion or insurrection; that standing armies in time of peace, are dangerous to liberty, and ought not to be kept up, except in cases of necessity; and that at all times the military should be under strict subordination to the civil power; that in time of peace no soldier ought to be quartered in any house without the consent of the owner, and in time of war only by the civil magistrate in such manner as the law directs.

Eighteenth. That any person religiously scrupulous of bearing arms, ought to be exempted upon payment of an equivalent to employ another to bear arms in his stead.

Under these impressions, and declaring that the rights aforesaid cannot be abridged or violated, and that the explanations aforesaid are consistent with the said Constitution, and in confidence that the amendments hereafter mentioned will receive an early and mature consideration, and conformably to the fifth article of said Constitution, speedily become a part thereof—We the said Delegates, in the name and in the behalf of the people of the state of Rhode-Island and Providence Plantations, do by these presents assent to and ratify the said Constitution. In full confidence nevertheless, that until the amendments hereafter proposed and undermentioned, shall be agreed to and ratified, pursuant to the aforesaid fifth article, the militia of this State will not be continued in service out of this State for a longer term than six weeks, without the consent of the legislature thereof; that the Congress will not make or alter any regulation in this State respecting the times, places and manner of holding elections for Senators or Representatives, unless the legislature of this State shall neglect or refuse to make laws or regulations for the purpose, or from any circumstance be incapable of making the same, and that in those cases such power will only be exercised until the legislature of this State shall make provision in the premises; that the Congress will not lay direct taxes within this State, but when the monies arising from the impost, tonnage and excise, shall be insufficient for the public exigencies, nor until the Congress shall have first made a requisition upon this State to assess, levy and pay the amount of such requisition made agreeable to the census fixed in the said constitution, in such way and manner as the legislature of this State shall judge best, and that the Congress will not lay any capitation or poll tax.

DONE in Convention at Newport, in the county of Newport, in the state of Rhode-Island and Providence Plantations, the twenty-ninth day of May, in the year of our Lord one thousand seven hundred and ninety, and in the fourteenth year of the Independence of the United States of America.

By order of the Convention,

(Signed)   DANIEL OWEN, President

Attest.   DANIEL UPDIKE, Secretary

AND the Convention do, in the name and behalf of the people of the state of Rhode-Island and Providence Plantations, enjoin it upon their Senators and Representative or Representatives which may be elected to represent this State in Congress, to exert all their influence and use all reasonable means to obtain a ratification of the following amendments to the said Constitution, in the manner prescribed therein, and in all laws to be passed by the Congress in the mean time, to conform to the spirit of the said amendments, as far as the Constitution will admit.

AMENDMENTS

First. The United States shall guarantee to each State its sovereignty, freedom and independence, and every power, jurisdiction and right, which is not by this Constitution expressly delegated to the United States.

Second. That Congress shall not alter, modify, or interfere in the times, places or manner of holding elections for Senators and Representatives, or either of them, except when the legislature of any State shall neglect, refuse, or be disabled by invasion or rebellion, to prescribe the same, or in case when the provision made by the State is so imperfect as that no consequent election is had, and then only until the legislature of such State shall make provision in the premises.

Third. It is declared by the Convention, that the judicial power of the United States, in cases in which a State may be a party, does not extend to criminal prosecutions, or to authorise any suit by any person against a State: but to remove all doubts or controversies respecting the same, that it be especially expressed as a part of the Constitution of the United States, that Congress shall not directly or indirectly, either by themselves, or through the judiciary, interfere with any one of the States, in the redemption of paper money already emitted, and now in circulation, or in liquidating or discharging the public securities of any one State; that each and every State shall have the exclusive right of making such laws and regulations for the before mentioned purpose as they shall think proper.

Fourth. That no amendments to the Constitution of the United States, hereafter to be made pursuant to the fifth article, shall take effect, or become a part of the Constitution of the United States, after the year one thousand seven hundred and ninety-three, without the consent of eleven of the States heretofore united under the confederation.

Fifth. That the judicial powers of the United States shall extend to no possible case where the cause of action shall have originated before the ratification of this Constitution; except in disputes between States about their territory, disputes between persons claiming lands under grants of different States, and debts due to the United States.

Sixth. That no person shall be compelled to do military duty otherwise than by voluntary enlistment, except in cases of general invasion; any thing in the second paragraph of the sixth article of the Constitution, or any law made under the Constitution, to the contrary notwithstanding.

Seventh. That no capitation or poll tax shall ever be laid by Congress.

Eighth. In cases of direct taxes, Congress shall first make requisitions on the several States to assess, levy and pay their respective proportions of such requisitions, in such way and manner as the legislatures of the several States shall judge best: and in case any State shall neglect or refuse to pay its proportion pursuant to such requisition, then Congress may assess and levy such State's proportion, together with interest at the rate of six per cent. per annum, from the time prescribed in such requisition.

Ninth. That Congress shall lay no direct taxes without the consent of the legislatures of three fourths of the States in the Union.

Tenth. That the journals of the proceedings of the Senate and House of

Representatives, shall be published as soon as conveniently may be, at least once in every year; except such parts thereof relating to treaties, alliances, or military operations, as in their judgment require secrecy.

Eleventh. That regular statements of the receipts and expenditures of all public monies, shall be published at least once a year.

Twelfth. As standing armies in time of peace are dangerous to liberty, and ought not to be kept up except in cases of necessity, and as at all times the military should be under strict subordination to the civil power, that therefore no standing army or regular troops shall be raised or kept up in time of peace.

Thirteenth. That no monies be borrowed on the credit of the United States, without the assent of two thirds of the Senators and Representatives present in each House.

Fourteenth. That the Congress shall not declare war without the concurrence of two thirds of the Senators and Representatives present in each House.

Fifteenth. That the words "without the consent of Congress," in the seventh clause in the ninth section of the first article of the Constitution, be expunged.

Sixteenth. That no judge of the supreme court of the United States, shall hold any other office under the United States, or any of them; nor shall any officer appointed by Congress, or by the President and Senate of the United States, be permitted to hold any office under the appointment of any of the States.

Seventeenth. As a traffic tending to establish or continue the slavery of any part of the human species, is disgraceful to the cause of liberty and humanity; that Congress shall as soon as may be, promote and establish such laws and regulations as may effectually prevent the importation of slaves of every description into the United States.

Eighteenth. That the State legislatures have power to recall, when they think it expedient, their federal Senators, and to send others in their stead.

Nineteenth. That Congress have power to establish a uniform rule of inhabitancy or settlement of the poor of the different States throughout the United States.

Twentieth. That Congress erect no company with exclusive advantages of commerce.

Twenty-first. That when two members shall move or call for the ayes and nays on any question, they shall be entered on the journals of the Houses respectively.

DONE in Convention, at Newport, in the county of Newport, in the State of Rhode-Island and Providence Plantations, the twenty-ninth day of

May, in the year of our Lord one thousand seven hundred and ninety, and the fourteenth year of the independence of the United States of America.

By order of the Convention,

(Signed) DANIEL OWEN, President

Attest. DANIEL UPDIKE, Secretary

A true copy.

TOBIAS LEAR, Secretary to the President of the United States

RATIFICATIONS OF THE AMENDMENTS
TO THE
CONSTITUTION OF THE UNITED STATES

BY THE STATE OF NEW-HAMPSHIRE

UNITED STATES, February 15th, 1790

GENTLEMEN of the SENATE and HOUSE of REPRESENTATIVES,

I HAVE directed my Secretary to lay before you the copy of a vote of the legislature of the state of New-Hampshire, to accept the articles proposed in addition to, and amendment of, the Constitution of the United States of America, except the second article. At the same time will be delivered to you, the copy of a letter from his Excellency the President of the state of New-Hampshire, to the President of the United States.

The originals of the above mentioned vote and letter will be lodged in the office of the Secretary of State.

G. WASHINGTON

DURHAM, in NEW-HAMPSHIRE, January 29th, 1790

SIR,

I HAVE the honor to inclose you, for the information of Congress, a vote of the assembly of this state to accept all the articles of amendments to the Constitution of the United States, except the second, which was rejected.

I have the honor to be,

With the most profound respect,

Sir, your most obedient, and

Very humble servant,

(Signed) JOHN SULLIVAN

The PRESIDENT of the UNITED STATES

STATE OF NEW-HAMPSHIRE

In the HOUSE of REPRESENTATIVES, January 25th, 1790

UPON reading and maturely considering the proposed Amendments to the federal Constitution,

VOTED, To accept the whole of said Amendments, except the second article, which was rejected.   Sent up for concurrence.

(Signed)   THOMAS BARTLETT, Speaker

In Senate, the same day, read and concurred.

(Signed)   J. PEARSON, Secretary

A true copy.   Attest,   JOSEPH PEARSON, Secretary

I certify the above to be a true copy of the copy transmitted to the President of the United States.

TOBIAS LEAR, Secretary to the President
of the United States

BY THE STATE OF NEW-YORK

THE PEOPLE of the STATE of NEW-YORK, by the grace of GOD free and independent

TO ALL TO WHOM THESE PRESENTS SHALL COME OR MAY CONCERN,
GREETING

KNOW YE, That we having inspected the records remaining in our secretary's office, do find there a certain act of our legislature, in the words following:

An Act ratifying certain Articles in addition to, and amendment of, the Constitution of the United States of America, proposed by the Congress

WHEREAS by the fifth article of the Constitution of the United States of America, it is provided, that the Congress, whenever two thirds of both Houses shall deem it necessary, shall propose amendments to the said Constitution, which shall be valid to all intents and purposes as part of the said Constitution, when ratified by the legislatures of three-fourths of the several States, or by conventions in three-fourths thereof, as the one or the other mode of ratification may be proposed by Congress.

And whereas in the session of the Congress of the United States of America, begun and held at the city of New-York, on Wednesday the fourth of March, one thousand seven hundred and eighty nine, it was resolved by the Senate and House of Representatives of the United States of America, in Congress assembled, two thirds of both Houses concurring, that the following articles be proposed to the Legislatures of the several States, as Amendments to the Constitution of the United States; all or any of which articles, when ratified by three-fourths of the said Legislatures, to be valid to all intents and purposes as a part of the said Constitution. VIZ.

ARTICLES in Addition to, and Amendment of, the Constitution of the United States of America, proposed by Congress and ratified by the Legislatures of the several States, pursuant to the fifth article of the original Constitution.

Article First. After the first enumeration required by the first article of the Constitution, there shall be one representative for every thirty thousand, until the number shall amount to one hundred, after which the proportion shall be so regulated by Congress, that there shall be not less than one hundred representatives, nor less than one representative for every forty thousand persons, until the number of representatives shall amount to two hundred, after which the proportion shall be so regulated by Congress, that there shall not be less than two hundred representatives, nor more than one representative for every fifty thousand persons.

Article the Second. No law varying the compensation for the services of the Senators and Representatives shall take effect until an election of Representatives shall have intervened.

Article the Third. Congress shall make no law respecting an establishment of religion, or prohibiting the free exercise thereof, or abridging the freedom of speech, or of the press, or the right of the people peaceably to assemble and to petition the government for a redress of grievances.

Article the Fourth. A well regulated militia being necessary to the security of a free state, the right of the people to keep and bear arms shall not be infringed.

Article the Fifth. No soldier shall, in time of peace, be quartered in any house without the consent of the owner, nor in time of war but in a manner to be prescribed by law.

Article the Sixth. The right of the people to be secure in their persons, houses, papers and effects against unreasonable searches and seizures shall not be violated, and no warrants shall issue but upon probable cause, supported by oath or affirmation, and particularly describing the place to be searched, and the persons or things to be seized.

Article the Seventh. No person shall be held to answer for a capital or otherwise infamous crime, unless on a presentment or indictment of a grand jury, except in cases arising in the land or naval forces, or in the militia when in actual service in time of war, or public danger; nor shall any person be subject for the same offence to be twice put into jeopardy of life or limb; nor shall be compelled in any criminal case, to be a witness against himself, nor be deprived of life, liberty or property, without due process of law, nor shall private property be taken for public use without just compensation.

Article the Eighth. In all criminal prosecutions the accused shall enjoy the right of a speedy and public trial, by an impartial jury of the state and district wherein the crime shall have been committed, which district shall have been previously ascertained by law, and to be informed of the nature and cause of the accusation; to be confronted with the witnesses against him; to have compulsory process for obtaining witnesses in his favour, and to have the assistance of counsel for his defence.

Article the Ninth. In suits of common law, where the value in controversy shall exceed twenty dollars, the right of trial by jury shall be preserved; and no fact tried by a jury shall be otherwise examined in any court of the United States, than according to the rules of the common law.

Article the Tenth. Excessive bail shall not be required, nor excessive fines imposed, nor cruel or unusual punishments inflicted.

Article the Eleventh. The enumeration in the Constitution of certain rights, shall not be construed to deny or disparage others retained by the people.

Article the Twelfth. The powers not delegated to the United States by the Constitution, nor prohibited by it to the States, are reserved to the States respectively, or to the people.

And whereas the Legislature of this State have considered the said articles, and do agree to the same, except the second article. Therefore,

BE *it enacted by the People of the State of New-York represented in Senate and Assembly, and it is hereby enacted by the authority of the same,* That the said articles, except the second, shall be and are hereby ratified by the Legislature of this State.

STATE of NEW-YORK, in ASSEMBLY, February 22, 1790

This bill having been read the third time—RESOLVED, That the bill do pass.

By order of the Assembly,
GULIAN VERPLANCK, Speaker

STATE of NEW-YORK, in SENATE, February 24, 1790

This bill having been read a third time—RESOLVED, That the bill do pass.
By order of the Senate,

ISAAC ROOSEVELT, President pro hac vice

COUNCIL of REVISION, February 27, 1790

RESOLVED, That it does not appear improper to the Council, that this bill, entitled, "An act ratifying certain articles in addition to, and amendment of the Constitution of the United States of America, proposed by the Congress, should become a law of this State."

GEORGE CLINTON

ALL which we have caused to be exemplified by these presents. In testimony whereof, we have caused these our letters to be made patent, and the great seal of our said State to be hereunto affixed. Witness our trusty and well beloved George Clinton, Esquire, Governor of our said State, General and Commander in chief of all the militia, and Admiral of the navy of the same, at our city of New-York, the twenty-seventh day of March, in the year one thousand seven hundred and ninety, and in the fourteenth year of our independence.

(Signed) GEORGE CLINTON

Passed the Secretary's Office, the 27th March, 1790.
(Signed) LEWIS A. SCOTT, Secretary

I HEREBY certify, that the foregoing is a true copy of the exemplification of an act transmitted to the President of the United States by the Governor of the State of New-York.

TOBIAS LEAR, Secretary to the President

UNITED STATES, April 5, 1790   of the United States[1]

BY THE STATE OF PENNSYLVANIA

UNITED STATES, March 16, 1790

GENTLEMEN of the SENATE and HOUSE of REPRESENTATIVES,

I HAVE directed my secretary to lay before you the copy of an act and the form of ratification, of certain articles of amendment to the Constitution of the United States, by the State of Pennsylvania; together with the copy of a letter which accompanied the said act, from the Speaker of the House of Assembly of Pennsylvania, to the President of the United States.

---

[1] These documents were enclosed with George Washington's message of April 5, 1790.

The originals of the above will be lodged in the office of the Secretary of State.

G. WASHINGTON

In ASSEMBLY of PENNSYLVANIA, March 11, 1790

SIR,

I HAVE the honor to transmit an exemplified copy of the act declaring the assent of this State to certain amendments to the Constitution of the United States, that you may be pleased to lay it before Congress.

With the greatest respect,
I have the honor to be,
Your obedient servant,
(Signed) RICHARD PETERS, Speaker

His Excellency the PRESIDENT of the UNITED STATES

IN GENERAL ASSEMBLY
STATE of PENNSYLVANIA, to wit.

IN pursuance of a resolution of the General Assembly of the State of Pennsylvania, being the legislature thereof; I do hereby certify that the paper hereunto annexed contains an exact and true exemplification of the act whereof it purports to be a copy, by virtue whereof the several amendments therein mentioned, proposed to the Constitution of the United States, were on the part of the Commonwealth of Pennsylvania, agreed to, ratified and confirmed.

GIVEN under my hand, and the seal of the State, this eleventh day of March, in the year of our Lord one thousand seven hundred and ninety.

(Signed) RICHARD PETERS, Speaker

(SEAL)

An Act declaring the Assent of this State to certain Amendments to the Constitution of the United States

Section 1. WHEREAS in pursuance of the fifth article of the Constitution of the United States, certain articles of amendment to the said Constitution, have been proposed by the Congress of the United States, for the consideration of the Legislatures of the several States: And whereas this House, being the Legislature of the State of Pennsylvania, having maturely deliberated thereupon, have resolved to adopt and ratify the articles hereafter enumerated, as part of the Constitution of the United States.

Section 2. Be it enacted therefore, and it is hereby enacted by the Repre-

sentatives of the Freemen of the Commonwealth of Pennsylvania, in General Assembly met, and by the authority of the same, That the following amendments to the Constitution of the United States, proposed by the Congress thereof, viz.

[Here follow the third, fourth, fifth, sixth, seventh, eighth, ninth, tenth, eleventh and twelfth articles, which were proposed by Congress to the legislatures of the several States, as amendments to the Constitution of the United States.]

Be, and they are hereby ratified on behalf of this State, to become, when ratified by the legislatures of three fourths of the several States, part of the Constitution of the United States.

Signed by order of the House,

RICHARD PETERS, Speaker of the General Assembly

I, Mathew Irwin, Esquire, master of the rolls for the State of Pennsylvania, do certify the preceding writing to be a true copy (or exemplification) of a certain law remaining in my office.

Witness my hand and seal of office, the 11th March, 1790.

(Signed) MATHEW IRWIN, M. R.

UNITED STATES, March 16th 1790

I CERTIFY the above to be a true copy from the original.

TOBIAS LEAR, Secretary to the President of the United States

By the STATE of DELAWARE

UNITED STATES, March 8th 1790

GENTLEMEN of the SENATE and HOUSE of REPRESENTATIVES,

I HAVE received from his Excellency Joshua Clayton, President of the State of Delaware, the articles proposed by Congress to the Legislatures of the several States, as amendments to the Constitution of the United States; which articles were transmitted to him for the consideration of the Legislature of Delaware, and are now returned with the following resolutions annexed to them, viz.

"THE General Assembly of Delaware having taken into their consideration the above amendments proposed by Congress, to the respective Legislatures of the several States:

"RESOLVED, That the first article be postponed.

"RESOLVED, That the General Assembly do agree to the second, third, fourth, fifth, sixth, seventh, eighth, ninth, tenth, eleventh and twelfth articles; and we do hereby assent to, ratify and confirm the same, as part of the Constitution of the United States.

"In Testimony whereof, we have caused the great seal of the State to be hereunto affixed, this twenty-eighth day of January, in the year of our Lord one thousand seven hundred and ninety, and in the fourteenth year of the Independence of the Delaware State.

"Signed by order of Council,

"GEORGE MITCHELL, Speaker

"Signed by order of the House of Assembly,

"JEHU DAVIS, Speaker"

I HAVE directed a copy of the letter which accompanied the said articles, from his Excellency Joshua Clayton to the President of the United States, to be laid before you.

The before-mentioned articles, and the original of the letter, will be lodged in the office of the Secretary of State.

G. WASHINGTON

SIR,

AGREEABLY to the directions of the General Assembly of this State, I do myself the honor to enclose your Excellency their ratification of the articles proposed by Congress to be added to the Constitution of the United States.

And am, with every sentiment of esteem, Sir, your Excellency's

Most obedient humble servant,

(Signed) JOSHUA CLAYTON

His Excellency GEORGE WASHINGTON,
PRESIDENT of the UNITED STATES

UNITED STATES, March 8th, 1790

I HEREBY certify that the above letter is a true copy from the original.

TOBIAS LEAR, Secretary to the President of the United States

BY THE STATE OF MARYLAND

UNITED STATES, January 25th, 1790

GENTLEMEN of the SENATE and HOUSE of REPRESENTATIVES,

I HAVE received from his Excellency John E. Howard, Governor of the state of Maryland, an act of the Legislature of Maryland, to ratify certain articles in addition to, and amendment of, the Constitution of the United States of America, proposed by Congress to the Legislatures of the several States; and have directed my Secretary to lay a Copy of the same before you, together with the copy of a letter accompanying the above act, from his Excellency the Governor of Maryland to the President of the United States. The originals will be deposited in the office of the Secretary of State.

G. WASHINGTON

ANNAPOLIS, January 15th, 1790

SIR,

I HAVE the honor to enclose a copy of an act of the Legislature of Maryland, to ratify certain articles in addition to, and amendment of the Constitution of the United States of America, proposed by Congress to the Legislatures of the several States.

I have the honor to be,
With the highest respect,
Sir, your most obedient servant,
(Signed) J. E. HOWARD

His Excellency the PRESIDENT of the UNITED STATES

I DO CERTIFY the foregoing to be a true copy from the original letter from John E. Howard, Governor of the State of Maryland, to the President of the United States.

TOBIAS LEAR, Secretary to the President of the United States

An act to ratify certain Articles in addition to, and amendment of, the Constitution of the United States of America, proposed by Congress to the Legislatures of the several States

WHEREAS it is provided by the fifth article of the Constitution of the United States of America, that Congress, whenever two-thirds of both Houses shall deem it necessary, shall propose Amendments to the said Constitution; or on the application of the Legislatures of two-thirds of the several States shall call a Convention for proposing Amendments, which in either case shall be valid to all intents and purposes as part of the said Constitution, when ratified by the Legislatures of three-fourths of the several States, or by Conventions in three-fourths thereof, as the one or the other mode of ratification may be proposed by the Congress.

And whereas at a session of the United States, in Congress assembled, begun and held at the city of New-York, on Wednesday the fourth day of

March, in the year of our Lord one thousand seven hundred and eighty-nine, it was resolved by the Senate and House of Representatives of the said United States in Congress assembled, two-thirds of both Houses concurring, that the following articles be proposed to the Legislatures of the several States, as Amendments to the Constitution of the United States, all or any of which articles, when ratified by three-fourths of the said Legislatures, to be valid to all intents and purposes, as part of the said Constitution, viz.

Article the First. After the first enumeration required by the first article of the Constitution, there shall be one representative for every thirty thousand, until the number shall amount to one hundred, after which the proportion shall be so regulated by Congress, that there shall be not less than one hundred representatives, nor less than one representative for every forty thousand persons, until the number of representatives shall amount to two hundred, after which the proportion shall be so regulated by Congress, that there shall not be less than two hundred representatives, nor more than one representative for every fifty thousand persons.

Article the Second. No law varying the compensation for the services of the Senators and Representatives shall take effect until an election of Representatives shall have intervened.

Article the Third. Congress shall make no law respecting an establishment of religion, or prohibiting the free exercise thereof, or abridging the freedom of speech, or of the press, or the right of the people peaceably to assemble and to petition the government for a redress of grievances.

Article the Fourth. A well regulated militia being necessary to the security of a free state, the right of the people to keep and bear arms shall not be infringed.

Article the Fifth. No soldier shall, in time of peace, be quartered in any house without the consent of the owner, nor in time of war but in a manner to be prescribed by law.

Article the Sixth. The right of the people to be secure in their persons, houses, papers and effects against unreasonable searches and seizures shall not be violated, and no warrants shall issue but upon probable cause, supported by oath or affirmation, and particularly describing the place to be searched, and the persons or things to be seized.

Article the Seventh. No person shall be held to answer for a capital or otherwise infamous crime, unless on a presentment or indictment of a grand jury, except in cases arising in the land or naval forces, or in the militia when in actual service in time of war, or public danger; nor shall any person be subject for the same offence to be twice put into jeopardy of life or limb; nor shall be compelled in any criminal case, to be a witness against himself, nor be deprived of life, liberty or property, without due process of law; nor shall private property be taken for public use without just compensation.

Article the Eighth. In all criminal prosecutions the accused shall enjoy the right of a speedy and public trial, by an impartial jury of the state and district wherein the crime shall have been committed, which district shall have been previously ascertained by law, and to be informed of the nature and cause of the accusation; to be confronted with the witnesses against him; to have compulsory process for obtaining witnesses in his favour, and to have the assistance of counsel for his defence.

Article the Ninth. In suits of common law, where the value in controversy shall exceed twenty dollars, the right of trial by jury shall be preserved; and no fact tried by a jury shall be otherwise re-examined in any court of the United States, than according to the rules of the common law.

Article the Tenth. Excessive bail shall not be required, nor excessive fines imposed, nor cruel and unusual punishments inflicted.

Article the Eleventh. The enumeration in the Constitution of certain rights, shall not be construed to deny or disparage others retained by the people.

Article the Twelfth. The powers not delegated to the United States by the Constitution, nor prohibited by it to the States, are reserved to the States respectively, or to the people.

Be it enacted by the General Assembly of Maryland, That the aforesaid articles and each of them be, and they are hereby confirmed and ratified.

By the HOUSE of DELEGATES, December 17th, 1789
(Signed) W. HARWOOD, Clerk

Read and Assented to. By order.

By the SENATE, December 19th, 1790

Read and assented to. By order.

H. RIDGELY, Clerk

(Signed) J. E. HOWARD (SEAL)

I HEREBY certify that the above is a true copy from the original engrossed act, as passed by the Legislature of the state of Maryland.
(Signed) T. JOHNSON, jun. Clerk Council

MARYLAND, ss.

IN testimony that Thomas Johnson, jun. is Clerk of the Executive Council for the state of Maryland, I have hereto affixed the great seal of the said state.

Witness my hand, this fifteenth day of January, Anno Domini, one thousand seven hundred and ninety.

(Signed) SAMUEL HARVEY HOWARD, Register Court Chancery

I CERTIFY the foregoing to be a true copy of the act transmitted to the President of the United States, by J. E. Howard, Governor of the state of Maryland.

TOBIAS LEAR, Secretary to the President of the United States

BY THE STATE OF SOUTH-CAROLINA

UNITED STATES, April 1st, 1790

GENTLEMEN of the SENATE and HOUSE of REPRESENTATIVES,

I HAVE directed my private Secretary to lay before you a copy of the adoption, by the Legislature of South-Carolina, of the Articles proposed by Congress to the Legislatures of the several States, as amendments to the Constitution of the United States, together with the copy of a letter from the Governor of the State of South-Carolina, to the President of the United States, which have lately come to my hands.

The originals of the foregoing will be lodged in the office of the Secretary of State.

G. WASHINGTON

CHARLESTON, January 28th, 1790

SIR,

I HAVE the honor to transmit you the entire adoption, by the Legislature of this State, of the amendments proposed to the Constitution of the United States.

I am, with most perfect
Esteem and Respect,
Your most obedient servant,
(Signed) CHARLES PINCKNEY

In the HOUSE of REPRESENTATIVES, January 18th, 1790

THE House took into consideration the report of the committee, to whom was referred the resolution of the Congress of the United States of the fourth day of March, one thousand seven hundred and eighty-nine, proposing Amendments to the Constitution of the United States, viz.

CONGRESS OF THE UNITED STATES
Begun and held at the City of New-York, on Wednesday, the Fourth of March, one thousand seven hundred and eighty-nine

THE Conventions of a number of the States, having at the time of their adopting the Constitution, expressed a desire, in order to prevent misconstruction or abuse of its powers, that further declaratory and restrictive clauses should be added. And as extending the ground of public confidence in the government will best ensure the beneficent ends of its institution:

RESOLVED, By the Senate and House of Representatives of the United States of America in Congress assembled, two-thirds of both Houses concurring, that the following Articles be proposed to the Legislatures of the several States, as Amendments to the Constitution of the United States, all or any of which Articles, when ratified by three-fourths of the said Legislatures, to be valid to all intents and purposes, as part of the said Constitution, viz.

ARTICLES in Addition to, and Amendment of, the Constitution of the United States of America, proposed by Congress and ratified by the Legislatures of the several States, pursuant to the fifth article of the original Constitution.

Article 1st. After the first enumeration required by the first article of the Constitution, there shall be one representative for every thirty thousand, until the number shall amount to one hundred, after which the proportion shall be so regulated, by Congress, that there shall not be less than one hundred representatives, nor less than one representative for every forty thousand persons, until the number of representatives shall amount to two hundred, after which the proportion shall be so regulated by Congress, that there shall not be less than two hundred representatives, nor more than one representative for every fifty thousand.

Article 2d. No law varying the compensation for services of the Senators and Representatives shall take effect, until an election of Representatives shall have intervened.

Article 3d. Congress shall make no law respecting an establishment of religion, or prohibiting the free exercise thereof, or abridging the freedom of speech, or of the press, or the right of the people peaceably to assemble, and to petition the government for a redress of grievances.

Article 4th. A well regulated militia being necessary to the security of a free state, the right of the people to keep and bear arms shall not be infringed.

Article 5th. No soldier shall, in time of peace, be quartered in any house, without the consent of the owner, nor in time of war, but in a manner prescribed by law.

Article 6th. The right of the people to be secure in their persons, Houses, papers and effects, against unreasonable searches and seizures, shall not be violated; and no warrants shall issue, but upon probable cause, supported by oath or affirmation, and particularly describing the place to be searched, and the persons or things to be seized.

Article 7th. No person shall be held to answer for a capital or otherwise infamous crime, unless on a presentment or indictment of a grand jury, except in cases arising in the land or naval forces, or in the militia when in actual service, in time of war or public danger; nor shall any person be subject for the same offence to be twice put in jeopardy of life or limb; nor shall be compelled in any criminal case to be a witness against himself; nor be deprived of life, liberty or property, without due process of law; nor shall private property be taken for public use without just compensation.

Article 8th. In all criminal prosecutions, the accused shall enjoy the right of a speedy and public trial, by an impartial jury of the State and district wherein the crime shall have been committed, which district shall have been previously ascertained by law; and to be informed of the nature and cause of the accusation; to be confronted with the witnesses against him; to have compulsory process for obtaining witnesses in his favor, and to have the assistance of counsel for his defence.

Article 9th. In suits at common law, where the value in controversy shall exceed twenty dollars, the right of trial by jury shall be preserved, and no fact tried by a jury shall be otherwise re-examined in any court of the United States, than according to the rules of the common law.

Article 10th. Excessive bail shall not be required, nor excessive fines imposed, nor cruel and unusual punishments inflicted.

Article 11th. The enumeration in the Constitution of certain rights, shall not be construed to deny or disparage others retained by the people.

Article 12th. The powers not delegated to the United States by the Constitution, nor prohibited by it to the States, are reserved to the States respectively, or to the people.

FREDERICK AUGUSTUS MUHLENBERG
Speaker of the House of Representatives
JOHN ADAMS, Vice-President of the United States,
and President of the Senate
Attest.   JOHN BECKLEY, Clerk of the House of Representatives
SAMUEL A. OTIS, Secretary of the Senate

Which being read through, was agreed to: Whereupon,
RESOLVED, That this House do adopt the said several Articles, and that they become a part of the Constitution of the United States.
RESOLVED, That the resolutions be sent to the Senate for their concurrence.
By order of the House,
JACOB READ, Speaker of the House of Representatives

In SENATE, January 19th, 1790
RESOLVED, That this House do concur with the House of Representatives in the foregoing resolutions.

By order of the Senate,

D. DE SAUSSURE, President of the Senate

BY THE STATE OF NORTH-CAROLINA

UNITED STATES, June 11th, 1790

GENTLEMEN of the SENATE and HOUSE of REPRESENTATIVES,

I HAVE directed my Secretary to lay before you a copy of the ratification of the Amendments to the Constitution of the United States by the State of North-Carolina; together with an extract from a letter, accompanying the said ratification, from the Governor of the State of North-Carolina to the President of the United States.

G. WASHINGTON

Extract of a letter from his Excellency Alexander Martin, Governor of the State of North-Carolina, to the PRESIDENT of the United States

ROCKINGHAM, May 25th, 1790

SIR,

I DO myself the honor to transmit you herewith enclosed, an Act of the General Assembly of this State, passed at their last session, entitled, "An act to ratify the Amendments to the Constitution of the United States."

STATE OF NORTH-CAROLINA

His Excellency ALEXANDER MARTIN, Esquire, Governor, Captain General and Commander in Chief in and over the said State

TO ALL TO WHOM THESE PRESENTS SHALL COME

IT is certified that the Honorable James Glasgow, Esquire, who hath attested the annexed copy of an act of the General Assembly of this State, was at the time thereof, and now is Secretary of the said State, and that full faith and credit are due to his official acts.

Given under my hand, and the great seal of the State, at Danbury, the fourteenth day of February, Anno Dom. 1790, and in the 14th year of our independence.

(Signed) ALEXANDER MARTIN

By His Excellency's command.

(Signed) THOMAS ROGERS, D. Sec.

An Act to ratify the Amendments to the Constitution of the United States

WHEREAS the Senate and House of Representatives of the United States of America in Congress assembled, on the fourth day of March, did resolve, two thirds of both houses concurring, that the following articles be proposed to the Legislatures of the several States, as amendments to the Constitution of the United States, all or any of which articles when ratified by three fourths of the said legislatures, to be valid to all intents and purposes as part of the said Constitution.

[Here follow the several articles of amendments, verbatim, as proposed by Congress to the legislatures of the several States.]

Be it therefore enacted by the General Assembly of the State of North-Carolina, and it is hereby enacted by the authority of the same, That the said amendments agreeable to the fifth article of the original Constitution, be held and ratified on the part of this State, as articles in addition to, and amendment of the Constitution of the United States of America.

(Signed)   CHA'S JOHNSON, S. S.

S. CABARRUS, C. H. C.

Read three times and ratified in General Assembly, this 22d day of December, Anno Domini 1789.

STATE OF NORTH-CAROLINA

I, James Glasgow, Secretary of the said State, do hereby certify the foregoing to be a true copy of the original act of the Assembly, filed in the Secretary's office. In testimony whereof, I have hereunto set my hand, this tenth day of February, 1790.

(Signed)   JAMES GLASGOW

UNITED STATES, June 11, 1790

I DO certify the preceding to be a true copy of the transcript of the act transmitted to the President of the United States by his Excellency Governor Martin.

TOBIAS LEAR, Secretary to the President of the United States

BY THE STATE OF RHODE-ISLAND AND
PROVIDENCE PLANTATIONS

UNITED STATES, June 30, 1790

GENTLEMEN of the SENATE and HOUSE of REPRESENTATIVES,

AN act of the Legislature of the State of Rhode-Island and Providence Plantations, for ratifying certain articles as amendments to the Constitution of the United States, was yesterday put into my hands; and I have directed my Secretary to lay a copy of the same before you.

G. WASHINGTON

By His Excellency ARTHUR FENNER, Esquire, Governor, Captain-General, and Commander in Chief of and over the State of Rhode-Island and Providence Plantations

BE IT KNOWN, That Henry Ward, Esquire, who hath under his hand certified the annexed paper, purporting an act of the General Assembly of the said State to be a true copy, is Secretary of the said State, duly elected and engaged according to law. Wherefore unto his certificate of that matter full faith is to be rendered.

Given under my Hand and the Seal of the said State, at Providence, this fifteenth day of June, A.D. 1790; and in the fourteenth year of Independence.

(Signed) ARTHUR FENNER

By His Excellency's command,
(Signed) HENRY WARD, Secretary

STATE OF RHODE-ISLAND AND PROVIDENCE PLANTATIONS
In GENERAL ASSEMBLY, June Session, A.D. 1790

An Act for ratifying certain articles as Amendments to the Constitution of the United States of America, and which were proposed by the Congress of the said States, at their session in March, A.D. 1789, to the Legislatures of the several States, pursuant to the fifth article of the aforesaid Constitution

BE *it enacted by the General Assembly, and by the authority thereof it is hereby enacted,* That the following articles, proposed by the Congress of the United States of America, at their session in March, A.D. 1789, to the Legislatures of the several States for ratification, as Amendments to the Constitution of the United States, pursuant to the fifth article of the said Constitution, be, and the same are hereby fully assented to, and ratified on the part of this State, to wit:

After the first enumeration required by the first article of the Constitution, there shall be one representative for every thirty thousand, until the number shall amount to one hundred; after which the proportion shall be so regulated by Congress, that there shall not be less than one hundred representatives, nor less than one representative for every forty thousand persons, until the number of representatives shall amount to two hundred; after which the proportion shall be so regulated by Congress, that there shall not be less than two hundred representatives, nor more than one representative for every fifty thousand persons.

Congress shall make no law respecting the establishment of religion, or prohibiting the free exercise thereof; or abridging the freedom of speech; or of the press; or to the right of the people peaceably to assemble, and to petition the government for a redress of grievances.

A well regulated militia being necessary to the security of a free state, the right of the people to keep and bear arms shall not be infringed.

No soldier shall in time of peace be quartered in any house without the consent of the owner; nor in time of war, but in a manner to be prescribed by law.

The right of the people to be secure in their persons, houses, papers and effects, against unreasonable searches and seizures, shall not be violated: And no warrants shall issue; but upon probable cause, supported by oath or affirmation, and particularly describing the place to be searched, and the persons or things to be seized.

No person shall be held to answer for a capital, or otherwise infamous crime, unless on a presentment or indictment of a grand jury; except in cases arising in the land and naval forces, or in the militia, when in actual service in time of war or public danger. Nor shall any person be subject for the same offence to be twice put in jeopardy of life or limb; nor shall be compelled in any criminal case, to be a witness against himself; nor be deprived of life, liberty or property, without due process of law: Nor shall private property be taken for public use without just compensation.

In all criminal prosecution, the accused shall enjoy the right to a speedy and public trial, by an impartial jury of the state and district wherein the crime shall have been committed, which district shall have been previously ascertained by law; and to be informed of the nature and cause of the accusation; to be confronted with the witnesses against him; to have compulsory process for obtaining witnesses in his favor; and to have the assistance of counsel for his defence.

In suits at common law, where the value in controversy shall exceed twenty dollars, the right of trial by jury shall be preserved: And no fact tried by a jury shall otherwise be re-examined in any court of the United States than according to the rules of the common law.

Excessive bail shall not be required; nor excessive fines imposed; nor cruel and unusual punishments inflicted.

The enumeration in the Constitution of certain rights, shall not be construed to deny or disparage others retained by the people.

The powers not delegated to the United States, by the Constitution, nor prohibited by it to the States, are reserved to the States respectively or to the people.

It is *ordered,* That his Excellency the Governor be, and he is hereby requested, to transmit to the President of the said United States, under the seal of this State, a copy of this act, to be communicated to the Senate and House of Representatives of the Congress of the said United States.

A true copy duly examined.

Witness, HENRY WARD, Secretary

BY THE STATE OF NEW-JERSEY

UNITED STATES, August 6, 1790

GENTLEMEN of the SENATE and HOUSE of REPRESENTATIVES,

I HAVE directed my Secretary to lay before you a copy of an exemplified copy of a law, to ratify, on the part of the State of New-Jersey, certain amendments to the Constitution of the United States; together with the copy of a letter which accompanied the said ratification, from the Honorable Elisha Lawrence, Esquire, Vice-President of the State of New-Jersey, to the President of the United States.

G. WASHINGTON

BURLINGTON, August 4, 1790

SIR,

I HAVE the honor to transmit an exemplified copy of a law of the State of New-Jersey, ratifying certain amendments to the Constitution of the United States.

I have the honor to be,

Your most obedient, humble servant,

(Signed) ELISHA LAWRENCE

The PRESIDENT of the UNITED STATES

A true copy.

TOBIAS LEAR, Secretary to the President of the United States

STATE OF NEW-JERSEY

The Honorable ELISHA LAWRENCE, Esquire, Vice-President, Captain-General and Commander in Chief in and over the State of New-Jersey, and territories thereunto belonging, Chancellor and Ordinary in the same

TO ALL TO WHOM THESE PRESENTS SHALL COME, GREETING

THESE are to certify, that Bowes Reed, Esquire, whose name is subscribed to the annexed certificate, certifying the annexed law to be a true copy taken from the original, enrolled in his office, is, and was at the time of signing thereof, Secretary of the State of New-Jersey; and that full faith and credit is, and ought to be due to his attestation as such.

In testimony whereof, I have hereunto subscribed my name, and caused the great seal of the State of New-Jersey to be hereunto affixed, at the city of Burlington, the third day of August, in the year of our Lord one thousand seven hundred and ninety, and of our independence the fifteenth.

(Signed)   ELISHA LAWRENCE

By his Honor's Command,

(Signed)   BOWES REED, Secretary

STATE OF NEW-JERSEY

An act to ratify on the part of this State certain Amendments to the Constitution of the United States

WHEREAS the Congress of the United States, begun and held at the city of New-York, on Wednesday the fourth day of March, one thousand seven hundred and eighty-nine, resolved, two thirds of both Houses concurring, That sundry articles be proposed to the Legislatures of the several States as Amendments to the Constitution of the United States, all or any of which articles, when ratified by three-fourths of the said legislatures, to be valid to all intents and purposes as part of the said constitution.

And whereas the President of the United States, did, in pursuance of a resolve of the Senate and House of Representatives of the United States of America, in Congress assembled, transmit to the Governor of this State the amendments proposed by Congress, which were by him laid before the legislature for their consideration.   Wherefore,

1. *Be it enacted by the Council and General Assembly of this State, and it is hereby enacted by the authority of the same*, That the following articles proposed by Congress, in addition to, and amendment of the constitution of the United States, to wit:

[Here follow, verbatim, the first, third, fourth, fifth, sixth, seventh, eighth, ninth, tenth, eleventh, and twelfth articles of the said amendments, proposed by Congress to the legislatures of the several states.]

Be, and the same are hereby ratified and adopted by the state of New-Jersey.

HOUSE OF ASSEMBLY, November 19th, 1789

This bill having been three times read in this House,

RESOLVED, That the same do pass.

By order of the House,

JOHN BEATTY, Speaker

COUNCIL-CHAMBER, November 20, 1789

This bill having been three times read in Council,

RESOLVED, That the same do pass.

By order of the House,

WILLIAM LIVINGSTON, President

CITY of BURLINGTON, STATE of NEW-JERSEY, August 3, 1790

THESE are to certify that the annexed law is a true copy taken from the original, inrolled in my office.

(Signed) BOWES REED, Secretary

I DO certify the foregoing to be a true copy of an exemplified copy of a law transmitted to the President of the United States, by the Honorable Elisha Lawrence.

TOBIAS LEAR, Secretary to the President of the United States

TREASURY OF THE UNITED STATES

NEW-YORK, January 28, 1790

SIR,

THE act of September 2d, 1789, requiring a statement of my accounts to be laid before Congress, I transmit the copy under cover, to be presented to the Honorable the House of Representatives.

I have the honor to be, with perfect respect,

Sir, your most humble servant,

SAMUEL MEREDITH, Treasurer of the United States

FREDERICK AUGUSTUS MUHLENBERG, Esq.

Speaker of the House of Representatives

TREASURY DEPARTMENT

AUDITOR'S OFFICE, January 22, 1790

I HAVE examined the accounts of Samuel Meredith, Esq. Treasurer of the United States, commencing at the time he entered on the duties of his office, and ending on the 31st day of December 1789, and find from his accounts, and the records of this department, that he is chargeable for the following sums, viz.

	Dols.	Cts.
To the president, directors and company of the bank of North-America, for monies borrowed of said bank	90,000.	
To the president, directors and company of the bank of New-York, for monies borrowed of said bank	80,000.	
To general account of monies arising from the acts of Congress, imposing duties on the tonnage of vessels, and on goods, wares and merchandize imported into the United States, for the amount of warrants drawn in favor of the Treasurer, on collectors, before 1st January, 1790	178,607.	24
To Joseph Howell, jun. paymaster-general, for cash paid by him into the general treasury	1,600.	
Amounting in the whole to, ...Dollars,	350,207.	24

I also find that warrants have been drawn on the Treasurer, during the period before stated, for the sum of 323,537. 91 hundredths dollars, which are charged in the Treasury books to the following general accounts.

To the appropriation of 216,000 dollars, granted to defray the expences of the civil list for the year 1789, under the late and present government, by an act passed the 29th day of September 1789	145,928.	89

Dols. Cts.

To the appropriation of 137,000 dollars granted to defray the
expences of the department of war for the year 1789, under
the late and present government, by an act passed the 29th
day of September, 1789 ....   49,216. 26

To the appropriation of 190,000 dollars granted for discharging warrants issued by the late Board of Treasury, and remaining unsatisfied, by an act passed the 29th day of September 1789 ....   7,449. 82

To the appropriation of 20,000 dollars granted for defraying
the expences of Indian treaties, by an act passed the 20th
day of August 1789 ....   20,000.

To the president, directors and company of the bank of North-
America, in part payment of monies borrowed of said bank   50,940.

To the president, directors and company of the bank of New-
York, in part payment of monies borrowed of said bank ...   48,402. 94

To Joseph Howell, jun. paymaster-general, for this sum borrowed of him and repaid ....   1,600.

Amounting, as before stated, to ....*Dollars,*   323,537. 91

Leaving a balance in the treasury, agreeably to the records of
this department, of 26,669. 33

Dollars,   350,207. 24

I find by the Treasurer's accounts, that the following warrants, registered
at the treasury, and included in the expenditures before stated, had not been
paid on the 31st December, 1789, viz.

Part of warrant, No. 1, for compensation to the members of the Senate.
For this sum due to Jonathan Elmer, Esq. ....*Dollars,*   966.

do.	Caleb Strong, Esq.	1,127.
do.	John Langdon, Esq.	754.

Amount of warrant No. 58 in favor of Jonathan Sturges, Esq..   1,107.

do.	157	Tobias Lear, Esq.	2,000.
do.	159	Will. Seton & Co. ...	2,000.
do.	161	President and directors of the bank of New-York	10,000.

Amounting in the whole to ....*Dollars,*   17,954.

Also, that the Treasurer has gained on a remittance of dollars 10,000, in gold, from Philadelphia, the sum of 6. 28

Which added to the last sum, will make 17,960. 28

It also appears that the following warrants have been drawn in favor of the Treasurer, on which he had not obtained payment, viz.

				Dols.	Cts.
Part of warrant No.	30	on Geo. Abbot Hall		7,500.	
do.	49	Benj. Lincoln		3,500.	
Amount of do.	56	William Lindsay		4,500.	
do.	57	Hudson Muse		600.	
do.	46	George Biscoe		290.	

	Dollars,	16,390.	
The balance of this statement being		1,570.	28

	Dollars,	17,960.	28

when added to the balance appearing to be in the treasury from the records of this department, amounts to the sum of twenty-eight thousand, two hundred and thirty-nine dollars, and sixty-one cents, for which the said Samuel Meredith, Esq. was accountable to the United States on the first day of January, 1790.

It appears from the treasurer's accounts, that this balance consisted of the following particulars, viz.

Payments for contingent expences of both Houses of Congress, which not having been included in the appropriations made by law, are suspended until legal warrants can be issued, viz.

	Dols.	Cts.	
Carter and Titlar's bill for cabinet work	138.	80	
Samuel A. Otis, for the use of the Senate	250.		
Do. do.	150.		
Gifford Dally, House of Representatives ...	250.		
Do. do.	100.		
Thomas Greenleaf, printer for do.	400.		

	1,288.	80

Charges of protest on three bills drawn upon William Lindsay, for which no appropriation has been made		41.	47
Money in the bank of North-America *Dollars,*	475. 53		
Notes of said bank in the bank of New-York	4,450.		
Money in the bank of New-York, including an error of 19$^{80}/_{100}$ dollars stated by the Treasurer	21,983. 81		

	26,909.	34

Amounting as before stated, to .... *Dollars,*	28,239.	61

The several warrants charged by the Treasurer are, except those numbered 58, 157, 159, and 161, which remained unpaid as before stated, herewith transmitted with the statement thereof for the decision of the Comptroller of the Treasury thereon.

(Signed)   OLIVER WOLCOTT, jun. Auditor
To NICHOLAS EVELEIGH, Esq. Comptroller of the Treasury

COMPTROLLER'S-OFFICE, 28th January, 1790
I ADMIT and certify the preceding statement: The Register will make entry accordingly.

(Signed)   NICHOLAS EVELEIGH, Comptroller

January 28th, 1790
ENTERED on record in conformity; the foregoing being true copies.

JOSEPH NOURSE, Register

TREASURY DEPARTMENT

AUDITOR'S-OFFICE, January 23d, 1790
I HAVE examined the accounts of Samuel Meredith, Esq. Treasurer of the United States, for indents of interest received and issued by him, from the time he entered on the duties of his office, to the 31st day of December, 1789, and find that he is chargeable for the following sums, viz.

To Michael Hillegas, Esq. late Treasurer for this sum in indents received per warrant No. 11.	937,257.
To fractional sums added by the Treasurer to indents issued on warrants for the payment of interest	6. 25
Amounting to ....*Dollars,*	937,263. 25

I also find that the said Treasurer has paid on legal warrants, for which he ought to have credit, the following sums, viz.

By Thomas Smith, Loan-Officer in Pennsylvania	53,400.
By William Imlay, do. in Connecticut	22,250.
By account of interest for payment of interest on the domestic debt	39,988. 25
Dollars,	115,638. 25
Leaving a balance in the hands of the said Treasurer, for which he was accountable to the United States, on the 1st January, 1790	821,625.
Dollars,	937,263. 25

Which from an examination of the books of indents in the hands of the said Treasurer, and an inspection of his accounts, appears to have actually been in the treasury on said day, agreeably to the statement and vouchers herewith transmitted for the decision of the Comptroller of the Treasury thereon.

(Signed) OLIVER WOLCOTT, jun. Auditor

To NICHOLAS EVELEIGH, Esq. Comptroller of the Treasury

COMPTROLLER'S-OFFICE, January 28th, 1790

I ADMIT and certify the preceding statement: The Register will make the entry accordingly.

(Signed) NICHOLAS EVELEIGH, Comptroller

January 28th, 1790

ENTERED on record in conformity; the foregoing being true copies.

JOSEPH NOURSE, Register

Receipts and Payments in Indents of Interest by the Treasurer of the United States

1789				Dols. Cts.	1789		Dols. Cts.
Nov. 23	Paid warrant No. 1	favor Thomas Smith, loan-officer for Pennsylvania		22,250.	Oct. 7.	Received per warrant No. 11 on Michael Hillegas	937,257.
Do.	2	William Imlay Connecticut		11,125.		Amount of fractions added to warrants for balances	6. 25
27	10	Comf. Sands, attorney for Wm. Johnson & Co.		1,081. 22			
	16	George Taylor		46. 58			
	25	James Gray		503. 27			
Dec. 12	3	William Imlay, loan-officer for Connecticut		11,125.			
19	26	Daniel Davis, attorney to Abel Seelye		19. 80			
	27	Charles Anderson		54. 40			
22	17	John Delafield		2,116. 15			
24	9	Do.		7,291. 30			
28	35	John Van Eps		4. 68			
	4	Thomas Smith, loan-officer for Pennsylvania		31,150.			
29	1	LeRoy and Bayard, attornies to L. Espinasse & Co.		28,153. 82			
	23	Do. do.		240. 86			
	29	James Burnside		259. 42			
31	36	Jonathan Lawrence, junior		216. 75			
		Balance this day in my hands		821,625.			
				937,263. 25			937,263. 25

January 1st, 1790

SAMUEL MEREDITH, Treasurer of the United States

Comptroller's Office

Admitted and certified this 28th January, 1790

NICHOLAS EVELEIGH, Comptroller

Register's Office, 28th January, 1790

I certify that the foregoing is a true copy from the original account filed on record in this office.

JOSEPH NOURSE, Register

TREASURY DEPARTMENT,

Auditor's Office, January 23, 1790

Examined by

OLIVER WOLCOTT, jun. Auditor

Comptroller's Office, January 25, 1790

Examined by

R. ROGERS

PAYMENTS on Warrants by the Treasurer of the United States

		No.	Dols. Cts.
Paid the compensations to the members of the Senate, pursuant to the Secretary of the Treasury's warrant		1.	26,009.
Fred. Aug. Muhlenberg, Esq. Speaker of the House of Representatives		2.	2,418.
Lamb. Cadwalader, Esq. Representative for New-Jersey ...		3.	1,125.
Isaac Coles, Esq. do.	Virginia	4.	1,455.
Peter Silvester, Esq. do.	New-York ...	5.	1,050.
John Brown, Esq. do.	Virginia	6.	1,182.
Daniel Hiester, Esq. do.	Pennsylvania ..	7.	1,212.
Jonath. Trumbull, Esq. do.	Connecticut ...	8.	1,182.
John Page, Esq. do.	Virginia	9.	1,446.
Fisher Ames, Esq. do.	Massachusetts .	10.	1,416.
Thomas Hartley, Esq. do.	Pennsylvania ..	11.	1,071.
Peter Muhlenberg, Esq. do.	do.	12.	1,332.
Andrew Moore, Esq. do.	Virginia	13.	1,440.
Thos. Fitzsimons, Esq. do.	Pennsylvania ..	14.	1,233.
George Clymer, Esq. do.	do.	15.	1,047.
Michael J. Stone, Esq. do.	Maryland	16.	1,005.
Thomas Scott, Esq. do.	Pennsylvania ..	17.	1,344.
Alex. White, Esq. do.	Virginia	18.	1,239.
George Gale, Esq. do.	Maryland	19.	1,290.
George Thatcher, Esq. do.	Massachusetts .	20.	1,479.
Daniel Carroll, Esq. do.	Maryland	21.	1,213.
Josiah Parker, Esq. do.	Virginia	22.	1,254.
William Floyd, Esq. do.	New-York	23.	990.
Abiel Foster, Esq. do.	N. Hampshire .	24.	474.
Samuel Livermore, Esq. do.	do.	25.	1,116.
James Jackson, Esq. do.	Georgia	26.	1,599.
Abraham Baldwin, Esq. do.	do.	27.	1,599.
George Partridge, Esq. do.	Massachusetts .	28.	1,242.
Thos. Sinnickson, Esq. do.	New-Jersey ...	29.	978.
James Schureman, Esq. do.	do.	30.	1,041.
George Leonard, Esq. do.	Massachusetts .	31.	1,050.
Benj. Goodhue, Esq. do.	do.	32.	1,425.
J. Van Rensselaer, Esq. do.	New-York	33.	960.
John Hathorn, Esq. do.	do.	34.	960.
Henry Wynkoop, Esq. do.	Pennsylvania ..	35.	1,092.
William Smith, Esq. do.	Maryland	36.	1,281.
Thomas Sumter, Esq. do.	S. Carolina ...	37.	1,278.
Elbridge Gerry, Esq. do.	Massachusetts .	38.	1,413.
Thos. T. Tucker, Esq. do.	S. Carolina ...	39.	1,806.
Joshua Seney, Esq. do.	Maryland	40.	1,140.
William Smith, Esq. do.	S. Carolina ...	41.	1,578.
Jonath. Grout, Esq. do.	Massachusetts .	42.	1,056.
Elias Boudinot, Esq. do.	New-Jersey ...	43.	1,134.

			No.	Dols.	Cts.
Paid Theod. Bland, Esq.	Representative for	Virginia	44.	1,428.	
Rich. Bland Lee, Esq.	do.	do.	45.	1,362.	
Roger Sherman, Esq.	do.	Connecticut ...	46.	1,266.	
Benjamin Contee, Esq.	do.	Maryland	47.	804.	
George Mathews, Esq.	do.	Georgia	48.	1,266.	
Jere. Wadsworth, Esq.	do.	Connecticut ...	49.	1,161.	
Ben. Huntington, Esq.	do.	do.	50.	1,350.	
Daniel Huger, Esq.	do.	S. Carolina ...	51.	1,578.	
Aedanus Burke, Esq.	do.	do.	52.	1,578.	
Samuel Griffin, Esq.	do.	Virginia	53.	1,443.	
J. Madison, jun. Esq.	do.	do.	54.	1,410.	
John Vining, Esq.	do.	Delaware	55.	990.	
Egbert Benson, Esq.	do.	New-York	56.	1,092.	
John Laurance, Esq.	do.	do.	57.	1,050.	
Jonathan Sturges, Esq.	do.	Connecticut ...	58.	1,107.	
Nicholas Gilman, Esq.	do.	N. Hampshire .	59.	1,447.	20
T. Sedgwick, Esq.	do.	Massachusetts .	60.	576.	

Salary to Samuel A. Otis, Esq. Secretary to the Senate 61. 1,069. 17
Joseph Wheaton, Serjeant at Arms to the House of Representatives .... 62. 564.
Benjamin Bankson, principal Clerk to the Senate ..... 63. 435.
William Lambert, principal Clerk to the House of Representatives .... 64. 546.
Robert Heysham, engrossing Clerk to the Senate ...... 65. 202.
George Sutton, engrossing Clerk to the House of Representatives .... 66. 248.
James Mathers, Doorkeeper to the Senate .... 67. 630.
Gifford Dally, Doorkeeper to the House of Representatives 68. 645. 66
Cornelius Maxwell, Messenger to the Senate .... 69. 350.
Do.   Messenger to the House of Representatives .... 70. 62.
Thomas Claxton, Assistant-Doorkeeper to do. .... 71. 358.
The Rev. William Linn, Chaplain to do. .... 72. 208.
Paid Robert Elliot and Elie Williams on account of their contract for supplying the army .... 73. 4,000.
Henry Knox, towards carrying into execution treaties with Indian tribes .... 74. 20,000.
Tobias Lear, on account of the President's compensation .. 75. 1,000.
John Beckley, his salary as Clerk to the House of Representatives .... 76. 1,114.
Tobias Lear, on account of the President's compensation ... 77. 2,000.
Do.   do. .... 78. 1,000.
Joseph Howell, jun. on account of forage, subsistence and pay due the troops the present year 79. 24,177. 54
Tobias Lear, on account of the President's compensation .. 80. 3,500.
Do.   do. .... 81. 200.

	No.	Dols.	Cts.
Paid John Meyer, for contingent expences of the Secretary of the Treasury's office	82.	200.	
Tobias Lear, on account of the President's compensation	83.	300.	
John Adams, on account of his compensation as Vice-President	84.	1,000.	
John Meyer, for contingent expences of the Secretary of the Treasury's office	85.	200.	
William Seton and Co. on account of Robert Elliot and Elie William's contract for supply of the army	86.	2,000.	
Patrick Ferrall, for contingent expences of the office for settling accounts with individual States	87.	200.	
Joseph Howell, jun. to reimburse him for the money borrowed of him by the Secretary of the Treasury	88.	1,600.	
Joseph Hardy, for contingent expences of the Comptroller's office	89.	200.	
Henry Remsen, for contingent expences of the office for foreign affairs	90.	50.	
John Adams, on account of his compensation as Vice-President	91.	2,000.	
Elizabeth Bergan, her pension to the 10th September	92.	8.	54
Do. do. 30th	93.	2.	91
Royal Flint, on account of a warrant, No. 1101, dated 3d March, 1789, on account of balance of his cloathing contract	94.	3,000.	
Tobias Lear, on account of the President's compensation	95.	1,000.	
William Hill, on account of a balance due him on his contract cloathing the troops	96.	6,500.	
Joseph Stretch, for contingent expences of the Register's office	97.	150.	
P. Dominique l'Eglize, his pension to 10th September	98.	23.	33
Do. do. 30th	99.	6.	67
Jos. Bindon, for Jos. Traversie's pension to 10th Sept.	100.	53.	33
Do. do. 30th	101.	6.	67
Samuel Provoost, for his salary as Chaplain to the Senate the 10th September	102.	188.	57
Samuel Provoost, for his salary as Chaplain to the Senate the 29th September	103.	26.	02
A. G. Fraunces, for board &c. of G. M. White Eyes	104.	110.	72
Joseph Nourse, salaries to the Register's office to the 10th September	105.	670.	83
Joseph Nourse, salaries to the Register's office to the 30th September	106.	194.	44
William Duer, salaries for the late Board of Treasury's office	107.	1,895.	82
Joseph Hardy, salaries for the Accountant's office	108.	418.	05
Henry Kuhl, his salary as late Clerk to the treasury	109.	88.	56
Joseph Howell, jun. salaries for the pay office to the 10th September	110.	1,328.	21
Joseph Howell, jun. salaries for the Pay-office to the 30th September	111.	375.	35

	No.	Dols.	Cts.

Paid Henry Knox, salaries for the War-office to the 10th September | 112. | 768. | 04

Henry Knox, salary for the War-office to the 30th September | 113. | 263. | 84

John Delafield, assignee to Arthur St. Clair, his salary as Governor of the Western Territory to the 10th September | 114. | 388. | 89

John Delafield, assignee to Arthur St. Clair, his salary as Governor of the Western Territory to the 30th September | 115. | 111. | 11

John Jay, salaries to the office of Secretary for Foreign Affairs to the 10th September . . . . | 116. | 1,088. | 87

John Jay, salaries to the office of Secretary for Foreign Affairs to the 30th September . . . . | 117. | 266. | 07

Royal Flint, on account of expences incurred for temporary residence of the President, and for furniture, &c. . . . . | 118. | 5,000. |

John Jay, for his salary as Chief Justice of the United States, to the 30th September . . . . | 119. | 54. | 79

John Paulding, on account of his pension to the 10th September . . . . | 120. | 71. | 04

John Paulding, on account of his pension to the 30th September . . . . | 121. | 10. | 95

John Ramsey, house-rent of the board of treasury to the 10th September . . . . | 122. | 162. | 50

John Ramsey, house-rent of the board of treasury to the 30th October . . . . | 123. | 62. | 50

Wm. Irvine, John T. Gilman and John Kean, Commissioners for settling accounts of individual States with the United States, salaries for their office to 10th September . . . . | 124. | 1,400. | 47

Wm. Irvine, John T. Gilman and John Kean, Commissioners for settling accounts of individual States with the United States, salaries for their office to 30th September . . . . | 125. | 477. | 88

Smith and Wyckoff, for provisions supplied the troops at West Point . . . . | 126. | 938. | 67

Smith and Wyckoff, for provisions supplied the troops at West Point . . . . | 127. | 52. | 55

Robert Gilchrist, assignee to James McKenzie, his pension to the 10th September . . . . | 128. | 17. | 78

Robert Gilchrist, assignee to James McKenzie, his pension to the 30th September . . . . | 129. | 2. | 22

Robert Gilchrist, assignee to Joseph Brussell, his pension to the 10th September . . . . | 130. | 17. | 78

Robert Gilchrist, assignee to Joseph Brussell, his pension to the 30th September . . . . | 131. | 2. | 22

Nicholas Eveleigh, for salaries for the Comptroller's office . . | 132. | 230. |

Oliver Wolcott, for salaries for the Auditor's office to the 30th September . . . . | 133. | 92. | 87

John Meyer, contingent expences for the Secretary of the Treasury's office . . . . | 135. | 150. |

Royal Flint, on account of expences incurred for the temporary residence of the President, and for furniture, &c. . . | 136. | 500. |

	No.	Dols.	Cts.

Paid Alexander Hamilton, salaries to the Secretary of the Treasury's office to the 30th September 137. 361. 08

David Williams, on account of his pension to the 10th September 137. 70. 44

David Williams, on account of his pension to the 30th September 138. 11. 10

William Seton and Co. on account of Robert Elliot and Elie Williams's contract supplying the army .... 139. 2,000.

Tobias Lear, on account of the President's compensation ... 140. 1,000.

Royal Flint, on account of expences incurred for the temporary residence of the President, and for furniture, &c. 141. 1,000.

William Hill, on account of his contract cloathing the troops 142. 5,000.

Royal Flint, in full for a balance due him on his cloathing contract 143. 3,449. 82

John Adams, on account of his compensation as Vice-President .... 144. 300.

Melancton Smith, for rations delivered the troops at West-Point, from the 1st to 31st July, 1789 .... 145. 175. 51

Melancton Smith, for rations delivered the troops, at West-Point, from the 1st to 31st October 146. 71. 99

Royal Flint, on account of expences incurred for the temporary residence of the President, and for furniture, &c. 147. 1,500.

Henry Knox, on account of two warrants, No. 317, 318, drawn by the late board of treasury .... 148. 1,000.

Tobias Lear, on account of the President's compensation ... 149. 2,000.

William Hill, on account of a balance due on his cloathing contract .... 150. 1,500.

Tobias Lear, on account of the President's compensation ... 151. 500.

Joseph Nourse, attorney for Richard Gridley, his pension to the 1st July last 152. 444. 40

Nicholas Eveleigh, on account salaries due the Comptroller's office .... 153. 60.

Joseph Nourse, attorney to the youngest children of the late General Warren, their pension to the 1st July last ...... 154. 450.

John Adams, on account of his compensation as Vice-President .... 155. 700.

William Smith, on account of his issues of provisions at the post of Springfield .... 156. 800.

President, directors, &c. of bank of North-America .... 158. 50,940.

  do.   New-York 160. 38,402. 94

  do.   do. .... 161. 10,000.

Will. Seton & Co. on account Rob. Elliot and Elie Williams's contract supplying the army .... 159. 2,000.

Tobias Lear, on account of the President's compensation ... 157. 2,000.

Balance carried forward, and accounted for in new account 26,669. 33

           Dollars, 350,207. 24

RECEIPTS on Warrants by the Treasurer of the United States

		No.	Dols.	Cts.
Received for the Secretary of the Treasury's warrant on				
Joseph Hiller	Collector of Salem	1.	350.	
Benjamin Lincoln	Boston	2.	4,753.	
Do.	do.	3.	800.	
Jedidiah Huntington	New-London	4.	2,000.	
Otho H. Williams	Baltimore	5.	3,184.	
Do.	do.	6.	267.	
Joseph Howell, jun. Paymaster-General		6.	1,600.	
Jas. McCubbin Lingan	collector of Georgetown	7.	750.	
William Lindsay	Norfolk	8.	300.	
William Heth	Bermuda-Hundred	9.	334.	
John Habersham	Savannah	10.	700.	
Jonathan Fitch	New-Haven	11.	900.	
Otho H. Williams	Baltimore	12.	400.	
Charles Lee	Alexandria	13.	750.	
George Abb. Hall	Charleston	14.	1,100.	
William Heth	Bermuda-Hundred	15.	333.	33
Benjamin Lincoln	Boston	16.	1,447.	20
Do.	do.	17.	1,070.	
Do.	do.	18.	500.	
Do.	do.	19.	2,000.	
William Lindsay	Norfolk	20.	500.	
Benjamin Lincoln	Boston	21.	2,500.	
Do.	do.	22.	500.	
George Burke	Wilmington	23.	400.	
Joseph Whipple	Portsmouth	24.	500.	
Jedidiah Huntington	New-London	25.	1,000.	
Samuel Smedly	Fairfield	26.	200.	
Benjamin Lincoln	Boston	27.	2,000.	
William Heth	Bermuda Hundred	28.	1,000.	
Hudson Muse	Tappahannock	29.	500.	
George Abbot Hall	Charleston	30.	10,000.	
Benjamin Lincoln	Boston	31.	1,500.	
Otho H. Williams	Baltimore	32.	1,230.	
Charles Lee	Alexandria	33.	115.	
Otho H. Williams	Baltimore	34.	450.	
Do.	do.	35.	2,500.	
John Scott	Chester Town	36.	75.	
Benjamin Lincoln	Boston	37.	500.	
George Bush	Wilmington	38.	225.	
Charles Lee	Alexandria	39.	270.	
Benjamin Lincoln	Boston	40.	6,500.	
Charles Lee	Alexandria	41.	150.	
Hudson Muse	Tappahannock	42.	846.	55
William Lindsay	Norfolk	43.	900.	

		No.	Dols.	Cts.
Received for the Secretary of Treasury's warrant on				
Otho H. Williams	collector of Baltimore	44.	1,000.	
Do.	do.	45.	2,000.	
George Biscoe	Nottingham	46.	290.	
Charles Lee	Alexandria	47.	305.	
William Heth	Bermuda-Hundred	48.	1,400.	
Benjamin Lincoln	Boston	49.	10,000.	
Otho H. Williams	Baltimore	50.	1,000.	
Benjamin Lincoln	Boston	51.	3,500.	
George Bush	Wilmington	52.	400.	
Benjamin Lincoln	Boston	53.	449.	82
Otho H. Williams	Baltimore	54.	1,000.	
Benjamin Lincoln	Boston	55.	300.	
William Lindsay	Norfolk	56.	4,500.	
Hudson Muse	Tappahannock	57.	600.	
Otho H. Williams	Baltimore	58.	1,000.	
Charles Lee	Alexandria	59.	150.	
William Lindsay	Norfolk	60.	1,000.	
Otho H. Williams	Baltimore	61.	1,000.	
Jedidiah Huntington	New-London	62.	600.	
Jonathan Fitch	New-Haven	63.	200.	
Sharp Delany	Philadelphia	64.	50,940.	
John Lamb	New-York	65.	38,402.	94
President, Directors, &c. of bank of	New-York	1.	20,000.	
Do.	North America	2.	50,000.	
Do.	New-York	3.	30,000.	
Do.	North America	4.	20,000.	
Do.	New-York	5.	20,000.	
Do.	do.	7.	10,000.	
Do.	North America	8.	20,000.	
Otho H. Williams, collector of	Baltimore	66.	475.	
Charles Lee	Alexandria	67.	800.	
Benjamin Lincoln	Boston	68.	994.	40
			350,207.	24

SAMUEL MEREDITH
Treasurer of the United States

PAYMENTS MADE UPON WARRANTS FOR WHICH THERE IS NO
APPROPRIATION

	Dols.	Cts.	Dols.	Cts.
To Carter and Titlar, cabinet-makers to the House of Representatives			138.	80

	Dols.	Cts.	Dols.	Cts.
Samuel A. Otis, for the use of the Senate	250.			
Do. do.	150.			
Gifford Dally, do. House of Representatives	250.			
Do. do.	100.			
Thomas Greenleaf, printing for do.	400.			
			1,288.	80
Warrant No. 30, on G. A. Hall, Collector of Charleston, 10,000.				
for which I have received only .... 2,500.				
			7,500.	
46, George Biscoe, collector of Notting-				
ham, wholly unpaid	290.			
49, Benjamin Lincoln, collector of Boston 10,000.				
for which I have received only .... 6,500.				
			3,500.	
56, William Lindsay, collector of				
Norfolk, wholly unpaid	4,500.			
Cost of protest and charges on three bills drawn upon William Lindsay				
(no appropriation)			41.	47
Pennsylvania bank post notes in the bank of New-York			4,450.	
Money in the bank of North-America			475.	53
Money in the bank of New-York			21,964.	01
Due by me, having by mistake paid specie for an indent warrant			19.	80
Warrant No. 57, on Hudson Muse, collector of Tappahannock, wholly				
unpaid			600.	
			44,629.	61

TREASURY DEPARTMENT

AUDITOR'S-OFFICE, January 22d, 1790

THE foregoing account of Samuel Meredith, Esq. Treasurer of the United States has been examined by

OLIVER WOLCOTT, jun. Auditor

COMPTROLLER'S-OFFICE, January 25th, 1790

EXAMINED by

R. ROGERS

COMPTROLLER'S-OFFICE, January 28th, 1790

ADMITTED,

NICHOLAS EVELEIGH, Comptroller

REGISTER'S-OFFICE, 28th January, 1790
I CERTIFY that the foregoing is a true copy from the original account filed
on record in this office.

JOSEPH NOURSE, Register

January 1, 1790
SAMUEL MEREDITH, Treasurer of the United States

	Dols.	Cts.
Balance brought forward from page 609	26,669.	33

Part of warrant No. 1, in favor of the members of the Senate
remaining unpaid, viz.

Compensation to Jonath. Elmer, Esq. Senator for New-Jersey	966.	
Caleb Strong, Esq. do. for Massachusetts	1,127.	

Part of do.

John Langdon, Esq. do. for New-Hampshire	754.	
		2,847.
Warrant No. 58, to Jonathan Sturges, Esq. Representative for Connecticut unpaid	1,107.	
157, Tobias Lear, Esq. on account of the President's compensation unpaid ..	2,000.	
159, Wm. Seton and Co. account Robert Elliot and Elie Williams contracts supplying the troops	2,000.	
161, President, Directors, &c. of bank of New-York for the loan unpaid ..	10,000.	
Gain in ten thousand dollars in gold brought by the Assist. Secretary from Philadelphia	6.	28
Dollars,	44,629.	61²

_____

² These documents were received in the House on January 29, 1790.

THIRD SESSION

JOURNAL

OF THE

HOUSE OF REPRESENTATIVES

OF THE

UNITED STATES

AT a Session of the Congress of the United States, begun and held at the city of Philadelphia, in the state of Pennsylvania, on Monday the sixth of December, one thousand seven hundred and ninety; pursuant to the act "for establishing the temporary and permanent seat of government of the United States;" being the third session of the first Congress held under the Constitution of Government of the United States:

On which day, being the day appointed by adjournment of the two Houses for the meeting of the present session, the following members of the House of Representatives appeared and took their seats, to wit:

From New-Hampshire
{
Abiel Foster
Nicholas Gilman and
Samuel Livermore
}

From Massachusetts
{
Fisher Ames
Benjamin Goodhue and
George Thatcher
}

From Connecticut
{
Benjamin Huntington
Roger Sherman and
Jonathan Sturges
}

From New-York
{
Egbert Benson
William Floyd
John Laurance and
Peter Silvester
}

From New-Jersey
{
Elias Boudinot
Lambert Cadwalader and
James Schureman
}

From Pennsylvania
{
George Clymer
Thomas Fitzsimons
Frederick Augustus Muhlenberg
Peter Muhlenberg and
Henry Wynkoop
}

From Maryland
{ Joshua Seney

From Virginia
{
John Brown
Samuel Griffin and
James Madison, junior
}

From North-Carolina
{
Timothy Bloodworth and
Hugh Williamson
}

From South-Carolina { William Smith

From Georgia { Abraham Baldwin

But a quorum of the whole number not being present, the House adjourned until to-morrow morning eleven o'clock.

TUESDAY, DECEMBER 7, 1790

The House met according to adjournment.

Several other members, to wit, from Pennsylvania, Daniel Hiester, and Thomas Scott; from Virginia, Richard Bland Lee; and from South-Carolina, Daniel Huger, appeared and took their seats:

And a quorum of the whole number being present,

A message was received from the Senate by Mr. Otis their Secretary.

MR. SPEAKER, I am directed to inform this House, that a quorum of the Senate is now assembled in the senate-chamber, and ready to proceed to business. And then he withdrew.

On motion,

ORDERED, That a message be sent to the Senate to inform them that a quorum of the House is assembled, and ready to proceed to business; and that the Clerk of this House do go with the said message.

Another member, to wit, William B. Giles, from Virginia, returned to serve in the room of Theodorick Bland, deceased, appeared, produced his credentials, and took his seat in the House; the oath to support the Constitution of the United States being administered to him by Mr. Speaker, according to law.

On motion,

RESOLVED, That Mr. Boudinot, Mr. Laurance, and Mr. Smith, of South-Carolina, be a committee, jointly with such committee as the Senate shall appoint, to wait on the President of the United States, and notify him that a quorum of the two Houses is assembled.[1]

ORDERED, That the Clerk of this House do acquaint the Senate therewith.

A message from the Senate by Mr. Otis their Secretary.

MR. SPEAKER, The Senate have agreed to a resolution, that Mr. Langdon and Mr. Morris be a committee on the part of the Senate, with such committee as this House shall appoint, to inform the President of the United States that a quorum of the two Houses is assembled, and will be ready in the

---

[1] A copy of the resolution is in House Joint and Concurrent Resolutions, SR, DNA.

senate-chamber, at such time as the President shall appoint, to receive any communications he may be pleased to make;[2] to which they desire the concurrence of this House.   And then he withdrew.

The House proceeded to consider the said resolution; and the same being read, was, on the question put thereupon, disagreed to.
ORDERED, That the Clerk of this House do acquaint the Senate therewith.
A message from the Senate by Mr. Otis their Secretary.

MR. SPEAKER,   The Senate have appointed a committee, jointly with the committee appointed by this House, to wait on the President of the United States, to inform him that a quorum of the two Houses has assembled.   And then he withdrew.

The several petitions of John Lewis, Francis Ackling, and Alexander Fowler, were presented to the House and read, respectively praying the liquidation and settlement of claims against the United States.   Also,
A petition of Jacob Bell, praying that the amount of certain duties to the payment of which he has been subjected by a mistake of the collector of the port of New-York, may be refunded to him.
ORDERED, That the said petitions do lie on the table.
Mr. Boudinot, from the joint committee appointed to wait on the President of the United States, and notify him that a quorum of the two Houses had assembled, reported, that the committee had, according to order, performed that service; and that the President was pleased to say, that he would attend, to make a communication to both Houses of Congress, to-morrow at twelve o'clock, in the senate-chamber.
And then the House adjourned until to-morrow morning eleven o'clock.

WEDNESDAY, DECEMBER 8, 1790

Several other members, to wit, from Massachusetts, Elbridge Gerry, and Jonathan Grout; from Virginia, Andrew Moore, and Alexander White; and from South-Carolina, Thomas Tudor Tucker, appeared and took their seats.
A message from the Senate by Mr. Otis their Secretary.

MR. SPEAKER,   The Senate are now ready in the senate-chamber, to attend this House in receiving the communication from the President of the United States, agreeably to his notification to both Houses yesterday.   And then he withdrew.

---

[2] The Senate resolution and appointment are noted on the House resolution in House Joint and Concurrent Resolutions, SR, DNA.

Mr. Speaker, attended by the members of this House, then withdrew to the senate-chamber, for the purpose expressed in the message from the Senate; and being returned,

Mr. Speaker laid before the House a copy of the speech delivered by the President of the United States to both Houses of Congress in the senate-chamber, as followeth:

FELLOW-CITIZENS of the SENATE and HOUSE of REPRESENTATIVES,

IN meeting you again I feel much satisfaction in being able to repeat my congratulations on the favorable prospects which continue to distinguish our public affairs. The abundant fruits of another year have blessed our country with plenty, and with the means of a flourishing commerce. The progress of public credit is witnessed by a considerable rise of American stock abroad as well as at home. And the revenues allotted for this and other national purposes, have been productive beyond the calculations by which they were regulated. This latter circumstance is the more pleasing, as it is not only a proof of the fertility of our resources, but as it assures us of a further increase of the national respectability and credit; and let me add, as it bears an honorable testimony to the patriotism and integrity of the mercantile and marine part of our citizens—The punctuality of the former in discharging their engagements has been exemplary.

In conformity to the powers vested in me by acts of the last session, a loan of three millions of florins, towards which some provisional measures had previously taken place, has been completed in Holland. As well the celerity with which it has been filled, as the nature of the terms (considering the more than ordinary demand for borrowing created by the situation of Europe) give a reasonable hope that the further execution of those powers may proceed with advantage and success. The Secretary of the Treasury has my direction to communicate such further particulars as may be requisite for more precise information.

Since your last sessions, I have received communications, by which it appears, that the district of Kentucky, at present a part of Virginia, has concurred in certain propositions contained in a law of that state; in consequence of which the district is to become a distinct member of the Union, in case the requisite sanction of Congress be added. For this sanction application is now made.

I shall cause the papers on this very important transaction to be laid before you. The liberality and harmony with which it has been conducted, will be found to do great honor to both the parties. And the sentiments of warm attachment to the Union, and its present government, expressed by our fellow-citizens of Kentucky, cannot fail to add an affectionate concern for their particular welfare, to the great national impressions under which you will decide on the case submitted to you.

It has been heretofore known to Congress, that frequent incursions have been made on our frontier settlements by certain banditti of Indians from the north-west side of the Ohio. These, with some of the tribes dwelling on and near the Wabash, have of late been particularly active in their depredations; and being emboldened by the impunity of their crimes, and aided by such parts of the neighbouring tribes as could be seduced to join in their hostilities, or afford them a retreat for their prisoners and plunder, they have, instead of listening to the humane invitations and overtures made on the part of the United States, renewed their violences with fresh alacrity and greater effect. The lives of a number of valuable citizens have thus been sacrificed, and some of them under circumstances peculiarly shocking; whilst others have been carried into a deplorable captivity.

These aggravated provocations rendered it essential to the safety of the western settlements, that the aggressors should be made sensible that the government of the Union is not less capable of punishing their crimes, than it is disposed to respect their rights and reward their attachments. As this object could not be effected by defensive measures, it became necessary to put in force the act which empowers the President to call out the militia for the protection of the frontiers. And I have accordingly authorized an expedition, in which the regular troops in that quarter are combined with such draughts of militia as were deemed sufficient. The event of the measure is yet unknown to me. The Secretary of War is directed to lay before you a statement of the information on which it is founded, as well as an estimate of the expense with which it will be attended.

The disturbed situation of Europe, and particularly the critical posture of the great maritime powers, whilst it ought to make us the more thankful for the general peace and security enjoyed by the United States, reminds us at the same time, of the circumspection with which it becomes us to preserve these blessings. It requires also that we should not overlook the tendency of a war, and even of preparations for a war, among the nations most concerned in active commerce with this country, to abridge the means, and thereby at least enhance the price of transporting its valuable productions to their proper markets. I recommend it to your serious reflections, how far, and in what mode, it may be expedient to guard against embarrassments from these contingencies, by such encouragements to our own navigation as will render our commerce and agriculture less dependent on foreign bottoms, which may fail us in the very moment most interesting to both of these great objects. Our fisheries, and the transportation of our own produce, offer us abundant means for guarding ourselves against this evil.

Your attention seems to be not less due to that particular branch of our trade which belongs to the Mediterranean. So many circumstances unite in rendering the present state of it distressful to us, that you will not think any deliberations misemployed which may lead to its relief and protection.

The laws you have already passed for the establishment of a judiciary system, have opened the doors of justice to all descriptions of persons. You will consider in your wisdom, whether improvements in that system may yet be made; and particularly, whether an uniform process of execution on sentences issuing from the federal courts, be not desirable through all the states.

The patronage of our commerce, of our merchants and seamen, has called for the appointment of consuls in foreign countries. It seems expedient to regulate by law the exercise of that jurisdiction, and those functions which are permitted them, either by express convention, or by a friendly indulgence in the places of their residence. The consular convention too with his Most Christian Majesty, has stipulated, in certain cases, the aid of the national authority to his consuls established here. Some legislative provision is requisite to carry these stipulations into full effect.

The establishment of the militia—of a mint—of standards of weights and measures—of the post-office and post-roads—are subjects which (I presume) you will resume of course, and which are abundantly urged by their own importance.

GENTLEMEN of the HOUSE of REPRESENTATIVES,

THE sufficiency of the revenues you have established, for the objects to which they are appropriated, leaves no doubt, but the residuary provisions will be commensurate to the other objects, for which the public faith stands now pledged. Allow me, moreover, to hope, that it will be a favorite policy with you, not merely to secure a payment of the interest of the debt funded, but as far and as fast as the growing resources of the country will permit, to exonerate it of the principal itself. The appropriations you have made of the western lands, explain your dispositions on this subject: And I am persuaded, that the sooner that valuable fund can be made to contribute, along with other means, to the actual reduction of the public debt, the more salutary will the measure be to every public interest, as well as the more satisfactory to our constituents.

GENTLEMEN of the SENATE and HOUSE of REPRESENTATIVES,

IN pursuing the various and weighty business of the present session, I indulge the fullest persuasion, that your consultations will be equally marked with wisdom, and animated by the love of your country. In whatever belongs to my duty, you shall have all the co-operation which an undiminished zeal for its welfare can inspire.

It will be happy for us both, and our best reward, if by a successful administration of our respective trusts, we can make the established government more and more instrumental in promoting the good of our fellow citizens, and more and more the objects of their attachment and confidence.

G. WASHINGTON

UNITED STATES, December 8th, 1790[3]

On motion,

RESOLVED, That the said speech be committed to the consideration of a committee of the whole House to-morrow.[4]

On motion,

RESOLVED, That two Chaplains, of different denominations, be appointed to Congress for the present session; one by each House, who shall interchange weekly.

ORDERED, That the Clerk of this House do carry the said resolution to the Senate, and desire their concurrence.[5]

A petition of John Carlile, was presented to the House and read, praying the liquidation and settlement of his accounts, as assistant adjutant-general to the late American army.

ORDERED, That the said petition, together with the petitions of Jacob Bell, and John Lewis, which were presented yesterday, be referred to the Secretary of the Treasury, with instruction to examine the same, and report his opinion thereupon to the House.

ORDERED, That the petition of Francis Ackling, which was presented yesterday, be referred to the Secretary at War, with instruction to examine the same, and report his opinion thereupon to the House.

ORDERED, That a committee be appointed to prepare and bring in a bill or bills for establishing the post-office and post-roads of the United States; and that Mr. Sherman, Mr. Clymer, and Mr. Williamson, be of the said committee.[6]

And then the House adjourned until to-morrow morning eleven o'clock.

THURSDAY, DECEMBER 9, 1790

Two other members, to wit; James Jackson and George Mathews, from Georgia, appeared and took their seats.

The House, according to the order of the day, resolved itself into a com-

---

[3] The speech is in President's Messages: Annual reports, SR, DNA. E–46076.

[4] On December 9 the state of the union address was considered in the COWH, and a committee was appointed to prepare an answer to it.

[5] On December 9 the Senate agreed to this resolution.

[6] On January 7, 1791, this committee presented a Post Office Bill [HR–113], which was read twice.

mittee of the whole House, on the speech of the President of the United States to both Houses of Congress; and after some time spent therein, Mr. Speaker resumed the chair, and Mr. Livermore reported, that the committee had, according to order, had the said speech under consideration, and come to a resolution thereupon, which he delivered in at the Clerk's table, where the same was twice read, and, on a question put thereupon, agreed to by the House as followeth:

RESOLVED, That it is the opinion of this committee, that an address ought to be presented by the House to the President of the United States, in answer to his speech to both Houses, with assurances that this House will, without delay, proceed to take into their serious consideration, the various and important matters recommended to their attention.

ORDERED, That Mr. Madison, Mr. Ames and Mr. Tucker, be appointed a committee to prepare an address pursuant to the said resolution.[7]

A message from the Senate by Mr. Otis their Secretary.

MR. SPEAKER, The Senate agree to the resolution of this House for the appointment of two Chaplains to Congress, for the present session; and have elected the Right Reverend Bishop White, on their part. And then he withdrew.

On motion,

ORDERED, That to-morrow be assigned as the day for the appointment of a Chaplain to Congress, on the part of this House.[8]

ORDERED, That the Clerk of this House cause the members to be furnished, during the present session, with three newspapers, such as the members respectively shall choose, to be delivered at their lodgings.

A message was received from the President of the United States, by Mr. Lear his Secretary, who delivered in the copy of certain official communications from the district of Kentucky, relative to the erection of the said district into an independent state,[9] as referred to in the President's speech to both Houses of Congress. And then withdrew.

The said official communications were read, and ordered to lie on the table.[10]

The Speaker laid before the House a letter from the Secretary at War, accompanied with a statement of the information, on which the expedition

---

[7] On December 10 this committee reported.

[8] On December 10 the House elected a chaplain.

[9] Copies of a petition, resolutions, and a covering letter are in Petitions and Memorials: Various subjects, SR, DNA. The documents are printed in the Appendix to the Third Session.

[10] On January 12 the Senate sent the Kentucky Statehood Bill [S–16] to the House. The bill was then read.

against the Indians north-west of the Ohio, has been founded; and also, the instructions to the Governor of the Western Territory, and the commanding officer of the troops relative to the same object; together with an estimate of the expense, with which the expedition will probably be attended.[11]

ORDERED, That the said letter and enclosures do lie on the table.

ORDERED, That a committee be appointed to prepare and bring in a bill or bills for registering ships or vessels, for regulating those employed in the coasting trade and fisheries, and for other purposes; and that Mr. Fitzsimons, Mr. Goodhue and Mr. Lee, be of the said committee.

ORDERED, That a committee be appointed to prepare and bring in a bill or bills, to amend the act, intituled, "An act to promote the progress of useful arts;" and that Mr. White, Mr. Seney, and Mr. Baldwin, be of the said committee.[12]

And then the House adjourned until to-morrow morning eleven o'clock.

FRIDAY, DECEMBER 10, 1790

Several other members, to wit; from Massachusetts, George Partridge; from Connecticut, Jonathan Trumbull and Jeremiah Wadsworth; from New-Jersey, Thomas Sinnickson; and from Maryland, William Smith, appeared and took their seats.

The House, according to the order of the day, proceeded by ballot to the appointment of a Chaplain to Congress, on the part of this House; and upon examining the ballots, a majority of the votes of the whole House was found in favor of the Reverend Mr. Blair.

ORDERED, That a committee be appointed to prepare and bring in a bill or bills for determining, agreeable to the provision in the first section of the second article of the Constitution, the time when the electors shall, in the year which will terminate on the third of March, one thousand seven hundred and ninety-three, and so in every fourth year thereafter, be chosen, and the day on which they shall give their votes; for declaring what officer shall, in case of vacancy both in the office of President and Vice-President, act as President; for assigning a public office, where the lists, mentioned in the second paragraph of the first section of the second article of the Constitution, shall, in case of vacancy in the office of President of the Senate, or his absence from the seat of government, be in the mean time deposited; and for directing the mode in which such lists shall be transmitted; and that Mr. Benson, Mr.

---

[11] The statement of information and instructions with an estimate of expenses are in Reports and Communications from the Secretary of War, HR, DNA. A copy of the letter and another copy of the enclosures are in A Record of the Reports of the Secretary of War, vol. 1, HR, DNA.

[12] On December 11 two members were added to this committee.

Huntington, Mr. Hiester, Mr. Moore, and Mr. Partridge, be of the said committee.[13]

ORDERED, That a committee be appointed to prepare and bring in a bill or bills, more effectually to provide for the national defence, by establishing an uniform militia throughout the United States; and that Mr. Boudinot, Mr. Peter Muhlenberg, Mr. Gilman, Mr. Floyd, Mr. Grout, Mr. Wadsworth, Mr. Smith (of Maryland), Mr. Bloodworth, Mr. Giles, Mr. Smith (of South-Carolina) and Mr. Mathews, be of the said committee.[14]

A message from the Senate by Mr. Otis their Secretary.

MR. SPEAKER, I am directed to bring to this House a letter from Monsieur Benier, President of the Commonalty of Paris, addressed to the President and Members of Congress of the United States, with twenty-six copies of a civic eulogium on Benjamin Franklin, pronounced the twenty-first of July, one thousand seven hundred and ninety, in the name of the Commonalty of Paris, by Monsieur the Abbe Fauchet, which were brought to the Senate by Mr. Lear, the Secretary of the President of the United States.[15] And he delivered in the same, and then withdrew.

Mr. Madison, from the committee appointed, presented, according to order, an address to the President of the United States, in answer to his speech to both Houses of Congress; which was read, and ordered to be committed to a committee of the whole House to-morrow.[16]

And then the House adjourned until to-morrow morning eleven o'clock.

SATURDAY, DECEMBER 11, 1790

The Speaker laid before the House a letter from the Commissioners of the city and county of Philadelphia, stating that they had fitted up, and made an appropriation of, their county court-house, for the accommodation of Congress;[17] which was read, and ordered to lie on the table.

The House, according to the order of the day, resolved itself into a commit-

---

[13] On December 20 this committee presented the Presidency Bill [HR–104], the Electors Bill [HR–105], and the Presidential Election Bill [HR–106], which were read.

[14] On December 14 this committee presented a Militia Bill [HR–102], which was read twice.

[15] The eulogy by Abbé Fauchet, printed in French, and entitled *Eloge Civique De Benjamin Franklin, LL.D.*, is in the RBkRm, DLC. An English translation is printed in *The Private Life of the Late Benjamin Franklin, LL.D.*, originally written by Franklin. It is also located in the RBkRm, DLC. On December 15 the House agreed to a resolution on the eulogium for Franklin.

[16] On December 11 the reply reported by the committee, which is printed in the Journal, was agreed to. A committee to confer with the president was then appointed. On the same day this committee reported.

[17] The letter is in Reports and Communications, SR, DNA.

tee of the whole House, on the address to the President of the United States, in answer to his speech to both Houses of Congress; and, after some time spent therein,

Mr. Speaker resumed the chair, and Mr. Livermore reported, that the committee had, according to order, had the said address under consideration, and made no amendment thereto.

RESOLVED UNANIMOUSLY, That this House doth agree to the said address in the words following.

SIR,

THE Representatives of the people of the United States have taken into consideration your address to the two Houses at the opening of the present session of Congress.

We share in the satisfaction inspired by the prospects which continue to be so auspicious to our public affairs. The blessings resulting from the smiles of Heaven on our agriculture; the rise of public credit, with the further advantages promised by it, and the fertility of resources which are found so little burdensome to the community, fully authorize our mutual congratulations on the present occasion. Nor can we learn without an additional gratification, that the energy of the laws for providing adequate revenues, have been so honorably seconded by those classes of citizens whose patriotism and probity were more immediately concerned.

The success of the loan opened in Holland, under the disadvantages of the present moment, is the more important as it not only denotes the confidence already placed in the United States, but as the effect of a judicious application of that aid, will still further illustrate the solidity of the foundation on which the public credit rests.

The preparatory steps taken by the state of Virginia, in concert with the district of Kentucky, towards the erection of the latter into a distinct member of the Union, exhibit a liberality mutually honorable to the parties. We shall bestow on this important subject the favorable consideration which it merits; and with the national policy which ought to govern our decision, shall not fail to mingle the affectionate sentiments which are awakened by those expressed on behalf of our fellow-citizens of Kentucky.

Whilst we regret the necessity which has produced offensive hostilities against some of the Indian tribes north-west of the Ohio, we sympathize too much with our western brethren, not to behold with approbation the watchfulness and vigor which have been exerted by the executive authority for their protection; and which we trust will make the aggressors sensible that it is their interest to merit by a peaceable behaviour, the friendship and humanity which the United States are always ready to extend to them.

The encouragement of our own navigation has at all times appeared to us highly important. The point of view under which you have recommended it to us, is strongly enforced by the actual state of things in Europe. It will be incumbent on us to consider in what mode our commerce and agriculture can be best relieved from an injurious dependence on the navigation of other nations, which the frequency of their wars renders a too precarious resource for conveying the productions of our country to market.

The present state of our trade to the Mediterranean seems not less to demand, and will accordingly receive, the attention which you have recommended.

Having already concurred in establishing a judiciary system, which opens the doors of justice to all, without distinction of persons, it will be our disposition to incorporate every improvement which experience may suggest. And we shall consider in particular, how far the uniformity, which, in other cases, is found convenient in the administration of the general government through all the states, may be introduced into the forms and rules of executing sentences issuing from the federal courts.

The proper regulation of the jurisdiction and functions, which may be exercised by consuls of the United States in foreign countries, with the provisions stipulated to those of his Most Christian Majesty established here, are subjects of too much consequence to the public interest and honor, not to partake of our deliberations.

We shall renew our attention to the establishment of the militia, and the other subjects unfinished at the last session, and shall proceed in them with all the dispatch, which the magnitude of all, and the difficulty of some of them, will allow.

Nothing has given us more satisfaction, than to find, that the revenues, heretofore established, have proved adequate to the purposes to which they were allotted. In extending the provision to the residuary objects, it will be equally our care, to secure sufficiency and punctuality in the payments due from the treasury of the United States. We shall, also, never lose sight of the policy of diminishing the public debt, as fast as the increase of the public resources will permit; and are particularly sensible of the many considerations, which press a resort to the auxiliary resource furnished by the public lands.

In pursuing every branch of the weighty business of the present session, it will be our constant study, to direct our deliberations to the public welfare. Whatever our success may be, we can at least answer for the fervent love of our country, which ought to animate our endeavors. In your co-operation, we are sure of a resource, which fortifies our hopes, that the fruits of the established government will justify the confidence which has been placed in it, and recommend it, more and more, to the affection and attachment of our fellow citizens.

RESOLVED, That Mr. Speaker, attended by the House, do present the said address; and that Mr. Madison, Mr. Ames, and Mr. Tucker, be a committee to wait on the President, to know when, and where, it will be convenient for him to receive the same.

ORDERED, That Mr. Williamson, and Mr. Sherman, be added to the committee appointed to prepare and bring in a bill or bills to amend the act, intituled, "An act to promote the progress of useful arts."[18]

Mr. Madison, from the committee appointed to wait on the President of the United States, to know when, and where, it will be convenient for him to receive the address of this House, in answer to his speech to both Houses of Congress, reported;

That the committee had, according to order, waited on the President, who signified to them, that it would be convenient to him to receive the said address, at two o'clock on Monday next, at his own house.[19]

And then the House adjourned until Monday morning eleven o'clock.

MONDAY, DECEMBER 13, 1790

Several other members, to wit; from Massachusetts, George Leonard; from Delaware, John Vining; from Virginia, Josiah Parker; from North-Carolina, John Baptista Ashe; and from South-Carolina, Aedanus Burke, appeared and took their seats.

The Speaker laid before the House a letter from the Secretary of the Treasury, accompanying his report of a farther provision for the establishment of the public credit, made pursuant to an order of the House of the ninth day of August last; which were read, and ordered to be committed to a committee of the whole House, on this day se'nnight.[20]

A petition of Jesse Holt, was presented to the House and read, praying to be placed on the list of pensioners, in consideration of wounds received in the service of the United States, during the late war.   Also,

A petition of Thomas McIntire, praying to be allowed the commutation of half-pay, as an officer in the army of the United States, during the late war.

Also, a petition of Joanna Gardener widow of Colonel Thomas Gardener,

---

[18] On February 7 this committee presented a Patents Bill [HR–121], which was read.

[19] On December 13 the House delivered its address to the president, and he made a response, which is printed in the Journal.

[20] The report is in Alexander Hamilton's Reports, HR, DNA. A copy of the report is in A Record of the Reports of the Secretary of the Treasury, vol. 1, HR, DNA. A copy of the report, probably made by ASP, is in Reports and Communications from the Secretary of the Treasury, HR, DNA. E–23006. On December 27 the COWH presented several resolutions on the secretary's report, which were agreed to by the House. A committee was appointed to bring in a bill on the resolutions, which are printed in the Journal.

late of Massachusetts, deceased, praying that the provision, made by an act of the late Congress, for the relief of the widows and children of officers who have died in the service of the United States, may be extended to her and to her children.

ORDERED, That the said petitions be referred to the Secretary at War, with instruction to examine the same, and report his opinion thereupon to the House.[21]

ORDERED, That the several petitions of Alexander Fowler, which were presented to the House on Tuesday last, be referred to the Secretary of the Treasury, with instruction to examine the same, and report his opinion thereupon to the House.

Mr. Speaker, attended by the House, then withdrew to the house of the President of the United States, and there presented to him the address of this House, in answer to his speech to both Houses of Congress; to which the President made the following reply:

GENTLEMEN,

THE sentiments expressed in your address are entitled to my particular acknowledgment.

Having no object but the good of our country, this testimony of approbation and confidence from its immediate Representatives, must be among my best rewards, as the support of your enlightened patriotism has been among my greatest encouragements. Being persuaded that you will continue to be actuated by the same auspicious principle, I look forward to the happiest consequences from your deliberations during the present session.

G. WASHINGTON

And then Mr. Speaker and the members being returned,
The House adjourned until to-morrow morning eleven o'clock.

TUESDAY, DECEMBER 14, 1790

Two other members, to wit; from New-York, Jeremiah Van Rensselaer; and from Pennsylvania, Thomas Hartley, appeared and took their seats.

A message in writing was received from the President of the United States, by Mr. Lear his Secretary, as followeth:

UNITED STATES, December 14, 1790
GENTLEMEN of the SENATE and HOUSE of REPRESENTATIVES,

HAVING informed Congress of the expedition which had been directed against certain Indians north-west of the Ohio, I embrace the earliest oppor-

---

[21] On February 15 the secretary reported on McIntire's petition.

tunity of laying before you the official communications, which have been received upon that subject.

G. WASHINGTON[22]

The official communications, referred to in the said message, were read, and ordered to lie on the table.[23]

The Speaker laid before the House a letter from the Secretary of the Treasury, accompanying his report, number two, of a plan for the institution of a national bank, as referred to in his letter of yesterday, which was read, and ordered to be committed to a committee of the whole House on this day se'nnight.[24]

ORDERED, That a committee be appointed to prepare and bring in a bill or bills directing the mode, in which the evidences of the debt of the United States, which have been or may be lost or destroyed, shall be renewed; and that Mr. Lee, Mr. Trumbull, and Mr. Cadwalader, be of the said committee.[25]

A petition of Anne Roberts, widow of Owen Roberts, late a colonel of artillery in the army of the United States, was presented to the House and read, praying to be allowed the seven years half-pay of a colonel, as the widow of the said Owen Roberts, who was slain in the service of his country.

ORDERED, That the said petition be referred to the Secretary at War, with instruction to examine the same, and report his opinion thereupon to the House.[26]

Mr. Boudinot, from the committee appointed, presented, according to order, a bill more effectually to provide for the national defence, by establishing a uniform militia throughout the United States;[27] which was received and read the first time.

On motion,

The said bill was read the second time, and ordered to be committed to a committee of the whole House on Thursday next.[28]

And then the House adjourned until to-morrow morning eleven o'clock.

---

[22] The message with enclosures is in President's Messages: Transmitting reports from the Secretary of War, SR, DNA. Copies of the enclosures are in Confidential Reports of the Secretary of War, HR, DNA.

[23] On December 15 the House made a resolution on this message, and the secretary of the treasury was ordered to report on appropriations for the expedition against the Indians.

[24] The report is in Alexander Hamilton's Reports, HR, DNA. A copy of the report is in A Record of the Reports of the Secretary of the Treasury, vol. 1, HR, DNA. On December 23 the House sent the secretary's report to the Senate.

[25] On December 20 a petition was referred to this committee.

[26] On February 15 the secretary reported on this petition.

[27] A printed copy of what is probably this bill is in the Broadside Collection, RBkRm, DLC.

[28] On December 16 this bill was considered by the COWH.

WEDNESDAY, DECEMBER 15, 1790

A petition of Henry Emanuel Lutterloh, was presented to the House and read, praying that his claim to a compensation for certain military services, which was exhibited to and rejected at the last session of Congress, may be re-considered.

A motion was made, and the question being put that the said petition be referred to the consideration of a committee,

It passed in the negative.

And so the said petition was rejected.

The several petitions of Timothy Mix, John Linn, Reuben Gould, and Josiah Simpson, attorney in fact for Dorcas Frost and others, were presented to the House and read, respectively praying to receive compensation for services rendered, or for losses or injuries sustained in the service of the United States, during the late war.

ORDERED, That the said petitions be referred to the Secretary at War, with instruction to examine the same, and report his opinion thereupon to the House.[29]

A petition of Thomas Randall, of the city of New-York, was presented to the House and read, praying to receive compensation for a sloop with her appurtenances, the property of the petitioner, which was impressed into the service of the United States, during the late war. Also,

A petition of Samuel Prioleau, junior, of the city of Charleston, praying to receive compensation for the value of certain wharves and houses, which were taken from him, and appropriated to the use of the American army, at the siege of that place.

ORDERED, That the said petitions be referred to the Secretary of the Treasury, with instruction to examine the same, and report his opinion thereupon to the House.

On a motion made and seconded, that the House do agree to the following resolution, to wit:

This House being highly sensible of the polite attention of the Commons of Paris, in directing copies of an eulogium lately pronounced before them, as a tribute to the illustrious memory of Benjamin Franklin, a citizen of the United States, to be transmitted to Congress:

RESOLVED, That the Speaker do accordingly communicate the sense of the House thereon, to the President of the Commons of Paris.

It was resolved in the affirmative.[30]

A petition of Amos Davis, was presented to the House and read, praying to be placed on the list of pensioners, in consideration of the fracture of his

---

[29] On February 15 the secretary reported on the Mix petition.
[30] On January 26 a tribute to Benjamin Franklin by the National Assembly of France was received.

hip, by a fall from his horse, after his discharge from the army in the year one thousand seven hundred and seventy-five.

A motion was made, and the question being put, that the said petition be referred to the consideration of a committee,

It passed in the negative.

And so the said petition was rejected.

ORDERED, That a committee be appointed to prepare and bring in a bill or bills to continue an act declaring the assent of Congress to certain acts of the states of Maryland, Georgia, and Rhode-Island and Providence Plantations; and that Mr. Jackson, Mr. Ames, and Mr. Sturges, be of the said committee.[31]

The House, according to the order of the day, resolved itself into a committee of the whole House on the state of the Union: and after some time spent therein, Mr. Speaker resumed the chair, and Mr. Livermore reported, that the committee had, according to order, had the state of the Union under consideration, and come to several resolutions thereupon, which he read in his place, and afterwards delivered in at the Clerk's table, where the same were again severally twice read, and agreed to by the House, as followeth:

RESOLVED, That it is the opinion of this committee, that immediate provision ought to be made for defraying the expenses incurred in the expedition against the Indians north-west of the Ohio.

RESOLVED, That it is the opinion of this committee, that a bill or bills ought to be brought in for the farther encouragement of the navigation of the United States.

RESOLVED, That it is the opinion of this committee, that so much of the speech of the President of the United States to both Houses of Congress, as relates to the trade of the United States in the Mediterranean, ought to be referred to the Secretary of State, with instruction to report thereupon to the House.

ORDERED, That the first resolution be referred to the Secretary of the Treasury, with instruction to report an appropriation pursuant thereto.

ORDERED, That a committee be appointed to prepare and bring in a bill or bills pursuant to the second resolution; and that Mr. Boudinot, Mr. Jackson, Mr. Tucker, Mr. Ashe, Mr. Parker, Mr. Smith, of Maryland, Mr. Clymer, Mr. Vining, Mr. Benson, Mr. Sherman, Mr. Goodhue, and Mr. Foster, be of the said committee.[32]

ORDERED, That the report of the Secretary of the Treasury of an uniform system for the disposition of lands, the property of the United States, which was made on the twenty-second of July last, be committed to a committee of the whole House on Friday next.[33]

---

[31] On December 16 this committee presented a Navigation Bill [HR-103], which was read.

[32] On January 13 another member was added to this committee.

[33] On December 27 this report was considered in the COWH on the state of the union.

ORDERED, That the report of the Secretary of State, of a proper plan or plans for establishing uniformity in the currency, weights and measures of the United States, which was made on the thirteenth of July last, be committed to a committee of the whole House on Wednesday next.

And then the House adjourned until to-morrow morning eleven o'clock.

THURSDAY, DECEMBER 16, 1790

A petition of the merchants and other inhabitants of the town of Baltimore, was presented to the House and read, praying that a health-office may be established, or other provision made by law, for protecting them from infectious and epidemical diseases, brought by passengers and others arriving from foreign countries.[34]   Also,

A petition of Isaac Mansfield, praying compensation for his services as a chaplain in the late army of the United States.   Also,

A petition of John Churchman, praying that the application he made at the first session of Congress, for permission to undertake a voyage to Baffin's Bay at the public expense, for the purpose of making magnetical experiments to ascertain the causes of the variation of the needle, and how near the longitude can be thereby ascertained, may now be determined.[35]

ORDERED, That the said petitions do lie on the table.

Mr. Jackson, from the committee appointed, presented, according to order, a bill to continue an act, intituled, "An act for declaring the assent of Congress to certain acts of the states of Maryland, Georgia, and Rhode-Island and Providence Plantations," which was received and read the first time.[36]

The House, according to the order of the day, resolved itself into a committee of the whole House, on the bill more effectually to provide for the national defence, by establishing a uniform militia throughout the United States; and after some time spent therein, Mr. Speaker resumed the chair, and Mr. Livermore reported, that the committee had, according to order, had the said bill under consideration, and made some progress therein.

RESOLVED, That this House will, to-morrow, again resolve itself into a committee of the whole House, on the said bill.[37]

And then the House adjourned until to-morrow morning eleven o'clock.

FRIDAY, DECEMBER 17, 1790

Two other members, to wit; from New-York, John Hathorn; and from North-Carolina, John Sevier, appeared and took their seats.

---

[34] On December 17 this petition was committed.
[35] On December 23 this petition was committed.
[36] On December 17 this bill was read again.
[37] On December 17 this bill was again considered by the COWH.

Benjamin Bourn, a member returned to serve in this House for the state of Rhode-Island and Providence Plantations, appeared, produced his credentials, and took his seat in the House, the oath to support the constitution of the United States being administered to him by Mr. Speaker, according to law.

ORDERED, That the petition of the merchants and other inhabitants of the town of Baltimore, which was presented yesterday, be referred to Mr. Seney, Mr. Vining and Mr. Parker; that they do examine the matter thereof, and report the same, with their opinion thereupon to the House.[38]

A petition of Francis Taylor, was presented to the House and read, praying compensation for military services rendered during the late war.

ORDERED, That the said petition, together with the petition of Isaac Mansfield, which was presented yesterday, be referred to the Secretary at War, with instruction to examine the same, and report his opinion thereupon to the House.

An address and memorial of the people called Quakers, convened at their yearly meeting for Pennsylvania, New-Jersey, Delaware, and the eastern part of Maryland and Virginia, lately held in Philadelphia, was presented to the House and read, representing their objections to certain provisions of a bill now depending, intituled, "A bill more effectually to provide for the national defence, by establishing a uniform militia throughout the United States."[39]

ORDERED, That the said address and memorial do lie on the table.

A bill to continue an act, intituled, "An act declaring the assent of Congress to certain acts of the states of Maryland, Georgia, and Rhode-Island and Providence Plantations," was read the second time, and ordered to be engrossed, and read the third time on Monday next.[40]

A message from the Senate by Mr. Otis their Secretary.

MR. SPEAKER, The Senate have passed a bill, intituled, "An act supplementary to the act, intituled, 'An act making farther provision for the payment of the debts of the United States,'"[41] to which they desire the concurrence of this House. And then he withdrew.

The said bill was read the first time.[42]

The House, according to the order of the day, again resolved itself into a committee of the whole House, on the bill more effectually to provide for the

---

[38] On December 21 this committee reported. The report, which is printed in the Journal, was agreed to. A committee to bring in a bill was then appointed.

[39] The petition is E–22517.

[40] On December 20 this bill was read again, agreed to, and sent to the Senate.

[41] The bill is in Engrossed Senate Bills and Resolutions, SR, DNA. The bill, as it passed the Senate and was agreed to in the House without amendments, is printed in the Appendix to the Third Session of the *Senate Legislative Journal*.

[42] On December 20 this bill was read again.

national defence, by establishing a uniform militia throughout the United States; and after some time spent therein, Mr. Speaker resumed the chair, and Mr. Livermore reported, that the committee had, according to order, again had the said bill under consideration, and made a farther progress therein.

RESOLVED, That this House will, on Monday next, again resolve itself into a committee of the whole House on the said bill.[43]

And then the House adjourned until Monday morning eleven o'clock.

MONDAY, DECEMBER 20, 1790

Another member, to wit; Michael Jenifer Stone, from Maryland, appeared and took his seat.

An engrossed bill to continue an act, intituled, "An act declaring the assent of Congress to certain acts of the states of Maryland, Georgia, and Rhode-Island and Providence Plantations," was read the third time, and the blank therein filled up.

RESOLVED, That the said bill do pass, and that the title be "An act to continue an act, intituled, 'An act declaring the assent of Congress to certain acts of the states of Maryland, Georgia, and Rhode-Island and Providence Plantations.' "[44]

ORDERED, That the Clerk of this House do carry the said bill to the Senate, and desire their concurrence.[45]

The bill sent from the Senate, intituled, "An act supplementary to the act, intituled, 'An act making farther provision for the payment of the debts of the United States,' " was read the second time, and ordered to be read the third time to-morrow.[46]

Mr. Benson, from the committee appointed, presented, according to order, a bill declaring the officer, who, in case of vacancies, both in the offices of President and Vice-President of the United States, shall act as President; also, a bill declaring the respective times when the electors to vote for a President of the United States shall be appointed or chosen, and shall give their votes; also, a bill directing the mode in which the lists of the votes for a President

---

[43] On December 20 the COWH considered this bill again.

[44] A copy of the bill, annotated by the Senate, is in House Bills, SR, DNA.

[45] The Senate read this bill on December 20 and 21. On December 21 the bill was committed, and on December 28 this committee reported an amendment, which was agreed to. The bill was then recommitted, and two members were added to the committee. On January 5, 1791, the committee reported amendments to the bill. Consideration of the amendments was postponed to consider a resolution, which was disagreed to. The Senate then agreed to several amendments reported by the committee, which are printed in the *Senate Legislative Journal*. On January 6 the bill was read again and agreed to with amendments. The amendments were sent to the House on the same day.

[46] On December 21 this bill was read again and agreed to.

shall be transmitted to the seat of the government of the United States; which were severally received, and read the first time.[47]

A petition from Barnabas Lucas, was presented to the House and read, praying relief in consideration of wounds received in the service of the United States, during the late war.

ORDERED, That the said petition be referred to the Secretary at War, with instruction to examine the same, and report his opinion thereupon to the House.

A petition of William Robinson, was presented to the House and read, praying the renewal of a final settlement certificate, the property of the petitioner, which was lost or destroyed some time in the year one thousand seven hundred and eighty-three.

ORDERED, That the said petition be referred to the committee appointed to prepare and bring in a bill or bills, declaring the mode in which the evidences of the debt of the United States, which have been or may be lost or destroyed, shall be renewed.[48]

A petition of John Miller Russel, was presented to the House and read, praying that the additional duty on hemp, imported from foreign countries, may be remitted to him on a quantity of hemp lately imported from Russia, and which was shipped from thence prior to the passing the act imposing the said additional duty. Also,

A petition of sundry merchants and traders of the city of Philadelphia, praying that pier-heads may be erected at the town of Chester, on the river Delaware, for the greater security and accommodation of the trade thereof.

ORDERED, That the said petitions be referred to the Secretary of the Treasury, with instruction to examine the same, and report his opinion thereupon to the House.

On a motion made and seconded, that the House do come to the following resolution, to wit;

RESOLVED, That provision be made for erecting a beacon at the entrance of the port of George-Town, in the state of South-Carolina:

ORDERED, That the said motion be referred to the Secretary of the Treasury, with instruction to examine the same, and report his opinion thereupon to the House.

The House, according to the order of the day, again resolved itself into a committee of the whole House, on the bill more effectually to provide for the national defence, by establishing a uniform militia throughout the United

---

[47] A printing, which probably represents these bills as introduced, is E–46017. On December 21 all of these bills were read again.

[48] On December 28 this committee presented an Evidences of Debt Bill [HR–108], which was read. On the same day William Robinson was given leave to withdraw his petition.

States; and after some time spent therein, Mr. Speaker resumed the chair, and Mr. Livermore reported, that the committee had, according to order, again had the said bill under consideration, and made a farther progress therein.

RESOLVED, That this House will, to-morrow, again resolve itself into a committee of the whole House on the said bill.[49]

And then the House adjourned until to-morrow morning eleven o'clock.

TUESDAY, DECEMBER 21, 1790

The bill sent from the Senate, intituled, "An act supplementary to the act, intituled, 'An act making farther provision for the payment of the debts of the United States,'" was read the third time; and, on the question that the said bill do pass,

It was resolved in the affirmative.

ORDERED, That the Clerk of this House do acquaint the Senate therewith.[50]

A bill declaring the officer, who, in case of vacancies both in the offices of President and Vice-President of the United States, shall act as President, was read the second time, and ordered to be committed to a committee of the whole House on Monday next.[51]

A bill declaring the respective times when the electors to vote for a President of the United States, shall be appointed or chosen, and shall give their votes, was read the second time, and ordered to be committed to a committee of the whole House on Monday next.[52]

A bill directing the mode in which the lists of the votes for a President shall be transmitted to the seat of the government of the United States, was read the second time, and ordered to be committed to a committee of the whole House on Monday next.[53]

A petition of the corporation of trustees of the public grammar school and academy of Wilmington, in the state of Delaware, was presented to the House and read, praying that compensation may be made for the use of, and the injuries done to, the buildings of the said academy, by the troops of the United States, during the late war.

ORDERED, That the said petition be referred to the Secretary of the Treasury, with instruction to examine the same, and report his opinion thereupon to the House.

A memorial and remonstrance of the public creditors who are citizens of

---

[49] On December 21 the COWH reported amendments to this bill.

[50] On December 23 the speaker signed this bill.

[51] From December 27 through January 7, 1791, consideration of this bill was postponed as an order of the day. On January 10 the COWH considered this bill.

[52] From December 27 through January 12, 1791, consideration of this bill was postponed as an order of the day. On January 13 it was considered by the COWH.

[53] This bill was not considered again in the First Congress.

the commonwealth of Pennsylvania, by their committee for that purpose appointed, was presented to the House and read, representing the insufficiency of the provision for the public creditors, made by an act passed at the last session of Congress, intituled, "An act making provision for the debt of the United States;" and praying that a more adequate provision may now be made.[54]

ORDERED, That the said memorial and remonstrance do lie on the table.

A petition of Robert Ford, was presented to the House and read, praying relief in consideration of wounds and injuries received in the service of the United States, during the late war.

ORDERED, That the said petition be referred to the Secretary at War, with instruction to examine the same, and report his opinion thereupon to the House.

Mr. Seney, from the committee to whom was referred the memorial of sundry inhabitants of the town of Baltimore, praying the establishment of a health-office, made a report,[55] which was twice read, and agreed to by the House, as followeth:

"Your committee have had under their consideration the subject matter of the said memorial, and are firmly persuaded that the same highly merits the attention of Congress: But being convinced that the regulation prayed by the memorialists, is not only essential for the port aforesaid, but for all others into which considerable imports are made, are of opinion that a law ought to be passed with general provisions in this respect."

ORDERED, That a bill or bills be brought in pursuant to the said report; and that Mr. Laurance, Mr. Seney, Mr. Fitzsimons, Mr. Vining, and Mr. Goodhue, do prepare and bring in the same.

The House, according to the order of the day, again resolved itself into a committee of the whole House, on the bill more effectually to provide for the national defence, by establishing a uniform militia throughout the United States; and after some time spent therein, Mr. Speaker resumed the chair, and Mr. Livermore reported, that the committee had, according to order, again had the said bill under consideration, and gone through the same, and made several amendments thereto, which he was ready to report whenever the House should think proper to receive the same.

ORDERED, That the said report be received to-morrow.[56]

The Speaker laid before the House a letter and report from the commissioners appointed by the act passed at the last session of Congress, intituled,

---

[54] The memorial is in Petitions and Memorials: Various subjects, SR, DNA. E–22983.

[55] A copy of the report is in A Record of the Reports of Select Committees, HR, DNA.

[56] On December 22 the amendments reported by the COWH were considered.

"An act making provision for the reduction of the public debt;" stating the amount of the purchases which have been made of the public debt, in pursuance of the powers vested in them by the said act.[57]

ORDERED, That the said letter and report do lie on the table.

And then the House adjourned until to-morrow morning eleven o'clock.

WEDNESDAY, DECEMBER 22, 1790

A petition of Simon Summers, was presented to the House and read, praying compensation for military services rendered during the late war.

ORDERED, That the said petition be referred to the Secretary at War, with instruction to examine the same, and report his opinion thereupon to the House.

A message from the Senate by Mr. Otis their Secretary.

MR. SPEAKER, The Senate have appointed Mr. Foster on their part, to be of the joint committee for inrolled bills. And then he withdrew.

ORDERED, That Mr. Floyd, and Mr. Peter Muhlenberg, be of the joint committee for inrolled bills, on the part of this House; and that the Clerk of this House do acquaint the Senate therewith.[58]

The House proceeded to consider the amendments agreed to yesterday by the committee of the whole House, to the bill more effectually to provide for the national defence, by establishing a uniform militia throughout the United States, and made some progress therein.

ORDERED, That the farther consideration of the said amendments be postponed until to-morrow.[59]

And then the House adjourned until to-morrow morning eleven o'clock.

THURSDAY, DECEMBER 23, 1790

Another member, to wit; Theodore Sedgwick, from Massachusetts, appeared and took his seat.

An address of the representatives of the religious society called Quakers, residing in the state of New-York, and western parts of New-England, was presented to the House and read, representing their objections to certain provisions of a bill now depending, intituled, "A bill more effectually to provide for the national defence, by establishing a uniform militia throughout the United States."

ORDERED, That the said address do lie on the table.

---

[57] The report is in Reports and Communications, SR, DNA. The report is printed in the *Senate Legislative Journal* on December 21.

[58] Copies of the Senate and House orders for committee are in Senate Joint and Concurrent Resolutions, SR, DNA.

[59] On December 23 these amendments were considered again.

ORDERED, That the petition of John Churchman, which was presented on Thursday last, be referred to Mr. Huntington, Mr. Madison, and Mr. Hiester; that they do examine the matter thereof, and report the same, with their opinion thereupon, to the House.[60]

ORDERED, That the Clerk of this House do communicate to the Senate, that this House has received a report from the Secretary of State, respecting coins, weights and measures; and also a report from the Secretary of the Treasury, containing a plan for a national bank; and that he carry attested copies of the said reports to the Senate.[61]

A message in writing was received from the President of the United States, by Mr. Lear, his Secretary, as follows:

UNITED STATES, December 23, 1790
GENTLEMEN of the SENATE and HOUSE of REPRESENTATIVES,

IT appearing, by the report of the Secretary of the government north-west of the Ohio, that there are certain cases respecting grants of land within that territory, which require the interference of the legislature of the United States.

I have directed a copy of said report and the papers therein referred to, to be laid before you; together with a copy of the report of the Secretary of State, upon the same subject.

G. WASHINGTON[62]

The report and papers referred to in the said message were read, and ordered to be sent to the Senate for their information.

The House resumed the consideration of the amendments agreed to by the committee of the whole House, to the bill "more effectually to provide for the national defence, by establishing a uniform militia throughout the United States," and made a farther progress therein.

ORDERED, That the farther consideration of the said amendments be postponed until to-morrow.[63]

---

[60] On January 6 this committee reported.

[61] A copy of this order is in Messages from the House, SR, DNA. On December 23 the Senate committed this report, and on January 3 this committee presented a Bank Bill [S–15], which was read. The bill was read again on January 6, 10, 11, 12, and 13. Amendments to the bill were considered on January 13 and 14. The second reading was continued on January 17 and 18. On January 18 the bill was recommitted for further amendments. Several amendments reported by the committee were agreed to on the same day. On January 19 the second reading was continued, and an amendment to the bill was disagreed to. On January 20 the bill was read, two more amendments were disagreed to, and the bill was agreed to. The bill was sent to the House on the same day.

[62] The message with enclosures is in President's Messages: Transmitting reports from the Secretary of State, SR, DNA.

[63] On December 24 the House acted on the COWH's amendments to the Militia Bill [HR–102], and the bill as amended was recommitted.

Mr. Floyd, from the joint committee for inrolled bills, reported, that the committee had examined an inrolled bill, intituled, "An act supplementary to the act, intituled, 'An act making farther provision for the payment of the debts of the United States,'"[64] and found the same to be truly inrolled: Whereupon,

Mr. Speaker signed the said inrolled bill.[65]

And then the House adjourned until to-morrow morning eleven o'clock.

FRIDAY, DECEMBER 24, 1790

The petitions of Alexander Nelson, attorney in fact for sundry persons, of James Alexander, and William Cottle, were presented to the House and read, respectively praying compensation for services rendered to the United States, during the late war.

ORDERED, That the said petitions be referred to the Secretary at War, with instruction to examine the same, and report his opinion thereupon to the House.

ORDERED, That a committee be appointed to prepare and bring in a bill or bills to ascertain how far owners of ships and vessels shall be liable to the freighters of goods shipped on board thereof; and that Mr. Fitzsimons, Mr. Foster, and Mr. Silvester, be of the said committee.[66]

A memorial of the people called Quakers, in their annual assembly for the Western Shore of Maryland, and the adjacent parts of Pennsylvania and Virginia, lately convened at Baltimore, was presented to the House and read, stating their objections to certain provisions of a bill now depending, intituled, "A bill more effectually to provide for the national defence, by establishing a uniform militia throughout the United States."

ORDERED, That the said memorial do lie on the table.

The House resumed the consideration of the amendments agreed to by the committee of the whole House, to the bill more effectually to provide for the national defence, by establishing a uniform militia throughout the United States; and having gone through the same, some were agreed to, others amended and agreed to, and others disagreed to.

On motion,

ORDERED, That the said bill, as now amended, be recommitted to Mr. Wadsworth, Mr. Giles, and Mr. Tucker.[67]

---

[64] The inspected enrolled bill is in Enrolled Acts, RG 11, DNA. E–23867, E–46059. The bill is printed in the Appendix to the Third Session of the *Senate Legislative Journal*.

[65] On December 24 this bill was signed by the vice president and delivered to the president.

[66] On December 27 this committee presented the Liability of Shipowners Bill [HR–107], which was read.

[67] On December 29 a motion to further instruct this committee was disagreed to.

Mr. Floyd, from the joint committee for inrolled bills, reported, that the committee did, this day, wait on the President of the United States, and present for his approbation, an inrolled bill, intituled, "An act supplementary to the act, intituled, 'An act making further provision for the payment of the debts of the United States.' "[68]

And then the House adjourned until Monday morning eleven o'clock.

MONDAY, December 27, 1790

The several petitions of Stephen Clapp, of Samuel Buffinton, attorney to Francis Suzor Debevere,[69] of Daniel Merrill, for himself and others, and of Joshua Orne, for himself and others, were presented to the House and read, respectively praying the settlement of claims against the United States.

ORDERED, That the said petitions be referred to the Secretary at War, with instruction to examine the same, and report his opinion thereupon to the House.[70]

A petition of Isaac Osgood and Sons, was presented to the House and read, praying that Congress would grant a sum of money, loan, bounty, or other encouragement, to the manufacture of malt-liquors in the United States.

ORDERED, That the said petition be referred to the Secretary of the Treasury, with instruction to examine the same, and report his opinion thereupon to the House.

Mr. Fitzsimons, from the committee appointed, presented, according to order, a bill to ascertain how far the owners of ships and vessels shall be answerable to the freighters; which was received and read the first time.[71]

The House, according to the order of the day, resolved itself into a committee of the whole House, on the report of the Secretary of the Treasury, of a farther provision for the establishment of the public credit; and after some time spent therein, Mr. Speaker resumed the chair, and Mr. Livermore reported, that the committee had, according to order, had the said report under consideration, and come to several resolutions thereupon, which he delivered in at the Clerk's table, where the same were severally twice read, and agreed to by the House, as follow:

RESOLVED, That an additional duty of eight cents per gallon, be imposed on all distilled spirits of common proof, and in the like proportion, for all other distilled spirits, which after the   day of   next, shall be imported into the United States.

---

[68] On December 27 the president signed this bill.

[69] This petition is in Miscellaneous Treasury Accounts, No. 2279, RG 217, DNA.

[70] On February 15 the secretary reported on the Buffinton petition.

[71] A printed copy of what is probably this bill is E–46314. On December 28 this bill was read again.

RESOLVED, That from and after the   day of   next, a duty of eleven cents per gallon be imposed on all spirits of the first class of proof, distilled within the United States, from molasses, sugar, or other foreign materials; and also a duty in like proportion, on like spirits, of all other classes of proof.

RESOLVED, That from and after the   day of   next, a duty of nine cents per gallon, be imposed on all spirits of the first class of proof, distilled within any city, town or village, from materials of the growth or production of the United States; and also a duty in like proportion, on like spirits of all other classes of proof.

RESOLVED, That upon each still employed in distilling spirits from materials of the growth or production of the United States, in any other place than a city, town or village, there be imposed a yearly tax or duty of sixty cents for every gallon, English wine measure, of the capacity of such still, including its head, in lieu of all other rates.

ORDERED, That a bill or bills be brought in pursuant to the said resolutions; and that Mr. Sedgwick, Mr. Trumbull, Mr. Laurance, Mr. Wynkoop, and Mr. Smith of Maryland, do prepare and bring in the same.[72]

ORDERED, That the committee of the whole House be discharged from farther proceeding on the said report.

ORDERED, That a committee be appointed to prepare and bring in a bill or bills to alter the mode of collecting the duties on wines and teas, and to grant a longer time for the payment of such duties thereon; and that Mr. Sedgwick, Mr. Trumbull, Mr. Laurance, Mr. Wynkoop, and Mr. Smith of Maryland, be of the said committee.[73]

The House, according to the standing order of the day, resolved itself into a committee of the whole House, on the state of the Union; and after some time spent therein, Mr. Speaker resumed the chair, and Mr. Livermore reported, that the committee had, according to order, had the state of the Union under consideration, and made some progress therein.[74]

A message from the Senate by Mr. Otis their Secretary.

MR. SPEAKER,   I am directed by the Senate to inform this House, that the President of the United States has this day approved and signed "An act sup-

---

[72] On December 30 this committee presented the Duties on Distilled Spirits Bill [HR–110], which was read twice.

[73] On February 22 this committee presented a Duties on Teas Bill [HR–130], which was read twice.

[74] According to the *Gazette of the United States*, December 29, 1790, the topic under discussion was the secretary of the treasury's report on a public land office. On December 28 this report was considered again in the COWH on the state of the union.

plementary to the act, intituled, 'An act making further provision for the payment of the debts of the United States.' "[75]   And then he withdrew.

ORDERED, That a committee be appointed to prepare and bring in a bill or bills to enable the collector of the district of Pennsylvania to permit the landing of goods at other places within his district than the port of Philadelphia, when the navigation of the river Delaware shall be obstructed by ice; and that Mr. Fitzsimons, Mr. White, and Mr. Bourn, be of the said committee.[76]

The several orders of the day were postponed until to-morrow.

And then the House adjourned until to-morrow morning eleven o'clock.

TUESDAY, DECEMBER 28, 1790

A bill to ascertain how far the owners of ships and vessels shall be answerable to the freighters, was read the second time, and ordered to be committed to a committee of the whole House on Friday next.[77]

A memorial and remonstrance of the public creditors, who are citizens of the county of Burlington, in the state of New-Jersey, and of the city of Trenton and its vicinity, in the same state, were presented to the House and read, stating the insufficiency of the provision for the public creditors made by an act of the last session, intituled, "An act making provision for the debt of the United States," and praying that a more adequate provision may now be made.

ORDERED, That the said memorial and remonstrance do lie on the table.

Mr. Lee, from the committee appointed, presented, according to order, a bill directing the mode in which the evidences of the debt of the United States, which have been or may be lost or destroyed, shall be renewed; which was received and read the first time.[78]

ORDERED, That the committee to whom was referred the petition of William Robinson, be discharged therefrom; and that the petitioner have leave to withdraw his said petition.

A petition of John Philip De Haas, was presented to the House and read, praying the settlement of a claim against the United States.

ORDERED, That the said petition be referred to the Secretary at War, with instruction to examine the same, and report his opinion thereupon to the House.

Mr. Fitzsimons, from the committee appointed, presented, according to

---

[75] The message is in Committee on Enrolled Bills, SR, DNA.

[76] On December 28 this committee presented a Collection Bill [HR–109], which was read twice.

[77] This bill was not considered again.

[78] A printed copy of what is probably this bill is in the Broadside Collection, RBkRm, DLC. On December 29 this bill was read again.

order, a bill to provide for the delivery of goods, wares and merchandize in the state of Pennsylvania, in cases of obstruction of the river Delaware by ice; which was received and read the first time.

On motion,

The said bill was read the second time, and ordered to be committed to a committee of the whole House to-morrow.[79]

The House then, according to the standing order of the day, again resolved itself into a committee of the whole House, on the state of the Union; and after some time spent therein, Mr. Speaker resumed the chair, and Mr. Boudinot reported, that the committee had, according to order, again had the state of the Union under consideration, and made a farther progress therein.[80]

The several orders of the day were further postponed until to-morrow.

And then the House adjourned until to-morrow morning eleven o'clock.

WEDNESDAY, DECEMBER 29, 1790

Another member, to wit; Daniel Carroll, from Maryland, appeared and took his seat.

A bill directing the mode in which the evidences of the debt of the United States, which have been or may be lost or destroyed, shall be renewed, was read the second time, and ordered to be committed to a committee of the whole House, on Monday next.[81]

A petition of Shubael Swain, was presented to the House and read, praying the remission of a penalty which he has incurred for a breach of the revenue laws of the United States.[82]

ORDERED, That the said petition be referred to Mr. Goodhue, Mr. Livermore, and Mr. Sinnickson; with instruction to prepare and bring in a bill or bills, pursuant to the prayer thereof.[83]

A petition of Philip Buck, was presented to the House and read, praying relief for an injury sustained in the service of the United States, during the late war; and also that compensation may be made him for a schooner impressed into the transport service, and lost during the same period.   Also,

A petition of Anna Wilhelmina Longcammer, praying relief as the widow of a soldier who was slain in the service of the United States, during the late war.

---

[79] On December 29 this bill was amended.

[80] According to the *Gazette of the United States*, January 1, 1791, the topic under discussion was the secretary of the treasury's report on a public land office. On December 29 this report was considered again in the COWH on the state of the union.

[81] From January 3–7 consideration of this bill was postponed as an order of the day. On January 10 this bill was considered in the COWH, amended, and recommitted.

[82] The petition is in Petitions and Memorials: Various subjects, SR, DNA.

[83] On December 31, 1790, this committee presented the Swain Bill [HR-111], which was read.

ORDERED, That the said petitions be referred to the Secretary at War, with instruction to examine the same, and report his opinion thereupon to the House.

A petition of Winthrop Sargent, Secretary of the Western Territory, was presented to the House and read, stating the insufficiency of the provision made by law for the support of his office; and praying that the same may be made adequate to his services and expenses.[84]

ORDERED, That the said petition be referred to the Secretary of the Treasury, with instruction to examine the same, and report his opinion thereupon to the House.

The House, according to the order of the day, resolved itself into a committee of the whole House, on the bill to provide for the delivery of goods, wares and merchandize, in the state of Pennsylvania, in cases of obstruction of the river Delaware by ice; and after some time spent therein, Mr. Speaker resumed the chair, and Mr. Boudinot reported, that the committee had, according to order, had the said bill under consideration, and made several amendments thereto, which he delivered in at the Clerk's table, where the same were severally twice read, and agreed to by the House.

ORDERED, That the said bill, with the amendments, be engrossed, and read the third time to-morrow.[85]

On a motion made and seconded, that it be an instruction to the committee to whom was re-committed the bill, "more effectually to provide for the national defence, by establishing a uniform militia throughout the United States," that they do insert the following clause; to wit, "Be it enacted, That the militia of the several states of the Union, consisting of such persons as are or may be enrolled by them, respectively, shall be organized, armed, and disciplined, in manner following;"

It passed in the negative— $\begin{cases} \text{AYES} & 8 \\ \text{NOES} & 43 \end{cases}$

The ayes and noes being demanded by one fifth of the members present;
Those who voted in the affirmative, are,

John Baptista Ashe	Samuel Livermore
Timothy Bloodworth	George Thatcher
William Floyd	Thomas Tudor Tucker and
Jonathan Grout	Hugh Williamson

Those who voted in the negative, are,

Fisher Ames	Egbert Benson
Abraham Baldwin	Elias Boudinot

---

[84] The petition is in the Sargent Papers, OHi.
[85] On December 30 this bill was read, agreed to, and sent to the Senate.

Benjamin Bourn
John Brown
Aedanus Burke
Lambert Cadwalader
Daniel Carroll
Thomas Fitzsimons
Abiel Foster
Elbridge Gerry
Nicholas Gilman
Benjamin Goodhue
Samuel Griffin
William B. Giles
John Hathorn
Daniel Hiester
Benjamin Huntington
John Laurance
Richard Bland Lee
James Madison, junior
George Mathews
Andrew Moore

Peter Muhlenberg
Josiah Parker
George Partridge
Jeremiah Van Rensselaer
Thomas Scott
Theodore Sedgwick
Joshua Seney
John Sevier
Roger Sherman
Peter Silvester
Thomas Sinnickson
William Smith (of Maryland)
William Smith (of South-Carolina)
Michael Jenifer Stone
Jonathan Sturges
Jonathan Trumbull
Jeremiah Wadsworth
Alexander White and
Henry Wynkoop[86]

The House, according to the standing order of the day, again resolved it-self into a committee of the whole House on the state of the Union; and after some time spent therein, Mr. Speaker resumed the chair, and Mr. Boudinot reported, that the committee had, according to order, again had the state of the Union under consideration, and made a farther progress therein.[87]

The several orders of the day were further postponed until to-morrow.

And then the House adjourned until to-morrow morning eleven o'clock.

THURSDAY, DECEMBER 30, 1790

An engrossed bill to provide for the delivery of goods, wares, and mer-chandize in the state of Pennsylvania, in cases of obstruction of the river Delaware by ice, was read the third time.

RESOLVED, That the said bill do pass, and that the title be, "An act to pro-vide for the unlading of ships or vessels, in cases of obstruction by ice."[88]

---

[86] On January 4 the committee that the Militia Bill [HR–102] was recommitted to presented a new Militia Bill [HR–112], which was read.

[87] According to the *Gazette of the United States*, January 1, 1791, the topic under discussion was the secretary of the treasury's report on a public land office. On December 31 the COWH considered this report again and came to several resolutions on it.

[88] The bill, as it passed the House and was agreed to in the Senate without amend-ments, is printed in the Appendix to the Third Session of the *Senate Legislative Journal*.

ORDERED, That the Clerk of this House do carry the said bill to the Senate, and desire their concurrence.[89]

A message, in writing, was received from the President of the United States, by Mr. Lear his Secretary, as followeth:

UNITED STATES, December 30th, 1790

GENTLEMEN of the SENATE and HOUSE of REPRESENTATIVES,

I LAY before you a report of the Secretary of State on the subject of the citizens of the United States in captivity at Algiers, that you may provide, on their behalf, what to you shall seem most expedient.

G. WASHINGTON[90]

The report referred to in the said message was read, and ordered to lie on the table.

Mr. Sedgwick, from the committee appointed, presented, according to order, a bill repealing after the last day of   next, the duties heretofore laid upon distilled spirits imported from abroad, and laying others in their stead, and also upon spirits distilled within the United States; as well to discourage the excessive use of those spirits and promote agriculture, as to provide for the support of the public credit, and for the common defence and general welfare, which was received and read the first time.

On motion,

The said bill was read the second time, and ordered to be committed to a committee of the whole House on Tuesday next.[91]

ORDERED, That the Secretary of the Treasury do report to this House the amount of the exports from the several districts within the United States, respectively; also of duties arising on imports and tonnage from the first of August, one thousand seven hundred and eighty-nine, to the thirtieth of September, one thousand seven hundred and ninety; and, as soon as may be, from thence to the end of the present year.[92]

A memorial of the college of physicians of the city of Philadelphia, was presented to the House, and read, praying that Congress will impose such heavy duties upon all distilled spirits imported into the United States, as will effectually prevent the intemperate use thereof.[93]

---

[89] The Senate read this bill on January 3, 4, and 5. On January 5 it was agreed to, and the House was notified.

[90] The message and report with enclosures are in President's Messages on Foreign Relations, Executive Proceedings, SR, DNA. A copy of the report is in A Record of the Reports of the Secretary of State, vol. 1, HR, DNA. The report with enclosures is printed in the *Senate Executive Journal* under United States Prisoners in Algiers.

[91] On January 4 consideration of this bill was postponed as an order of the day. It was considered by the COWH on January 5.

[92] On January 7 the secretary sent his report on revenue from duties to the House. On February 15 the secretary sent the report on exports to the House.

[93] The petition is in Petitions and Memorials: Various subjects, SR, DNA.

ORDERED, That the said memorial do lie on the table.

A petition of Simeon Thayre, was presented to the House and read, praying to be placed on the list of pensioners in consideration of a wound received in the service of the United States during the late war.

ORDERED, That the said petition be referred to the Secretary at War, with instruction to examine the same, and report his opinion thereupon to the House.

The Speaker laid before the House a letter from the Secretary of State, accompanying his report upon so much of the speech of the President of the United States, as relates to the trade of the United States in the Mediterranean,[94] which were read, and ordered to lie on the table.

The several orders of the day were further postponed until to-morrow.

And then the House adjourned until to-morrow morning eleven o'clock.

FRIDAY, DECEMBER 31, 1790

Another member, to wit; John Steele, from North-Carolina, appeared and took his seat in the House.

The several petitions of Nathaniel Porter, Lewis Prahl, John Hodge, William Paine, and Henry Laurens (of South Carolina),[95] were presented to the House and read, respectively praying compensation for services rendered, supplies furnished, or injuries sustained in the service of the United States, during the late war.

ORDERED, That the said petitions be referred to the Secretary at War, with instruction to examine the same, and report his opinion thereupon to the House.[96]

A petition of John S. Hunn, attorney to the executrix of John H. W. D. Smith, late of Charleston, South-Carolina, deceased, was presented to the House and read, praying the settlement of a claim against the United States.

Also a petition of William Paine, praying the renewal of a certificate heretofore granted him for sundry articles furnished a deputy quarter-master, for the use of the United States, during the late war, which certificate has been defaced and destroyed.

ORDERED, That the said petitions be referred to the Secretary of the Treasury, with instruction to examine the same, and report his opinion thereupon to the House.

A petition of Seth Harding, was presented to the House and read, praying

---

[94] The report with enclosures is in Reports from the Secretary of State, SR, DNA. A copy of the report is in A Record of the Reports of the Secretary of State, vol. 1, HR, DNA.

[95] The petition of Henry Laurens with supporting documents is in Petitions and Memorials: Claims, SR, DNA.

[96] On March 3 the secretary of war made a report on this Laurens petition.

compensation for services rendered in the navy of the United States, during the late war.

ORDERED, That the said petition be referred to Mr. Laurance, Mr. Huntington, and Mr. Schureman; that they do examine the matter thereof, and report the same, with their opinion thereupon, to the House.[97]

A petition of Henry Laurens, of the state of South-Carolina, as guardian to and in behalf of his grand-daughter Frances Eleanor Laurens, the orphan daughter of the late Lieutenant-Colonel John Laurens; was presented to the House and read, praying that interest may be granted on an allowance made by a resolution of the late Congress, for the services and expenses of the said John Laurens, on an embassy to France.[98]

ORDERED, That the said petition be referred to Mr. Smith (of South-Carolina), Mr. Gerry, and Mr. Carroll; that they do examine the matter thereof, and report the same, with their opinion thereupon, to the House.[99]

The Speaker laid before the House a letter from the Attorney-General, accompanying his report, on such matters relative to the administration of justice under the authority of the United States, as may require to be remedied; and also such provisions in the respective cases as he deems advisable; made pursuant to an order of this House of the fifth of August last;[100] which were read, and ordered to be committed to a committee of the whole House on Wednesday se'nnight.

Mr. Goodhue, from the committee appointed, presented, according to order, a bill for the relief of Shubael Swain, which was received, and read the first time.[101]

The House, according to the standing order of the day, again resolved itself into a committee of the whole House on the state of the Union; and after some time spent therein, Mr. Speaker resumed the chair, and Mr. Boudinot reported, that the committee had, according to order, again had the state of the Union under consideration, and agreed to several resolutions thereupon, which he delivered in at the Clerk's table, where the same were severally read, and ordered to lie on the table.[102]

The several orders of the day were further postponed until Monday next.

And then the House adjourned until Monday morning eleven o'clock.

---

[97] On January 22 this committee reported.

[98] The petition is in Petitions and Memorials: Claims, SR, DNA.

[99] On January 28 this committee reported.

[100] A copy of the letter and report is in A Record of the Reports of the Attorney General of the United States, vol. 1, HR, DNA. A copy, probably made by ASP, is in Reports and Communications from the Attorney General, HR, DNA. E–23908, E–23909.

[101] On January 3, 1791, this bill was read again.

[102] These resolutions concerned a land office for the Western Territory. On January 3, 1791, these resolutions were considered.

MONDAY, JANUARY 3, 1791

A bill for the relief of Shubael Swain, was read the second time, and ordered to be engrossed, and read the third time to-morrow.[1]

The petitions of Joseph Hugg, and William Reynolds, were presented to the House and read, respectively praying relief in consideration of wounds and injuries received in the service of the United States, during the late war.

ORDERED, That the said petitions be referred to the Secretary at War, with instruction to examine the same, and report his opinion thereupon to the House.

A message, in writing, was received from the President of the United States, by Mr. Lear his Secretary, as follows:

UNITED STATES, January 3d, 1791

GENTLEMEN of the SENATE and HOUSE of REPRESENTATIVES,

I LAY before you a copy of an exemplified copy of an act passed by the legislature of the state of New-Jersey, for vesting in the United States of America the jurisdiction of a lot of land at Sandy-Hook, in the county of Monmouth; and a copy of the letter which accompanied said act, from the Governor of the state of New-Jersey, to the President of the United States.

G. WASHINGTON[2]

The papers referred to in the said message, were read and ordered to lie on the table.

The House proceeded to consider the resolutions agreed to on Friday last, by the committee of the whole House on the state of the Union, and made some progress therein.[3]

The several orders of the day were further postponed until to-morrow.

And then the House adjourned until to-morrow morning eleven o'clock.

TUESDAY, JANUARY 4, 1791

An engrossed bill for the relief of Shubael Swain, was read the third time. RESOLVED, That the said bill do pass, and that the title be, "An act for the relief of Shubael Swain."[4]

---

[1] On January 4 this bill was read again, agreed to, and sent to the Senate.

[2] Copies of the letter and act are in Transcribed Reports and Communications from the Executive Departments, 1789–1814, Records of the Secretary, SR, DNA.

[3] On January 4 these resolutions, which concerned a land office for the Western Territory, were agreed to. They are printed in the Journal for that date. A committee was then appointed to bring in a bill.

[4] The bill is in Engrossed House Bills, HR, DNA. It is printed in the *Senate Legislative Journal* on February 25.

ORDERED, That Clerk of this House do carry the said bill to the Senate, and desire their concurrence.[5]

A petition of sundry freeholders of the counties of Albany and Washington, in the state of New-York, was presented to the House and read, representing that the pension granted by an act of the last session to John Younglove, as a disabled major in colonel Van Voert's regiment of New-York militia, during the late war, was obtained by misrepresentation, and praying that the said act, so far as respects the said John Younglove, may be repealed.

ORDERED, That the said petition be referred to Mr. Sturges, Mr. Van Rensselaer, and Mr. Thatcher; that they do examine the matter thereof, and report the same, with their opinion thereupon, to the House.[6]

The House then, according to the order of the day, resumed the consideration of the resolutions agreed to on Friday last by the committee of the whole House on the state of the Union, and the said resolutions, being severally read at the Clerk's table, were amended and agreed to by the House, as followeth:

RESOLVED, That it is the opinion of this committee, that it is expedient that a general land-office be established and opened at the seat of the government of the United States.

That two subordinate land-offices be established and opened; one in the government north-west of the Ohio, and the other in the government south of the Ohio.

That all contracts for the sale of land above the quantity of   acres, shall be exclusively made at the general land office.

That no land shall be sold, except such in respect to which the titles of the Indian tribes shall have been previously extinguished.

That the seven ranges already surveyed, be sold in lots as laid out.

That any quantities may be sold by special contract comprehended either within natural boundaries or lines, or both, but no survey shall in any case be made on a river, but in the proportion of   chains back from such river for every chain along the bank thereof.

That the price shall be thirty cents per acre.

That warrants for military services be put on the same footing with warrants issuing from the land office, and that the exclusive right of locating the same in districts set apart for the army, cease after the   day of

That no credit shall be given for any quantity less than a township of six miles square, nor more than two years credit for any quantity.

---

[5] The Senate read this bill on January 4 and 5. It was committed on January 5, and the committee reported on January 6. On the same day the Senate read the bill again and disagreed to it, and the House was notified. On February 25 Shubael Swain submitted another petition to the Senate. The Senate tabled the petition.

[6] On January 28 this committee reported.

That in every instance of credit, at least one quarter part of the consideration shall be paid down, and security, other than the land itself, shall be
required for the residue. And that no title shall be given for any tract or part
of a purchase, beyond the quantity for which the consideration shall be
actually paid.

That the   of each subordinate office, shall have the management of
all sales, and the issuing of warrants for all locations in the tracts to be set
apart for the accommodation of individual settlers, subject to the superin-
tendency of the   of the general land office, who may also commit to
them the management of any other sales or locations, which it may be found
expedient to place under their direction.

That preference be given for a limited time to those actual settlers, whose
titles are not secured by the former governments of that country, and the
existing ordinances and acts of Congress.

That there shall be a surveyor-general, who shall have power to appoint a
deputy surveyor-general in each of the western governments, and a competent number of deputy surveyors, to execute in person all warrants to them
directed by the surveyor-general, or the deputy surveyor-generals, within
certain districts to be assigned to them respectively. That the surveyor-general
shall also have in charge all the duties committed to the geographer-general
by the several resolutions of Congress.

That all warrants issued at the general land-office, shall be signed by
and shall be directed to the surveyor-general. That all warrants issued at a
subordinate office, shall be signed by   and shall be directed to the
deputy surveyor-general within the government. That the priority of locations upon warrants shall be determined by the times of the applications to
the deputy surveyors: and in case of two applications for the same land at
one time, the priority may be determined by lot.

That the treasurer of the United States shall be the receiver of all payments
for sales made at the general land-office, and may also receive deposits of
money for purchases intended to be made at the subordinate offices; his
receipt or certificate for which shall be received in payments at those offices.

That the secretary of each of the western governments shall be the receiver
of all payments arising from sales at the office of such government.

That controversies concerning rights to patents or grants of land, shall be
determined by the   of that office, under whose immediate direction or
jurisdiction the locations, in respect to which they may arise, shall have been
made.

That the   of the general land-office, surveyor-general, deputy surveyor-general, and the   of the land-office in each of the western govern-

ments, shall not purchase, nor shall others purchase for them in trust, any public lands.

That the secretaries of the western governments, shall give security for the faithful execution of their duty as receivers of the land-office.

That all patents shall be signed by the President of the United States, and shall be recorded in the office of the Secretary of State.

That all officers, acting under the laws establishing the land-office, shall make oath or affirmation, faithfully to discharge their respective duties, previously to their entering upon the execution thereof.

That all surveys of land shall be at the expense of the purchasers or grantees.

That the fees shall not exceed certain rates to be specified in the law, affording equitable compensations for the services of surveyors, and establishing reasonable and customary charges for patents and other office papers, for the benefit of the United States.

That the   of the general land-office, shall, as soon as may be, from time to time, cause all the rules and regulations which they may establish to be published in one gazette at least, in each state, and in each of the western governments where there is a gazette, for the information of the citizens of the United States.

ORDERED, That a bill or bills be brought in pursuant to the said resolutions; and that Mr. White, Mr. Scott, and Mr. Bloodworth, do prepare and bring in the same.[7]

The several petitions of Andrew Colton and Lydia his wife,[8] Joseph Anderson, and Ebenezer A. Smith, were presented to the House and read, respectively praying compensation for services rendered, supplies furnished, or injuries sustained in the service of the United States, during the late war.

ORDERED, That the said petitions be referred to the Secretary at War, with instruction to examine the same, and report his opinion thereupon to the House.[9]

Mr. Wadsworth, from the committee to whom was re-committed the bill more effectually to provide for the national defence, by establishing a uniform militia throughout the United States, presented an amendatory bill, which was received and read the first time.[10]

The Speaker laid before the House a letter from the Treasurer of the United States, accompanying a statement of accounts for the receipts and

---

[7] On January 14 this committee presented a Land Office Bill [HR–114], which was read twice.

[8] This petition was submitted on behalf of the children of William White.

[9] On February 15 the secretary reported on the Colton petition.

[10] On January 5 this bill was read again.

expenditures of the public monies, from the first of July to the thirtieth of September last inclusive;[11] which were read, and ordered to lie on the table.

The several orders of the day were further postponed until to-morrow.

And then the House adjourned until to-morrow morning eleven o'clock.

WEDNESDAY, JANUARY 5, 1791

An amendatory bill more effectually to provide for the national defence, by establishing a uniform militia throughout the United States, was read the second time, and ordered to be committed to a committee of the whole House on this day se'nnight.[12]

A message from the Senate by Mr. Otis their Secretary.

MR. SPEAKER,   The Senate have passed the bill, intituled, "An act to provide for the unlading of ships or vessels, in cases of obstruction by ice."[13] And then he withdrew.

The House, according to the order of the day, resolved itself into a committee of the whole House, on the bill, "repealing, after the last day of next, the duties heretofore laid upon distilled spirits imported from abroad, and laying others in their stead; and also upon spirits distilled within the United States, as well to discourage the excessive use of those spirits, and promote agriculture, as to provide for the support of the public credit, and for the common defence and general welfare;" and after some time spent therein, Mr. Speaker resumed the chair, and Mr. Boudinot reported, that the committee had, according to order, had the said bill under consideration, and made some progress therein.

RESOLVED, That this House will, to-morrow, again resolve itself into a committee of the whole House on the said bill.[14]

A petition of Patrick Colvin, was presented to the House and read, praying compensation for losses and injuries in his property sustained by the army of the United States, during the late war.

ORDERED, That the said petition be referred to the Secretary of the Treasury, with instruction to examine the same, and report his opinion thereupon to the House.

Several petitions of the Baptist Associations of New-Hampshire, Massachusetts, Rhode-Island and Vermont, were presented to the House and read,

---

[11] The letter and accounts are in Transcribed Reports and Communications from the Executive Departments, 1789–1814, Records of the Secretary, SR, DNA. Copies of the letter and accounts are in Accounts of the Treasurer of the United States, vol. 1, HR, DNA. These documents are printed in the Appendix to the Third Session.

[12] This bill was not considered again.

[13] On January 6 this bill was signed by the speaker.

[14] On January 6 this bill was again considered by the COWH.

praying that Congress will adopt measures to prevent the publication of any inaccurate editions of the holy bible.

ORDERED, That the said petitions do lie on the table.

The several orders of the day were further postponed until to-morrow.

And then the House adjourned until to-morrow morning eleven o'clock.

THURSDAY, JANUARY 6, 1791

A petition of Jacob Philips, was presented to the House and read, praying to be reimbursed the amount of certain advances of money, which he made for supplies furnished for the use of the United States, during the late war.

ORDERED, That the said petition be referred to the Secretary of the Treasury, with instruction to examine the same, and report his opinion thereupon to the House.

A petition of William Cook, was presented to the House and read, praying the renewal of certain loan-office certificates issued by the loan-officer of Pennsylvania, which being the property of the petitioner, have been lost or stolen from his possession.

ORDERED, That the said petition do lie on the table.

The several petitions of John Post, John M. Charlesworth, Nathan Davis, and Donald McDonald, were presented to the House and read, respectively praying compensation for services rendered, supplies furnished, or injuries sustained in the service of the United States, during the late war.

ORDERED, That the said petitions be referred to the Secretary at War, with instruction to examine the same, and report his opinion thereupon to the House.

Mr. Madison, from the committee to whom was referred the petition of John Churchman, made a report, which was read, and ordered to lie on the table.[15]

A message from the Senate by Mr. Otis their Secretary.

MR. SPEAKER, The Senate have passed the bill, intituled, "An act to continue the act, intituled, 'An act declaring the assent of Congress to certain acts of the states of Maryland, Georgia, and Rhode-Island and Providence Plantations;'" with several amendments, to which they desire the concurrence of this House.[16]   And then he withdrew.

---

[15] A copy of the report is in A Record of the Reports of Select Committees, HR, DNA. On January 28 this report was considered, and a motion on the petition was disagreed to.

[16] The Senate committee report on the bill, with amendments, is in Various Select Committee Reports, SR, DNA. Senate amendments are noted on the bill in House Bills, SR, DNA, and are printed in the Senate Legislative Journal on January 5. On January 7 the House agreed to these amendments.

The House, according to the order of the day, again resolved itself into a committee of the whole House on the bill repealing after the last day of next, the duties heretofore laid upon distilled spirits imported from abroad, and laying others in their stead, and also upon spirits distilled within the United States, as well to discourage the excessive use of those spirits, and promote agriculture, as to provide for the support of the public credit, and for the common defence and general welfare; and after some time spent therein, Mr. Speaker resumed the chair, and Mr. Boudinot reported, that the committee had, according to order, again had the said bill under consideration, and made a farther progress therein.

RESOLVED, That this House will, to-morrow, again resolve itself into a committee of the whole House on the said bill.[17]

The Speaker laid before the House a letter from the Secretary of the Treasury, enclosing an abstract-return of the amount of tonnage in the United States, and of the duties arising thereon, between the first day of October, one thousand seven hundred and eighty-nine, and the thirtieth day of September one thousand seven hundred and ninety;[18] which was read, and ordered to lie on the table.

The Speaker laid before the House a letter and report from the Secretary of the Treasury, stating such farther appropriations of money, as will be necessary for the support of civil government for the current year; which were read and ordered to lie on the table.[19]

Mr. Floyd, from the joint committee for inrolled bills, reported, that the committee had examined an inrolled bill, intituled, "An act to provide for the unlading of ships or vessels in cases of obstruction by ice,"[20] and found the same to be truly inrolled: Whereupon,

Mr. Speaker signed the said inrolled bill.[21]

A message from the Senate by Mr. Otis their Secretary.

---

[17] On January 7 and 10 consideration of this bill was postponed as an order of the day. It was considered in the COWH on January 11.

[18] A copy of the letter is in A Record of the Reports of the Secretary of the Treasury, vol. 2, HR, DNA. Copies of the letter and the report, probably made by ASP, are in Reports and Communications from the Secretary of the Treasury, HR, DNA. The letter is E–23926.

[19] Copies of the letter and report are in A Record of the Reports of the Secretary of the Treasury, vol. 2, HR, DNA. Copies of the letter and report, probably made by ASP, are in Reports and Communications from the Secretary of the Treasury, HR, DNA. E–23925. On January 26 a committee was appointed to prepare an appropriations bill.

[20] The inspected enrolled bill is in Enrolled Acts, RG 11, DNA. E–23877, E–46329. The bill is printed in the Appendix to the Third Session of the *Senate Legislative Journal*.

[21] On January 7 this bill was signed by the vice president and the president.

MR. SPEAKER, I am directed to inform this House, that the Senate have rejected the bill sent for their concurrence, intituled, "An act for the relief of Shubael Swain." And then he withdrew.

The several orders of the day were further postponed until to-morrow. And then the House adjourned until to-morrow morning eleven o'clock.

FRIDAY, JANUARY 7, 1791

A petition of Simeon Noes, was presented to the House and read, praying relief as a disabled soldier in the service of the United States during the late war.

ORDERED, That the said petition be referred to the Secretary at War, with instruction to examine the same, and report his opinion thereupon to the House.

A petition of William Simmons, was presented to the House and read, praying an augmentation of his salary, as principal clerk in the office of the Auditor of the Treasury.

ORDERED, That the said petition be referred to the Secretary of the Treasury, with instruction to examine the same, and report his opinion thereupon to the House.[22]

The House proceeded to consider the amendments proposed by the Senate to the bill, intituled, "An act to continue an act, intituled, 'An act declaring the assent of Congress to certain acts of the states of Maryland, Georgia, and Rhode-Island and Providence Plantations:'" Whereupon,

RESOLVED, That this House doth agree to the said amendments.

ORDERED, That the Clerk of this House do acquaint the Senate therewith.[23]

Mr. Sherman, from the committee appointed, presented, according to order, a bill for establishing the post-office and post-roads of the United States; which was received and read the first time.

On motion,

The said bill was read the second time, and ordered to be committed to a committee of the whole House, on Wednesday se'nnight.[24]

The House, according to the order of the day, resolved itself into a committee of the whole House on the bill directing the mode in which the evidences of the debt of the United States, which have been or may be lost or destroyed, shall be renewed; and after some time spent therein, Mr. Speaker resumed the chair, and Mr. Boudinot reported, that the committee had, ac-

[22] On February 24 the secretary reported on this petition, and a committee was appointed to prepare a bill on the report.
[23] On January 10 this bill was signed.
[24] From January 14–28 consideration of this bill was postponed as an order of the day. On January 31 it was considered by the COWH.

cording to order, had the said bill under consideration, and made some progress therein.

RESOLVED, That this House will, on Monday next, again resolve itself into a committee of the whole House on the said bill.[25]

Mr. Floyd, from the joint committee for inrolled bills, reported, that the committee did, this day, wait on the President of the United States, and present for his approbation an inrolled bill, intituled, "An act to provide for the unlading of ships or vessels, in cases of obstruction by ice."

The Speaker laid before the House a letter from the Secretary of the Treasury, covering abstract returns of the amount of duties on imports into the United States; one exhibiting the sum received from the commencement of the operation of the impost act, to the thirtieth of September, one thousand seven hundred and eighty-nine; and the other shewing, as far as the returns have been transmitted, the sum received for one year following that day;[26] which were read, and ordered to lie on the table.

A message was received from the President of the United States, by Mr. Lear his Secretary, notifying that the President did, this day, approve and sign an act, intituled, "An act to provide for the unlading of ships or vessels, in cases of obstruction by ice."[27]

ORDERED, That the Clerk of this House do acquaint the Senate therewith.

The several orders of the day were further postponed until Monday next.

And then the House adjourned until Monday morning eleven o'clock.

MONDAY, JANUARY 10, 1791

The petitions of Lawrance Allman, and Anthony Musgenug, attorney for Nicholas Haugendobler, were presented to the House and read, praying compensation for military services rendered to the United States, during the late war.

ORDERED, That the said petitions be referred to the Secretary at War, with instruction to examine the same, and report his opinion thereupon to the House.

The House, according to the order of the day, again resolved itself into a committee of the whole House on the bill directing in what manner the evidences of the debt of the United States, which have been or may be lost or destroyed, shall be renewed; and after some time spent therein, Mr.

---

[25] On January 10 amendments to this bill were agreed to, and the bill was recommitted.

[26] A copy of the letter and a copy of the report are in A Record of the Reports of the Secretary of the Treasury, vol. 2, HR, DNA. Copies of the letter and report, probably made by ASP, are in Reports and Communications from the Secretary of the Treasury, HR, DNA. E–23926.

[27] The message is in Committee on Enrolled Bills, SR, DNA.

Speaker resumed the chair, and Mr. Boudinot reported, that the committee had, according to order, again had the said bill under consideration, and made several amendments thereto, which he delivered in at the Clerk's table, where the same were severally twice read, and agreed to by the House.

ORDERED, That the said bill as amended, be recommitted to Mr. Laurance, Mr. Sedgwick, Mr. Carroll, Mr. Clymer, Mr. Williamson, Mr. Sherman, and Mr. Sturges.[28]

The House, according to the order of the day, resolved itself into a committee of the whole House, on the bill declaring the officer who, in case of vacancies both in the offices of President and Vice-President of the United States, shall act as President; and after some time spent therein, Mr. Speaker resumed the chair, and Mr. Boudinot reported, that the committee had, according to order, had the said bill under consideration, and made some progress therein.

RESOLVED, That this House will, to-morrow, again resolve itself into a committee of the whole House on the said bill.[29]

Mr. Floyd, from the joint committee for inrolled bills, reported, that the committee had examined an inrolled bill, intituled, "An act to continue an act, intituled, 'An act declaring the assent of Congress to certain acts of the states of Maryland, Georgia, and Rhode-Island and Providence Plantations,' so far as the same respects the states of Georgia, and Rhode-Island and Providence Plantations," and had found the same to be truly inrolled:[30] Whereupon,

Mr. Speaker signed the said inrolled bill.

ORDERED, That the Clerk of this House do acquaint the Senate therewith.

ORDERED, That a committee be appointed to prepare and bring in a bill or bills to prevent invalids who are pensioners of the United States, from selling or transferring their respective pensions before the same shall become due; and that Mr. Williamson, Mr. Bourn, and Mr. Griffin, be of the said committee.[31]

Mr. Floyd, from the joint committee for inrolled bills, reported, that the committee did, this day, wait on the President of the United States, and present for his approbation, an inrolled bill, intituled, "An act to continue an act, intituled, 'An act declaring the assent of Congress to certain acts of the

---

[28] On January 25 this committee presented a new Evidences of Debt Bill [HR–118], which was read.

[29] Consideration of this bill was postponed as an order of the day on January 11 and 12. On January 13 it was considered by the COWH.

[30] The inspected enrolled bill is in Enrolled Acts, RG 11, DNA. E–23870. The bill is printed in the Appendix to the Third Session of the *Senate Legislative Journal*. The committee report is in Committee on Enrolled Bills, SR, DNA.

[31] On January 21 this committee presented the Transfer of Pensions Bill [HR–117], which was read twice.

states of Maryland, Georgia, and Rhode-Island and Providence Plantations,'
so far as the same respects the states of Georgia, and Rhode-Island and
Providence Plantations."[32]

A petition of the inspectors for the port of Philadelphia, was presented to
the House and read, praying an augmentation of the allowances granted by
law for their services.

ORDERED, That the said petition do lie on the table.

A message was received from the President of the United States, by Mr.
Lear his Secretary, notifying that the President did, this day, approve and sign
an act, intituled, "An act to continue an act, intituled, 'An act declaring the
assent of Congress to certain acts of the states of Maryland, Georgia, and
Rhode-Island and Providence Plantations,' so far as the same respects the
states of Georgia, and Rhode-Island and Providence Plantations."[33]

ORDERED, That the Clerk of this House do acquaint the Senate therewith.

The several orders of the day were further postponed until to-morrow.

And then the House adjourned until to-morrow morning eleven o'clock.

TUESDAY, JANUARY 11, 1791

A petition of John Haverd and others, was presented to the House and
read, praying compensation for losses and injuries sustained by the army of
the United States, during the late war.

ORDERED, That the said petition be referred to the Secretary of the Treasury, with instruction to examine the same, and report his opinion thereupon
to the House.

The petitions of sundry merchants and others of the towns of Fayetteville
and Wilmington, in the state of North-Carolina, were presented to the
House and read, praying that the district and circuit courts of the said state
may be held alternately at the said town of Fayetteville, and at Newbern.

ORDERED, That the said petitions be referred to Mr. Jackson, Mr. Burke,
Mr. Bloodworth, Mr. Giles, and Mr. Moore; that they do examine the matter
thereof, and report the same, with their opinion thereupon, to the House.

The House, according to the order of the day, again resolved itself into a
committee of the whole House on the bill, repealing, after the last day of
next, the duties heretofore laid upon distilled spirits imported from
abroad, and laying others in their stead; and also upon spirits distilled within
the United States, as well to discourage the excessive use of those spirits and
promote agriculture, as to provide for the support of the public credit, and
for the common defence and general welfare; and after some time spent

---

[32] The report is in Committee on Enrolled Bills, SR, DNA.
[33] A copy of the message is in Committee on Enrolled Bills, SR, DNA.

therein, Mr. Speaker resumed the chair, and Mr. Boudinot reported, that the committee had, according to order, again had the said bill under consideration, and made a farther progress therein.

RESOLVED, That this House will, to-morrow, again resolve itself into a committee of the whole House on the said bill.[34]

A message from the Senate by Mr. Otis their Secretary.

MR. SPEAKER,   The Senate have passed a bill, intituled, "An act for granting lands to the inhabitants and settlers at Vincennes and the Illinois country, in the territory north-west of the Ohio, and for confirming them in their possessions;"[35] to which they desire the concurrence of this House.   And then he withdrew.

The said bill was read the first time.[36]

The several orders of the day were further postponed until to-morrow.

And then the House adjourned until to-morrow morning eleven o'clock.

WEDNESDAY, JANUARY 12, 1791

The bill sent from the Senate, intituled, "An Act for granting lands to the inhabitants and settlers at Vincennes and the Illinois country in the territory north west of the Ohio, and for confirming them in their possessions," was read the second time, and ordered to be committed to a committee of the whole House on Wednesday next.[37]

The several petitions of Caleb Chadwick, Abner Pier, Jabez Bill, Job Priest, Nathaniel Alexander, Wardwell Green, James Easton, John Chadwick, and Patrick McLaughlen, were presented to the House and read, respectively praying compensation for services rendered, supplies furnished, or injuries sustained in the service of the United States during the late war.

ORDERED, That the said petitions be referred to the Secretary at War, with instruction to examine the same, and report his opinion thereupon to the House.

A petition of Joshua Barney, was presented to the House and read, praying to be allowed certain expenses, and also the commutation of half-pay, for services as a captain in the navy of the United States during the late war. Also,

---

[34] On January 12 the COWH considered this bill again.

[35] The bill with annotations is in Engrossed Senate Bills and Resolutions, SR, DNA. The bill is printed in the *Senate Legislative Journal* on March 2.

[36] On January 12 this bill was read again.

[37] From January 19 through February 25 consideration of this bill was postponed as an order of the day. On February 26 the COWH was discharged from considering the bill, and the bill was committed.

A memorial of sundry officers in the late navy of the state of Pennsylvania, praying compensation for services rendered during the late war.

ORDERED, That the said petition and memorial be referred to Mr. Fitzsimons, Mr. Smith (of Maryland), Mr. Trumbull, Mr. Goodhue, and Mr. Cadwalader; that they do examine the matter thereof, and report the same, with their opinion thereupon, to the House.[38]

A petition of the tradesmen employed in the various arts of constructing, repairing, fitting, equipping and furnishing ships and vessels, in and near the port of Philadelphia, was presented to the House and read, praying that an act of Congress may pass, creating a lien upon the body, tackle, apparel and furniture of all ships and vessels while they remain in port, for all repairs and materials furnished by the respective tradesmen employed therein, and giving them a remedy for the same, by admiralty-process in the circuit and district courts of the United States.

ORDERED, That the said petition do lie on the table.

A memorial and remonstrance of the public creditors of the county of Gloucester, in the state of New-Jersey, was presented to the House and read, representing the insufficiency of the provision for the public creditors, made by an act passed at the last session of Congress, intituled, "An act making provision for the debt of the United States," and praying that a more adequate provision may now be made.

ORDERED, That the said memorial and remonstrance do lie on the table.

On a motion made and seconded,

ORDERED, That so much of the standing rules and orders of this House, as directs that, "No bill amended by the Senate shall be committed," be rescinded.

A message from the Senate by Mr. Otis their Secretary.

MR. SPEAKER,   The Senate have passed a bill, intituled, "An act declaring the consent of Congress, that a new state be formed within the jurisdiction of the commonwealth of Virginia, and admitted into this Union by the name of the state of Kentucky,"[39] to which they desire the concurrence of this House.   And then he withdrew.

The said bill was read the first time.[40]

---

[38] On January 14 this committee reported on the petition of the officers of the navy, and the petitioners were given leave to withdraw their petition. On January 19 the committee reported on the Barney petition.

[39] The bill is in Engrossed Senate Bills and Resolutions, SR, DNA. The bill, as it passed the Senate and later was agreed to by the House without amendments, is printed in the *Senate Legislative Journal* on February 25.

[40] On January 13 this bill was read again.

The House, according to the order of the day, again resolved itself into a committee of the whole House on the bill, repealing, after the last day of next, the duties heretofore laid upon distilled spirits imported from abroad, and laying others in their stead; and also upon spirits distilled within the United States, as well to discourage the excessive use of those spirits, and promote agriculture, as to provide for the support of the public credit, and for the common defence and general welfare; and after some time spent therein, Mr. Speaker resumed the chair, and Mr. Boudinot reported, that the committee had, according to order, again had the said bill under consideration, and made a farther progress therein.

RESOLVED, That this House will, to-morrow, again resolve itself into a committee of the whole House on the said bill.[41]

The several orders of the day were further postponed until to-morrow.

And then the House adjourned until to-morrow morning eleven o'clock.

THURSDAY, JANUARY 13, 1791

The bill sent from the Senate, intituled, "An act declaring the consent of Congress, that a new state be formed within the jurisdiction of the commonwealth of Virginia, and admitted into this Union, by the name of the state of Kentucky," was read the second time, and ordered to be committed to a committee of the whole House on Monday next.[42]

The House, according to the order of the day, again resolved itself into a committee of the whole House on the bill, repealing, after the last day of next, the duties heretofore laid upon distilled spirits imported from abroad, and laying others in their stead; and also upon spirits distilled within the United States, as well to discourage the excessive use of those spirits, and promote agriculture, as to provide for the support of the public credit, and for the common defence and general welfare; and after some time spent therein, Mr. Speaker resumed the chair, and Mr. Boudinot reported, that the committee had, according to order, again had the said bill under consideration, and made several amendments thereto; which he delivered in at the Clerk's table.

ORDERED, That the said amendments be taken into consideration on Monday next.[43]

The House, according to the order of the day, again resolved itself into a committee of the whole House, on the bill declaring what officer shall, in

---

[41] On January 13 the COWH presented amendments to this bill.

[42] From January 17–27 consideration of this bill was postponed as an order of the day. On January 28 the bill was considered in the COWH, read again, and agreed to.

[43] On January 17 the House agreed to the amendments introduced by the COWH. A further amendment to the bill was defeated.

case of vacancies both in the offices of President and Vice-President of the United States, act as President; and after some time spent therein, Mr. Speaker resumed the chair, and Mr. Boudinot reported, that the committee had, according to order, again had the said bill under consideration, and made a farther progress therein.

RESOLVED, That this House will, to-morrow, again resolve itself into a committee of the whole House on the said bill.[44]

The House, according to the order of the day, resolved itself into a committee of the whole House, on the bill declaring the respective times when the electors to vote for a President of the United States shall be appointed or chosen, and shall give their votes; and after some time spent therein, Mr. Speaker resumed the chair, and Mr. Boudinot reported, that the committee had, according to order, had the said bill under consideration, and made some progress therein.

RESOLVED, That this House will, to-morrow, again resolve itself into a committee of the whole House on the said bill.[45]

On a motion made and seconded, "That a committee be appointed to consider and report, whether any and what farther compensation is necessary to be made to the commissioners of loans, to defray the extraordinary expense occasioned to them, in the first instance, in the execution of the act making farther provision for the debt of the United States."

ORDERED, That the said motion be referred to the Secretary of the Treasury, with instruction to examine the same, and report his opinion thereupon to the House.[46]

ORDERED, That Mr. Bourn, be added to the committee appointed to prepare and bring in a bill or bills concerning the trade and navigation of the United States.[47]

The several orders of the day were further postponed until to-morrow.

And then the House adjourned until to-morrow morning eleven o'clock.

FRIDAY, JANUARY 14, 1791

A petition of Joseph Wheaton, late an officer in the continental army, was presented to the House and read, praying to be reimbursed the amount of a judgment obtained against him in the state of Rhode-Island for a quantity of forage impressed for the army of the United States, during the late war.

ORDERED, That the said petition be referred to the Secretary of the Treas-

---

[44] This bill was not considered again in the First Congress.
[45] On January 14 this bill was amended.
[46] On February 15 the secretary of the treasury reported on this matter.
[47] On February 11 a petition was referred to this committee.

ury, with instruction to examine the same, and report his opinion thereupon to the House.

A petition of Andrew Brown, was presented to the House and read, praying that Congress will adopt some mode of authenticating a new edition of the laws of the United States, which he is now about to publish.

ORDERED, That the said petition do lie on the table.[48]

Mr. White, from the committee appointed, presented, according to order, a bill to establish offices for the purpose of granting lands within the territories of the United States, which was received and read the first time.

On motion,

The said bill was read the second time, and ordered to be committed to a committee of the whole House on Thursday next.[49]

A petition of Thomas Boyd, was presented to the House and read, praying to be placed on the list of pensioners, in consideration of wounds received whilst a soldier in the service of the United States, during the late war.

ORDERED, That the said petition be referred to the Secretary at War, with instruction to examine the same, and report his opinion thereupon to the House.

Mr. Fitzsimons, from the committee to whom was referred the petition of sundry officers of the navy of the state of Pennsylvania, made a report,[50] which was twice read, and agreed to by the House, as followeth:

"That it will not be advisable to grant the prayer of the petitioners, and therefore, that they have leave to withdraw their petition."

On motion,

ORDERED, That a committee be appointed to prepare and bring in a bill or bills to authorize the President of the United States, to cause the debt due to foreign officers, the interest whereof is now payable in Paris, at the rate of six per cent. per annum, to be paid and discharged; and that Mr. Sedgwick, Mr. Benson, and Mr. Sevier, be of the said committee.[51]

A member from Virginia presented to the House a memorial from the General Assembly of that State, stating certain objections to the act passed at the last session of Congress, intituled, "An act making provision for the debts of the United States;"[52] which was read, and ordered to lie on the table.

The House, according to the order of the day, again resolved itself into a

---

[48] On January 17 this petition was referred to the secretary of state.

[49] From January 20 through February 9 consideration of this bill was postponed as an order of the day. On February 10 it was considered by the COWH.

[50] A copy of the report is in A Record of the Reports of Select Committees, HR, DNA.

[51] On January 19 this committee presented the Foreign Officers Bill [HR–116], which was read twice.

[52] An annotated copy of what is probably the representation is in the Papers of the House of Delegates, Archives Division, Vi.

committee of the whole House, on the bill declaring the respective times when the electors to vote for a President of the United States shall be appointed or chosen, and shall give their votes; and after some time spent therein, Mr. Speaker resumed the chair, and Mr. Boudinot reported, that the committee had, according to order, again had the said bill under consideration, and made several amendments thereto, which he delivered in at the Clerk's table, where the same were severally twice read, and agreed to by the House.

ORDERED, That the said bill, with the amendments, do lie on the table.[53]

The several orders of the day were further postponed until Monday next.

And then the House adjourned until Monday morning eleven o'clock.

MONDAY, JANUARY 17, 1791

ORDERED, That the petition of Andrew Brown, which was presented on Friday last, be referred to the Secretary of State, with instruction to examine the same, and report his opinion thereupon to the House.[54]

Another member, to wit; George Gale, from Maryland, appeared and took his seat in the House.

A memorial of George Glentworth, was presented to the House and read, praying compensation for services rendered, as senior physician and surgeon-general of the general hospital of the United States, during the late war. Also,

A petition of Ebenezer Nash, praying relief in consideration of wounds received, whilst a soldier in the service of the United States, during the late war.

ORDERED, That the said memorial and petition be referred to the Secretary at War, with instruction to examine the same, and report his opinion thereupon to the House.

A petition of Daniel Ellis and John How, executors of Samuel How, late of the city of Burlington, deceased, was presented to the House and read, praying to receive payment for a quantity of pork, which was impressed from the said Samuel How, for the use of the army of the United States, during the late war. Also,

A petition of Israel Jones, in behalf of Joshua Ashbridge, praying compensation for sundry articles impressed from the said Joshua Ashbridge for the use of the army of the United States, during the late war.

ORDERED, That the said petitions be referred to the Secretary of the Treasury, with instruction to examine the same, and report his opinion thereupon to the House.

---

[53] This bill was not considered again by the First Congress.

[54] On February 7 the secretary of state reported on this petition.

A petition of Donald Campbell, was presented to the House and read, praying a liquidation and payment of certain claims against the United States.

And on the question, that the said petition be referred to the consideration of a committee,

It passed in the negative.

RESOLVED, That the said petition be rejected.

A message, in writing, was received from the President of the United States, by Mr. Lear his Secretary, as followeth:

UNITED STATES, January 17th, 1791

GENTLEMEN of the SENATE and HOUSE of REPRESENTATIVES,

I LAY before you an official statement of the appropriation of ten thousand dollars, granted to defray the contingent expenses of government by an act of the twenty-sixth of March, one thousand seven hundred and ninety.

A copy of two resolutions of the legislature of Virginia, and of a petition of sundry officers, and assignees of officers and soldiers of the Virginia line on continental establishment, on the subject of bounty-lands allotted to them on the north-west side of the Ohio; and a copy of an act of the legislature of Maryland, to empower the wardens of the port of Baltimore to levy and collect the duty therein mentioned.

G. WASHINGTON[55]

The House proceeded to consider the amendments agreed to by the committee of the whole House on Thursday last, to the bill, repealing, after the last day of   next, the duties heretofore laid upon distilled spirits imported from abroad, and laying others in their stead; and also upon spirits distilled within the United States, as well to discourage the excessive use of those spirits, and promote agriculture, as to provide for the support of the public credit, and for the common defence and general welfare: And the said amendments being twice read at the Clerk's table, were, on the question severally put thereupon, agreed to.

A motion was then made, and the question being put, further to amend the said bill, by striking out the thirteenth section thereof, in the words following, to wit:

"And be it further enacted, That upon all spirits which, after the said last day of   next, shall be distilled within the United States, from any article of the growth or production of the United States, in any city, town or village, there shall be paid for their use the duties following; that is to say,

---

[55] The message with enclosures is in President's Messages: Suggesting legislation, SR, DNA. The statement of appropriation is printed in the Appendix to the Third Session of the *Senate Legislative Journal*. On January 18 a committee was appointed to prepare a bill assenting to the Maryland act. On the same day the committee presented the Maryland Bill [HR–115], which was read.

"For every gallon of those spirits more than ten per cent. below proof, according to Dicas's hydrometer, nine cents.

"For every gallon of those spirits under five and not more than ten per cent. below proof, according to the same hydrometer, ten cents.

"For every gallon of those spirits of proof, and not more than five per cent. below proof, according to the same hydrometer, eleven cents.

"For every gallon of those spirits above proof, but not exceeding twenty per cent. according to the same hydrometer, thirteen cents.

"For every gallon of those spirits more than twenty and not more than forty per cent. above proof, according to the same hydrometer, seventeen cents.

"For every gallon of those spirits more than forty per cent. above proof, according to the same hydrometer, twenty-five cents."

It passed in the negative—$\begin{cases} \text{AYES} & 16 \\ \text{NOES} & 36 \end{cases}$

The ayes and noes being demanded by one fifth of the members present; Those who voted in the affirmative, are,

Abraham Baldwin	Peter Muhlenberg
Timothy Bloodworth	Josiah Parker
John Brown	Thomas Scott
Aedanus Burke	John Sevier
Daniel Hiester	John Steele
James Jackson	Michael Jenifer Stone
George Mathews	Thomas Tudor Tucker and
Andrew Moore	Hugh Williamson

Those who voted in the negative, are,

Fisher Ames	William B. Giles
Egbert Benson	John Laurance
Elias Boudinot	Richard Bland Lee
Benjamin Bourn	George Leonard
Lambert Cadwalader	Samuel Livermore
George Clymer	James Madison, junior
Thomas Fitzsimons	George Partridge
William Floyd	Jeremiah Van Rensselaer
Abiel Foster	James Schureman
Nicholas Gilman	Theodore Sedgwick
Benjamin Goodhue	Joshua Seney
Samuel Griffin	Roger Sherman
Jonathan Grout	Peter Silvester

Thomas Sinnickson
William Smith (of Maryland)
William Smith (of South-Carolina)
Jonathan Sturges
George Thatcher

Jonathan Trumbull
John Vining
Jeremiah Wadsworth
Alexander White and
Henry Wynkoop

The House proceeded further to consider the said bill;[56] and an adjournment being called for,

The several orders of the day were further postponed until to-morrow.

And then the House adjourned until to-morrow morning eleven o'clock.

TUESDAY, JANUARY 18, 1791

The several papers referred to in the President's message of yesterday, were read, and ordered to lie on the table.

ORDERED, That a committee be appointed to prepare and bring in a bill or bills, for declaring the assent of Congress to a certain act of the state of Maryland; and that Mr. Seney, Mr. Smith (of Maryland), and Mr. Mathews, be of the said committee.

The Speaker laid before the House a letter from the Secretary of State, covering a postscript to his former report on the subject of the coins, weights and measures of the United States;[57] which were read, and ordered to lie on the table.

On motion,

ORDERED, That the Secretary of the Treasury be directed to report to this House, his opinion whether any, and what further compensation ought to be made to the respective officers employed in the collection of the revenue.

A memorial of sundry inhabitants of the state of Connecticut, was presented to the House and read, praying that foreign vessels may not be allowed to participate in the coasting trade, or to go to other ports than those specially permitted by law, except in cases of distress.

ORDERED, That the said memorial be referred to the committee appointed to prepare and bring in a bill or bills for registering ships or vessels, for regulating those employed in the coasting trade and fisheries, and for other purposes; that they do examine the matter thereof, and report the same, with their opinion thereupon, to the House.

---

[56] On January 18 the Duties on Distilled Spirits Bill [HR–110] was considered again.

[57] This letter, addressed to the Senate, is in Reports and Communications from the Secretary of State, SR, DNA. A copy of the letter with the postscript to the report is in A Record of the Reports of the Secretary of State, vol. 1, HR, DNA. E–22995, E–22996, and E–23910 are printings of the original report and the postscript.

A petition of Margaret Fisher, Administratrix of Henry Fisher, late of Sussex county in the state of Delaware, deceased, was presented to the House and read, praying that a claim against the United States, for sundry expenditures and services of the deceased, during the late war, may be liquidated and allowed.

ORDERED, That the said petition, together with the petition of the inspectors of the port of Philadelphia, which lay on the table, be referred to the Secretary of the Treasury, with instruction to examine the same, and report his opinion thereupon to the House.

The several petitions of Samuel Kearsley, John Cardiff, and Michael Gabriel Houdin, were presented to the House and read, respectively praying compensation for services rendered in the army of the United States, during the late war.

ORDERED, That the said petitions be referred to the Secretary at War, with instruction to examine the same, and report his opinion thereupon to the House.

A petition of Charles Collins, was presented to the House and read, praying compensation for services rendered in the navy of the United States, during the late war.

ORDERED, That the said petition do lie on the table.

Mr. Seney, from the committee appointed, presented, according to order, a bill, declaring the assent of Congress to a certain act of the state of Maryland; which was received and read the first time.[58]

The House resumed the further consideration of the bill, repealing, after the last day of   next, the duties heretofore laid upon distilled spirits imported from abroad, and laying others in their stead; and also upon spirits distilled within the United States, as well to discourage the excessive use of those spirits, and promote agriculture, as to provide for the support of the public credit, and for the common defence and general welfare; and after some debate thereon, an adjournment being called for,[59]

The several orders of the day were further postponed until to-morrow.

And then the House adjourned until to-morrow morning eleven o'clock.

WEDNESDAY, JANUARY 19, 1791

A bill to declare the assent of Congress to a certain act of the state of Maryland, was read the second time, and ordered to be committed to a committee of the whole House on Monday next.[60]

---

[58] On January 19 this bill was read again.
[59] On January 19 this bill was considered again.
[60] From January 24–27 consideration of this bill was postponed as an order of the day. On January 28 the House agreed to amendments to this bill from the COWH.

Mr. Sedgwick, from the committee appointed, presented, according to order, a bill authorizing the President of the United States to cause the debt due to foreign officers to be paid and discharged; which was received and read the first time.

On motion,

The said bill was read the second time, and ordered to be committed to a committee of the whole House to-morrow.[61]

A petition of the Baptist Stonington Association, was presented to the House and read, praying that Congress will adopt measures to prevent the publication of any inaccurate editions of the holy bible.

ORDERED, That the said petition do lie on the table.

A petition of James Latham, was presented to the House and read, praying to be placed on the list of pensioners in consideration of the loss of his left arm in the service of the United States, during the late war.

ORDERED, That the said petition do lie on the table.

A petition of William Dewees, was presented to the House and read, praying compensation for losses and injuries sustained in the service of the United States, during the late war. Also,

A petition of Richard Blackledge, praying compensation for a quantity of coffee and sugar supplied to the troops of the late North-Carolina line and militia in continental service.

ORDERED, That the said petitions be referred to the Secretary of the Treasury, with instruction to examine the same, and report his opinion thereupon to the House.

A memorial of sundry surgeons and mates in the medical department of the late army, was presented to the House and read, praying a farther compensation for their services, during the late war.[62] Also,

A petition of Richard Blackledge, praying compensation for a quantity of leather furnished for the service of the United States, during the late war.

ORDERED, That the said petition and memorial be referred to the Secretary at War, with instruction to examine the same, and report his opinion thereupon to the House.

Mr. Fitzsimons, from the committee to whom was referred the petition of Joshua Barney, made a report, which was read, and ordered to lie on the table.[63]

---

[61] From January 20 through February 9 consideration of this bill was postponed as an order of the day. On February 10 the bill was considered in the COWH.

[62] The memorial is in Petitions and Memorials: Claims, SR, DNA. When the secretary of war reports on February 16, this petition is referred to under the names of two of the petitioners, William W. Smith and John Keehmle.

[63] A copy of the report is in A Record of the Reports of Select Committees, HR, DNA. On February 15 this report was considered, and a committee was appointed to prepare a bill.

The House resumed the consideration of the bill, repealing, after the last day of   next, the duties heretofore laid upon distilled spirits imported from abroad, and laying others in their stead; and also upon spirits distilled within the United States, as well to discourage the excessive use of those spirits, and promote agriculture, as to provide for the support of the public credit, and for the common defence and general welfare; and after farther debate thereon, an adjournment being called for,[64]

The several orders of the day were further postponed until to-morrow.[65]

And then the House adjourned until to-morrow morning eleven o'clock.

THURSDAY, JANUARY 20, 1791

A memorial of the merchants of Philadelphia, trading to India and China, was presented to the House and read, praying that an additional duty may be laid upon goods imported from thence in foreign bottoms; and also on articles the growth and produce of India or China, which are imported from Europe either in American or foreign bottoms.[66]   Also,

A petition of Robert Neil, praying relief against the determination of the Auditor and Comptroller of the Treasury on a claim which he has exhibited against the United States.   Also,

A petition of Comfort Sands and others, praying that the proceedings of the former Congress upon a claim of the petitioners against the United States, may now be confirmed, and payment of the said claim granted to them.

ORDERED, That the said memorial and petitions be referred to the Secretary of the Treasury, with instruction to examine the same, and report his opinion thereupon to the House.[67]

A message from the Senate by Mr. Otis their Secretary.

MR. SPEAKER,   The Senate have passed a bill, intituled, "An act to incorporate the subscribers to the bank of the United States," to which they desire the concurrence of this House.[68]   And he delivered in the same, and then withdrew.

On motion,

ORDERED, That a committee be appointed to join a committee of the Senate, to consider and report what time will be proper for the commencement

---

[64] On January 20 the House made further amendments to this bill.

[65] Although not journalized, the House received a letter from the directors of the Library Company of Philadelphia, offering Congress the use of their books on this date. The letter is in Reports and Communications, SR, DNA.

[66] The memorial is in Petitions and Memorials: Various subjects, SR, DNA.

[67] On February 25 the secretary reported on this petition. This report was then committed.

[68] The bill is in Engrossed Senate Bills and Resolutions, SR, DNA. On January 21 this bill was read twice.

of the next Congress; to the end that timely notice may be given to the members who are to serve for the ensuing two years:

And a committee was appointed of Mr. Tucker, Mr. Lee, and Mr. Partridge.[69]

ORDERED, That the Clerk of this House do acquaint the Senate therewith.[70]

The House resumed the consideration of the bill, repealing, after the last day of   next, the duties heretofore laid upon distilled spirits imported from abroad, and laying others in their stead; and also upon spirits distilled within the United States, as well to discourage the excessive use of those spirits, and promote agriculture, as to provide for the support of the public credit, and for the common defence and general welfare; and having made some additional amendments thereto, an adjournment was called for:[71] Whereupon,

The several orders of the day were further postponed until to-morrow.

And then the House adjourned until to-morrow morning eleven o'clock.

FRIDAY, JANUARY 21, 1791

The bill sent from the Senate, intituled, "An act to incorporate the subscribers to the bank of the United States," was read the first time.

On motion,

The said bill was read the second time, and ordered to be committed to a committee of the whole House on Wednesday next.[72]

A petition of William C. Webb and Conyers White, was presented to the House and read, praying compensation for a number of beef-cattle, which were supplied to a commissary of the southern army, during the late war.

ORDERED, That the said petition be referred to the Secretary of the Treasury, with instruction to examine the same, and report his opinion thereupon to the House.

Mr. Williamson, from the committee appointed, presented, according to order, a bill to prevent invalids who are pensioners of the United States, from selling or transferring their respective pensions before the same shall become due; which was received and read the first time.

On motion,

---

[69] A copy of the order is in Messages from the House, SR, DNA. Another copy of the order, with the Senate committee appointments noted, is in Joint Committee Reports, SR, DNA.

[70] On January 21 the Senate notified the House that they had appointed members to this committee.

[71] On January 21 an amendment to this bill was disagreed to, and the bill was further amended.

[72] From January 26–28 consideration of this bill in the COWH was postponed as an order of the day. On January 31 it was considered in the COWH.

The said bill was read the second time, and ordered to be committed to a committee of the whole House on Thursday next.[73]

ORDERED, That a committee be appointed to prepare and bring in a bill or bills making provision for the compensations to inspectors and officers of inspection to be appointed to collect the duties imposed on distilled spirits, and to secure the collection thereof; and that Mr. Sedgwick, Mr. Madison, and Mr. Laurance be of the said committee.[74]

A message from the Senate by Mr. Otis their Secretary.

MR. SPEAKER, The Senate have appointed a committee on their part, jointly with the committee appointed on the part of this House, to consider and report what time it will be proper the next Congress should commence.[75] And then he withdrew.

The House resumed the consideration of the bill, repealing, after the last day of   next, the duties heretofore laid upon distilled spirits imported from abroad, and laying others in their stead; and also upon spirits distilled within the United States, as well to discourage the excessive use of those spirits, and promote agriculture, as to provide for the support of the public credit, and for the common defence and general welfare: Whereupon,

A motion being made and seconded, further to amend the said bill, by inserting the following clause:

"And be it further enacted, That if any inspector, or other officer or person concerned in the collection of the revenue to be raised by this act, shall, by word, message or writing, or in any other manner whatsoever, persuade or endeavor to persuade any elector to give, or dissuade or endeavor to dissuade any elector from giving his vote for the choice of any person to be a member of the House of Representatives, member of the Senate, or President of the United States, such inspector or other person so offending shall be forever disabled from holding an office under this act, and shall be subject to a penalty of   dollars;"

It passed in the negative— $\begin{cases} \text{AYES} & 21 \\ \text{NOES} & 37 \end{cases}$

The ayes and noes being demanded by one fifth of the members present; Those who voted in the affirmative, are,

John Baptista Ashe	John Brown
Abraham Baldwin	Aedanus Burke
Timothy Bloodworth	William Floyd

---

[73] This bill was not considered again in the First Congress.

[74] On January 26 this committee presented the Salaries of Inspectors Bill [HR–119], which was read.

[75] On January 25 this committee reported.

Elbridge Gerry
Jonathan Grout
John Hathorn
Daniel Hiester
James Jackson
Samuel Livermore
George Mathews
Andrew Moore

Josiah Parker
Jeremiah Van Rensselaer
Joshua Seney
Peter Silvester
Michael Jenifer Stone
Thomas Tudor Tucker and
Alexander White

Those who voted in the negative, are,

Fisher Ames
Egbert Benson
Elias Boudinot
Benjamin Bourn
Lambert Cadwalader
Daniel Carroll
George Clymer
Thomas Fitzsimons
Abiel Foster
George Gale
Nicholas Gilman
Benjamin Goodhue
Samuel Griffin
William B. Giles
Thomas Hartley
Benjamin Huntington
John Laurance
Richard Bland Lee
George Leonard

James Madison, junior
Peter Muhlenberg
James Schureman
Thomas Scott
Theodore Sedgwick
John Sevier
Roger Sherman
Thomas Sinnickson
William Smith (of Maryland)
William Smith (of South-Carolina)
John Steele
Jonathan Sturges
George Thatcher
Jonathan Trumbull
John Vining
Jeremiah Wadsworth
Hugh Williamson and
Henry Wynkoop

The said bill was then further amended at the Clerk's table; and an adjournment being called for,[76]

The several orders of the day were further postponed until to-morrow.

And then the House adjourned until to-morrow morning eleven o'clock.

SATURDAY, JANUARY 22, 1791

Mr. Laurance, from the committee to whom was referred the petition of Seth Harding, made a report, which was read, and ordered to lie on the table.[77]

---

[76] On January 22 further amendments to the Duties on Distilled Spirits Bill [HR–110] were considered.

[77] A copy of the report is in A Record of the Reports of Select Committees, HR, DNA. On February 26 this committee report was disagreed to.

The House resumed the consideration of the bill, repealing, after the last day of   next, the duties heretofore laid upon distilled spirits imported from abroad, and laying others in their stead; and also upon spirits distilled within the United States, as well to discourage the excessive use of those spirits, and promote agriculture, as to provide for the support of the public credit, and for the common defence and general welfare; and several propositions of amendment thereto being offered, and debate arising thereon, an adjournment was called for:[78]   Whereupon,

The several orders of the day were further postponed until Monday next.

And then the House adjourned until Monday morning eleven o'clock.

MONDAY, JANUARY 24, 1791

A petition of Peter Johnson, was presented to the House and read, praying to be placed on the list of pensioners, in consideration of a wound received in the service of the United States, during the late war.   Also,

A petition of John Cockley, praying that a bounty of lands may be granted him for military services in the army of the United States, during the late war.

ORDERED, That the said petitions be referred to the Secretary at War, with instruction to examine the same, and report his opinion thereupon to the House.

A petition of William Lane, was presented to the House and read, praying compensation for damages sustained in his property by the army of the United States, during the late war.

ORDERED, That the said petition be referred to the Secretary of the Treasury, with instruction to examine the same, and report his opinion thereupon to the House.

A petition of George Gibson, was presented to the House and read, praying compensation for services rendered to the United States, during the late war, in various stations.

ORDERED, That the said petition be referred to Mr. Giles, Mr. Vining, Mr. Peter Muhlenberg, Mr. Mathews, and Mr. Wadsworth; that they do examine the matter thereof, and report the same, with their opinion thereupon, to the House.[79]

A message, in writing, was received from the President of the United States, by Mr. Lear his Secretary, as followeth:

---

[78] On January 24 the House made further amendments to this bill.
[79] On January 28 this committee reported.

UNITED STATES, January 24th, 1791

GENTLEMEN of the SENATE and HOUSE of REPRESENTATIVES,

IN execution of the powers with which Congress were pleased to invest me by their act, intituled, "An act for establishing the temporary and permanent seat of the government of the United States," and on mature consideration of the advantages and disadvantages of the several positions, within the limits prescribed by the said act, I have, by a proclamation, bearing date this day, a copy of which is herewith transmitted, directed commissioners, appointed in pursuance of the act, to survey and limit a part of the territory of ten miles square, on both sides the river Potowmac, so as to comprehend George-Town in Maryland, and to extend to the eastern branch.

I have not by this first act, given to the said territory the whole extent of which it is susceptible, in the direction of the river; because I thought it important that Congress should have an opportunity of considering whether, by an amendatory law, they would authorize the location of the residue at the lower end of the present, so as to comprehend the eastern branch itself, and some of the country on its lower side, in the state of Maryland, and the town of Alexandria in Virginia—if however, they are of opinion that the federal territory should be bounded by the water edge of the eastern branch, the location of the residue will be to be made at the upper end of what is now directed.

I have thought best to await a survey of the territory, before it is decided on what particular spot on the north-eastern side of the river, the public buildings shall be erected.

GEORGE WASHINGTON[80]

The proclamation referred to in the said message, was read, and ordered to lie on the table.

The petition and remonstrance of sundry inhabitants of the city of Philadelphia, was presented to the House and read, stating their objections to the principles of excise laws in general, and praying that no such law may be passed or sanctioned by the general government.

ORDERED, That the said petition and remonstrance do lie on the table.

The House resumed the consideration of the bill, repealing, after the last day of   next, the duties heretofore laid upon distilled spirits imported from abroad, and laying others in their stead; and also upon spirits distilled within the United States, as well to discourage the excessive use of those spirits, and promote agriculture, as to provide for the support of the public credit, and for the common defence and general welfare: Whereupon,

---

[80] A copy of the proclamation mentioned in the message is in Transcribed Reports and Communications from the Executive Departments, 1789–1814, Records of the Secretary, SR, DNA. E–46332.

The said bill was further amended at the Clerk's table; and the following section, which was offered on Saturday last, to be added to the said bill by way of amendment; to wit,

"And be it further enacted, That the several duties imposed by this act, shall continue to be collected and paid, until the debts and purposes for which they are pledged and appropriated, shall be fully discharged and satisfied, and no longer," being under debate,

A motion was made, and the question being put, to amend the same, by striking out from the word "paid," to the end thereof, and inserting in lieu thereof, the following words;

"Until the   day of   in the year   and until the end of the next session of Congress, and no longer, the faith of the United States being hereby pledged, that timely and adequate provision shall be made for the full accomplishment of all the purposes, for which the monies arising under the operation of this act, are pledged and appropriated:"

It passed in the negative— $\begin{cases} \text{AYES} & 19 \\ \text{NOES} & 39 \end{cases}$

The ayes and noes being demanded by one fifth of the members present;
Those who voted in the affirmative, are,

John Baptista Ashe	Andrew Moore
Abraham Baldwin	Peter Muhlenberg
Timothy Bloodworth	Josiah Parker
John Brown	Thomas Scott
Aedanus Burke	Joshua Seney
William B. Giles	John Sevier
Thomas Hartley	John Steele
Daniel Hiester	Thomas Tudor Tucker and
James Jackson	Hugh Williamson
George Mathews	

Those who voted in the negative, are,

Fisher Ames	George Gale
Egbert Benson	Elbridge Gerry
Elias Boudinot	Nicholas Gilman
Benjamin Bourn	Benjamin Goodhue
Lambert Cadwalader	Samuel Griffin
George Clymer	Jonathan Grout
Thomas Fitzsimons	John Hathorn
William Floyd	Benjamin Huntington
Abiel Foster	John Laurance

Richard Bland Lee

George Leonard

Samuel Livermore

James Madison, junior

George Partridge

Jeremiah Van Rensselaer

James Schureman

Theodore Sedgwick

Roger Sherman

Peter Silvester

Thomas Sinnickson

William Smith (of Maryland)

William Smith (of South-Carolina)

Michael Jenifer Stone

Jonathan Sturges

George Thatcher

Jonathan Trumbull

John Vining

Jeremiah Wadsworth

Alexander White and

Henry Wynkoop

And then the main question being put, that the House do agree to the said section, as originally moved;

It was resolved in the affirmative.[81]

An adjournment was then called for: Whereupon,

The several orders of the day were further postponed until to-morrow.[82]

And then the House adjourned until to-morrow morning eleven o'clock.

TUESDAY, JANUARY 25, 1791

The several petitions of sundry citizens of the state of Pennsylvania; of sundry citizens of the state of North-Carolina, and of Abiel Smith, were presented to the House and read, respectively praying compensation for property destroyed by the troops of the United States, or supplies furnished them during the late war.   Also,

A petition of Alexander Contee Hanson, praying compensation for expenses incurred in consequence of an appointment of the late Congress.

ORDERED, That the said petitions be referred to the Secretary of the Treasury, with instruction to examine the same, and report his opinion thereupon to the House.

A petition of Sarah Leitch, and James Frisby Leitch, infants and children of Major Andrew Leitch, deceased, was presented to the House and read, praying that the half pay of the commission possessed by their said father, who was slain in the service of the United States, may be extended to them.[83]

---

[81] On January 25 the Duties on Distilled Spirits Bill [HR–110] was amended again.

[82] A presidential message and three reports from the secretary of war concerning the state of the frontiers were received in secret session on this date. The message and reports with enclosures are in President's Messages: Transmitting reports from the Secretary of War, SR, DNA. Copies of the three reports are in A Record of the Reports of the Secretary of War, vol. 1, HR, DNA.

[83] The petition is in the Miscellaneous Vertical File, MdHi.

ORDERED, That the said petition be referred to the Secretary at War, with instruction to examine the same, and report his opinion thereupon to the House.[84]

A petition of sundry inhabitants of the county of Lancaster, in the state of Pennsylvania, was presented to the House and read, praying that the excise-bill, now before Congress, may be so modified, as to prevent inconvenience or oppression to the farmers and tradesmen.[85]

ORDERED, That the said petition do lie on the table.

Mr. Laurance, from the committee to whom was recommitted the bill directing the mode in which the evidences of the debt of the United States, which have been or may be lost or destroyed, shall be renewed, presented an amendatory bill, which was received and read the first time.[86]

Mr. Jackson, from the committee to whom were referred the petitions of the merchants of the towns of Wilmington and Fayetteville in the state of North-Carolina, made a report,[87] which was read, and ordered to lie on the table.

The House resumed the consideration of the bill, repealing, after the last day of   next, the duties heretofore laid upon distilled spirits imported from abroad, and laying others in their stead; and also upon spirits distilled within the United States, as well to discourage the excessive use of those spirits, and promote agriculture, as to provide for the support of the public credit, and for the common defence and general welfare: Whereupon,

The said bill was further amended at the Clerk's table.

And then the question, "that the said bill be engrossed, and read the third time," being put,

It was resolved in the affirmative— $\begin{cases} \text{AYES} & 35 \\ \text{NOES} & 20 \end{cases}$

The ayes and noes being demanded by one fifth of the members present; Those who voted in the affirmative, are,

Fisher Ames	Thomas Fitzsimons
Egbert Benson	William Floyd
Elias Boudinot	Abiel Foster
Benjamin Bourn	George Gale
Lambert Cadwalader	Elbridge Gerry
Daniel Carroll	Nicholas Gilman
George Clymer	Benjamin Goodhue

---

[84] On February 15 the secretary reported on this petition.

[85] The petition is in Petitions and Memorials: Various subjects, SR, DNA.

[86] On January 26 this bill was read again.

[87] A copy of the report is in A Record of the Reports of Select Committees, HR, DNA.

Jonathan Grout
Benjamin Huntington
John Laurance
Richard Bland Lee
George Leonard
Samuel Livermore
James Madison, junior
George Partridge
James Schureman
Thomas Scott
Theodore Sedgwick

Roger Sherman
Peter Silvester
Thomas Sinnickson
Jonathan Sturges
George Thatcher
Jonathan Trumbull
John Vining
Jeremiah Wadsworth
Alexander White and
Henry Wynkoop

Those who voted in the negative, are,

John Baptista Ashe
Abraham Baldwin
Timothy Bloodworth
John Brown
Aedanus Burke
Samuel Griffin
William B. Giles
Thomas Hartley
John Hathorn
Daniel Hiester

James Jackson
George Mathews
Peter Muhlenberg
Josiah Parker
Jeremiah Van Rensselaer
Joshua Seney
John Sevier
John Steele
Michael Jenifer Stone and
Thomas Tudor Tucker

ORDERED, That Thursday next be assigned for the third reading of the said bill.[88]

Mr. Tucker, from the committee "appointed to confer with a committee of the Senate, respecting the time for the commencement of the next session of Congress," made a report, which was read, and ordered to lie on the table.[89]

The several orders of the day were further postponed until to-morrow.

And then the House adjourned until to-morrow morning eleven o'clock.

WEDNESDAY, JANUARY 26, 1791

Mr. Sedgwick, from the committee appointed, presented, according to order, a bill providing compensations for inspectors, and other officers of inspection, and for other purposes, which was received and read the first time.[90]

---

[88] On January 27 the Duties on Distilled Spirits Bill [HR–110] was read again, agreed to, and sent to the Senate.

[89] The report is in Joint Committee Reports, SR, DNA. A copy of the report is in A Record of the Reports of Select Committees, HR, DNA. On January 28 this report was agreed to, and a committee was appointed to bring in a bill.

[90] On January 27 this bill was read again.

An amendatory bill, "directing the mode in which the evidences of the debt of the United States, which have been or may be lost or destroyed, shall be renewed," was read the second time, and ordered to be committed to a committee of the whole House on Thursday se'nnight.[91]

A message, in writing, was received from the President of the United States, by Mr. Lear his Secretary, as followeth:

UNITED STATES, January 26th, 1791

GENTLEMEN of the SENATE and HOUSE of REPRESENTATIVES,

I LAY before you the copy of a letter from the President of the National Assembly of France, to the President of the United States, and of a decree of that Assembly, which was transmitted with the above mentioned letter.

G. WASHINGTON[92]

The papers referred to in the said message, were read, and ordered to lie on the table.[93]

A petition of the inspectors of the district of Baltimore, was presented to the House and read, praying farther compensation for their services: Also,

A petition of John Crumpton, of the State of New-York, praying compensation for thirty hogs, which were taken from him for the use of the army, during the late war.

ORDERED, That the said petitions be referred to the Secretary of the Treasury, with instruction to examine the same, and report his opinion thereupon to the House.

A petition of Albert Roux, late a captain in the second continental regiment of South Carolina, was presented to the House and read, praying to be placed on the list of pensioners, in consideration of a wound received in the service of the United States, during the late war.[94]

ORDERED, That the said petition be referred to the Secretary at War, with instruction to examine the same, and report his opinion thereupon to the House.

ORDERED, That a committee be appointed to prepare and bring in a bill or bills, for making compensation to widows, orphans and invalids, in certain cases; and that Mr. Smith (of South Carolina), Mr. Stone, and Mr. Trumbull, be of the said committee.[95]

---

[91] This bill was not considered again in the First Congress.

[92] The message with enclosures is in President's Messages: Suggesting legislation, SR, DNA. The letter and decree mentioned in this message concerned tributes to Benjamin Franklin.

[93] On February 22 the Senate sent the House a resolution on these tributes.

[94] The petition is in Petitions and Memorials: Claims, SR, DNA.

[95] On February 26 two resolutions on petitions were referred to this committee.

ORDERED, That a committee be appointed to prepare and bring in a bill or bills, making appropriations for the service of the current year, and that Mr. Laurance, Mr. Clymer, and Mr. Boudinot, be of of the said committee.[96]

The House proceeded to consider the report of the committee, to whom were referred the petitions of the merchants of Wilmington and Fayetteville, in the State of North-Carolina; and the said report being twice read at the Clerk's table, was agreed to, as followeth.

RESOLVED, That a bill or bills ought to be brought in, to repeal so much of the act, intituled, "An act for giving effect to an act, intituled, 'An act to establish the judicial courts of the United States, within the State of North-Carolina,' " as relates to the holding the stated district and circuit courts at the town of Newbern only.

The several orders of the day were further postponed until to-morrow.

And then the House adjourned until to-morrow morning eleven o'clock.

THURSDAY, JANUARY 27, 1791

A bill providing compensation for inspectors, and other officers of inspection, and for other purposes, was read the second time, and ordered to be committed to a committee of the whole House on Friday se'nnight.[97]

A memorial of the people called Quakers, in New-England, was presented to the House and read, stating their objections to certain provisions of a bill now depending, intituled, "A bill more effectually to provide for the national defence, by establishing a uniform militia throughout the United States."

ORDERED, That the said memorial do lie on the table.

The several petitions of Ezekiel Johnston, William Dade,[98] Joel Phelps and Timothy Lane, were presented to the House and read, respectively praying to be placed on the list of pensioners, in consideration of wounds received in the service of the United States, during the late war.

ORDERED, That the said petitions be referred to the Secretary at War, with instruction to examine the same, and report his opinion thereupon to the House.

A petition of Levy Bartleson, was presented to the House and read, praying compensation for supplies furnished for the use of the United States, during the late war.

ORDERED, That the said petition be referred to the Secretary of the Treasury, with instruction to examine the same, and report his opinion thereupon to the House.

---

[96] On January 31 this committee presented an Appropriations Bill [HR-120], which was read.

[97] This bill was not considered again in the First Congress.

[98] This petition later is referred to as that of William McDade. The correct spelling has not been established.

A message, in writing, was received from the President of the United States, by Mr. Lear his Secretary, as followeth:

UNITED STATES, January 27th, 1791

GENTLEMEN of the SENATE and HOUSE of REPRESENTATIVES,

IN order that you may be fully informed of the situation of the frontiers, and the prospect of hostility in that quarter, I lay before you the intelligence of some recent depredations, received since my message to you upon this subject of the twenty-fourth instant.

G. WASHINGTON[99]

The papers referred to in the said message, were read, and ordered to be referred to Mr. Ames, Mr. Wadsworth, Mr. Fitzsimons, Mr. Vining, Mr. Brown, Mr. Williamson, and Mr. Jackson.

A memorial of the Boston marine society, in the commonwealth of Massachusetts, was presented to the House and read, praying that Congress will establish three marine hospitals in the United States, for the care and support of aged and disabled seamen, one for the southern, one for the middle, and one for the eastern States.

ORDERED, That the said memorial do lie on the table.

A message from the Senate by Mr. Otis their Secretary.

MR. SPEAKER, The Senate have passed a bill, intituled "An act concerning consuls and vice-consuls," to which they desire the concurrence of this House.[100] And he delivered in the same, and then withdrew.

An engrossed bill, repealing, after the last day of   next, the duties heretofore laid upon distilled spirits imported from abroad, and laying others in their stead; and also upon spirits distilled within the United States, as well to discourage the excessive use of those spirits, and promote agriculture, as to provide for the support of the public credit, and for the common defence and general welfare, was read the third time, and the blanks therein filled up, and the question being put, that the said bill do pass,

It was resolved in the affirmative— $\begin{cases} \text{AYES} & 35 \\ \text{NOES} & 21 \end{cases}$

---

[99] The message with enclosures is in President's Messages: Transmitting reports from the Secretary of War, SR, DNA. As a result of this message and one received on January 24, 1791, the House drafted a Military Establishment Bill [HR–126A]. This bill passed the House in secret session on February 12.

[100] An incomplete bill is in Engrossed Senate Bills and Resolutions, SR, DNA. The bill is printed in the *Senate Legislative Journal* on March 2. E–46321. On January 28 this bill was read twice.

The ayes and noes being demanded by one fifth of the members present;
Those who voted in the affirmative, are,

Fisher Ames
Egbert Benson
Elias Boudinot
Benjamin Bourn
Lambert Cadwalader
Daniel Carroll
George Clymer
Thomas Fitzsimons
William Floyd
Abiel Foster
Elbridge Gerry
Nicholas Gilman
Benjamin Goodhue
Samuel Griffin
Jonathan Grout
Benjamin Huntington
John Laurance
Richard Bland Lee

George Leonard
Samuel Livermore
James Madison, junior
George Partridge
James Schureman
Theodore Sedgwick
Roger Sherman
Peter Silvester
Thomas Sinnickson
William Smith (of South-Carolina)
Jonathan Sturges
George Thatcher
Jonathan Trumbull
John Vining
Jeremiah Wadsworth
Alexander White and
Henry Wynkoop

Those who voted in the negative, are,

John Baptista Ashe
Abraham Baldwin
Timothy Bloodworth
John Brown
Aedanus Burke
William B. Giles
Thomas Hartley
John Hathorn
Daniel Hiester
James Jackson
George Mathews

Andrew Moore
Peter Muhlenberg
Josiah Parker
Jeremiah Van Rensselaer
Joshua Seney
William Smith (of Maryland)
John Steele
Michael Jenifer Stone
Thomas Tudor Tucker and
Hugh Williamson

RESOLVED, That the title of the said bill be, "An act, repealing, after the last day of June next, the duties heretofore laid upon distilled spirits imported from abroad, and laying others in their stead; and also upon spirits distilled within the United States, and for appropriating the same."[101]

---

[101] The bill is E–46327. It is printed in the *Senate Legislative Journal* on February 10.

ORDERED, That the Clerk of this House do carry the said bill to the Senate, and desire their concurrence.[102]

The several orders of the day were further postponed until to-morrow.

And then the House adjourned until to-morrow morning eleven o'clock.

FRIDAY, JANUARY 28, 1791

The bill sent from the Senate, intituled, "An act concerning consuls and vice-consuls," was read the first time.

On motion,

The said bill was read the second time, and ordered to be committed to a committee of the whole House on Wednesday next.[103]

A petition of the public creditors, holding loan-office certificates for money lent the United States to carry on the late war, was presented to the House and read, representing the insufficiency of the provision for the public creditors, made by an act of the last session of Congress, intituled, "An act making provision for the debt of the United States," and praying that a more adequate provision may now be made.

ORDERED, That the said petition do lie on the table.[104]

Mr. Smith (of South-Carolina), from the committee to whom was referred the petition of Henry Laurens, in behalf of the orphan daughter of the late Colonel John Laurens, made a report;[105] which was read, and ordered to lie on the table.

A petition of the inspectors of the state of New-York, was presented to the House and read, praying an increase of the compensation allowed by law for their services.

---

[102] The Senate read this bill on January 28, 31, and February 2. On February 2 it was committed, and on February 7 this committee reported amendments to the bill. The committee's amendment to the fourth section was agreed to on February 8. The entire report was agreed to on February 9. On February 10 the bill, as it passed the House, is printed in the *Senate Legislative Journal*. On the same day several amendments to it were defeated, and the fourth section was recommitted. On February 11 the committee reported an amendment to the fourth section, which was agreed to. The bill and the amendments were then recommitted to conform the bill to the amendments. On February 12 this committee reported, and the bill was agreed to after a further amendment was disagreed to. The Senate amendments are printed in the *Senate Legislative Journal* for that date. On February 14 the House was notified of the Senate amendments.

[103] From February 2 through March 1 consideration of this bill was postponed as an order of the day. On March 2 this bill was considered in the COWH, amended, read, and agreed to. On the same day the Senate disagreed to the amendments, and the House insisted on them.

[104] On February 7 this petition was committed.

[105] A copy of the report is in A Record of the Reports of Select Committees, HR, DNA. A copy, probably made by ASP, is in Select Committee on Claims, HR, DNA.

ORDERED, That the said petition do lie on the table.

Mr. Sturges, from the committee to whom were referred the petitions of the freeholders of the counties of Albany and Washington, in the state of New-York, respecting the pension granted to John Younglove, made a report;[106] which was read, and ordered to lie on the table.

Mr. Giles, from the committee to whom was referred the petition of George Gibson, made a report; which was read, and ordered to lie on the table.[107]

The House proceeded to consider the report of the committee to whom was referred the petition of John Churchman: Whereupon,

A motion being made and seconded, "That the petition of the said John Churchman be complied with, so far as to enable him to make a voyage to Baffins Bay, for ascertaining his discoveries relating to the magnetic circles;"

It passed in the negative.

ORDERED, That a bill or bills be brought in to encrease the penalties provided by the act for the encouragement of learning, &c. so far as the said penalties apply to maps and charts, and to books of calculation; and that Mr. Huntington, Mr. Madison, and Mr. Hiester, do prepare and bring in the same.[108]

The House, according to the order of the day, resolved itself into a committee of the whole House on the bill sent from the Senate, intituled, "An act declaring the consent of Congress, that a new state be formed within the jurisdiction of the commonwealth of Virginia, and admitted into this Union, by the name of the state of Kentucky;" and after some time spent therein, Mr. Speaker resumed the chair, and Mr. Boudinot reported, that the committee had, according to order, had the said bill under consideration, and made no amendment thereto.

On motion,

The said bill was read the third time; and the question being put that the same do pass,

It was resolved in the affirmative.

ORDERED, That the Clerk of this House do acquaint the Senate therewith.[109]

The Speaker laid before the House a letter from the Secretary of the Treasury, accompanying his report on the subject of the establishment of a mint,

---

[106] A copy of the report is in A Record of the Reports of Select Committees, HR, DNA.

[107] On February 16 this report was considered, and part of it was disagreed to.

[108] On February 9 this committee presented a Copyright Bill [HR–123], which was read.

[109] On January 31 this bill was signed by the speaker and the vice president.

made pursuant to an order of the House of the fifteenth of April last; which were read, and ordered to lie on the table.[110]

The House proceeded to consider the report of the committee appointed to confer with a committee of the Senate, respecting the time for the commencement of the next session of Congress: Whereupon,

RESOLVED, That this House doth agree to the said report, in the words following, to wit:

That it is the opinion of the joint committee, that a revenue-bill may be passed, and such other business, as is of immediate importance, accomplished before the fourth day of March next, and that it will therefore not be necessary that a new session should commence immediately thereafter.

That the joint committee are also of opinion, that a bill should pass to alter the next annual meeting of Congress to an earlier day than that expressed in the Constitution.

ORDERED, That a bill or bills be brought in pursuant to the said report; and that Mr. Tucker, Mr. Lee, and Mr. Partridge, do prepare and bring in the same.[111]

The House, according to the order of the day, resolved itself into a committee of the whole House on the bill, declaring the assent of Congress to a certain act of the state of Maryland; and after some time spent therein, Mr. Speaker resumed the chair, and Mr. Boudinot reported, that the committee had, according to order, had the said bill under consideration, and made several amendments thereto; which he delivered in at the Clerk's table, where the same were severally twice read, and agreed to by the House.

ORDERED, That the said bill, with the amendments, be engrossed, and read the third time on Monday next.[112]

The several orders of the day were further postponed until Monday next.

And then the House adjourned until Monday morning eleven o'clock.

MONDAY, JANUARY 31, 1791

Another member, to wit; Benjamin Contee, from Maryland, appeared and took his seat in the House.

Mr. Floyd, from the joint committee for inrolled bills, reported, that the committee had, according to order, examined an inrolled bill, intituled, "An act declaring the consent of Congress that a new State be formed within the

---

[110] The report is in Alexander Hamilton's Reports, HR, DNA. A copy of the report is in A Record of the Reports of the Secretary of the Treasury, vol. 2, HR, DNA. E–23920. On February 5 the House sent this report to the Senate.

[111] A copy of the resolution and order is in Messages from the House, SR, DNA. On February 8 this committee presented a Time of Meeting Bill [HR–122], which was read twice.

[112] On January 31 this bill was read again, agreed to, and sent to the Senate.

jurisdiction of the commonwealth of Virginia, and admitted into the Union, by the name of the State of Kentucky,"[113] and had found the same to be truly inrolled: Whereupon,

Mr. Speaker signed the said inrolled bill.[114]

An engrossed bill, to declare the assent of Congress to a certain act of the State of Maryland, was read the third time, and the blanks therein filled up.

RESOLVED, That the said bill do pass, and that the title be, "An act declaring the consent of Congress to a certain act of the State of Maryland."[115]

ORDERED, That the Clerk of this House do carry the said bill to the Senate, and desire their concurrence.[116]

Mr. Laurance, from the committee appointed, presented, according to order, a bill making appropriations for the support of government, during the year one thousand seven hundred and ninety one, and for other purposes, which was received and read the first time.[117]

A petition of Thomas Hobby, was presented to the House and read, praying to be placed on the list of pensioners, in consideration of wounds received in the service of the United States, during the late war.

ORDERED, That the said petition be referred to the Secretary at War, with instruction to examine the same, and report his opinion thereupon to the House.

The House, according to the order of the day, resolved itself into a committee of the whole House, on the bill sent from the Senate, intituled, "An act to incorporate the subscribers to the bank of the United States;" and after some time spent therein, Mr. Speaker resumed the chair, and Mr. Boudinot reported, that the committee had, according to order, had the said bill under consideration, and made no amendment thereto.

ORDERED, That the said bill be read the third time to-morrow.[118]

The House, according to the order of the day, resolved itself into a committee of the whole House, on the bill for establishing the post-office and post-roads of the United States, and after some time spent therein, Mr. Speaker resumed the chair, and Mr. Boudinot reported, that the committee had, according to order, had the said bill under consideration, and made some progress therein.

---

[113] The inspected enrolled bill is in Enrolled Acts, RG 11, DNA. E–23850.

[114] On February 2 this bill was presented to the president.

[115] The bill, in the form that it passed the House and was agreed to by the Senate without amendments, is printed in the Appendix to the Third Session of the *Senate Legislative Journal.*

[116] The Senate read this bill on January 31, February 1, and 2. On February 2 it was agreed to.

[117] On February 1 this bill was read again.

[118] On February 1 this bill was read again, and a motion to recommit it was defeated.

RESOLVED, That this House will, to-morrow, again resolve itself into a committee of the whole House on the said bill.[119]

The several orders of the day were further postponed until to-morrow.

And then the House adjourned until to-morrow morning eleven o'clock.

---

[119] From February 1–23 consideration of this bill was postponed as an order of the day. On February 24 it was considered by the COWH.

TUESDAY, February 1, 1791

A bill making appropriations for the support of government for the year one thousand seven hundred and ninety one, was read the second time, and ordered to be engrossed, and read the third time to-morrow.[1]

The bill sent from the Senate, intituled, "An act to incorporate the subscribers to the bank of the United States," was read the third time.

A motion was made, and the question being put, that the said bill be recommitted to the consideration of a committee of the whole House,

It passed in the negative—$\left\{\begin{array}{l}\text{AYES } 23 \\ \text{NOES } 34\end{array}\right.$

The ayes and noes being demanded by one fifth of the members present; Those who voted in the affirmative, are,

John Baptista Ashe	Richard Bland Lee
Abraham Baldwin	James Madison, junior
Timothy Bloodworth	George Mathews
Benjamin Bourn	Andrew Moore
John Brown	Josiah Parker
Aedanus Burke	William Smith (of Maryland)
Daniel Carroll	William Smith (of South-Carolina)
Benjamin Contee	Michael Jenifer Stone
George Gale	Thomas Tudor Tucker
Jonathan Grout	Alexander White and
William B. Giles	Hugh Williamson
James Jackson	

Those who voted in the negative, are,

Fisher Ames	Abiel Foster
Egbert Benson	Elbridge Gerry
Elias Boudinot	Nicholas Gilman
Lambert Cadwalader	Benjamin Goodhue
George Clymer	Thomas Hartley
Thomas Fitzsimons	John Hathorn
William Floyd	Daniel Hiester

---

[1] Although the Journal does not record the third reading and passage of this bill, the Senate received it on February 2. Thus, the third reading and passage occurred on that date. The Senate read the Appropriations Bill [HR–120] on February 2 and 3. On February 3 the bill was committed along with the petition of James Mathers. On February 5 this committee reported amendments to the bill. This report was disagreed to on February 7, and on February 8 the bill was read again and agreed to. The bill, as it passed the House and was agreed to by the Senate without amendments, is printed in the Appendix to the Third Session of the *Senate Legislative Journal.*

Benjamin Huntington	Roger Sherman
John Laurance	Peter Silvester
George Leonard	Thomas Sinnickson
Samuel Livermore	John Steele
Peter Muhlenberg	Jonathan Sturges
George Partridge	George Thatcher
Jeremiah Van Rensselaer	Jonathan Trumbull
James Schureman	John Vining
Thomas Scott	Jeremiah Wadsworth and
Joshua Seney	Henry Wynkoop

ORDERED, That the said bill do lie on the table.[2]

The several orders of the day were farther postponed until to-morrow.

And then the House adjourned until to-morrow morning eleven o'clock.[3]

WEDNESDAY, FEBRUARY 2, 1791

A petition of Gosuinus Erkelens, was presented to the House and read, praying compensation for services rendered to the United States, during the late war.   Also,

A petition of John Edgar, of Kaskaskies village, in the Illinois country, praying the settlement of a claim against the United States.

ORDERED, That the said petitions be referred to the Secretary of the Treasury, with instruction to examine the same, and report his opinion thereupon to the House.

The several petitions of Daniel Lollar, Samuel Sheppard, Robert King, and Cornelius Vanslyck, agent and attorney in fact for sundry officers in the late army,[4] were presented to the House and read, respectively praying to be placed on the list of pensioners, in consideration of wounds received and injuries sustained in the service of the United States, during the late war.

ORDERED, That the said petitions be referred to the Secretary at War, with instruction to examine the same, and report his opinion thereupon to the House.[5]

A message from the Senate by Mr. Otis their Secretary.

---

[2] On February 2 the Bank Bill [S–15] was considered again.

[3] Sometime before the House adjourned, they considered a committee report on a confidential message from the president concerning southwestern frontiers. The message was not journalized, but according to the report, it was received in the House on January 24 and referred to the committee on January 26. The report is in A Record of the Reports of Select Committees, HR, DNA.

[4] The Vanslyck petition was presented in behalf of several Oneida and Tuscarora Indian officers.

[5] On February 21 the secretary reported on the King petition.

MR. SPEAKER,   The Senate have passed the bill, intituled, "An act declaring the consent of Congress to a certain act of the State of Maryland."[6]   And then he withdrew.

Mr. Floyd, from the joint committee for inrolled bills, reported, that the committee did, this day, wait on the President of the United States, and present for his approbation, an inrolled bill, intituled, "An act declaring the consent of Congress, that a new State be formed within the jurisdiction of the commonwealth of Virginia, and admitted into the Union, by the name of the State of Kentucky."[7]

The House resumed the consideration of the bill sent from the Senate, intituled, "An act to incorporate the subscribers to the bank of the United States;" upon the question that the said bill do pass, and some time being spent in debate thereon, an adjournment was called for:[8]   Whereupon,

The several orders of the day were further postponed until to-morrow.

And then the House adjourned until to-morrow morning eleven o'clock.

THURSDAY, FEBRUARY 3, 1791

The petitions of Francis Shaffner, and James Swaine, were presented to the House and read, respectively praying compensation for services rendered to the United States, during the late war.   Also,

A petition of Anna Emmerson, widow of Oliver Emmerson, deceased, who died in the service of the United States, during the late war, praying some provision for her support.

ORDERED, That the said petitions be referred to the Secretary at War, with instruction to examine the same, and report his opinion thereupon to the House.

A petition of sundry widows, who are creditors of the United States, for money loaned during the late war, was presented to the House and read, praying that a more adequate provision may be made for the payment of their respective claims.

ORDERED, That the said petition do lie on the table.

The petitions of Richard Dale, and John Jones, were presented to the House and read, respectively praying the settlement of a claim against the United States.[9]   Also,

---

[6] On February 8 this bill was signed by the speaker and the vice president and presented to the president.

[7] The president signed this bill on February 4.

[8] On February 3 this bill was considered again, and a motion to recommit the first section was disagreed to.

[9] The Dale petition is in Miscellaneous Treasury Accounts, No. 2286, RG 217, DNA. The Jones petition is in Petitions and Memorials: Claims, SR, DNA.

A petition of the merchants of Philadelphia, praying that public piers may be erected at Newcastle, in the state of Delaware, for the better accommodation of the trade in the port of Philadelphia.

ORDERED, That the said petitions be referred to the Secretary of the Treasury, with instruction to examine the same, and report his opinion thereupon to the House.

ORDERED, That a committee be appointed to prepare and bring in a bill or bills to establish a temporary provision for the clerks of the several judicial courts of the United States, for the marshals of districts, and for the attendance and services of jurors in the circuit and district courts; and that Mr. Sedgwick, Mr. Sturges, and Mr. Contee be of the said committee.[10]

On a motion made and seconded, that the House do come to the following resolution:

Whereas certain certificates or evidences of debt dated after the first of January, one thousand seven hundred and ninety, have been issued by one or more of the States, which certificates purport that they were issued in lieu of certain other certificates dated prior to the first of January, one thousand seven hundred and ninety; and the certificates of the first description are, on account of their date, not received by the loan-officers, as subscriptions to the loan proposed by the United States, although the certificates, in lieu of which they were issued, are clearly within the description of the law, and would, if not cancelled, be recoverable at the loan-office: Therefore,

RESOLVED, That all certificates of the first description above, be received at the loan-offices, as other evidences of the debt of the several states are by law receivable.

ORDERED, That the said motion be referred to the Secretary of the Treasury, with instruction to examine the same, and report his opinion thereupon to the House.[11]

The House resumed the consideration of the bill sent from the Senate, intituled, "An act to incorporate the subscribers to the bank of the United States:" upon the question that the said bill do pass;   whereupon,

A motion being made and seconded, that the first section of the said bill be recommitted to a committee of the whole House "for the purpose of altering the time or manner of subscribing, so that the holders of state securities assumed to be paid by the United States, may be on a footing with the holders of other securities formerly called national securities,"

It passed in the negative— $\begin{cases} \text{AYES} & \text{21} \\ \text{NOES} & \text{38} \end{cases}$

---

[10] On February 11 this committee presented a Judicial Officers Bill [HR–126], which was read twice.

[11] On February 25 the secretary made his report.

The ayes and noes being demanded by one fifth of the members present; Those who voted in the affirmative, are,

Abraham Baldwin
Timothy Bloodworth
John Brown
Aedanus Burke
Daniel Carroll
Benjamin Contee
George Gale
Jonathan Grout
William B. Giles
James Jackson
Richard Bland Lee

James Madison, junior
George Mathews
Andrew Moore
John Sevier
William Smith (of South-Carolina)
John Steele
Michael Jenifer Stone
Thomas Tudor Tucker
Alexander White and
Hugh Williamson

Those who voted in the negative, are,

Fisher Ames
Egbert Benson
Elias Boudinot
Benjamin Bourn
Lambert Cadwalader
George Clymer
Thomas Fitzsimons
William Floyd
Abiel Foster
Elbridge Gerry
Nicholas Gilman
Benjamin Goodhue
Samuel Griffin
Thomas Hartley
John Hathorn
Daniel Hiester
Benjamin Huntington
John Laurance
George Leonard

Samuel Livermore
Peter Muhlenberg
Josiah Parker
George Partridge
Jeremiah Van Rensselaer
James Schureman
Thomas Scott
Theodore Sedgwick
Joshua Seney
Roger Sherman
Peter Silvester
Thomas Sinnickson
William Smith (of Maryland)
Jonathan Sturges
George Thatcher
Jonathan Trumbull
John Vining
Jeremiah Wadsworth and
Henry Wynkoop

After which, further debate arising on the said bill, an adjournment was called for:[12] Whereupon,

The several orders of the day were further postponed until to-morrow.

And then the House adjourned until to-morrow morning eleven o'clock.

---

[12] On February 4 the Bank Bill [S–15] was considered again.

FRIDAY, February 4, 1791

A petition of Andrew Ohe, was presented to the House and read, praying the settlement of a claim against the United States. Also,

A petition of John Hollins, praying an abatement of the additional duties, which took place the first of January last, arising on a cargo imported in a vessel, which, although she arrived before that period, was prevented by the ice from getting to her port of entry till some time after.

ORDERED, That the said petitions be referred to the Secretary of the Treasury, with instruction to examine the same, and report his opinion thereupon to the House.

The Speaker laid before the House a letter from the Secretary of State, to whom was referred on the ninth of August last, the representation of the general court of the commonwealth of Massachusetts, respecting the whale and cod fisheries, accompanying his report on that subject;[13] which was read, and ordered to be sent to the Senate for their information.

The House resumed the consideration of the bill sent from the Senate, intituled, "An act to incorporate the subscribers to the bank of the United States:" on the question that the said bill do pass, and after farther debate thereon, an adjournment being called for,[14]

The several orders of the day were further postponed until to-morrow.

And then the House adjourned until to-morrow morning eleven o'clock.

SATURDAY, February 5, 1791

A petition of James Norris, was presented to the House and read, praying compensation for military services rendered to the United States, during the late war. Also,

A petition of Isaac Vincent, praying relief in consideration of a wound received in the service of the United States, during the late war.

ORDERED, That the said petitions be referred to the Secretary at War, with instruction to examine the same, and report his opinion thereupon to the House.

A petition of Abraham Skinner, was presented to the House and read, praying to be reimbursed for monies advanced whilst commissary-general of prisoners, during the late war.

ORDERED, That the said petition be referred to the Secretary of the Treasury, with instruction to examine the same, and report his opinion thereupon to the House.

---

[13] The letter and report with enclosures are in Reports from the Secretary of State, SR, DNA. A copy of the report is in A Record of the Reports of the Secretary of State, vol. 1, HR, DNA. E–23911, E–23912.

[14] On February 5 this bill was considered again.

On motion,

ORDERED, That a committee be appointed to prepare and bring in a bill or bills, further to continue in force an act passed the first session of Congress, intituled, "An act to regulate civil processes in the courts of the United States:"

And a committee was appointed of Mr. Sedgwick, Mr. Sturges, and Mr. Contee.[15]

On motion,

ORDERED, That the report of the Secretary of the Treasury, relative to the establishment of a mint, which was made to this House on Friday the twenty-eighth ultimo, be sent to the Senate for their information.[16]

The House resumed the consideration of the bill sent from the Senate, intituled, "An act to incorporate the subscribers to the bank of the United States:" Upon the question that the said bill do pass, and further debates arising thereon, after some time spent therein, an adjournment was called for:[17] Whereupon,

The several orders of the day were further postponed until Monday next.

And then the House adjourned until Monday morning ten o'clock.

MONDAY, FEBRUARY 7, 1791

The Speaker laid before the House a letter and report from the Secretary of State, on the petition of Andrew Brown, which were read, and ordered to lie on the table.[18]

A petition of Benoni Shipman, was presented to the House and read, praying to receive compensation for a number of guns and warlike implements which he purchased for the use of the army of the United States, during the late war.

ORDERED, That the said petition be referred to the Secretary at War, with instruction to examine the same, and report his opinion thereupon to the House.

Mr. White, from the committee appointed, presented, according to order,

---

[15] On February 9 this committee presented a Courts Bill [HR–124], which was read.

[16] A copy of the order is in Messages from the House, SR, DNA. The Senate committed this report on February 7, and on March 1 this committee reported. On March 2 the Senate agreed to resolutions empowering the president to establish a mint, and the resolutions were sent to the House on March 3. On the same day the House agreed to the resolutions with an amendment, which was then agreed to by the Senate. The resolutions were signed on the same day.

[17] On February 8 this bill was agreed to, and the Senate was notified.

[18] A copy of the report is in A Record of the Reports of the Secretary of State, vol. 1, HR, DNA. On February 12 the House passed a resolution on the petition of Andrew Brown.

a bill to amend an act, intituled, "An act to promote the progress of useful arts;" which was received and read the first time.[19]

A petition of sundry merchants and others, of the town of New-Bedford, in the county of Bristol, in the state of Massachusetts, was presented to the House and read, praying that a weekly post may be established by law from Boston, through Taunton, to the said town of New-Bedford.

ORDERED, That the said petition do lie on the table.

ORDERED, That the memorial of the public creditors holding loan-office certificates, which lay on the table, be referred to Mr. Sherman, Mr. Gerry, Mr. Hiester, Mr. Benson, and Mr. Gale; that they do examine the matter thereof, and report the same, with their opinion thereupon, to the House.[20]

The House resumed the consideration of the bill sent from the Senate, intituled, "An act to incorporate the subscribers to the bank of the United States:" Upon the question that the said bill do pass, and after farther debate thereon, an adjournment being called for,[21]

The several orders of the day were further postponed until to-morrow.

And then the House adjourned until to-morrow morning ten o'clock.

TUESDAY, FEBRUARY 8, 1791

Mr. Floyd, from the joint committee for inrolled bills, reported,[22] that the committee had examined an inrolled bill, intituled, "An act declaring the consent of Congress to a certain act of the state of Maryland,"[23] and had found the same to be truly inrolled: Whereupon,

Mr. Speaker signed the said inrolled bill.

ORDERED, That the Clerk of this House do acquaint the Senate therewith.

A bill to amend an act, intituled, "An act to promote the progress of useful arts," was read the second time, and ordered to be committed to a committee of the whole House on Saturday next.[24]

The petitions of Charles Lockman, and Sylvester Springer, were presented to the House and read, respectively praying compensation for services rendered as surgeon's mates in the hospital department of the United States, during the late war.   Also,

A petition of Peter Sheffner, praying to be placed on the list of pensioners,

---

[19] A printed copy of what is probably the bill is E–23848. On February 8 this bill was read again.

[20] On February 12 this committee reported.

[21] On February 7 this bill was considered again.

[22] The report is in Committee on Enrolled Bills, SR, DNA.

[23] The inspected enrolled bill is in Enrolled Acts, RG 11, DNA. E–23851, E–46328. The bill is printed in the Appendix to the Third Session of the *Senate Legislative Journal.*

[24] This bill was not considered again in the First Congress.

as a disabled lieutenant in the service of the United States, during the late war.

ORDERED, That the said petitions be referred to the Secretary at War, with instruction to examine the same, and report his opinion thereupon to the House.

ORDERED, That the petition of the marine society of Boston, which lay on the table, be referred to the Secretary of the Treasury, with instruction to examine the same, and report his opinion thereupon to the next session of Congress.

Mr. Tucker, from the committee appointed, presented, according to order, a bill to alter the time of the next meeting of Congress; which was received and read the first time.

On motion,

The said bill was read the second time, and ordered to be engrossed, and read the third time to-morrow.[25]

A message from the Senate by Mr. Otis their Secretary.

MR. SPEAKER,   The Senate have passed the bill, intituled, "An act making appropriations for the support of government, for the year one thousand seven hundred and ninety-one, and for other purposes."[26]   And then he withdrew.

On motion,

ORDERED, That the Secretary at War be discharged from considering the petition of Richard Blackledge, which was referred to him on the nineteenth of January last; and that the said petition be referred to the Secretary of the Treasury, with instruction to examine the same, and report his opinion thereupon to the House.

Mr. Floyd, from the joint committee for inrolled bills, reported, that the committee did, this day, wait on the President of the United States, and present for his approbation, an inrolled bill, intituled, "An act declaring the consent of Congress to a certain act of the state of Maryland."[27]

A petition of Ezekiel Conklin and others, inhabitants of the county of Orange, in the state of New-York, by Ebenezer Hazard their attorney, was presented to the House and read, praying compensation for damages sustained in their property, by the army of the United States, during the late war.

ORDERED, That the said petition be referred to the Secretary of the Treas-

---

[25] On February 11 this bill was read again, agreed to, and sent to the Senate.

[26] On February 9 this bill was signed by the speaker and the vice president and delivered to the president.

[27] On February 9 this bill was signed by the president.

ury, with instruction to examine the same, and report his opinion thereupon to the House.

A petition of George Le Roy, late a captain in the army of the United States, by his agents, Vanuxem and Lombaert, was presented to the House and read, praying that Congress will direct the interest on the certificates which he received for his services, to be paid him by a banker in Paris.

ORDERED, That the said petition do lie on the table.

The House resumed the consideration of the bill sent from the Senate, intituled, "An act to incorporate the subscribers to the bank of the United States:" upon the question "that the said bill do pass;" whereupon,

The previous question being called for by five members; to wit, "Shall the main question be now put?"

It was resolved in the affirmative— $\begin{cases} \text{AYES} & 38 \\ \text{NOES} & 20 \end{cases}$

The ayes and noes being demanded by one fifth of the members present; Those who voted in the affirmative, are,

Fisher Ames	Peter Muhlenberg
Egbert Benson	George Partridge
Elias Boudinot	Jeremiah Van Rensselaer
Benjamin Bourn	James Schureman
Lambert Cadwalader	Thomas Scott
George Clymer	Theodore Sedgwick
Thomas Fitzsimons	Joshua Seney
William Floyd	John Sevier
Abiel Foster	Roger Sherman
Elbridge Gerry	Peter Silvester
Nicholas Gilman	Thomas Sinnickson
Benjamin Goodhue	William Smith (of Maryland)
Thomas Hartley	William Smith (of South-Carolina)
John Hathorn	John Steele
Daniel Hiester	Jonathan Sturges
Benjamin Huntington	George Thatcher
John Laurance	Jonathan Trumbull
George Leonard	Jeremiah Wadsworth and
Samuel Livermore	Henry Wynkoop

Those who voted in the negative, are,

John Baptista Ashe	Aedanus Burke
Abraham Baldwin	Daniel Carroll
Timothy Bloodworth	Benjamin Contee
John Brown	George Gale

Jonathan Grout
William B. Giles
James Jackson
Richard Bland Lee
James Madison, junior
George Mathews

Andrew Moore
Josiah Parker
Michael Jenifer Stone
Thomas Tudor Tucker
Alexander White and
Hugh Williamson

And then the main question being put, That the said bill do pass,

It was resolved in the affirmative— $\begin{cases} \text{AYES} & 39 \\ \text{NOES} & 20 \end{cases}$

The ayes and noes being demanded by one fifth of the members present; Those who voted in the affirmative, are,

Fisher Ames
Egbert Benson
Elias Boudinot
Benjamin Bourn
Lambert Cadwalader
George Clymer
Thomas Fitzsimons
William Floyd
Abiel Foster
Elbridge Gerry
Nicholas Gilman
Benjamin Goodhue
Thomas Hartley
John Hathorn
Daniel Hiester
Benjamin Huntington
John Laurance
George Leonard
Samuel Livermore
Peter Muhlenberg

George Partridge
Jeremiah Van Rensselaer
James Schureman
Thomas Scott
Theodore Sedgwick
Joshua Seney
John Sevier
Roger Sherman
Peter Silvester
Thomas Sinnickson
William Smith (of Maryland)
William Smith (of South-Carolina)
John Steele
Jonathan Sturges
George Thatcher
Jonathan Trumbull
John Vining
Jeremiah Wadsworth and
Henry Wynkoop

Those who voted in the negative, are,

John Baptista Ashe
Abraham Baldwin
Timothy Bloodworth
John Brown
Aedanus Burke
Daniel Carroll

Benjamin Contee
George Gale
Jonathan Grout
William B. Giles
James Jackson
Richard Bland Lee

James Madison, junior   Michael Jenifer Stone
George Mathews   Thomas Tudor Tucker
Andrew Moore   Alexander White and
Josiah Parker   Hugh Williamson

ORDERED, That the Clerk of this House do acquaint the Senate therewith.[28]
The several orders of the day were further postponed until to-morrow.
And then the House adjourned until to-morrow morning ten o'clock.

WEDNESDAY, FEBRUARY 9, 1791

A message was received from the President of the United States, by Mr.
Lear his Secretary, notifying that the President did, this day, approve and sign
an act, intituled, "An act declaring the consent of Congress to a certain act
of the state of Maryland."[29]
The said messenger also delivered in a written message from the President,
in the words following, to wit:

UNITED STATES, February 9th, 1791
GENTLEMEN of the SENATE and HOUSE of REPRESENTATIVES,
I HAVE received from the Governor of Vermont, authentic documents,
expressing the consent of the Legislatures of New-York and of the Territory
of Vermont, that the said Territory shall be admitted to be a distinct member
of our Union; and a memorial of Nathaniel Chipman and Lewis R. Morris,
Commissioners from the said Territory, praying the consent of Congress to
that admission, by the name and stile of the State of Vermont, copies of
which I now lay before Congress, with whom the Constitution has vested the
object of these proceedings.

G. WASHINGTON[30]

ORDERED, That the said written message, together with the papers accompanying the same, be referred to Mr. Laurance, Mr. Boudinot, and Mr.
Carroll.[31]
Mr. Huntington, from the committee appointed, presented, according to
order, a bill for increasing the penalty contained in an act passed the second
session of Congress, intituled, "An act for the encouragement of learning, by
securing the copies of maps, charts and books, to the authors and proprietors

---

[28] On February 12 this bill was signed by the speaker and the vice president.
[29] A copy of the message is in Committee on Enrolled Bills, SR, DNA.
[30] The documents referred to in this message are printed in the Appendix to the
Third Session.
[31] On February 12 the Senate sent the Vermont Statehood Bill [S–19] to the House.
The bill was then read twice.

of such copies, during the times therein mentioned;" which was received and read the first time.[32]

Mr. Sedgwick, from the committee appointed, presented, according to order, a bill to continue in force, for a limited time, an act passed at the first session of Congress, intituled, "An act to regulate processes in the courts of the United States;" which was received and read the first time.[33]

Mr. Floyd, from the joint committee for inrolled bills, reported, that the committee had examined an inrolled bill, intituled, "An act making appropriations for the support of government, for the year one thousand seven hundred and ninety-one, and for other purposes,"[34] and had found the same to be truly inrolled: Whereupon,

Mr. Speaker signed the said inrolled bill.

ORDERED, That the Clerk of this House do acquaint the Senate therewith.

A petition of Michael Jackson, late colonel of the eighth Massachusetts regiment, was presented to the House and read, praying to be placed on the list of pensioners, in consideration of a wound received in the service of the United States, during the late war.

ORDERED, That the said petition be referred to the Secretary at War, with instruction to examine the same, and report his opinion thereupon to the House.

ORDERED, That a committee be appointed to prepare and bring in a bill or bills, supplementary to an act, intituled, "An act to incorporate the subscribers to the bank of the United States;" and that Mr. Smith (of South-Carolina), Mr. Williamson, and Mr. Vining, be of the said committee.[35]

Mr. Floyd, from the joint committee for inrolled bills, reported, that the committee did, this day, wait on the President of the United States, and present, for his approbation, an inrolled bill, intituled, "An act making appropriations for the support of government, for the year one thousand seven hundred and ninety-one, and for other purposes."[36]

The several orders of the day were further postponed until to-morrow.

And then the House adjourned until to-morrow morning ten o'clock.

THURSDAY, FEBRUARY 10, 1791

A bill for increasing the penalty contained in an act passed the second session of Congress, intituled, "An act for the encouragement of learning, by

---

[32] On February 10 this bill was read again.

[33] On February 10 this bill was read again.

[34] The inspected enrolled bill is in Enrolled Acts, RG 11, DNA. E–23860. The bill is printed in the Appendix to the Third Session of the *Senate Legislative Journal.*

[35] On February 10 this committee presented a Bank Bill [HR–125], which was read.

[36] On February 11 the president signed this bill.

securing the copies of maps, charts and books to the authors and proprietors of such copies, during the times therein mentioned," was read the second time, and ordered to be committed to a committee of the whole House on Saturday next.[37]

A bill to continue for a limited time, the act regulating processes in the courts of the United States, was read the second time, and ordered to be engrossed, and read the third time to-morrow.[38]

A petition and remonstrance of John Fitch, was presented to the House and read, complaining of the injurious operation which the bill now depending before Congress, intituled, "A bill to amend the act to promote the progress of useful arts," will have on his interest, should the same be passed into a law.

ORDERED, That the said petition and remonstrance do lie on the table.

A petition of sundry masters of vessels in the port of Charleston, South-Carolina, was presented to the House and read, praying that Congress will adopt measures to relieve them from the injury they suffer, by the preference given in that place to foreign vessels, in the carrying trade.[39]

ORDERED, That the said petition do lie on the table.[40]

On a motion made and seconded, "That a committee be appointed to prepare and bring in a bill or bills repealing so much of the act, intituled, "An act to provide more effectually for the collection of the duties imposed by law on goods, wares, and merchandize imported into the United States, and on the tonnage of ships or vessels," as hath rated the rix dollar of Denmark at one hundred cents."

ORDERED, That the said motion be committed to Mr. Bourn, Mr. Sherman, and Mr. Thatcher.[41]

ORDERED, That a committee be appointed to prepare and bring in a bill or bills, supplementary to the act, intituled, "An act to establish the treasury department;" and that Mr. Boudinot, Mr. Fitzsimons, and Mr. Ames, be of the said committee.[42]

The House, according to the order of the day, resolved itself into a committee of the whole House, on the bill authorizing the President of the United States to cause the debt due to foreign officers to be paid and discharged; and after some time spent therein, Mr. Speaker resumed the chair, and Mr. Boudinot reported, that the committee had, according to order, had the said bill under consideration, and made no amendment thereto.

---

[37] This bill was not considered again.

[38] On February 11 this bill was read, agreed to, and sent to the Senate.

[39] The petition is in Petitions and Memorials: Various subjects, SR, DNA.

[40] On February 11 this petition was referred to the committee on trade.

[41] On February 24 this committee presented a Collection Bill [HR–134], which was read.

[42] On February 22 this committee presented a Treasury Bill [HR–131], which was read twice.

ORDERED, That the said bill be engrossed, and read the third time to-morrow.[43]

The House, according to the order of the day, resolved itself into a committee of the whole House, on the bill to establish offices for the purpose of granting lands within the territory of the United States; and after some time spent therein, Mr. Speaker resumed the chair, and Mr. Boudinot reported, that the committee had, according to order, had the said bill under consideration, and made some progress therein.

RESOLVED, That this House will, to-morrow, again resolve itself into a committee of the whole House, on the said bill.[44]

Mr. Smith (of South-Carolina), from the committee appointed, presented, according to order, a bill supplementary to the act, intituled, "An act to incorporate the subscribers to the bank of the United States," which was received and read the first time.[45]

The Speaker laid before the House, a letter from the Secretary of the Treasury, covering his report on the petition of the merchants of Philadelphia, trading to India and China,[46] made pursuant to an order of this House, of the 20th of January last, which were read and ordered to lie on the table.

The several orders of the day were further postponed until to-morrow.

And then the House adjourned until to-morrow morning ten o'clock.

FRIDAY, FEBRUARY 11, 1791

An engrossed bill to continue in force, for a limited time, an act, intituled, "An act to regulate processes in the courts of the United States," was read the third time.

RESOLVED, That the said bill do pass; and that the title be, "An act to continue in force, for a limited time, an act to regulate processes in the courts of the United States."

ORDERED, That the Clerk of this House do carry the said bill to the Senate, and desire their concurrence.[47]

An engrossed bill, authorising the President of the United States to cause the debt due to foreign officers to be paid and discharged, was read the third time.

RESOLVED, That the said bill do pass; and that the title be, "An act au-

---

[43] On February 11 this bill was read again, agreed to, and sent to the Senate.

[44] On February 11 the COWH reported amendments to this bill.

[45] On February 11 this bill was read again.

[46] A copy of the report is in A Record of the Reports of the Secretary of the Treasury, vol. 2, HR, DNA.

[47] On February 11 the Senate read this bill, which is printed in the *Senate Legislative Journal*. It was read again on February 12, and on February 14 it was read again and agreed to.

thorising the President of the United States to cause the debt due to foreign officers to be paid and discharged."[48]

ORDERED, That the Clerk of this House do carry the said bill to the Senate, and desire their concurrence.[49]

A bill supplementary to the act, intituled, "An act to incorporate the subscribers to the bank of the United States," was read the second time, and ordered to be committed to a committee of the whole House to-morrow.[50]

A message was received from the President of the United States, by Mr. Lear his Secretary, notifying that the President did, this day, approve and sign an act, intituled, "An act making appropriations for the support of government, for the year one thousand seven hundred and ninety-one, and for other purposes."[51]

ORDERED, That the Clerk of this House do acquaint the Senate therewith.

A petition of Ebenezer Fielding, was presented to the House and read, praying to be placed on the list of pensioners, as a disabled soldier in the service of the United States, during the late war. Also,

The petitions of Francis Procter, and John Henderson, respectively praying compensation for services rendered to the United States, during the late war.

ORDERED, That the said petitions be referred to the Secretary at War, with instruction to examine the same, and report his opinion thereupon to the House.

Mr. Sedgwick, from the committee appointed, presented, according to order, a bill providing compensations for clerks, marshals and jurors; which was received and read the first time.

On motion,

The said bill was read the second time, and ordered to be committed to a committee of the whole House on Tuesday next.[52]

The House, according to the order of the day, again resolved itself into a committee of the whole House, on the bill to establish offices for the purpose of granting lands, within the territories of the United States; and after some time spent therein, Mr. Speaker resumed the chair, and Mr. Boudinot reported, that the committee had, according to order, again had the said bill under consideration, and made several amendments thereto, which he de-

---

[48] The bill is in Engrossed House Bills, HR, DNA. This bill is printed in the *Senate Legislative Journal* on February 11.

[49] On February 11 the Senate read this bill, and on February 12 the bill was read again and committed. On February 22 this committee reported, and on February 23 the Senate resolved not to read this bill again.

[50] From February 12–21 consideration of this bill in the COWH was postponed as an order of the day. On February 22 the COWH presented several amendments to the bill, which were agreed to by the House.

[51] A copy of the message is in Committee on Enrolled Bills, SR, DNA.

[52] On February 12 a petition from John Tucker was referred to the COWH on the Judicial Officers Bill [HR–126].

livered in at the Clerk's table, where the same were read, and ordered to lie on the table.[53]

An engrossed bill to alter the time of the meeting of the next session of Congress, was read the third time, and the blank therein filled up.

RESOLVED, That the said bill do pass, and that the title be, "An act to alter the time of the meeting of the next session of Congress."[54]

ORDERED, That the Clerk of this House do carry the said bill to the Senate, and desire their concurrence.[55]

ORDERED, That the petition of the masters of vessels employed in the carrying trade in the port of Charleston, South-Carolina, which was presented yesterday, be referred to the committee appointed to prepare and bring in a bill or bills to amend the laws concerning the trade and navigation of the United States.[56]

A memorial of Thomas Walley, William Smith and Joseph Ward, was presented to the House and read, praying that certain bills issued under authority of the former Congress, of which the petitioners are possessed, the interest whereof was payable in sterling bills of exchange in Europe, may be liquidated, and the arrears of interest paid, or the principal and interest of the said bills funded in like manner with loan-office certificates.

ORDERED, That the said memorial do lie on the table.

ORDERED, That a committee be appointed to report whether any and what farther provision is necessary to secure the due accounting for the monies expended in the department of war:

And a committee was appointed of Mr. Fitzsimons, Mr. Parker, and Mr. Gilman.[57]

The several orders of the day were further postponed until to-morrow.

And then the House adjourned until to-morrow morning ten o'clock.

SATURDAY, FEBRUARY 12, 1791

A petition of Aquila Giles, on behalf of sundry inhabitants of Long-Island, in the State of New-York, was presented to the House and read, praying the liquidation and payment of certain claims against the United States.   Also,

A petition of the gaugers of the city of New-York, praying compensation for certain services which they have rendered, and for which no provision hath been made by law.   Also,

---

[53] On February 12 the amendments reported by the committee were considered.

[54] The bill is in Engrossed House Bills, HR, DNA. It is printed in the *Senate Legislative Journal* on February 11.

[55] The Senate read this bill on February 11. It was read again on February 12. On February 22 a motion to amend the bill was defeated, and the Senate voted not to read the bill again.

[56] On February 12 this committee was discharged.

[57] On February 22 this committee reported.

A petition of Peter Miller, of Vincent township, Chester county, and State of Pennsylvania, praying compensation for damages sustained in his property, by the army of the United States, during the late war. Also,

The petitions of the ministers and trustees of the Lutheran church, Pikeland township, Chester county, and of the wardens of the Calvinist church, in Vincent township, Chester county, in the State of Pennsylvania, respectively praying compensation for damages done to their churches, by the army of the United States, during the late war.

ORDERED, That the said petitions, together with the petition of the inspectors of New-York, which lay on the table, be referred to the Secretary of the Treasury, with instruction to examine the same, and report his opinion thereupon to the House.

A petition of Ebenezer Stevens, late a lieutenant-colonel in the army of the United States, was presented to the House and read, praying, that the resolution of the late Congress of the twenty-eighth of February, one thousand seven hundred and seventy-nine, granting an extra allowance to a certain description of officers of artillery, may be extended to him. Also,

A petition of John Knight, praying compensation for services rendered to the United States, as surgeon's mate, during the late war.

ORDERED, That the said petitions be referred to the Secretary at War, with instruction to examine the same, and report his opinion thereupon to the House.

The petitions of Thomas Barclay, and of Jacob Winey, on behalf of himself and others, were presented to the House and read, respectively praying that depreciation may be allowed on certain paper money payments, made them by order of the late Congress, for the freight and valuation of two ships, the property of the petitioners, which were chartered for public service, and afterwards taken by the enemy.

ORDERED, That the said petitions be referred to Mr. Clymer, Mr. Smith (of Maryland), and Mr. Partridge, that they do examine the matter thereof, and report the same, with their opinion thereupon, to the House.[58]

A petition of John Tucker, was presented to the House and read, praying compensation for his past services and expences, as clerk to the supreme court of the United States.

ORDERED, That the said petition be referred to the committee of the whole House, to which is committed the bill, providing compensations for clerks, marshals and jurors.[59]

---

[58] On February 19 this committee was discharged, and the petitions were referred to the secretary of the treasury.

[59] On February 28 the Tucker petition was committed. From February 15–18 consideration of the Judicial Officers Bill [HR–126] was postponed as an order of the day. On February 19 it was considered by the COWH.

A petition of David Brubaker, of Lancaster county, in the state of Pennsylvania, was presented to the House and read, praying compensation for a quantity of timber, furnished for the purpose of building stockades, huts, &c. for the use of the British prisoners, during the late war.

ORDERED, That the said petition do lie on the table.

On motion,

ORDERED, That the committee appointed to prepare and bring in a bill or bills, concerning the trade and navigation of the United States, be discharged from further proceeding thereon.

The House proceeded to consider the report of the Secretary of State, on the petition of Andrew Brown; Whereupon,

RESOLVED, That Andrew Brown, or any other printer, be permitted (under the direction of the Secretary of State) to collate with and correct by the original rolls, the laws, resolutions, and treaties of the United States, to be by him printed; and that a certificate of their having been so collated and corrected, be annexed to the said edition. PROVIDED, That such collation and correction be at the expense of the said Andrew Brown, or such other printer, and that the person or persons to be by him or them employed in that service, be approved by the Secretary of State.[60]

ORDERED, That the Clerk of this House do carry the said resolution to the Senate, and desire their concurrence.[61]

Mr. Floyd, from the joint committee for inrolled bills, reported, that the committee had examined an inrolled bill, intituled, "An act to incorporate the subscribers to the bank of the United States,"[62] and had found the same to be truly inrolled: Whereupon,

Mr. Speaker signed the said inrolled bill.[63]

ORDERED, That the Clerk of this House do acquaint the Senate therewith.

Mr. Sherman, from the committee to whom was referred the memorial of the public creditors holding loan-office certificates for money lent to the United States, between September, one thousand seven hundred and seventy-seven, and March, one thousand seven hundred and seventy-eight, made a report, which was read, and ordered to lie on the table.[64]

The Speaker laid before the House a letter from the Secretary of the Treasury, covering his report on the petition of John Hollins, of the town of Balti-

---

[60] A copy of the resolution is in Messages from the House, SR, DNA.

[61] The Senate agreed to this resolution on February 15.

[62] The inspected enrolled bill is in Enrolled Acts, RG 11, DNA. E-23875.

[63] On February 14 this bill was presented to the president.

[64] A copy of the report is in A Record of the Reports of Select Committees, HR, DNA. On February 24 the House resolved not to grant the various petitions from public creditors.

more,[65] referred to him pursuant to an order of this House, of the fourth instant, which was read: Whereupon,

ORDERED, That the petitioner have leave to withdraw his said petition.

A message from the Senate by Mr. Otis their Secretary.

MR. SPEAKER, The Senate have passed a bill, intituled, "An act for the admission of the state of Vermont into this Union;"[66] they have also passed a bill, intituled, "An act regulating the number of Representatives to be chosen by the states of Kentucky and Vermont;"[67] to which bills they desire the concurrence of this House. I am also directed to inform this House, that the President of the United States did, on the fourth instant, affix his signature to an act which originated in the Senate, intituled, "An act declaring the consent of Congress, that a new State be formed within the jurisdiction of the commonwealth of Virginia, and admitted into this Union, by the name of the State of Kentucky." And then he withdrew.

The bill sent from the Senate, intituled, "An act for the admission of the state of Vermont into this Union," was read the first time.

On motion,

The said bill was read the second time, and ordered to be committed to a committee of the whole House on Monday next.[68]

The bill sent from the Senate, intituled, "An act regulating the number of Representatives to be chosen by the states of Kentucky and Vermont," was read the first time.

On motion,

The said bill was read the second time, and ordered to be committed to a committee of the whole House on Monday next.[69]

The House proceeded to consider the amendments agreed to by the committee of the whole House, to the bill to establish offices for the purpose of granting lands within the territories of the United States, and made some progress therein.[70]

---

[65] A copy of the report is in A Record of the Reports of the Secretary of the Treasury, vol. 2, HR, DNA.

[66] The bill is in Engrossed Senate Bills and Resolutions, SR, DNA.

[67] The bill is in Engrossed Senate Bills and Resolutions, SR, DNA. The bill, as introduced in the Senate and passed without amendments, is printed in the *Senate Legislative Journal* on February 11.

[68] On February 14 this bill was considered by the COWH, read again, and agreed to without amendments.

[69] From February 14–18 consideration of this bill was postponed as an order of the day. On February 19 the bill was considered in the COWH, read again, and agreed to.

[70] On February 14 these amendments were considered again.

The several orders of the day were further postponed until Monday next.[71] And then the House adjourned until Monday morning ten o'clock.

MONDAY, FEBRUARY 14, 1791

A message, in writing, was received from the President of the United States, by Mr. Lear his Secretary, as followeth, to wit:

UNITED STATES, February 14th, 1791

GENTLEMEN of the SENATE and HOUSE of REPRESENTATIVES,

SOON after I was called to the administration of the government, I found it important to come to an understanding with the court of London, on several points interesting to the United States; and particularly to know, whether they were disposed to enter into arrangements, by mutual consent, which might fix the commerce between the two nations, on principles of reciprocal advantage. For this purpose, I authorised informal conferences with their ministers; and from these, I do not infer any disposition on their part, to enter into any arrangements merely commercial. I have thought it proper to give you this information, as it might, at some time, have influence on matters under your consideration.

G. WASHINGTON

ORDERED, That the said message do lie on the table.[72]

The several petitions of David Cook, Moses Sanderson, Thomas Haven, Elizabeth Parker, Charles Clingen, William Copeland and others, by Michael Connelly their agent, Mary Ripley, and Stephen Drayton,[73] were presented to the House and read, respectively praying compensation for services rendered or injuries sustained in the service of the United States, during the late war.

ORDERED, That the said petitions be referred to the Secretary at War, with instruction to examine the same, and report his opinion thereupon to the House.[74]

ORDERED, That a bill or bills be brought in to explain so much of the act, intituled, "An act making further provision for the payment of the debts of

---

[71] On this date the House passed the Military Establishment Bill [HR–126A] in secret session. A printed copy of the bill, annotated by the Senate, is in House Bills, SR, DNA. On February 12 the Senate read this bill, which is printed in the *Senate Legislative Journal*. On February 14 the bill was read again and committed. On February 17 the committee reported. The report was considered and the bill amended on February 19. On February 21 the bill was read and agreed to with amendments, which are printed in the *Senate Legislative Journal* on this date.

[72] On February 15 this message was committed.

[73] The Drayton petition is in Petitions and Memorials: Claims, SR, DNA.

[74] On February 22 the secretary of war reported on the petition of David Cook.

the United States," as imposes a duty on imported lead and on calicoes; and that Mr. Madison, Mr. Wadsworth, and Mr. Leonard, do prepare and bring in the same.[75]

The House, according to the order of the day, resolved itself into a committee of the whole House on the bill sent from the Senate, intituled, "An act for the admission of the state of Vermont into this Union;" and after some time spent therein, Mr. Speaker resumed the chair, and Mr. Boudinot reported, that the committee had, according to order, had the said bill under their consideration, and made no amendment thereto.

On motion,

The said bill was read the third time; and on the question that the same do pass,

It was resolved in the affirmative.

ORDERED, That the Clerk of this House do acquaint the Senate therewith.[76]

ORDERED, That a committee be appointed to prepare and bring in a bill or bills, to give effect to the laws of the United States within the state of Vermont; and that Mr. Sedgwick, Mr. Benson, and Mr. Sturges, be of the said committee.[77]

A message from the Senate by Mr. Otis their Secretary.

MR. SPEAKER,   The Senate have passed the bill, intituled, "An act repealing, after the last day of June next, the duties heretofore laid upon distilled spirits imported from abroad, and laying others in their stead; and also upon spirits distilled within the United States, and for appropriating the same," with several amendments, to which they desire the concurrence of this House.[78]   And then he withdrew.

Mr. Floyd, from the joint committee for inrolled bills, reported, that the committee did, this day, wait on the President of the United States, and present, for his approbation, an inrolled bill, intituled, "An act to incorporate the subscribers to the bank of the United States."[79]

A message from the Senate by Mr. Otis their Secretary.

---

[75] On February 21 this committee presented a Ways and Means Bill [HR–129], which was read twice.

[76] On February 16 this bill was signed by the speaker and the vice president.

[77] On February 17 this committee presented the Vermont Bill [HR–128], which was read twice.

[78] The Senate committee report on this bill, with amendments, is in Various Select Committee Reports, SR, DNA. Annotations on the printed bill in American Imprints, 1791 folio, U.S. Laws and Statutes, RBkRm, DLC, correspond to some Senate actions in regard to amendments. The amendments are printed in the *Senate Legislative Journal* on February 12. On February 15 the Senate amendments, together with the bill, were ordered committed to the COWH.

[79] On February 25 the president signed this bill. On the same day the bill is printed in the *Senate Legislative Journal*.

MR. SPEAKER, The Senate have passed the bill, intituled, "An act to continue in force, for a limited time, an act passed at the first session of Congress, intituled, 'An act to regulate processes in the courts of the United States.' "[80] And then he withdrew.

The House resumed the consideration of the amendments reported from the committee of the whole House, to the bill to establish offices for the purpose of granting lands within the territories of the United States, and made a farther progress therein.[81]

The several orders of the day were farther postponed until to-morrow.

And then the House adjourned until to-morrow morning ten o'clock.

TUESDAY, FEBRUARY 15, 1791

Another member, to wit; Thomas Sumter, from South-Carolina, appeared and took his seat in the House.

The several petitions of Nathan Stacey and others, Esther Mix, Elizabeth Kuhn, and Ann Harold, were presented to the House and read, respectively praying compensation for services rendered to the United States, during the late war.

ORDERED, That the said petitions be referred to the Secretary at War, with instruction to examine the same, and report his opinion thereupon to the House.

The Speaker laid before the House a letter from the Secretary at War, accompanying his reports on the several petitions of Joseph Anderson, Abraham Hunt, Samuel Sheppard, George Glentworth, Anne Roberts, the orphan children of Andrew Leitch, the orphan children of William White, Michael G. Houdin, Samuel Buffinton attorney of Frances S. Debevere, Moses Rawlings, Joseph Pannill, Thomas McIntire, Timothy Mix, and Abel Turney, which were read, and ordered to lie on the table.[82]

The House proceeded to consider the report of the committee to whom was referred the petition of Joshua Barney: Whereupon,

---

[80] On February 16 the speaker and the vice president signed this bill.

[81] On February 15 the COWH's amendments plus other amendments to this bill were agreed to.

[82] Copies of all of these reports are in A Record of the Reports of the Secretary of War, vol. 2, HR, DNA. Transcripts of two of these reports, one on Roberts, Leitch, and White, and the other on Buffinton, are in Reports and Communications from the Secretary of War, HR, DNA. These copies were probably made by ASP. On February 26 all of these reports, except the first four and the one on the petition of Moses Rawlings, were considered, and the committee on widows, orphans, and invalids was instructed to include all of these people, except Michael Houdin, in the bill they were writing. A motion on the Houdin petition was disagreed to on the same day.

ORDERED, That a committee be appointed to prepare and bring in a bill or bills to authorize the payment of   dollars to captain Barney for expenses incurred in obtaining his release from captivity, and in returning to the United States; and that Mr. Fitzsimons, Mr. Smith (of Maryland), Mr. Trumbull, Mr. Goodhue, and Mr. Cadwalader, be of the said committee.[83]

The Speaker laid before the House a letter from the Secretary of the Treasury, covering his report respecting farther compensation to commissioners of the several loan-offices, made pursuant to an order of the House of the thirteenth of January last; which was read, and ordered to lie on the table.[84]

ORDERED, That Mr. Stone have leave to be absent from the service of this House from Monday next until the end of the session.

On motion,

ORDERED, That the written message of yesterday, from the President of the United States, be referred to Mr. Goodhue, Mr. Madison, Mr. Fitzsimons, Mr. Bourn, Mr. Laurance, Mr. Vining, and Mr. Smith (of South-Carolina).[85]

A message from the Senate by Mr. Otis their Secretary.

MR. SPEAKER, The Senate have agreed to the resolution for authorizing Andrew Brown, or any other printer, to collate with and correct by the original rolls, the laws, resolutions and treaties of the United States, for the purpose of publishing new editions thereof.[86]   And then he withdrew.

On motion,

ORDERED, That the amendments proposed by the Senate to the bill, intituled, "An act repealing, after the last day of June next, the duties heretofore laid upon distilled spirits imported from abroad, and laying others in their stead; and also upon spirits distilled within the United States, and for appropriating the same," together with the said bill, be committed to a committee of the whole House to-morrow.[87]

The Speaker laid before the House a letter from the Secretary of the Treasury, accompanied with a return of the exports of the United States between

---

[83] On February 16 this committee presented the Barney Bill [HR–127], which was read twice.

[84] A copy of the report is in A Record of the Reports of the Secretary of the Treasury, vol. 2, HR, DNA. On February 23 a committee was appointed to prepare a bill on this report.

[85] On February 21 this committee reported on the president's message, which concerned commercial relations with Great Britain.

[86] On February 16 this resolution was signed by the speaker and the vice president.

[87] Consideration of this bill was postponed as an order of the day on February 16. On February 17 the COWH was discharged from considering the Senate amendments, and the House agreed to some of them and disagreed to others.

the month of August, one thousand seven hundred and eighty-nine, and the thirtieth of September, one thousand seven hundred and ninety, which were read and ordered to lie on the table.[88]

The House resumed the consideration of the amendments made by the committee of the whole House, to the bill to establish offices for the purpose of granting lands within the territories of the United States; and having gone through and agreed to the same, and further amended the said bill at the Clerk's table,

A motion was made, and the question being put, to add to the end of the second section the following proviso,

Provided always, That any purchaser of lands, when the payment thereof shall be due, may proffer in payment any of the certificates of the funded debt of the United States, at the same rates as the Treasurer shall have allowed for such certificates respectively, in the last purchase which he shall have made thereof, prior to such payment;

It was resolved in the affirmative— $\begin{cases} \text{Ayes} & 34 \\ \text{Noes} & 21 \end{cases}$

The ayes and noes being demanded by one fifth of the members present; Those who voted in the affirmative, are,

Fisher Ames	Daniel Hiester
John Baptista Ashe	James Jackson
Abraham Baldwin	Richard Bland Lee
Timothy Bloodworth	Samuel Livermore
Elias Boudinot	James Madison, junior
Benjamin Bourn	George Mathews
Aedanus Burke	Andrew Moore
Lambert Cadwalader	John Sevier
Daniel Carroll	Roger Sherman
Thomas Fitzsimons	Thomas Sinnickson
George Gale	William Smith (of Maryland)
Elbridge Gerry	Thomas Sumter
Nicholas Gilman	George Thatcher
Benjamin Goodhue	Thomas Tudor Tucker
Samuel Griffin	Alexander White
William B. Giles	Hugh Williamson and
John Hathorn	Henry Wynkoop

---

[88] The report is in Reports and Communications from the Secretary of the Treasury, HR, DNA. The letter with an abbreviated version of the report is E–23927. On February 19 this report was committed.

Those who voted in the negative, are,

Egbert Benson

John Brown

George Clymer

Benjamin Contee

William Floyd

Abiel Foster

Thomas Hartley

Benjamin Huntington

John Laurance

George Leonard

Peter Muhlenberg

George Partridge

Jeremiah Van Rensselaer

Thomas Scott

Theodore Sedgwick

Joshua Seney

Peter Silvester

William Smith (of South-Carolina)

Michael Jenifer Stone

Jonathan Trumbull and

John Vining

ORDERED, That the said bill, with the amendments, be engrossed, and read the third time to-morrow.[89]

The several orders of the day were further postponed until to-morrow.

And then the House adjourned until to-morrow morning eleven o'clock.

WEDNESDAY, FEBRUARY 16, 1791

The several petitions of Jacob Garigues, Ludwig Kuhn, by Levi Rubin his attorney, and of Joseph Ball, acting executor of John Ball, deceased, and Isaac Ledyard, were presented to the House and read, praying the liquidation and settlement of claims against the United States.

ORDERED, That the said petitions be referred to the Secretary of the Treasury, with instruction to examine the same, and report his opinion thereupon to the House.

A petition of Tarlton Woodson, was presented to the House and read, praying to be allowed the commutation of half pay, in consideration of services rendered in the army of the United States, during the late war; and also the payment of a balance due to him on the public books. Also,

A petition of Reuben Spencer, praying an addition to his pension as a disabled soldier in the service of the United States, during the late war.

ORDERED, That the said petitions be referred to the Secretary at War, with instruction to examine the same, and report his opinion thereupon to the House.

The Speaker laid before the House a letter from the Secretary at War, accompanying his reports on the petitions of John Chadwick, Nicholas Haugen-

---

[89] On February 16 the Land Office Bill [HR-114] was read again, agreed to, and sent to the Senate.

dobler, Nathaniel Alexander, Daniel Merrill for himself and others, Joseph Hugg, John Post, Joshua Orne for himself and others, Lewis Prahl, Stephen Clapp, Josiah Simpson attorney for Dorcas Frost and others, Nathaniel Porter, Lawrence Allman, James Easton, Samuel Kearsley, William W. Smith, John Keehmle, and John Linn, which were read, and ordered to lie on the table.[90]

Mr. Madison, from the committee appointed to enquire into the administration of the late Superintendant of Finance, made a report,[91] which was read, and ordered to lie on the table.

Mr. Fitzsimons, from the committee appointed, presented, according to order, a bill to compensate Joshua Barney, which was received and read the first time.

On motion,

The said bill was read the second time, and ordered to be committed to a committee of the whole House to-morrow.[92]

A petition of Nicholas Ferdinand Westfall, was presented to the House and read, praying a gratuity of lands and other advantages, promised by the late Congress to those who should quit the British service, in consideration of his having left that service and joined the American army, during the late war.

ORDERED, That the said petition be referred to the Secretary of State, with instruction to examine the same, and report his opinion thereupon to the House.[93]

A petition of sundry merchants of the city of Philadelphia, was presented to the House and read, stating sundry reasons in opposition to a petition of sundry other merchants of the said city, trading to India and China, praying an increase of the duties on all China and East-India goods, imported into the United States, from Europe.

ORDERED, That the said petition do lie on the table.

An engrossed bill, to establish offices for the purpose of granting lands within the territories of the United States, was read the third time, and the blanks therein filled up.

---

[90] Copies of these reports are in A Record of the Reports of the Secretary of War, vol. 2, HR, DNA. The report on William W. Smith and John Keehmle is actually a report on the petition of the surgeons and surgeons' mates, which was received in the House on January 19.

[91] A copy of the report is in A Record of the Reports of Select Committees, HR, DNA. A copy, probably made by ASP, is in Various Select Committees, HR, DNA. This committee is the committee on the petition of Robert Morris, introduced on February 8, 1790.

[92] From February 17–20 consideration of this bill was postponed as an order of the day. On February 21 the COWH reported an amendment, which was agreed to. The bill was then disagreed to by the House.

[93] On February 25 the secretary reported on the petition.

RESOLVED, That the said bill do pass, and that the title be, "An act to establish offices for the purpose of granting lands, within the territories of the United States."[94]

ORDERED, That the Clerk of this House do carry the said bill to the Senate, and desire their concurrence.[95]

Mr. Floyd, from the joint committee for inrolled bills, reported, that the committee had examined two inrolled bills, one intituled, "An act for the admission of the State of Vermont into this Union,"[96] the other, intituled, "An act to continue in force for a limited time, an act passed at the first session of Congress, intituled, 'An act to regulate processes in the courts of the United States:' "[97] Also,

An inrolled resolve, "Authorizing Andrew Brown, or any other printer, to collate with, and correct by the original rolls, the laws, resolutions and treaties of the United States, for the purpose of publishing new editions thereof;"[98] and had found them to be truly inrolled: Whereupon,

Mr. Speaker signed the said inrolled bills and resolve.[99]

ORDERED, That the Clerk of this House do acquaint the Senate therewith.

The House proceeded to consider the report of the committee, to whom was referred the petition of George Gibson; and the first part of the said report, in the words following, to wit; "That the petitioner, George Gibson is, in justice, entitled to the sum of   dollars from the United States, as a commutation for half pay of a continental colonel, agreeably to former resolutions of Congress;" was on the question put thereupon, disagreed to by the House.[100]

An adjournment being then called for,

The several orders of the day were further postponed until to-morrow.

And then the House adjourned until to-morrow morning eleven o'clock.

---

[94] The bill is in Engrossed House Bills, HR, DNA. It is printed in the *Senate Legislative Journal* on February 16. E–46310.

[95] On February 16 the Senate read this bill. The bill was considered on February 17, 18, and 21. It was committed on February 21, and on February 26 the committee reported that the bill should be postponed until the next Congress. This report was postponed, and the bill was recommitted. On March 1 this committee presented a resolution, which was agreed to. The resolution is printed in the *Senate Legislative Journal.* The Senate then agreed to postpone consideration of the Land Office Bill [HR–114] until the next session. The House was notified of these actions on March 2, and on the same day the resolution was agreed to with an amendment.

[96] The inspected enrolled bill is in Enrolled Acts, RG 11, DNA. E–23856.

[97] The inspected enrolled bill is in Enrolled Acts, RG 11, DNA. E–23872.

[98] The inspected enrolled resolution is in Enrolled Acts, RG 11, DNA. E–23878.

[99] On February 17 the bills and resolution were presented to the president.

[100] On February 26 the second part of the committee's report was agreed to, and a committee was appointed to bring in a bill.

THURSDAY, FEBRUARY 17, 1791

Mr. Sedgwick, from the committee appointed, presented, according to order, a bill giving effect to the laws of the United States within the State of Vermont, which was received and read the first time.

On motion,

The said bill was read the second time, and ordered to be committed to a committee of the whole House, to-morrow.[101]

A petition of John Nicholason, was presented to the House and read, praying compensation for services rendered to the United States, during the late war, as an Indian interpreter and guide.

ORDERED, That the said petition be referred to the Secretary of the Treasury, with instruction to examine the same, and report his opinion thereupon to the House.

Mr. Floyd, from the joint committee for inrolled bills, reported, that the committee did, this day, wait on the President of the United States, and present for his approbation, two inrolled bills, to wit; one intituled, "An act for the admission of the state of Vermont into this Union;" the other intituled, "An act to continue in force, for a limited time, an act passed at the first session of Congress, intituled, 'An act to regulate processes in the courts of the United States;'" also, an inrolled resolve, "To authorize Andrew Brown, or any-other printer, to collate with, and correct by the original rolls, the laws, resolutions and treaties of the United States, for the purpose of publishing new editions thereof."[102]

On motion,

ORDERED, That the committee of the whole House be discharged from further proceeding on the amendments proposed by the Senate to the bill, intituled, "An act repealing, after the last day of June next, the duties heretofore laid upon distilled spirits imported from abroad, and laying others in their stead; and also upon spirits distilled within the United States, and for appropriating the same."

The House then proceeded to consider the amendments to the said bill: Whereupon,

Some were agreed to, others amended and agreed to, and others disagreed to.

ORDERED, That the farther consideration of the said amendments be postponed until to-morrow.[103]

---

[101] On February 18 consideration of this bill was postponed as an order of the day. On February 19 an amendment proposed by the COWH was agreed to by the House.
[102] On February 18 the president signed the bills and resolution.
[103] On February 18 the House further considered the Senate amendments.

The several orders of the day were further postponed until to-morrow. And then the House adjourned until to-morrow morning eleven o'clock.

FRIDAY, FEBRUARY 18, 1791

A message was received from the President of the United States, by Mr. Lear his Secretary, notifying that the President did, this day, approve and sign an act, intituled, "An act to continue in force, for a limited time, an act passed at the first session of Congress, intituled, 'An act to regulate processes in the courts of the United States;'" also, an inrolled resolve, to authorize Andrew Brown, or any other printer, to collate with, and correct by the original rolls, the laws, resolutions and treaties of the United States, for the purpose of publishing new editions thereof.[104] The said messenger also delivered in a written message from the President, as followeth:

UNITED STATES, February 18th, 1791
GENTLEMEN of the SENATE and HOUSE of REPRESENTATIVES,

I HAVE received from the Secretary of State, a report on the proceedings of the Governor of the North-Western Territory, at Kaskaskia, Kahokia, and Prairie, under the resolution of Congress, of August twenty-ninth, one thousand seven hundred and eighty-eight, which containing matter proper for your consideration, I lay the same before you.

GEORGE WASHINGTON[105]

The said written message, and the report therein referred to, were read, and ordered to lie on the table.

ORDERED, That the Secretary at War be discharged from further proceeding on the petition of Peter Shaffner, referred to him by an order of this House of the eighth instant; and that the petitioner have leave to withdraw his said petition.

A petition of Charles McClane, was presented to the House and read, praying to be placed on the list of pensioners, in consideration of wounds received in the service of the United States, during the late war. Also,

A petition of Rosina Jones, widow of Abel Jones, deceased, praying that the allowance granted to the widows of those who died in the service of the United States, during the late war, may be extended to her.

ORDERED, That the said petitions be referred to the Secretary at War, with

---

[104] A copy of the message is in Committee on Enrolled Bills, SR, DNA.

[105] The message and report with enclosures are in President's Messages: Transmitting reports from the Secretary of State, SR, DNA. A copy of the report to the president is in A Record of the Reports of the Secretary of State, vol. 1, HR, DNA.

instruction to examine the same, and report his opinion thereupon to the House.

A message from the Senate by Mr. Otis their Secretary.

MR. SPEAKER, I am directed to inform this House, that the President of the United States did, this day, approve and sign, an act which originated in the Senate, intituled, "An act for the admission of the State of Vermont into this Union." And then he withdrew.

The House resumed the consideration of the amendments proposed by the Senate, to the bill, intituled, "An act repealing, after the last day of June next, the duties heretofore laid upon distilled spirits imported from abroad, and laying others in their stead; and also upon spirits distilled within the United States, and for appropriating the same:" Whereupon,

The amendment to the sixty-first section, for striking out the words *"any justice of the peace, or court of any state of competent jurisdiction;"* and also the proviso, and to substitute the word *"the,"* in lieu of the words first stricken out, being read,

A motion was made, and the question being put, to amend the said amendment, by striking out the whole of the said sixty-first section, in the words following, to wit;

And be it further enacted, That the prosecution for all fines, penalties and forfeitures incurred by force of this act, and for all duties payable in virtue thereof, and which shall not be duly paid, shall and may be had before any justice of the peace, or court of any state of competent jurisdiction, or court of the United States, of the district in which the cause of action shall arise, with an appeal as in other cases: Provided, That where the cause of action shall exceed in value fifty dollars, the same shall not be cognizable before a justice of the peace only.

It was resolved in the affirmative.

And then the main question being put, "That the House do agree to the said amendment of the Senate, as now amended?"

It was resolved in the affirmative— $\begin{cases} \text{AYES} & 35 \\ \text{NOES} & 21 \end{cases}$

The ayes and noes being demanded by one fifth of the members present;

Those who voted in the affirmative, are,

Fisher Ames	Lambert Cadwalader
Abraham Baldwin	Daniel Carroll
Egbert Benson	George Clymer
Benjamin Bourn	Benjamin Contee

Thomas Fitzsimons
Abiel Foster
George Gale
Elbridge Gerry
Nicholas Gilman
Benjamin Goodhue
Samuel Griffin
William B. Giles
Benjamin Huntington
John Laurance
Richard Bland Lee
George Leonard
James Madison, junior
James Schureman

Theodore Sedgwick
Joshua Seney
John Sevier
Roger Sherman
Peter Silvester
Thomas Sinnickson
William Smith (of Maryland)
William Smith (of South-Carolina)
Jonathan Sturges
Thomas Sumter
Jonathan Trumbull
Jeremiah Wadsworth and
Henry Wynkoop

Those who voted in the negative, are,

John Baptista Ashe
Timothy Bloodworth
Elias Boudinot
Aedanus Burke
William Floyd
Thomas Hartley
John Hathorn
Daniel Hiester
Samuel Livermore
George Mathews
Andrew Moore

Peter Muhlenberg
Josiah Parker
George Partridge
Jeremiah Van Rensselaer
Thomas Scott
John Steele
George Thatcher
Thomas Tudor Tucker
Alexander White and
Hugh Williamson

And then the House having proceeded further in the consideration of the Senate's amendments, an adjournment was called for:[106]   Whereupon,

The several orders of the day were further postponed until to-morrow.

And then the House adjourned until to-morrow morning eleven o'clock.

SATURDAY, FEBRUARY 19, 1791

A petition of Valentine Wizick, was presented to the House and read, praying compensation for military services rendered to the United States, during the late war.

ORDERED, That the said petition be referred to the Secretary at War, with

---

[106] On February 19 the House further considered the Senate amendments to the Duties on Distilled Spirits Bill [HR–110], and the Senate was notified of the House actions on their amendments.

instruction to examine the same, and report his opinion thereupon to the House.

A petition of Joseph Tatlow, was presented to the House and read, praying compensation for the hire and valuation of a sloop which was impressed from him for the service of the United States, during the late war.[107]   Also,

A petition of Benjamin Fuller, praying compensation for injuries done to his property by the army of the United States, during the late war.   Also,

A petition of Coningham, Nesbitt and Company, and James Crawford, of the city of Philadelphia, praying to be relieved against the payment of second tonnage on certain vessels, the double entry of which was occasioned by the mistake of the deputy-collector at Newcastle.   Also,

A petition of Frederick W. Starman, and sundry other persons, holding certificates of the registered debt of the United States, which have not been duly transferred to them agreeable to the regulations of the treasury, praying to be permitted to deliver in the said certificates, and to receive others in their own names for the amount thereof.

ORDERED, That the said petitions be referred to the Secretary of the Treasury, with instruction to examine the same, and report his opinion thereupon to the House.

ORDERED, That the committee to whom were referred the petitions of Jacob Winey, and Thomas Barclay, be discharged from further proceeding thereon; and that the said petitions be referred to the Secretary of the Treasury, with instruction to examine the same, and report his opinion thereupon to the House.

ORDERED, That the return of the Secretary of the Treasury, of the amount of exports of the United States, for one year, made to this House on Tuesday last, be committed to Mr. Carroll, Mr. Bourn, and Mr. Sedgwick.[108]

The House, according to the order of the day, resolved itself into a committee of the whole House, on the bill for giving effect to the laws of the United States, within the state of Vermont; and after some time spent therein, Mr. Speaker resumed the chair, and Mr. Boudinot reported, that the committee had, according to order, had the said bill under consideration, and made an amendment thereto; which he delivered in at the Clerk's table, where the same was twice read, and agreed to by the House.

ORDERED, That the said bill, with the amendment, be engrossed, and read the third time on Monday next.[109]

The House, according to the order of the day, resolved itself into a com-

---

[107] The petition is in Petitions and Memorials: Claims, SR, DNA.

[108] On February 24 this committee made a report, which is printed in the Journal. It was then agreed to, and the secretary of the treasury was ordered to report any additions to the report.

[109] On February 21 this bill was read again, agreed to, and sent to the Senate.

mittee of the whole House, on the bill sent from the Senate, regulating the number of Representatives to be chosen by the states of Kentucky and Vermont; and after some time spent therein, Mr. Speaker resumed the chair, and Mr. Boudinot reported, that the committee had, according to order, had the said bill under consideration, and made no amendment thereto.

On motion,

The said bill was read the third time; and the question being put that the same do pass,

It was resolved in the affirmative.

ORDERED, That the Clerk of this House do acquaint the Senate therewith.[110]

The House, according to the order of the day, resolved itself into a committee of the whole House, on the bill providing compensations for clerks, marshals and jurors; and after some time spent therein, Mr. Speaker resumed the chair, and Mr. Boudinot reported, that the committee had, according to order, had the said bill under consideration, and made some progress therein.

RESOLVED, That this House will, on Monday next, again resolve itself into a committee of the whole House on the said bill.[111]

The House resumed the consideration of the amendments proposed by the Senate to the bill, "repealing, after the last day of June next, the duties heretofore laid upon distilled spirits imported from abroad, and laying others in their stead; and also upon spirits distilled within the United States, and for appropriating the same:" Whereupon,

A motion was made; and the question being put to amend the section proposed by the Senate to be inserted in the said bill by way of amendment, after the sixty-first section, by striking out the following words, "five per cent. of the said product computed throughout the United States; and such allowances shall continue to be paid until altered by law;" and inserting in lieu thereof the words, "seven per cent. of the whole product of the duties arising from the spirits distilled within the United States; and such allowances shall continue to be paid for the space of two years, unless sooner altered by law;"

It was resolved in the affirmative— $\begin{cases} \text{AYES} & 34 \\ \text{NOES} & 20 \end{cases}$

The ayes and noes being demanded by one fifth of the members present;

Those who voted in the affirmative, are,

John Baptista Ashe	Benjamin Bourn
Abraham Baldwin	John Brown
Timothy Bloodworth	Aedanus Burke
Elias Boudinot	Daniel Carroll

---

[110] On February 22 this bill was signed by the speaker.

[111] On February 21 the House agreed to an amendment to this bill, and the bill was recommitted.

Benjamin Contee
William Floyd
Nicholas Gilman
Samuel Griffin
Jonathan Grout
William B. Giles
Thomas Hartley
John Hathorn
Daniel Hiester
James Jackson
Richard Bland Lee
Samuel Livermore
George Mathews

Andrew Moore
Peter Muhlenberg
Josiah Parker
Jeremiah Van Rensselaer
Thomas Scott
Joshua Seney
John Sevier
Peter Silvester
William Smith (of Maryland)
Thomas Sumter
Thomas Tudor Tucker
John Vining and
Alexander White

Those who voted in the negative, are,

Fisher Ames
Egbert Benson
Lambert Cadwalader
George Clymer
Thomas Fitzsimons
Abiel Foster
Elbridge Gerry
Benjamin Goodhue
Benjamin Huntington
John Laurance

George Leonard
George Partridge
James Schureman
Roger Sherman
Thomas Sinnickson
William Smith (of South-Carolina)
Jonathan Sturges
George Thatcher
Jonathan Trumbull and
Henry Wynkoop

And then the main question being put, "That the House do agree to the said amendment of the Senate, as now amended?"

It was resolved in the affirmative.

RESOLVED, That this House doth agree to all the other amendments proposed by the Senate to the said bill.

ORDERED, That the Clerk of this House do acquaint the Senate therewith.[112]

The several orders of the day were further postponed until Monday next.

And then the House adjourned until Monday morning eleven o'clock.

MONDAY, FEBRUARY 21, 1791

The Speaker laid before the House, a letter from the Secretary at War, accompanying his report on the several petitions of James Alexander, Wil-

---

[112] On February 22 the House was notified of further Senate actions on this bill and considered the Senate message.

liam Paine, Simon Summers, Jeremiah Ocain, Benoni Shipman, Robert King, Lemuel Sherman,[113] John Hodge, Alexander Neilson, John Falconer, and sundry inhabitants of West-Chester county, in the state of New-York, John Baylor, executor of colonel George Baylor, deceased, Stephen Steward, junior, executor of the late colonel John Steward, deceased, and Anthony Walton White: which were read, and ordered to lie on the table.[114]

An engrossed bill, giving effect to the laws of the United States within the State of Vermont, was read the third time, and the blanks therein filled up.

RESOLVED, That the said bill do pass, and that the title be, "An act giving effect to the laws of the United States, within the state of Vermont."

ORDERED, That the Clerk of this House do carry the said bill to the Senate, and desire their concurrence.[115]

Mr. Goodhue, from the committee to whom was referred the written message from the President of the United States, of the fourteenth instant, made a report, which was read, and ordered to lie on the table.[116]

The House, according to the order of the day, again resolved itself into a committee of the whole House, on the bill providing compensations for clerks, marshals and jurors; and after some time spent therein, Mr. Speaker resumed the chair, and Mr. Boudinot reported, that the committee had, according to order, again had the said bill under consideration, and made an amendment thereto, which he delivered in at the Clerk's table, where the same was twice read, and agreed to by the House.

ORDERED, That the said bill, together with the amendment, be re-committed to Mr. Sherman, Mr. Benson, Mr. Seney, Mr. White, and Mr. Livermore.[117]

Mr. Madison, from the committee appointed, presented, according to order, a bill to explain and amend the act, intituled, "An act making further provision for the payment of the debts of the United States;" which was received, and read the first time.

On motion,

---

[113] On February 26 the King and Sherman petitions were referred to the committee to prepare the Widows, Orphans, and Invalids Bill [HR–139].

[114] Copies of all of these reports are in A Record of the Reports of the Secretary of War, vol. 2, HR, DNA.

[115] On February 21 the Senate read this bill. It is printed in the *Senate Legislative Journal* on this date. On February 22 the Senate read the bill again and amended it, and on February 23 it was read again and agreed to with one amendment, which is printed in the *Senate Legislative Journal.*

[116] A copy of the report is in A Record of the Reports of Select Committees, HR, DNA. The president's message concerned commercial relations with Great Britain. On February 23 the committee's report was considered and referred to the secretary of state.

[117] On February 24 this committee presented a new Judicial Officers Bill [HR–133], which was read twice.

The said bill was read the second time, and ordered to be engrossed, and read the third time to-morrow.[118]

The House, according to the order of the day, resolved itself into a committee of the whole House, on the bill to compensate Joshua Barney; and after some time spent therein, Mr. Speaker resumed the chair, and Mr. Boudinot reported, that the committee had, according to order, had the said bill under consideration, and made an amendment thereto, which he delivered in at the Clerk's table, where the same was twice read, and agreed to by the House.

And then the question being put, that the said bill, with the amendment, be engrossed, and read the third time;

It passed in the negative.

And so the bill was rejected.

The several orders of the day were further postponed until to-morrow.[119]

And then the House adjourned until to-morrow morning eleven o'clock.

TUESDAY, FEBRUARY 22, 1791

The Speaker laid before the House a letter from the Secretary at War, accompanying his reports on the several petitions of Richard Lloyd, Francis Taylor, Ebenezer A. Smith, James Norris, William Cottle, and David Cook, which were read, and ordered to lie on the table.[120]

An engrossed bill to explain and amend the act making further provision for the payment of the debts of the United States, was read the third time.

RESOLVED, That the said bill do pass, and that the title be, "An act to explain and amend the act making further provision for the payment of the debts of the United States."

ORDERED, That the Clerk of this House do carry the said bill to the Senate, and desire their concurrence.[121]

Mr. Sedgwick, from the committee appointed, presented, according to order, a bill making further provision for the collection of the duties imposed on teas; which was received, and read the first time.

---

[118] On February 22 this bill was read again, agreed to, and sent to the Senate.

[119] On this date the Senate passed the Military Establishment Bill [HR–126A] with amendments. Senate amendments are filed with the bill in House Bills, SR, DNA. They are printed in the *Senate Legislative Journal* on February 21. On February 26 the House agreed to the Senate amendments with amendments. The House amendments are printed in the *Senate Legislative Journal* on February 28.

[120] Copies of these reports are in A Record of the Reports of the Secretary of War, vol. 2, HR, DNA. On February 26 the report on David Cook's petition was considered, and a committee to prepare a bill was appointed.

[121] On February 22 the Senate read this bill. It is printed in the *Senate Legislative Journal* on that date. It was read again on February 23 and read and agreed to on February 24.

On motion,

The said bill was read the second time, and ordered to be committed to a committee of the whole House to-morrow.[122]

Mr. Boudinot, from the committee appointed, presented, according to order, a bill, supplementary to the act establishing the treasury department; which was received, and read the first time.

On motion,

The said bill was read the second time, and ordered to be committed to a committee of the whole House to-morrow.[123]

Mr. Fitzsimons, from the committee appointed to report, "whether any farther provision is necessary to secure the due accounting for the monies expended in the department of war," made a report,[124] which was read, and ordered to lie on the table.

The House, according to the order of the day, resolved itself into a committee of the whole House, on the bill, supplementary to the act, intituled, "An act to incorporate the subscribers to the bank of the United States;" and after some time spent therein, Mr. Speaker resumed the chair, and Mr. Boudinot reported, that the committee had, according to order, had the said bill under consideration, and made several amendments thereto, which he delivered in at the Clerk's table, where the same were severally twice read, and agreed to by the House.

ORDERED, That the said bill, with the amendments, be engrossed, and read the third time to-morrow.[125]

A message from the Senate by Mr. Otis their Secretary.

MR. SPEAKER, The Senate do recede from their amendment disagreed to by this House, to the bill, intituled, "An act repealing, after the last day of June next, the duties heretofore laid upon distilled spirits imported from abroad, and laying others in their stead; and also upon spirits distilled within the United States, and for appropriating the same:" And do agree to all the amendments proposed by this House, to their other amendments to the said bill, with an amendment to the amendment to the amendment which is proposed to follow the sixty-first section, by striking out the words *"for the space of two years, unless sooner altered by law,"* in the amendment to the amendment, and substituting in lieu thereof, the words, *"until altered by law."* The

---

[122] From February 23 through March 1 consideration of this bill was postponed as an order of the day. On March 2 this bill was considered in the COWH, amended, read again, agreed to, and sent to the Senate.

[123] On February 23 consideration of this bill was postponed as an order of the day. On February 24 amendments presented by the COWH were agreed to.

[124] A copy of the report is in A Record of the Reports of Select Committees, HR, DNA.

[125] On February 23 this bill was read again, agreed to, and sent to the Senate.

Senate have also agreed to some farther amendments to the said bill, to which they desire the concurrence of this House. And then he withdrew.

The House proceeded to consider the said message: Whereupon,

RESOLVED, That this House doth disagree to the amendment to the amendment to the amendment, which is proposed to follow the sixty-first section of the before mentioned bill, and doth insist on the amendment to the said amendment, as originally proposed on the part of this House. AYES 36: NOES 24.

The ayes and noes being demanded by one fifth of the members present; Those who voted in the affirmative, are,

John Baptista Ashe	Samuel Livermore
Abraham Baldwin	James Madison, junior
Timothy Bloodworth	George Mathews
Elias Boudinot	Andrew Moore
Benjamin Bourn	Peter Muhlenberg
John Brown	Josiah Parker
Aedanus Burke	Jeremiah Van Rensselaer
Daniel Carroll	Thomas Scott
Benjamin Contee	Joshua Seney
William Floyd	Peter Silvester
Samuel Griffin	William Smith (of Maryland)
Jonathan Grout	John Steele
William B. Giles	Michael Jenifer Stone
Thomas Hartley	Thomas Sumter
John Hathorn	Thomas Tudor Tucker
Daniel Hiester	John Vining
James Jackson	Alexander White and
Richard Bland Lee	Hugh Williamson

Those who voted in the negative, are,

Fisher Ames	Benjamin Huntington
Egbert Benson	John Laurance
Lambert Cadwalader	George Leonard
George Clymer	George Partridge
Thomas Fitzsimons	James Schureman
Abiel Foster	Theodore Sedgwick
George Gale	John Sevier
Elbridge Gerry	Roger Sherman
Benjamin Goodhue	Thomas Sinnickson

William Smith (of South-   Jonathan Trumbull
    Carolina)   Jeremiah Wadsworth and
Jonathan Sturges   Henry Wynkoop
George Thatcher

RESOLVED, That this House doth agree to the farther amendments proposed by the Senate, to the said bill.

ORDERED, That the Clerk of this House do acquaint the Senate therewith.[126]

Mr. Floyd, from the joint committee for inrolled bills, reported, that the committee had examined an inrolled bill, intituled, "An act regulating the number of Representatives to be chosen by the states of Kentucky and Vermont,"[127] and had found the same to be truly inrolled: Whereupon,

Mr. Speaker signed the said inrolled bill.[128]

ORDERED, That the Clerk of this House do acquaint the Senate therewith.

A message from the Senate by Mr. Otis their Secretary.

MR. SPEAKER,   I am directed to inform this House, that the Senate have resolved that the bill sent from this House, intituled, "An act to alter the time of the next meeting of Congress," do not pass to the third reading.[129] They have also agreed to a resolution, that the President of the United States be requested to cause to be communicated to the National Assembly of France, the peculiar sensibility of Congress to the tribute paid to the memory of Benjamin Franklin, by the enlightened and free Representatives of a great nation, in their decree of the eleventh of June, seventeen hundred and ninety; to which they desire the concurrence of this House.[130]   And then he withdrew.

The several orders of the day were further postponed until to-morrow.

And then the House adjourned until to-morrow morning eleven o'clock.

WEDNESDAY, FEBRUARY 23, 1791

An engrossed bill supplementary to the act, intituled, "An act to incorporate the subscribers to the bank of the United States," was read the third time.

---

[126] On February 23 the Senate requested a conference on the Duties on Distilled Spirits Bill [HR–110], and the House agreed.

[127] The inspected enrolled bill is in Enrolled Acts, RG 11, DNA. E–23863.

[128] On February 23 the vice president signed this bill, and it was presented to the president on February 24.

[129] On February 23 a committee was appointed and presented a Time of Meeting Bill [HR–132], which was read twice.

[130] On February 23 the House agreed to this resolution.

RESOLVED, That the said bill do pass; and that the title be, "An act supplementary to the act, intituled, 'An act to incorporate the subscribers to the bank of the United States.'"

ORDERED, That the Clerk of this House do carry the said bill to the Senate, and desire their concurrence.[131]

The House proceeded to consider the resolution sent from the Senate yesterday; and the same being twice read, was agreed to as followeth:

RESOLVED, by the Senate and House of Representatives of the United States of America in Congress assembled, That the President of the United States be requested to cause to be communicated to the National Assembly of France, the peculiar sensibility of Congress to the tribute paid to the memory of Benjamin Franklin, by the enlightened and free Representatives of a great nation, in their decree of the eleventh of June, one thousand seven hundred and ninety.[132]

ORDERED, That the Clerk of this House do acquaint the Senate therewith.[133]

The House proceeded to consider the report of the Secretary of the Treasury, respecting farther compensation to commissioners of the several loan-offices; and the same being twice read, was agreed to as followeth:

That provision should be made by law for admitting to the credit of the several commissioners of loans in the settlement of their respective accounts, all such sums as shall appear to have been necessarily expended by them in the purchase of stationary, and for the hire of clerks in relation to the execution of their offices, from the commencement of the same to the first day of October next, deducting the salary of one clerk in respect to each of the commissioners of Massachusetts, New-York, Pennsylvania and Virginia.

ORDERED, That a bill or bills be brought in pursuant to the said report; and that Mr. Williamson, Mr. Partridge, and Mr. White, do prepare and bring in the same.[134]

A message from the Senate by Mr. Otis their Secretary.

MR. SPEAKER, The Senate have come to a resolution, that the bill sent from this House, intituled, "An act to authorize the President of the United States to cause the debt due to foreign officers to be paid and discharged," do

---

[131] On February 23 the Senate read this bill. It is printed in the *Senate Legislative Journal* on that date. The bill was read again on February 24 and 25, and it was agreed to on February 25, after two amendments were disagreed to. The House was notified of the passage of the bill on February 26.

[132] A copy of the resolution is in Senate Joint and Concurrent Resolutions, SR, DNA.

[133] On February 24 this resolution was signed by the speaker and the vice president.

[134] On February 24 this committee presented the Commissioners of Loans Bill [HR–135], which was read.

not pass to the third reading: And they have passed the bill, intituled, "An act giving effect to the laws of the United States within the state of Vermont," with an amendment, to which they desire the concurrence of this House.[135] And then he withdrew.

ORDERED, That a committee be appointed to prepare and bring in a bill or bills, fixing the time for the next annual meeting of Congress, and that Mr. Smith (of South-Carolina), Mr. Laurance, and Mr. Van Rensselaer, be of the said committee.

A message from the Senate by Mr. Otis their Secretary.

MR. SPEAKER, The Senate insist on their amendment disagreed to by this House, to the amendment to the amendment which is proposed to follow the sixty-first section of the bill, intituled, "An act repealing, after the last day of June next, the duties heretofore laid upon distilled spirits imported from abroad, and laying others in their stead; and also upon spirits distilled within the United States, and for appropriating the same;" and desire a conference with this House on the subject matter thereof, to which they have appointed managers on their part. And then he withdrew.

On motion,

RESOLVED, That this House doth agree to the conference desired by the Senate; and that Mr. Boudinot, Mr. White, and Mr. Livermore, be appointed managers at the said conference on the part of this House.

ORDERED, That the Clerk of this House do acquaint the Senate therewith.[136]

The House proceeded to consider the report of the committee to whom was referred the written message from the President of the United States, of the fourteenth instant:[137] Whereupon,

ORDERED, That the said report be referred to the Secretary of State; and that he be directed to report to Congress the nature and extent of the privileges and restrictions of the commercial intercourse of the United States with foreign nations, and such measures as he shall think proper to be adopted for the improvement of the commerce and navigation of the same.

Mr. Smith (of South-Carolina), from the committee appointed, presented, according to order, a bill fixing the time for the next annual meeting of Congress; which was received and read the first time.

---

[135] The Senate amendment is in House Bills, SR, DNA. The amendment is printed in the *Senate Legislative Journal* on February 23. On February 24 the Senate amendment was agreed to.

[136] On February 25 this conference reported, and the House resolved to agree to the disputed Senate amendment with an amendment.

[137] This message concerns commercial relations with Great Britain.

On motion,

The said bill was read the second time, and ordered to be engrossed and read the third time to-morrow.[138]

The several orders of the day were further postponed until to-morrow.

And then the House adjourned until to-morrow morning eleven o'clock.

THURSDAY, FEBRUARY 24, 1791

The several petitions of Peter Stoy, Thomas Alexander and John Turner, were presented to the House and read, respectively praying to be placed on the list of pensioners, in consideration of wounds received or injuries sustained in the service of the United States, during the late war. Also,

A petition of William Middleton, praying compensation for military services rendered to the United States, during the late war.

ORDERED, That the said petitions be referred to the Secretary at War, with instruction to examine the same, and report his opinion thereupon to the House.

A petition of George Webb, was presented to the House and read, praying farther compensation for his services, and also to be reimbursed for the loss of a sum of the public money, whilst receiver of continental taxes, for the state of Virginia.

ORDERED, That the said petition be referred to the Secretary of the Treasury, with instruction to examine the same, and report his opinion thereupon to the House.

The Speaker laid before the House a letter from the Secretary of the Treasury, accompanying his report on the petition of William Simmons,[139] referred to him by an order of this House of the seventh of January last, which was twice read, and agreed to as followeth:

That it would be expedient, in the opinion of the Secretary, to raise the salary of the chief clerk of the Auditor, to the same standard with the salary of the chief clerk of the Comptroller.

ORDERED, That a bill or bills be brought in pursuant to the said report; and that Mr. Trumbull, Mr. Bourn, and Mr. Foster, do prepare and bring in the same.[140]

The House proceeded to consider the amendment of the Senate to the bill,

---

[138] On February 24 this bill was read again, agreed to, and sent to the Senate.

[139] A copy of the report is in A Record of the Reports of the Secretary of the Treasury, vol. 2, HR, DNA.

[140] According to the *Gazette of the United States*, March 2, 1791, and the manuscript journal, this committee presented a Salaries Bill [HR–136A], which was read twice on February 26. On March 2 the bill was considered in the COWH. Later on the same day, the bill was read again, agreed to, and sent to the Senate.

intituled, "An act giving effect to the laws of the United States, within the state of Vermont;" and the same being twice read, was agreed to.

ORDERED, That the Clerk of this House do acquaint the Senate therewith.[141]

Mr. Floyd, from the joint committee for inrolled bills, reported, that the committee did, this day, wait on the President of the United States, and present for his approbation, an inrolled bill, intituled, "An act regulating the number of Representatives to be chosen by the States of Kentucky and Vermont:"[142] Also, that they had examined an inrolled resolve, which originated in the Senate, requesting the President of the United States to communicate to the National Assembly of France, the peculiar sensibility of Congress, to the tribute paid to the memory of Benjamin Franklin,[143] and had found the same to be truly inrolled: Whereupon,

Mr. Speaker signed the said inrolled resolve.[144]

ORDERED, That the Clerk of this House do acquaint the Senate therewith.

Mr. Sherman, from the committee to whom was re-committed the bill, making compensation to clerks, marshals and jurors, presented an amendatory bill, providing compensations for the officers of the several courts of law, and for jurors and witnesses; which was received and read the first time.

On motion,

The said bill was read the second time, and ordered to be committed to a committee of the whole House to-morrow.[145]

Mr. Bourn, from the committee appointed, presented, according to order, a bill repealing so much of an act as establishes the rate of the rix dollar of Denmark; which was received and read the first time.[146]

Mr. Carroll, from the committee to whom was referred the letter of the Secretary of the Treasury, of the fifteenth instant, accompanying a return of the exports of the United States, between the month of August, one thousand seven hundred and eighty-nine, and the thirtieth of September, one thousand seven hundred and ninety, made a report,[147] which was twice read, and agreed to by the House as followeth:

That the said return of exports ought to be printed for the information of the citizens of the United States, in such manner as to shew the names, quan-

---

141 On March 1 this bill was signed by the speaker and the vice president and presented to the president.

142 On February 25 this bill was signed by the president.

143 The inspected enrolled resolution is in Enrolled Acts, RG 11, DNA. E–23879.

144 On March 1 this resolution was sent to the president.

145 On February 25 and 26 consideration of this bill was postponed as an order of the day. On February 28 the bill was considered by the COWH and amended.

146 On February 25 this bill was read again.

147 A copy of the report is in A Record of the Reports of Select Committees, HR, DNA.

tity and value of the articles exported, the dominions to which the same were carried, and the amount in value so carried.

Mr. Williamson, from the committee appointed, presented, according to order, a bill for making compensations to the commissioners of loans for extraordinary expenses and services; which was received and read the first time.[148]

On motion,

ORDERED, That the Secretary of the Treasury report, whether any, and what additions are to be made to his return of the exports of the United States.

An engrossed bill, fixing the time for the next annual meeting of Congress, was read the third time, and the blanks therein filled up.

RESOLVED, That the said bill do pass; and that the title be, "An act fixing the time for the next annual meeting of Congress."

ORDERED, That the Clerk of this House do carry the said bill to the Senate, and desire their concurrence.[149]

The House, according to the order of the day, resolved itself into a committee of the whole House, on the bill, supplementary to the act establishing the treasury department; and after some time spent therein, Mr. Speaker resumed the chair, and Mr. Boudinot reported, that the committee had, according to order, had the said bill under consideration, and made several amendments thereto, which he delivered in at the Clerk's table, where the same were severally twice read, and agreed to by the House.

ORDERED, That the said bill, with the amendments, be engrossed, and read the third time to-morrow.[150]

The House proceeded to consider the several petitions and memorials of the public creditors, which lay on the table: Whereupon,

A motion being made and seconded, that the House do come to the following resolution;

"RESOLVED, That it would be inexpedient to alter the system for funding the public debt, established during the last session of Congress; and that the petition of Thomas McKean and others, stiling themselves a committee of the public creditors of the commonwealth of Pennsylvania, and also the other petitions on that subject, cannot be granted:"

---

[148] The manuscript journal correctly includes a paragraph following this line. It reads:

On motion, the said bill was read the second time, and ordered to be committed to a Committee of the whole House tomorrow.

On February 28 this bill was considered, and an amendment to it was disagreed to.

[149] On February 24 the Senate read this bill. It is printed in the *Senate Legislative Journal* on that date. On February 25 the bill was read again, and a motion to amend it was defeated. It was read again and agreed to on February 26. The House was notified on February 28.

[150] On February 25 this bill was read again, agreed to, and sent to the Senate.

It was resolved in the affirmative— $\begin{cases} \text{AYES} & 53 \\ \text{NOES} & 2 \end{cases}$

The ayes and noes being demanded by one fifth of the members present; Those who voted in the affirmative, are,

Fisher Ames	George Mathews
John Baptista Ashe	Andrew Moore
Abraham Baldwin	Peter Muhlenberg
Egbert Benson	Josiah Parker
Elias Boudinot	George Partridge
Benjamin Bourn	Jeremiah Van Rensselaer
John Brown	James Schureman
Aedanus Burke	Theodore Sedgwick
Lambert Cadwalader	Joshua Seney
George Clymer	Roger Sherman
Benjamin Contee	Peter Silvester
Thomas Fitzsimons	Thomas Sinnickson
William Floyd	William Smith (of Maryland)
Abiel Foster	William Smith (of South-Carolina)
George Gale	John Steele
Nicholas Gilman	Michael Jenifer Stone
Benjamin Goodhue	Jonathan Sturges
Samuel Griffin	Thomas Sumter
Jonathan Grout	George Thatcher
William B. Giles	Jonathan Trumbull
Benjamin Huntington	Thomas Tudor Tucker
James Jackson	John Vining
John Laurance	Jeremiah Wadsworth
Richard Bland Lee	Alexander White
George Leonard	Hugh Williamson and
Samuel Livermore	Henry Wynkoop
James Madison, junior	

Those who voted in the negative, are,

Elbridge Gerry and   Thomas Scott

A message from the Senate by Mr. Otis their Secretary.

MR. SPEAKER, The Senate have passed the bill, intituled, "An act to explain and amend an act making farther provision for the payment of the debts of the United States."[151]   And then he withdrew.

---

[151] On March 1 this bill was signed by the speaker and the vice president and presented to the president.

The House, according to the order of the day, again resolved itself into a committee of the whole House, on the bill for establishing the post-office and post-roads of the United States; and after some time spent therein, Mr. Speaker resumed the chair, and Mr. Boudinot reported, that the committee had, according to order, again had the said bill under their consideration, and made a farther progress therein.[152]

The several orders of the day were further postponed until to-morrow.

And then the House adjourned until to-morrow morning eleven o'clock.

FRIDAY, FEBRUARY 25, 1791

An engrossed bill, supplementary to the act establishing the treasury department, was read the third time, and the blanks therein filled up.

RESOLVED, That the said bill do pass; and that the title be, "An act supplementary to the act establishing the treasury department."[153]

ORDERED, That the Clerk of this House do carry the said bill to the Senate, and desire their concurrence.[154]

A petition of Jacob Isaacs, of Newport, in the State of Rhode-Island, was presented to the House and read, praying that some adequate reward or gratuity may be made to him, for the discovery of an art or secret which he possesses, of converting salt water into fresh, so as to render it proper for every purpose for which spring or fresh river water is wanted, by a process simple, easy, and unexpensive.

ORDERED, That the said petition be referred to the Secertary of State, with instruction to examine the same, and report his opinion thereupon to the House.

A petition of Aaron Vail, was presented to the House and read, praying that two vessels employed under contract of the petitioner, to carry the mail between the United States and France, may be exempted from the duties of tonnage on foreign vessels.   Also,

---

[152] The manuscript journal correctly includes a paragraph following this line. It reads:

Resolved that this House will tomorrow again resolve itself into a Committee of the whole House on the said Bill.

On February 25 the COWH was discharged from considering the Post Office Bill [HR–113].

[153] A printed copy of the bill, annotated by the Senate, is in House Bills, SR, DNA. The bill is printed in the *Senate Legislative Journal* on February 25.

[154] The Senate read this bill on February 25. On February 26 this bill was committed to a committee on motions concerning expenses for officers of the department of the treasury and the attorney general. On the same day this committee reported amendments to the Treasury Bill [HR–131], and the amendments were agreed to. On February 28 the Senate read the bill again, and agreed to it with amendments, which are printed in the *Senate Legislative Journal,* and the amendments were sent to the House.

A petition of Christian Harner, praying compensation for damages sustained in his property by the army of the United States, during the late war. Also,

A petition of Christian Knipe, praying payment for a waggon which was impressed into the service of the United States, during the late war. Also,

A petition of Brown and Francis, praying to be reimbursed the amount of the second duty paid by the petitioners, on sundry goods of foreign manufacture, which were exported by them from the United States, and afterwards imported into the same. Also,

A petition of Dorsey Pentecost, praying the pre-emption of a certain tract of land in the western territory of the United States.

ORDERED, That the said petitions be referred to the Secretary of the Treasury, with instruction to examine the same, and report his opinion thereupon to the House.

The Speaker laid before the House a letter from the Secretary of the Treasury, covering his report respecting the loan negociated in Holland, on the part of the United States, of three millions of florins; which was read, and ordered to be referred to Mr. Fitzsimons, Mr. Laurance, and Mr. Smith (of South-Carolina), with instruction to prepare and bring in a bill or bills, pursuant to the tenor thereof.[155]

A message from the Senate by Mr. Otis their Secretary.

MR. SPEAKER, I am directed by the Senate to inform this House, that the President of the United States did, this day, approve and sign two acts, which originated in the Senate, one intituled, "An act to incorporate the subscribers to the bank of the United States;" the other intituled, "An act regulating the number of Representatives to be chosen by the states of Kentucky and Vermont." And then he withdrew.

The Speaker laid before the House a letter from the Secretary of the Treasury, covering his report on the petition of Comfort Sands and others; which was read, and ordered to be referred to Mr. Sedgwick, Mr. Williamson, and Mr. Benson.[156]

The Speaker laid before the House a letter from the Secretary of State,

---

[155] The report is in Reports of the Secretary of the Treasury, SR, DNA. A copy of the report is in A Record of the Reports of the Secretary of the Treasury, vol. 2, HR, DNA. This report is printed in the *Senate Legislative Journal* on February 25. This committee presented the Sinking Fund Bill [HR–136], which deals with the loan from Holland, on this same date.

[156] A copy of the report is in A Record of the Reports of the Secretary of the Treasury, vol. 2, HR, DNA. On February 26 the committee reported.

covering his report on the petition of Nicholas Ferdinand Westphall; which was read, and ordered to lie on the table.[157]

Mr. Boudinot, from the managers appointed on the part of this House, to attend the conference with the Senate, agreeable to the order of yesterday, made a report:[158] Whereupon,

On a motion made and seconded,

That this House doth recede from their disagreement to the amendment last proposed by the Senate, to the amendment of this House to the amendment of the Senate, which is proposed to follow the sixty-first section of the bill, intituled, "An act repealing, after the last day of June next, the duties heretofore laid upon distilled spirits imported from abroad, and laying others in their stead; and also upon spirits distilled within the United States, and for appropriating the same;" and doth agree to the said amendment to the amendment to the amendment, amended to read as followeth—"Seven per cent. of the whole product of the duties arising from the spirits distilled within the United States: AND PROVIDED ALSO, That such allowances shall not exceed the annual amount of forty-five thousand dollars, until the same shall be further ascertained by law."[159]

It was resolved in the affirmative— $\begin{cases} \text{AYES} & 30 \\ \text{NOES} & 29 \end{cases}$

The ayes and noes being demanded by one fifth of the members present;

Those who voted in the affirmative, are,

Fisher Ames	George Leonard
Egbert Benson	George Partridge
Elias Boudinot	James Schureman
Benjamin Bourn	Thomas Scott
Lambert Cadwalader	Theodore Sedgwick
George Clymer	John Sevier
Thomas Fitzsimons	Roger Sherman
Abiel Foster	Thomas Sinnickson
George Gale	William Smith (of South-Carolina)
Elbridge Gerry	Jonathan Sturges
Nicholas Gilman	George Thatcher
Benjamin Goodhue	Jonathan Trumbull
Thomas Hartley	John Vining
Benjamin Huntington	Jeremiah Wadsworth and
John Laurance	Henry Wynkoop

[157] A copy of the letter and a copy of the report are in A Record of the Reports of the Secretary of State, HR, DNA. On February 28 this report was considered, and a resolution on the petition was referred to the committee to prepare a widows, orphans, and invalids bill.

[158] The report is in Joint Committee Reports, SR, DNA.

[159] A copy of the resolution is in Messages from the House, SR, DNA.

Those who voted in the negative, are,

John Baptista Ashe	George Mathews
Abraham Baldwin	Andrew Moore
Timothy Bloodworth	Peter Muhlenberg
John Brown	Josiah Parker
Aedanus Burke	Jeremiah Van Rensselaer
Daniel Carroll	Joshua Seney
Benjamin Contee	Peter Silvester
William Floyd	William Smith (of Maryland)
Samuel Griffin	John Steele
Jonathan Grout	Michael Jenifer Stone
William B. Giles	Thomas Sumter
James Jackson	Thomas Tudor Tucker
Richard Bland Lee	Alexander White and
Samuel Livermore	Hugh Williamson
James Madison, junior	

ORDERED, That the Clerk of this House do acquaint the Senate therewith.[160]

The several petitions of Thomas Campbell, Caleb Ferris, Thomas Brush, junior, and Paul Bowman, were presented to the House and read, respectively praying to be placed on the list of pensioners, in consideration of wounds received in the service of the United States, during the late war. Also,

A petition of Thaddeus Reed, late a soldier in the coast guards, in the State of Connecticut, praying relief in consideration of an injury sustained in his health, in the service of the United States, during the late war. Also,

A petition of Benjamin Fuller, praying payment of certain arrearages of wages and clothing, which he alleges are still due to him, as a soldier in the Massachusetts line, during the late war. Also,

The petitions of Joseph Cox, and Ebenezer Kent, respectively praying to be allowed commutation of five years half-pay, in lieu of half-pay for life, as ensigns in the service of the United States, during the late war. Also,

A petition of commodore Abraham Whipple, praying to be allowed commutation, and all other emoluments as an officer in the late navy of the United States.[161]

ORDERED, That the said petitions be referred to the Secretary at War, with instruction to examine the same, and report his opinion thereupon to the House.

The Speaker laid before the House a letter from the Secretary of the Treas-

---

[160] On February 28 the House was notified that the Senate had agreed to the House amendment to their amendment. On the same day the speaker signed the Duties on Distilled Spirits Bill [HR-110].

[161] A copy of the petition is in the American Manuscripts, RPJCB.

ury, covering his report respecting certificates or evidences of debt issued after the first of January one thousand seven hundred and ninety; which were read, and ordered to lie on the table.[162]

On motion,

ORDERED, That the committee of the whole House be discharged from further proceeding on the bill for establishing post-offices and post-roads of the United States.[163]

A bill repealing so much of an act as establishes the rate of the rix-dollar of Denmark, was read the second time, and ordered to be engrossed, and read the third time to-morrow.[164]

Mr. Fitzsimons, from the committee appointed, presented, according to order, a bill supplemental to the act making provision for the reduction of the public debt; which was received and read the first time.

On motion,

The said bill was read the second time, and ordered to be committed to a committee of the whole House to-morrow.[165]

The several orders of the day were further postponed until to-morrow.

And then the House adjourned until to-morrow morning eleven o'clock.

S A T U R D A Y, FEBRUARY 26, 1791

A message from the Senate by Mr. Otis their Secretary.

MR. SPEAKER, The Senate have passed the bill sent from this House, intituled, "An act supplementary to the act to incorporate the subscribers to the bank of the United States:"[166] The Senate have also passed a bill, intituled, "An act to amend the act, intituled, 'An act to establish the temporary and permanent seat of the government of the United States;' "[167] to which they desire the concurrence of this House.   And then he withdrew.

The said bill was read the first time.
On motion,

---

[162] On March 1 this report was referred to a committee to prepare a bill.

[163] On February 28 a committee to prepare another post office bill was appointed, and the committee presented a Post Office Bill [HR–137], which was read on the same day.

[164] On February 26 this bill was read, agreed to, and sent to the Senate.

[165] On February 26 and 28 consideration of this bill was postponed as an order of the day. On March 1 the bill was considered in the COWH. On the same day this bill was read again, agreed to, and sent to the Senate.

[166] On March 1 this bill was signed by the speaker and the vice president and delivered to the president.

[167] The bill is in Engrossed Senate Bills and Resolutions, SR, DNA. The bill, as introduced and later agreed to without amendments, is printed in the *Senate Legislative Journal* on February 17.

The said bill was read the second time, and ordered to be committed to a committee of the whole House on Monday next.[168]

Mr. Sedgwick, from the committee to whom was referred the report of the Secretary of the Treasury on the petition of Comfort Sands and others, made a report; which was read, and ordered to lie on the table.[169]

A petition of Elias Hasket Derby, was presented to the House and read, praying relief in the payment of the impost on certain cargoes of tea, imported by the petitioner.

ORDERED, That the said petition be referred to the Secretary of the Treasury, with instruction to examine the same, and report his opinion thereupon to the House.

The House proceeded to consider the report of the committee to whom was referred the petition of Seth Harding: Whereupon,

It being moved and seconded, that the House do agree to the said report in the words following, to wit:

"That Congress pass an act granting to captain Harding the sum of dollars, as a gratuity for his services and losses occasioned by leaving his estate and employment within the British dominions, and for the active, beneficial and meritorious part he has taken in securing the rights and independence of America:"

It passed in the negative.

The House proceeded to consider the reports of the Secretary at War, on the several petitions of the children of captain Robert Lewis, deceased, of Hannah Douglass, widow of the late colonel William Douglass, of Anne Roberts, of the orphan children of the late major Andrew Leitch, of the orphan children of the late captain William White, of Samuel Buffinton, attorney to Francis Suzor Debevere, of Joseph Pannill, of Thomas McIntire, of Robert King, and of Lemuel Sherman: Whereupon,

RESOLVED, That the prayer of the said petitions, respectively, be granted, in conformity to the tenor of the said reports: and that it be an instruction to the committee appointed to prepare and bring in a bill or bills "for making compensation to widows, orphans and invalids, in certain cases," that they do insert a clause or clauses, making provision for the said cases respectively.

The House proceeded to consider the report of the Secretary at War, on the petitions of Timothy Mix, and Abel Turney: Whereupon,

---

[168] On February 28 this bill was read again.

[169] The manuscript journal correctly includes a paragraph following this line. It reads: Mr. Trumbull from the Committee appointed, presented according to order, a Bill in addition to the Act intituled an Act for establishing the salaries of the Executive Officers of Government, with their assistants and clerks; which was received and read the first time; On motion, the said Bill was read the second time, and ordered to be committed to a Committee of the whole House on Monday next.

On March 2 this bill was considered in the COWH.

RESOLVED, That the said Timothy Mix, be intitled, as an invalid, to the half-pay of a lieutenant, upon his returning his commutation; and that the said Abel Turney be placed on the pension-list, agreeable to the said report.

ORDERED, That the committee appointed to prepare and bring in a bill or bills "for making compensations to widows, orphans and invalids, in certain cases," do insert a clause or clauses pursuant to the said resolution.[170]

The House proceeded to consider the report of the Secretary at War, on the petition of Michael Gabriel Houdin: Whereupon,

A motion being made and seconded, "That there be granted to the petitioner, as a foreign officer, a gratuity of two hundred dollars, to reimburse him for expenses incurred in coming to and returning from America;"

It passed in the negative.

The House proceeded to consider the report of the Secretary at War, on the petition of David Cook: Whereupon,

ORDERED, That the said report be referred to Mr. Burke, Mr. Thatcher, and Mr. Mathews, with instruction to prepare and bring in a bill or bills pursuant to the tenor thereof.[171]

The Speaker laid before the House a letter and report from the Secretary at War, on the several petitions of Thaddeus Beebe, Robert Connelly, Francis Ackling, Jesse Holt, Reuben Gould, Barnabas Lucas, Robert Ford, Philip Buck, John Miles Charlesworth, Nathan Davis, Patrick McLaughlin, Thomas Boyd, Donald McDonald, Simeon Noyes, John Cardiff, Caleb Chadwick, Jabez Bill, Abner Pier, Job Priest, Wardwell Green, William Reynolds, Albert Roux, Anna Emmerson, Anna W. Longcammer, Peter Johnson, Ezekiel Johnston, William McDade, Joel Phelps, Timothy Lane, Thomas Hobby, Isaac Vincent, Ebenezer Nash, Daniel Lollar, Ebenezer Fielding, and Simeon Thayer; which were read, and ordered to lie on the table.[172]

An engrossed bill, repealing so much of an act as establishes the rate of the rix dollar of Denmark, was read the third time.

RESOLVED, That the said bill do pass; and that the title be, "An act concerning the rates of foreign coin."

ORDERED, That the Clerk of this House do carry the said bill to the Senate, and desire their concurrence.[173]

---

[170] On February 28 three more resolutions on petitions were referred to this committee. On the same day the committee presented the Widows, Orphans, and Invalids Bill [HR–139], which was read.

[171] On March 2 this committee presented the Cook Bill [HR–140], which was read.

[172] A copy of the report on all of these petitions is in A Record of the Reports of the Secretary of War, vol. 2, HR, DNA.

[173] On February 28 the Senate read this bill. It is printed in the Senate Legislative Journal on that date. On March 1 this bill was read and committed. On the same day this committee reported amendments, which were agreed to and are printed in the Senate Legislative Journal. The bill was then read again and agreed to. The House was notified of the Senate amendments on March 2 and agreed to them on the same day.

ORDERED, That the committee of the whole House be discharged from further considering the bill sent from the Senate, intituled, "An act for granting lands to the inhabitants and settlers at Vincennes and the Illinois country, in the territory north-west of the Ohio, and for confirming them in their possessions," and that the said bill be referred to Mr. White, Mr. Carroll, and Mr. Brown.[174]

The House proceeded to the farther consideration of the report of the committee to whom was referred the petition of George Gibson; Whereupon,

The latter part of the said report in the words following, to wit, "That in a most critical period during the late revolution, the petitioner undertook a fatiguing, hazardous, and important expedition of a secret nature, and by his fidelity and masterly management in the execution thereof, procured advantages to the United States, singularly important, without incurring any, or but a very trivial expense, for which he has hitherto received no compensation; and therefore the committee are of opinion that he is justly and equitably intitled to the sum of   dollars, as a reasonable compensation for his said services;" was, on the question put thereupon agreed to by the House.

ORDERED, That a bill or bills be brought in pursuant thereto, and that Mr. Giles, Mr. Vining, Mr. Peter Muhlenberg, Mr. Mathews and Mr. Wadsworth, do prepare and bring in the same.[175]

The several orders of the day were further postponed until Monday next.[176]

And then the House adjourned until Monday morning eleven o'clock.

MONDAY, FEBRUARY 28, 1791

A message from the Senate by Mr. Otis their Secretary.

MR. SPEAKER, The Senate have passed the bill sent from this House, intituled, "An act fixing the time for the next annual meeting of Congress:"[177]

---

[174] According to the *Federal Gazette* of March 1 and 2, this committee reported amendments on March 1, and the House agreed to the amendments on March 2. The bill was then read again, agreed to with the amendments, and returned to the Senate. The Senate committed the amendments on March 2. They are printed in the *Senate Legislative Journal* on that date. On March 3 the committee reported, and the Senate agreed to the amendments with an amendment, which is printed in the *Senate Legislative Journal* on March 3. The House agreed to the amendment, and the bill was signed later on the same date.

[175] On February 28 this committee presented the Gibson Bill [HR–138], which was read.

[176] On this date the House passed amendments to the Senate amendments to the Military Establishment Bill [HR–126A]. The Senate was notified on February 28. The House amendments are filed with the bill in House Bills, SR, DNA. These amendments are printed in the *Senate Legislative Journal* on February 28. On March 1 the Senate considered the House amendments and agreed to all but the last two.

[177] On March 1 this bill was signed by the speaker and the vice president and delivered to the president.

The Senate have also agreed to the amendment last proposed on the part of this House to their amendment to the bill repealing, after the last day of June next, the duties heretofore laid upon distilled spirits imported from abroad, and laying others in their stead; and also upon spirits distilled within the United States, and for appropriating the same. And then he withdrew.

The bill sent from the Senate, intituled, "An act to amend the act for establishing the temporary and permanent seat of the government of the United States," was read the second time, and ordered to be read the third time to-morrow.[178]

ORDERED, That a committee be appointed to prepare and bring in a bill or bills to continue in force, for a limited time, an act, intituled, "An act for the temporary establishment of the post-office;" and that Mr. Smith (of South-Carolina), Mr. Sherman, and Mr. Scott, be of the said committee.

The House proceeded to consider the report of the Secretary at War, on the petition of the orphan-children of John Harris, deceased: Whereupon,

RESOLVED, That there be paid to the petitioners the sum of one thousand one hundred and twenty dollars, being the amount of a lieutenant's half-pay for seven years, agreeably to the resolve of Congress of the twenty-fourth of August, one thousand seven hundred and eighty.

ORDERED, That it be an instruction to the committee appointed to prepare and bring in a bill or bills for making compensation to widows, orphans and invalids, in certain cases, to insert a clause or clauses pursuant to the said resolution.

The Speaker laid before the House a letter from the Secretary at War, enclosing his report on the petition of Philip De Haas:[179] Whereupon,

RESOLVED, That the prayer of the petition of the said Philip De Haas be so far granted, as that the comptroller of the treasury be directed to adjust his accounts, and to admit such sums as by evidence shall appear to have been advanced by him for public service.

ORDERED, That it be an instruction to the committee appointed to prepare and bring in a bill or bills for making compensation to widows, orphans and invalids, in certain cases, to insert a clause or clauses pursuant to the said resolution.

The House proceeded to consider the report of the Secretary of State, on the petition of Nicholas Ferdinand Westfall: Whereupon,

RESOLVED, That one hundred acres of unappropriated lands be granted to the said Nicholas Ferdinand Westfall, free of all charges, and that there be

---

[178] On March 1 this bill was read again and agreed to, and the Senate was notified.
[179] A copy of the report is in A Record of the Reports of the Secretary of War, vol. 2, HR, DNA.

paid to him as a farther reward, the sum of three hundred and thirty-six dollars and eighty-four cents.

ORDERED, That it be an instruction to the committee appointed to prepare and bring in a bill or bills for making compensation to widows, orphans and invalids, in certain cases, to insert a clause or clauses pursuant to the said resolution.

A message from the Senate by Mr. Otis their Secretary.

MR. SPEAKER,   The Senate have passed the bill, intituled, "An act supplemental to the act establishing the treasury department," with several amendments, to which they desire the concurrence of this House.[180]   And then he withdrew.

The House, according to the order of the day, resolved itself into a committee of the whole House, on the bill providing compensations for the officers of the several courts of law, and for jurors and witnesses; and after some time spent therein, Mr. Speaker resumed the chair, and Mr. Boudinot reported, that the committee had, according to order, had the said bill under consideration, and made no amendment thereto.

The said bill was then amended at the Clerk's table, and, together with the amendments, ordered to be engrossed, and read the third time to-morrow.[181]

The House, according to the order of the day, resolved itself into a committee of the whole House, on the bill for making compensations to the commissioners of loans, for extraordinary expenses and services; and after some time spent therein, Mr. Speaker resumed the chair, and Mr. Boudinot reported, that the committee had, according to order, had the said bill under consideration, and made an amendment thereto, which he delivered in at the Clerk's table.

The House proceeded to consider the said amendment; and the same being read as followeth:

"Strike out the last clause of the bill in the words following, 'excepting only the hire of one clerk for the several commissioners in the states of Massachusetts, New-York, Pennsylvania and Virginia,' " was, on the question put thereupon, disagreed to by the House—AYES 23: NOES 27.

The ayes and noes being demanded by one fifth of the members present;

---

[180] Senate amendments are noted on the bill in House Bills, SR, DNA. A separate amendment is also in the above location. The amendments are printed in the *Senate Legislative Journal* on February 28. On March 1 the House agreed to the Senate amendments.

[181] On March 1 this bill was read again, agreed to, and sent to the Senate.

Those who voted in the affirmative, are,

Fisher Ames	John Hathorn
Egbert Benson	Benjamin Huntington
Aedanus Burke	John Laurance
Lambert Cadwalader	Peter Muhlenberg
Daniel Carroll	Jeremiah Van Rensselaer
George Clymer	Thomas Scott
Thomas Fitzsimons	Theodore Sedgwick
William Floyd	Michael Jenifer Stone
Elbridge Gerry	Jonathan Trumbull
William B. Giles	Jeremiah Wadsworth and
Samuel Griffin	Henry Wynkoop
Thomas Hartley	

Those who voted in the negative, are,

John Baptista Ashe	George Partridge
Abraham Baldwin	James Schureman
Timothy Bloodworth	Joshua Seney
Elias Boudinot	Roger Sherman
Benjamin Bourn	Thomas Sinnickson
John Brown	William Smith (of Maryland)
Benjamin Contee	William Smith (of South-Carolina)
Abiel Foster	Jonathan Sturges
Nicholas Gilman	Thomas Sumter
Jonathan Grout	George Thatcher
James Jackson	Thomas Tudor Tucker
George Leonard	Alexander White and
Samuel Livermore	Hugh Williamson[182]
George Mathews	

ORDERED, That the petition of John Tucker, which lay on the table, be referred to Mr. Gerry, Mr. Hartley, and Mr. Seney; that they do examine the matter thereof, and report the same, with their opinion thereupon, to the House.[183]

---

[182] The passage of the Commissioners of Loans Bill [HR–135] is not noted in the Journal. It was agreed to and sent to the Senate on March 1. On the same day the Senate read this bill, and it is printed in the *Senate Legislative Journal*. On March 2 the Senate read the bill and committed it. An amendment reported by this committee was agreed to on the same day. On March 3 the Senate agreed to the bill with the amendment, and the House disagreed to the amendment. The Senate then insisted on the amendment, and the House receded from its disagreement. The bill was signed on the same day.

[183] On March 3 this committee reported, and its report was agreed to and printed.

Mr. Floyd, from the joint committee for inrolled bills, reported, that the committee had examined an inrolled bill, intituled, "An act repealing, after the last day of June next, the duties heretofore laid upon distilled spirits imported from abroad, and laying others in their stead; and also upon spirits distilled within the United States, and for appropriating the same,"[184] and had found the same to be truly inrolled: Whereupon,

Mr. Speaker signed the said inrolled bill.[185]

ORDERED, That the Clerk of this House do acquaint the Senate therewith.

Mr. Smith (of South-Carolina), from the committee appointed, presented, according to order, a bill to continue in force, for a limited time, an act, intituled, "An act for the temporary establishment of the post-office;" which was received and read the first time.[186]

Mr. Giles, from the committee appointed, presented, according to order, a bill to compensate George Gibson; which was received and read the first time.[187]

Mr. Smith (of South-Carolina), from the committee appointed, presented, according to order, a bill for making compensation to the widows and orphan children of certain officers who were killed, or who died while in the service of the United States, during the late war, and for the relief of certain invalids and other persons therein mentioned; which was received and read the first time.[188]

The several orders of the day were further postponed until to-morrow.

And then the House adjourned until to-morrow morning eleven o'clock.

---

[184] The inspected enrolled bill is in Enrolled Acts, RG 11, DNA. E–23865, E–46325.

[185] The vice president signed this bill on March 1. It was presented to the president on the same day.

[186] On March 1 this bill was read again and amended from the COWH. Later on the same day the bill was read again, agreed to, and sent to the Senate.

[187] On March 1 this bill was read again and considered in the COWH.

[188] On March 1 this bill was read again and considered in the COWH.

TUESDAY, MARCH 1, 1791

A petition of James Adams, was presented to the House and read, praying compensation for services rendered and injuries sustained in the navy of the United States, during the late war. Also,

A petition of John Paul Schott, praying compensation for services rendered as a captain in the army of the United States, during the late war. Also,

A petition of Patrick Sullivan, praying compensation for services rendered as an assistant-commissary of military stores, and clothier to the western expedition under General Sullivan. Also,

A petition of William Adams, praying to be placed on the list of pensioners, in consideration of injuries sustained in his health as a surgeon in the late army of the United States, during the late war.

ORDERED, That the said petitions be referred to the Secretary at War, with instruction to examine the same, and report his opinion thereupon to the House.

A petition of John Jones, of Berks county in the state of Pennsylvania, was presented to the House and read, praying compensation for damages done to his property, by the army of the United States, during the late war. Also,

A petition of Joseph Henry, assignee of Matthias Bush, praying compensation for wood furnished the British prisoners at Winchester, by the said Matthias Bush, during the late war.

ORDERED, That the said petitions be referred to the Secretary of the Treasury, with instruction to examine the same, and report his opinion thereupon to the House.

Mr. Floyd, from the joint committee for inrolled bills, reported, that the committee had examined four inrolled bills—to wit, one intituled, "An act supplementary to the act, intituled, 'An act to incorporate the subscribers to the bank of the United States;' "[1] another intituled, "An act giving effect to the laws of the United States within the state of Vermont;"[2] another intituled, "An act to explain and amend an act, intituled, 'An act making farther provision for the payment of the debts of the United States;' "[3] and another intituled, "An act fixing the time for the next annual meeting of Congress;"[4] and had found the same to be truly inrolled: Whereupon,

Mr. Speaker signed the said inrolled bills.

ORDERED, That the Clerk of this House do acquaint the Senate therewith.

On a motion made and seconded,

RESOLVED, That the Clerk of the House of Representatives of the United States, shall be deemed to continue in office until another be appointed.

---

[1] The inspected enrolled bill is in Enrolled Acts, RG 11, DNA. E–23876.
[2] The inspected enrolled bill is in Enrolled Acts, RG 11, DNA. E–23857.
[3] The inspected enrolled bill is in Enrolled Acts, RG 11, DNA. E–23874.
[4] The inspected enrolled bill is in Enrolled Acts, RG 11, DNA. E–23852.

An engrossed bill providing compensations to the officers of the several courts of law, and to jurors and witnesses, was read the third time, and the blanks therein filled up; and on the question that the said bill do pass,

It was resolved in the affirmative— $\begin{cases} \text{AYES} & 30 \\ \text{NOES} & 23 \end{cases}$

The ayes and noes being demanded by one fifth of the members present; Those who voted in the affirmative, are,

Fisher Ames	John Laurance
Egbert Benson	Richard Bland Lee
Benjamin Bourn	Samuel Livermore
Aedanus Burke	James Madison, junior
Lambert Cadwalader	Thomas Scott
Daniel Carroll	Theodore Sedgwick
George Clymer	Joshua Seney
Benjamin Contee	Roger Sherman
Thomas Fitzsimons	William Smith (of Maryland)
Abiel Foster	William Smith (of South-Carolina)
George Gale	Jonathan Sturges
Elbridge Gerry	Jonathan Trumbull
Samuel Griffin	Jeremiah Wadsworth
Thomas Hartley	Alexander White and
Benjamin Huntington	Henry Wynkoop

Those who voted in the negative, are,

John Baptista Ashe	Andrew Moore
Abraham Baldwin	Peter Muhlenberg
Timothy Bloodworth	Josiah Parker
Elias Boudinot	George Partridge
John Brown	Jeremiah Van Rensselaer
William Floyd	James Schureman
Nicholas Gilman	Peter Silvester
Jonathan Grout	Thomas Sinnickson
William B. Giles	Michael Jenifer Stone
John Hathorn	Thomas Sumter and
James Jackson	George Thatcher
George Leonard	

RESOLVED, That the title of the said bill be, "An act providing compensations to the officers of the judicial courts of the United States, and to jurors and witnesses, and for other purposes."[5]

---

[5] A printed copy of the bill, annotated by the Senate, is in House Bills, SR, DNA. The bill is printed in the *Senate Legislative Journal* on March 1.

ORDERED, That the Clerk of this House do carry the said bill to the Senate, and desire their concurrence.[6]

The bill sent from the Senate, intituled, "An act to amend an act, intituled, 'An act to establish the temporary and permanent seat of the government of the United States,'" was read the third time;   and on the question that the said bill do pass,

It was resolved in the affirmative— $\left\{ \begin{array}{l} \text{AYES } 39 \\ \text{NOES } 18 \end{array} \right.$

The ayes and noes being demanded by one fifth of the members present;
Those who voted in the affirmative, are,

John Baptista Ashe	Andrew Moore
Abraham Baldwin	Josiah Parker
Timothy Bloodworth	James Schureman
John Brown	Thomas Scott
Aedanus Burke	Roger Sherman
Lambert Cadwalader	Peter Silvester
Daniel Carroll	Thomas Sinnickson
George Clymer	William Smith (of Maryland)
Benjamin Contee	William Smith (of South-Carolina)
Thomas Fitzsimons	John Steele
George Gale	Michael Jenifer Stone
Elbridge Gerry	Thomas Sumter
Samuel Griffin	Jonathan Trumbull
William B. Giles	Thomas Tudor Tucker
John Hathorn	John Vining
James Jackson	Jeremiah Wadsworth
John Laurance	Alexander White
Richard Bland Lee	Hugh Williamson and
James Madison, junior	Henry Wynkoop
George Mathews	

Those who voted in the negative, are,

Fisher Ames	Abiel Foster
Egbert Benson	Nicholas Gilman
Elias Boudinot	Jonathan Grout
William Floyd	Thomas Hartley

---

[6] On March 1 this bill was read by the Senate, and on March 2 the bill was read again and committed. On March 3 this committee reported amendments to the bill, which were agreed to. The bill was then read a third time and agreed to with amendments, which are printed in the *Senate Legislative Journal.* On the same day the House agreed to some of the amendments and disagreed to others. The Senate then receded from the amendments disagreed to, and the bill was signed.

Benjamin Huntington	Jeremiah Van Rensselaer
George Leonard	Theodore Sedgwick
Samuel Livermore	Joshua Seney
Peter Muhlenberg	Jonathan Sturges and
George Partridge	George Thatcher

ORDERED, That the Clerk of this House do acquaint the Senate therewith.[7]

The House proceeded to consider the amendments proposed by the Senate to the bill supplemental to the act establishing the treasury department; and the same being read, were agreed to.

ORDERED, That the Clerk of this House do acquaint the Senate therewith.[8]

The House, according to the order of the day, resolved itself into a committee of the whole House, on the bill supplementary to the act making provision for the reduction of the public debt; and after some time spent therein, Mr. Speaker resumed the chair, and Mr. Boudinot reported, that the committee had, according to order, had the said bill under consideration, and made no amendment thereto.

ORDERED, That the said bill be engrossed, and read the third time.

A bill to continue in force, for a limited time, an act, intituled, "An act for the temporary establishment of the post-office," was read the second time, and ordered to be committed to a committee of the whole House immediately.

The House accordingly resolved itself into a committee of the whole House on the said bill; and after some time spent therein, Mr. Speaker resumed the chair, and Mr. Boudinot reported, that the committee had, according to order, had the said bill under consideration, and agreed to several amendments thereto; which he delivered in at the Clerk's table, where the same were severally twice read, and agreed to by the House.

ORDERED, That the said bill, with the amendments, be engrossed, and read the third time.

Mr. Floyd, from the committee for inrolled bills, reported, that the committee did, this day, wait on the President of the United States, and present for his approbation five inrolled bills; one intituled, "An act repealing, after the last day of June next, the duties heretofore laid upon distilled spirits imported from abroad, and laying others in their stead; and also upon spirits distilled within the United States, and for appropriating the same;" another intituled, "An act supplementary to the act, intituled, 'An act to incorporate the subscribers to the bank of the United States;'" another intituled, "An act giving effect to the laws of the United States within the state of Vermont;"

---

[7] On March 2 the Residence Bill [S-21] was signed by the speaker and the vice president and presented to the president.

[8] On March 2 this bill was signed by the speaker and the vice president and delivered to the president.

another intituled, "An act to explain and amend an act, intituled, 'An act making further provision for the payment of the debts of the United States;' " and another intituled, "An act fixing the time for the next annual meeting of Congress;" also, an inrolled resolve, which originated in the Senate, expressive of the high sense of Congress on the decree of the National Assembly of France, respecting the late Benjamin Franklin.[9]

A bill for making compensation to the widows and orphan children of certain officers who were killed, or who died while in the service of the United States, during the late war, and for the relief of certain invalids and other persons therein mentioned, was read the second time, and ordered to be committed to a committee of the whole House immediately.

The House accordingly resolved itself into a committee of the whole House on the said bill; and after some time spent therein, Mr. Speaker resumed the chair, and Mr. Boudinot reported, that the committee had, according to order, had the said bill under consideration, and made no amendment thereto.

ORDERED, That the said bill be engrossed and read the third time to-morrow.[10]

ORDERED, That the report of the Secretary of the Treasury which was made on Friday last, respecting certificates or evidences of debt issued after the first day of January, one thousand seven hundred and ninety, be referred to Mr. Laurance, Mr. Tucker, and Mr. Wadsworth, with instruction to prepare and bring in a bill or bills pursuant thereto.[11]

A bill to compensate George Gibson, was read the second time, and ordered to be committed to a committee of the whole House to-morrow.[12]

An engrossed bill to continue in force, for a limited time, an act, intituled, "An act for the temporary establishment of the post-office," was read the third time.

RESOLVED, That the said bill do pass; and that the title be, "An act to continue in force, for a limited time, an act, intituled, 'An act for the temporary establishment of the post-office,' and for other purposes."

ORDERED, That the Clerk of this House do carry the said bill to the Senate, and desire their concurrence.[13]

---

[9] The resolution and the above bills, except the Duties on Distilled Spirits Bill [HR–110], were signed by the president on March 2. On March 3 the Duties on Distilled Spirits Bill [HR–110] was signed.

[10] On March 2 this bill was read again, agreed to, and sent to the Senate.

[11] On March 2 this committee presented an Evidences of Debt Bill [HR–141], which was read.

[12] On March 2 this bill was amended, read again, and agreed to.

[13] On March 2 the Senate read this bill, and it is printed in the *Senate Legislative Journal.* Later on the same day, the bill was read again, and it was agreed to delete the second section. On March 3 the Senate read the bill again, amended, and agreed to it. The Senate amendments are printed in the *Senate Legislative Journal* for March 3. On the same day the House agreed to the Senate amendments, and the bill was signed.

An engrossed bill supplementary to the act making provision for the reduction of the public debt, was read the third time.

RESOLVED, That the said bill do pass; and that the title be, "An act supplementary to the act making provision for the reduction of the public debt."

ORDERED, That the Clerk of this House do carry the said bill to the Senate, and desire their concurrence.[14]

A petition of Thomas Claxton, assistant-doorkeeper to the House of Representatives, was presented to the House and read, praying a farther compensation for his services.

ORDERED, That the said petition do lie on the table.

The several orders of the day were further postponed until to-morrow.[15]

And then the House adjourned until to-morrow morning ten o'clock.

WEDNESDAY, MARCH 2, 1791

A message from the Senate by Mr. Otis their Secretary.

MR. SPEAKER, I am directed to inform this House, that the Senate have postponed the consideration of the bill sent from this House, intituled, "An act to establish offices for the purpose of granting lands within the territories of the United States," until the next session. I am also directed to inform this House, that the Senate have passed the bill, intituled, "An act repealing so much of an act as establishes the rate of the rix-dollar of Denmark," with several amendments,[16] to which they desire the concurrence of this House. And then he withdrew.

An engrossed bill for making compensation to the widows and orphan children of certain officers who were killed, or who died while in the service of the United States, during the late war, and for the relief of certain invalids and other persons therein mentioned, was read the third time.

RESOLVED, That the said bill do pass; and that the title be, "An act for making compensation to the widows and orphans of certain officers who were

---

[14] On March 2 the Senate read this bill twice. It is printed in the *Senate Legislative Journal* for that date. On March 3 the Senate read the bill again and agreed to it with amendments, which are printed in the *Senate Legislative Journal*. On the same day the House agreed to the Senate amendments, and the bill was signed.

[15] On this date the House probably was notified that the Senate had agreed to all but the last two House amendments to the Military Establishment Bill [HR–126A]. On March 2 the House receded from the last two amendments, and the bill was signed by the speaker and vice president.

[16] The Senate committee report on this bill, with amendments, is in Various Select Committee Reports, SR, DNA. The amendments are printed in the *Senate Legislative Journal* on March 1.

killed, or who died while in the service of United States, during the late war, and for the relief of certain invalids and other persons therein mentioned."

ORDERED, That the Clerk of this House do carry the said bill to the Senate, and desire their concurrence.[17]

Mr. Floyd, from the joint committee for inrolled bills, reported, that the committee had examined two inrolled bills—to wit; one intituled, "An act supplemental to the act establishing the treasury department, and for a farther compensation to certain officers;"[18] and another which originated in the Senate, intituled, "An act to amend an act for establishing the temporary and permanent seat of the government of the United States,"[19] and had found the same to be truly inrolled:[20]   Whereupon,

Mr. Speaker signed the said inrolled bills.

ORDERED, That the Clerk of this House do acquaint the Senate therewith.

The House, according to the order of the day, resolved itself into a committee of the whole House on the bill, in addition to the act for establishing the salaries of the executive officers of government, with their assistants and clerks; and after some time spent therein, Mr. Speaker resumed the chair, and Mr. Livermore reported, that the committee had, according to order, had the said bill under consideration, and made no amendment thereto.

ORDERED, That the said bill be engrossed, and read the third time.

Mr. Burke, from the committee appointed, presented, according to order, a bill for the relief of David Cook; which was received and read the first time.[21]

The House proceeded to consider the amendments of the Senate to the bill, intituled, "An act repealing so much of an act as establishes the rate of the rix-dollar of Denmark;" and the same being twice read, were agreed to.

ORDERED, That the Clerk of this House do acquaint the Senate therewith.[22]

The House, according to the order of the day, resolved itself into a committee of the whole House, on the bill making farther provision for the collec-

---

[17] On March 2 the Senate read this bill. It is printed in the *Senate Legislative Journal* on this date. On the same day the bill was read again and committed. On March 3 this committee reported, and consideration of this bill was postponed until the next session.

[18] The inspected enrolled bill is in Enrolled Acts, RG 11, DNA. E–23866.

[19] The inspected enrolled bill is in Enrolled Acts, RG 11, DNA. E–23869.

[20] This committee also reported on the Military Establishment Bill [HR–126A]. The inspected enrolled bill is in Enrolled Acts, RG 11, DNA. E–23855.

[21] On March 3 this bill was read twice, agreed to, and sent to the Senate. On the same date the Senate postponed this bill to the next session.

[22] On March 3 this bill was signed by the speaker, vice president, and president. The message from the House to the Senate concerning these amendments to the Collection Bill [HR–134] also noted that the House receded from the amendments disagreed to by the Senate on the "Bill founded on certain confidential communications," which is the Military Establishment Bill [HR–126A]. The message is in Messages from the House, SR, DNA.

tion of the duties by law imposed on teas; and after some time spent therein, Mr. Speaker resumed the chair, and Mr. Boudinot reported, that the committee had, according to order, had the said bill under consideration, and made no amendment thereto.

On motion,

ORDERED, That the said bill be re-committed to a committee of the whole House immediately.

The House accordingly resolved itself into the said committee; and after some time spent therein, Mr. Speaker resumed the chair, and Mr. Boudinot reported, that the committee had, according to order, again had the said bill under consideration, and made an amendment thereto; which he delivered in at the Clerk's table, where the same was twice read, and agreed to.

ORDERED, That the said bill, with the amendment, be engrossed, and read the third time.

A message was received from the President of the United States, by Mr. Lear his Secretary, notifying that the President did, this day, approve and sign the following acts—to wit:

"An act giving effect to the laws of the United States within the state of Vermont."

"An act to explain and amend an act, intituled, 'An act making farther provision for the payment of the debts of the United States.'"

"An act supplementary to the act, intituled, 'An act to incorporate the subscribers to the bank of the United States.'" And

"An act fixing the time for the next annual meeting of Congress."

A message from the Senate by Mr. Otis their Secretary.

MR. SPEAKER, The Senate have agreed to a resolution, "That the President of the United States be, and he hereby is requested to cause a return to be made to Congress at their next session, of the quantity and situation of the lands not claimed by the Indians, nor granted to, nor claimed by any citizens of the United States, within the territory ceded to the United States, by the state of North-Carolina, and within the territory of the United States north-west of the river Ohio," to which they desire the concurrence of this House. And then he withdrew.

The House proceeded to consider the said resolution; and the same being amended by striking out the words "*a return to be made to*," and inserting in lieu thereof the words, "*an estimate to be laid before*," was, on the question put thereupon, agreed to by the House.[23]

---

[23] Copies of the Senate resolution and the House amendment are in Senate Joint and Concurrent Resolutions, SR, DNA. The Senate committee report of this resolution is in Various Select Committee Reports, SR, DNA.

ORDERED, That the Clerk of this House do acquaint the Senate therewith.[24]

Mr. Laurance, from the committee to whom was referred the report of the Secretary of the Treasury respecting certificates or evidences of debt issued since the first day of January, one thousand seven hundred and ninety, presented a bill concerning certain certificates or evidences of the public debt; which was received and read the first time.[25]

The House, according to the order of the day, resolved itself into a committee of the whole House, on the bill sent from the Senate, "concerning consuls and vice-consuls;" and after some time spent therein, Mr. Speaker resumed the chair, and Mr. Boudinot reported, that the committee had, according to order, had the said bill under consideration, and made several amendments thereto;[26] which he delivered in at the Clerk's table, where the same were severally twice read, and agreed to.

The said bill, as amended, was then read the third time; and, on the question that the same do pass,

It was resolved in the affirmative.

ORDERED, That the Clerk of this House do acquaint the Senate therewith.

A message from the Senate by Mr. Otis their Secretary.

MR. SPEAKER, The Senate have passed a bill, intituled, "An act making an appropriation for the purpose therein mentioned;"[27] to which they desire the concurrence of this House. And then he withdrew.

The said bill was read the first time.

On motion,

The said bill was read the second time.

On motion,

The said bill was read the third time; and, on the question that the same do pass,

It was resolved in the affirmative.

ORDERED, That the Clerk of this House do acquaint the Senate therewith.[28]

The Speaker laid before the House a letter from the Secretary of the Treasury, covering his reports on the several petitions of Gosuinus Erkelens, Elias Hasket Derby, and of Coninghame, Nesbitt and Company, and James Crawford; which were read, and ordered to lie on the table.[29]

---

[24] On March 3 the Senate agreed to the House amendment, and the resolution was signed.

[25] This bill was not considered again in the First Congress.

[26] The amendments are filed with the bill in Senate Bills, SR, DNA. They are printed in the *Senate Legislative Journal* on March 2.

[27] The Moroccan Treaty Bill [S–23] is in Engrossed Senate Bills and Resolutions, SR, DNA. The bill is printed in the *Senate Legislative Journal* on March 1.

[28] On March 3 this bill was signed.

[29] Copies of all of these reports are in A Record of the Reports of the Secretary of the Treasury, vol. 2, HR, DNA.

An engrossed bill in addition to the act for establishing the salaries of the executive officers of government, with their assistants and clerks, was read the third time.

RESOLVED, That the said bill do pass; and that the title be, "An act in addition to the act for establishing the salaries of the executive officers of government with their assistants and clerks."

ORDERED, That the Clerk of this House do carry the said bill to the Senate, and desire their concurrence.[30]

The House, according to the order of the day, resolved itself into a committee of the whole House, on the bill to compensate George Gibson; and after some time spent therein, Mr. Speaker resumed the chair, and Mr. Boudinot reported, that the committee had, according to order, had the said bill under consideration, and made an amendment thereto; which he delivered in at the Clerk's table, where the same was twice read, and agreed to.

And then the question being put, that the said bill, with the amendment, be engrossed, and read the third time;

It was resolved in the affirmative— $\begin{cases} \text{AYES} & 33 \\ \text{NOES} & 14 \end{cases}$

The ayes and noes being demanded by one fifth of the members present; Those who voted in the affirmative, are,

John Baptista Ashe	John Laurance
Abraham Baldwin	Richard Bland Lee
Egbert Benson	James Madison, junior
Elias Boudinot	Peter Muhlenberg
John Brown	Thomas Scott
Aedanus Burke	Joshua Seney
Lambert Cadwalader	John Sevier
Daniel Carroll	William Smith (of Maryland)
George Clymer	William Smith (of South-Carolina)
Benjamin Contee	Thomas Sumter
Thomas Fitzsimons	Jonathan Trumbull
William Floyd	Thomas Tudor Tucker
Nicholas Gilman	John Vining
William B. Giles	Jeremiah Wadsworth
Thomas Hartley	Alexander White and
Benjamin Huntington	Henry Wynkoop
James Jackson	

---

[30] On March 2 the Senate read this bill twice. It is printed in the *Senate Legislative Journal* on this date. On March 3 the bill was read again and agreed to with amendments. On the same day the House agreed to the amendments, and the bill was signed.

Those who voted in the negative, are,

Fisher Ames	Jeremiah Van Rensselaer
Benjamin Bourn	James Schureman
Abiel Foster	Theodore Sedgwick
John Hathorn	Roger Sherman
George Leonard	Peter Silvester
Samuel Livermore	George Thatcher and
George Partridge	Hugh Williamson

An engrossed bill, making farther provision for the collection of the duties by law imposed on teas, was read the third time, and the blanks therein filled up.

RESOLVED, That the said bill do pass; and that the title be, "An act making farther provision for the collection of the duties by law imposed on teas, and for prolonging the term for the payment of the duties on wines."

ORDERED, That the Clerk of this House do carry the said bill to the Senate, and desire their concurrence.[31]

An engrossed bill to compensate George Gibson, was read the third time.

RESOLVED, That the said bill do pass; and that the title be, "An act to compensate George Gibson."[32]

ORDERED, That the Clerk of this House do carry the said bill to the Senate, and desire their concurrence.[33]

A message from the Senate by Mr. Otis their Secretary.

MR. SPEAKER,   The Senate disagree to the amendments proposed by this House to the bill sent from the Senate, intituled, "An act concerning consuls and vice-consuls."   And then he withdrew.

The House proceeded to re-consider the amendments to the said bill: Whereupon,

RESOLVED, That this House doth insist on their said amendments.

ORDERED, That the Clerk of this House do acquaint the Senate therewith.[34]

Mr. Floyd, from the joint committee for inrolled bills, reported, that the committee did, this day, wait on the President of the United States, and pre-

---

[31] On March 2 the Senate read this bill twice. It is printed in the *Senate Legislative Journal* on this date. It was then committed. This committee reported, and the bill was agreed to without amendments on March 3. On the same day the bill was signed.

[32] The bill is in Engrossed House Bills, HR, DNA. It is printed in the *Senate Legislative Journal* on March 2.

[33] On March 2 the Senate read this bill. On March 3 it was postponed until the next session.

[34] On March 3 the Senate adhered to its disagreement to the amendments, and the House insisted on them.

sent for his approbation two inrolled bills—to wit; one intituled, "An act supplementary to an act establishing the treasury department, and for a farther compensation to certain officers;" and another intituled, "An act to amend an act for establishing the temporary and permanent seat of the government of the United States."[35]

On a motion made and seconded,

RESOLVED, That Gifford Dally be authorized to take the care of the rooms appropriated for the use of the House of Representatives, until the next meeting of Congress, and to make the necessary provision of fire-wood for the next session.

The several orders of the day were further postponed until to-morrow.[36]

And then the House adjourned until to-morrow morning ten o'clock.

THURSDAY, MARCH 3, 1791

The Speaker laid before the House a letter from the Secretary at War, accompanying his report on the petition of Henry Laurens; also, his report on the petitions of several Oneida and Tuscarora Indians, by their attorney Cornelius Vanslyk; which were read, and ordered to lie on the table.[37]

The House proceeded to consider the petition of Thomas Claxton, which lay on the table: Whereupon,

ORDERED, That the expenses incurred by the said Thomas Claxton, as stated in his petition, not exceeding one hundred dollars, be included in the account of the Clerk of this House, when rendered, for the contingent expenses of the present session.

Mr. Cadwalader, from the committee to whom was referred the petition of John Tucker, made a report;[38] which was read, and agreed to by the House as followeth:

"That the petition being unaccompanied with a stated account of the petitioner's expenses, and the petitioner being absent, the committee cannot ascertain with precision the amount of his claim, and therefore recommend that the farther consideration of the said petition be deferred until the next session of Congress."

A message from the Senate by Mr. Otis their Secretary.

---

[35] The report, which includes the Military Establishment Bill [HR–126A], is in Committee on Enrolled Bills, SR, DNA. On March 3 the president signed these bills.

[36] Although not journalized on this date, the Senate probably notified the House that the president had signed the resolution thanking the National Assembly of France for its resolution on Benjamin Franklin. This message is in Committee on Enrolled Bills, SR, DNA.

[37] Copies of these reports are in A Record of the Reports of the Secretary of War, vol. 2, HR, DNA. A copy of the Vanslyk report, probably made by ASP, is in Reports and Communications from the Secretary of War, HR, DNA.

[38] A copy of the report is in A Record of the Reports of Select Committees, HR, DNA.

MR. SPEAKER, The Senate adhere to their disagreement to the amendments proposed by this House to the bill, intituled, "An act concerning consuls and vice-consuls." The Senate have also passed the bill, intituled, "An act making farther provision for the collection of the duties by law imposed on teas, and for prolonging the term for the payment of the duties on wines." The Senate have also agreed to two resolutions, to which they desire the concurrence of this House, as follow:

"That a mint shall be established, under such regulations as shall be directed by law."

"That the President of the United States be, and he is hereby authorized to cause to be engaged, such artists[39] as shall be necessary to carry the preceding resolution into effect, and to stipulate the terms and conditions of their service; and also to cause to be procured such apparatus as shall be requisite for the same purpose."

The House proceeded to consider the said resolutions; and the second resolution being amended by inserting after the word "*such*," the word "*principal*;" the same were, on the question put thereupon, agreed to by the House.[40] AYES 25: NOES 21.

The ayes and noes being demanded by one fifth of the members present;

Those who voted in the affirmative, are,

Elias Boudinot	Thomas Scott
Lambert Cadwalader	Theodore Sedgwick
George Clymer	Joshua Seney
Benjamin Contee	John Sevier
Thomas Fitzsimons	Peter Silvester
William Floyd	William Smith (of Maryland)
George Gale	William Smith (of South-Carolina)
Nicholas Gilman	John Steele
Samuel Griffin	Jonathan Trumbull
Thomas Hartley	John Vining
John Laurance	Jeremiah Wadsworth and
Richard Bland Lee	Henry Wynkoop
Peter Muhlenberg	

[39] At this point the words "and workmen" have been omitted from the Senate resolution by the House. This omission probably occurred because of a House amendment that expunged the words "and workmen." This amendment was also agreed to on March 3, although it is not journalized. Both the House and the Senate refer to the two House changes in the resolution as one amendment.

[40] Copies of the Senate resolution and the House amendments are in Senate Joint and Concurrent Resolutions, SR, DNA. The Senate committee report of these two resolutions is in Various Select Committee Reports, SR, DNA.

Those who voted in the negative, are,

John Baptista Ashe	Andrew Moore
Abraham Baldwin	George Partridge
Aedanus Burke	Jeremiah Van Rensselaer
Abiel Foster	James Schureman
William B. Giles	Roger Sherman
John Hathorn	Thomas Sinnickson
Daniel Hiester	Thomas Sumter
Benjamin Huntington	Thomas Tudor Tucker
James Jackson	Alexander White and
George Leonard	Hugh Williamson
Samuel Livermore	

The House proceeded to re-consider the amendments insisted on by this House, and to their disagreement to which the Senate doth adhere, to the bill, intituled, "An act concerning consuls and vice-consuls:" Whereupon, RESOLVED, That this House doth adhere to their said amendments.

ORDERED, That the Clerk of this House do acquaint the Senate therewith.

A message from the Senate by Mr. Otis their Secretary.

MR. SPEAKER,   The Senate have passed the bill, intituled, "An act making compensations to the commissioners of loans, for extraordinary expenses," with an amendment,[41] to which they desire the concurrence of this House. And then he withdrew.

The House proceeded to consider the said amendment; and the same being read, as followeth: "Strike out the last clause in the words following; 'excepting only the hire of one clerk for the several commissioners in the states of Massachusetts, New-York, Pennsylvania and Virginia;'" was, on the question put thereupon, disagreed to.   AYES 20: NOES 22.

The ayes and noes being demanded by one fifth of the members present; Those who voted in the affirmative, are,

Lambert Cadwalader	William B. Giles
Daniel Carroll	Thomas Hartley
George Clymer	John Hathorn
Thomas Fitzsimons	Daniel Hiester
William Floyd	Benjamin Huntington
George Gale	John Laurance
Samuel Griffin	Richard Bland Lee

[41] The amendment is printed in the *Senate Legislative Journal* on March 3.

Thomas Scott   Peter Silvester
Theodore Sedgwick   Jonathan Trumbull and
Roger Sherman   Henry Wynkoop

Those who voted in the negative, are,

Abraham Baldwin   James Madison, junior
Elias Boudinot   Peter Muhlenberg
Benjamin Bourn   George Partridge
John Brown   James Schureman
Aedanus Burke   Thomas Sinnickson
Benjamin Contee   William Smith (of Maryland)
Abiel Foster   William Smith (of South-Carolina)
Nicholas Gilman   Thomas Sumter
James Jackson   John Vining
George Leonard   Alexander White and
Samuel Livermore   Hugh Williamson

A message from the Senate by Mr. Otis their Secretary.

MR. SPEAKER, The Senate have agreed to the amendments proposed by this House to the resolution respecting the ungranted lands within the territories of the United States. The Senate have also passed the bill, intituled, "An act in addition to the act establishing the salaries of the executive officers of government, with their assistants and clerks," with several amendments,[42] to which they desire the concurrence of this House. The Senate do also adhere to their amendment disagreed to by this House, to the bill, intituled, "An act making compensations to the commissioners of loans, for extraordinary expenses." And then he withdrew.

The House proceeded to consider the said message: Whereupon,

RESOLVED, That this House doth recede from their disagreement to the amendment adhered to by the Senate to the bill last mentioned. AYES 23: NOES 20.

The ayes and noes being demanded by one fifth of the members present; Those who voted in the affirmative, are,

Lambert Cadwalader   Samuel Griffin
George Clymer   William B. Giles
Thomas Fitzsimons   Thomas Hartley
William Floyd   John Hathorn
George Gale   Benjamin Huntington

---

[42] Senate amendments are in House Bills, SR, DNA. They are printed in the *Senate Legislative Journal* on March 3.

John Laurance   Roger Sherman
Richard Bland Lee   Peter Silvester
Peter Muhlenberg   Jonathan Trumbull
George Partridge   John Vining
Thomas Scott   Jeremiah Wadsworth and
Theodore Sedgwick   Henry Wynkoop
John Sevier

Those who voted in the negative, are,

John Baptista Ashe   Jeremiah Van Rensselaer
Abraham Baldwin   James Schureman
Timothy Bloodworth   Joshua Seney
Elias Boudinot   Thomas Sinnickson
Benjamin Contee   William Smith (of Maryland)
Abiel Foster   William Smith (of South-Carolina)
James Jackson   John Steele
George Leonard   Thomas Sumter
Samuel Livermore   Alexander White and
George Mathews   Hugh Williamson

RESOLVED, That this House doth agree to all the amendments proposed by the Senate to the bill, intituled, "An act in addition to the act establishing the salaries of the executive officers of government, with their assistants and clerks."

ORDERED, That the Clerk of this House do acquaint the Senate therewith.

A message from the Senate by Mr. Otis their Secretary.

MR. SPEAKER, The Senate have passed the bill, intituled, "An act for granting lands to the inhabitants and settlers at Vincennes and the Illinois country, in the territory north-west of the Ohio, and for confirming them in their possessions," with several amendments,[43] to which they desire the concurrence of this House. The Senate have also passed the bill, intituled, "An act to continue in force, for a limited time, an act for the temporary establishment of the post-office," with several amendments,[44] to which they also desire the concurrence of this House.   And then he withdrew.

---

[43] This message is incorrect. The Northwest Territory Bill [S–17] had already been agreed to by the Senate, and the House had returned it to the Senate with amendments. According to the *Senate Legislative Journal* of March 3, the Senate agreed to the House amendments with an amendment on this date. A copy of the Senate resolution with an amendment is filed with the bill in Engrossed Senate Bills and Resolutions, SR, DNA. The amendment is printed in the *Senate Legislative Journal* on March 3.

[44] A Senate amendment is in House Bills, SR, DNA. The amendments are printed in the *Senate Legislative Journal* on March 3.

The House proceeded to consider the said message: Whereupon,

RESOLVED, That this House doth agree to all the amendments proposed by the Senate to the said two last mentioned bills.

ORDERED, That the Clerk of this House do acquaint the Senate therewith.

A message from the Senate by Mr. Otis their Secretary.

MR. SPEAKER,   The Senate have passed the bill, intituled, "An act providing compensations for the officers of the judicial courts of the United States, and for jurors and witnesses, and for other purposes," with several amendments,[45] to which they desire the concurrence of this House.   And then he withdrew.

The House proceeded to consider the said amendments; and the same being read, some were agreed to, and others disagreed to.

ORDERED, That the Clerk of this House do acquaint the Senate therewith.

A message from the Senate by Mr. Otis their Secretary.

MR. SPEAKER,   The Senate have deferred until the next session of Congress, the consideration of two bills sent from this House; the one intituled, "An act making compensation to the widows and orphan children of certain officers who were killed, or who died while in the service of the United States, during the late war, and for the relief of certain invalids and other persons therein mentioned;" the other intituled, "An act to compensate George Gibson." The Senate have also agreed to the amendment proposed by this House to the resolutions respecting the establishment of a mint. They have also passed the bill, intituled, "An act supplementary to the act making provision for the reduction of the public debt," with several amendments,[46] to which they desire the concurrence of this House.   And then he withdrew.

The House proceeded to consider the amendments proposed by the Senate to the said last mentioned bill; and the same being read, were agreed to.

ORDERED, That the Clerk of this House do acquaint the Senate therewith.

A message.   The Senate recede from such of their amendments as were disagreed to by this House, to the bill, intituled, "An act providing compensations for the officers of the judicial courts of the United States, and for jurors and witnesses, and for other purposes." The Senate have also passed the bill,

---

[45] Senate amendments are noted on and filed with the bill in House Bills, SR, DNA. A separate list of amendments is also in the above location. The amendments are printed in the *Senate Legislative Journal* on March 3.

[46] The Senate amendments are in House Bills, SR, DNA. They are printed in the *Senate Legislative Journal* on March 3.

intituled, "An act to continue in force the act therein mentioned, and to make further provision for the payment of pensions to invalids, and for the support of light-houses, beacons, buoys and public piers;"[47] to which they desire the concurrence of this House.   And then he withdrew.

The said bill was read the first time.
On motion,
The said bill was read the second time.

On a motion made and seconded, that the following clauses of amendment to the Constitution of the United States, be proposed by Congress to the Legislatures of the several States, to wit:

THAT the Congress shall, either by declaring the superior or supreme common law-court of the state to be the court, or by creating a new court for the purpose, establish A GENERAL JUDICIAL COURT in each state, the judges whereof shall hold their commissions during good behavior, and without any other limitation whatsoever, and shall be appointed and commissioned by the state, and shall receive their compensations from the United States only; and the compensations shall not be diminished during their continuance in office.

The number of judges of the general judicial court in a state, unless the same should be altered by the consent of the Congress and the legislature of the state, shall be in the proportion of one judge for every   persons in the state, according to the enumeration for apportioning the Representatives among the several states; but there shall always be at least three judges in each state.

The general judicial court shall, in all cases to which the judicial power of the United States doth extend, have original jurisdiction, either exclusively or concurrently with other courts in the respective states, and otherwise regulated as the Congress shall prescribe; and, in cases where the judicial power is reserved to the several states, as the legislature of each state shall prescribe: but shall have, and exclusively, *immediate* appellate jurisdiction, in all cases, from every other court within the state, under such limitations, exceptions and regulations, however, as shall be made with the consent of the Congress, and the legislature of the state: there may, notwithstanding, be in each state a court of appeals or errors in the last resort, under the authority of the state, from the general judicial court, in cases and on questions only, where the supreme court of the United States hath not appellate jurisdiction from the general judicial court.

The Congress may provide that the judges of the general judicial court shall hold circuit courts within the state; and the legislature of the state may,

---

[47] This bill is the Mitigation of Forfeitures Bill [S–24]. The bill is in Engrossed Senate Bills and Resolutions, SR, DNA.

in addition to the times and places to be assigned by the Congress for holding the general judicial court or the circuit courts, assign other times and places.

The Congress may determine the number of judges which shall be a quorum to hold a general judicial court, or a circuit court, in each respective state.

The Congress may, in the cases to which the judicial power of the United States doth extend, and the legislature of the state may, in the other cases, regulate the fees and proceedings in the several courts, and the jurisdiction of the circuit courts, within the state.

The ministerial officers of the general judicial court shall be appointed and commissioned in such manner as the legislature of the state shall prescribe.

All writs, issuing out of the general judicial court, shall be in the name of *the Judges* thereof.

The judges of the general judicial court may be impeached by the House of Representatives of the United States, and also by the most numerous branch of the state legislature.

The impeachment shall not be tried by the Senate of the United States, or by any judicature under the authority of the state, but the Congress shall, by law, establish a court to be held in each state, for the trial of such impeachments, to consist only of Senators of the United States, judges of the supreme court of the United States, and judges of general judicial courts—The trial shall be in the state where the person impeached shall reside; and every law, designating the judges of a court for the trial of impeachments, shall be passed previous to the impeachment; and the designation shall be, not by naming the persons, but by describing the offices, the persons in which offices for the time being, and elected or appointed previous to the impeachment, shall be the judges; and no person shall be convicted without the concurrence of two thirds of the judges present.

Judgments by the courts so to be established for the trial of impeachments, shall not extend further than is provided by the Constitution of the United States, in cases of impeachments, and the party, nevertheless, to be liable and subject to indictment, trial, judgment and punishment according to law.

In every state where the Congress shall declare the superior or supreme common law-court, to be the general *judicial court*, the judges shall, by force of their appointments as judges of the superior or supreme common law-court, become judges of the general judicial court: and all the powers and duties of the judges of the superior or supreme common law-court, either by the Constitution or the laws of the state, shall devolve on the judges of the general judicial court.

If on the establishment of the general judicial courts, the Congress shall deem proper to discontinue any of the district courts of the United States, the judges of the courts so discontinued shall, thereupon, by force of their appointments as district judges, become judges of the general judicial courts in the respective states, and shall continue to receive their compensations as theretofore established.

The judges of the supreme or superior common law-courts, and the district judges, may, on the first establishment of the general judicial courts, become judges thereof, notwithstanding the limitation of the number of the judges of the general judicial courts in the respective states, but as vacancies happen they shall not afterwards be filled up beyond the number limited.

For avoiding of doubts, it is declared, that all officers, as well ministerial as judicial, in the *administration of justice* under the authority of a state, shall also be held to execute their respective offices, for carrying into effect the laws of the United States; and, in addition to the duties assigned to them by the laws of the state, the Congress may assign to them such farther duties as they shall deem proper for that purpose.

RESOLVED, That the consideration of the said amendments be deferred until the next session of Congress; and that one hundred copies thereof be printed for the use of the members of both Houses.[48]

On a motion made and seconded, that the House do come to the following resolution:

Whereas Congress did, by a resolution of the twenty-third of September, one thousand seven hundred and eighty-nine, recommend to the several states to pass laws, making it expressly the duty of the keepers of their gaols, to receive and safe keep therein all prisoners committed under the authority of the United States:

In order therefore to insure the administration of justice,

RESOLVED by the SENATE and HOUSE of REPRESENTATIVES of the UNITED STATES of AMERICA in CONGRESS assembled, That in case any state shall not have complied with the said recommendation, the marshal in such state, under the direction of the judge of the district, be authorized to hire a convenient place to serve as a temporary gaol, and to make the necessary provision for the safe keeping of prisoners committed under the authority of the United States, until permanent provision shall be made by law for that purpose; and the said marshal shall be allowed his reasonable expenses incurred for the above purposes, to be paid out of the treasury of the United States.

It was resolved in the affirmative.

ORDERED, That the Clerk of this House do carry the said resolution to the Senate, and desire their concurrence.

ORDERED, That leave be given to bring in a bill or bills for carrying into effect a consular convention between His Most Christian Majesty and the

---

[48] The resolution with the proposed amendments is E-23883.

United States; and that Mr. Smith (of South-Carolina), Mr. Madison, and Mr. Vining, do prepare and bring in the same.

The bill sent from the Senate, intituled, "An act to continue in force the act therein mentioned, and to make farther provision for the payment of pensions to invalids, and for the support of light-houses, beacons, buoys and public piers,"[49] was read the third time; and on the question that the said bill do pass,

It was resolved in the affirmative.

ORDERED, That the Clerk of this House do acquaint the Senate therewith.

Mr. Smith (of South-Carolina), from the committee appointed, presented, according to order, a bill for carrying into effect the consular convention between His Most Christian Majesty and the United States; which was received and read the first time.

On motion,

The said bill was read the second time, and ordered to be engrossed, and read the third time to-day.

A bill for the relief of David Cook, was read the second time, and ordered to be engrossed, and read the third time to-day.

An engrossed bill for carrying into effect the consular convention between His Most Christian Majesty and the United States, was read the third time.

RESOLVED, That the said bill do pass; and that the title be, "An act for carrying into effect the consular convention between His Most Christian Majesty and the United States."[50]

ORDERED, That the Clerk of this House do carry the said bill to the Senate, and desire their concurrence.

An engrossed bill for the relief of David Cook, was read the third time.

RESOLVED, That the said bill do pass; and that the title be, "An act for the relief of David Cook."[51]

ORDERED, That the Clerk of this House do carry the said bill to the Senate, and desire their concurrence.

A message from the Senate by Mr. Otis their Secretary.

MR. SPEAKER, The Senate have agreed to the resolution respecting the safe-keeping of prisoners committed under the authority of the United States. The Senate have also deferred until the next session of Congress, the consideration of the two bills sent from this House; one intituled, "An act for carrying into effect the consular convention between His Most Christian Ma-

---

[49] This bill is the Mitigation of Forfeitures Bill [S–24].

[50] The bill is in Engrossed House Bills, HR, DNA. It is printed in the *Senate Legislative Journal* on March 3.

[51] The bill is in Engrossed House Bills, HR, DNA. It is printed in the *Senate Legislative Journal* on March 3.

jesty and the United States;" the other intituled, "An act for the relief of David Cook." And then he withdrew.

Mr. Floyd, from the joint committee for inrolled bills, reported, that the committee had examined the following inrolled bills and resolves—to wit;

An act, intituled, "An act making compensations to the commissioners of loans, for extraordinary expenses."[52]

An act, intituled, "An act in addition to an act, intituled, 'An act for establishing the salaries of the executive officers of government, with their assistants and clerks.' "[53]

An act, intituled, "An act to continue in force, for a limited time, an act, intituled, 'An act for the temporary establishment of the post-office.' "[54]

An act, intituled "An act relative to the rix-dollar of Denmark."[55]

An act, intituled, "An act supplementary to the act making provision for the reduction of the public debt."[56]

An act, intituled, "An act providing compensations for the officers of the judicial courts of the United States, and for jurors and witnesses, and for other purposes."[57]

An act, intituled, "An act making farther provision for the collection of the duties by law imposed on teas, and to prolong the term for the payment of the duties on wines."[58]

An act, intituled, "An act to continue in force the act therein mentioned, and to make farther provision for the payment of pensions to invalids, and for the support of light-houses, beacons, buoys and public piers."[59]

An act, intituled, "An act for granting lands to the inhabitants and settlers at Vincennes and the Illinois country, in the territory north-west of the Ohio, and for confirming them in their titles."[60]

And an act, intituled, "An act for making an appropriation for the purpose therein mentioned."[61]

A resolve respecting the establishment of a mint.[62]

---

[52] The inspected enrolled bill is in Enrolled Acts, RG 11, DNA. E–23854.
[53] The inspected enrolled bill is in Enrolled Acts, RG 11, DNA. E–23858.
[54] The inspected enrolled bill is in Enrolled Acts, RG 11, DNA. E–23871.
[55] The inspected enrolled bill is in Enrolled Acts, RG 11, DNA. E–23964.
[56] The inspected enrolled bill is in Enrolled Acts, RG 11, DNA. E–23868.
[57] The inspected enrolled bill is in Enrolled Acts, RG 11, DNA. E–23862.
[58] The inspected enrolled bill is in Enrolled Acts, RG 11, DNA. E–23861.
[59] This bill is the Mitigation of Forfeitures Bill [S–24]. The inspected enrolled bill is in Enrolled Acts, RG 11, DNA. E–23873.
[60] The inspected enrolled bill is in Enrolled Acts, RG 11, DNA. E–23853.
[61] The inspected enrolled bill is in Enrolled Acts, RG 11, DNA. E–23859. Reports on all of these bills, except the first and second, are in Committee on Enrolled Bills, SR, DNA.
[62] The inspected enrolled resolution is in Enrolled Acts, RG 11, DNA. E–23880.

A resolve respecting the ungranted lands within the territory of the United States.[63]   And

A resolve respecting the safe-keeping of prisoners committed under the authority of the United States—[64]

And had found the same to be truly inrolled: Whereupon,

Mr. Speaker signed the said inrolled bills and resolves.

A petition of sundry officers and soldiers of the old flying camp, was presented to the House and read, praying compensation for military services rendered during the late war.

ORDERED, That the said petition do lie on the table.

Mr. Floyd, from the joint committee for inrolled bills, reported, that the committee did, this day, wait on the President of the United States, and present for his approbation the following inrolled bills and resolves, to wit:

An act, intituled, "An act making compensations to the commissioners of loans, for extraordinary expenses."

An act, intituled, "An act in addition to the act, intituled, 'An act for establishing the salaries of the executive officers of government, with their assistants and clerks.'"

An act, intituled, "An act to continue in force for a limited time, an act, intituled, 'An act for the temporary establishment of the post-office.'"

An act, intituled, "An act relative to the rix dollar of Denmark."

An act, intituled, "An act supplementary to the act making provision for the reduction of the public debt."

An act, intituled, "An act providing compensations to the officers of the judicial courts of the United States, and for jurors and witnesses, and for other purposes."

An act, intituled, "An act making farther provision for the collection of the duties by law imposed on teas, and to prolong the term of the payment of the duties on wines."

An act, intituled, "An act to continue in force the act therein mentioned, and to make farther provision for the payment of pensions to invalids, and for the support of light-houses, beacons, buoys, and public piers."[65]

An act, intituled, "An act for granting lands to the inhabitants and settlers at Vincennes and the Illinois country, in the territory north-west of the Ohio, and for confirming them in their titles."

An act, intituled, "An act making an appropriation therein mentioned."

A resolve respecting the establishment of a mint.

A resolve respecting the ungranted lands within the territories of the United States.   And

---

[63] The inspected enrolled resolution is in Enrolled Acts, RG 11, DNA. E-23882.

[64] The inspected enrolled resolution is in Enrolled Acts, RG 11, DNA. E-23881.

[65] This bill is the Mitigation of Forfeitures Bill [S-24].

A resolve respecting the safe-keeping of prisoners committed under the authority of the United States.[66]

On a motion made and seconded,

RESOLVED UNANIMOUSLY, That the Speaker communicate the thanks of the House of Representatives to the Mayor and Corporation of this city, and the Commissioners of the county of Philadelphia, for the elegant and convenient accommodations provided for their present session.

A message was received from the President of the United States, by Mr. Lear his Secretary, notifying that the President did, this day, approve and sign the following acts and resolve—to wit:[67]

"An act repealing, after the last day of June next, the duties heretofore laid upon distilled spirits imported from abroad, and laying others in their stead; and also upon spirits distilled within the United States, and for appropriating the same."

"An act supplemental to the act establishing the treasury department, and for a farther compensation to certain officers."

"An act relative to the rix-dollar of Denmark."

"An act in addition to an act, intituled, 'An act for establishing the salaries of the executive officers of government, with their assistants and clerks.' "

"An act making compensations to the commissioners of loans, for extraordinary expenses."

"An act providing compensations for the officers of the judicial courts of the United States, and for jurors and witnesses, and for other purposes."

"An act to continue in force, for a limited time, an act, intituled, 'An act for the temporary establishment of the post-office.' "

"An act supplementary to the act making provision for the reduction of the public debt."

"An act making farther provision for the collection of the duties by law imposed on teas, and to prolong the term for the payment of the duties on wines."   And

A resolve respecting the safe-keeping of prisoners committed under the authority of the United States.[68]

A message from the Senate by Mr. Otis their Secretary.

MR. SPEAKER,   I am directed to inform this House, that the President of the United States did, this day, approve and sign the following inrolled bills and resolves, which originated in the Senate—to wit:

---

[66] Reports on all of these bills and resolutions, except the fourth bill, are in Committee on Enrolled Bills, SR, DNA.

[67] Included in the president's messages for this date was the approval of the Military Establishment Bill [HR-126A]. It was received by the House in secret session. This message is in Committee on Enrolled Bills, SR, DNA.

[68] Three messages from the president, concerning the signing of these bills and resolutions, are in Committee on Enrolled Bills, SR, DNA.

"An act making an appropriation for the purpose therein mentioned."

"An act to amend an act for establishing the temporary and permanent seat of the government of the United States."

"An act to continue in force the act therein mentioned, and to make further provision for the payment of pensions to invalids, and for the support of light houses, beacons, buoys and public piers."[69]

"An act for granting lands to the inhabitants and settlers at Vincennes and the Illinois country, in the territory north-west of the Ohio, and for confirming them in their possessions."

"A resolve respecting the ungranted lands within the territories of the United States."   And

"A resolve respecting the establishment of a mint."[70]   And then he withdrew.

On a motion made and seconded,

"That the thanks of the House of Representatives of the United States, be presented to FREDERICK AUGUSTUS MUHLENBERG, in testimony of their approbation of his conduct in the chair, and in the execution of the difficult and important trust reposed in him, as Speaker of the said House:"

It was resolved unanimously: Whereupon,

Mr. Speaker made his acknowledgments to the House, in manner following:

GENTLEMEN of the HOUSE of REPRESENTATIVES,

THIS unexpected mark of your approbation of my conduct has made so deep an impression on my mind, that I cannot find words to express the high sense of gratitude I entertain on this occasion.

I have not vanity sufficient to suppose that my feeble though well-meant endeavors merit so great a reward; for it was your kind indulgence and support alone which enabled me to go through the duties of the station which you were pleased to assign me; but I shall ever consider this distinguished and honorable testimony as the most fortunate circumstance of my life.

Gentlemen, I most sincerely thank you. May every possible happiness attend you and every individual of this body—and may your zealous endeavors to promote the welfare of our beloved country, which I have so long and so often been a witness to, be crowned with unbounded success.

---

[69] This bill is the Mitigation of Forfeitures Bill [S–24].

[70] Three messages from the president, concerning the signing of these bills and resolutions, are in Committee on Enrolled Bills, SR, DNA.

ORDERED, That a message be sent to the Senate, to inform them that this House, having completed the business before them, are now about to adjourn without day, and that the Clerk of this House do go with the said message.

The Clerk accordingly went with the said message; and being returned,

A message was received from the Senate by Mr. Otis their Secretary, notifying that the Senate, having completed the legislative business before them, are now about to adjourn: Whereupon,

Mr. Speaker adjourned the House *sine die.*

APPENDIX to the THIRD SESSION

PROCEEDINGS of the DISTRICT of KENTUCKY for ADMISSION into the UNION as an INDEPENDENT STATE

(Copy)

DANVILLE, October 4th, 1790

SIR,

By order of Convention, I now enclose to you a copy of the resolutions of Convention, respecting the separation of the district of Kentucky from the state of Virginia; and their address to the President and Congress of the United States.

I have the honor to be,

With the highest respect,

SIR,

Your most humble Servant,

(Signed) GEORGE MUTER, President of Convention

The PRESIDENT of the UNITED STATES

UNITED STATES, December 9, 1790

A TRUE COPY.

TOBIAS LEAR, Secretary to the President of the United States

(Copy)

DISTRICT OF KENTUCKY (TO WIT)

IN CONVENTION, July 28th, 1790

RESOLVED, That it is expedient for, and the will of, the good people of the district of Kentucky, that the same be erected into an independent state, on the terms and conditions specified in an act of the Virginia Assembly, passed the eighteenth day of December, one thousand seven hundred and eighty-nine, intituled, "An act concerning the erection of the district of Kentucky into an independent state."

RESOLVED, That We, the representatives of the people of Kentucky, duly elected in pursuance of an act of the legislature of Virginia, passed the eighteenth day of December, one thousand seven hundred and eighty-nine, intituled, "An act concerning the erection of the district of Kentucky into an independent state," and now met in convention, having, with full powers, maturely investigated the expediency of the proposed separation on the terms and conditions specified in the above recited act; do by these presents, and in behalf of the people of Kentucky accept the terms and conditions, and do declare that on the first day of June, one thousand seven hundred and ninety-two, the said district of Kentucky shall become a state separate from, and independent of, the government of Virginia, and that the said articles become a solemn compact binding on the said people.

To the President, and the Honorable the Congress of the United States of America

The MEMORIAL of the Representatives of the People of Kentucky, in Convention assembled, pursuant to an act of the Legislature of Virginia, passed the eighteenth day of December, one thousand seven hundred and eighty-nine, intituled, "An act concerning the erection of the District of Kentucky into an independent State,"

HUMBLY SHEWETH,

THAT the inhabitants of this country are as warmly devoted to the American Union, and as firmly attached to the present happy establishment of the federal government as any of the citizens of the United States. That migrating from thence, they have with great hazard and difficulty effected their present settlements. The hope of increasing numbers could alone have supported the early adventurers under those arduous exertions; they have the satisfaction to find that hope verified. At this day, the population and strength of this country, render it fully able, in the opinion of your memorialists, to form and support an efficient domestic government.

The inconveniences resulting from its local situation as a part of Virginia, at first but little felt, have for some time been objects of their most serious attention; which occasioned application to the legislature of Virginia for redress.

Here your memorialists would acknowledge, with peculiar pleasure, the benevolence of Virginia in permitting them to remove the evils arising from that source by assuming upon themselves a state of independence.

This they have thought expedient to do on the terms and conditions stipulated in the above recited act; and have fixed on the first day of June, one thousand seven hundred and ninety-two, as the period when the said independence shall commence.

It now remains with the President and the Congress of the United States to sanction these proceedings, by an act of their honorable Legislature prior to the first day of November, one thousand seven hundred and ninety-one, for the purpose of receiving into the Federal Union the people of Kentucky, by the name of THE STATE OF KENTUCKY.

Should this determination of your memorialists meet the approbation of the General Government, they have to call a convention to form a constitution, subsequent to the act of Congress, and prior to the day fixed for the independence of this country.

When your memorialists reflect on the present comprehensive system of Federal Government; and when they also recollect the determination of a former Congress on this subject, they are left without a doubt that the object of their wishes will be accomplished. And your memorialists as in duty bound shall forever pray.

(Signed)   GEORGE MUTER, President

Attest,

THOMAS TODD, Clerk Convention

UNITED STATES, December 9th, 1790

A TRUE COPY.

TOBIAS LEAR, Secretary to the President of the United States[1]

UNITED STATES, February the 9th, 1791

GENTLEMEN of the SENATE and HOUSE of REPRESENTATIVES,

I HAVE received from the Governor of Vermont, authentic documents expressing the consent of the legislatures of New-York, and of the territory of Vermont, that the said territory shall be admitted to be a distinct member of our Union; and a memorial of Nathaniel Chipman and Lewis R. Morris, commissioners from the said territory, praying the consent of Congress to that admission by the name and stile of the State of Vermont, copies of which I now lay before Congress, with whom the Constitution has vested the object of these proceedings.

GEORGE WASHINGTON

PROCEEDINGS OF THE LEGISLATURES OF NEW-YORK AND OF THE TERRITORY OF VERMONT, RELATIVE TO THE ADMISSION OF THE SAID TERRITORY INTO THE UNION BY THE NAME OF THE STATE OF VERMONT

---

[1] These documents were received by the House on December 9, 1790.

(Copy)

THE PEOPLE OF THE STATE OF NEW-YORK, BY THE GRACE OF GOD, FREE
AND INDEPENDENT

To all to whom these Presents shall come, greeting

KNOW YE, That we having inspected the records remaining in our Secretary's office, do find there a certain original act in the words and figures following—to wit: "An act appointing commissioners with power to declare the consent of the legislature of this state, that a certain territory within the jurisdiction thereof, should be formed or erected into a new State:" *Be it enacted by the People of the State of New-York, represented in Senate and Assembly, and it is hereby enacted by the authority of the same,* That Robert Yates, Robert R. Livingston, John Lansing, junior, Gulian Verplanck, Simeon De Witt, Egbert Benson, Richard Sill, and Melancton Smith, shall be, and hereby are appointed commissioners, with full power to them, or any four or more of them, in their discretion, as they shall judge the peace and interest of the United States in general, and of this state in particular, to require the same, and on such terms and conditions, and in such manner and form as they shall judge necessary and proper, to declare the consent of the legislature of this state, that such district or territory within the jurisdiction, and in the north-eastern and northern parts thereof, as the said commissioners shall judge most convenient, should be formed and erected into a new State; and with farther full power to treat, conclude, and agree with any person or persons, or any assemblies or bodies of people, touching the premises, or touching the ceding or relinquishing the jurisdiction of this state over such district or territory, or touching the securing or confirming of rights, titles or possessions of land within such district or territory, held or claimed under grants from the state of New-Hampshire, while a colony, or under grants, sales or locations made by the authority of the government or jurisdiction now existing and exercised in the north-eastern parts of this state, under the name or stile of the state of Vermont, against persons claiming the same lands under grants from this state, while a colony, or since the independence thereof; and every act of any four or more of the commissioners hereby appointed, in the execution of the powers aforesaid, shall be as effectual to every purpose as if the same were an immediate act of the legislature of this state: *Provided,* Such grants, sales or locations, by or under Vermont, do not extend to the westward of the towns granted, located or occupied under the late colony of New-Hampshire, which lay in that part of the country aforesaid, between the north boundary of the commonwealth of Massachusetts, continued from the northwest corner thereof towards Hudson's river, and a parallel line extended eastward from the point of land where Fort Edward formerly stood, until it meets with the west bounds of any of the said granted, located or occupied towns. *And be it further enacted by the authority aforesaid,* That whatever stipulations shall be made by the commissioners appointed by this act, with any person or persons, or any assemblies or bodies of people, touching the premises, or touching the ceding or relinquishing the jurisdiction of this state over such district or territory, or touching the securing of rights, titles or possessions of lands within such district, for a compensation for extinguishing the claims to lands within such district, as derived under the late colony of New-York, shall be for the use of such claimants, although in such stipulations such compensation should be declared to be for the use of this state, or for the people thereof; and that nothing in this act contained shall be intended or construed to give any such claimant any right to any further compensation whatsoever from this state, other than such compensation which may be so stipulated as aforesaid. *And be it further enacted by the authority aforesaid,* That the act, intituled, "An act appointing commissioners with power to declare the consent of the legislature of this state of New-York, that a certain territory within the jurisdiction thereof, should be formed or erected into a new state:" passed the sixteenth day of July, in the year one thousand seven hundred and eighty-nine, shall be, and hereby is repealed.

STATE OF NEW-YORK

IN ASSEMBLY, February 20th, 1790

This bill having been read the third time;
RESOLVED, That the bill do pass.

By order of the Assembly,
GULIAN VERPLANCK, Speaker

STATE OF NEW-YORK

IN SENATE, February 27th, 1790

This bill having been read a third time;
RESOLVED, That the bill do pass.

By order of the Senate:
ISAAC ROOSEVELT, President pro hac vice

IN COUNCIL OF REVISION, 6th of March, 1790

RESOLVED, That it does not appear improper to the Council, that this bill, intituled, "An act appointing commissioners with power to declare the consent of the legislature of this state that a certain territory within the jurisdiction thereof, should be formed or erected into a new state," should become a law of this state.

GEO. CLINTON

All which we have exemplified by these presents. In testimony whereof, we have caused these our letters to be made patent, and the great seal of our said state to be hereunto affixed. Witness our trusty and well beloved GEORGE CLINTON, Esquire, Governor of our said State, General and Commander in Chief of all the militia, and Admiral of the navy of the same, at our city of New-York, this first day of February, one thousand seven hundred and ninety-one, and in the fifteenth year of our independence.

GEO. CLINTON

PASSED the Secretary's office the 2d February, 1791
ROBERT HARPUR, Deputy Secretary

(Copy)

To all to whom these Presents shall come

BE IT KNOWN, That Robert Yates, John Lansing, junior, Gulian Verplank, Simeon De Witt, Egbert Benson, and Melancton Smith, commissioners appointed by an act of the legislature of the state of New-York, intituled, "An act appointing commissioners with power to declare the consent of the legislature of this state that a certain territory within the jurisdiction thereof should be formed into a new state," passed the sixth day of March last, Do hereby, by virtue of the powers to them granted for the purpose, declare the consent of the legislature of the state of New-York, that the community now actually exercising independent jurisdiction as The State of Vermont, be admitted into the Union of the United States of America, and that immediately from such admission all claim of jurisdiction of the state of New-York within the state of Vermont shall cease; and thenceforth the perpetual boundary line between the state of New-York and the state of Vermont shall be as follows, viz. Beginning at the north-west corner of the state of Massachusetts, thence westward along the south boundary of the township of Pownall to the south-west corner thereof, thence northerly along the western boundaries of the townships of Pownall, Bennington, Shaftsbury, Arlington, Sandgate, Rupert, Pawlett, Wells, and Poultney, as the said townships are now held or possessed, to the river commonly called Poultney River, thence down the same through the middle of the deepest channel thereof to East Bay, thence through the middle of the deepest channel of East Bay and the waters thereof to where the same communicate with Lake Champlain, thence through the middle of the deepest channel of Lake Champlain to the eastward of the islands called the Four Brothers, and the westward of the islands called Grand Isle and Long Isle, or the Two Heroes, and to the westward of the Isle La Motte to the forty-fifth degree of north latitude. And the said commissioners do hereby declare the will of the legislature of the state of New-York, that if the legislature of the state of Vermont shall, on or before the first day of January, in the year one thousand seven hundred and ninety-two, declare that the state of Vermont shall, on or before the first day of June, in the year one thousand seven hundred and ninety-four, pay to the state of New-York the sum of thirty thousand dollars, that immediately from such declaration by the legislature of the state of Vermont, all rights and titles to lands within the state of Vermont, under grants from the government of the late colony of New-York, or from the state of New-York, except as herein after excepted, shall cease. Or if the legislature of the state of Vermont shall not elect to make such declaration, then that, except in cases where the grants from New-York were intended as confirmations of grants from New-Hampshire, all rights and titles under grants from the government of the late colony of New-York, or from the state of New-York, to lands within the state of Vermont, which may have been granted by the government of the colony of New-Hampshire, shall cease, and the boundaries, according to which such grants from the government of the late colony of New-Hampshire have been held or possessed, shall be deemed to be the true boundaries. And the said commissioners do hereby further declare the will of the legislature of the state of New-York, that all rights and titles to lands within the state of Vermont, under grants from the government of the late colony of New-York, or from the state of New-York, and not granted by the government of the late colony of New-Hampshire, shall be suspended until the expiration of three years after the governor of the state of Vermont, for the time being, shall have been notified, that a commissioner, to be appointed by the state of New-York, after the first day of January, in the year one thousand seven hundred and ninety-two, and to reside and hold a public office at the city of Albany, shall have entered upon the execution of his office. And if within one year after such notification, there shall be delivered to such commissioner, either the original or a certified abstract, containing the date, the names of the grantees, and the boundaries of a grant from New-York, and if, thereupon, at any time before the expiration of the said term of three years above mentioned, there shall be paid to such commissioner, at the rate of ten cents per acre, for the whole or any parcel of the lands contained in such grant from New-York, all right and title under such grant, shall, in respect to the lands for which payment shall so be made, cease; and a receipt under the hand and seal of such commissioner, specifying the land for which payment shall be made, shall be evidence of the payment; and in default of delivering the original, or such certified abstract of the grant, to the commissioner, within the said term of one year, for that purpose above limited, all right and title under the grant, in respect of which there shall be such default of delivery, shall cease; but where the original or certified abstract of the grant shall be duly delivered to the commissioner, and if thereupon payment shall not be duly made to the commissioner, the right and title under the grant in respect to the lands for which payment shall not be made, shall remain; and suits for the recovery of such lands may be prosecuted in the ordinary course of law, provided the suit be commenced within ten years after the state of Vermont shall have been admitted into the Union of the United States, otherwise the right and title under the grant from New-York shall in such case also cease. In testimony whereof the said commissioners have hereunto set their hands, and affixed their seals, the seventh day of October, in the fifteenth year of the independence of the United States of America, one thousand seven hundred and ninety.

		EGBERT BENSON	(L.S.)
RICHARD VARICK		GULIAN VERPLANCK	(L.S.)
ALEXANDER HAMILTON		ROBERT YATES	(L.S.)
SAMUEL JONES	Witnesses	MELANCTON SMITH	(L.S.)
ROBERT BENSON		SIMEON DE WITT	(L.S.)
		JOHN LANSING, junior	(L.S.)

An ACT directing the Payment of thirty thousand Dollars to the State of New-York, and declaring what shall be the Boundary Line between the State of Vermont and the State of New-York, and declaring certain Grants therein mentioned extinguished.

WHEREAS Robert Yates, John Lansing, junior, Gulian Verplank, Simeon De Witt, Egbert Benson, and Melancton Smith, Esquires, commissioners, appointed by an act of the legislature of the state of New-York, intituled, "An act appointing commissioners with power to declare the consent of the legislature of the state of New-York, that a certain territory within the jurisdiction thereof, should be formed into a new State;" passed the fifth day of March, in the year of our Lord one thousand seven hundred and ninety, did, by their certain act, on the seventh day of October instant, at New-York, by virtue of the powers to them granted for that purpose, among other things, declare the consent of the legislature of the state of New-York, that the state of Vermont be admitted into the Union of the United States of America. And that immediately from such admission, all claims of jurisdiction of the state of New-York, within the state of Vermont should cease; and thenceforth the perpetual boundary line between the state of New-York and the state of Vermont should be as follows—viz: Beginning at the north-west corner of the state of Massachusetts, thence westward along the south boundary of Pownall, to the south-west corner thereof; thence northerly along the western boundaries of the townships of Pownall, Bennington, Shaftsbury, Arlington, Sandgate, Rupert, Pawlett, Wells, and Poultney, as the said townships are now held or possessed, to the river commonly called Poultney river; thence down the same through the middle of the deepest channel thereof, to East Bay; thence through the middle of the deepest channel of East Bay, and the waters thereof, to where the same communicate with Lake Champlain, thence through the middle of the deepest channel of Lake Camplain to the eastward of the islands called the Four Brothers, and the westward of the islands called the Grand Isle, and Long Isle, or the Two Heroes, and to the westward of the Isle La Motte, to the forty-fifth degree of north latitude. And the said commissioners, by virtue of the powers to them granted, did declare the will of the legislature of the state of New-York, that if the legislature of the state of Vermont, should on or before the first day of January, one thousand seven hundred and ninety-two, declare, that on or before the first day of June, one thousand seven hundred and ninety-four, the said state of Vermont would pay to the state of New-York, the sum of thirty thousand dollars; that immediately from such declaration by the legislature of the state of Vermont, all rights and titles to lands within the state of Vermont, under grants from the government of the late colony of New-York, or from the state of New-York, (except as is therein excepted) should cease:

Wherefore, *It is hereby enacted by the General Assembly of the State of Vermont*, That the state of Vermont shall, on or before the first day of June, one thousand seven hundred and ninety-four, pay the state of New-York thirty thousand dollars. And the treasurer of this state, for, and in behalf of this state, and for the purposes mentioned in the act of the commissioners aforesaid, shall pay to the state of New-York, the sum of thirty thousand dollars, on or before the first day of June, one thousand seven hundred and ninety-four. And,

It is hereby further enacted, That the said line described in the said act of the said commissioners, shall henceforth be the perpetual boundary line between the state of Vermont and the state of New-York. And all grants, charters or patents of land lying within the state of Vermont, made by or under the government of the late colony of New-York, except such grants, charters or patents as were made in confirmation of grants, charters or patents, made by or under the government of the late province or colony of New-Hampshire, are hereby declared null and void, and incapable of being given in evidence in any court of law within this state.

STATE OF VERMONT

SECRETARY'S OFFICE, BENNINGTON
January 21, 1791

THE preceding is a true copy of an act passed by the legislature of the state of Vermont, the twenty-eighth day of October, in the year of our Lord one thousand seven hundred and ninety.

Attest.   ROSWELL HOPKINS, Secretary of State

An ACT to authorize the People of this State to meet in Convention to deliberate upon and agree to the Constitution of the United States

WHEREAS, in the opinion of this legislature, the future interest and welfare of this state, render it necessary that the Constitution of the United States of America, as agreed to by the convention at Philadelphia, on the seventeenth day of September, in the year of our Lord, one thousand seven hundred and eighty-seven, with the several amendments and alterations, as the same has been since established by the United States, should be laid before the people of this state for their approbation.

It is hereby enacted by the General Assembly of the State of Vermont, That the first constable in each town shall warn the inhabitants who by law are entitled to vote for representatives in general assembly, in the same manner as they warn freemens' meetings, to meet in their respective towns on the first Tuesday of December next, at ten o'clock forenoon, at the several places fixed by law for holding the annual election, and when so met they shall proceed in the same manner as in the election of representatives, to choose some suitable person from each town to serve as a delegate in a state convention, for the purpose of deliberating upon and agreeing to the Constitution of the United States as now established; and the said constable shall certify to the state convention the person so chosen in manner aforesaid.   And,

It is hereby further enacted by the authority aforesaid, That the persons so elected to serve in state convention as aforesaid, do assemble and meet together on the first Thursday of January next, at Bennington, in the county of Bennington, then and there to deliberate upon the aforesaid Constitution of the United States, and if approved of by them, finally to assent to, and ratify the same in behalf and on the part of the people of this state, and make report thereof to the governor of this state, for the time being, to be by him communicated to the President of the United States, and the legislature of this state.

STATE OF VERMONT

SECRETARY'S OFFICE, BENNINGTON
January 21, 1791

THE preceding is a true copy of an act passed by the legislature of the state of Vermont, the twenty-seventh day of October, in the year of our Lord, one thousand seven hundred and ninety.

Attest.   ROSWELL HOPKINS, Secretary of State

IN CONVENTION OF THE DELEGATES OF THE PEOPLE OF THE STATE OF VERMONT

WHEREAS by an act of the commissioners of the state of New-York, done at New-York, the seventeenth day of October, in the fifteenth year of the independence of the United States of America, one thousand seven hundred and ninety, every impediment, as well on the part of the state of New-York, as on the part of the state of Vermont, to the admission of the state of Vermont into the Union of the United States of America, is removed. In full faith and assurance that the same will stand approved and ratified by Congress.

This Convention having impartially deliberated upon the Constitution of the United States of America, as now established, submitted to us by an act of the General Assembly of the state of Vermont, passed October twenty-seventh, one thousand seven hundred and ninety, do, in virtue of the power and authority to us given for that purpose, fully and entirely approve of, assent to and ratify the said Constitution; and declare, that immediately from and after this state shall be admitted by the Congress into the Union, and to a full participation of the benefits of the government now enjoyed by the states in the Union, the same shall be binding on us, and the people of the state of Vermont forever.

DONE at Bennington, in the county of Bennington, the tenth day of January, in the fifteenth year of the independence of the United States of America, one thousand seven hundred and ninety-one. In testimony whereof we have hereunto subscribed our names.

(Signed)   THOMAS CHITTENDEN, President

Signed by one hundred and five members—Dissented four.

Attest.   ROSWELL HOPKINS, Secretary of Convention

STATE OF VERMONT

SECRETARY'S OFFICE, BENNINGTON
January 21, 1791

THE preceding is a true copy of the original act of the Convention of the state of Vermont. DONE at Bennington, the tenth day of January, one thousand seven hundred and ninety-one.

Attest.   ROSWELL HOPKINS, Secretary of State

BY HIS EXCELLENCY
THOMAS CHITTENDEN, ESQUIRE,
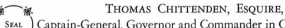 (SEAL) Captain-General, Governor and Commander in Chief in and over
the State of Vermont

THIS certifies, that ROSWELL HOPKINS, Esquire, is Secretary to the State of Vermont, and that all due faith and credence ought to be given to attestations by him officially made.

In testimony whereof we have caused the Seal of this State to be affixed, in Council this twenty-second day of January, one thousand seven hundred and ninety-one.

(Signed)   THOMAS CHITTENDEN

By his Excellency's command,
JOSEPH FAY, Secretary

BENNINGTON, January 22, 1791

SIR,

I HAVE the honor to transmit to you copies of two acts of the legislature of this state; the one directing the payment of thirty thousand dollars to the state of New-York, and declaring the boundary line between the state of Vermont and the state of New-York, and extinguishing certain grants therein mentioned; the other, an act authorizing the people of this state to meet in convention, to deliberate upon and agree to the Constitution of the United States; and also a copy of the proceeding of the convention.

This will be delivered by the Honorable Nathaniel Chipman, and Lewis R. Morris, Esquires, who are appointed commissioners to apply to the Congress of the United States, for the admission of this state into the Union, whom I beg leave to recommend to your favorable notice.

I have the honor to be,
With the greatest consideration and respect,
SIR,
Your most obedient, and
Very humble Servant,
(Signed)   THOMAS CHITTENDEN

The PRESIDENT of the UNITED STATES

BY HIS EXCELLENCY
THOMAS CHITTENDEN, ESQUIRE,

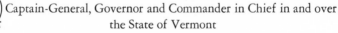

(SEAL) Captain-General, Governor and Commander in Chief in and over
the State of Vermont

To the Honorable NATHANIEL CHIPMAN, Esquire, and LEWIS R. MORRIS, Esquire, greeting

YOU being elected by the legislature of this state, commissioners to the Congress of the United States, to apply for the admission of the state of Vermont into the Union, are hereby authorized and empowered to proceed to the Congress of the United States, now in session at the city of Philadelphia, and negociate on behalf of this state, agreeable to your said appointment.

In testimony whereof we have caused the Seal of this State to be affixed, in Council at Bennington, this twenty-fourth day of January, one thousand seven hundred and ninety-one, and in the fifteenth year of the independence of this State.

(Signed)   THOMAS CHITTENDEN

By his Excellency's command,
JOSEPH FAY, Secretary

THE PRESIDENT AND CONGRESS OF THE UNITED STATES OF AMERICA

NATHANIEL CHIPMAN and LEWIS R. MORRIS, Commissioners, authorized and appointed by the state of Vermont, most respectfully represent, that the citizens of that state having shared, in common with those of the other states, in the hazards and burthens of establishing the American revolution, have long anxiously desired to be united with them, under the same General Government. They have seen with great satisfaction a new and more perfect union of the people of America, and the unanimity with which they have recently approved the National Constitution, manifests their attachment to it, and the zeal with which they desire to participate in its benefits.

Questions of interfering jurisdiction between them and the state of New-York, have heretofore delayed this application; these points being now happily adjusted, the memorialists, on behalf of their constituents, most respectfully petition, that the Congress will consent to the admission of the state of Vermont, by that name and stile, as a new and entire member of the United States.

They have the honor to accompany this memorial with such papers and documents as have relation to the same; and with the highest deference for the wisdom of Congress, the memorialists repeat their solicitations, that during their present session, they would be pleased to adopt such measures, as will include within the National Government, a people zealous to support and defend it.

(Signed)   NATHANIEL CHIPMAN
LEWIS R. MORRIS

PHILADELPHIA, February 7th, 1791

TREASURY of the UNITED STATES, January 3, 1791

SIR,

MY accounts having lain a considerable time in the offices for settlement, and being now passed, permit me, through you, to lay them before the Honorable the House of Representatives; and to assure you,

That I am,

With perfect respect,

SIR,

Your most humble Servant,

SAMUEL MEREDITH, Treasurer of the United States

The Honorable F. A. MUHLENBERG

Speaker of the House of Representatives

TREASURER'S ACCOUNT OF THE RECEIPTS AND EXPENDITURES OF THE PUBLIC MONEY, BETWEEN THE 1ST OF JULY, 1790, AND THE 30TH OF SEPTEMBER FOLLOWING

TREASURY DEPARTMENT

AUDITOR'S OFFICE, December 2d, 1790

I HEREBY certify, that I have examined and adjusted an account between the United States and Samuel Meredith, Esq. Treasurer of said States, for indents of interest received and issued by him from July 1st to September 30th, 1790, and find that he is chargeable on said account for the following sums, viz.

	Dols.	Cts.
To balance of indents remaining in his hands on settlement of his account, ending 30th June, 1790, per report No. 553, dated July 20th, 1790	477,986.	98
To John Cochran, loan-officer for the state of New-York, for this sum in indents, received per warrant No. 33	1	
To amount of fractional parts added to the indents issued on warrants for the payment of interest	19.	81
Amounting in the whole to . . . . *Dollars,*	478,007.	79

I also find that the said Treasurer has paid on warrants, for which he is entitled to have credit, the following sums, viz.

Dols. Cts.

By Thomas Smith, Esq. loan-officer for the state of Pennsylvania, for amount of indents paid to him on warrant
No. 9   400,000

By account of interest, for payment of interest on the domestic debt 69,442. 81

Leaving a balance in the hands of the said Treasurer on the
1st day of October, 1790, the sum of 8,564. 98

                                    Dollars,   478,007. 79

For which balance of eight thousand five hundred and sixty four dollars
and ninety-eight cents in indents of interest, he is to be debited in a future
settlement of his accounts, as appears from the statement and vouchers herewith transmitted for the decision of the Comptroller of the Treasury thereon.

                              OLIVER WOLCOTT, jun. Auditor
To NICHOLAS EVELEIGH, Esq. Comptroller of the Treasury

                        COMPTROLLER'S OFFICE, 6th December, 1790
                                             Dols. Cts.

Balance as stated above brought down 8,564. 98

To which add amount of warrant No. 319 in favour of John
C. Freeke, not paid 28. 34

Balance for which the Treasurer is accountable ....*Dollars,*   8,593. 32

Admitted as above and certified:

                              NICHOLAS EVELEIGH, Comptroller

                           REGISTER'S OFFICE, 31st December 1790
   THE preceding statement of Samuel Meredith, Treasurer of the United
States, his amount of indents of interest received and paid, commencing on
the first day of July, one thousand seven hundred and ninety, and ending on
the thirtieth day of September following, is a true copy of the original, transmitted to me by the Comptroller of the Treasury, to be entered in the treasury books, and to be filed in this office.

                                    JOSEPH NOURSE, Register

                         AUDITOR'S OFFICE, December 16th, 1790
   I HAVE examined the accounts of Samuel Meredith, Esquire, Treasurer of
the United States, commencing on the 1st day of July, and ending on the
30th day of September, 1790, and find that by the statement of his accounts

to the 1st day of July last, it appeared that he was accountable to the United
States for the sum of ....*Dollars,* 155,320. 23

And that warrants had been drawn in his favor on collectors
which remained unpaid, as particularized in said statement, amounting to .... 11,290.

Dollars,	166,610. 23

                                         Dols. Cts.

I also find that since the 1st day of July, 1790, the Treasurer
has paid sundry warrants which were drawn on him before that day, and included in the former settlement, to
the amount of 125. 79

Which sum being deducted from the amount last mentioned, will leave the balance which appeared to be due to
the United States, by the records of the treasury, on the
1st day of July, 1790, agreeably to the statement of the
Treasurer's accounts to that period 166,484. 44

Dollars,	166,610. 23

On examining the treasury records, it appears that the Treasurer is charg-
able in his accounts from June 30th till 30th September, 1790, for the following sums—viz.

                                         Dols. Cts.

To the balance due the United States, by the books of the
treasury, on the 1st day of July, 1790 .... 166,484. 44

                       Dols. Cts.

To contingent funds for the amount of a warrant on James Blanchard 394. 10

For the amount of do. on Nathaniel Gilman 800

For interest received on Theodosius Fowler and
Company's note 8. 98

                                 1,203. 08

To general account of monies arising from the acts imposing duties on merchandize and tonnage, for the amount of
warrants drawn in favor of the Treasurer on collectors,
from 30th June to 30th of September, 1790, inclusive,
agreeably to the Register's account 444,283. 06

Amounting in the whole to ....*Dollars,* 611,970. 58

It also appears that warrants have been drawn on the Treasurer, from July
1st till September 30th, 1790, which were charged as expenditures on account
of the following appropriations—to wit:

Upon the appropriation granted to defray the expences in-
    cident to the sessions of Congress, anno 1790, as specified   *Dols. Cts.*
    in the statement herewith—the sum of 65,578. 29

Upon the appropriation of	*Dols.*	147,169. 54	as per do.	5,901. 77
Upon the appropriation of		155,537. 72	as per do.	33,625. 20
Upon the appropriation of		141,492. 73	as per do.	39,383. 87
Upon the appropriation of		190,000	as per do.	75,038. 32
Upon the appropriation of		96,000	as per do.	11,827. 33
Upon the appropriation of		96,979. 72	as per do.	1,008
Upon the appropriation of		216,000	as per do.	400
Upon the appropriation of		104,327. 22	as per do.	20,926. 52
Upon the appropriation of		20,000	as per do.	7,000
Upon the appropriation of		50,000	as per do.	541. 75
Upon the appropriation of		1,309. 71	as per do.	1,309. 71
Upon the appropriation of		10,000	as per do.	1,165. 58
Upon the appropriation of		200	as per do.	200
Upon the appropriation of		120	as per do.	120

       Amounting in the whole to ....*Dollars*, 264,026. 34

Leaving a balance due to the United States on the first day of
    October, 1790, agreeably to the records of the treasury,
    (including 8 dollars and 98 cents, not yet charged in the
    public books) of 347,944. 24

                    Total Dollars, 611,970. 58

I find that to ascertain the actual balance for which the Treasurer was accountable on the first day of October, 1790, the following sums ought to be
added to the balance appearing due by the foregoing statement, being the
amount of warrants drawn on the Treasurer, which had not been discharged
by him—viz.

Warrant No.   *Dols. Cts.*

577	in favor of Geo. Bush, not produced .	1,008
614	J. Elmer	924
669	B. Harrison	24
671	M. Smith	57. 28
672	LeRoy and Bayard	3,087. 71

                                      Dols. Cts.
                                      5,100. 99

Which when added to the balance due by the foregoing statement, will amount to ....Dollars, 353,045. 23

From the foregoing balance the following sums are to be deducted, being the amount of warrants in favor of the Treasurer, on account of which he had not received payment—viz.

Warrant No. 267 on William Heth ...... Dols. 3,000
485 on Benjamin Lincoln 358
524 on do. 17
Amounting in the whole to ...... Dollars, 3,375

Which will leave the sum for which the Treasurer was accountable to the United States on the 1st day of Oct. 1790
Dols. 349,670. 23

It appears from the accounts rendered by the Treasurer, and the records of the treasury, that said sum of three hundred and forty-nine thousand six hundred and seventy dollars, and twenty-three cents, consisted of the following particulars—viz.

	Dols.	Cts.
Commissions charged by the bank of Massachusetts in this and the preceding quarters, on deposits not admitted to his credit	90.	52
Charge for transporting money in the last quarter's account, including 8 cents balance of errors not admitted	1.	46
Protests of drafts on William Lindsay not admitted	41.	47
Warrant in favor of Geo. Bush, No. 577, said to be paid by the Treasurer, but not produced	1,008	
Cash in the hands of Samuel Meredith, Esquire, as agent to the trustees for reducing the public debt	51,477.	90
Cash in the bank of North-America	89,533.	66
Do. in the bank of New-York	197,097.	41
Do. in the bank of Massachusetts	10,419.	81
Amounting as before stated to ....Dollars,	349,670.	23

The statement and vouchers on which this report is founded, are herewith transmitted for the decision of the Comptroller of the Treasury thereon.

(Signed) OLIVER WOLCOTT, jun. Auditor
To NICHOLAS EVELEIGH, Esq. Comptroller of the Treasury

From the foregoing balance is now to be deducted No. 577 warrant, in favor of George Bush, of 1008 dollars, which is since produced, making the balance ....*Dollars*,   348,662. 23

N. B. The above warrant No. 577 is to be charged as an expenditure upon the appropriation of 96,979 dollars and 72 cents.

COMPTROLLER'S OFFICE, 27th Dec. 1790

ADMITTED and certified.

(Signed)   NICHOLAS EVELEIGH, Comptroller

To JOSEPH NOURSE, Esq. Register

REGISTER'S OFFICE, Dec. 31, 1790

THE foregoing statement of Samuel Meredith, Treasurer of the United States, his account of monies received and paid, commencing on the first day of July, one thousand seven hundred and ninety, and ending on the thirtieth day of September following, is a true copy of the original, transmitted to me by the Comptroller of the Treasury, to be entered in the treasury books, and to be filed in this office.

JOSEPH NOURSE, Register

PAYMENTS and RECEIPTS in INDENTS by the TREASURER of the United States

Paid	Warrant		*Dols.*	*Cts.*		*Dols.*	*Cts.*
No.	9 to	Thomas Smith ..	400,000		Balance in my		
	21	William Rogers .	1,800		hands 30th		
	95	J. Tichenor	518.	92	last June,		
	108	Andrew Craigie .	1,379.	18	per account		
	157	J. F. Sebor and Co.	1,697.	80	furnished to		
	166	Richard Cornell .	18.	95	that time	477,986.	98
	194	T. Fowler and Co.	670.	33	Received for		
	217	Ditto	567.	06	warrant No.		
	222	Andrew Craigie .	446.	73	33, on John		
	223	T. Fowler and Co.	2,383.	15	Cochran		1
	234	James F. Sebor ..	4,063.	97			
	235	Ditto	3,200.	05			
	236	T. Fowler and Co.	208.	97			
	237	Abijah Hammond	3,231.	71			
	242	T. Fowler and Co.	2,900.	39			
	254	Robert Gilchrist .	1,019.	35			
	256	Anspach & Rogers	837.	56			
	259	Ditto	274.	25			

PAYMENTS and RECEIPTS in INDENTS by the TREASURER of the United States

Paid Warrant		Dols. Cts.	Dols. Cts.
No. 267 to	T. Fowler and Co.	1,074. 69	
268	Daniel Penfield ..	801. 91	
276	Robert Gilchrist .	2,866. 93	
279	T. Fowler and Co.	1,656. 92	
286	Benj. S. Judah ..	13. 43	
288	Andrew Craigie .	1,928. 16	
292	Robert Colfax ...	196. 27	
294	Joseph Howell, jun.	421. 35	
296	Thomas McEwen.	863. 24	
301	Andrew Dunscomb	588. 36	
304	J. C. Freeke	334. 90	
305	Anspach & Rogers	203. 13	
308	Joshua Mersereaux	927. 73	
309	J. Freeke	1,822. 32	
310	John Polhelmus .	46. 08	
312	Thomas Barclay .	1,233. 91	
314	Joseph Hardy ...	212. 55	
316	William Kenyon .	2,880	
317	Robert Gilchrist .	818. 12	
319	J. C. Freeke	28. 34	
323	Dorcas Lee	73. 08	
324	Nicholas Low ...	2,799. 60	
332	John Polhelmus .	509. 19	
340	J. C. Freeke	604. 77	
341	Anspach & Rogers	531. 30	
342	Robert Gilchrist .	1,019. 25	
343	Samuel Hay	130. 21	
346	Robert Gilchrist .	896. 30	Amount of
353	William Wilsher .	65. 41	fractions
358	John Quackenbos .	26. 76	added to the
359	Thomas Speer ...	318. 59	several war-
361	A. G. Fraunces ..	637. 82	rants per contra 19. 81
367	Jabes Johnson ...	259. 16	
369	John and C. Shaw	557. 63	
371	Andrew Hageman	37. 67	
376	Benj. S. Judah ...	7,254. 05	
379	Henry Van Pelt .	58. 08	

PAYMENTS and RECEIPTS in INDENTS by the TREASURER of the United States

Paid Warrant	Dols. Cts.		Dols. Cts.
No. 384 to Anspach & Rogers	263. 07		
385 David Reedy	235. 71		
389 Benj. S. Judah ...	224. 07		
391 D. Penfield	855. 58		
393 Richard Platt ...	1,189. 55		
397 Mary Ross	21. 38		
401 John Stryker	33. 42		
403 Leonard Bleecker .	1,929. 47		
412 Thomas Hook ...	32. 02		
414 Thomas Van Pelt .	230. 18		
417 John Simmons ..	957. 42		
421 John Conway ...	157. 83		
426 Andrew Craigie .	3,310. 55		
435 Stephen Rabbit ..	86. 98		
Balance in my hands this day	8,564. 98		
Dollars,	478,007. 79	Dollars,	478,007. 79

J. C. Freeke's warrant, No. 319, was paid August 12th, 1790, to John Bush, with eight others, as the undermentioned entry will shew, (but not receipted).

				Dols. Cts.
No. 237 A. Hammond	1st June	for		3,231. 71
254 R. Gilchrist	7th	for		1,019. 35
304 J. C. Freeke	13th July	for		334. 90
309 Ditto	15th	for		1,822. 32
317 R. Gilchrist	23d	for		818. 12
319 J. C. Freeke	26th	for		28. 34
340 Ditto	9th August	for		604. 77
342 R. Gilchrist		for		1,019. 25
346 Ditto	11th	for		896. 30
			Dollars,	9,775. 06

Indents paid for the above warrants	Dols. Cts.
No. 18,001 to 18,024 is 24, at 13 dollars each .	312
18,025	1
18,001 to 18,017 is 17, at 165 dollars each .	2,805
18,018	40
18,126 to 18,150 a whole book	4,450

	Dols.	*Cts.*
No. 18,163 to 18,175 is 13, at 165 dollars each .	2,145	
18,175	13	
18,174	9	
Fraction,	6	
Dollars,	9,775.06	

The warrant is given up and cancelled, and therefore no injury can arise to the public.

TREASURY of the UNITED STATES, NEW-YORK, October 1, 1790

SAMUEL MEREDITH, Treasurer of the United States

PAYMENTS AND RECEIPTS BY THE

Paid warrant	*Dols. Cts.*

No. 522 to Reuben Burnley, for warrant No. 1109, dated 26th
March, 1789 . . . . 101. 83

523	Ditto No. 1111	23. 96
524	Amasa Learned, attorney for Richard Law, his salary .	250
525	John Paulding, his pension	50
526	Dominick L'Eglize, ditto	30
527	Oliver Wolcott, salaries for his office	2,470. 03
528	Henry Knox ditto ditto	1,295. 98
529	Tench Coxe, salaries for Secretary of Treasury's office	1,764. 28
530	Wm. Houston, attorney for Rich. Wylley, his salary .	678. 28
531	Nicholas Eveleigh, salaries for his office	1,138. 73
532	William Irvine, and others, salaries for their office . .	2,275
533	Joseph Nourse, salaries for his office	1,312. 50
534	Jos. Bindon, attorney for Joseph Traversie, his pension	60
535	John Ramsey, attorney for Arthur St. Clair, his salary	500
536	Jos. Stanton, his attendance and travelling expences .	62
537	Benjamin Hawkins, ditto	546
538	Joseph Nourse, assignee of Eliz. Bergen, her pension .	13. 33
539	Cyrus Griffin, his salary	450
540	Nich. Gilman, attorney for John Sullivan, his salary . .	250
541	Jehoiakim McToksin, his compensation as interpreter	120
542	John McCord, for balance of his account	1,309. 71
543	Samuel Meredith, for salaries for his office	650
544	Ditto, attorney for James Wilson, his salary	875
545	Samuel A. Otis, his salary	375
546	Joseph Nourse, for balance of contingent account for treasury department	17. 31
547	Ditto account of contingent expenses of treasury department	517. 39
548	Thomas Sinnickson, attorney for David Brearly, for his salary	250
549	John Bard, jun. attorney for Nathaniel Pendleton, his salary	375
550	Mel. Smith, for provisions at West-Point from 1st to 30th June, 1790	55. 44
551	Thomas Jefferson, salaries for his office, &c.	1,584. 72
552	Geo. Thatcher, attorney for David Sewall, his salary .	500

Treasurer of the United States

			Dols.	Cts.
Balance of account furnished to the 30th last June			166,540.	55
Received for warrant				
No. 377 on Joseph Hiller collector of Salem			2,061	
378	William Heth	Bermuda-Hundred ...	500	
379	John Halsted	Perth-Amboy	575	
380	Otho H. Williams	Baltimore	300	
381	George Bush	Wilmington (Delaware)	1,008	
382	Charles Lee	Alexandria	1,000	
383	Eli Elmer	Bridgetown	550.	10
384	George Bush	Wilmington (Delaware)	139	
385	William Heth	Bermuda-Hundred ...	4,033.	33
386	John Lamb	New-York	5,656.	68
387	John Habersham	Savannah	500	
388	William Lindsay	Norfolk	500	
390	John Muir	Vienna	300	
391	Benjamin Lincoln	Boston	1,000	
392	George Abb. Hall	Charleston	2,000	
393	Charles Lee	Alexandria	1,000	
394	Benjamin Lincoln	Boston	7,000	
395	Hudson Muse	Tappahannock	500	
396	George Abb. Hall	Charleston	8,000	
397	Jedidiah Huntington	New-London	1,000	
398	William Lindsay	Norfolk	3,000	
399	George Abb. Hall	Charleston	3,000	
400	Benjamin Lincoln	Boston	9,000	
401	Jonathan Fitch	New-Haven	550	
402	George Abb. Hall	Charleston	2,000	
403	Jedidiah Huntington	New-London	2,000	
404	William Heth	Bermuda-Hundred ...	500	
405	Benjamin Lincoln	Boston	1,000	
406	Otho H. Williams	Baltimore	446.	66
407	Ditto	ditto	2,372.	31
408	Benjamin Lincoln	Boston	2,083	

Payments and Receipts by the

Paid warrant		Dols.	Cts.
No. 553 to	John Adams, account his compensation	500	
554	Joseph Howell, jun. for warrant No. 1045, dated 31st December, 1788	6,000	
555	Tobias Lear, account the President's compensation . .	1,000	
556	Samuel Meredith, attorney for Francis Hopkinson his salary	400	
557	Ditto, attorney for John Rutledge, his salary	875	
558	James Gunn, attendance and travelling expenses	866	
559	Ralph Izard ditto	636	
560	John Jay, his salary	1,000	
561	Thomas T. Tucker, agent for J. Neufville, his salary .	1,500	
562	William Constable, assignee of Ph. Audibert, for warrant No. 191, dated 28th August, 1787	2,000	
563	William Constable, assignee of James O'Hara, for warrant No. 1154, dated 19th May, 1789	4,223.	32
564	Ditto, ditto 457 20th	2,133.	63
565	F. A. Muhlenberg, for the House of Representatives .	8,000	
566	Tobias Lear, account the President's compensation . .	500	
567	Pierce Butler, his attendance and travelling expences	636	
568	William Maclay, ditto	759	
569	Samuel Meredith, attorney for John Blair, his salary	875	
570	Ditto, assignee of T. L. Moore, attorney to George Turner, for his salary	158.	70
571	Richard Bassett, agent for G. Bedford, his salary	610.	86
572	Ditto, for his attendance and travelling expenses . . .	754.	50
573	Sam. Sterret and Co. agents for Wm. Paca, his salary .	375	
574	Jos. Nourse, agent for Richard Gridley, his Pension . .	444.	40
575	Samuel Meredith, agent of D. Delozier, administrator to the estate of John White, his salary	430.	40
576	John Beckley, for contingent expenses of House of Representatives	1,000	
577	Geo. Bush, to pay invalid pensions for Delaware state	1,008	
578	Edmund Randolph, account of his salary	145.	38
579	Ditto his salary	375	
580	John Adams, account of his compensation	500	
581	Rob. Morris, agent for John C. Symmes, his salary . . .	400	
582	Sam. A. Otis, for contingent expenses of the Senate . .	1,500	

Treasurer of the United States

Received for warrant			Dols.	Cts.
No. 409 on Otho H. Williams	collector of Baltimore		2,091.	86
410	George Bush	Wilmington (Delaware)	1,287.	18
411	Ditto	ditto	75.	63
412	John Ross	Burlington	240	
413	William Heth	Bermuda-Hundred .	20	
414	Benjamin Lincoln	Boston	455	
415	Richard Harris	Marblehead	396	
416	Nath. F. Fosdick	Portland	410	
417	Ditto	ditto	200	
418	Joseph Hiller	Salem	1,200	
419	Jer. Hill	Biddeford & Pepperelboro'	149.	33
420	Stephen Cross	Newburyport	475	
421	Jer. Hill	Biddeford & Pepperelboro'	170	
422	Stephen Cross	Newburyport	645	
423	Fr. Cook	Wiscasset	200	
424	Epes Sargent	Gloucester	400	
425	Joseph Hiller	Salem	1,138.	66
426	Stephen Cross	Newburyport	326.	20
427	Ditto	ditto	525	
428	Benjamin Lincoln	Boston	7,000	
429	James Read	Wilmington (N.C.)	500	
430	Benjamin Lincoln	Boston	700	
431	William Lindsay	Norfolk	41,800	
432	John Habersham	Savannah	3,000	
433	Thomas Benbury	Edenton	500	
434	James Read	Wilmington (N.C.)	800	
435	John Daves	Newbern	700	
436	R. M. Scott	Dumfries	3,300	
437	Hudson Muse	Tappahannock	2,000	
438	James M. C. Lingan	Georgetown	1,050	
439	Charles Lee	Alexandria	4,072.	59

Payments and Receipts by the

Paid Warrant		*Dols.*	*Cts.*
No. 583 to John Beckley, attorney to Harry Innes, for his salary .		13.	58
584 Ditto ditto ditto		250	
585 William Cushing, for his salary		875	
586 John Page, attorney for Gen. Weedon, executor to the estate of the late Gen. Mercer, for his youngest son		400	
587 Tobias Lear, account the President's compensation ..		1,500	
588 T. Foster, his attendance and travelling expenses		285	
589 John Adams, account his compensation		1,000	
590 Joseph Howell, jun. salaries for his office		1,628.	13
591 Pat. Ferrall, for balance of contingent expences of office for settling accounts		29.	51
592 James Iredell, for his salary		875	
593 William Heth, to pay invalid pensions for Virginia ..		4,033.	33
594 John Lamb ditto New York ..		5,656.	68
595 John Langdon, account his compensation		876	
596 F. A. Muhlenberg, for House of Representatives		12,000	
597 Ditto ditto		15,911.	69
598 Richard Bassett, attendance and travelling expenses ..		78	
599 Paine Wingate, attendance and travelling expenses ..		886.	50
600 F. A. Muhlenberg, for House of Representatives		670	
601 Benj. Walker, attorney for Baron Steuben, his pension		1,250	
602 F. C. Mantel, attorney to Le Ray de Chaumont the younger, attorney to the elder, due him		9,051.	33
603 Tench Coxe, attorney for Richard Butler executor to the estate of William Butler, deceased, for his pay		788.	35
604 Ditto, ditto, balance due him		337.	67
605 Thomas Jefferson, for use of his office		500	
606 S. Harding, his services on board the Alliance frigate		200	
607 Thomas Tudor Tucker, agent for Richard Winn, for balance due him		75	
608 Samuel Provoost, his salary		295.	80
609 Tobias Lear, account the President's compensation ..		1,000	
610 P. R. Maverick, for engraving		91.	08
611 Thomas Randal, for salaries for himself, &c.		415.	80
612 Joseph Howell, jun. two months pay and subsistence of Burbeck's company of artillery for the year 1790		811	
613 Henry Knox, account the Indian treaty		7,000	

Treasurer of the United States

Received for warrant			Dols.	Cts.
No. 440 on George Abb. Hall collector of Charleston		....	6,991.	31
441	Jonathan Fitch	New-Haven	1,220	
442	Otho H. Williams	Baltimore	6,092.	72
443	Burrall Devereaux, deputy	Marblehead	370	
444	Stephen Hussey	Nantucket	448.	17
445	John Lee		130	
446	William Watson		400	
447	Stephen Cross	Newburyport	333.	33
448	Nath. F. Fosdick	Portland	412.	40
449	Joseph Hiller	Salem	787	
450	Stephen Cross	Newburyport	195.	29
451	Jer. Hill	Biddeford & Pep-		
		perelboro'	265.	92
452	Joseph Hiller	Salem	897	
453	Fr. Cook	Wiscasset	125	
454	Ditto	ditto	100	
455	William Webb		500	
456	Richard Trevett		300	
457	M. Jordan		490	
458	Jos. Otis		100	
459	B. Devereaux, deputy	Marblehead	200	
460	Edward Pope		284	
461	Richard Trevett		200	
462	John Lee		120	
463	John Pease		100	
464	Stephen Hussey	Nantucket	100	
465	William Watson		200	
466	William Webb		120	
467	Stephen Cross	Newburyport	1,075	
468	Joseph Hiller	Salem	1,610	
469	John Lamb	New-York	66,388.	93
470	Ditto	ditto	2,137.	32

PAYMENTS AND RECEIPTS BY THE

Paid Warrant		Dols.	Cts.
No. 615 to Joseph Howell, jun. for warrant 1046, dated 31st December, 1788		6,000	
616	Ditto, agent for Andrew Ellicott, account of surveys .	1,200	
617	Pat. Ferrall, for contingent expenses for office of settling accounts	300	
618	William Bayard, substitute for Thomas L. Moore attorney for George Turner, his salary	241.	30
619	Walter Nicols, for sundry articles for household of late President of Congress	22.	12
620	Cob. Myers, for wood ditto	13.	84
621	Rich. Platt, attorney for Winth. Sargent, his salary ..	187.	50
622	William Houston, attorney to Richard Wylley, balance due him	804.	26
623	Cons. Freeman, account a bill of exchange and drafts thereon	3,123.	28
624	Dan. Dennison, administrator to the estate of Hugh Smith, balance due him	120.	65
625	M. Ogden, assignee of Alb. Cox, for dyes for medals	140	
626	Joseph Howell, for warrant No. 1046, dated 31st December, 1788	6,000	
627	W. Edgar, assignee of J. Rankin, his pay as interpreter	416	
628	Ditto ditto messenger	878.	78
629	Samuel A. Otis, his pay	268	
630	Benjamin Bankson, ditto	402	
631	Robert Heysham, ditto	268	
632	James Mathers, ditto	402	
633	Cornelius Maxwell, ditto	268	
634	Henry Knox, salaries, &c.	1,300	
635	S. and J. Smith, agents for Robert Elliott and Elie Williams for rations and provisions, &c.	15,000	
636	Shedden Patrick, and Co. for a bill of exchange on B. Franklin, returned	200	
637	Tobias Lear, on account of President's compensation	1,000	
638	J. D. Mercier, agent for Thos. Leaming, jun. for two bills exchange on commissioners at Paris, returned	36	
639	Royal Flint, agent for J. Wadsworth, for apprehending the Cranes	1,061	

Treasurer of the United States

Received for warrant			Dols.	Cts.
No. 471 on	Sharp Delany collector of	Philadelphia	63,500	
472	George Bush	Wilmington	188	
473	Eli Elmer	Bridgetown	216	
474	Joseph Whipple	Portsmouth	1,500	
475	George Biscoe	Nottingham	200	
476	John Cogdell		600	
477	George Abb. Hall	Charleston	2,000	
478	Ditto	ditto	2,000	
479	Jedidiah Huntington	New-London	1,000	
480	Benjamin Lincoln	Boston	1,000	
481	George Abb. Hall	Charleston	1,600	
482	Ditto	ditto	2,000	
483	Ditto	ditto	2,000	
484	Benjamin Lincoln	Boston	16,020.	80
486	Ditto	ditto	930	
487	Joseph Whipple	Portsmouth	1,350	
488	George Abb. Hall	Charleston	15,804.	34
489	Ditto	ditto	5,100	
490	Ditto	ditto	1,000	
491	Ditto	ditto	250	
492	Benjamin Lincoln	Boston	296	
493	Jedidiah Huntington	New-London	3,700	
494	Ditto	ditto	800	
495	William Lindsay	Norfolk	1,000	
496	Thomas Benbury	Edenton	500	
497	John Cogdell		400	
498	George Abb. Hall	Charleston	237.	36
499	George Biscoe	Nottingham	4,000	
500	Benjamin Lincoln	Boston	2,000	
501	Ditto	Ditto	1,800	
502	John Habersham	Savannah	1,500	
503	Ditto	ditto	1,906.	20

PAYMENTS AND RECEIPTS BY THE

Paid Warrant		*Dols.*	*Cts.*
No. 640 to	Tobias Lear, on account of President's compensation	2,000	
641	Joseph Howell, jun. assignee of M. Hillegas for warrant No. 447, dated 6th Nov. 1788	4,000	
642	Tench Coxe, balance of salaries due the office of Secretary of the Treasury	71.	42
643	Thomas Jefferson balance of salaries due the office of Secretary of State	22.	25
644	M. Leavenworth, agent for A. Doolittle, for a seal . .	8	
645	E. Prior, attorney to W. Wilson, his pay as messenger	958.	80
646	P. R. Maverick, for engraving	5.	50
647	John Beckley, for contingent expenses of his office .	1,500	
648	Joseph Nourse, ditto ditto	500	
649	Joseph Howell, jun. for warrant No. 1049, dated 31st December, 1788	6,000	
650	Mel. Smith, for provisions issued at West-Point from 1st to 30th July, 1790	57.	28
651	T. Jefferson, to pay an interpreter of the French language	302.	75
652	Tobias Lear, on account the President's compensation	1,000	
653	Joseph Howell, jun. for warrant 1048, dated 31st December, 1788	6,000	
654	Samuel Meredith, agent for Jacob Drayton, executor to the estate of Wm. Drayton, his salary	237.	36
656	Wm. Maclay, his attendance and travelling expenses	18	
655	Samuel Meredith, agent for several members of the Senate, for their attendance and travelling expenses	14,556.	80
657	Caleb Strong, his attendance and travelling expenses	834	
658	J. Howell, jun. pay and subsistence of troops on the Ohio	8,438	
659	R. Philips, steward to the late President of Congress	234.	22
660	I. Ludlow, balance due to him for executing a survey	541.	75
661	Joseph Howell, jun. for warrant No. 1050, dated 31st Dec. 1788	4,000	
662	Ditto, pay and subsistence of the troops for the present year	1,906.	20
663	Richard Rogers, for his salary	103.	26
664	W. Hill, agent for R. Flint, account his clothing contract	6,000	

Treasurer of the United States

Received for warrant			Dols.	Cts.
No. 504 on Jedidiah Huntington collector of New-London			2,000	
505	Otho H. Williams	Baltimore	876	
506	Benjamin Lincoln	Boston	894	
507	Abraham Archer	York-Town	964	
508	Hudson Muse	Tappahannock ...	891	
509	R. M. Scott	Dumfries	131	
510	William Lindsay	Norfolk	18,049.	51
511	Charles Lee	Alexandria	2,178	
512	Joseph Whipple	Portsmouth	706	
513	William Heth	Bermuda-Hundred	400	
514	John Halsted	Perth-Amboy	350	
515	George Bush	Wilmington	1,257.	56
516	Eli Elmer	Bridgetown	36	
517	John Ross	Burlington	430	
518	Sharp Delany	Philadelphia	40,000	
519	George Bush	Wilmington	100.	37
520	Benjamin Lincoln	Boston	500	
521	Jedidiah Huntington	New-London	700	
522	George Abb. Hall	Charleston	2,000	
523	John Habersham	Savannah	450	

Payments and Receipts by the

Paid Warrant		Dols.	Cts.
No. 665 to Tobias Lear, on account of President's compensation		1,000	
666 John Adams, on account of his compensation		1,000	
667 Joseph Howell, jun. for warrant No. 1085 for 3500, No. 1086 for 3000, No. 1087 for 2000, No. 1088 for $2422\frac{17}{90}$, No. 1089 for $1626\frac{78}{90}$, No. 1090 for 3102, No. 1091 for $3539\frac{31}{90}$, No. 1092 for $3490\frac{60}{90}$, all dated 28th February, 1788		22,681.	37
668 Ditto, for warrant No. 1043, dated 31st Dec. 1788 ..		6,000	
670 John Lamb, to pay invalid pensions at New-York ..		2,137.	32
Commissions charged by Massachusetts bank on receiving deposits		22.	30
		260,081.	44
Balance to the 30th Sept. 1790, as explained at foot		351,570.	25
		611,651.	69

No. 267, on William Heth, unpaid		3,000	
Protests on drafts on Wm. Lindsay (no warrant issued)		41.	47
Trustees for reduction of public debt		51,477.	90
In the bank of North America	89,533. 66		
New-York	197,097. 41	297,050.	88
Massachusetts	10,419. 81		
	Dollars,	351,570.	25

TREASURER OF THE UNITED STATES

Received for warrant	*Dols.*	*Cts.*
No. 525 on George Abb. Hall, collector of Charleston	2,000	
389 John Habersham Savannah	500	
42 James Blanchard	394.	10
43 Nathaniel Gilman	800	
Interest received on Theodosius Fowler and Co.'s note	8.	98
	611,651.	69

TREASURY of the UNITED STATES

New-York, 1st October, 1790

SAMUEL MEREDITH, Treasurer of the United States

Mr. Bush was written to the 9th July, to send forward his receipt for warrant No. 577; but it was not obtained till after the Auditor had passed the account.[2]

---

[2] These documents were received by the House on January 4, 1791.

No.	Short Title	Long Title	Date Introduced	Date Signed by President

No.	Short Title	Long Title	Date Introduced	Date Signed by President
1	OATH	A Bill to regulate the taking the oath or affirmation prescribed by the sixth article of the Constitution	Apr. 14	June 1
		An Act to regulate the time and manner of administering certain oaths		
2	IMPOST	An Act for laying a duty on goods, wares, and merchandizes, imported into the United States	May 5	July 4
3	COLLECTION	A Bill for collecting duties on goods, wares, and merchandizes, imported into the United States	May 8	Tabled—HR See [HR–6]
4	No bill so numbered			
5	TONNAGE	An Act imposing duties on tonnage	May 25	July 20
6	COLLECTION	A Bill to regulate the collection of duties, imposed on goods, wares, and merchandizes, imported into the United States	May 27	Recommitted See [HR–11]
7	WAR DEPARTMENT	An Act to establish an Executive Department, to be denominated the Department of War	June 2	Aug. 7
8	FOREIGN AFFAIRS	An Act for establishing an Executive Department, to be denominated the Department of Foreign Affairs	June 2	July 27
9	TREASURY	A Bill to establish an Executive Department, to be denominated the Treasury Department	June 4	Sept. 2
		An Act to establish the Treasury Department		
10	COPYRIGHT (AND PATENTS)	A Bill to promote the progress of science and useful	June 23	Postponed— HR

No.	Short Title	Long Title	Date Introduced	Date Signed by President
		arts, by securing to authors and inventors the exclusive right to their respective writings and discoveries		
11	COLLECTION	A Bill to regulate the collection of duties imposed on goods, wares, and merchandizes, imported into the United States	June 29	July 31
		An Act to regulate the collection of the duties imposed by law on the tonnage of ships or vessels, and on goods, wares, and merchandizes, imported into the United States		
12	LIGHTHOUSES	A Bill for the Establishment and support of lighthouses, beacons, and buoys; and for authorising the several states to provide and regulate pilots	July 1	Aug. 7
		An Act for the establishment and support of Light-Houses, Beacons, and Buoys		
		An Act for the Establishment and support of Light-Houses, Beacons, Buoys, and Public Piers		
13	SETTLEMENT OF ACCOUNTS	An Act for settling the accounts between the United States and individual States	July 16	Aug. 5
14	NORTHWEST TERRITORY	An Act to provide for the government of the territory north west of the River Ohio	July 16	Aug. 7
15	COMPENSATION	An Act for allowing [making] a compensation to the President and Vice President of the United States	July 22	Sept. 24

No.	Short Title	Long Title	Date Introduced	Date Signed by President
16	COASTING	A Bill for registering and clearing vessels, ascertaining their tonnage, and for regulating the coasting trade An Act for registering and clearing Vessels, regulating the Coasting Trade, and for other purposes	July 24	Sept. 1
17	LAND OFFICE	A Bill establishing a Land Office in and for the Western Territory	July 31	Postponed—HR
18	RECORDS	A Bill to provide for the safekeeping of the acts, records, and seal of the United States; for the due publication of the acts of Congress; for the authentication of copies of records; for making out, and recording commissions, and prescribing their form, and for establishing the fees of office to be taken for making such commissions, and for copies of records and papers An Act to provide for the safekeeping of the Acts, Records, and Seal of the United States, and for other Purposes	July 31	Sept. 15
19	SALARIES-LEGISLATIVE	An Act for allowing compensation to the members of the Senate and House of Representatives of the United States, and to the officers of both Houses	Aug. 4	Sept. 22
20	INDIAN TREATIES	An Act providing for the Expenses which may attend Negotiations or Treaties with the Indian Tribes, and the Appointment of Commissioners for managing the same	Aug. 10	Aug. 20

No.	Short Title	Long Title	Date Introduced	Date Signed by President
21	SALARIES-EXECUTIVE	An Act for establishing the Salaries of the Executive Officers of Government, with their Assistants and Clerks	Aug. 24	Sept. 11
22	HOSPITALS AND HARBORS	A Bill providing for the establishment of hospitals for the relief of sick and disabled seamen, and prescribing regulations for the harbours of the United States	Aug. 27	Postponed—HR
23	COLLECTION	An Act to suspend part [obliging vessels bound up the Potomac to stop at St. Mary's or Yeocomico, to report a manifest of their cargoes] of an Act, entitled, "An Act to regulate the Collection of the Duties imposed by Law on the Tonnage of Ships or Vessels, and on Goods, Wares, and Merchandizes, imported into the United States"	Aug. 28	Sept. 16
24	TONNAGE	A Bill for suspending the operations of part of an Act, entitled "An Act imposing duties on tonnage"	Sept. 9	Not passed—S See [HR–23]
25	SEAT OF GOVERNMENT	An Act to establish the Seat of Government of the United States	Sept. 14	Postponed—S
26	COLLECTION	An Act for amending part of an Act, entitled, "An Act to regulate the Collection of the Duties imposed by Law on the Tonnage of Ships or Vessels and on Goods, Wares, and Merchandizes, imported into the United States"	Sept. 17	Not passed—S
27	TROOPS	An Act to recognize and adapt to the Constitution	Sept. 17	Sept. 29

No.	Short Title	Long Title	Date Introduced	Date Signed by President
		of the United States, the establishment of the Troops raised under the Resolves of the United States in Congress assembled, and for other Purposes therein mentioned		
28	SALARIES-JUDICIARY	An Act for allowing certain Compensation to the Judges of the Supreme and other Courts, and to the Attorney General of the United States	Sept. 17	Sept. 23
29	INVALID PENSIONERS	An Act providing for the payment of the invalid Pensioners of the United States	Sept. 18	Sept. 29
30	SLAVE TRADE	A Bill concerning the importation of certain persons prior to the year 1808	Sept. 19	Postponed—HR
31	TIME OF MEETING	A Bill to alter the time of the annual meeting of Congress An Act to alter the Time for the next meeting of Congress	Sept. 21	Sept. 29
32	APPROPRIATIONS	An Act making appropriations for the service of the present year	Sept. 21	Sept. 29
33	COASTING	An Act to explain and amend an Act, entitled, "An Act for registering and clearing Vessels, regulating the Coasting Trade, and for other Purposes"	Sept. 23	Sept. 29

SECOND SESSION: JANUARY 4, 1790–AUGUST 12, 1790

No.	Short Title	Long Title	Date Introduced	Date Signed by President
34	ENUMERATION	An Act providing for the actual enumeration of the inhabitants of the United States	Jan. 18	Mar. 1

No.	Short Title	Long Title	Date Introduced	Date Signed by President
35	FOREIGN INTERCOURSE	A Bill providing the means of intercourse between the United States and foreign nations	Jan. 21	Recommitted See [HR–52]
36	NORTH-CAROLINA	An Act for giving effect to the several acts therein mentioned, in respect to the State of North Carolina, and other purposes	Jan. 25	Feb. 8
37	NATURALIZA-TION	A Bill establishing an uniform rule of naturalization	Jan. 25	Recommitted See [HR–40]
38	MITIGATION OF FINES	A Bill to provide for the remission or mitigation of fines, forfeitures, and penalties in certain cases	Jan. 26	Recommitted See [HR–45]
39	COPYRIGHT	A Bill for securing the copyright of books to authors and proprietors	Jan. 28	Recommitted See [HR–43]
40	NATURALIZA-TION	A Bill to establish an uniform rule of naturalization, and to enable aliens to hold lands under certain restrictions An Act to establish a uniform rule of naturalization	Feb. 16	Mar. 26
41	PATENTS	An Act to promote the progress of useful arts	Feb. 16	Apr. 10
42	POST OFFICE	A Bill for regulating the post-office of the United States	Feb. 23	Recommitted See [HR–74]
43	COPYRIGHT	A Bill for the encouragement of learning, by securing the copies of maps, charts, books, and other writings, to the authors and proprietors of such copies, during the times therein mentioned An Act for the encouragement of learning, by securing the copies of maps, charts, books, to the authors and proprie-	Feb. 25	May 31

No.	Short Title	Long Title	Date Introduced	Date Signed by President
		tors of such copies, during the times therein mentioned		
44	BAILEY	An Act to vest in Francis Bailey, the exclusive privilege of making, using, and vending to others, punches for stamping the matrices of types, and impressing marks on plates, or any other substance, to prevent counterfeits, upon a principle by him invented, for a term of years	Feb. 26	Not passed— S See [HR–41]
45	MITIGATION OF FINES	An Act to provide for the remission or mitigation of fines, forfeitures, and penalties, in certain cases	Mar. 3	Not passed See [HR–57]
46	SALARIES OF CLERKS	An Act for encreasing the salaries of clerks in the office of the Commissioners for settling accounts, between the United States and individual states	Mar. 8	Not passed— S
47	APPROPRIATIONS	An Act making appropriations for the support of government for the year one thousand seven hundred and ninety	Mar. 8	Mar. 26
48	INSPECTION	An Act to prevent the exportation of goods not duly inspected according to the laws of the several States	Mar. 8	Apr. 2
49	ELY	A Bill to allow compensation to John Ely, for his services and expences as a regimental surgeon in the late army of the United States	Mar. 11	Not passed— HR See [HR–56]
50	COLLECTION	An Act further to suspend part of an Act, entitled, "An Act to regulate the collection of the duties imposed by law on the	Mar. 26	Apr. 15

No.	Short Title	Long Title	Date Introduced	Date Signed by President
		tonnage of ships or vessels, and on goods, wares, and merchandizes, imported into the United States"		
		An Act, further to suspend part of an Act, entitled, "An Act to regulate the collection of the duties imposed by law on the tonnage of ships or vessels, and on goods, wares, and merchandizes, imported into the United States;" and to amend the said Act		
[50a]	MILITARY ESTABLISHMENT	An Act for regulating the military establishment of the United States	Mar. 25, passed by House	Apr. 30
[50b]	INDIAN TREATY	An Act providing for holding a treaty or treaties, to establish peace with certain Indian tribes	Mar. 29, received by Senate	July 22
51	INDIAN TRADE	A Bill to regulate trade and intercourse with the Indian Tribes	Mar. 30	Recommitted See [HR–65]
52	FOREIGN INTERCOURSE	An Act providing the means of intercourse between the United States and foreign nations	Mar. 31	July 1
53	OFFICERS	An Act for the relief of a certain description of officers therein mentioned	Apr. 5	Not passed See [HR–59]
54	SALARIES-EXECUTIVE	An Act supplemental to the Act for establishing the salaries of the executive officers of government, with their assistants and clerks	Apr. 13	June 4
55	See [HR–50a]			
56	ELY	An Act to allow compensation to John Ely, for his attendance as a physician and surgeon on the prisoners of the United States	Apr. 22	Not passed— S

No.	Short Title	Long Title	Date Introduced	Date Signed by President
57	MITIGATION OF FORFEITURES	An Act to provide for mitigating or remitting the forfeitures and penalties accruing under the revenue laws, in certain cases therein mentioned	Apr. 27	May 26
58	AUTHENTICATION	An Act to prescribe the mode in which the public acts, records, and judicial proceedings in each State shall be authenticated, so as to take effect in every other State	Apr. 28	May 26
59	INVALID OFFICERS	An Act to authorize the issuing of certificates to a certain description of invalid officers	Apr. 30	Not passed— S
60	STEUBEN	An Act for finally adjusting and satisfying the claims of Frederick William de Steuben	Apr. 30	June 4
61	MERCHANT SEAMEN	An Act for the government and regulation of seamen in the merchants service	May 3	July 20
62	DUTIES ON DISTILLED SPIRITS	A Bill for repealing, after the last day of ———— next, the duties heretofore laid upon distilled spirits imported from abroad, and laying others in their stead, and also upon spirits distilled within the United States, as well to discourage the excessive use of those spirits, and promote agriculture, as to provide for the support of the public credit, and for the common defence and general welfare	May 5	Not passed See [HR–83]
63	FUNDING	An Act making provision for the debt of the United States	May 6	Aug. 4
64	DUTIES ON WINES	A Bill repealing, after the last day of ———— next,	May 11	Not passed See [HR–83]

No.	Short Title	Long Title	Date Introduced	Date Signed by President
		the duties heretofore laid upon wines imported from foreign ports or places, and laying others in their stead		
65	INDIAN TRADE	An Act to regulate trade and intercourse with the Indian tribes	May 14	July 22
66	TRADE AND NAVIGATION	A Bill concerning the navigation and trade of the United States	May 17	Not passed— HR
67	JENKINS	An Act for the relief of Thomas Jenkins and company	May 20	June 14
68	NORTH CAROLINA JUDICIARY	An Act for giving effect to an Act, entitled, "An Act to establish the Judicial Courts of the United States," within the State of North-Carolina	May 21	June 4
69	SETTLEMENT OF ACCOUNTS	A Bill to provide for the settlement of the accounts between the United States, and the individual States	May 27	Recommitted —HR See [HR–77]
70	MCCORD	An Act to satisfy the claims of John McCord, against the United States	June 2	July 1
71	RHODE ISLAND	An Act for giving effect to the several Acts therein mentioned, in respect to the State of Rhode-Island and Providence Plantations	June 2	June 14
72	TWINING	An Act for the relief of Nathaniel Twining	June 3	July 1
73	RHODE ISLAND JUDICIARY	An Act for giving effect to an Act, entitled, "An Act to establish the Judicial Courts of the United States" within the State of Rhode-Island and Providence Plantations	June 4	June 23
74	POST OFFICE	An Act to establish the Post-Office and Post-Roads within the United States	June 7	Not passed

No.	Short Title	Long Title	Date Introduced	Date Signed by President
75	RHODE ISLAND ENUMERATION	An Act for giving effect to an Act, entitled, "An Act, providing for the enumeration of the inhabitants of the United States," in respect to the State of Rhode-Island and Providence Plantations	June 7	July 5
76	WEST POINT	An Act to authorize the purchase of a tract of land [at West Point] for the use of the United States	June 15	July 5
77	SETTLEMENT OF ACCOUNTS	An Act to provide more effectually for the settlement of the accounts between the United States and individual States	June 17	Aug. 5
78	TONNAGE	An Act imposing duties on the tonnage of ships or vessels	June 22	July 20
79	GOULD	An Act to satisfy the claim of the representatives of David Gould, deceased, against the United States	June 23	Not passed— S
80	INVALID PENSIONERS	An Act further to provide for the payment of the invalid pensioners of the United States	June 29	July 16
81	MILITIA	A Bill more effectually to provide for the national defence, by establishing a uniform militia throughout the United States	July 1	Not passed— HR
82	COLLECTION	An Act to provide more effectually for the collection of the duties imposed by law on goods, wares, and merchandize, imported into the United States, and on the tonnage of ships or vessels	July 8	Aug. 4
83	WAYS AND MEANS	An Act making further provision for the payment of	July 13	Aug. 10

No.	Short Title	Long Title	Date Introduced	Date Signed by President
		the debts of the United States		
84	LIGHTHOUSES	An Act to amend the Act for the establishment and support of light-houses, beacons, buoys and public piers	July 14	July 22
85	VIRGINIA CESSION	An Act to enable the officers and soldiers of the Virginia line, on the continental establishment, to obtain titles to certain lands lying north-west of the river Ohio, between the Little Miami and Sciota	July 15	Aug. 10
86	CONSULS AND VICE CONSULS	A Bill for establishing the fees and perquisites to be received by Consuls and Vice-Consuls of the United States in foreign parts, and for other purposes	July 15	Postponed— S
		An Act concerning consuls and vice consuls of the United States, in foreign parts		
87	See [HR–50b]			
88	DISABLED SOLDIERS AND SEAMEN	An Act for the relief of disabled soldiers and seamen lately in the service of the United States, and of certain other persons	July 16	Aug. 11
89	COASTING	A Bill for registering ships or vessels, for regulating those employed in the coasting trade and fisheries, and for other purposes	July 22	Postponed— HR
90	STEWART AND DAVIDSON	An Act for the relief of John Stewart and John Davidson	July 27	Aug. 4
91	BARCLAY	An Act to compensate Thomas Barclay for various public services	July 28	Not passed

No.	Short Title	Long Title	Date Introduced	Date Signed by President
92	POST OFFICE	An Act to continue in force for a limited time, an Act, entitled, "An Act for the temporary establishment of the post-office"	July 28	Aug. 4
93	NAVIGATION	An Act declaring the assent of Congress to certain Acts of the States of Maryland, Georgia, and Rhode-Island	Aug. 3	Aug. 11
94	GEORGIA	A Bill making further provision for the debt of the United States, so far as respects the assumption of the debt of the State of Georgia	Aug. 3	Not passed— HR
95	SETTLING ACCOUNTS	An Act for adding two Commissioners to the board established for settling the accounts between the United States and the individual States	Aug. 4	Not passed— S
96	STIRLING	An Act making an appropriation for discharging the claim of Sarah Alexander, the widow of the late Major General Lord Stirling, who died in the services of the United States	Aug. 4	Aug. 11
		An Act for the relief of the persons therein mentioned or described		
97	PORTLAND HEAD LIGHTHOUSE	An Act authorizing the Secretary of the Treasury to finish the lighthouse on Portland Head in the district of Maine	Aug. 5	Aug. 10
98	SURVEYOR GENERAL	A Bill providing for the appointment of a surveyor-general for the United States	Aug. 6	Not passed— HR
99	CALDWELL	An Act for the relief of Adam Caldwell	Aug. 6	Postponed— S

No.	Short Title	Long Title	Date Introduced	Date Signed by President
100	SPECIAL APPROPRIA- TIONS	An Act making certain ap- propriations therein men- tioned	Aug. 9	Aug. 12
101	SINKING FUND	An Act making provision for the reduction of the public debt	Aug. 9	Aug. 12

THIRD SESSION: DECEMBER 6, 1790–MARCH 3, 1791

No.	Short Title	Long Title	Date Introduced	Date Signed by President
102	MILITIA	A Bill more effectually to provide for the national defence, by establishing a uniform militia through- out the United States	Dec. 14	Recommitted See [HR– 112]
103	NAVIGATION	An Act to continue an Act, entitled, "An Act declar- ing the assent of Con- gress to certain Acts of the States of Maryland, Georgia, and Rhode-Is- land and Providence Plantations"	Dec. 16	Jan. 10
104	PRESIDENCY	A Bill declaring the officer, who, in case of vacancies, both in the offices of President and Vice-Presi- dent of the United States, shall act as President	Dec. 20	Not passed— HR
105	ELECTORS	A Bill declaring the respec- tive times when the elec- tors to vote for a Presi- dent of the United States shall be appointed or chosen, and shall give their votes	Dec. 20	Not passed— HR
106	PRESIDENTIAL ELECTION	A Bill directing the mode in which the lists of the votes for a President shall be transmitted to the seat of the government of the United States	Dec. 20	Not passed— HR
107	LIABILITY OF SHIPOWNERS	A Bill to ascertain how far the owners of ships and vessels shall be answer- able to the freighters	Dec. 27	Not passed— HR

No.	Short Title	Long Title	Date Introduced	Date Signed by President
108	EVIDENCES OF DEBT	A Bill directing the mode in which the evidences of the debt of the United States, which have been or may be lost or destroyed, shall be renewed	Dec. 28	Recommitted See [HR–118]
109	COLLECTION	A Bill to provide for the delivery of goods, wares, and merchandize, in the state of Pennsylvania, in cases of obstruction of the river Delaware by ice An Act to provide for the unlading of ships or vessels in cases of obstruction by ice	Dec. 28	Jan. 7
110	DUTIES ON DISTILLED SPIRITS	A Bill repealing after the last day of ——— next, the duties heretofore laid upon distilled spirits imported from abroad, and laying others in their stead, and also upon spirits distilled within the United States; as well to discourage the excessive use of those spirits and promote agriculture, as to provide for the support of the public credit, and for the common defence and general welfare An Act repealing, after the last day of June next, the duties heretofore laid upon distilled spirits imported from abroad, and laying others in their stead; also upon spirits distilled within the United States, and for appropriating the same	Dec. 30	Mar. 3
111	SWAIN	An Act for the relief of Shubael Swain	Dec. 31	Not passed— S
112	MILITIA	A Bill more effectually to provide for the national	Jan. 4	Not passed— HR

No.	Short Title	Long Title	Date Introduced	Date Signed by President
		defence, by establishing a uniform militia throughout the United States		
113	POST OFFICE	A Bill for establishing the post-office and post-roads of the United States	Jan. 7	Not passed— HR
114	LAND OFFICE	An Act to establish offices for the purpose of granting lands within the territories of the United States	Jan. 14	Postponed— S
115	MARYLAND	An Act declaring the assent of Congress to a certain Act of the State of Maryland	Jan. 18	Feb. 9
116	FOREIGN OFFICERS	An Act authorizing the President of the United States, to cause the debt due to foreign officers, to be paid and discharged	Jan. 19	Not passed— S
117	TRANSFER OF PENSIONS	A Bill to prevent invalids who are pensioners of the United States, from selling or transferring their respective pensions before the same shall become due	Jan. 21	Not passed— HR
118	EVIDENCES OF DEBT	A Bill directing the mode in which the evidences of the debt of the United States, which have been or may be lost or destroyed, shall be renewed	Jan. 25	Not passed— HR See [HR– 141]
119	SALARIES OF INSPECTORS	A Bill providing compensations for inspectors, and other officers of inspection, and for other purposes	Jan. 26	Not passed— HR
120	APPROPRIATIONS	An Act making appropriations for the support of government during the year one thousand seven hundred and ninety-one, and for other purposes	Jan. 31	Feb. 11

No.	Short Title	Long Title	Date Introduced	Date Signed by President
121	PATENTS	A Bill to amend an Act, intituled, "An Act to promote the progress of useful arts"	Feb. 7	Not passed— HR
122	TIME OF MEETING	An Act to alter the time of the next meeting of Congress	Feb. 8	Not passed— S See [HR–132]
123	COPYRIGHT	A Bill for increasing the penalty contained in an Act, passed the second session of Congress, intituled, "An Act for the encouragement of learning, by securing the copies of maps, charts, and books, to the authors and proprietors of such copies, during the times therein mentioned"	Feb. 9	Not passed— HR
124	COURTS	An Act to continue in force for a limited time, an Act passed at the first session of Congress, entitled, "An Act to regulate processes in the courts of the United States"	Feb. 9	Feb. 18
125	BANK	An Act supplementary to the Act, entitled, "An Act to incorporate the subscribers to the bank of the United States"	Feb. 10	Mar. 2
126	JUDICIAL OFFICERS	A Bill providing compensations for clerks, marshals, and jurors	Feb. 11	Recommitted See [HR–133]
126A	MILITARY ESTABLISHMENT	An Act for raising and adding another regiment to the military establishment of the United States, and for making further provision for the protection of the frontiers	Feb. 12, passed by House	Mar. 3
127	BARNEY	A Bill to compensate Joshua Barney	Feb. 16	Not passed— HR

No.	Short Title	Long Title	Date Introduced	Date Signed by President
128	VERMONT	An Act for giving effect to the laws of the United States, within the State of Vermont	Feb. 17	Mar. 2
129	WAYS AND MEANS	An Act to explain and amend an Act, entitled, "An Act making further provision for the payment of the debts of the United States"	Feb. 21	Mar. 2
130	DUTIES ON TEAS	A Bill making further provision for the collection of the duties imposed on teas An Act making further provision for the collection of duties by law imposed on teas, and to prolong the term for the payment of duties on wines	Feb. 22	Mar. 3
131	TREASURY	An Act supplemental to the Act establishing the Treasury Department	Feb. 22	Mar. 3
132	TIME OF MEETING	An Act fixing the time for the next annual meeting of Congress	Feb. 23	Mar. 2
133	JUDICIAL OFFICERS	A Bill providing compensations for the officers of the several courts of law, and for jurors and witnesses An Act providing compensations for the officers of the judicial courts of the United States, and for jurors and witnesses, and for other purposes	Feb. 24	Mar. 3
134	COLLECTION	A Bill repealing so much of an act [i.e., collection] as establishes the rate of the rix dollar of Denmark An Act concerning the rates of foreign coins An Act relative to the rix dollar of Denmark	Feb. 24	Mar. 3

No.	Short Title	Long Title	Date Introduced	Date Signed by President
135	COMMISSIONERS OF LOANS	An Act for making compensations to the Commissioners of loans, for extraordinary expenses	Feb. 24	Mar. 3
136	SINKING FUND	An Act supplementary to the Act making provision for the reduction of the public debt	Feb. 25	Mar. 3
136A	SALARIES	An Act in addition to an Act, entitled, "An Act for establishing the salaries of the executive officers of government with their assistants and clerks"	[Feb. 26]	Mar. 3
137	POST OFFICE	An Act to continue in force for a limited time, an Act, entitled, "An Act for the temporary establishment of the Post-Office"	Feb. 28	Mar. 3
138	GIBSON	An Act to compensate George Gibson	Feb. 28	Postponed— S
139	WIDOWS, ORPHANS, AND INVALIDS	An Act for making compensation to the widows and orphan children of certain officers who were killed, or who died in the service of the United States, during the late war; and for the relief of certain invalids, and other persons therein mentioned	Feb. 28	Postponed— S
140	COOK	An Act for the relief of David Cook	Mar. 2	Not passed— HR
141	EVIDENCES OF DEBT	A Bill concerning certificates or evidences of the public debt	Mar. 2	Not passed— HR
142	See [HR–136A]			
143	CONSULAR CONVENTION	An Act for carrying into effect the Convention between His Most Christian Majesty and the United States	Mar. 3	Not passed— S

No.	Short Title	Long Title	Date Introduced	Date Signed by President

FIRST SESSION: MARCH 4, 1789–SEPTEMBER 29, 1789

No.	Short Title	Long Title	Date Introduced	Date Signed by President
1	JUDICIARY	An Act to establish the Judicial Courts of the United States	June 12	Sept. 24
2	PUNISHMENT OF CRIMES	An Act for the punishment of certain crimes against the United States	July 28	Postponed— HR
3	POST OFFICE	An Act for the temporary establishment of the Post-Office	Sept. 11	Sept. 22
4	COURTS	An Act to regulate Processes in the Courts of the United States	Sept. 17	Sept. 29
5	GLAUBECK	An Act to allow the Baron de Glaubeck the Pay of a Captain in the Army of the United States	Sept. 24	Sept. 29

SECOND SESSION: JANUARY 4, 1790–AUGUST 12, 1790

No.	Short Title	Long Title	Date Introduced	Date Signed by President
6	PUNISHMENT OF CRIMES	A Bill defining the crimes and offences that shall be cognizable under the authority of the United States, and their punishment An Act for the punishment of certain crimes against the United States	Jan. 26	Apr. 30
7	NORTH CAROLINA CESSION	An Act to accept a cession of the claims of the State of North-Carolina, to a certain district of western territory	Mar. 3	Apr. 2
8	SOUTHERN TERRITORY	An Act for the government of the territory of the United States south of the River Ohio	Apr. 9	May 26
9	COURTS	An Act to continue in force an Act passed at the last session of Congress, entitled, "An Act to regulate processes in the courts of the United States"	Apr. 23	May 26

No.	Short Title	Long Title	Date Introduced	Date Signed by President
10	NORTH CAROLINA JUDICIARY	An Act for giving effect to the Acts therein mentioned, in respect to the State of North-Carolina, and to amend the said Act	Apr. 29	Not passed See [HR–68]
11	RHODE ISLAND TRADE	An Act to prevent bringing goods, wares, and merchandizes from the State of Rhode-Island and Providence Plantations, into the United States, and to authorize a demand of money from the said State	May 13	Not passed— HR
12	RESIDENCE	A Bill to determine the permanent seat of Congress, and the government of the United States An Act for establishing the temporary and permanent seat of the Government of the United States	May 31	July 16
13	CIRCUIT COURTS	A Bill for altering the time of holding the courts in South Carolina and Georgia An Act to alter the times for holding the Circuit Courts of the United States in the districts of South-Carolina and Georgia, and providing that the District Court of Pennsylvania shall in future be held in the city of Philadelphia only	Aug. 7	Aug. 11

THIRD SESSION: DECEMBER 6, 1790–MARCH 3, 1791

No.	Short Title	Long Title	Date Introduced	Date Signed by President
14	WAYS AND MEANS	An Act supplementary to the Act, entitled, "An Act making further provision for the payment of the debts of the United States"	Dec. 16	Dec. 27

No.	Short Title	Long Title	Date Introduced	Date Signed by President
15	BANK	An Act to incorporate the subscribers to the bank of the United States	Jan. 3	Feb. 25
16	KENTUCKY STATEHOOD	An Act providing that the district of Kentucky should become an independent State, and be admitted as a member of the United States of America	Jan. 4	Feb. 4
		An Act declaring the consent of Congress that a new State be formed within the jurisdiction of the Commonwealth of Virginia, and admitted into this union by the name of the State of Kentucky		
17	NORTHWEST TERRITORY	An Act for granting lands to the inhabitants and settlers at Vincennes and the Illinois country, in the territory northwest of the Ohio, and for confirming them in their possessions	Jan. 7	Mar. 3
18	CONSULS AND VICE CONSULS	An Act concerning Consuls and Vice Consuls	Jan. 7	Not passed
19	VERMONT STATEHOOD	An Act for the admission of the State of Vermont into this union	Feb. 10	Feb. 18
20	KENTUCKY AND VERMONT REPRESENTATIVES	An Act regulating the number of Representatives to be chosen by the States of Kentucky and Vermont	Feb. 11	Feb. 25
21	RESIDENCE	An Act to amend an Act, entitled, "An Act for establishing the temporary and permanent seat of government of the United States"	Feb. 17	Mar. 3
22	PAYMENT OF BALANCES	An Act concerning the payment of balances due to	Feb. 26	Postponed— S

No.	Short Title	Long Title	Date Introduced	Date Signed by President
		the United States in certain cases		
23	MOROCCAN TREATY	An Act making an appropriation for the purposes therein mentioned [effecting a recognition of the treaty of the United States with the new Emperor of Morocco]	Mar. 1	Mar. 3
24	MITIGATION OF FORFEITURES	An Act to continue in force the Act therein mentioned [to provide for mitigating . . . forfeitures], and to make further provision for the payment of pensions to invalids, and for the support of lighthouses, beacons, buoys, and public piers	Mar. 2	Mar. 3

INDEX

This index utilizes the short titles and numbers of bills given in the preceding List of Bills. For the full title as given in the text, the reader should consult this list.

I

K

L